D0079320

THE ESSENTIAL MARGARET FULLER

AMERICAN WOMEN WRITERS SERIES

Joanne Dobson, Judith Fetterley, and Elaine Showalter, series editors

ALTERNATIVE ALCOTT
Louisa May Alcott
Elaine Showalter, editor

MOODS
Louisa May Alcott
Sarah Elbert, editor

STORIES FROM THE COUNTRY OF
LOST BORDERS
Mary Austin
Marjorie Pryse, editor

CLOVERNOOK SKETCHES AND
OTHER STORIES
Alice Cary
Judith Fetterley, editor

HOBOMOK AND OTHER WRITINGS
ON INDIANS
Lydia Maria Child
Carolyn L. Karcher, editor

"HOW CELIA CHANGED HER MIND"
AND SELECTED STORIES
Rose Terry Cooke
Elizabeth Ammons, editor

THE LAMPLIGHTER
Maria Susanna Cummins
Nina Baym, editor

RUTH HALL AND OTHER
WRITINGS
Fanny Fern
Joyce Warren, editor

THE ESSENTIAL
MARGARET FULLER
Jeffrey Steele, editor

GAIL HAMILTON: SELECTED WRITINGS
Susan Coultrap-McQuin, editor

A NEW HOME, WHO'LL FOLLOW?
Caroline M. Kirkland
Sandra A. Zagarell, editor

QUICKSAND AND PASSING
Nella Larsen
Deborah E. McDowell, editor

HOPE LESLIE
Catharine Maria Sedgwick
Mary Kelley, editor

THE HIDDEN HAND
E.D.E.N. Southworth
Joanne Dobson, editor

"THE AMBER GODS" AND
OTHER STORIES
Harriet Prescott Spofford
Alfred Bendixen, editor

OLDTOWN FOLKS
Harriet Beecher Stowe
Dorothy Berkson, editor

WOMEN ARTISTS, WOMEN
EXILES: "MISS GRIEF"
AND OTHER STORIES
Constance Fenimore Woolson
Joan Myers Weimer, editor

AMERICAN WOMEN POETS
OF THE NINETEENTH CENTURY:
AN ANTHOLOGY
Cheryl Walker, editor

THE ESSENTIAL
MARGARET FULLER

MARGARET FULLER

Edited and with an Introduction by

JEFFREY STEELE

RUTGERS UNIVERSITY PRESS

New Brunswick, New Jersey

HOUSTON PUBLIC LIBRARY

R0163944289
humca

HOUSTON PUBLIC LIBRARY

Library of Congress Cataloging-in-Publication Data

Fuller, Margaret, 1810–1850.
  The essential Margaret Fuller / edited and with an introduction by Jeffrey Steele.
    p.   cm.—(American women writers series)
  Includes bibliographical references (p.   ).
  ISBN 0-8135-1777-X (cloth)—ISBN 0-8135-1778-8 (pbk.)
  I. Steele, Jeffrey, 1947–   . II. Title. III. Series.
PS2502.S68 1992
818'.309—dc20   91-29962
                                                                              CIP

British Cataloging-in-Publication information available

Copyright © 1992 by Rutgers, The State University
All rights reserved
Manufactured in the United States of America

For Jocelyn, Doran, and Brendan

"These not only know themselves more, but *are* more for having met, and regions of their being, which would else have laid sealed in cold obstruction, burst into leaf and bloom and song."
—Margaret Fuller, "Autobiographical Romance"

CONTENTS

Contents

ACKNOWLEDGMENTS

Every scholar and student of Margaret Fuller is indebted to the work of three pioneers in the field: Joel Myerson, Robert N. Hudspeth, and Bell Gale Chevigny. Without their example and scholarship this anthology would not have been possible. I found especially helpful Hudspeth's annotation of Fuller's letters and Myerson's annotation of *Woman in the Nineteenth Century,* which I used as models in my own efforts to track down Fuller's myriad success. Dale Bauer, Susan Friedman, Leslie Mitchner, Elaine Showalter, Jocelyn Riley, and the members of the "Draft Group" at the University of Wisconsin made much appreciated comments and suggestions on the introduction. Thomas Pfau provided assistance in tracking down and translating some of Fuller's German sources. I am grateful to Jane Dieckmann for her meticulous editing. Over the past several years, I have been particularly fortunate in having three indefatigable research assistants: Melissa Fuller, Paul Dudenhefer, and Amor Kohli. For the hours spent together discussing Fuller's work, I thank my student, Barbara Korbal. My colleague Annis Pratt served as a model of humane scholarship. I wish to thank the National Endowment of the Humanities, the Graduate School of the University of Wisconsin, and the Vilas Foundation for financial support during this project. Excerpts from Fuller's unpublished papers are reprinted by permission of the Houghton Library; by courtesy of the Trustees of the Boston Public Library; by permission of the Fruitlands Museum Library, Harvard MA; and by permission of Reverend Allie Perry. Finally, to Jocelyn Riley, whose own researches in American women's writing have been a continual source of information and inspiration, I am most indebted of all.

"When I write," Margaret Fuller declared in an 1840 letter, "it is into another world, not a better one perhaps, but one with very dissimilar habits of thought to this where I am domesticated" (*L* 2 : 125). Like most women of her day, Fuller grew up in a world in which men and women occupied separate spheres. Three of her five surviving brothers graduated from Harvard, an educational resource not open to her. With the exception of Lloyd, who was mentally handicapped, all of her brothers pursued careers outside of the home—as teachers, a businessman, and a lawyer. Two brothers, Arthur and Richard, earned postgraduate degrees from Harvard—in Divinity and Law, respectively. In contrast, Margaret—the oldest of seven surviving children—became expert at sewing, housework, and child care. Especially after her father was elected to Congress when she was seven, she was expected to play a central role in the daily management of her family. In her mid twenties, after her father moved the family from Cambridge to a farm in western Massachusetts, she spent much of her time as a tutor and surrogate mother for her younger siblings. Her mother was often ill, and Margaret complained in her journal that as "the only grown up daughter" her time was "considerably taxed" (MH). Yet, unlike nearly every other woman of her generation, Fuller ultimately achieved in her life the ability to balance the demands of domesticity against a professional accomplishment ordinarily expected of men. When she died with her husband and child in a shipwreck at the age of forty,[1] she had been the best literary critic in America, a successful editor, a teacher who pioneered new forms of educational practice, one of the country's first columnists and war correspondents, and the author of the most influential book on woman's rights. In her life, the demands of traditional domesticity coexisted with "another world" in which she was a pioneer.

In many respects, Margaret Fuller's unique blend of domesticity and professional accomplishment resulted from the extraordinary education she received from her father. A distinguished graduate of Harvard College, Timothy Fuller was active in various branches of Massachusetts state government, a four-term U.S. congressman, and chairman of the House Committee on Naval Affairs. According to all acounts, he was an affectionate but demanding parent who held Margaret, his oldest child, to an unusually high standard of intellectual and personal discipline. Her education, dress, and even social life were strictly controlled by the man whom Thomas Wentworth Higginson, a personal friend of the family, described as a "strong-willed spouse" who dominated his "self-effacing" wife (Margarett Crane Fuller) and his daughter (17). Timothy Fuller trained Margaret in an intellectual discipline unique among women of the age, leaving her with the difficult challenge of balancing the demands of analytical rigor against the emotional necessities of her experience. This difficulty, however, also became a source of strength for America's first feminist theorist. Inhabiting the worlds of both mother and father, but totally at home in neither, she was in the perfect position to understand the strengths and limitations of both masculinity and femininity in the nineteenth century. Ultimately, this sense of gender duality led Fuller to define herself in bisexual terms. "Will there never be a being to combine a man's mind and a woman's heart," she once lamented; while, in *Woman in the Nineteenth Century,* she asserted that men and women possess both masculine and feminine traits (*WM* 58).

By depicting excursions into other "worlds," Fuller drew attention to the ways in which she and other Americans—both men and women— had been "domesticated." Sometimes, as in the portrait of her mother's garden in her "Autobiographical Romance," she found another world in the maternalized image of a pastoral retreat that offered an escape from masculine America. At other times, the language of mythology and dreams provided her with visionary landscapes in which female figures were able to achieve a nobility and heroism unavailable in contemporary religious narratives. When she traveled in 1843 to Chicago and the Wisconsin Territory, she documented that excursion in *Summer on the Lakes,* a book evoking a frontier world that disturbed the settled existence of her eastern readers. Her 1844 poetry articulated a mythologized realm in which she transformed the self into a powerful goddess, while in *Woman in the Nine-*

teenth Century she combined the world of myth with the domains of history and literature to provide her readers with a pantheon of potential identities. Some of her best *New-York Tribune* essays recounted journeys into the prisons and asylums of New York—a realm largely unknown to her audience. Finally, her travels in Europe, culminating in her personal involvement with the Italian Revolution of 1848, enabled her to portray a revolutionary fervor challenging the imperialistic complacency of an 1840s America that had recently invaded Mexico.

Fuller's depictions of other worlds pulled her in contradictory directions. On the one hand, she was an idealist at home in the realms of Greek literature, Shakespeare, and German philosophy. On the other, she was a careful observer of contemporary manners and morals whose portraits of the West, New York, and Europe competed with Caroline Kirkland's survey of the Michigan frontier in *A New Home, Who'll Follow* (1839) and Lydia Maria Child's account of the "urban frontier" in *Letters from New York* (1843).[2] Such a blend of idealism and realism was one of the hallmarks of Romantic literature, merging a fascination with the imaginary with the desire for a closer proximity to "experience." But in Fuller's work, it contributed as well to double-voiced patterns of analysis. In her "Autobiographical Romance," for example, she constructed a dialogue between the masculinized language of "common sense" and a feminized language of transcendence which had been appropriated by men and thus muted for women. In opposition to the imperialism of "Rome" (a familiar and even cherished image of America in the nineteenth century), she placed maternal images centered on her mother's garden and goddess figures derived from classical mythology. At first a sanctuary that enabled her to escape from oppressive masculine authority, this maternal realm became, by the time of *Woman in the Nineteenth Century,* an image focusing the possibility of cultural change.

Such depictions of gender difference involved Fuller in a difficult process of self-interpretation. In her writing, ironic critical detachment contended with imaginative fervor, as she searched for a literary mode that would allow expression of the dualities of her being. At the same time, her sense of personal disjunction helped her interpret the ways in which the victims of racial and sexual oppression had been compartmentalized into categories that isolated them from effective political sympathy. In the conclusion of *Summer on the Lakes,* for example, she confronted aestheticized views of "picturesque" American Indian culture by uncovering the cultural imperialism of such representations. One of the pivotal moments in *Woman in the Nineteenth Century* was a dialogue staged between a slaveholder and a woman who challenges his conflation of the ideology of slavery with that of masculine domination. In similar fashion, Fuller's New York essays and Italian letters measured aesthetic detachment against the demands of political, and even revolutionary, involvement.

The competing voices of Fuller's writing allowed her to measure the personal and cultural expense of what she called "idolatry." "I wish woman to live, *first* for God's sake," she observes in *Woman in the Nineteenth Century;* "Then she will not make an imperfect man her god, and thus sink to idolatry." Significantly, the ex-slave Frederick Douglass also associated bondage with idolatry, suggesting that "slavishness" was reinforced by an internalized oppression that manifested itself as reverence for distant 'god-like' masters. Even in the North, Douglass confessed in *My Bondage and My Freedom,* he found it difficult to escape from the tendency to be a "hero worshipper," entranced by the spectacle of white male power. Fuller's struggle for mental liberation followed an analogous path, as she labored to free herself from patriarchal ideologies threatening to submerge her personality. Writing in an age when the languages of westward expansion, of domesticity, even of reform had been permeated by the pervasive assumption of masculine superiority, she learned to diagnose the sexual, racial, and class prejudices that marred the efforts of many women to achieve personal independence.

On a personal level, Fuller's recognition of the dangers of idolatry dated from her complicated reaction to her father's death from cholera in October 1835. She seems to have experienced what has been called "disordered mourning," a process in which "grief becomes *frozen,* or blocked" until "the mourner works though the conflicts he or she feels toward the deceased" (Tolchin 5). The immediate result of Timothy Fuller's death was the cancellation of Margaret's plans to travel and study in Europe. Instead, she was forced to sacrifice her own plans for the good of her family, now sorely pressed for money, and in need of leadership.[3] Committing herself to a life of renunciation, she struggled "to try to forget myself, and act for others' sakes" (*L* 1: 254). Over the next three years, she accepted paid positions as a teacher—first in Bronson Alcott's Temple School and then in the Greene Street School in Providence. But teaching, which Fuller found laborious and draining, only added to the conflicts that she felt over her father's death. It made her more self-sufficient and yet also tied her financially to her family. Over the next five years, her unresolved mourning inscribed itself in a succession of ailments, as each subsequent autumn and winter became for her a time of isolation, depression, and sickness.[4]

Yet, despite her ill health, Fuller in the years immediately following her father's death greatly expanded her personal horizons. In 1836 she met Ralph Waldo Emerson, whose theory of "self-reliance" quickly became for her an important stimulus toward independence. In 1839 she continued her translation of German literature with the publication of *Eckermann's Conversations with Goethe*.[5] Beginning in the fall of 1839, she initiated a series of "Conversations" for Boston women—an experiment in alternative education which lasted until the spring of 1844. She joined the Transcendental Club and, in 1840, became the first editor of the new Transcendentalist journal—the *Dial*.

But this apparent tranquillity was shattered in 1840 by the engagement and marriage of two of her closest friends, Samuel Ward and Anna Barker. Fuller's grief over her estrangement from Ward and Barker, both of whom she deeply loved, brought into focus an emotional pattern with which she had been grappling since her father's death in 1835. Confronting the psychological expense of this loss, as well as her growing distance from her mentor Ralph Waldo Emerson, she returned to the ghost of her unmourned father, measuring the hidden powers that had been repressed by his influence and then frozen by her failure to mourn. This time, something—perhaps the coincidence of a double grief, the echo of the previous loss of her father combined with a fresh cycle of bereavement—precipitated an emotional "winter" out of which, she hoped, "Phenix like rises the soul into the tenderest spring" (*L* 2: 169).

Fuller later characterized this emotional crisis, which lasted during the fall and winter of 1840–41, as "the era of illumination in my mental life" (*L* 3: 55). Up to this moment, her public writing had been marked by an almost exclusive attention to male writers and images of masculine "genius," but in 1840 she began to shift attention to issues of *female* creativity. Displacing the act of mourning from external to internal objects, she came to understand the ways in which her psychological dependence upon the image of her dead father recapitulated the dependence of women in general upon patriarchal values. In many ways, American women at this time seem to have been more deeply affected than men by the mourning process. Not only did the "burden of mourning" fall upon them, they were also expected to assume elaborate mourning costumes that turned them into "a public symbol of restrained grief."[6] In contrast to the male mourner, who often used the act of mourning as a gateway to personal independence, the female mourner found that her ceremonialized grief replicated patterns of dependence and filiation that filtered through all aspects of female existence. The image of the mourning woman, the weeping maiden draped over the tomb of husband or father, was a familiar icon; her suffering, passive, and silent posture validated the monument of patriarchal power that depended upon the presence of an abject female worshiper.

Coming to terms with her sense of loss, Fuller began to see that her position *as a mourner* replicated roles occupied by numerous other women. Learning how to grieve for herself and not for an absent male figure whose image was sustained by such homage, she displaced attention from the power of the "buried" Father to the damage experienced by his mourners. From this perspective, her "Autobiographical Romance" (begun in 1840) becomes the founding document of her feminism, for it marks the moment at which she begins to grieve for herself as a representative woman. Assessing the damage caused by her father's instruction, she turns the portrait of his ideas into a critique of some of the most cherished masculinist assumptions of American culture.

Like many nineteenth-century men, Timothy Fuller had been intoxicated with the image of the great man who embodied a "Roman" fortitude and exercised "an indomitable will, self-command, and force of expression." Even Emerson had argued in *Nature* for the forceful expansion of a masculine "dominion" modeled in part upon the example of Julius Caesar. But as a woman writing in nineteenth-century America, Fuller was unable to assume Roman character as a model without an ensuing alienation. Denied the means to achieve political or social power, she came to see that such "Roman" imperialism ignored the needs of women. The result of a pedagogy founded upon such principles, she argued, was the silencing of the "feminine" side of her being, which was repressed deep within by her father's demand for common sense and accuracy. In the place of reverie, her father had taught her a "heroic" but self-denying discipline.

Although Fuller "steadily loved this ideal in my childhood," she realized in 1840 that it threatened the nurture of her imagination. Recognizing the extent to which she had incorporated into her personality the powerful voice of Timothy Fuller, she saw that this act of identification had alienated her from the maternal side of her personality. By dedicating herself to her father's memory, she had neglected to mourn the side of her self that had been blighted and distorted by his rule. But in 1840 she began to restore the psychological equilibrium disrupted by her earlier grief. She freed herself from her idolatry of the Father (both Timothy Fuller and the other male leaders of America). In the process, she rediscovered the existence of a core of maternal values—an "atmosphere of ample grace"—corresponding to a submerged aspect of her self and her culture.

Fuller's discovery of this maternal realm in 1840 and 1841 led her to espouse a new model of libidinal and literary energy. Men such as Timothy Fuller and Emerson, she concluded, "impoverish the treasury to build the palace"—evoking the economy of scarcity that motivated Emerson's lament that "talent sucks the substance of the man . . . the accumulation of one point has drained the trunk" (Porte 280). In contrast to this scene of loss, Fuller envisioned an economy based upon the "free flow of life" and the interconnection of friends.[7] Her definition of a maternal economy of writing and being marked her conscious departure from Emerson's style of "self-reliance," which valued individual development over communal being. Emerson himself recognized this difference in a letter to Fuller when he contrasted his unitary style of writing with "the dins & combinations which enrich you whose name is Polyanthos."[8] The two of them, he felt, used "a different rhetoric" (*LE* 2: 353), a comment reflecting his inability to appreciate the "mother tongue" that Fuller was developing in 1840. At first her exploration of this maternal economy focused on three areas: a model of friendship opposed to Emerson's vision of solitary self-reliance, a mythical image of the maternal realm, and representations of female selfhood lying outside of patriarchal definitions.

Re-creating her first friendship in her "Autobiographical Romance," Fuller analyzes the ways in which "a whole region of new life" was opened to her. The value of the friend, she suggests, is not that he or she suggests new thoughts (Emerson's position) but that his or her presence allows the expansion of the self in directions that otherwise would have lain fallow. In contrast to Emerson's model of solitary self-development, Fuller advocates both a multiple connection with others and a multiple sense of selfhood, declaring that "we are not merely one another's priests or gods, but ministering angels, exercising in the past the same function as the Great Soul in the whole of seeing the perfect through the imperfect nay, making it come there" (*L* 2: 214). While Emerson had promoted personal independence and a sense of moral and intellectual superiority, Fuller began to advocate ideals of friendship and community that connected her with such contemporary writers as Caroline Kirkland and with utopian communities that attempted to realize forms of power lacking in competitive, capitalist society.[9]

A second aspect of the maternal language that Fuller discovered in 1840 and 1841 involves her mythological image of a female realm, which received its first full formulation in her description of the mother's garden.[10] In this fecund place her "thoughts could lie callow in the nest," while the presence of her mother's flowers allowed the release of hidden passions: "I kissed them, I pressed them to my bosom with passionate emotions, such as I have never dared to express to any human being. An ambition swelled my heart to be as beautiful, as perfect as they." Fuller "valued, of course, the significance of flowers," Emerson later noted (*M* 1: 221), without really exploring the profound meaning that they held for her. Emblems of organic unfolding, flowers possessed in Fuller's imagination a symbolic richness analogous to that found in the art of Judy Chicago and Georgia O'Keeffe.

The third and perhaps the most striking aspect of Fuller's new language is found in the images of female selfhood she constructs during this period. Challenging traditional definitions of womanhood, she explores what Nancy Chodorow has called a "more permeable" sense of "ego boundaries" (93). Women, Fuller argues, embody an "electricity" that both frightens men and draws individuals together. At such moments the self becomes the vehicle of a connective power, emerging from outside patriarchal law and threatening it. "There is some magic about me," she observes, "which draws other spirits into my circle whether I will or they will or no" (*L* 2: 175). Constructing images of an instinctive force that she intuited within, she evokes a female creative energy that had been consigned to a political "unconscious" outside of masculine dominion.[11]

Over the next three years, from 1841 to 1843, Fuller explored these ideas in a series of essays she published in the *Dial*. Her mystical sketches, "The Magnolia of Lake Pontchartrain" and "Leila," both dramatized the discovery of a maternal power outside of the realm of the Father; while her essay "Bettine Brentano and Her Friend Günderode" analyzed female roles that offered an alternative to masculinized models of female being. Although many readers assume that Fuller developed her feminist insights when she finished *Woman in the Nineteenth Century,* a close reading of these essays reveals that she had developed many of her most important arguments *before* her travels in the West and the composition of *Summer on the Lakes.* The culmination of this feminist development was the 1843 essay

"The Great Lawsuit," which formed the nucleus of the critique that Fuller later expanded into *Woman in the Nineteenth Century*.

In "The Magnolia of Lake Pontchartrain" Fuller constructs a dialogue between the masculinized consciousness she absorbed from her father and an emerging mother tongue. The essay opens with a male rider whose meditation on "nobleness" is disrupted by an encounter with the Magnolia, a figure "beyond anything [he] had ever known." Telling her story to the rider, the Magnolia recounts her transformation from being an "orange tree," a true woman valued for her cheerful self-sacrifice and "beautiful gifts." One day, she remembers, a cold wind arose and turned her into something "black, stiff, and powerless." The Magnolia's transformation into an isolated "vestal" made her aware of the ways in which her self-image (and by extension, the self-images of all "true women") had been dependent upon masculine standards of beauty. No longer perceived as beautiful or useful, she was cast out by "men":

> Sealed were my fountains and all my heart-beats still. I felt that I had been that beauteous tree, but now only was—what—I knew not; yet I was, and the voices of men said, It is dead; cast it forth and plant another in the costly vase.

But at the very moment she was rejected by a masculinized society, the Magnolia gained access to a previously buried realm of female power—the region of "the queen and guardian of the flowers."

Expanding the image of the mother's garden, Fuller uses the language of flowers to construct a psychological and social allegary about her changed sense of self. In the popular lexicons of the day—works such as Sarah Hale's *Flora's Interpreter* (1833)—each variety of flower was paired with a different emotion or faculty in a discursive system enabling women writers to examine ranges of feeling not easily approached through the medium of ordinary language. While Emily Dickinson was later to use the language of flowers to examine the aggressive dynamics of American gender relations, Fuller here uses this code to evoke a "wild zone" of maternal power that had been suppressed by masculine culture. "Of this being," the Magnolia tells her male auditor, "I cannot speak in any language now possible betwixt us," for this "goddess" is "not such a being as men love to paint." Instead, the Magnolia can only obliquely suggest the existence of a region of "secret, radiant, profound" maternal power: "All the secret powers are 'Mothers.' There is but one paternal power." Opposed to the image of masculine quest with which the sketch opens, Fuller's speaker suggests the possibility of a female quest into the self: "Take a step inward" and "become a vestal priestess and bide thy time in the Magnolia." An important aspect of this reorientation, the Magnolia asserts, is the rejection of patriarchal terminology: "nor shall I again subject myself to be questioned by an alien spirit to tell the tale of my being in words that divide it from itself." The essay closes with the male figure, left to muse on the meaning of the strange being he has just encountered—a conclusion that stages a confrontation between the dominant values of American culture and a mythologized image of female self-reliance.

In "Leila" Fuller took her feminist mythmaking even further. This sketch presents a full-blown description of a goddess figure who is presented both as the narrator's dream-self and as a female savior.[12] Appearing in the narrator's dreams and in her meditations, Leila embodies a transcendent center of maternal power that threatens men and, presumably, male-identified women: "Most men, as they gazed on Leila were pained; they left her at last baffled and well-nigh angry." A preliminary version of the "electrical" self that Fuller associates with the "Muse" in "The Great Lawsuit" and in *Woman in the Nineteenth Century,* the figure of Leila enables Fuller to explore an image of divine and dangerous female power—a being suppressed in mainstream American culture. At times Leila embodies a volcanic energy, a female anger, equivalent to that explored in some of Emily Dickinson's poems. At other moments she symbolizes the damage experienced by the unconventional woman who is punished for her unconventionality. Both aspects are contained in the following characterization: "Leila, with wild hair scattered to the wind, bare and often bleeding feet, opiates and divining rods in each over-full hand, walked amid the habitations of mortals as a Genius, visited their consciences as a Demon." A figure experienced as "demonic" by those who have suppressed maternal power, Leila becomes—in Fuller's mythology—her most significant symbol of woman's buried creativity.

While Fuller's mystical essays expand the mythmaking later underlying *Woman in the Nineteenth Century,* "Bettine Brentano and Her Friend Günderode" introduces several of her most important feminist arguments. Centering on two relationships—between Goethe and Bettine Brentano and between Bettine and Günderode—this essay becomes an extended analysis of the advantages for women of female over male friendship. In Fuller's discussion, Goethe's relationship with Bettine is "unequal" and exploitative, for Bettine is trapped in a position of idolatry, worshiping a distant male figure who relates to her with "the cold pleasure of an observer." Fuller's Goethe is "willing to make a tool of this fresh, fervent being" but is incapable of moving from a visual economy that objectifies Bettine. Anticipating twentieth-century feminists, she details the ways in which such exploitative relationships inhibit female self-development. The antidote to such passive victimization, she insists, is female friendship founded upon "equal expense." In contrast to a masculine aggression that encourages the release of aggressive and competitive urges, she imagines a female intimacy in which young women are able to walk "hand in hand . . . in some garden, laughing, singing, chatting in low tones of mystery, cheek to cheek and brow to brow."

In addition to developing an important concept of female community, this essay refines the dialogic method of "The Magnolia of Lake Pontchartrain." As in the earlier work, Fuller stages a confrontation between male and female figures (in this case, Goethe and Bettine), at the same time she supplements that contrast with two female figures who embody contrasting forms of womanhood—"true woman" and "new woman." Like the "orange tree" in "The Magnolia of Lake Pontchartrain," Bettine is the natural woman often admired by men for her beauty. But instead of portraying Bettine only as a victim, Fuller supplements her beauty with the wild, inspirational power previously associated with the "queen of the flowers" and Leila. Corresponding to this change in Fuller's figure of the true woman is a transformation of the new woman, Günderode. No longer portrayed as the victim of men who "cast" her out (like the Magnolia), she possesses the intellectual capacity to "interpret" Bettine, the natural woman of beauty. The conjunction of Bettine and Günderode sets up the central dynamic of Fuller's feminist model of interpretation. On the one hand, Fuller argues, women must emulate Bettine by finding roles that allow them to jump over "the fences of society as easily as over the fences of the field." But on the other, they must cultivate Günderode's capacity to interpret their being; for without such self-consciousness, they will be trapped in roles written by others, replicating the passivity and subordination of the domesticated woman.

The next year, in 1843, Fuller's "The Great Lawsuit" (the nucleus of *Woman in the Nineteenth Century*) moved even further from dependency with the striking assertion that "the time is come when Euridice is to call for an Orpheus, rather than Orpheus for Euridice." Journeying into the underworld in order to rescue his beloved wife Eurydice from Death, Orpheus was celebrated by male Romantic artists as an image of mastery over Nature, the unconscious, and woman (Richardson 55–60). But in

Fuller's hands, this figure takes on a complexity lacking in the more celebratory allusions of male writers. She knew that Orpheus's great flaw was lack of faith in Eurydice. Having been told by Death that he could only rescue her if he did not look back until after they returned above, Orpheus succumbed to curiosity, only to lose her once again. Interpreting Orpheus as a symbol of man in general, she suggests that he failed to raise Eurydice (woman) up to his level; instead, he left her in the underworld of a half-completed psychological process. Since man has failed to rescue woman, Fuller suggests, it is time to reverse the process and allow woman to rescue man from his own underworld—patriarchal prejudice. But before she can call Orpheus, a woman must recuperate that part of her self that has been trapped with him in the underworld. Having been forced by unforeseen circumstances to work through the disordered mourning of her father, Fuller had learned that the process of mourning could be a source of strength as well as weakness. Only by facing the "death" encrypted within themselves, she came to see, could women learn to free their latent powers. Instead of worshiping monuments of male authority, they needed to find a complementary energy within themselves.

BY THE SPRING OF 1843, after the completion of "The Great Lawsuit," Fuller was ready for a change. Three years of literary self-examination had given her the opportunity to assess her position as an American woman. Her essays and reviews were read and admired by her circle of New England friends. She had reached the point where Emerson, Thoreau, and Hawthorne—three of America's leading writers—treated her as a literary equal if not an intimidating antagonist. Her "Conversations" for Boston women had placed her at the center of an influential and important circle of female intellectuals. But the fervor of 1840–41—the period when Fuller had been animated by a "power" that reshaped her vision of the world—was missing. For the moment, no one had taken the place of either Samuel Ward or Anna Barker. Thus, the opportunity to travel west provided her with a much needed change of situation. With the financial assistance of her friends Sarah Shaw and James Freeman Clarke, Fuller spent the summer of 1843 traveling from Niagara Falls through the Great Lakes to Chicago and into the Wisconsin Territory.

This journey also helped to set the pattern for much of Fuller's mature writing. The immediate literary fruit of her western travels was the volume *Summer on the Lakes, in 1843*, which she finished early in 1844. But many of her succeeding texts—*Woman in the Nineteenth Century*, her New

Introduction

York essays, and her Italian dispatches—were also shaped by the model of travel writing. In many respects these works were also "excursions," taking Fuller through the different realms of female America, urban poverty, and revolutionary Italy. In the process, she self-consciously examined the ways in which the people she encountered were often constrained by the attitudes that travelers like herself often carried with them. Writing to Emerson from the West, Fuller complained of her sense that she lacked a "home," a "place for me to live" (*L* 3: 142, 143). This sense of homelessness, of uprootedness, sensitized her to the precarious efforts of others at settlement. While white male American writers were able to boast of the ways in which they felt "at home," Fuller was learning to see those people who were prevented from achieving such a sense of entitlement.[13]

Summer on the Lakes extends the argument begun in "The Great Lawsuit" by linking the analysis of gender differences to that of racial difference. In this transitional text Fuller moves even further from her middle-class, New England perspective to a wider viewpoint that demystifies the bourgeois complacency of white Americans, with their easy assumption of Manifest Destiny and their sense of superiority to American Indian cultures. Combining the "objectivity" of the travel sketch with the "subjectivity" of autobiography, poetry, and book reviews, she constructs a literary excursion that is an amalgam of genres linked by a common thread—their self-consciousness. In each case the focus falls upon the narrator's reactions to the persons, places, and texts she encounters. As a whole, *Summer on the Lakes* presents models of response to the landscape, to women, and to American Indians—all linked in Fuller's day by gendered fantasies binding them together as available objects of exploitation. By representing her changing reactions to imperialistic, sexist, and racist attitudes, she challenges the ideologies that made the land, women, and racial minorities exploitable commodities.

Her text engages itself with such imperialistic ideologies by adopting and, ultimately, mimicking two familiar modes of landscape writing: the "sublime" and the "picturesque." Each aesthetic mode, she knew, carried with it a set of ideological assumptions that pattern reactions of the individual encountering the sublime or picturesque scene. In this regard, Fuller's depiction of her visit to Niagara Falls takes on interest as a subtle revision of the aesthetics of sublimity celebrated by male artists. Popularized by the theories of Edmund Burke and Immanuel Kant, the poetry of William Wordsworth, and the paintings of Frederick Jackson Turner and Washington Allston, the sublime landscape was expected to shatter the viewer's complacency by exposing him or her to an overpowering scene that evoked wonder and fear. The sheer magnitude or expanse of the spectacle paralyzed normal patterns of response, allowing the release of deeply buried feelings from the unconscious. Since—for the Romantic artist—the unconscious was viewed as the site of transcendent power, experiences of sublimity were cultivated by Fuller's generation either as gateways to the divine or as expressions of the infinite potential of the human mind. In Europe, Mont Blanc became famous as a stimulus to sublimity; while in America, Niagara Falls was the tourist attraction renowned for its sublime effect upon the susceptible viewer. Generations of writers and painters had visited Niagara, recording their experiences of available transcendence.

Encountering the Falls, Fuller found the expected "grandeur—somewhat eternal, if not infinite." But the emphasis of her opening chapter falls less on the experience of transcendence—the typical experience of male viewers—than on her sense of vulnerability. Typically, she was filled with "undefined dread," one of the hallmarks of the sublime. But this dread quickly resolved into the unexpected fantasy of "naked savages stealing behind me with uplifted tomahawks." Her feelings scripted by the familiar discourse of the sublime, which encouraged passivity in the face of overpowering stimuli, Fuller is trapped in the position of victimization. She is not culturally authorized to see the sublime experience as the analogue of creative powers within herself, as are the men who visit the falls. As a woman, she is encouraged to identify with the victims of power not with powerful agency. Instead of being empowered by her visit to Niagara, she finds herself closer to the position of a chained eagle she encounters: "Probably, he listened to the voice of the cataract, and felt that congenial powers flowed free, and was consoled, though his own wing was broken." Like her, this eagle is a victim of a sublime aesthetic that celebrates the image of wildness at the same time that it attempts to control it. As her narrative proceeds, Fuller's attention will fall increasingly on those—for example, women and American Indians—who are perceived as wild by masculinized American culture at the same time that they are "enchained" and have their "wings" broken.

Fuller's discovery of the difficulties of representing the sublime reinforces her sense of vulnerability in the face of imperialistic masculine discourses. Over and over again, she finds herself inhibited by earlier (male) texts that narrow the range of her feelings. As a result, she must struggle for new words to communicate her own experience, which has been contaminated by the ideologically laden representations of others. "Happy were the first discoverers of Niagara," she exclaims at the end of the first chapter, "those who could come unawares upon this view and upon that, whose feelings were entirely their own." If Fuller's fantasy of Indian attack is one example of feelings overwritten by masculine discourse, her recurrent digressions throughout this book remind the reader of the ways in which her experience is inscribed. Her longing for an unmediated connection with her experience—a direct sense of "presence"—thus becomes an impossible ideal that is undercut by the structure of her text. With its surfeit of quotations, *Summer on the Lakes* enacts the process of cultural inscription, while it embodies the desire to regain control of experience. Unable to escape the discourses of others, Fuller *can* revise them—by drawing attention to their ideological effects.

As a nineteenth-century American, Fuller was to varying degrees enmeshed within genres and assumptions that linked her to the very attitudes that she elsewhere critiques. This is nowhere more apparent than in her depictions of "picturesque" places. The nineteenth-century viewer valued the picturesque scene, which was varied, beautiful, light and dark, and marked by a "pleasing" irregularity that motivated aesthetic appreciation. In Fuller's words, "a picturesque and pleasing" scene has "that mixture of culture and rudeness in the aspect of things to give a pleasing effect"; such scenes are "lovely," "beautiful," "friendly," "noble," "pleasant," and "entertaining." But the great liability of the picturesque is its "dissociation of visual, pictorial, or generally aesthetic elements from other values in contemplating a scene," the net result being the isolation of aesthetic enjoyment from moral or political involvement (Price 260). The picturesque gaze detaches the viewer from persons or places, which are judged solely in terms of their appropriation within a specular pleasure. The ugly, the vulgar, and the politically disturbing are either dismissed outright or appreciated for their "irregular" aesthetic qualities. The result—in the words of one of Fuller's characters—is the removal of details "from the demesne of coarse utilities into that of picture."

Such aestheticism motivates much of Fuller's narration in the second and third chapters, which detail her journey into the prairie west of Chicago. Evincing "distaste" at the confusion of western settlement, she attempts to redeem her image of the West with a "sweetness . . . shed over all thoughts." From this viewpoint, the most pleasing moments are visits with settlers who offer her a picturesque beauty set apart from the general "vulgarities" of city life. From the standpoint of aesthetic pleasure, even a site of warfare could be a scene of "romance." But the tendency for Fuller's descriptions to resolve themselves into picturesque moments generates an increasing suspense for the reader. Despite her apparent commitment to a bourgeois aesthetic of picturesque pleasure, she engages herself—at times—with the political and material realities of the persons and places she visits. Early on, for example, she recognizes the "clash of material interests" in the West and the importance of "the position of men's lives, not the state of their minds." But such insights are for the most part submerged in the second chapter beneath an aestheticism that compels her to seek picturesque pleasure at the expense of political awareness.

The tension between aestheticism and sympathetic political engagement, however, finally disrupts the narrative in the third chapter. Continuing her journey into the region of the Rock River, Fuller extols the loveliness and freedom found in the pastoral retreats of some of the region's new landed gentry, who display "unobtrusive good taste" in contrast to "the grossest material wants." Enacting a domesticated sensibility worthy of the most genteel "true woman," she is repelled by the "slovenliness" and "repulsive" quality of other settlers' dwellings, left in a state of ugliness "when so little care would have presented a charming whole." But at a decisive moment, she begins to decenter such middle-class gentility by bringing it into contact with a different mode of apprehension, arising from her contact with the harsh realities of pioneer life for women. Abruptly switching voices in the middle of the chapter, Fuller stops her catalogue of picturesque details to observe:

> The great drawback upon the lives of these settlers, at present, is the unfitness of the women for their new lot. It has generally been the choice of the men, and the women follow, as women will, doing their best for affection's sake, but too often in heartsickness and weariness.

Forced to adopt the "hardest" part, these women find wholly unsuitable a training designed "to make them 'ornaments of society.'" In the place of "fashionable delicacy" they need a resolute strength. If they are to play a domestic role, Fuller concludes, it should be a domesticity that is "new, original" and "different from that of the city belle."

A few pages later, she seems to reassume an aestheticism that allows her to criticize a ferry girl for her "most unpicturesque appearance." But her narrative has been permanently realigned in its perspective. She closes the chapter with a poetic elegy for Washington Allston, perhaps the most famous American painter in the picturesque mode—an ending that leaves the reader with a sweet nostalgia for a pictorial mode that seems to be vanishing: "A tender blessing lingers o'er the scene, / Like some young mother's thought, fond yet serene." In the next two chapters the scene shifts and with it the narrator's perspective, as lengthy digressions interrupt Fuller's description of the West with portraits of two extraordinary women. The first, the story of Mariana, has often been read as a thinly veiled autobiography. The second, an account of the Seeress of Prevorst, tells the story of a European mystic. Notably, the introduction of these accounts coincides with significant changes in the narrator's viewpoint. She recognizes in chapter four, for example, that her almost exclusive "attention" to "the picturesque beauty of this scene" has blinded her to the realities of pioneer women's lives. Similarly, in the next chapter, the picturesque appreciation of the American Indians' romance vanishes in the face of a sympathetic anger at the wrongs they have suffered: "I scarcely see how they can forbear to shoot the white man where he stands." The central challenge for any reader of *Summer on the Lakes* is to explain the way this shift in perspective is linked to the stories of Mariana and the Seeress.

On one level, Fuller's perception of the losses experienced by Mariana and the Seeress allows her to reframe her narrative as an act of mourning. The account of Mariana's transformation at school from a wild, self-centered theatricality into a sympathy for others is marked by the moment when she despairs at the self she has become. Mariana cradles her "grief," holding it "in the arms and to the heart, like a child which makes it wretched, yet is indubitably its own." Mourning her self, she begins to realize the damaging limitations of her earlier position. At the same time, Fuller's representation of Mariana's grief expands into a recognition of the losses experienced by other women. Commenting on a poem "written" by Mariana, a work in which the speaker characterizes herself as a "mourner for . . . martyred love," she observes: "It marks the defect in the position of women that one like Mariana should have found reason to write thus. To a man of equal power, equal sincerity, no more!—many resources would have presented themselves." At this moment, Fuller explicitly links mourning for the self (one's own self and the damaged selves of others) with her feminism. Beginning to be cured of the self-centered enjoyment of its picturesque aesthetic, the narrative opens out into a more involved consideration of marginalized groups—here, suffering women, and in several chapters, persecuted Indians.

But the chastening of Mariana creates a problem Fuller cannot immediately resolve, her gain in "character" at the expense of creativity. If

Introduction

Mariana's unruly energy led her into self-destructive relationships, it was also a momentary source of strength. But she was forced to tame this "wild fire" in her "hour of penitence"—a renunciation that "prevented the world from hearing much of her." By the end of *Summer on the Lakes,* Fuller needs to recover the qualities sacrificed by Mariana. Without them, she will be forced to endorse the outer world of physical realities, sacrificing any connection with the spiritual center that she believes lies at the heart of the self-reliant individual. This is an especially urgent problem, because she has shown the reader that the physical world cannot be viewed "objectively." It has been contaminated by powerful cultural narratives, such as those found in the discourse of the picturesque. Only a countervailing subjectivity founded on a strong faith in the self can offset prevailing cultural myths. Fuller finds such an enabling subjectivity in the story of the Seeress of Prevorst, a narrative that she had alluded to a year earlier in "The Great Lawsuit" as the best example she knew of the "electrical" or "Cassandra" side of woman. Accompanied by the mystical vein that had animated "The Magnolia of Lake Pontchartrain" and "Leila," the extended discussion of the Seeress reestablishes a counterpoise to the cultural pressures documented in earlier chapters.

Significantly, the account of the Seeress is prefaced by a "dialogue" in which appear—among the four characters—Fuller herself (identified as Free Hope) and a parody of Emerson (Self-Poise). Like Emerson, she defends the priority of the inner self as a source of spiritual insight and moral authority. Without this anchor in the "hidden springs of life," she suggests, the person will lack "poise" and can be overwhelmed by external events, which are filtered through ideologically shaped modes of perception. Although neither Emerson nor Fuller can escape from ideology, each cultivates a strong inner self as the source of a potentially liberating consciousness able to differentiate itself from areas of cultural determination. But Fuller parts company with Emerson over her faith in the occult as a source of insight. "I find not in your theory," Free Hope (Fuller) tells Self-Poise (Emerson), "room enough for the lyric inspirations, or the mysterious whispers of life. To me it seems that it is madder never to abandon oneself, than often to be infatuated; better to be wounded, a captive, a slave, than always to walk in armor." This passage provides Fuller with what the Seeress desperately seeks—a new language that is not "broken" and "hackneyed by ages of conventional use." Representing within the self "the presence" of "unseen powers," it establishes a myth of independent female selfhood counterbalancing dominant cultural myths of female sub-ordination and passivity. Although the Seeress is destroyed in the end, Fuller's account of her life demonstrates the possibility that unconventional female spirituality might counteract the cultural imperialism embedded in sublime and picturesque aesthetics.

Fuller's presentation of the Seeress of Prevorst has an important effect upon the narrator's standpoint in *Summer on the Lakes*. Representing a sustained engagement with the subjectivity of another, it necessitates an act of identification that foreshadows later—more sympathetic—portrayals of immigrants and American Indians. Just after the conclusion of the Seeress section, the narrator signals her movement from an earlier, distancing aestheticism by her evocation of the manifold dreams of the immigrants she has been reading about in the paper. Her recognition that the imagination of each person, no matter how foreign, has a validity of its own will be matched by later acceptance of the essential truth of Indian legends. On another level, the story of the Seeress leads to the recognition that the perception of physical phenomena is a blend of the imaginary and the real, of ideology and sense perception. This understanding of the ways dreams and perceptions blend with one another enables Fuller to depict, in the next chapter, both the dreams of American Indian culture and the white nightmares projected onto them.

Recapitulating the structure of the excursion as a whole, Fuller's account in the sixth chapter of her visit with the Chippewa and Ottawa Indians at Mackinaw Island pairs descriptions of their life with narratives cited from numerous texts. Although it begins with portraits of the Indians' "domestic pleasures," this chapter quickly seems to take on the character of an extended book review. But the density of citation combined with the incisiveness of Fuller's commentary makes it clear that her intention is not merely to survey popular accounts of Indian culture but to take this literature as an index of American racism. Although some of the literature provides glimpses of the "beauty and grandeur" of Indian character, many texts—in her eyes—are skewed by prejudices that prevent their authors or readers from taking the "position of the Indians." Distinguishing her own sympathetic viewpoint from such blindness, Fuller accumulates instances of Indian heroism, faith, nobility, and self-sacrifice, which she provides as "a collection of genuine fragments" giving "a glimpse of what was great in Indian life and Indian character." The Indian, she concludes, must be "looked at by his own standard"—not through the eyes of "inherited prejudices" or from the perspective of an imperialistic "civilization."

As the chapter continues, Fuller blends together her critiques of the sexism and racism of American ideology. Resisting the appropriative and masculinized gaze of the picturesque, she asserts a connection between herself and American Indians—a viewpoint that she finally labels a "clear view." Such clarification of vision, the reader comes to see in this penultimate chapter, is one of the primary goals of *Summer on the Lakes,* revealed—for example—at the moment when Fuller links the positions of Indians, Indian women, and white women, all of whom occupy "an inferior position to that of man." Resisting the appropriation of the picturesque gaze, Fuller provides a catalogue of instances revealing the ways in which white Americans, and especially white men, have mystified their brutal power relations with the Indian behind "a veil of subtle evasions." Rather than replicating this "veil," Fuller rends the deceptive tissue of an ideology that has subordinated Indians to masculinized patterns of thought. As in the cases of Mariana and the Seeress of Prevorst, she sees that the American Indians have lost "harmony of being" because they are victimized by a culture that values material gain over nobility of character or spiritual intensity.

The final chapter of *Summer on the Lakes* is marked throughout by a tone of "wasted resources, disjunction, and disappointment" (Adams 252). In recounting her journey back from Mackinaw through Sault St. Marie to the edge of Buffalo, Fuller expresses regret for the many extracts she will not have space to include and the experiences that seem just out of reach. Accentuating her position in a world of absence, she asserts the need for a "more equal, more thorough, more harmonious development," while recognizing that her experiences "did not depend on me." This gap—between the dream of harmony and the awareness of loss—measures the distance opened up by Fuller's critique in the preceding chapters. For one final time, on a day when she takes a canoe ride down some rapids, experience takes on a "power" and a "dewy freshness." But such access to a power of being, *Summer on the Lakes* has shown, is a momentary occurrence often blocked for those trapped within exploitative aesthetics. As "a woman," Fuller has not been granted the authority to diagnose the alienation and oppression marring the lives of many Americans. But as "a person with common sense and good eyesight," she has been able to suggest the ways in which her vision—as well as that of many white Americans—was clouded by modes of writing that assumed the disposability of "broken and degraded" beings.

FULLER completed *Summer on the Lakes* on her thirty-fourth birthday—May 23, 1844—and then "passed the afternoon at Mt Auburn [Cemetery]" (*L* 3: 197) where she "walked gently among the graves" (202). Commenting upon this moment in a letter two days later, she compared the birth of her new book with the child that her sister Ellen delivered on May 22, an event recalling an earlier birth and death—that of her "youngest brother Edward, who died while I held him" (*L* 3: 197). This conjunction of birth and death, of creativity and mourning, echoed the terms of her 1840–41 spiritual crisis, suggesting that Fuller was returning to mourning as a gateway to her deepest psychological energies. But once again, the image of mourning was transformed in her writing into a transcendent vision of female power, especially in the poems Fuller wrote in 1844 while completing *Woman in the Nineteenth Century*.

The earliest of these poems are marked by an almost suicidal melancholy.[14] But as the year progressed, Fuller's poetry gained in spiritual depth and security. Leila, the most profound symbol of her muse, reappeared after a three-year absence, accompanied by Io, Isis, Diana, Mercury, the Sphynx—a weave of mythical figures that concretized the "idea of Woman" celebrated in "The Great Lawsuit" and *Woman in the Nineteenth Century*. Many of these poems function as prayers in which Fuller attempts to define a symbol of wholeness that might resolve the contradictions of her existence. As a whole, they remind us that her deepest moments of introspection, as well as her most effective political actions, were directed by a fervent—although unorthodox—faith. "Yes, others are purer, chaster, kinder than I," she once wrote, "but none more religious. All my life is aspiration."[15]

In her 1844 poetry Fuller refines the psychological symbolism that she first used in "The Magnolia of Lake Pontchartrain" and "Leila." In the "radiant ruby heart" of "My Seal Ring" and the "rosy light" in "Sub Rosa—Crux," she reproduces the symbol of the shining red gemstone or carbuncle, which stands for spiritual purity and fervor. She uses again the image of the serpent (modeled in part on the dragon Typhon from the myth of Isis and Osiris[16]) as an emblem of self-destructive instinctual energies that must be controlled in order for her to advance in spiritual being. In this regard, many of these poems function like the sistrum of Isis, a rattle used by the goddess to frighten away Typhon. Helping the author to control her unruly moods, they allow her to define a sense of personal harmony expressed in part through images of powerful goddesses—Leila, Diana, Sphynx, and Isis. But other images of harmony abound as well—the mandala (in "Double Triangle, Serpent and Rays"), the transfigured being (in "Winged Sphynx"), the sacred marriage. Striving for a balance between the different sides of her personality—father and mother, sun and moon, masculinity and femininity—Fuller works out in these poems many of the symbols and themes that will appear in *Woman in the Nineteenth Century.*

Fuller's finest poem, "Raphael's Deposition from the Cross," suggests the extent to which she was returning in 1844 to the imagery of her earlier spiritual crisis. Once again, she dramatizes a rebirth of the self that involves a transformation of grief, a process preparing the way for vision, what she elsewhere calls winning "the secrets of the tomb."[17] The goal she longs for is a moment of purification and apotheosis—her old self dying into a renewed being in a phoenix-like rebirth. Taking as its occasion Mary's grief for the dead Christ, Fuller represents her own grief for "the heavenly child, / Crucified within my heart." But in the second part of the poem, she realizes the necessity of such suffering—that "power" is reached through the "deepest of distress." By focusing upon the "blight" hidden in the "coffin," she learns how to "escape and bathe in God." In the concluding stanzas the figure of Leila reappears as the embodiment of unconscious energies that have been transformed from dragonish instinct into creative power. Coinciding with this reappearance, death ceases to be a specter—the hiding place of either father or muse—but becomes a source of release: "Planted in a senseless sod / The life is risen to flower a God." At this triumphant moment, all sense of entrapment, frustration, and enclosure falls away. Resurrected from the ashes of her former existence, the Poet rises with a godlike power, fulfilling the Transcendentalist dream of the essential divinity of the self.

As Fuller's mythic poems of 1844 replaced mourning with a renewed assurance, her self-image took on a new maternal quality. It is clear from her journals and letters that the recent births of children to her sister Ellen, Hawthorne's wife Sophia, and Emerson's wife Lydia deeply affected her. But during 1844, while she was composing her best poetry and finishing *Woman in the Nineteenth Century,* she was able to translate her ambivalence about motherhood into powerful mythic images of maternity. Cut off by personal circumstances from the actual experience of bearing and nurturing a child, she imagined herself as sharing maternal qualities, acting as a "Mother" toward one of her female friends (*L* 3: 225) and even comparing herself to the goddess Ceres seeking her lost child, Persephone (*L* 3: 220). Once Fuller released what she called in one of her poems the "prisoned queen," she was able to manifest in public ways the nurturing, maternal qualities that she found through her image of the Goddess.

Near the end of 1844, this quality of maternal care was marked by two significant events in Fuller's life. In October she visited the female inmates at Sing Sing Prison—the first of many visits with the incarcerated women of New York. In November she completed *Woman in the Nineteenth Century* (published in February 1845). Fuller's concern for the fallen and imprisoned women of New York is especially evident in the second half of her text, which she added as she expanded "The Great Lawsuit." "Seek out these degraded women," she exhorts, "give them tender sympathy, counsel, employment. Take the place of mothers, such as might have saved them originally." Several pages later, she argues that the "divine birds" (of human potential) "need to be brooded into life and song by mothers." Such maternal care had been the tie that had bound Fuller's close circle of female friends and which had animated her Boston "Conversations"; now it became a principle of political action, allowing her to focus an ideal of public female nurturance.

Fuller's care for the women of America was matched by an anger at the attitudes binding them. The women that she saw around her had lost "harmony" with themselves and others because they had been corrupted and "enslaved" by a society whose values facilitated female dependence and passivity. Like the Scandinavian goddess Iduna evoked near the end of *Woman in the Nineteenth Century,* they had been "seized and carried away captive" by an ideology that had imprisoned them. Since the minds of Americans had been clouded, Fuller saw the need for a process of clarification that would liberate a "clear, independent judgment" and a "clear-sightedness" enabling men and women to see the damage done to their lives. This process of "disclosure"—as she terms it—reveals the ways in which Americans, and American women especially, have fallen from the "power of self-poise." As she defines this ideal, Fuller once more establishes a dialogue with the model of self-reliance advocated by Emerson. The fault of most women, "Miranda" asserts in a direct paraphrase of Emerson's central tenet, was that they "are taught to learn their rule from without, not to unfold it from within." While challenging Emerson's easy assumption of an independence that was beyond the ability of most nineteenth-century women to attain, Fuller also reveals the way women have been victimized by the patriarchal ideology implicit in his portrait of "self-reliant" existence. Men such as Emerson had been able to define themselves in spiritual terms, but women and slaves were unable to escape the materialistic definition of their selves as commodities.

But while Emerson validates an independent *male* activity, Fuller argues that the fates of men and women are intertwined. A man's marriage is not "a trifle" but rather involves "the closest relations with another soul, which . . . must eternally affect his growth." Rather than defending a society in which men and women occupy different spheres and hold competing values, she envisions a world in which independence and domesticity can be shared by both sexes. "If men look straitly to it, they will find that, unless their lives are domestic, those of the women will not be." Conversely, women need to achieve "a much greater range of occupation than they have, to rouse their latent powers." At the heart of this vision of reform is a radical revision of gender difference. Challenging the widespread nineteenth-century assumption that men and women are essentially different beings, Fuller asserts that they both share masculinity and femininity in differing proportions: "There is no wholly masculine man, no purely feminine woman."[18]

As might be expected, the most difficult and contradictory aspect of Fuller's essay involves her search for a new language to define the masculine and the feminine. Trying to balance the man and woman within, she is "groping toward some sense of identity in a world that had no categories for the particulr mixture she embodied" (Allen 135). She both desires to "exchange" the gendered vocabulary of her culture for "words . . . of a larger sense" and recognizes, near the end of the essay, that "we have not language primitive and pure enough to express such ideas with precision." For most of her discussion she addresses this problem of language by deriving a psychological terminology from classical mythology. Men, she argues, have both a "Vulcan" (masculine) and an "Apollo" (feminine) side; while women combine the feminine qualities of the "Muse" with the masculine qualities of "Minerva."

In important ways, Fuller's definitions of the Muse and Minerva sides of woman challenge some of the most cherished gender assumptions of her culture. The image of the Muse, for example, partially recapitulates the nineteenth-century image of the "true woman" (Welter 21). But if the "true woman" was pious, pure, domestic, and submissive, Fuller's Muse retains primarily vestiges of the first two qualities—piety and purity—at the same time that she embodies a power threatening domesticity and submissiveness. Attacking the image of what she calls the "model-woman of bride-like beauty and gentleness," Fuller directly confronts those who would "mark out with precision the limits of woman's sphere." Her Muse—like the figures of the Queen in "The Magnolia of Lake Pontchartrain," of Leila, of the Seeress of Prevorst, and of Cassandra—expresses an innate female power that she sees as being "electrical in movement, intuitive in function, spiritual in tendency." Rather than articulating a reassuring domesticity, these figures suggest that beneath the civilized veneer of female selfhood exists a powerful creative energy that has the capacity to disrupt conventional definitions of femininity.

Ostensibly a model of female psychology, the paradigm of Muse and Minerva is also an instrument of political analysis. For example, the act of balancing the subversive potential of the Muse's passionate energy against the intellectual discipline of Minerva comments directly upon the repressive limitations of conventional female roles. One of the most warlike of the classical goddesses, Minerva (known to the Greeks as Athena) embodies a fierce and self-reliant independence—what Fuller calls a "virgin," steadfast soul."[19] "Grant her, then, for a while," she asserts, "the armor and the javelin. Let her put from her the press of other minds and meditate in virgin loneliness." Given the nineteenth-century's worship of the mother as the embodiment of a domesticated femininity, this figure strikes at the very heart of middle-class conceptions of gender, which inscribed women with an overlay of "other minds" as thick as the texture of prejudice that Fuller had critiqued in *Summer on the Lakes*. Her portrait of Minerva defined a vision of independent womanhood so threatening that it evoked the misunderstanding and anger of many of her reviewers, one of whom attacked the unmarried Fuller in March 1845 for presuming to discuss the proper role of women. "Woman is nothing but as a wife," Charles F. Briggs pontificated. "How, then, can she truly represent the female character who has never filled it? No woman can be a true woman, who has not been a wife and mother."[20]

At its most ecstatic, Fuller's vision of female independence culminates in what she calls "sacred marriage" (the title of the poem concluding *Woman in the Nineteenth Century*). This image of psychological harmony, a "Union in the Soul," conjoins what Fuller once called the "Woman in me" and the "Man in me." From "the union of this tragic king and queen," she believed, "shall be born a radiant sovereign self" balancing masculinity and femininity, Minerva and Muse, what she had characterized in the "Autobiographical Romance" as the realms of the father's study and the mother's garden. Embodying such psychological harmony, the dominant figure of *Woman in the Nineteenth Century* is the Madonna-like woman of "vestal loveliness" who is "betrothed to the Sun." Escaping from the position of "idolatry," this figure achieves a sense of female selfhood incorporating "masculine" features as *part* of her psyche, instead of subordinating her to an external male world (Harding 153, 187).

At the same time, the symbol of the "sacred marriage" provides Fuller with a paradigm for measuring the shortcomings of mutually exclusive ideals of masculinity and femininity associated with separate and unequal spheres. "Man," she observes near the end of her essay, ". . . was developed first," but "he misunderstood and abused his advantages" and became the "master" of woman rather than her guide. Perpetuating an "unequal union," he "educated woman more as a servant than a daughter, and found himself a king without a queen." The result of masculine domination was a psychological and social disharmony founded upon an oppressive model of gender difference. Ultimately, *Woman in the Nineteenth Century* illustrates the ways in which the misconstruction of gender in America had led to a society that limited woman's self-development both inside and outside the home, leading to paternalistic conceptions of marriage, restricted roles, and sinister forms of sexual exploitation. As she dissects the disproportionate gender roles of men and women, Fuller analyzes women's lack of property rights, the difficulty they faced in escaping abusive or drunken husbands, the hardships of female factory workers and slaves, the absence of educational and vocational opportunities, the lack of effective role models, and their developing "selfish coquetry and petty power" at the expense of political awareness.

In addressing such issues, Fuller infuriated many of her readers by challenging the prevailing hegemony of masculinized values. This is nowhere more clear than in her analysis of the twin issues of "pollution" and prostitution—new elements added in 1844 as she revised and expanded "The Great Lawsuit" into *Woman in the Nineteenth Century*. American men, she argued, had become "degraded" by failing to exercise control "over the lower self." Indulging their "brute nature," they defended a self-serving double standard that allowed them to seduce women and frequent prostitutes. Instead of looking at prostitution as a social evil, they saw it as a necessary sexual outlet, so that in New York "legislators admit that ten thousand prostitutes are a fair proportion to one city." Confronting the repressive, middle-class decorum that declared sexual topics off limits for "respectable" women, Fuller asserts first-hand acquaintance with sexual evil: "I have seen the husband who has stained himself by a long course of low vice." In her concern for the plight of the poor and victimized women of New York, she allied herself with the New York Female Moral Reform Society, which fought to eliminate prostitution and to assist poor and imprisoned women. Recognizing a bond of sisterhood between herself and the "fallen" women of New York, she addressed in November the female inmates at Sing Sing Prison, telling them: "Your angels stand forever there to intercede for you; and to you they call to be gentle and good. Nothing can so grieve and discourage those heavenly friends as when you mock the suffering" (*M* 1: 147). This note of compassion, which was to characterize her *New-York Tribune* essays over the next two years, represents one of the most important fruits of Fuller's years of turmoil. Having wrestled with her own demons, she was now ready to help those less fortunate ones who seemed to have perished in the battle.

AT THE END of 1844 Fuller reached a moment of personal reconciliation. Many of her family responsibilities were coming to an end. Four of her five surviving brothers were in their twenties; her sister Ellen was settling into marriage and motherhood; the old family home in Cambridgeport had just been sold (*L* 3: 228). The composition of her 1844 poems and the completion of *Woman in the Nineteenth Century* embodied her deepest anxieties and her most cherished dreams, while representing the culmination of the mythical strain of her thought. Thus, when Horace Greeley offered her a position as book reviewer and columnist on his *New-York Tribune,* she could not resist the chance at steady employment and a secure public stage reaching thousands of readers. Fuller had played a central role in her family's life and in Boston's literary culture. But her position had changed. "I want that my friends should *wish* me now to act in my public career rather than towards them personally," she wrote to her brother Richard; "I have given almost all my young energies to personal relations. I no longer feel inclined to do this, and wish to share and impel the general stream of thought" (*L* 4: 54). This impetus was evident in the two hundred and fifty articles that Fuller published in the *Tribune* over the next two years, a body of writing ranging from reviews of important American and European writers to commentaries on the contemporary social and political scene. While many of Fuller's *Tribune* pieces consist of brief notices, her best work directly addressed the attitudes of her readers toward contemporary social dilemmas: the institutionalization of the mentally ill, urban poverty, slavery, and the changing status of women.

The first piece that Fuller published after her move to New York in December 1844 was a review of Emerson's *Essays*. Measuring the extent to which she had moved beyond Emerson's influence, this article defined the changes taking place in her literary practice. Emerson had provided her with the impetus to define her own vision of self-reliance, but he had not given her an effective model of social and political change. Despite great merit as America's best "representative of the claims of individual culture," he failed—Fuller argues—to address the whole person. Missing from his writing is the very quality that was to prove central to the literary practices of both female moral reformers and domestic novelists—an articulation of "the deeper needs of the human heart." Lacking the "glow" that can only come from the "free circulation of the heart's blood," Fuller's Emerson provides a brilliant exposition of "spiritual laws," but he misses in the process "the heart and genius of human life." Failing to "lie along the ground long enough to hear the secret whispers of our parent life," he accepts an intellectualized vision of "Truth" as a substitute for the rich complexity of human experience. Like many female reformers of her day, Fuller suggests that the cause of reform can be advanced only by basing it upon the expression of sympathetic feeling—a model of reform culminating, less than a decade later, in the "sentimental power" of such domestic novelists as Harriet Beecher Stowe (Tompkins 141).

Rather than continuing to detail along with Emerson the glories of an ideal realm, Fuller began to turn instead to witness the vicissitudes of life in the metropolis. What she saw shocked her. Her visits with the women in New York's correctional institutions brought her face to face with an urban underclass that had fallen below the threshold of respectability into a purgatory where the simplest domestic details could be maintained only with difficulty. Organized as a brief literary excursion, Fuller's survey "Our City Charities" tackles the problem of moral response that had structured *Summer on the Lakes* and which was to be the topic of Fuller's letter No. XVIII written in Italy—the conflict between a picturesque gaze imposing standards of middle-class respectability and the felt need for sympathetic involvement with its aestheticized victims. At this time, urban correctional institutions were prominent tourist attractions, often visited by those who merely wanted to gawk at the poor, the insane, and the criminal, all of whom functioned as embodiments of an urban picturesque equivalent to aestheticized American Indians. While Fuller admonishes male visitors who examine nursing mothers with "careless scrutiny" and expose new-born infants to the "gaze of the stranger," she herself succumbs to the temptation to see picturesque qualities in some of the inmates—in a Dutch girl with "glowering wizard eye," for example, and in an insane Catholic woman who takes on a "high poetical interest." But at the same time that Fuller partially gives in to an aestheticizing perspective, she recognizes the need to shift public opinion, what she calls "public attention." By addressing the attitudes of her reading audience (and, implicitly, her own viewpoint), she finds a way out of the aesthetic bind, for such critical awareness allows her to defamiliarize her reader's (and her own) ideological complacency.

One of Fuller's most direct examinations of such self-satisfaction is the essay "Prevalent Idea that Politeness is too great a Luxury to be given to the Poor." Positioning herself as a member of the middle-class crowd on one of the city's ferry boats, she addresses the behavior and attitudes of one of her compatriots—a "well-dressed woman" who accosts a poor boy with a series of rude and patronizing questions. Challenging this woman's sense of class superiority, Fuller asserts in the face of her condescension the existence of shared human qualities that cross class barriers and necessitate a "universal obligation of politeness." Such an assertion of shared human identity was characteristic of many reformers during this period. Criticizing the social stratification of individuals according to race, gender, and national origin, new reform societies began to emphasize the "likeness between themselves and the social outcasts with whom they worked" (Berg 218). In the process, they struggled against the ideologically laden representations contained within popular genres such as the emerging domestic novel, the urban excursion, and popular newspaper columns. Challenging the ideology of a middle-class reading audience that could laugh at Irish immigrants or weep at the poor, Fuller labored to de-aestheticize such persons by erasing the artistic frame that kept them safely at arm's length.

At the same time, she began to realign her readers' attitudes by redefining their historical context as one marked by a new "Spirit." By the summer of 1845, Fuller's *Tribune* articles suggested that new literary voice was being given to the claims of "the people" and the "working classes."[21] In August she translated a lengthy review of the recent European social theorists who advanced "Socialism" as "the great Idea of the Age."[22] In "1st January, 1846," she condemned the "lust of gain" that had become the "ruling passion" of America. If "the pure blood shown in the time of our Revolution still glows in the heart," she lamented, America "has scarce achieved a Roman nobleness, a Roman liberty" that might allow it to rise from the ashes like a "Phenix." Using symbols that in 1840 and 1844 had been applied to herself ("glowing" heart, "Phenix"), she began to displace the language of transformation to "those larger individuals, the Nations"—a pattern that she later repeated in Italy when she transposed to the Italian people "qualities that were defined as feminine in *Woman in the Nineteenth Century*" (Ellison 291). Particularly striking is her longing for a rebirth of "Roman nobleness." During 1840 Fuller had achieved a sense of independence as she distanced herself from the "Roman" values of her dead father, values that as late as *Woman in the Nineteenth Century* were portrayed as oppressive to women. But by 1846 the image of Rome stood before her as a beacon luring her to Europe, to a revolutionary fervor she was to find in 1848 in the Roman Republic.

A complicated blend of motives led Fuller to Europe and eventually to Italy. She had dreamed of traveling abroad since her childhood, but her plans for such an excursion had been interrupted in 1835 by the death of her father. Recent American political events, such as the annexation of Texas and the extension of slavery, seemed to reinforce her sense that Europe, not America, might be the place to find a democratic idealism lacking in her own country. She had been reading, translating, and reviewing European writing since the beginning of her career. But a personal incident in New York seems to have been the most significant catalyst behind her decision to travel abroad. Throughout 1845 and 1846 her private life was complicated by a serious romantic involvement with James Nathan, a German businessman who eventually left her to travel Europe with another woman.

Functioning as Fuller's muse, the idealized image of Nathan had promised to bind their "twin spirits" in a "heavenly union" (*L* 4: 75) that would realize the harmony she had imagined at the end of *Woman in the Nineteenth Century*. Her love letters to Nathan expressed her deep longing for a relationship reuniting the surfaces and depths of her self. Since 1840 she had felt the anguish of feeling that her "true life . . . was secluded and veiled over by a thick curtain of available intellect." Despite the mastery of her critical side, she had felt most whole at those moments when her critical temperament was conjoined with spiritual ecstasy. Once again, it seemed, a private occasion presented itself in which she was able to infuse her persona with the energy of both sides—pulling together head and heart, critical consciousness and a sense of divinely inspired creativity. "I wish," she exclaimed to Nathan, "I long to be hunan, but divinely human. Let the soul invest every act of its abode with somewhat of its own lightness and subtlety" (*L* 4: 95). Nathan seems to have offered Fuller a concrete basis for her spiritual intensity, allowing the language of her soul to be "rooted on earth" (96). Significantly, this very union is something that she felt was missing in most of her New York writings, for she complained that the "deep passages" of her "inward life" were not "making any show outwardly" (132). Only in Italy, three years later, would she find a public occasion that provided an adequate vehicle for her pent-up enthusiasm.

When Fuller sailed for England in August of 1846 in the company of her Quaker friends Marcus and Rebecca Spring, she had made arrangements with Horace Greeley to send back regular dispatches for his *New-York Tribune*. Altogether, thirty-six of these travel letters were published on the front page under the heading *Things and Thoughts in Europe*. While the overall significance of Fuller's European dispatches is still the subject of critical debate, there is general agreement that the Italian letters (five of them reprinted here) are among her best work. In Europe she felt once again as if the depths of her being were able to rise to the surface. "It was no false instinct," she wrote from London in November 1846, "that said I might here find an atmosphere needed to develope me in ways *I* need" (*L* 4: 239). At their best, Fuller's accounts of England, Scotland, and France are punctuated with vivid descriptions of working-class life and oppressive social conditions that suggest an emerging involvement with the persons and places she was visiting. But on the whole, her early letters are marked with a touristic detachment that finally vanished in Rome where she found herself personally and politically engaged in a way that she had never been before. "Italy," she exclaimed in September 1847, "receives me as a long lost child and I feel myself at home here" (*L* 4: 293).

Fuller's sense of belonging was fostered by a fortuitous conjunction of political and personal circumstances. Drawn into Italian politics by her friendship with the Italian revolutionary Giuseppe Manzini, whom she met in London, her tie with Italy was cemented by her love affair with one of his followers, Giovanni Ossoli, who would become the father of her son. For the first time in her life, Fuller's personal and political relationships joined to place her at the center of a world in which love and revolutionary fervor could reinforce each other. Since her youth Fuller had been searching for a secure relationship that would allow her to grow from within, instead of being forced to respond to outward stimuli. Ossoli, a deeply devoted and caring person, provided that domestic context. Although she kept her involvement with Ossoli a secret, Fuller's letters home reflected the change in her situation. In Italy she felt that the lure of the picturesque was giving way to a profound and sympathetic engagement. Rather than skirting over the surfaces of things, she began by October 1847 "to live in tranquil companionship, not in the restless impertinence of sight-seeing" (*L* 4: 298). Instead of merely giving "a passing stare at the beautiful body of Italy," she was learning to "come in contact with its soul" (306).

Fuller's desire for "contact" is evident throughout her Letter No. XVIII, written in December 1847 and published in the *Tribune* on 1 January 1848. Placing the three "species" of American travelers on a scale ranging from self-indulgence to empathy, it evaluates the capacity of Americans to appreciate the "mighty idea" of "genuine Democracy" moving the Italian people. In the process, Fuller's depiction of Italy illustrates a "clarification" analogous to that portrayed in *Woman in the Nineteenth Century*. Just as she had challenged her readers to lift the fog of gender stereotypes in order to see the "idea of Woman," she advocates a similar clearing away of political prejudices so that her readers can see the progressive "idea" of Italy. This process shifts both Fuller and her readers from the distanced aestheticism of the tourist, a perspective that frames experience as a quaint "picture" and not as a "reality" animated by political ideals. "What was but picture to us becomes reality," she observes near the beginning of Letter No. XVIII, "remote allusions and derivations trouble no more; we see the *pattern* of the stuff, and *understand the whole tapestry*" (emphasis added). Fuller's experience is meaningful in Italy, because it is part of a political "cause" that illuminates the details of her daily existence and makes the "world intelligible." [23]

As she had done in *Summer on the Lakes*, Fuller differentiates political engagement from an aesthetic view that threatens to turn the Italian people into tourist attractions. Avoiding the tendency of the "servile American" who comes to Europe to "indulge his tastes," she struggles against the middle-class tendency to appropriate the experiences of other cultures. [24] Instead, she argues for a dialogue between the viewpoint of American observers and the political values of the Italian people—a confrontation that would result in the planting of seeds "from the past" in "a new climate and a new culture." Such seeds, the remainder of Letter No. XVIII demonstrates, are not aestheticized museum pieces or souvenirs, but rather the beginnings of political transformation. Audaciously, Fuller breaks down the distance between Italy and America by suggesting that her readers back home had lost touch with a spirit of "Democracy" now to be found in Italy.[25] America, she complains, has become greedy and rapacious, the American "Eagle" having changed into a "vulture" rending the slave population of America and also Mexico. In the face of this corruption of American democratic idealism, she appeals to her audience to be "true" to the "new world" appearing in Italy.

This world was realized during the early months of 1848 when a wave of revolution swept across Europe. Popular uprisings occurred in Sicily, Naples, and Vienna, leading to the hope that the separate states of Italy might be united into one country; while in France the people deposed Louis Philippe, whose rule had seemed to Fuller like "an iron vice."[26] Sharing the enthusiasm of many Boston "literati" who "rejoiced at the 'glorious tidings from Europe,'" she believed that the new wave of democratic idealism emerging in these revolutions had the potential to reshape the political landscape of America as well.[27] In Letter No. XXIII, written in March 1848, Fuller expresses her enthusiasm over the transformation of the Italian people, who seem to her "kindling into pure flame at the touch of a ray from the Sun of Truth." Motivating her American audience to emulate the political commitment of this moment, she provides—in the penultimate passage of her letter—a portrait of a world appearing to come to life before her (and our) eyes: "A million birds sang; the woods teemed with blossoms . . . the surf rushed in . . . I felt the calm of thought, the sublime hopes of the Future, Nature, Man."

Fuller had personal reasons as well for her enthusiasm at the new "emotions . . . swelling the hearts of men." Now three months pregnant, she perceived the quickening of new energies both in the people and in herself. In late May she hid her pregnancy by leaving Rome. Whether or not she had married Giovanni Ossoli by this point (or whether she ever formally married him) remains an open question. On September 5 she gave birth to a son, Angelo, in Rieti; then, in mid-November, she was forced to leave her new-born child in the care of a nurse so that she could return to Ossoli. Giovanni had been with Fuller for the birth of Angelo, but as an officer in the Civic Guard he was recalled to Rome because of the increasingly tense political situation. Austrian troops had already invaded northern Italy in order to quell the uprisings in Milan, Venice, and Lombardy. As they moved closer to Rome, the people eagerly awaited the Pope's response.

Initially, Pius IX had seemed to support the cause of Italian reunification. But in the face of open war in Italy, he wavered and then shifted to a conservative position, going so far as to appoint as his minister Pellegrino Rossi, an ambassador of the deposed French king (*WM* 384–86). Returning to Rome at this politically dramatic moment, Fuller captures the excitement of history in the making of her Letter No. XXVI. Shortly after her arrival, Rossi—a symbol of oppression for the Roman people—was assassinated, an event which precipitated the flight of Pope Pius IX from Rome and paved the way for the eventual declaration of the Roman Republic. Zooming in to the precise moment when she learned of the assassination, Fuller presents what seems to be an eye-witness account of the scene of Rossi's death in a passage so vivid that it is difficult to believe that she was not present. Then, in the remainder of her letter, she presents an almost cinematic portrait of an unfolding historical moment that is anchored—at the end—by a plea for American support of the emerging Roman Republic. Near the opening of this dispatch, Fuller comments upon the difficulty of capturing "the truest life of our day." But her careful blending of detail and political generalization epitomizes the new style of history writing that she was shaping in Italy. Both *Summer on the Lakes* and *Woman in the Nineteenth Century* had been slowed by a dense fabric of allusions and references.[28] But in her representation of the Italian revolutionary movement, Fuller found a political context that gave life to the details of her experience, "rooting" her writing "in the material and the actual" (*WM* 374).

The expense of revolution was brought home, however, after French troops, in order to restore the Pope to power, surrounded Rome and began bombing the city. Fuller, who had accepted a position as the director of the Hospital of the Fate Bene Fratelli, now saw firsthand the agonies of wounded and dying soldiers. Finally, on 30 June 1849, French troops, commanded by General Oudinot, entered Rome and began their occupation. In Letter No. XXXIII, Fuller dramatizes her reaction to the fall and occupation of Rome. Griefstricken by the slaughter around her, she identifies herself and the women of Rome with the mythical figure of Niobe, a mother whose pride was punished by the killing of her seven sons and seven daughters.[29] This image of mourning received its full expression five months later in a letter Fuller wrote in December. Recalling the destruction of Rome and the death of its heroic youth, she once again cast herself in the role of grieving Mary, the weeping mother: "But when I saw the beautiful fair young men bleeding to death, or mutilated for life, I felt all the wo of all the mothers who had nursed each to that full flower to see it thus cut down. I felt the consolation too for those youths died worthily. I was the Mater Dolorosa" (*L* 5: 293).

In the economy of Fuller's creative rhythms, mourning always seemed to lead to insight, defeat to a sense of victory. "O, it has ever been thus," she wrote in October 1840, "from the darkest comes my brightness, from Chaos depths my love" (*L* 2: 168). Thus, in her spiritual crisis of 1840–41, the "snowy shroud" of Fuller's "Northern winter" transformed into a renewed energy. During the tumultuous summer and fall of 1844, she again moved from a period of mourning to the triumphant resurrection of her buried self in the conclusion of "Raphael's Deposition from the Cross." One final time, in her last published work—"Special Correspondence of The Tribune, Jan. 6, 1850"—she defined a rhythm of grief and transformation. But this time, the object of hope was not her damaged self but the Italian nation. The dispatch opens with a somber image of Italy, "shrouded with snow," undergoing a harsh winter in which the "houseless wanderer" suffers. But as in 1840 and 1844, wintry despair gives way to a vision of fiery energy that will be reborn phoenix-like from the ashes of the failed Roman revolution. Transforming the image of defeat into a "fierce visionary beauty,"[30] she prophesies that the failure of the Roman Republic will be only a momentary setback in a larger revolutionary struggle. Ultimately, she predicts, a "New Era" will be "born," as the spirit of democratic equality triumphs over arbitrary authority.

This final blend of personal engagement and political commitment, of experience and vision, seems exemplary of Fuller's entire career. Measuring both her life and—eventually—the lives of others against fervently held ideals, she articulated in her writing the conscience of America. It was a conscience sorely missed after she, Ossoli, and their child drowned in a shipwreck off Fire Island on 19 July 1850. After her death Emerson lamented that "I have lost in her my audience" (*JMN* 11: 258). Two years later, in 1852, Emerson, along with James Freeman Clarke and William Henry Channing, commemorated Fuller in the *Memoirs of Margaret Fuller Ossoli*. This work was deeply flawed by the editors' tendency to mythologize Fuller and by their felt need to legitimize her relationship with Ossoli. Still, it remains to this day one of the most important sources of information about her life. Unavoidably, the image of Margaret Fuller had already started to pass into American folklore. Hawthorne used her ideas and her charismatic personality as the model for Zenobia in *The Blithedale Romance* (also published in 1852). As late as 1903, Henry James referred to the "haunting Margaret-ghost" in *William Wetmore Story and His Friends.*

But the impact of Fuller's life and death was most clearly felt in the woman's movement in America. With her pioneering literary career as an editor, journalist, and essayist, she proved an inspiring model for later women writers, some of them—such as Lydia Maria Child, Elizabeth Peabody, and Caroline Healey Dall—her students in the Boston "Conversations." Paulina Wright Davis, the organizer of the 1850 woman's rights convention, expressed the regret that Fuller had not lived to assume control of the emerging movement.[31] After her death, however, Fuller left behind a legacy that led Elizabeth Cady Stanton and Susan B. Anthony to declare, in their monumental *History of Woman Suffrage,* that she "possessed more influence upon the thought of American women than any woman previous to her time."[32] Today, we can see that influence in Fuller's published writings and in her more private texts, which together portray her struggle for self-definition during an age that seemed to provide no adequate models for her multifaceted vision.

1. While it has been the source of enormous and unresolved controversy as to whether or not Margaret Fuller and Giovanni Ossoli were ever married, their relationship—at the very least—fulfilled the requirements of a common-law marriage.

2. Judith Fetterly connects Kirkland's depiction of the "western rural frontier" with Child's portrayal of the "eastern urban frontier" (163).

3. None of Fuller's brothers seems to have been capable of supporting her family, so that—after her father's death—she was forced to assume financial leadership of the household.

4. During the months of October and November between 1837 and 1839, for example, Fuller was "miserably unwell" (*L* 1: 303), so ill that she "could attend to nothing that was not absolutely necessary" (*L* 1: 310), convinced that "the secret of all things is pain" (*L* 1: 347), praying that she might find some peace in "vestal solitudes" (*L* 1: 351), hoping that she might recover her "natural tone of health and spirits" (*L* 1: 352), and victimized by a three-week long headache (*L* 2: 98).

5. Fuller translated a succession of German works, focusing upon Goethe and his circle. She translated Goethe's drama *Torquato Tasso* "sometime around 1833" (Zwarg, "Feminism" 471). She published *Eckermann's Conversations with Goethe* in 1839 and *Correspondence of Fräulein Günderode with Bettine von Arnim* in 1842. Christina Zwarg argues persuasively that Fuller's German translations "enabled her to decanonize her literary fathers without destroying them" (465). In a sense they provided Fuller with a countertradition—a different route into the German literature that was an important source of American Romanticism.

6. Pike 310; Tolchin xii.

7. One might compare Fuller's position with Cixous's assertion: "She has

never 'held still'; explosion, diffusion, effervescence, abundance, she takes pleasure in being boundless, outside self, outside same, far from a 'center,' from any
capital of her 'dark continent'. . . . Masculine energy, with its limited oil reserves,
questions itself. Whereas, the fact that feminine energy has vast resources is not
without consequences—still very rarely analyzed—for exchange in general, for
love-life, and for the fate created for woman's desire" (Cixous and Clément 91).

 8. *LE* 2: 258. Polyanthos, adapted from the Greek, "having many flowers or
blossoms."

 9. These alternative forms of community were theorized in the works of
Robert Owen and Charles Fourier, as well as in the works of Karl Marx, who
wrote in the 1840s: "Only in community has each individual the means of cultivat-
ing his gifts in all directions; only in the community . . . is personal freedom
possible" (193).

 10. For an evocative discussion of the way Fuller transformed the image of
the mother's garden in her 1843 book, *Summer on the Lakes,* see Annette Kolodny's
chapter "Margaret Fuller: Recovering Our Mother's Garden."

 11. Compare with Julia Kristeva: "It is thus that female specificity defines
itself in patrilinear society: woman is a specialist in the unconscious, a witch, a
baccanalian, taking her *jouissance* in an anti-Apollonian, Dionysian orgy" (154).

 12. The idea of a female savior appeared in England with Joanna Southcott,
"the Woman clothed with the sun," who became the focus of a cult that worshiped the image of liberated woman as the bride of Christ (Taylor 162–66); in
America, the Shakers followed a female Redeemer "Mother Ann" Lee, who
preached that "God had a dual nature, part male and part female" (Welter 87).

 13. While the phrase "at home" is cited from Walt Whitman's "Song of
Myself," which was published after Fuller's death, she encountered similar attitudes in the writings of Emerson, Thoreau, and Bronson Alcott.

 14. This vein is most noticeable in the following verses, which Fuller wrote
on 22 April: "Death / Opens her sweet white arms and whispers, peace! / Come
say thy sorrows in this bosom! This / Will never close against thee; and my
heart / Though cold cannot be colder much than man's" (MB).

 15. Journal fragments included at the end of MHi, 1844 Commonplace
Book 173.

 16. Associating the figure of Typhon with instinct and irrationality, Fuller
once observed "I have a great share of Typhon to the Osiris, wild rush and leap,
blind force for the sake of force" (*M* 1: 230).

 17. "To the Face seen in the Moon."

 18. One might compare Fuller's position with that of Hélène Cixous, who
argues in favor of what she terms "bisexuality"—"the location within oneself of
the presence of both sexes" (Cixous and Clément 85).

 19. Plutarch, in the *Morals,* associated Minerva with the Egyptian goddess
Isis. The Egyptians, Plutarch notes, "oftentimes call Isis by the name of Minerva,

which in their languages expresseth this sentence, 'I came from myself,' and is significative of a motion proceeding from herself" (4: 120–21).

20. Charles F. Briggs, review of *Woman in the Nineteenth Century* (*Broadway Journal,* Mar. 1845), rpt. in Myerson ed., *Critical Essays on Margaret Fuller* 9–10.

21. These phrases come from "The Poets of the People," *New-York Daily Tribune,* 26 July 1845, and "Prince's Poems," *New-York Daily Tribune,* 13 Aug. 1845.

22. "The Social Movement in Europe," *New-York Daily Tribune,* 5 Aug. 1845. Fuller's involvement with utopian socialism had dated back to her days at Brook Farm, a community modeled in part on the theories of Charles Fourier, whose ideas also informed both *Summer on the Lakes* and *Woman in the Nineteenth Century.*

23. Chevigny, "To the Edges of Ideology" 179.

24. Dean MacCannell writes: "It is the middle class that systematically scavenges the earth for new experiences to be woven into a collective, touristic vision of other peoples and other places." The goal is "to coordinate the differentiations of the world into a single ideology" (13).

25. According to Chevigny, Fuller hoped "to repatriate the American project" by demonstrating that "the essence of America is to be found in Europe" ("To the Edges of Ideology" 189).

26. Julia Kristeva discusses the antiauthoritarian and populist aspects of the "carnivalesque" in her essay "Word, Dialogue and Novel" (36, 48, 49).

27. Reynolds 15; the phrase "glorious tidings from Europe" is Longfellow's.

28. According to Julie Ellison, the rhetoric of *Woman in the Nineteenth Century* is impeded by this "flood of cultural associations" (277).

29. Ovid's account of Niobe in book 8 of the *Metamorphoses* concludes with the transformation of Niobe into a stone statue surrounded by the dead bodies of her children—a passage echoed in Fuller's image of a "marble nymph, with broken arm" gazing at the corpses of thirty-seven soldiers. According to Ellison, this figure embodies "the look of sadness that Rome casts over itself and that Fuller casts over Rome" (297). Shakespeare's Hamlet compares his mother's grief to that of "Niobe, all tears" (I.ii.149)—a reference suggesting that Fuller's choice of Niobe here connects her grief for Rome with that for her father, the man who taught her to admire Roman heroism.

30. Reynolds 72–73.

31. Flexnor, *Century of Struggle* 246n.

32. *The History of Women's Suffrage* 1: 801 (cited in Flexnor 347).

SELECTED BIBLIOGRAPHY

The following abbreviations are used in the introduction:

JMN *The Journals and Miscellaneous Notebooks of Ralph Waldo Emerson.* Ed. William H. Gilman, Alfred R. Ferguson, George P. Clark, et al. Cambridge, MA: Harvard UP, 1960–82.

L *The Letters of Margaret Fuller.* Ed. Robert N. Hudspeth. Ithaca: Cornell UP, 1983–.

LE *The Letters of Ralph Waldo Emerson.* Ed. Ralph L. Rusk. New York: Columbia UP, 1939.

M *The Memoirs of Margaret Fuller Ossoli.* Ed. Ralph Waldo Emerson, James Freeman Clarke, and William Henry Channing. Boston: Phillips, Sampson, 1852.

MB Fuller papers, Boston Public Library.

MH Fuller papers, Houghton Library, Harvard University.

MHi Fuller papers, Massachusetts Historical Society.

WM Chevigny, Bell Gale. *The Woman and the Myth: Margaret Fuller's Life and Writings.* Old Westbury, NY: Feminist Press, 1976.

OTHER WORKS BY MARGARET FULLER

Goethe, Johann Wolfgang. *Torquato Tasso* (trans. c. 1833). Pub. posthumously as "Tasso" in *Art, Literature, and the Drama,* ed. Arthur B. Fuller. Boston: Crosby, Nichols, 1856.

1

Selected Bibliography

Eckermann's Conversations with Goethe (trans.). Boston: Hilliard, Gray, 1839.
"A Short Essay on Critics." The *Dial* July 1840.
"A Record of Impressions Produced by the Exhibition of Allston's Pictures in the Summer of 1839." The *Dial* July 1840.
"Menzel's View of Goethe." The *Dial* Jan. 1841.
"A Dialogue: Poet and Critic." The *Dial* Apr. 1841.
"Goethe." The *Dial* July 1841.
"Lives of the Great Composers: Haydn, Mozart, Handel, Bach, Beethoven." The *Dial* Oct. 1841.
"Hawthorne's 'Twice-Told Tales.'" The *Dial* July 1842.
"Romaic and Rhine Ballads." The *Dial* Oct. 1842.
Correspondence of Fräulein Günderode with Bettine von Arnim (trans. pub. as *Günderode*). Boston: E. P. Peabody, 1842.
"The Great Lawsuit." The *Dial* July 1843.
"Dialogue." The *Dial* April 1844.
"Miss Barrett's Poems." *New-York Daily Tribune* 4 Jan. 1845.
"St. Valentine's Day—Bloomingdale Asylum for the Insane." *New-York Daily Tribune* 22 Feb. 1845.
"Frederick Douglass." *New-York Daily Tribune* 10 June 1845.
"The Poets of the People." *New-York Daily Tribune* 26 July 1845.
"Prince's Poems." *New-York Daily Tribune* 13 Aug. 1845.
"L. M. Child's *History of Women*." *New-York Daily Tribune* 20 Nov. 1845.
"First of January, 1846." *New-York Daily Tribune* 1 Jan. 1846.
"The Rich Man—An Ideal Sketch." *New-York Daily Tribune* 6 Feb. 1846.
"Mistress of herself, though china fall." *New-York Daily Tribune* 15 Apr. 1846.
Papers on Literature and the Arts (a collection of articles and reviews). New York: Wiley and Putnam, 1846.

WORKS CITED AND FURTHER READING

Adams, Stephen. "'That Tidiness We Always Look For in Woman': Fuller's *Summer on the Lakes* and Romantic Aesthetics." *Studies in the American Renaissance* (1987): 247–64.
Allen, Margaret Vanderhaar. *The Achievement of Margaret Fuller.* University Park, PA: Pennsylvania State UP, 1979.
Berg, Barbara J. *The Remembered Gate: Origins of American Feminism.* Oxford and New York: Oxford UP, 1978.

Selected Bibliography

Berkson, Dorothy. "'Born and Bred in Different Nations': Margaret Fuller and Ralph Waldo Emerson." *Patrons and Protégées: Gender, Friendship, and Writing in Nineteenth-Century America.* Ed. Shirley Marchalonis. New Brunswick and London: Rutgers UP, 1988.

Blanchard, Paula. *Margaret Fuller: From Transcendentalism to Revolution.* New York: Dell, 1979.

Buell, Lawrence. *Literary Transcendentalism: Style and Vision in the American Renaissance.* Ithaca and London: Cornell UP, 1973.

Capper, Charles. "Margaret Fuller as Cultural Reformer: The Conversations in Boston." *American Quarterly* 39 (1987): 509–28.

Chevigny, Bell Gale. "Daughters Writing: Toward a Theory of Women's Biography." *Feminist Studies* 9 (1983): 79–102.

——. "Growing Out of New England: The Emergence of Margaret Fuller's Radicalism," *Women's Studies* 5 (1977): 65–100.

——. "To the Edges of Ideology: Margaret Fuller's Centrifugal Evolution." *American Quarterly* 38 (1986): 173–201.

Chodorow, Nancy. *The Reproduction of Mothering: Psychoanalysis and the Sociology of Gender.* Berkeley and Los Angeles: U. of California P, 1978.

Cixous, Hélène and Catherine Clément, *The Newly Born Woman.* Trans. Betsy Wing & introd. Sandra Gilbert. Minneapolis: U of Minnesota P, 1986.

Ellison, Julie. *Delicate Subjects: Romanticism, Gender, and the Ethics of Understanding.* Ithaca and London: Cornell UP, 1990.

Fetterly, Judith, ed. & introd. *Provisions: A Reader from 19th-Century American Women.* Bloomington: Indiana UP, 1985.

Flexnor, Eleanor. *Century of Struggle: The Woman's Rights Movement in the United States.* 1959. Rpt. New York: Atheneum, 1973.

Hale, Sarah Josepha. *Flora's Interpreter: or, the American Book of Flowers and Sentiments.* Boston: Thomas H. Webb, 1833.

Harding, Esther. *Women's Mysteries: Ancient and Modern.* New York: Longmans, Green, 1935.

Higginson, Thomas Wentworth. *Margaret Fuller Ossoli.* 1884. Rpt. New York: Confucian P, 1980.

Hudspeth, Robert, ed. *The Letters of Margaret Fuller.* 5 vols. to date. Ithaca: Cornell UP, 1983–.

Kolodny, Annette. *The Land before Her: Fantasy and Experience of the American Frontiers, 1630–1860.* Chapel Hill: U of North Carolina P, 1984.

Kristeva, Julia. *The Kristeva Reader.* Ed. Toril Moi. New York: Columbia UP, 1986.

Selected Bibliography

Leverenz, David. *Manhood and the American Renaissance.* Ithaca and London: Cornell UP, 1989.

MacCannell, Dean. *The Tourist: A New Theory of the Leisure Class.* New York: Schocken, 1976.

Marx, Karl. *The Portable Karl Marx.* Ed. Eugene Kamenka. New York: Penguin, 1983.

Myerson, Joel, ed. *Critical Essays on Margaret Fuller.* Boston: G. K. Hall, 1980.

————. *Margaret Fuller: A Descriptive Bibliography.* Pittsburgh: U of Pittsburgh P, 1978.

————, ed. *Margaret Fuller: Essays on American Life and Letters.* New Haven: College & University P, 1978.

Plutarch's Morals: Translated from the Greek by Several Hands. Ed. William W. Goodwin, 5 vols. Boston: Little, Brown, 1878.

Porte, Joel. *Representative Man: Ralph Waldo Emerson in His Time.* New York: Oxford UP, 1979.

Price, Martin. "The Picturesque Moment." In *From Sensibility to Romanticism.* Ed. Frederick W. Hilles and Harold Bloom. London and New York: Oxford UP, 1965. 259–92.

Reynolds, Larry J. *European Revolutions and the American Literary Renaissance.* New Haven and London: Yale UP, 1988.

Richardson, Robert D., Jr. *Myth and Literature in the American Renaissance.* Bloomington and London: Indiana UP, 1978.

Schorsch, Anita. *Mourning Becomes America: Mourning Art in the New Nation.* Clinton, NJ: Main Street P, 1976.

Smith-Rosenberg, Carroll. *Disorderly Conduct: Visions of Gender in Victorian America.* New York: Knopf, 1985.

————. "Writing History: Language, Class, and Gender." *Feminist Studies/ Critical Studies.* Ed. Teresa de Lauretis. Bloomington: Indiana UP, 1986.

Stansell, Christine. *City of Women: Sex and Class in New York, 1789–1860.* Urbana and Chicago: U of Illinois P, 1987.

Steele, Jeffrey. "The Call of Eurydice: Mourning and Intertextuality in Margaret Fuller's Writing." In *Influence and Intertextuality in Literary History.* Ed. Eric Rothstein and Jay Clayton. Madison: U of Wisconsin P, 1991.

————. "Freeing the 'Prisoned Queen': The Development of Margaret Fuller's Poetry." *Studies in the American Renaissance,* 1992.

————. *The Representation of the Self in the American Renaissance.* Chapel Hill and London: U of North Carolina P, 1987.

Selected Bibliography

Taylor, Barbara. *Eve and the New Jerusalem: Socialism and Feminism in the Nineteenth Century*. New York: Pantheon, 1983.

Tolchin, Neal. *Mourning, Gender, and Creativity in the Art of Herman Melville*. New Haven & London: Yale UP, 1988.

Tompkins, Jane. *Sensational Designs: The Cultural Work of American Fiction 1790–1860*. New York and Oxford: Oxford UP, 1985.

Welter, Barbara. *Dimity Convictions: The American Woman in the Nineteenth Century*. Athens: Ohio UP, 1976.

Zwarg, Christina. "Feminism in Translation: Margaret Fuller's *Tasso*." *Studies in Romanticism* 29 (1990): 463–90.

———. "Womanizing Margaret Fuller: Theorizing a Lover's Discourse." *Cultural Critique* 16 (Fall 1990): 161–91.

CHRONOLOGY

1810   May 23, Margaret Fuller born in Cambridgeport, MA, the first child of Timothy Fuller and Margarett Crane Fuller.

1813   Her 18-month-old sister Julia dies.

1815   Brother Eugene is born.

1817   Brother William Henry is born; Timothy Fuller begins serving the first of four terms in the U.S. House of Representatives.

1818   Meets Ellen Kilshaw, the "first friend" described in the "Autobiographical Romance."

1820   Sister Ellen is born.

1821   Attends the school of Dr. John Park in Boston.

1822   Brother Arthur is born.

1824   Brother Richard is born.

1824–25   Attends Miss Prescott's Young Ladies Seminary at Groton, MA, the setting of the "Mariana" episode in *Summer on the Lakes*.

1826   Brother Lloyd is born.

1828   Brother Edward is born on her 18th birthday.

1829   September 15, her brother Edward dies in her arms.

1833   Timothy Fuller moves his family from Cambridge to Groton; she translates Goethe's drama, *Torquato Tasso*.

1834   Publishes her first essay, "In Defense of Brutus," in the *Boston Daily Advertiser & Patriot*.

Chronology

1835   March, plans to write a series of tragedies and short stories; June, her friend James Freeman Clarke becomes an editor of the *Western Messenger,* a liberal journal that publishes seven of Fuller's early reviews and articles over the next three years; October 1, Timothy Fuller dies of cholera—an event canceling Margaret's planned European trip with John and Eliza Farrar.

1836   July, meets Ralph Waldo Emerson; teaches at Bronson Alcott's Temple School; September, Emerson publishes *Nature.*

1837   Begins teaching at the Greene Street School in Providence.

1838   July, Emerson delivers his controversial "Divinity School Address."

1839   May, publishes *Eckermann's Conversations with Goethe;* agrees to edit the *Dial;* November, begins first series of "Conversations" with the topic "Greek Mythology."

1840   July, the first issue of the *Dial* appears; begins her "Autobiographical Romance" (probably while visiting Emerson in August); October, the marriage of Samuel Gray Ward and Anna Barker precipitates a spiritual crisis lasting through the winter; November, starts writing "The Magnolia of Lake Pontchartrain" and begins series of "Conversations" on the "Fine Arts."

1841   January, publishes "The Magnolia of Lake Pontchartrain"; March, Emerson publishes *Essays: First Series* in which the essay "Friendship" borrows liberally from his correspondence with Fuller; April, publishes "Leila"; July, publishes critical essay "Goethe"; September, sister Ellen marries William Ellery Channing after a tempestuous courtship; November, begins series of "Conversations" on "Ethics."

1842   January, publishes "Bettine Brentano and Her Friend Günderode"; March, publishes translation of *Correspondence of Fräulein Günderode with Bettine von Arnim* and resigns editorship of the *Dial;* November, begins series of "Conversations" on religion, education, and the position of women.

1843   May, finishes "The Great Lawsuit"; May–September, with the financial assistance of Sarah Shaw and James Freeman Clarke, travels through the Great Lakes to Wisconsin

Chronology

Territory with Sarah Freeman Clarke; November, begins series of "Conversations" on "Education."

1844   April, concludes final class in her "Conversations"; May, publishes *Summer on the Lakes, in 1843;* May, her sister Ellen gives birth to a daughter; April–November, writes over thirty poems; November, visits female prisoners at Sing Sing and finishes *Woman in the Nineteenth Century* at Fishkill, NY; December, moves to Horace Greeley's household in New York and takes a position as a book reviewer and social analyst for his *New-York Tribune.*

1845   February, publishes *Woman in the Nineteenth Century;* meets and falls in love with James Nathan, a German businessman who eventually leaves her.

1846   Publishes *Papers on Literature and Art,* an anthology of literary criticism; August, sails to Europe with Marcus and Rebecca Spring as a foreign correspondent for the *New-York Tribune;* visits England, Scotland, and Paris.

1847   Travels to Italy; meets Giovanni Ossoli.

1848   Uprisings in Italy, Austria, and France; September 5, gives birth to her son Angelo Ossoli in Rieti; November, assassination of Pellegrino Rossi and flight of the Pope Pius IX from Rome.

1849   February, Roman Republic declared; June, the French general Oudinot bombs and invades Rome, restoring the Pope to power; September, moves to Florence with her family.

1850   January 6, publishes her final work, "Special Correspondence of The Tribune"; May, sails for America in the *Elizabeth;* July 19, drowns with Ossoli and Angelo in a shipwreck off Fire Island, NY.

A NOTE ON THE TEXT

Margaret Fuller's writing presents special textual difficulties. After her death, some texts were published in corrupt versions edited by her brother, Arthur Fuller. Many of her manuscripts were dismembered by the editors of the posthumous *Memoirs of Margaret Fuller Ossoli*. In some cases journals were cut apart and excised selections were pasted into the hand-written draft of the *Memoirs* sent to the printer. Many of these texts were destroyed, although fragments of Fuller's journals (and in some cases, complete journals) exist in the Houghton Library, the Boston Public Library, the Massachusetts Historical Society, and the Fruitlands Museum.

The texts in this anthology were compiled from manuscripts and editions of Fuller's work at the Boston Public Library, Fruitlands Museum, Harvard University, Massachusetts Historical Society, and the University of Wisconsin. I have retained Fuller's punctuation and spelling including the following idiosyncratic usages: "develope" for "develop," "hight" for "height," "recal" for "recall," "phenix" for "phoenix," and "wo" for "woe." Obvious misspellings of persons' names and missing punctuation marks in published works have been silently corrected. Punctuation has not been added to or changed in journal entries, where periods are occasionally missing. An obvious printer's error in Mariana's song in *Summer on the Lakes* ("burd" for "lyred") has been corrected through comparison with Fuller's manuscript of the poem. Bibliographical information is as follows:

Self-Definitions, 1835–1842. *Memoirs of Margaret Fuller Ossoli*. Boston: Phillips, Sampson, 1852; manuscripts at Houghton Library, Harvard University, and the Boston Public Library.

A Note on the Text

"Autobiographical Romance." *Memoirs of Margaret Fuller Ossoli.*

"The Magnolia of Lake Pontchartrain." The *Dial* Jan. 1841.

"Leila." The *Dial* Apr. 1841.

"Bettine Brentano and Her Friend Gunderode." The *Dial* Jan. 1842.

Summer on the Lakes, in 1843. 2d ed. Boston: Charles C. Little and James Brown, 1844.

1844 Poetry. Manuscripts at Boston Public Library, Fruitlands Museum, Houghton Library, and Massachusetts Historical Society.

Woman in the Nineteenth Century. 1st ed. New York: Greeley & McElrath, 1845.

New York essays and *Things and Thoughts in Europe.* Articles in the *New-York Daily Tribune* and *New-York Weekly Tribune* Dec. 1844–Jan. 1850.

THE ESSENTIAL MARGARET FULLER

SELF-DEFINITIONS, 1835–42

TO A.H.B.[1]

On our meeting, on my return from N.Y.
to Boston, August 1835. — *Written Jany 1836*

Brief was the meeting,—tear-stained, full of fears
  For future days, and sad thoughts of the past,—
  Thou, seeing thy horizon overcast,
Timid, didst shrink from the dark-coming years;
And I, (though less ill in mine appears,)
    Was haunted by a secret dread of soul,
    That Fate had something written in her scroll
Which soon must ope again the fount of tears;
    Oh could we on the waves have lingered then,
Or in that bark, together borne away,
    Have sought some isle far from the haunts of men,
Ills left behind which cloud the social day,
    What grief I had escaped; yet left untried
    That holy faith by which, now fortified,
    I feel a peace to happiness allied;—
And thou, although for thee my loving heart
Would gladly some Elysium set apart,
From treachery's pestilence, and passion's strife,
Where thou might'st lead a pure untroubled life,
Sustained and fostered by hearts like thy own,
The conflicts which thy friend must brave, unknown,—
Yet I feel deeply, that it may be best
For thee as me, that fire the gold should test,
And that in God's good time we shall know perfect rest!

TO THE SAME. A FEVERISH VISION.

After a day of wearying, wasting pain,
  At last my aching eyes I think to close;—
  Hoping to win some moments of repose,
Though I must wake to suffering again.

1

But what delirious horrors haunt my brain!
   In a deep ghastly pit, bound down I lie,—
   About me flows a stream of crimson dye,
Amid its burning waves I strive in vain;
   Upward I stretch my arms,—aloud I cry
   In frantic anguish,—"raise me, or I die!"[2]
When with soft eyes, beaming the tenderest love,
I see thy dear face, Anna! far above,—
By magnet drawn up to thee I seem,
And for some moments was dispelled the fever's frightful dream!—

Sept. 1835

❧

[On the Death of Her Father]

Journal, 1835

On the evening of the 30th of September, 1835, ever memorable era—my father was seized with cholera and on the 2d of October was a corpse. For the first two days, my grief under this calamity was such as I dare not speak of. But since my father's head is laid in the dust, I feel an awful calm, and am becoming familiar with the thought of being an orphan. I have prayed to God that *Duty* may now be the first object and self sit aside. May I have light and strength to do what is right in the highest sense for my Mother, brothers and sister.

It has been a gloomy week indeed. The children have all been ill, and dearest Mother is overpowered with sorrow, fatigue and anxiety. I suppose she must be ill too. When the children recover I shall endeavor to keep my mind steady by remembering that there is a God, and that grief is but for a season. Grant, Oh Father, that neither the joys and sorrows of this past season shall have visited my heart in vain. Make me wise and strong for the performance of immediate duties, and ripen me, by what means Thou seest best for those which lie beyond.

My father's image follows me constantly, whenever I am in my room he seems to open the door and look on me with a complacent tender smile. What would I not give to have it in my power to make that heart beat once more with joy. The saddest feeling is the remembrance of little things, in which I have fallen short of love and duty. I never sympathized in his liking for this farm, and secretly wondered how a mind which had for thirty years been so widely engaged in the affairs of men could care so much for trees and crops.[3] But now, amidst the beautiful autumn days, I walk over the grounds and look with painful emotions at every little improvement. He had selected a spot to place a seat where I might go to read alone and had asked me to visit it. I contented myself with "where you please, Father," but we never went; what would I not now give, if I had fixed a time, and shown more interest. A day or two since I went there. The tops of the distant blue hills were veiled in delicate autumn haze, soft silence brooded over the landscape, on one side a brook gave to the gently sloping meadow spring-like verdure, on the other a grove—which he had named for me—lay softly glowing in the gorgeous hues of October. It was very sad; may this sorrow give me a higher sense of duty in the relationships which remain!

∿

Journal, 1835–36

The occupations of the coming months I have settled   Some duties come first to parents, brothers and sister but these will not consume above one sixth of the time— The family is so small now Mother will have little need of my sewing— We shall probably receive very little company— The visits required of me by civility will be few— When the Farrars return I hope to see them frequently—and E. Woodward I may possibly know if she comes. But I shall not, of free-will look out of door for a moment's pleasure— I shall have no one to stay here any time except Eliz— I love her and she is never in the way— All hopes of travelling I have dismissed—[4] All youthful hopes of every kind I have pushed from my thoughts— I will not, if I can help it, lose an hour in castle-building and repining— Too much of that already! I have now a pursuit of immediate importance to the German language and literature I will give my undivided attention— I have made rapid progress for one quite unassisted— I have always hitherto been too constantly distracted by childish feelings to acquire any thing properly but have snatched a little here and there to feed my restless fancy therewith— Please God now to keep my mind composed, that I may atone it with all that may be conducive hereafter to the best good of others—

Oh! keep me steady in an honorable ambition. Favored by this calm, this obscurity of life I might learn every-thing, did not these feelings lavish away my strength— Let it be no longer thus— Teach me to think justly and act firmly— Stifle in my breast those feelings which pouring forth so aimlessly did indeed water but the desert and offend the sun's clear eye by producing weeds of rank luxuriance. Thou art my only Friend, thou hast not seen fit to interpose one feeling, understanding breast between me and a rude, woful world, vouchsafe then thy protection that I may "hold on in courage of soul."

∾

[On Her Childhood]

Journal, March 1839

What did Elizabeth's father gain by forcing her young mind—by constraining her attention long after the physical sense was weary—by keeping her, a delicate child up till midnight whenever it suited him?—[5] He did, as he proposed, sharpen her faculties, give her the power of attention, and bestow an intellectual tinge on a being born only to love eagerly and feel keenly— But the time gained then has been lost since fifty times over in the indulgence of a morbid sensibility created by this unnatural taxing of her faculties—her imagination is disordered; she is doomed to nervous horrors through life, her soul is constantly shaken by too aspiring thoughts on subjects she has not strength to comprehend— Had she grown up an unmolested flower by the side of some secret stream she had been a thing all natural life, softness, bloom and fragrance—

What have I gained by my precocity? I have never been happy—my faculties have always been rather intensely in action and produced no harmonious result. I was more robust by nature than E.[6] Therefore the results have been different. But I am confident that I should have been much superior to my present self had sense, intellect, passion been brought out in the natural order. . . .

Many observations in this book give me new light upon myself— From my *own* experience merely I should go great lengths with him— In childhood I was a somnambulist— I was very subject to attacks of delirium— I perceive I had what are now called spectral illusions— For a long time I dreaded excessively going to bed for as soon as I was left alone— huge shapes—usually faces advanced from the corners of the room and pressed upon me growing larger and larger till they seemed about to crush me— Then I would scream and sit up in bed to get out of the way— Sometimes eyes would detach themselves from the faces and come upon me—I had peculiar horror of this. I told these things sometimes but little notice was taken— I thought other children felt the same for I knew they generally dreaded going to bed— Mother seemed ashamed of my sleep-walking and I had an idea something ridiculous was attached to it— I was twice found in convulsions in consequence of dreadful dreams— One of these dreams I shall never forget— I was wading in a sea of blood— I caught at twigs and rocks to save myself: they all streamed blood on me— This fancy was attributed at the time to my incessant reading of Virgil.— When I was about twelve all these things left me—but were succeeded by a determination of the blood to the head— My Father attributed it to my overheating myself, my Mother to an unfortunate cold—both were much mortified to see the fineness of my complexion destroyed— My own vanity was for a time severely wounded but I recovered and made up my mind to be bright and ugly— My father could not be so easily reconciled but was always scolding me for getting my forehead so red when excited.

If Brigham's theory [7] were correct it would be curious to trace the singular traits of mind I exhibited up to my twenty first year to this ugly and very painful flush in the forehead— The summer of that year my forehead and indeed my whole system was pretty fairly exhausted of the vital fluid under the care of Dr Robbins— Thanks to his medicines, my nerves became calmed, flushes and headaches gradually disappeared— I craved sleep, so long almost impossible to me— My wakefulness had always been troublesome to myself and others— I would now lie down in the middle of the day and sleep for hours. . . .

∽

[On Samuel Ward's and Anna Barker's Engagement]

Journal, c. 1839

The son of the Gods has sold his birthright. He has received therefor one, not merely the fairest, but the sweetest and holiest of earth's daughters. Yet is it not a fit exchange. His pinions droop powerless, he must no longer soar amid the golden stars. No matter, he thinks—I will take her to some green and flowering isle. I will pay the penalty for Adam for the sake of the daughter of Eve. For her I will make the earth fruitful by the sweat of my brow.[8] No longer shall my hands bear the coal to the lips of the inspired singer,[9] no longer my voice modulate its tones to the accompaniment of spheral harmonies. My hands lift the clod of the valley which now dares cling to them with brotherly familiarity. And for my soiling dreary task-work all the day I receive—food.

But the smile with which she greets me at the set of sun, is it not worth all that sun has seen me endure. Can angelic delights surpass those I possess when pacing the shore with her watched by the quiet Moon, we listen to the tide of the world surging up impatiently against the Eden it cannot conquer. Truly, the joys of heaven were gregarious and low in comparison. This alone is exquisite, because exclusive and peculiar.

Ah Seraph—but the winter's frost must nip thy vine. A viper lurks beneath the flowers to sting the foot of thy child, and pale decay must steal over the cheek thou dost adore. In the realm of Ideas all was imperishable. Be blest, while thou canst; —I love thee, fallen Seraph, but thou shouldst not have sold thy birthright.[10]

All for love and the world well lost. That sounds so true. But Genius when it sells itself gives up not only the world but the universe.

Yet does not Love comprehend the universe? The universe is Love: Why should I weary my eye with scanning the parts, when I can clasp the whole this moment to my beating heart?

But if the intellect be repressed, the idea will never be brought out from the feeling The amaranth wreath[11] will in thy grasp be changed to one of roses, more fragrant, indeed, but withering with a single sun.

. . . .

[A Dream]

Went to bed with pain in the right side of my head. Could not get to sleep for a long time, when I did, dreamt that the Egyptian, who has so often tormented me into the nervous headache, sat by my side and kept alluring a gigantic butterfly who was hovering near to rest upon her finger. He approached, but, declining her skinny fingers, flapped his crimson wings for a moment, then settled on the *left* side of my forehead; I tried in vain to drive him away; he plunged his feet, bristling with feelers, deeper and deeper into my forehead till my pain rose to agony. I awoke with my hand on the left side of my forehead to which the pain had changed. After the usual applications had been made I again fell asleep. Now I was in a room of a large hotel, very ill. On the bed was a pink counterpane, such as was in the little room where I endured so many weeks of nervous headache without complaining to any body. I wandered out, I know not why, and could not find my way back. I went through the usual distresses of going into strange rooms, & at last, in despair and quite exhausted, lay down in an entry. Many persons passed by, some looked scornfully at me, others tried to lift me but I was too heavy and at last was left lying on the floor. I was in great pain in the back. I was wrapt in a long robe, but my feet were bare They seemed growing cold as marble. I thought I must die in this forlorn condition, and tried to resign myself to bear it well. At last a sweet female form approached she sat down by me on the cold, damp, brick floor. I cried, O Amy, and laid my head on her bosom. I wept long and bitterly. She had dark eyes and regular features the face I never saw before, but the feeling I had was the same as when Anna in the fever drew me up out of the pit of blood. It is the true feeling of feminine influence, the same which Goethe wished to illustrate by his tale of the child charming the lion, the influence of benignity, purity and faith. As I have masculine traits, I am naturally often relieved by the women in my imaginary distresses. When I awoke the warmth was gone from the stone + (+ not a tombstone) which had been placed at my feet. They were marble cold, the pain had gone, into the spine and my pillow was drenched with tears.

This dream seems, as mine, from the nature of my illness must be, very illustrative of the influence of the body on the mind when will and understanding are not on the alert to check it. Let those who undervalue the moral powers of will analyze their dreams and see what they become without it.

≫

Journal fragment, 183—?

But I love many a good deal, and see some way into their eventual beauty. I am myself growing better, and shall by and by be a worthy object of love, one that will not anywhere disappoint or need forbearance. Meanwhile I have no fetter on me, no engagement, and as I look on others almost every other, can I fail to feel this great privilege? I have no way tied my hands or feet. And yet the varied calls on my sympathy have been such that I hope not to be made partial, cold or ignorant by this isolation. I have no child, and the woman in me has so craved this experience that it has seemed the want of it must paralyze me. But now as I look on these lovely children of a human birth what slow and neutralizing cares they bring with them to the mother. The children of the muse come quicker, with less pain and disgust, rest these lightly on the bosom. . . .

≫

[Mystical Experiences]

Journal, Autumn 1839

Second moonlight. A lonely one. A sweeping, voluptuous breeze. A cloud car for the moon. My ridge of rocks and trysting tree. The singing grove. The distant hills and sweeping fields across which the eye of Raphael steals.[12] Sympathy with between Nature and Man.

Thoughts of Makaria and her stellar correspondences[13] But I cannot think of other souls now. Mine is too fresh and living   Understood wreaths of stars and the wandering in the Elysian grove.

My head wrapped in my shawl I would listen to the music of earth then raise it and look straight into the secrets of the heaven. I fail the moon. Thoughts on lunacy. How could Swedenborg think children were in the moon.[14] She makes me understand the attraction Sand finds in un front impassible[15]   I need to go wild when she rose and shriek   No bliss for me. But now Nature suffices me, and often I rest in her centre as in the bosom of God!

Shapes move across the valley. Abandon thyself to second sight[16]. . . .

DISTANT SHOUTS of laughter. Reflexions on kindred. Michel Angelo's Sybils.[17] Where is my tripod? Clearest moon. Heaven without a fleck or mark.

. . . .

7th   High rapture of solitude. Full moon. Presence of my Daemon. I cannot yet touch its hand. . . .

∾

10 Dec 39

. . . Yet O it seems almost no mortal before me can know such a rapture as mine in the pine wood. Alas that I cannot paint it, only tell the feeling. I envied God, as the last flush of the sun light fell. Then rose the silver bow amid the gorgeous clouds and then again I saw it, a diamond of shivering sparks, trembling in the brook!

∾

Journal, 17 April 1840

Then a woman of tact and brilliancy like me has an undue advantage in conversation with men. They are astonished at our instincts   They do not see where we got our knowledge and while they tramp on in their clumsy way we wheel and fly and dance hither and thither and seize with ready eye all the weak points (like Saladin in the desert)[18] It is quite another thing when we are come to write and without suggestions from another mind to declare the *positive* amount of thought that is in us. Because we seemed to know all they think we can tell all—and finding we can tell so little lose faith in their first opinion of us *which naturally was true*

Then these gentlemen are surprised that I write no better because I talk so well. But I have served a long apprenticeship to the one, none to the other. I will write well yet, but never I think so well as I talk for then I feel inspired and the means are pleasant; my voice excites me, my pen never.

I shall by no means be discouraged, nor take what they say for gospel, but try to sift from it all the truth & use it. I feel within myself the strength to dispense with all illusions and I will manifest it. I will stand steady and rejoice in the severest probations!

∾

Then all earth is sanctified
Upsprings Paradise around.

Then shall come the Eden days
    Guardian watch from seraph eyes,
Angels on the slanting rays
    Voices from the opening skies.

From this spirit land afar
    All disturbing force shall flee,
Sin nor toil nor *hope,* shall mar
    Its immortal unity.

Summer 1840.

∾

[Mystical Experience at Age 21]

Journal, 1840

It was Thanksgiving day, (Nov., 1831,) and I was obliged to go to church or exceedingly displease my father. I almost always suffered much in church from a feeling of disunion with the hearers and dissent from the preacher; but to-day, more than ever before, the services jarred upon me from their grateful and joyful tone. I was wearied out with mental conflicts, and in a mood of most childish, child-like sadness. I felt within myself great power, and generosity, and tenderness; but it seemed to me as if they were all unrecognized, and as if it was impossible that they should be used in life. I was only one-and-twenty; the past was worthless, the future hopeless; yet I could not remember ever voluntarily to have done a wrong thing, and my aspiration seemed very high. I looked round the church, and envied all the little children; for I supposed they had parents who protected them, so that they could never know this strange anguish, this dread uncertainty. I knew not, then, that none could have any father but God. I knew not, that I was not the only lonely one, that I was not the selected Oedipus, the special victim of an iron law. I was in haste for all to be over, that I might get into the free air.

I walked away over the fields as fast as I could walk. This was my custom at that time, when I could no longer bear the weight of my feelings, and fix my attention on any pursuit; for I do believe I never voluntarily gave way to these thoughts one moment. The force I exerted I think, even now, greater than I ever knew in any other character. But when I could bear myself no longer, I walked many hours, till the anguish was wearied out, and I returned in a state of prayer. To-day all seemed to have reached its height. It seemed as if I could never return to a world in which I had no place,—to the mockery of humanities. I could not act a part, nor seem to live any longer. It was a sad and sallow day of the late autumn. Slow processions of sad clouds were passing over a cold blue sky; the hues of earth were dull, and gray, and brown, with sickly struggles of late green here and there; sometimes a moaning gust of wind drove late, reluctant leaves across the path;—there was no life else. In the sweetness of my present peace, such days seem to me made to tell man the worst of his lot; but still that November wind can bring a chill of memory.

I paused beside a little stream, which I had envied in the merry fulness of its spring life. It was shrunken, voiceless, choked with withered leaves. I marvelled that it did not quite lose itself in the earth. There was no stay for me, and I went on and on, till I came to where the trees were thick about a little pool, dark and silent. I sat down there. I did not think; all was dark, and cold, and still. Suddenly the sun shone out with that transparent sweetness, like the last smile of a dying lover, which it will use when it has been unkind all a cold autumn day. And, even then, passed into my thought a beam from its true sun, from its native sphere, which has never since departed from me. I remembered how, a little child, I had stopped myself one day on the stairs, and asked, how came I here? How is it that I seem to be this Margaret Fuller? What does it mean? What shall I do about it? I remembered all the times and ways in which the same thought had returned. I saw how long it must be before the soul can learn to act under these limitations of time and space, and human nature; but I saw, also, that it MUST do it,—that it must make all this false true,—and sow new and immortal plants in the garden of God, before it could return again. I saw there was no self; that selfishness was all folly, and the result of circumstance; that it was only because I thought self real that I suffered; that I had only to live in the idea of the ALL, and all was mine. This truth came to me, and I received it unhesitatingly; so that I was for that hour taken up into God. In that true ray most of the relations of earth seemed mere films, phenomena.

My earthly pain at not being recognized never went deep after this hour. I had passed the extreme of passionate sorrow; and all check, all failure, all ignorance, have seemed temporary ever since. When I consider that this will be nine years ago next November, I am astonished that I have not gone on faster since; that I am not yet sufficiently purified to be taken back to God. Still, I did but touch then on the only haven of Insight. You know what I would say. I was dwelling in the ineffable, the unutterable. But the sun of earth set, and it grew dark around; the moment came for me to go. I had never been accustomed to walk alone at night, for my father was very strict on that subject, but now I had not one fear. When I came back, the moon was riding clear above the houses. I went into the churchyard, and there offered a prayer as holy, if not as deeply true, as any I know now; a prayer, which perhaps took form as the guardian angel of my life. If that word in the Bible, Selah, means what gray-headed old men think it does, when they read aloud, it should be written here,—Selah!

Since that day, I have never more been completely engaged in self; but the statue has been emerging, though slowly, from the block. Others may not see the promise even of its pure symmetry, but I do, and am learning to be patient. I shall be all human yet; and then the hour will come to leave humanity, and live always in the pure ray.

This first day I was taken up; but the second time the Holy Ghost descended like a dove.[19] I went out again for a day, but this time it was spring. I walked in the fields of Groton. But I will not describe that day; its music still sounds too sweetly near. Suffice it to say, I gave all into our Father's hands, and was no stern-weaving Fate more, but one elected to obey, and love, and at last know. Since then I have suffered, as I must suffer again, till all the complex be made simple, but I have never been in discord with the grand harmony.

&

Journal fragment, 1840

I grow more and more what they will call a mystic. Nothing interests me except listening to the secret harmonies of nature. . . .

The oar has fallen from hand, the sail has sent away. I have no means to steer my boat. There shines the polestar, I keep my eye fixed upon it; friendly waves,—will ye not drift me to the needed haven!

If I meet men for a brief time, they check and veil the music, like heavy draperies near an instrument, but if they stay near me long I fill them till they vibrate.

But this music is sweet in my soul to very pain. I cannot alter it, and the hour when I should do so seems afar, yet it swells my heart painfully, thoughts move and push forth from my heart like young birds from the nest, but as yet, if any tries to take wing it falls back into the nest ruffled and trembling with cold.

We mortals live too imperfectly to be happy. While brooding on our birds we famish and our bright plumes fall off. I would brood a beautiful lark into life every night and let it soar with the morning sun. I would let loose whole flights of little birds with every new fleece of snow. I would drop them numerous as hail, gentle as manna, upon the harvest field. There is no need of an Inferno, it will be punishment enough for every fault, if we never become creators!

&

To Caroline Sturgis

8 Sept. 1840

. . . I live, I am— *The carbuncle is found* [20] And at present the mere sight of my talisman is enough. The hour may come when I wish to charm with it, but not yet. I have no future, as no past. . . .

∾

To Caroline Sturgis

26 Sept. 1840

. . . Of the mighty changes in my spiritual life I do not wish to speak, yet surely you cannot be ignorant of them. All has been revealed, all foreshown yet I know it not. Experiment has given place to certainty, pride to obedience, thought to love, and truth is lost in beauty. . . . When we meet you will find me at home. Into that home cold winds may blow, keen lightnings dart their bolts, but I cannot be driven from it more. . . .

∾

To Ralph Waldo Emerson

29 Sept. 1840

. . . All things I have given up to the central power, you also; yet, I cannot forbear adding, dear friend. I am now so at home, I know not how again to wander and grope, seeking my place in another Soul. I need to be recognized. After this, I shall be claimed, rather than claim, yet if I speak of facts, it must be as I see them. . . .

∾

To Caroline Sturgis

22 Oct. 1840

. . . But I can say very little now, scarce a word that is not absolutely drawn from me at the moment. I cannot plunge into myself enough. I cannot dedicate myself sufficiently. The life that flows in upon me from so many quarters is too beautiful to be checked. I would not check a single pulsation. It all ought to be;—if caused by any apparition of the Divine in me I could bless myself like the holy Mother.[21] But like her I long to be virgin. I would fly from the land of my birth. I would hide myself in night and poverty. Does a star point out the spot. The gifts I must receive, yet for my child, not me. I have no words, wait till he is of age, then hear *him*

Oh Caroline, my soul swells with the future. The past, I know it not. . . .

∾

To William H. Channing

25/28 Oct. 1840

. . . The old religionists did talk about "grace, conversion," and the like, technically, without striving to enter into the idea, till they quite lost sight of it. Undervaluing the intellect, they became slaves of a sect, instead of organs of the Spirit. . . . Yet the time seems now to have come for reinterpreting the old dogmas. I would now preach the Holy Ghost as zealously as they have been preaching Man, and faith instead of the understanding, and mysticism &c. . . .

∾

To William H. Channing

3 Dec. 1840

. . . My brother Edward was born on my birth-day, and they said he should be my child. But he sickened and died just as the bud of his existence showed its first bright hues. He was some weeks wasting away, and I took care of him always half the night. He was a beautiful child, and became very dear to me then. Still in lonely woods the upturned violets show me the pleading softness of his large blue eyes, in those hours when I would have given worlds to prevent his suffering, and could not. I used to carry him about in my arms for hours; it soothed him, and I loved to feel his gentle weight of helpless purity upon my heart, while night listened around. At last, when death came, and the soul took wing like

an overtasked bird from his sweet form, I felt what I feel now. Might I
free —————, as that angel freed him! . . .

⁓

1st Jany 1841.

      River of beauty flowing through the life
        How joyful were thy smiles in plain and vale,
   Flower, Star, Swan, graceful tree and golden sands
        Decked thy long course in its successive thoughts
   It seemed could know no end. Soft spread the meadow
        Nobly the tenderness of heavenly blue
   And o'er thy mirror the fair clouds were happy
        Alike in coming and in vanishing,
   And canst thou pause, Oh poem of the world,
        Oh lyre once strung, how canst thou fail a note?
   If music be the food of love, play on,[22]
        Love pauses not; how can its accents cease?
        Alas! there was a chasm in the earth,
        Down plunged my stream, astonished, where stern rocks
        Repelled its sweetness, and refused its depths,
          Foam blurred its amber clearness, and its tones
   Of happy faith are roused to beg and chide
        "Impede me not, my brethren of the Earth;
        Still let me, blissful, deck his gentle breast."
        —But no! the wild cleft opens, wilder still,
        And draws her into a cold silent rush
          Through caverns dark, unvisited, unthought of,
   Where never look of love from moon nor star,
          Where never thought of power from nearest Sun,
   Nor bird, nor falling flower with mute caress
   Shall cheer the longing waves from weariness
        Of following, following—whither no wave knows.

   And yet, they shrink not from thee, solemn cave
        Forbidding, yet inviting this dimmed love
   The Suns and Moons which flatter need them not,
        And faithfully have they adorned the vale;
   Has now the moment come to live with thee,
        Thou must not be left lonely. Doth the light

The cheerful light refuse to follow—
    Yet music hangs upon the darkened course
Of Echoes silvery plaintive, and, indeed,
    In the faint wooing winning tenderer
Than the full voices of triumphant day;
    And we will dress the hall where they abide
With diamond sheen which asks not to be seen,
    But, conscious of its worth, for centuries
Can wait the flashing torch, unless indeed
    The inmost powers a strange convulsion cause
And give the glorious secrets of sad love,
    Of darkened, chilled, but changeless love to day;
Then shall, perchance, be seen
    From this dim grotto to the crystal heights
    Of those serenest heavens is but a step
      For winged feet elastic.

    The pilgrim angels wandered on the plain
Long, long had most been absent from their home,
    All suffered, and all strove for their return,
Melodia suffered most, much would have striven,
    Had but her way been clear.
Her heart was large with love, her ear was keen,
Her hand was strong upon the golden wires,
But through her flowed such endless wishing sweetness
As dimmed here eye with tears; she asked a guide,
    Or else to have that sweetness harmonized,
That she might pause in thought, kneel in the shrine,
    And see, clear eyed, the Virgin Mother smile.

    One day she wandered lonely in the grove,
Lonely she long had been, thus was the best;
    For other pilgrims saw not why she wept,
And, walking in their paths, she sang to them
    Of their own hope, but none had ear for hers,
Nor cleared her eye, nor prophesied the song
    In which the key of all her being lay;
True they were hers, because they were from God,
    But none her ministrants, companions none,
Their office different, hopeless deep; *less wild*
    Melodia sometimes felt, but never thought.

    And now she sang a song, a full-voiced descant song,
But often lost the key and changed the strain

For the key-note was placed in other spheres
  Whose echo her soul knew, but her ear missed;
When lo! a note sent back, vibration felt,
  Startled her soul to sudden revelation,
And near her stood her angel and her friend,
  Receptive, bounteous, radiant, and profound.

  Not quite unknown the form;—
For in a marble quarry wandering,
Once her keen voice startled it from the rock;
But she in childish marvel silent grew
And paused to gaze,—as ceased her heavenward song
  The form drew back into its cradle tomb,
For ages to await the sculptor's thought,
  Nor could her voluntary song recal,
And haunting hope grew sister to despair.

  But now the hour had come;—
And, through the skilful wounds and splintering blows
  Which Nature uses most, loving the most,
Slowly he had come forth, of godlike mould.
  The Paria, from Paros' whiteness named [23]
Sepulchral whiteness of the holiest tomb.

  How met that music and that purity
They knew not; meetings never can be known
  As separations are; it was; it lived;
It is, and what is known, in being known, is not.

  But not a moment could they be detained,
When thus united, from their proper home;
  One marble gleam, one short and lovely note,
The dazzling gate was passed; the robe of primal life put on.

  Too soon, too keen! The work of Love is still
To antedate our Fates; this union pure,
  This wedlock of the two Eternities
Meeting in God has for its child a Man.

  Close in the bosom of the only Love,
Birds drawn back to the nest, one moment full
  They felt the pulse of the creative heart,
And were the key-note of Concordia,
  They lived the multiple of Unity,
Revolved, the all-embracing Sun and Moon,

Shed forth in that one look of mutual love,
All stars, flowers, rivers, Angels, Gods and Thoughts,
    And brooding, trembling, hovered into life;
Such was the smile of God which these two angels meant,
    The fullest utterance One has ever made,
The much that calls for more, the light of final shade.

    Oh words weak wondrous words! Night listened round
The Spheral Music singing without sound,
    All that was ever lost that instant found,
All that was ever loosed that life-pulse bound,
Speech wedded silence, Death life crowning crowned;
    It is and yet has ceased to be.
    Melodia was again, and being so
Paria had fled into the secret caves
    To purify anew a second life
And from the marble centre to the diamond.
    But she, Melodia!
How can she wait, a voice, which was a life?
    Oh reassure, Eternal Harmony,
This wandering vestal of herself bereft,
    And veil in prayers the breast without a heart,
And bind with truth the wound that truth has made,
And calm in faithful death the broken life of Love.

&

Journal, Jan. 1841

Each moment is an age between me, and the consummation of my existence. I have realized the phenomenal nature of outward action, and can there find refuge and rest never again, only by deepening the fountains of Spirit can I obtain any peace. At present I can only wait as I may. I die daily, yet cannot plunge down to rise again into heaven. I rest with heavenward, though languid eye, with broad and gloomy pinion upon the surface of myself. Seeing thee, Sun, far and bright, though wild, I trust thou will enable me to wait the fertilizing beam. Permit not that I say "Why hast thou forsaken me?"[24]

I wandered in the subterranean recesses, the light was darkness; my feet bled with the sharp stones I could not see to avoid; cliffs pierced my ardent breast; cold and foreign substances slid on either side from my seeking hands. Gleams of light came sometimes only to show me that the path wound on and on. Suddenly a wide blaze, of meteoric light? showed me the cave with its diamond pillars and river path, which had been waiting for ages the seeker who must try the depths as well as scale the heights   I looked around a moment at the glittering walls, then plunged in with brow serene; the waters were cold but I did not shrink, beside they rushed onward with a force I felt, the stern chill and the sudden darkness into which they drew me were nothing—but now they have left me on this unknown lake, how shall I pass the moments, till I am seized and borne once more toward the eternal sea. How —I ask not why is it, but *how* I shall bear it? . . .

. . . .

My head is very sensitive, and as they described the Spina Christi,[25] I shuddered all over, and could have fainted only at the thought of its pressure on his head. Yet if he had experienced the sufferings of humanity and believed that by "thy will be done"[26] a steady feeling in his breast during these hours of torture from an ungrateful race, he could free them from suffering & sin. I feel how he might have borne it.— It seems to me I might be educated through suffering to the same purity. . .

. . . .

Return Madonna, for none since thee has been the mother of a perfectly holy child.[27] Why have not all women since been dedicate and pure, then he would not have been left alone. Is there not one, one whose heart is free from idolatry? not one worthy of a miracle? Ah there were buds of promise, yet not one that I know would dare to invoke the Angel, or arm her hand with the palm branch

❧

Journal, Feb. 1841

I wish I were a man, and then there would be one. I weary in this playground of boys, proud and happy in their balls and marbles. Give me heroes, poets, lawgivers, then.

There are women much less unworthy to love than you, men. The best are so unripe, the wisest, so ignoble, the truest so cold!

Divine Spirit, I pray thee, grow out into our age before I leave it. I pray, I prophesy, I trust, yet I pine.

❧

[Notes for Autobiography][28]

c. 1840–41

LILLO

New England village. Father a lawyer. Much engrossment in his profession. Upright and kind, but sharp outward and Martinet. Aunts hardened a vulgarized representation of himself   Mother died early. The child's heart pious for the rainbow of beauty and love. The sign of an eternal covenant that the Mother's face affords as she bends over her sobbing child. She stoops to him as the rainbow of the heavens over the earth— Nature always avenges herself and these feelings, if not indulged at their natural season vindicate their claims at another. My anguish at a later day on seeing the Madonna of the chair   At 17 I elected a Mother, but this comes in a later chapter. My first view of society. Gossips that visit my Aunt   Marriage and domestic life made hateful by their profaning talk. My tutor, also a Martinet— His influence. Good and bad. My life is twofold— The Roman chapter & the Garden. What flowers were to me. The little door that opened beneath the vine to the sunset. Objects breathing and growing in the moonlight. Modern European influences   English lady known at 7 years old. Gaze at her in church. Her dress, her hazle eyes and clustering locks. My visit to her. Her harp, and all it gave rise to in my mind. She gives me the bunch of golden flowers which come, she says from Madeira. Greek phantasy Islands of the blest. Meads of Asphodel, and lives passed in playing on golden harps. How my father's library was formed. On the whole how good for me. Elegant extracts, Pope and Spectator on Sunday. I steal the keys quite destitute of moral compunction. First night of Shakspeare   Chapter on Shakspeare. My good thus brought me also Moliere and Cervantes. My bad Lesage and Smollet— Critique— English novelists— State of the body and brain at this too until lecture period— when my father hid the keys. He should have given me active games in their place. What daily contact with boys teaches easily and pleasantly I had to learn afterwards with care and pain at the university and too late for the good influences on my bodily constitution. First influence of society   When I was brought into contact with it. Makes me a coxcomb, or bully, and an intriguer. French period. Frederick the Great. De Retz. Rousseau. My Mother Elect. Arminians. Beauty & truth are the same   The Italian poets. The German philosophers   Many intimacies follow one another. They cultivate the intellect and develope the passions but speak not to the soul. My life is for years social, polite and various, but shallow music raises me in some measure from this   Then comes love, Ella   I give her up to another   Renunciation hallows and clarifies. My life begins to be musical. I am one string on the great harp. I go abroad. Art. A tropical nature   Rafaello[29] & Marc ———— Pictures. Goethe. My father's death recals me to N England. Episode of my cousin Annette   Ce n'est que le premier pas que coute[30]   I encounter practical life— I teach. Buy and sell. I know men as citizens   Meet Lillo   The crisis of soul and final & N England life   Transcendentalism. Crudeness of reform— Vulgarity of reformers   Pas encore[31]   Yet Geere saved the Capital. Bettine.[32] The silver time, how it had spoken to me since my childhood. By that I abide. The church, quite set aside   Jesus Christ. Elizabeth's Children   Swedenborg   Lillo. Crisis of my life. My heart breaks. The soul chooses its own. I go to the western forest to think it out. Thou art strong O Bettine   Live in the world and wait for me. I will return.

∽

A Credo

Summer 1842

There is a spirit uncontainable and uncontained. —Within it all manifestation is contained, whether of good (accomplishment) or evil (obstruction).   To itself its depths are unknown. By living it seeks to know itself. Thus evolving plants, animals, men, suns, stars, angels, and, it is to be presumed an infinity of forms not yet visible in the horizon of this being who now writes.

Its modes of operation are two-fold. First as genius inspires genius,—love love,—angel mother brings forth angel-child. This is the uninterrupted generation or publication of spirit taking upon itself congenial forms.

—Second
Conquering obstruction, finding the like in the unlike. This is a secondary generation, a new dynasty, as virtue for simplicity, faith for oneness, charity for pure love.

Then begins the genesis of Man, as through his consciousness he attests the laws which regulated the divine genesis. The Father is justified in the Son.

The mind of man asks "why was this second development? —Why seeks the divine to exchange best for better, bliss for hope, domesticity for knowledge? We reject the plan in the universe which the Spirit permitted as the condition of conscious life.

We reject it in the childhood of the soul's life. —The cry of infancy is why should we seek God when he is always there, why seek what is ours as soul's through indefinite pilgrimages, and burdensome cultures.

The intellect has no answer to this question, yet as we through faith and purity of deed enter into the nature of the Divine it is answered from our own experience. We understand though we cannot explain the mystery of something gained where all already is.

God we say is Love,[33] if we believe this we must trust him. Whatever has been permitted by the law of being must be *for* good, and only *in time* not *good*. We do trust him and are led forward by experience. Light gives experience of outward life, faith of inward. We then discern however faintly the necessary harmony of the true lives. The moment we have broken through an obstruction, not accidentally but by the aid of Faith we begin to realize why any was permitted. We begin to interpret the Universe and deeper depths are opened with each soul that is convinced. For it would seem that the Divine expressed his meaning to himself more distinctly in man than in the other forms of our sphere, and through him uttered distinctly the Hallelujah which the other forms of nature only intimate.

Whenever man remains imbedded in nature, whether from sensuality or because he is not yet awakened to consciousness, the purpose of the whole remains unfulfilled, hence our displeasure when man is not, in a sense, *above* nature. Yet when he is not so closely bound with all other manifestations, as duly to express their spirit, we are also displeased. He must be at once the highest form of nature and conscious of the meaning she has been striving successively to unfold through those below him. . . .

∾

[On Anna Barker]

Journal, October 1842

Many things interested me at the time which are not worth writing about, but nothing fixed my attention so much, as a large engraving of Me Recamier in her boudoir.[34] I have so often thought over the intimacy between her and Me de Stael. It is so true that a woman may be in love with a woman, and a man with a man. It is so pleasant to be sure of it because undoubtedly it is the same love that we shall feel when we are angels when we ascend to the only place fit for the Mignon's where

Sie fragen nicht nach Mann und Weib— [35]

It is regulated by the same law as that of love between persons of different sexes, only it is purely intellectual and spiritual, unprofaned by any mixture of lower instincts, undisturbed by any need of consulting temporal interests, its law is the desire of the spirit to realize a whole which makes it seek in another being for what it finds not in itself. Thus the beautiful seeks the strong, and the strong the beautiful, the mute seek the eloquent &c the butterfly settles always on the dark flower. Why did Socrates love Alcibiades?—why did Korner love Schneider? how natural is the love of Wallenstein for Max, that of Me de Stael for de Recamier, mine for Anna Barker[.][36] I loved Anna for a time I think with as much passion as I was then strong enough to feel— Her face was always gleaming before me, her voice was echoing in my ear, all poetic thoughts clustered round the dear image. This love was a key which unlocked for me many a treasure which I still possess, it was the carbuncle (emblematic gem) which cast light into many of the darkest caverns of human nature.[37] —She loved me, too, though not so much, because her nature was "less high, less grave, less large, less deep" but she loved more tenderly, less passionately[.] She loved me, for I well remember her suffering when she first would feel my faults and knew one part of the exquisite veil rent away, how she wished to stay apart and weep the whole day. Then again that night when she leaned on me and her eyes were such a deep violet blue, so like night, as they never were before, and we both felt such a strange mystic thrill and knew what we had never known before. Now well too can I now account for that desire which I often had to get away from her and be alone with nature, which displeased her so, for she wished to be with me all the time. I do not love her now with passion, for I have exhausted her idea, and she does not stimulate my fancy, she does not represent the Beautiful to me now, she is only one beautiful object. Then she has never had a chance to get a hold on my heart by the thousand links of intimacy, we have been so little together; all was from the elective affinities.[38] But still I love her with a sort of pallid, tender romance and feel towards her as I can to no other woman. I thought of all this as I looked at Me Recamier and had one thought beside which has often come into my mind, but I will not write it down; it is so singular that I have often thought I would never express it in any way; I am sure no human being but myself would understand it—

Parents

MY FATHER was a lawyer and a politician. He was a man largely endowed with that sagacious energy, which the state of New England society, for the last half century, has been so well fitted to develop. His father was a clergyman, settled as pastor in Princeton, Massachusetts, within the bounds of whose parish-farm was Wachuset. His means were small, and the great object of his ambition was to send his sons to college. As a boy, my father was taught to think only of preparing himself for Harvard University, and when there of preparing himself for the profession of Law. As a Lawyer, again, the ends constantly presented were to work for distinction in the community, and for the means of supporting a family. To be an honored citizen, and to have a home on earth, were made the great aims of existence. To open the deeper fountains of the soul, to regard life here as the prophetic entrance to immortality, to develop his spirit to perfection,—motives like these had never been suggested to him, either by fellow-beings or by outward circumstances. The result was a character, in its social aspect, of quite the common sort. A good son and brother, a kind neighbor, an active man of business—in all these outward relations he was but one of a class, which surrounding conditions have made the majority among us. In the more delicate and individual relations, he never approached but two mortals, my mother and myself.

His love for my mother was the green spot on which he stood apart from the common-places of a mere bread-winning, bread-bestowing existence. She was one of those fair and flower-like natures, which sometimes spring up even beside the most dusty highways of life—a creature not to be shaped into a merely useful instrument, but bound by one law with the blue sky, the dew, and the frolic birds. Of all persons whom I have known, she had in her most of the angelic,—of that spontaneous love for every living thing, for man, and beast, and tree, which restores the golden age.

Death in the House

MY EARLIEST recollection is of a death,—the death of a sister, two years younger than myself. Probably there is a sense of childish endearments, such as belong to this tie, mingled with that of loss, of wonder, and mystery; but these last are prominent in memory. I remember coming home and meeting our nursery-maid, her face streaming with tears. That strange sight of tears made an indelible impression. I realize how little I was of stature, in that I looked up to this weeping face;—and it has often seemed since, that—full-grown for the life of this earth, I have looked up just so, at times of threatening, of doubt, and distress, and that just so has some being of the next higher order of existences looked down, aware of a law unknown to me, and tenderly commiserating the pain I must endure in emerging from my ignorance.

She took me by the hand and led me into a still and dark chamber,— then drew aside the curtain and showed me my sister. I see yet that beauty of death! The highest achievements of sculpture are only the reminder of its severe sweetness. Then I remember the house all still and dark,—the people in their black clothes and dreary faces,—the scent of the newly-made coffin,—my being set up in a chair and detained by a gentle hand to hear the clergyman,—the carriages slowly going, the procession slowly doling out their steps to the grave. But I have no remembrance of what I have since been told I did,—insisting, with loud cries, that they should not put the body in the ground. I suppose that my emotion was spent at the time, and so there was nothing to fix that moment in my memory.

I did not then, nor do I now, find any beauty in these ceremonies. What had they to do with the sweet playful child? Her life and death were alike beautiful, but all this sad parade was not. Thus my first experience of life was one of death. She who would have been the companion of my life was severed from me, and I was left alone. This has made a vast difference in my lot. Her character, if that fair face promised right, would have been soft, graceful and lively; it would have tempered mine to a gentler and more gradual course.

Overwork

MY FATHER,—all of whose feelings were now concentred on me,—instructed me himself. The effect of this was so far good that, not passing through the hands of many ignorant and weak persons as so many do at preparatory schools, I was put at once under discipline of considerable severity, and, at the same time, had a more than ordinarily high standard presented to me. My father was a man of business, even in literature; he had been a high scholar at college, and was warmly attached to all he had learned there, both from the pleasure he had derived in the exercise of his faculties and the associated memories of success and good repute. He was, beside, well read in French literature, and in English, a Queen Anne's man.[1] He hoped to make me the heir of all he knew, and of as much more as the income of his profession enabled him to give me means of acquiring. At the very beginning, he made one great mistake, more common, it is to be hoped, in the last generation, than the warnings of physiologists will permit it to be with the next. He thought to gain time, by bringing forward the intellect as early as possible. Thus I had tasks given me, as many and various as the hours would allow, and on subjects beyond my age; with the additional disadvantage of reciting to him in the evening, after he returned from his office. As he was subject to many interruptions, I was often kept up till very late; and as he was a severe teacher, both from his habits of mind and his ambition for me, my feelings were kept on the stretch till the recitations were over. Thus frequently, I was sent to bed several hours too late, with nerves unnaturally stimulated. The consequence was a premature development of the brain, that made me a "youthful prodigy" by day, and by night a victim of spectral illusions, nightmare, and somnambulism, which at the time prevented the harmonious development of my bodily powers and checked my growth, while, later, they induced continual headache, weakness and nervous affections, of all kinds. As these again re-acted on the brain, giving undue force to every thought and every feeling, there was finally produced a state of being both too active and too intense, which wasted my constitution, and will bring me,—even although I have learned to understand and regulate my now morbid temperament,—to a premature grave.

No one understood this subject of health then. No one knew why this child, already kept up so late, was still unwilling to retire. My aunts cried out upon the "spoiled child, the most unreasonable child that ever was,—if brother could but open his eyes to see it,—who was never willing to go to bed." They did not know that, so soon as the light was taken away, she seemed to see colossal faces advancing slowly towards her, the eyes dilating, and each feature swelling loathsomely as they came, till at last, when they were about to close upon her, she started up with a shriek which drove them away, but only to return when she lay down again. They did not know that, when at last she went to sleep, it was to dream of horses trampling over her, and to awake once more in fright, or, as she had just read in her Virgil, of being among trees that dripped with blood, where she walked and walked and could not get out, while the blood became a pool and plashed over her feet, and rose higher and higher, till soon she dreamed it would reach her lips. No wonder the child arose and walked in her sleep, moaning all over the house, till once, when they heard her, and came and waked her, and she told what she had dreamed, her father sharply bid her "leave off thinking of such nonsense, or she would be crazy,"—never knowing that he was himself the cause of all these horrors of the night. Often she dreamed of following to the grave the body of her mother, as she had done that of her sister, and woke to find the pillow drenched in tears. These dreams softened her heart too much, and cast a deep shadow over her young days; for then, and later, the life of dreams,— probably because there was in it less to distract the mind from its own earnestness,—has often seemed to her more real, and been remembered with more interest, than that of waking hours.

Poor child! Far remote in time, in thought, from that period, I look back on these glooms and terrors, wherein I was enveloped, and perceive that I had no natural childhood!

Books

THUS PASSED my first years. My mother was in delicate health, and much absorbed in the care of her younger children. In the house was neither dog nor bird, nor any graceful animated form of existence. I saw no persons who took my fancy, and real life offered no attraction. Thus my already over-excited mind found no relief from without, and was driven for refuge from itself to the world of books. I was taught Latin and English grammar at the same time, and began to read Latin at six years old, after which, for some years, I read it daily. In this branch of study, first by my father, and afterwards by a tutor, I was trained to quite a high degree of precision. I was expected to understand the mechanism of the language thoroughly, and in translating to give the thoughts in as few well-arranged words as possible, and without breaks or hesitation,—for with these my father had absolutely no patience.

Indeed, he demanded accuracy and clearness in everything: you must not speak, unless you can make your meaning perfectly intelligible to the person addressed; must not express a thought, unless you can give a reason for it, if required; must not make a statement, unless sure of all particulars—such were his rules. "But," "if," "unless," "I am mistaken," and "it may be so," were words and phrases excluded from the province where he held sway. Trained to great dexterity in artificial methods, accurate, ready, with entire command of his resources, he had no belief in minds that listen, wait, and receive. He had no conception of the subtle and indirect motions of imagination and feeling. His influence on me was great, and opposed to the natural unfolding of my character, which was fervent, of strong grasp, and disposed to infatuation, and self-forgetfulness. He made the common prose world so present to me, that my natural bias was controlled. I did not go mad, as many would do, at being continually roused from my dreams. I had too much strength to be crushed,—and since I must put on the fetters, could not submit to let them impede my motions. My own world sank deep within, away from the surface of my life; in what I did and said I learned to have reference to other minds. But my true life was only the dearer that it was secluded and veiled over by a thick curtain of available intellect, and that coarse, but wearable stuff woven by the ages,—Common Sense.

In accordance with this discipline in heroic common sense, was the influence of those great Romans, whose thoughts and lives were my daily food during those plastic years. The genius of Rome displayed itself in Character, and scarcely needed an occasional wave of the torch of thought to show its lineaments, so marble strong they gleamed in every light. Who, that has lived with those men, but admires the plain force of fact, of thought passed into action? They take up things with their naked hands. There is just the man, and the block he casts before you,—no divinity, no demon, no unfulfilled aim, but just the man and Rome, and what he did for Rome. Everything turns your attention to what a man can become, not by yielding himself freely to impressions, not by letting nature play freely through him, but by a single thought, an earnest purpose, an indomitable will, by hardihood, self-command, and force of expression. Architecture was the art in which Rome excelled, and this corresponds with the feeling these men of Rome excite. They did not grow,—they built themselves up, or were built up by the fate of Rome, as a temple for Jupiter Stator. The ruined Roman sits among the ruins; he flies to no green garden; he does not look to heaven; if his intent is defeated, if he is less than he meant to be, he lives no more. The names which end in *"us,"* seem to speak with lyric cadence. That measured cadence,—that tramp and march,—which are not stilted, because they indicate real force, yet which seem so when compared with any other language,—make Latin a study in itself of mighty influence. The language alone, without the literature, would give one the *thought* of Rome. Man present in nature, commanding nature too sternly to be inspired by it, standing like the rock amid the sea, or moving like the fire over the land, either impassive, or irresistible; knowing not the soft mediums or fine flights of life, but by the force which he expresses, piercing to the centre.

We are never better understood than when we speak of a "Roman virtue," a "Roman outline." There is somewhat indefinite, somewhat yet unfulfilled in the thought of Greece, of Spain, of modern Italy; but ROME! it stands by itself, a clear Word. The power of will, the dignity of a fixed purpose is what it utters. Every Roman was an emperor. It is well that the infallible church should have been founded on this rock, that the presumptuous Peter should hold the keys, as the conquering Jove did before his thunderbolts, to be seen of all the world. The Apollo tends flocks with Admetus,[2] Christ teaches by the lonely lake, or plucks wheat as he wanders through the fields some Sabbath morning. They never come to this stronghold; they could not have breathed freely where all became stone as soon as spoken, where divine youth found no horizon for its all-promising glance, but every thought put on, before it dared issue to the day in action, its *toga virilis*.[3]

Suckled by this wolf,[4] man gains a different complexion from that which is fed by the Greek honey. He takes a noble bronze in camps and battle-fields; the wrinkles of council well beseem his brow, and the eye cuts its way like the sword. The Eagle should never have been used as a symbol by any other nation: it belonged to Rome.

The history of Rome abides in mind, of course, more than the literature. It was degeneracy for a Roman to use the pen; his life was in the day. The "vaunting" of Rome, like that of the North American Indians, is her proper literature. A man rises; he tells who he is, and what he has done; he speaks of his country and her brave men; he knows that a conquering god is there, whose agent is his own right hand; and he should end like the Indian, "I have no more to say."

It never shocks us that the Roman is self-conscious. One wants no universal truths from him, no philosophy, no creation, but only his life, his Roman life felt in every pulse, realized in every gesture. The universal heaven takes in the Roman only to make us feel his individuality the more. The Will, the Resolve of Man!—it has been expressed,—fully expressed!

I steadily loved this ideal in my childhood, and this is the cause, probably, why I have always felt that man must know how to stand firm on the ground, before he can fly. In vain for me are men more, if they are less, than Romans. Dante was far greater than any Roman, yet I feel he was right to take the Mantuan as his guide through hell, and to heaven.

Horace was a great deal to me then, and is so still. Though his words do not abide in memory, his presence does: serene, courtly, of darting hazel eye, a self-sufficient grace, and an appreciation of the world of stern realities, sometimes pathetic, never tragic. He is the natural man of the world; he is what he ought to be, and his darts never fail of their aim. There is a perfume and raciness, too, which makes life a banquet, where the wit sparkles no less that the viands were bought with blood.

Ovid [5] gave me not Rome, nor himself, but a view into the enchanted gardens of the Greek mythology. This path I followed, have been following ever since; and now, life half over, it seems to me, as in my childhood, that every thought of which man is susceptible, is intimated there. In those young years, indeed, I did not see what I now see, but loved to creep from amid the Roman pikes to lie beneath this great vine, and see the smiling and serene shapes go by, woven from the finest fibres of all the elements. I knew not why, at that time,—but I loved to get away from the hum of the forum, and the mailed clang of Roman speech, to these shifting shows of nature, these Gods and Nymphs born of the sunbeam, the wave, the shadows on the hill.

As with Rome I antedated the world of deeds, so I lived in those Greek forms the true faith of a refined and intense childhood. So great was the force of reality with which these forms impressed me, that I prayed earnestly for a sign,—that it would lighten in some particular region of the heavens, or that I might find a bunch of grapes in the path, when I went forth in the morning. But no sign was given, and I was left a waif stranded upon the shores of modern life!

Of the Greek language, I knew only enough to feel that the sounds told the same story as the mythology;—that the law of life in that land was beauty, as in Rome it was a stern composure. I wish I had learned as much of Greece as of Rome,—so freely does the mind play in her sunny waters, where there is no chill, and the restraint is from within out; for these Greeks, in an atmosphere of ample grace, could not be impetuous, or stern, but loved moderation as equable life always must, for it is the law of beauty.

With these books I passed my days. The great amount of study exacted of me soon ceased to be a burden, and reading became a habit and a passion. The force of feeling, which, under other circumstances, might have ripened thought, was turned to learn the thoughts of others. This was not a tame state, for the energies brought out by rapid acquisition gave glow enough. I thought with rapture of the all-accomplished man, him of the many talents, wide resources, clear sight, and omnipotent will. A Caesar seemed great enough. I did not then know that such men impoverish the treasury to build the palace. I kept their statues as belonging to the hall of my ancestors, and loved to conquer obstacles, and fed my youth and strength for their sake.

STILL, though the bias was so great that in earliest years I learned, in these ways, how the world takes hold of a powerful nature, I had yet other experiences. None of these were deeper than what I found in the happiest haunt of my childish years,—our little garden. Our house, though comfortable, was very ugly, and in a neighborhood which I detested,—every dwelling and its appurtenances having a *mesquin*⁶ and huddled look. I liked nothing about us except the tall graceful elms before the house, and the dear little garden behind. Our back door opened on a high flight of steps, by which I went down to a green plot, much injured in my ambitious eyes by the presence of the pump and tool-house. This opened into a little garden, full of choice flowers and fruit-trees, which was my mother's delight, and was carefully kept. Here I felt at home. A gate opened thence into the fields,—a wooden gate made of boards, in a high, unpainted board wall, and embowered in the clematis creeper. This gate I used to open to see the sunset heaven; beyond this black frame I did not step, for I liked to look at the deep gold behind it. How exquisitely happy I was in its beauty, and how I loved the silvery wreaths of my protecting vine! I never would pluck one of its flowers at that time, I was so jealous of its beauty, but often since I carry off wreaths of it from the wild-wood, and it stands in nature to my mind as the emblem of domestic love.

Of late I have thankfully felt what I owe to that garden, where the best hours of my lonely childhood were spent. Within the house everything was socially utilitarian; my books told of a proud world, but in another temper were the teachings of the little garden. There my thoughts could lie callow in the nest, and only be fed and kept warm, not called to fly or sing before the time. I loved to gaze on the roses, the violets, the lilies, the pinks; my mother's hand had planted them, and they bloomed for me. I culled the most beautiful. I looked at them on every side. I kissed them, I pressed them to my bosom with passionate emotions, such as I have never dared express to any human being. An ambition swelled my heart to be as beautiful, as perfect as they. I have not kept my vow. Yet, forgive, ye wild asters, which gleam so sadly amid the fading grass; forgive me, ye golden autumn flowers, which so strive to reflect the glories of the departing distant sun; and ye silvery flowers, whose moonlight eyes I knew so well, forgive! Living and blooming in your unchecked law, ye know nothing of the blights, the distortions, which beset the human being; and which at such hours it would seem that no glories of free agency could ever repay!

THERE WAS, in the house, no apartment appropriated to the purpose of a library, but there was in my father's room a large closet filled with books, and to these I had free access when the task-work of the day was done. Its window overlooked wide fields, gentle slopes, a rich and smiling country, whose aspect pleased without much occupying the eye, while a range of blue hills, rising at about twelve miles distance, allured to reverie. "Distant mountains," says Tieck, "excite the fancy, for beyond them we place the scene of our Paradise."" Thus, in the poems of fairy adventure, we climb the rocky barrier, pass fearless its dragon caves, and dark pine forests, and find the scene of enchantment in the vale behind. My hopes were never so definite, but my eye was constantly allured to that distant blue range, and I would sit, lost in fancies, till tears fell on my cheek. I loved this sadness; but only in later years, when the realities of life had taught me moderation, did the passionate emotions excited by seeing them again teach how glorious were the hopes that swelled my heart while gazing on them in those early days.

Melancholy attends on the best joys of a merely ideal life, else I should call most happy the hours in the garden, the hours in the book closet. Here were the best French writers of the last century; for my father had been more than half a Jacobin,[8] in the time when the French Republic cast its glare of promise over the world. Here, too, were the Queen Anne authors, his models, and the English novelists; but among them I found none that charmed me. Smollet, Fielding, and the like, deal too broadly with the coarse actualities of life. The best of their men and women—so merely natural, with the nature found every day—do not meet our hopes. Sometimes the simple picture, warm with life and the light of the common son, cannot fail to charm,—as in the wedded love of Fielding's Amelia,[9]—but it is at a later day, when the mind is trained to comparison, that we learn to prize excellence like this as it deserves. Early youth is prince-like: it will bend only to "the king, my father." Various kinds of excellence please, and leave their impression, but the most commanding, alone, is duly acknowledged at that all-exacting age.

Three great authors it was my fortune to meet at this important period,—all, though of unequal, yet congenial powers,—all of rich and wide, rather than aspiring genius,—all free to the extent of the horizon their eye took in,—all fresh with impulse, racy with experience; never to be lost sight of, or superseded, but always to be apprehended more and more.

Ever memorable is the day on which I first took a volume of SHAKSPEARE in my hand to read. It was on a Sunday.

—This day was punctiliously set apart in our house. We had family prayers, for which there was no time on other days. Our dinners were different, and our clothes. We went to church. My father put some limitations on my reading, but—bless him for the gentleness which has left me a pleasant feeling for the day!—he did not prescribe what was, but only what was *not,* to be done. And the liberty this left was a large one. "You must not read a novel, or a play;" but all other books, the worst, or the best, were open to me. The distinction was merely technical. The day was pleasing to me, as relieving me from the routine of tasks and recitations; it gave me freer play than usual, and there were fewer things occurred in its course, which reminded me of the divisions of time; still the church-going, where I heard nothing that had any connection with my inward life, and these rules, gave me associations with the day of empty formalities, and arbitrary restrictions; but though the forbidden book or walk always seemed more charming then, I was seldom tempted to disobey.—

This Sunday—I was only eight years old—I took from the bookshelf a volume lettered SHAKSPEARE. It was not the first time I had looked at it, but before I had been deterred from attempting to read, by the broken appearance along the page, and preferred smooth narrative. But this time I held in my hand "Romeo and Juliet" long enough to get my eye fastened to the page. It was a cold winter afternoon. I took the book to the parlor fire, and had there been seated an hour or two, when my father looked up and asked me what I was reading so intently. "Shakspeare," replied the child, merely raising her eye from the page. "Shakspeare,—that won't do; that's no book for Sunday; go put it away and take another." I went as I was bid, but took no other. Returning to my seat, the unfinished story, the personages to whom I was but just introduced, thronged and burnt my brain. I could not bear it long; such a lure it was impossible to resist. I went and brought the book again. There were several guests present, and I had got half through the play before I again attracted attention. "What is that child about that she don't hear a word that's said to her?" quoth my aunt. "What are you reading?" said my father. "Shakspeare" was again the reply, in a clear, though somewhat impatient, tone. "How?" said my father angrily,—then restraining himself before his guests,—"Give me the book and go directly to bed."

Into my little room no care of his anger followed me. Alone, in the dark, I thought only of the scene placed by the poet before my eye, where the free flow of life, sudden and graceful dialogue, and forms, whether grotesque or fair, seen in the broad lustre of his imagination, gave just what I wanted, and brought home the life I seemed born to live. My fancies swarmed like bees, as I contrived the rest of the story;—what all would do, what say, where go. My confinement tortured me. I could not go forth from this prison to ask after these friends; I could not make my pillow of the dreams about them which yet I could not forbear to frame. Thus was I absorbed when my father entered. He felt it right, before going to rest, to reason with me about my disobedience, shown in a way, as he considered, so insolent. I listened, but could not feel interested in what he said, nor turn my mind from what engaged it. He went away really grieved at my impenitence, and quite at a loss to understand conduct in me so unusual.

—Often since I have seen the same misunderstanding between parent and child,—the parent thrusting the morale, the discipline, of life upon the child, when just engrossed by some game of real importance and great leadings to it. That is only a wooden horse to the father,—the child was careering to distant scenes of conquest and crusade, through a country of elsewhere unimagined beauty. None but poets remember their youth; but the father who does not retain poetical apprehension of the world, free and splendid as it stretches out before the child, who cannot read his natural history, and follow out its intimations with reverence, must be a tyrant in his home, and the purest intentions will not prevent his doing much to cramp him. Each new child is a new Thought, and has bearings and discernings, which the Thoughts older in date know not yet, but must learn.—

My attention thus fixed on Shakspeare, I returned to him at every hour I could command. Here was a counterpoise to my Romans, still more forcible than the little garden. My author could read the Roman nature too,—read it in the sternness of Coriolanus, and in the varied wealth of Caesar. But he viewed these men of will as only one kind of men; he kept them in their place, and I found that he, who could understand the Roman, yet expressed in Hamlet a deeper thought.

In CERVANTES, I found far less productive talent,—indeed, a far less powerful genius,—but the same wide wisdom, a discernment piercing the shows and symbols of existence, yet rejoicing in them all, both for their own life, and as signs of the unseen reality. Not that Cervantes philosophized,—his genius was too deeply philosophical for that; he took things as they came before him, and saw their actual relations and bearings. Thus the work he produced was of deep meaning, though he might never have expressed that meaning to himself. It was left implied in the whole. A Coleridge comes and calls Don Quixote the pure Reason, and Sancho the Understanding.[10] Cervantes made no such distinctions in his own mind; but he had seen and suffered enough to bring out all his faculties, and to make him comprehend the higher as well as the lower part of our nature. Sancho is too amusing and sagacious to be contemptible; the Don too noble and clear-sighted towards absolute truth, to be ridiculous. And we are pleased to see manifested in this way, how the lower must follow and serve the higher, despite its jeering mistrust and the stubborn realities which break up the plans of this pure-minded champion.

The effect produced on the mind is nowise that described by Byron:—

"Cervantes smiled Spain's chivalry away," &c.[11]

On the contrary, who is not conscious of a sincere reverence for the Don, prancing forth on his gaunt steed? Who would not rather be he than any of the persons who laugh at him?—Yet the one we would wish to be is thyself, Cervantes, unconquerable spirit! gaining flavor and color like wine from every change, while being carried round the world; in whose eye the serene sagacious laughter could not be dimmed by poverty, slavery, or unsuccessful authorship. Thou art to us still more the Man, though less the Genius, than Shakspeare; thou dost not evade our sight, but, holding the lamp to thine own magic shows, dost enjoy them with us.

My third friend was MOLIÉRE, one very much lower, both in range and depth, than the others, but, as far as he goes, of the same character. Nothing secluded or partial is there about his genius,—a man of the world, and a man by himself, as he is. It was, indeed, only the poor social world of Paris that he saw, but he viewed it from the firm foundations of his manhood, and every lightest laugh rings from a clear perception, and teaches life anew.

These men were all alike in this,—they loved the *natural history* of man.[12] Not what he should be, but what he is, was the favorite subject of their thought. Whenever a noble leading opened to the eye new paths of light, they rejoiced; but it was never fancy, but always fact, that inspired them. They loved a thorough penetration of the murkiest dens, and most tangled paths of nature; they did not spin from the desires of their own special natures, but reconstructed the world from materials which they collected on every side. Thus their influence upon me was not to prompt me to follow out thought in myself so much as to detect it everywhere, for each of these men is not only a nature, but a happy interpreter of many natures. They taught me to distrust all invention which is not based on a wide experience. Perhaps, too, they taught me to overvalue an outward experience at the expense of inward growth; but all this I did not appreciate till later.

It will be seen that my youth was not unfriended, since those great minds came to me in kindness. A moment of action in one's self, however, is worth an age of apprehension through others; not that our deeds are better, but that they produce a renewal of our being. I have had more productive moments and of deeper joy, but never hours of more tranquil pleasure than those in which these demi-gods visited me,—and with a smile so familiar, that I imagined the world to be full of such. They did me good, for by them a standard was early given of sight and thought, from which I could never go back, and beneath which I cannot suffer patiently my own life or that of any friend to fall. They did me harm, too, for the child fed with meat instead of milk becomes too soon mature. Expectations and desires were thus early raised, after which I must long toil before they can be realized. How poor the scene around, how tame one's own existence, how meagre and faint every power, with these beings in my mind! Often I must cast them quite aside in order to grow in my small way, and not sink into despair. Certainly I do not wish that instead of these masters I had read baby books, written down to children, and with such ignorant dulness that they blunt the senses and corrupt the tastes of the still plastic human being. But I do wish that I had read no books at all till later,—that I had lived with toys, and played in the open air. Children should not cull the fruits of reflection and observation early, but expand in the sun, and let thoughts come to them. They should not through books antedate their actual experiences, but should take them gradually, as sympathy and interpretation are needed. With me, much of life was devoured in the bud.

First Friend

FOR A FEW MONTHS, this bookish and solitary life was invaded by interest in a living, breathing figure. At church, I used to look around with a feeling of coldness and disdain, which, though I now well understand its causes, seems to my wiser mind as odious as it was unnatural. The puny child sought everywhere for the Roman or Shakspeare figures, and she was met by the shrewd, honest eye, the homely decency, or the smartness of a New England village on Sunday. There was beauty, but I could not see it then; it was not of the kind I longed for. In the next pew sat a family who were my especial aversion. There were five daughters, the eldest not above four-and-twenty,—yet they had the old fairy, knowing look, hard, dry, dwarfed, strangers to the All-Fair,—were working-day residents in this beautiful planet. They looked as if their thoughts had never strayed beyond the jobs of the day, and they were glad of it. Their mother was one of those shrunken, faded patterns of woman who have never done anything to keep smooth the cheek and dignify the brow. The father had a Scotch look of shrewd narrowness, and entire self-complacency. I could not endure this family, whose existence contradicted all my visions; yet I could not forbear looking at them.

As my eye one day was ranging about with its accustomed coldness, and the proudly foolish sense of being in a shroud of thoughts that were not their thoughts, it was arrested by a face most fair, and well-known as it seemed at first glance,—for surely I had met her before and waited for her long. But soon I saw that she was a new apparition foreign to that scene, if not to me. Her dress,—the arrangement of her hair, which had the graceful pliancy of races highly cultivated for long,—the intelligent and full picture of her eye, whose reserve was in its self-possession, not in timidity,—all combined to make up a whole impression, which, though too young to understand, I was well prepared to feel.

How wearisome now appears that thorough-bred *millefleur*[13] beauty, the distilled result of ages of European culture! Give me rather the wild heath on the lonely hill-side, than such a rose-tree from the daintily clipped garden. But, then, I had but tasted the cup, and knew not how little it could satisfy; more, more, was all my cry; continued through years, till I had been at the very fountain. Indeed, it was a ruby-red, a perfumed draught, and I need not abuse the wine because I prefer water, but merely say I have had enough of it. Then, the first sight, the first knowledge of such a person was intoxication.

She was an English lady,[14] who, by a singular chance, was cast upon this region for a few months. Elegant and captivating, her every look and gesture was tuned to a different pitch from anything I had ever known. She was in various ways "accomplished," as it is called, though to what degree I cannot now judge. She painted in oils;—I had never before seen any one use the brush, and days would not have been too long for me to watch the pictures growing beneath her hand. She played the harp; and its tones are still to me the heralds of the promised land I saw before me then. She rose, she looked, she spoke; and the gentle swaying motion she made all through life has gladdened memory, as the stream does the woods and meadows.

As she was often at the house of one of our neighbors, and afterwards at our own, my thoughts were fixed on her with all the force of my nature. It was my first real interest in my kind, and it engrossed me wholly. I had seen her,—I should see her,—and my mind lay steeped in the visions that flowed from this source. My task-work I went through with, as I have done on similar occasions all my life, aided by pride that could not bear to fail, or be questioned. Could I cease from doing the work of the day, and hear the reason sneeringly given,—"Her head is so completely taken up with ———— that she can do nothing"? Impossible.

Should the first love be blighted, they say, the mind loses its sense of eternity. All forms of existence seem fragile, the prison of time real, for a god is dead. Equally true is this of friendship. I thank Heaven that this first feeling was permitted its free flow. The years that lay between the woman and the girl only brought her beauty into perspective, and enabled me to see her as I did the mountains from my window, and made her presence to me a gate of Paradise. That which she was, that which she brought, that which she might have brought, were mine, and over a whole region of new life I ruled proprietor of the soil in my own right. Her mind was sufficiently unoccupied to delight in my warm devotion. She could not know what it was to me, but the light cast by the flame through so delicate a vase cheered and charmed her. All who saw admired her in their way; but she would lightly turn her head from their hard or oppressive looks, and fix a glance of full-eyed sweetness on the child, who, from a distance, watched all her looks and motions. She did not say much to me—not much to any one; she spoke in her whole being rather than by chosen words. Indeed, her proper speech was dance or song, and what was less expressive did not greatly interest her. But she saw much, having in its perfection the woman's delicate sense for sympathies and attractions. We walked in the fields, alone. Though others were present, her eyes were gliding over all the field and plain for the objects of beauty to which she was of kin. She was not cold to her seeming companions; a sweet courtesy satisfied them, but it hung about her like her mantle that she wore without thinking of it; her thoughts were free, for these civilized beings can really live two lives at the same moment. With them she seemed to be, but her hand was given to the child at her side; others did not observe me, but to her I was the only human presence. Like a guardian spirit she led me through the fields and groves, and every tree, every bird greeted me, and said, what I felt, "She is the first angel of your life."

One time I had been passing the afternoon with her. She had been playing to me on the harp, and I sat listening in happiness almost unbearable. Some guests were announced. She went into another room to receive them, and I took up her book. It was Guy Mannering, then lately published, and the first of Scott's novels I had ever seen. I opened where her mark lay, and read merely with the feeling of continuing our mutual existence by passing my eyes over the same page where hers had been. It was the description of the rocks on the sea-coast where the little Harry Bertram was lost.[15] I had never seen such places, and my mind was vividly stirred to imagine them. The scene rose before me, very unlike reality, doubtless, but majestic and wild. I was the little Harry Bertram, and had lost her,—all I had to lose,—and sought her vainly in long dark caves that had no end, plashing through the water; while the crags beetled above, threatening to fall and crush the poor child. Absorbed in the painful vision, tears rolled down my cheeks. Just then she entered with light step, and full-beaming eye. When she saw me thus, a soft cloud stole over her face, and clothed every feature with a lovelier tenderness than I had seen there before. She did not question, but fixed on me inquiring looks of beautiful love. I laid my head against her shoulder and wept,—dimly feeling that I must lose her and all,—all who spoke to me of the same things,—that the cold wave must rush over me. She waited till my tears were spent, then rising, took from a little box a bunch of golden amaranths or everlasting flowers,[16] and gave them to me. They were very fragrant. "They came," she said, "from Madeira." These flowers stayed with me seventeen years. "Madeira" seemed to me the fortunate isle, apart in the blue ocean from all of ill or dread. Whenever I saw a sail passing in the distance,—if it bore itself with fulness of beautiful certainty,—I felt that it was going to Madeira. Those thoughts are all gone now. No Madeira exists for me now,—no fortunate purple isle,—and all these hopes and fancies are lifted from the sea into the sky. Yet I thank the charms that fixed them here so long,—fixed them till perfumes like those of the golden flowers were drawn from the earth, teaching me to know my birth-place.

I can tell little else of this time,—indeed, I remember little, except the state of feeling in which I lived. For I *lived,* and when this is the case, there is little to tell in the form of thought. We meet—at least those who are true to their instincts meet—a succession of persons through our lives, all of whom have some peculiar errand to us. There is an outer circle, whose existence we perceive, but with whom we stand in no real relation. They tell us the news, they act on us in the offices of society, they show us kindness and aversion; but their influence does not penetrate; we are nothing to them, nor they to us, except as a part of the world's furniture. Another circle, within this, are dear and near to us. We know them and of what kind they are. They are to us not mere facts, but intelligible thoughts of the divine mind. We like to see how they are unfolded; we like to meet them and part from them; we like their action upon us and the pause that succeeds and enables us to appreciate its quality. Often we leave them on our path, and return no more, but we bear them in our memory, tales which have been told, and whose meaning has been felt.

But yet a nearer group there are, beings born under the same star, and bound with us in a common destiny. These are not mere acquaintances, mere friends, but, when we meet, are sharers of our very existence. There is no separation; the same thought is given at the same moment to both,—indeed, it is born of the meeting, and would not otherwise have been called into existence at all! These not only know themselves more, but *are* more for having met, and regions of their being, which would else have laid sealed in cold obstruction, burst into leaf and bloom and song.

The times of these meetings are fated, nor will either party be able ever to meet any other person in the same way. Both seem to rise at a glance into that part of the heavens where the word can be spoken, by which they are revealed to one another and to themselves. The step in being thus gained, can never be lost, nor can it be re-trod; for neither party will be again what the other wants. They are no longer fit to interchange mutual influence, for they do not really need it, and if they think they do, it is because they weakly pine after a past pleasure.

To this inmost circle of relations but few are admitted, because some prejudice or lack of courage has prevented the many from listening to their instincts the first time they manifested themselves. If the voice is once disregarded it becomes fainter each time, till, at last, it is wholly silenced, and the man lives in this world, a stranger to its real life, deluded like the maniac who fancies he has attained his throne, while in reality he is on a bed of musty straw. Yet, if the voice finds a listener and servant the first time of speaking, it is encouraged to more and more clearness. Thus it was with me,—from no merit of mine, but because I had the good fortune to be free enough to yield to my impressions. Common ties had not bound me; there were no traditionary notions in my mind; I believed in nothing merely because others believed in it; I had taken no feelings on trust. Thus my mind was open to their sway.

This woman came to me, a star from the east, a morning star, and I worshipped her.[17] She too was elevated by that worship, and her fairest self called out. To the mind she brought assurance that there was a region congenial with its tendencies and tastes, a region of elegant culture and intercourse, whose object, fulfilled or not, was to gratify the sense of beauty, not the mere utilities of life. In our relation she was lifted to the top of her being. She had known many celebrities, had roused to passionate desire many hearts, and became afterwards a wife; but I do not believe she ever more truly realized her best self than towards the lonely child whose heaven she was, whose eye she met, and whose possibilities she predicted. "He raised me," said a woman inspired by love, "upon the pedestal of his own high thoughts, and wings came at once, but I did not fly away. I stood there with downcast eyes worthy of his love, for he had made me so."

Thus we do always for those who inspire us to expect from them the best. That which they are able to be, they become, because we demand it of them. "We expect the impossible—and find it."

My English friend went across the sea. She passed into her former life, and into ties that engrossed her days. But she has never ceased to think of me. Her thoughts turn forcibly back to the child who was to her all she saw of the really New World. On the promised coasts she had found only cities, careful men and women, the aims and habits of ordinary life in her own land, without that elegant culture which she, probably, overestimated, because it was her home. But in the mind of the child she found the fresh prairie, the untrodden forests for which she had longed. I saw in her the storied castles, the fair stately parks and the wind laden with tones from the past, which I desired to know. We wrote to one another for many years;—her shallow and delicate epistles did not disenchant me, nor did she fail to see something of the old poetry in my rude characters and stammering speech. But we must never meet again.

When this friend was withdrawn I fell into a profound depression. I knew not how to exert myself, but lay bound hand and foot. Melancholy enfolded me in an atmosphere, as joy had done. This suffering, too, was out of the gradual and natural course. Those who are really children could not know such love, or feel such sorrow. "I am to blame," said my father, "in keeping her at home so long merely to please myself. She needs to be with other girls, needs play and variety. She does not seem to me really sick, but dull rather. She eats nothing, you say. I see she grows thin. She ought to change the scene."

I was indeed *dull*. The books, the garden, had lost all charm. I had the excuse of headache, constantly, for not attending to my lessons. The light of life was set, and every leaf was withered. At such an early age there are no back or side scenes where the mind, weary and sorrowful, may retreat. Older, we realize the width of the world more, and it is not easy to despair on any point. The effort at thought to which we are compelled relieves and affords a dreary retreat, like hiding in a brick-kiln till the shower be over. But then all joy seemed to have departed with my friend, and the emptiness of our house stood revealed. This I had not felt while I every day expectd to see or had seen her, or annoyance and dulness were unnoticed or swallowed up in the one thought that clothed my days with beauty. But now she was gone, and I was roused from habits of reading or reverie to feel the fiery temper of the soul, and to learn that it must have vent, that it would not be pacified by shadows, neither meet without consuming what lay around it. I avoided the table as much as possible, took long walks and lay in bed, or on the floor of my room. I complained of my head, and it was not wrong to do so, for a sense of dulness and suffocation, if not pain, was there constantly.

But when it was proposed that I should go to school, that was a remedy I could not listen to with patience for a moment. The peculiarity of my education had separated me entirely from the girls around, except that when they were playing at active games, I would sometimes go out and join them. I liked violent bodily exercise, which always relieved my nerves. But I had no success in associating with them beyond the mere play. Not only I was not their school-mate, but my book-life and lonely habits had given a cold aloofness to my whole expression, and veiled my manner with a hauteur which turned all hearts away. Yet, as this reserve was superficial, and rather ignorance than arrogance, it produced no deep dislike. Besides, the girls supposed me really superior to themselves, and did not hate me for feeling it, but neither did they like me, nor wish to have me with them. Indeed, I had gradually given up all such wishes myself; for they seemed to me rude, tiresome, and childish, as I did to them dull and strange. This experience had been earlier, before I was admitted to any real friendship; but now that I had been lifted into the life of mature years, and into just that atmosphere of European life to which I had before been tending, the thought of sending me to school filled me with disgust.[18]

Yet what could I tell my father of such feelings? I resisted all I could, but in vain. He had no faith in medical aid generally, and justly saw that this was no occasion for its use. He thought I needed change of scene, and to be roused to activity by other children. "I have kept you at home," he said, "because I took such pleasure in teaching you myself, and besides I knew that you would learn faster with one who is so desirous to aid you. But you will learn fast enough wherever you are, and you ought to be more with others of your own age. I shall soon hear that you are better, I trust."

THE STARS tell all their secrets to the flowers, and, if we only knew how to look around us, we should not need to look above. But man is a plant of slow growth, and great heat is required to bring out his leaves. He must be promised a boundless futurity, to induce him to use aright the present hour. In youth, fixing his eyes on those distant worlds of light, he promises himself to attain them, and there find the answer to all his wishes. His eye grows keener as he gazes, a voice from the earth calls it downward, and he finds all at his feet.

I was riding on the shore of Lake Pontchartrain, musing on an old English expression, which I had only lately learned to interpret. "He was fulfilled of all nobleness." Words so significant charm us like a spell long before we know their meaning. This I had now learned to interpret. Life had ripened from the green bud, and I had seen the difference, wide as from earth to heaven, between nobleness, and the fulfillment of nobleness.

A fragrance beyond anything I had ever known came suddenly upon the air and interrupted my meditation. I looked around me, but saw no flower from which it could proceed. There is no word for it; exquisite and delicious have lost all meaning now. It was of a full and penetrating sweetness, too keen and delicate to be cloying. Unable to trace it, I rode on, but the remembrance of it pursued me. I had a feeling that I must forever regret my loss, my want, if I did not return and find the poet of the lake, which could utter such a voice. In earlier days I might have disregarded such a feeling; but now I have learned to prize the monitions of my nature as they deserve, and learn sometimes what is not for sale in the market-place. So I turned back and rode to and fro at the risk of abandoning the object of my ride.

I found her at last, the Queen of the South, singing to herself in her lonely bower. Such should a sovereign be, most regal when alone; for then there is no disturbance to prevent the full consciousness of power.[1] All occasions limit, a kingdom is but an occasion, and no sun ever saw itself adequately reflected on sea or land.

Nothing at the south had affected me like the Magnolia. Sickness and sorrow, which have separated me from my kind, have requited my loss by making known to me the loveliest dialect of the divine language. "Flowers," it has been truly said, "are the only positive present made us by nature." Man has not been ungrateful, but consecrated the gift to adorn the darkest and brightest hours. If it is ever perverted, it is to be used as a medicine, and even this vexes me. But no matter for that. We have pure intercourse with these purest creations; we love them for their own sake, for their beauty's sake. As we grow beautiful and pure, we understand them better. With me knowledge of them is a circumstance, a habit of my life, rather than a merit. I have lived with them, and with them almost alone, till I have learned to interpret the slightest signs by which they manifest their fair thoughts. There is not a flower in my native region, which has not for me a tale, to which every year is adding new incidents, yet the growths of this new climate brought me new and sweet emotions, and, above all others, was the Magnolia a revelation. When I first beheld her, a stately tower of verdure, each cup, an imperial vestal,[2] full-displayed to the eye of day, yet guarded from the too hasty touch even of the wind by its graceful decorums of firm, glistening, broad, green leaves, I stood astonished as might a lover of music, who after hearing in all his youth only the harp or the bugle, should be saluted on entering some vast cathedral by the full peal of its organ.

After I had recovered from my first surprise, I became acquainted with the flower, and found all its life in harmony. Its fragrance, less enchanting than that of the rose, excited a pleasure more full of life, and which could longer be enjoyed without satiety. Its blossoms, if plucked from their home, refused to retain their dazzling hue, but drooped and grew sallow, like princesses captive in the prison of a barbarous foe.

But there was something quite peculiar in the fragrance of this tree; so much so, that I had not at first recognized the Magnolia. Thinking it must be of a species I had never yet seen, I alighted, and leaving my horse, drew near to question it with eyes of reverent love.

"Be not surprised," replied those lips of untouched purity, "stranger, who alone hast known to hear in my voice a tone more deep and full than that of my beautiful sisters. Sit down, and listen to my tale, nor fear, that I will overpower thee by too much sweetness. I am indeed of the race you love, but in it I stand alone. In my family I have no sister of the heart, and though my root is the same as that of the other virgins of our royal house, I bear not the same blossom, nor can I unite my voice with theirs in the forest choir. Therefore I dwell here alone, nor did I ever expect to tell the secret of my loneliness. But to all that ask there is an answer, and I speak to thee.

"Indeed, we have met before, as that secret feeling of home, which makes delight so tender, must inform thee. The spirit that I utter once inhabited the glory of the most glorious climates. I dwelt once in the orange tree."

"Ah?" said I! "then I did not mistake. It is the same voice I heard in the saddest season of my youth, a time described by the prophetic bard.

'Sconosciuto pur cammina avanti
Per quella via ch'è piu deserta e sola,
E rivolgendo in se quel che far deggia,
In gran tempesta di pensieri on deggia.'

"I stood one evening on a high terrace in another land, the land where 'the plant man has grown to greatest size.' It was an evening, whose unrivalled splendor demanded perfection in man, answering to that he found in nature, a sky 'black-blue,' deep as eternity, stars of holiest hope, a breeze promising rapture in every breath. To all I might have answered, applying still farther the prophecy,

'Una ombra oscura al mondo toglie.
I varj aspetti e i color tinge in negro.'

"I could not long endure this discord between myself and such beauty, I retired within my window, and lit the lamp. Its rays fell on an orange tree, full clad in its golden fruit and bridal blossoms. How did we talk together then, fairest friend; thou didst tell me all; and yet thou knowest, that even then, had I asked any part of thy dower, it would have been to bear the sweet fruit, rather than the sweeter blossoms. My wish had been expressed by another.

'O that I were an orange tree,
That busy plant!

The Magnolia of Lake Pontchartrain

Then should I ever laden be
And never want
Some fruit for him that dresseth me.'

"Thou didst seem to me the happiest of all spirits in wealth of nature, in fulness of utterance. How is it that I find thee now in another habitation?"

"How is it, Man, that thou art now content that thy life bears no golden fruit?"

"It is," I replied, "that I have at last, through privation, been initiated into the secret of peace. Blighted without, unable to find myself in other forms of nature, I was driven back upon the centre of my being, and there found all being. For the wise, the obedient child from one point can draw all lines, and in one germ read all the possible disclosure of successive life."

"Even so," replied the flower, "and ever for that reason am I trying to simplify my being. How happy I was in the 'spirit's dower when first it was wed,' I told thee in that earlier day. But after a while I grew weary of that fulness of speech, I felt a shame at telling all I knew and challenging all sympathies. I was never silent. I was never alone. I had a voice for every season, for day and night. On me the merchant counted, the bride looked to me for her garland, the nobleman for the chief ornament of his princely hall, and the poor man for his wealth. All sang my praises, all extolled my beauty, all blessed my beneficence. And, for a while, my heart swelled with pride and pleasure. But as years passed, my mood changed. The lonely moon rebuked me as she hid from the wishes of man, nor would return till her due change was passed. The inaccessible sun looked on me with the same ray as on all others; my endless profusion could not bribe him to one smile sacred to me alone. The mysterious wind passed me by to tell its secret to the solemn pine. And the nightingale sang to the rose, rather than me, though she was often silent, and buried herself yearly in the dark earth.

"I had no mine or thine, I belonged to all, I could never rest, I was never at one. Painfully I felt this want, and from every blossom sighed entreaties for some being to come and satisfy it. With every bud I implored an answer, but each bud only produced—an orange.

"At last this feeling grew more painful and thrilled my very root. The earth trembled at the touch with a pulse so sympathetic, that ever and anon it seemed, could I but retire and hide in that silent bosom for one calm winter, all would be told me, and tranquillity, deep as my desire, be mine. But the law of my being was on me, and man and nature seconded it. Ceaselessly they called on me for my beautiful gifts; they decked themselves with them, nor cared to know the saddened heart of the giver. O how cruel they seemed at last, as they visited and despoiled me, yet never sought to aid me, or even paused to think that I might need their aid; yet I would not hate them. I saw it was my seeming riches that bereft me of sympathy. I saw they could not know what was hid beneath the perpetual veil of glowing life. I ceased to expect aught from them, and turned my eyes to the distant stars. I thought, could I but hoard from the daily expenditure of my juices, till I grew tall enough, I might reach those distant spheres, which looked so silent and consecrated, and there pause a while from these weary joys of endless life, and in the lap of winter, find my spring.

"But not so was my hope to be fulfilled. One starlight night I was looking, hoping, when a sudden breeze came up. It touched me, I thought, as if it were a cold white beam from those stranger worlds. The cold gained upon my heart, every blossom trembled, every leaf grew brittle, and the fruit began to seem unconnected with the stem. Soon I lost all feeling, and morning found the pride of the garden black, stiff, and powerless.

"As the rays of the morning sun touched me, consciousness returned, and I strove to speak, but in vain. Sealed were my fountains and all my heart-beats still. I felt that I had been that beauteous tree, but now only was—what—I knew not; yet I was, and the voices of men said, It is dead; cast it forth and plant another in the costly vase. A mystic shudder of pale joy then separated me wholly from my former abode.

"A moment more and I was before the queen and guardian of the flowers. Of this being I cannot speak to thee in any language now possible betwixt us. For this is a being of another order from thee, an order whose presence thou mayest feel, nay, approach step by step, but which cannot be known till thou art it, nor seen nor spoken of till thou hast passed through it.

"Suffice it to say, that it is not such a being as men love to paint, a fairy,—like them, only lesser and more exquisite than they, a goddess, larger and of statelier proportion, an angel,—like still, only with an added power. Man never creates, he only recombines the lines and colors of his own existence; only a deific fancy could evolve from the elements the form that took me home.

"Secret, radiant, profound ever, and never to be known, was she; many forms indicate and none declare her. Like all such beings she was feminine. All the secret powers are 'Mothers.'[5] There is but one paternal power.

"She had heard my wish while I looked at the stars, and in the silence of fate prepared its fulfilment. 'Child of my most communicative hour,' said she, 'the full pause must not follow such a burst of melody. Obey the gradations of nature, nor seek to retire at once into her utmost purity of silence. The vehemence of thy desire at once promises and forbids its gratification. Thou wert the keystone of the arch and bound together the circling year; thou canst not at once become the base of the arch, the centre of the circle. Take a step inward, forget a voice, lose a power; no longer a bounteous sovereign, become a vestal priestess and bide thy time in the Magnolia.'

"Such is my history, friend of my earlier day. Others of my family that you have met, were formerly the religious lily, the lonely dahlia, fearless decking the cold autumn, and answering the shortest visits of the sun with the brightest hues, the narcissus, so wrapt in self-contemplation, that it could not abide the usual changes of a life. Some of these have perfume, others not, according to the habit of their earlier state, for as spirits change, they still bear some trace, a faint reminder of their latest step upwards or inwards. I still speak with somewhat of my former exuberance, and over-ready tenderness to the dwellers on this shore, but each star sees me purer, of deeper thought, and more capable of retirement into my own heart. Nor shall I again detain a wanderer, luring him from afar, nor shall I again subject myself to be questioned by an alien spirit to tell the tale of my being in words that divide it from itself. Farewell stranger, and believe that nothing strange can meet me more. I have atoned by confession; further penance needs not, and I feel the Infinite possess me more and more. Farewell, to meet again in prayer, in destiny, in harmony, in elemental power."

The Magnolia left me, I left not her, but must abide forever in the thought to which the clue was found in the margin of that lake of the South.

YUCA FILAMENTOSA

"The Spirit builds his house, in the least flowers,—
A beautiful mansion. How the colours live,
Intricately delicate. Every night
An angel for this purpose from the heavens,
With his small urn of ivory-like hue, drops
A globular world of the purest element
In the flower's midst, feeding its tender soul
With a lively inspiration. I wonder
That a man wants knowledge; is there not here
Spread in amazing wealth, a form too rare,
A soul so inward, that with an open heart
Tremulous and tender, we all must fear,
Not to see near enough, of these deep thoughts?"—MS.

OFTEN, as I looked up to the moon, I had marvelled to see how calm she was in her loneliness. The correspondences between the various parts of this universe are so perfect, that the ear, once accustomed to detect them, is always on the watch for an echo. And it seemed that the earth must be peculiarly grateful to the orb whose light clothes every feature of her's with beauty. Could it be that she answers with a thousand voices to each visit from the sun, who with unsparing scrutiny reveals all her blemishes, yet never returns one word to the flood of gentleness poured upon her by the sovereign of the night?

I was sure there must be some living hieroglyphic to indicate that class of emotions which the moon calls up. And I perceived that the all-perceiving Greeks had the same thought, for they tell us that Diana loved once and was beloved again.[1]

In the world of gems, the pearl and opal answered to the moonbeam, but where was the Diana-flower?—Long I looked for it in vain. At last its discovery was accidental, and in the quarter where I did not expect it.

For several years I had kept in my garden two plants of the Yuca Filamentosa, and bestowed upon them every care without being repaid by a single blossom. Last June, I observed with pleasure that one was preparing to flower. From that time I watched it eagerly, though provoked at the slowness with which it unfolded its buds.

A few days after, happening to look at the other, which had not by any means so favorable an exposure, I perceived flower-buds on that also. I was taking my walk as usual at sunset, and, as I returned, the slender crescent of the young moon greeted me, rising above a throne of clouds, clouds of pearl and opal.

Soon, in comparing the growth of my two plants, I was struck by a singular circumstance. The one, which had budded first, seemed to be waiting for the other, which, though, as I said before, least favorably placed of the two, disclosed its delicate cups with surprising energy.

At last came the night of the full moon, and they burst into flower together. That was indeed a night of long-sought melody.

The day before, looking at them just ready to bloom, I had not expected any farther pleasure from the fulfilment of their promise, except the gratification of my curiosity. The little greenish bells lay languidly against the stem; the palmetto-shaped leaves which had, as it were, burst asunder to give way to the flower-stalk, leaving their edges rough with the filaments from which the plant derives its name, looked ragged and dull in the broad day-light.

But now each little bell had erected its crest to meet the full stream of moonlight, and the dull green displayed a reverse of silvery white. The filaments seemed a robe, also of silver, but soft and light as gossamer. Each feature of the plant was now lustrous and expressive in proportion to its former dimness, and the air of tender triumph, with which it raised its head towards the moon, as if by worship to thank her for its all, spoke of a love, bestowed a loveliness beyond all which I had heretofore known of beauty.

As I looked on this flower my heart swelled with emotions never known but once before. Once, when I saw in woman what is most womanly, the love of a seraph shining through death.[2] I expected to see my flower pass and melt as she did in the celestial tenderness of its smile.

I longed to have some other being share a happiness which seemed to me so peculiar and so rare, and called Alcmeon from the house. The heart and mind of Alcmeon are not without vitality, but have never been made interpreters between nature and the soul. He is one who could travel amid the magnificent displays of the tropical climates, nor even look at a flower, nor do I believe he ever drew a thought from the palm tree more than the poplar.

But the piercing sweetness of this flower's look in its nuptial hour conquered even his obtuseness. He stood before it a long time, sad, soft, and silent. I believe he realized the wants of his nature more than ever he had done before, in the course of what is called a life.

Next day I went out to look at the plants, and all the sweet glory had vanished. Dull, awkward, sallow stood there in its loneliness the divinity of the night before.—Oh Absence!—Life was in the plant; birds sang and insects hovered around; the blue sky bent down lovingly, the sun poured down nobly over it,—but the friend, to whom the key of its life had been given in the order of nature, had begun to decline from the ascendant, had retired into silence, and the faithful heart had no language for any other.

At night the flowers were again as beautiful as before.—Fate! let me never murmur more. There is an hour of joy for every form of being, an hour of rapture for those that wait most patiently.—Queen of night!—Humble Flower!—how patient were ye, the one in the loneliness of bounty,—the other in the loneliness of poverty. The flower brooded on her own heart; the moon never wearied of filling her urn, for those she could not love as children. Had the eagle waited for her, she would have smiled on him as serenely as on the nightingale. Admirable are the compensations of nature. As that flower, in its own season, imparted a dearer joy than all my lilies and roses, so does the Aloes in its concentrated bliss know all that has been diffused over the hundred summers through which it kept silent.—Remember the Yuca; wait and trust; and either Sun or Moon, according to thy fidelity, will bring thee to love and to know.

LEILA

"In a deep vision's intellectual scene."

I HAVE OFTEN but vainly attempted to record what I know of Leila.[1] It is because she is a mystery, which can only be indicated by being reproduced. Had a Poet or Artist met her, each glance of her's would have suggested some form of beauty, for she is one of those rare beings who seem a key to all nature. Mostly those we know seem struggling for an individual existence. As the procession passes an observer like me, one seems a herald, another a basket-bearer, another swings a censer, and oft-times even priest and priestess suggest the ritual rather than the Divinity. Thinking of these men your mind dwells on the personalities at which they aim. But if you looked on Leila she was rather as the *fetiche*[2] which to the mere eye almost featureless, to the thought of the pious wild man suggests all the elemental powers of nature, with their regulating powers of conscience and retribution. The eye resting on Leila's eye, felt that it never reached the heart. Not as with other men did you meet a look which you could define as one of displeasure, scrutiny, or tenderness. You could not turn away, carrying with you some distinct impression, but your glance became a gaze from a perception of a boundlessness, of depth below depth, which seemed to say "in this being (couldst thou but rightly apprehend it) is the clasp to the chain of nature." Most men, as they gazed on Leila were pained; they left her at last baffled and well-nigh angry. For most men are bound in sense, time, and thought. They shrink from the overflow of the infinite; they cannot a moment abide in the coldness of abstractions; the weight of an idea is too much for their lives. They cry, "O give me a form which I may clasp to the living breast, fuel for the altars of the heart, a weapon for the hand." And who can blame them; it is almost impossible for time to bear this sense of eternity. Only the Poet, who is so happily organized as continually to relieve himself by reproduction, can bear it without falling into a kind of madness. And men called Leila mad, because they felt she made them so.[3] But I, Leila, could look on thee;—to my restless spirit thou didst bring a kind of peace, for thou wert a bridge between me and the infinite; thou didst arrest the step, and the eye as the veil hanging before the Isis.[4] Thy nature seemed large enough for boundless suggestion. I did not love thee, Leila, but the desire for love was soothed in thy presence. I would fain have been nourished by some of thy love, but all of it I felt was only for the all.

We grew up together with name and home and parentage. Yet Leila ever seemed to me a spirit under a mask, which she might throw off at any instant. That she did not, never dimmed my perception of the unreality of her existence among us. She *knows* all, and *is* nothing. She stays here, I suppose, as a reminder to man of the temporary nature of his limitations. For she ever transcends sex, age, state, and all the barriers behind which man entrenches himself from the assaults of Spirit.[5] You look on her, and she is the clear blue sky, cold and distant as the Pole-star; suddenly this sky opens and flows forth a mysterious wind that bears with it your last thought beyond the verge of all expectation, all association.[6] Again, she is the mild sunset, and puts you to rest on a love-couch of rosy sadness, when on the horizon swells up a mighty sea and rushes over you till you plunge on its waves, affrighted, delighted, quite freed from earth.

When I cannot look upon her living form, I avail myself of the art magic. At the hour of high moon, in the cold silent night, I seek the centre of the park. My daring is my vow, my resolve my spell. I am a conjurer, for Leila is the vasty deep. In the centre of the park, perfectly framed in by solemn oaks and pines, lies a little lake, oval, deep, and still it looks up steadily as an eye of earth should to the ever promising heavens which are so bounteous, and love us so, yet never give themselves to us. As that lake looks at Heaven, so look I on Leila. At night I look into the lake for Leila.[7]

If I gaze steadily and in the singleness of prayer, she rises and walks on its depths. Then know I each night a part of her life; I know where she passes the midnight hours.

In the days she lives among men; she observes their deeds, and gives them what they want of her, justice or love. She is unerring in speech or silence, for she is disinterested, a pure victim, bound to the altar's foot; God teaches her what to say.

Leila

In the night she wanders forth from her human investment, and travels amid those tribes, freer movers in the game of spirit and matter, to whom man is a supplement. I know not then whether she is what men call dreaming, but her life is true, full, and more single than by day.

I have seen her among the Sylphs' faint florescent forms that hang in the edges of life's rainbows. She is very fair, thus, Leila; and I catch, though edgewise, and sharp-gleaming as a sword, that bears down my sight, the peculiar light which she will be when she finds the haven of herself. But sudden is it, and whether king or queen, blue or yellow, I never can remember; for Leila is too deep a being to be known in smile or tear. Ever she passes sudden again from these hasty glories and tendernesses into the back-ground of being, and should she ever be detected it will be in the central secret of law. Breathless is my ecstasy as I pursue her in this region. I grasp to detain what I love, and swoon and wake and sigh again. On all such beauty transitoriness has set its seal. This sylph nature pierces through the smile of childhood. There is a moment of frail virginity on which it has set its seal, a silver star which may at any moment withdraw and leave a furrow on the brow it decked. Men watch these slender tapers which seem as if they would burn out next moment. They say that such purity is the seal of death. It is so; the condition of this ecstasy is, that it seems to die every moment, and even Leila has not force to die often; the electricity accumulates many days before the wild one comes, which leads to these sylph nights of tearful sweetness.

After one of these, I find her always to have retreated into the secret veins of earth. Then glows through her whole being the fire that so baffles men, as she walks on the surface of earth; the blood-red, heart's-blood-red of the carbuncle.[8] She is, like it, her own light, and beats with the universal heart, with no care except to circulate as the vital fluid; it would seem waste then for her to rise to the surface. There in these secret veins of earth she thinks herself into fine gold, or aspires for her purest self, till she interlaces the soil with veins of silver.[9] She disdains not to retire upon herself in the iron ore. She knows that fires are preparing on upper earth to temper this sternness of her silent self. I venerate her through all this in awed silence. I wait upon her steps through the mines. I light my little torch and follow her through the caves where despair clings by the roof, as she trusts herself to the cold rushing torrents, which never saw the sun nor heard of the ocean. I know if she pauses, it will be to diamond her nature, transcending generations. Leila! thou hast never yet, I believe, penetrated to the central ices, nor felt the whole weight of earth. But thou searchest and searchest. Nothing is too cold, too heavy, nor too dark for the faith of the being whose love so late smiled and wept itself into the rainbow, and was the covenant of an only hope. Am I with thee on thy hours of deepest search? I think not, for still thou art an abyss to me, and the star which glitters at the bottom, often withdraws into newer darknesses. O draw me, Star, I fear not to follow; it is my eye and not my heart which is weak. Show thyself for longer spaces. Let me gaze myself into religion, then draw me down,—down.

As I have wished this, most suddenly Leila bursts up again in the fire. She greets the sweet moon with a smile so haughty, that the heavenly sky grows timid, and would draw back; but then remembering that the Earth also is planetary, and bound in one music with all its spheres, it leans down again and listens softly what this new, strange voice may mean. And it seems to mean wo, wo! for, as the deep thought bursts forth, it shakes the thoughts in which time was resting; the cities fall in ruins; the hills are rent asunder; and the fertile valleys ravaged with fire and water.[10] Wo, wo! but the moon and stars smile denial, and the echo changes the sad, deep tone into divinest music. Wait thou, O Man, and walk over the hardened lava to fresh wonders. Let the chain be riven asunder; the gods will give a pearl to clasp it again.

Since these nights, Leila, Saint of Knowledge, I have been fearless, and utterly free. There are to me no requiems more, death is a name, and the darkest seeming hours sing Te Deum.

See with the word the form of earth transfused to stellar clearness, and the Angel Leila showers down on man balm and blessing. One downward glance from that God-filled eye, and violets clothe the most ungrateful soil, fruits smile healthful along the bituminous lake, and the thorn glows with a crown of amaranth. Descend, thou of the silver sandals, to thy weary son; turn hither that swan-guided car. Not mine but thine, Leila. The rivers of bliss flow forth at thy touch, and the shadow of sin falls separate from the form of light. Thou art now pure ministry, one arrow from the quiver of God; pierce to the centre of things, and slay Dagon for evermore.[11] Then shall be no more sudden smiles, nor tears, nor searchings in secret caves, nor slow growths of centuries. But floating, hovering, brooding, strong-winged bliss shall fill eternity, roots shall not be clogged with earth, but God blossom into himself for evermore.

Straight at the wish the arrows divine of my Leila ceased to pierce. Love retired back into the bosom of chaos, and the Holy Ghost descended on the globes of matter. Leila, with wild hair scattered to the wind, bare and often bleeding feet, opiates and divining rods in each over-full hand, walked amid the habitations of mortals as a Genius, visited their consciences as a Demon.[12]

At her touch all became fluid, and the prison walls grew into Edens. Each ray of particolored light grew populous with beings struggling into divinity. The redemption of matter was interwoven into the coronal of thought, and each serpent form soared into a Phenix.

Into my single life I stooped and plucked from the burning my divine children.[13] And ever, as I bent more and more with an unwearied benignity, an elected pain, like that of her, my wild-haired Genius; more beauteous forms, unknown before to me, nay, of which the highest God had not conscience as shapes, were born from that suddenly darting flame, which had threatened to cleave the very dome of my being. And Leila, she, the moving principle; O, who can speak of the immortal births of her unshrinking love. Each surge left Venus Urania at her feet; from each abjured blame, rose floods of solemn incense, that strove in vain to waft her to the sky. And I heard her voice, which ever sang, "I shrink not from the baptism, from slavery let freedom, from parricide piety, from death let birth be known."

COULD I but write this into the words of earth, the secret of moral and mental alchymy[14] would be discovered, and all Bibles have passed into one Apocalypse; but not till it has all been lived can it be written.

Meanwhile cease not to whisper of it, ye pines, plant here the hope from age to age; blue dome, wait as tenderly as now; cease not, winds, to bear the promise from zone to zone; and thou, my life, drop the prophetic treasure from the bud of each day,—Prophecy.

Of late Leila kneels in the dust, yea, with her brow in the dust. I know the thought that is working in her being. To be a child, yea, a human child, perhaps man, perhaps woman, to bear the full weight of accident and time, to descend as low as ever the divine did, she is preparing. I also kneel. I would not avail myself of all this sight. I cast aside my necromancy, and yield all other prowess for the talisman of humility. But Leila, wondrous circle, who hast taken into thyself all my thought, shall I not meet thee on the radius of human nature? I will be thy fellow pilgrim, and we will learn together the bliss of gratitude.

Should this ever be, I shall seek the lonely lake no more, for in the eye of Leila I shall find not only the call to search, but the object sought. Thou hast taught me to recognize all powers; now let us be impersonated, and traverse the region of forms together. *Together,* CAN that be, thinks Leila, can one be with any but God? Ah! it is so, but only those who have known the one can know the two. Let us pass out into nature, and she will give us back to God yet wiser, and worthier, than when clinging to his footstool as now. "Have I ever feared," said Leila. Never! but the hour is come for still deeper trust. Arise! let us go forth!

BETTINE BRENTANO AND HER FRIEND GÜNDERODE

BETTINE BRENTANO'S letters to Goethe, published under the title of Goethe's correspondence with a Child,[1] are already well known among us and met with a more cordial reception from readers in general than could have been expected. Even those who are accustomed to measure the free movements of art by the conventions that hedge the path of daily life, who, in great original creations, seek only intimations of the moral character borne by the author in his private circle, and who, had they been the contemporaries of Shakspeare, would have been shy of visiting the person who took pleasure in the delineation of a Falstaff;—even those whom Byron sneers at as "the garrison people," suffered themselves to be surprised in their intrenchments, by the exuberance and wild, youthful play of Bettine's genius, and gave themselves up to receive her thoughts and feelings in the spirit which led her to express them. They felt that here was one whose only impulse was to live,—to unfold and realize her nature, and they forgot to measure what she did by her position in society.

There have been a few exceptions of persons who judged the work unworthily, who showed entire insensibility to its fulness of original thought and inspired fidelity to nature, and vulgarized by their impure looks the innocent vagaries of youthful idolatry. But these have been so few that, this time, the vulgar is not the same with the mob, but the reverse.

If such was its reception from those long fettered by custom, and crusted over by artificial tastes, with what joy was it greeted by those of free intellect and youthful eager heart. So very few printed books are in any wise a faithful transcript of life, that the possession of one really sincere made an era in many minds, unlocking tongues that had long been silent as to what was dearest and most delicate in their experiences, or most desired for the future, and making the common day and common light rise again to their true value, since it was seen how fruitful they had been to this one person. The meteor playing in our sky diffused there an electricity and a light, which revealed unknown attractions in seemingly sluggish substances, and lured many secrets from the dim recesses in which they had been cowering for years, unproductive, cold, and silent.

Yet, while we enjoyed this picture of a mind tuned to its highest pitch by the desire of daily ministering to an idolized object; while we were enriched by the results of the Child's devotion to him, hooted at by the Philistines as the "Old Heathen," but to her poetic apprehension "Jupiter, Apollo, all in one," we must feel that the relation in which she stands to Goethe is not a beautiful one. Idolatries are natural to youthful hearts noble enough for a passion beyond the desire for sympathy or the instinct of dependence, and almost all aspiring natures can recall a period when some noble figure, whether in life or literature, stood for them at the gate of heaven, and represented all the possible glories of nature and art. This worship is in most instances, a secret worship; the still, small voice constantly rising in the soul to bid them harmonize the discords of the world, and distill beauty from imperfection, for another of kindred nature has done so. This figure whose achievements they admire is their St. Peter, holding for them the keys of Paradise, their model, their excitement to fulness and purity of life, their external conscience. When this devotion is silent, or only spoken out through our private acts, it is most likely to make the stair to heaven, and lead men on till suddenly they find the golden gate will open at their own touch, and they need neither mediator nor idol more. The same course is observable in the religion of nations, where the worship of Persons rises at last into free thought in the minds of Philosophers.

But when this worship is expressed, there must be singular purity and strength of character on the part both of Idol and Idolater, to prevent its degenerating into a mutual excitement of vanity or mere infatuation. "Thou art the only one worthy to inspire me;" cries one.

"Thou art the only one capable of understanding my inspiration," smiles back the other.

And clouds of incense rise to hide from both the free breath of heaven!

But if the idol stands there, grim and insensible, the poor votary will oftentimes redouble his sacrifices with passionate fervor, until the scene becomes as sad a farce as that of Juggernaut,[2] and all that is dignified in human nature lies crushed and sullied by one superstitious folly.

An admiration restrained by self-respect; (I do not mean pride, but a sense that one's own soul is, after all, a regal power and a precious possession, which, if not now of as apparent magnificence, is of as high an ultimate destiny as that of another) honors the admirer no less than the admired. But humility is not groveling weakness, neither does bounty consist in prodigality; and the spendthrifts of the soul deserve to famish on husks for many days; for, if they had not wandered so far from the Father, he would have given them bread.[3]

In short we are so admirably constituted, that excess anywhere must lead to poverty somewhere[4]; and though he is mean and cold, who is incapable of free abandonment to a beautiful object, yet if there be not in the mind a counterpoising force, which draws us back to the centre in proportion as we have flown from it, we learn nothing from our experiment, and are not vivified but weakened by our love.

Something of this we feel with regard to Bettine and Goethe. The great poet of her nation, and representative of half a century of as high attainment as mind has ever made, was magnet strong enough to draw out the virtues of many beings as rich as she. His greatness was a household word, and the chief theme of pride in the city of her birth. To her own family he had personally been well known in all the brilliancy of his dawn. She had grown up in the atmosphere he had created. Seeing him up there on the mountain, he seemed to her all beautiful and majestic in the distant rosy light of its snow-peaks. Add a nature, like one of his own melodies, as subtle, as fluent, and as productive of minute flowers and mosses, we could not wonder if one so fitted to receive him, had made of her whole life a fair sculptured pedestal for this one figure.

All this would be well, or rather, not ill, if he were to her only an object of thought; but when the two figures are brought into open relation with one another; it is too unequal. Were Bettine, indeed, a child, she might bring her basket of flowers and strew them in his path without expecting even a smile in return. But to say nothing of the reckoning by years, which the curious have made, we constantly feel that she is not a child. She is so indeed when compared with him as to maturity of growth, but she is not so in their relation, and the degree of knowledge she shows of life and thought compels us to demand some conscious dignity of her as a woman. The great art where to stop is not evinced in all passages. Then

Goethe is so cold, so repulsive, diplomatic, and courteously determined not to compromise himself. Had he assumed truly the paternal attitude, he might have been far more gentle and tender, he might have fostered all the beauteous blossoms of this young fancy, without ever giving us a feeling of pain and inequality. But he does not; there is an air as of an elderly guardian flirting cautiously with a giddy, inexperienced ward, or a Father Confessor, who, instead of through the holy office raising and purifying the thoughts of the devotee, uses it to gratify his curiosity. We cannot accuse him of playing with her feelings. He never leads her on. She goes herself, following the vision which gleams before her. "I will not," he says, "wile the little bird from its nest," and he does not. But he is willing to make a tool of this fresh, fervent being; he is unrelenting as ever in this. What she offers from the soul the artist receives,—to use artistically. Indeed we see, that he enjoyed as we do the ceaseless bee-like hum of gathering from a thousand flowers, but only with the cold pleasure of an observer; there is no genuine movement of a grateful sensibility. We often feel that Bettine should perceive this, and that it should have modified the nature of her offerings. For now there is nothing kept sacred, and no balance of beauty maintained in her life. Impatiently she has approached where she was not called, and the truth and delicacy of spiritual affinities has been violated. She has followed like a slave where she might as a pupil. Observe this, young idolaters. Have you chosen a bright particular star for the object of your vespers? you will not see it best or revere it best by falling prostrate in the dust; but stand erect, though with upturned brow and face pale with devotion.

An ancient author says, "it is the punishment of those who have honored their kings as gods to be expelled from the gods," and we feel this about Bettine, that her boundless abandonment to one feeling must hinder for a time her progress and that her maturer years are likely to lag slowly after the fiery haste of her youth. She lived so long, not for truth, but for a human object, that the plant must have fallen into the dust when its prop was withdrawn, and lain there long before it could economize its juices enough to become a tree where it had been a vine.

We also feel as if she became too self-conscious in the course of this intimacy. There being no response from the other side to draw her out naturally, she hunts about for means to entertain a lordly guest, who brings nothing to the dinner but a silver fork. Perhaps Goethe would say his questions and answers might be found in his books; that if she knew what he was, she knew what to bring. But the still human little maiden wanted to excite surprise at least if not sympathy by her gifts, and her simplicity was perverted in the effort. We see the fanciful about to degenerate into the fantastic, freedom into lawlessness, and are reminded of the fate of Euphorion in Goethe's great Rune.[5]

Thus we follow the course of this intimacy with the same feelings as the love of Tasso, and, in the history of fiction, of Werther, and George Douglas, as also those of Sappho, Eloisa, and Mlle. de L'Espinasse.[6] There is a hollowness in the very foundation, and we feel from the beginning,

"It will not, nor it cannot come to good."

Yet we cannot but be grateful to circumstances, even if not in strict harmony with our desires, to which we owe some of the most delicate productions of literature, those few pages it boasts which are genuine transcripts of private experience. They are mostly tear-stained;—by those tears have been kept living on the page those flowers, which the poets present to us only when distilled into essences. The few records in this kind that we possess remind us of the tapestries woven by prisoners and exiles, pathetic heir-looms, in noble families.

Of these letters to Goethe some have said they were so pure a product, so free from any air of literature, as to make the reader feel he had never seen a genuine book before.

Another, "She seems a spirit in a mask of flesh, to each man's heart revealing his secret wishes and the vast capacities of the narrowest life."

But the letters to Goethe are not my present subject; and those before me with the same merits give us no cause however trifling for regret. They are letters which passed between Bettine, and the Canoness Günderode, the friend to whom she was devoted several years previous to her acquaintance with Goethe.

The readers of the Correspondence with a Child will remember the history of this intimacy, and of the tragedy with which it closed, as one of the most exquisite passages in the volumes. The filling out of the picture is not unworthy the outline there given.

Günderode was a Canoness in one of the orders described by Mrs. Jameson,[7] living in the house of her order, but mixing freely in the world at her pleasure. But as she was eight or ten years older than her friend, and of a more delicate and reserved nature, her letters describe a narrower range of outward life. She seems to have been intimate with several men of genius and high cultivation, especially in philosophy, as well as with

Bettine; these intimacies afforded stimulus to her life, which passed, at the period of writing, either in her little room with her books and her pen, or in occasional visits to her family and to beautiful country-places.

Bettine, belonging to a large and wealthy family of extensive commercial connexions, and seeing at the house of grandmother Me. La Roche, most of the distinguished literati of the time, as well as those noble and princely persons who were proud to do honor to letters, if they did not professedly cultivate them, brings before us a much wider circle. The letters would be of great interest, if only for the distinct pictures they present of the two modes of life; and the two beautiful figures which animate and portray these modes of life are in perfect harmony with them.

I have been accustomed to distinguish the two as Nature and Ideal. Bettine, hovering from object to object, drawing new tides of vital energy from all, living freshly alike in man and tree, loving the breath of the damp earth as well as that of the flower which springs from it, bounding over the fences of society as easily as over the fences of the field, intoxicated with the apprehension of each new mystery, never hushed into silence by the highest, flying and singing like the bird, sobbing with the hopelessness of an infant, prophetic, yet astonished at the fulfilment of each prophecy, restless, fearless, clinging to love, yet unwearied in experiment—is not this the pervasive vital force, cause of the effect which we call nature?

And Günderode, in the soft dignity of each look and gesture, whose lightest word has the silvery spiritual clearness of an angel's lyre, harmonizing all objects into their true relations, drawing from every form of life its eternal meaning, checking, reproving, and clarifying all that was unworthy by her sadness at the possibility of its existence. Does she not meet the wild, fearless bursts of the friendly genius, to measure, to purify, to interpret, and thereby to elevate? As each word of Bettine's calls to enjoy and behold, like a free breath of mountain air, so each of Günderode's comes like the moonbeam to transfigure the landscape, to hush the wild beatings of the heart and dissolve all the sultry vapors of day into the pure dewdrops of the solemn and sacred night.

The action of these two beings upon one another, as representing classes of thoughts, is thus of the highest poetical significance. As persons, their relation is not less beautiful. An intimacy between two young men is heroic. They call one another to combat with the wrongs of life; they buckler one another against the million; they encourage each other to ascend the steeps of knowledge; they hope to aid one another in the administration of justice, and the diffusion of prosperity. As the life of man is to be active, they have still more the air of brothers in arms than of fellow students. But the relation between two young girls is essentially poetic. What is more fair than to see little girls, hand in hand, walking in some garden, laughing, singing, chatting in low tones of mystery, cheek to cheek and brow to brow. Hermia and Helena, the nymphs gathering flowers in the vale of Enna, sister Graces and sister Muses rise to thought,[8] and we feel how naturally the forms of women are associated in the contemplation of beauty and the harmonies of affection. The correspondence between very common-place girls is interesting, if they are not foolish sentimentalists, but healthy natures with a common groundwork of real life. There is a fluent tenderness, a native elegance in the arrangement of trifling incidents, a sincere childlike sympathy in aspirations that mark the destiny of women. She should be the poem, man the poet.

The relation before us presents all that is lovely between woman and woman, adorned by great genius and beauty on both sides. The advantage in years, the higher culture, and greater harmony of Günderode's nature is counterbalanced, by the ready spring impulse, richness and melody of the other.

And not only are these letters interesting as presenting this view of the interior of German life, and of an ideal relation realized, but the high state of culture in Germany which presented to the thoughts of those women themes of poesy and philosophy as readily, as to the English or American girl come the choice of a dress, the last concert or assembly, has made them expressions of the noblest aspirations, filled them with thoughts and oftentimes deep thoughts on the great subjects. Many of the poetical fragments from the pen of Günderode are such as would not have been written had she not been the contemporary of Schelling and Fichte, yet are they native and original, the atmosphere of thought reproduced in the brilliant and delicate hues of a peculiar plant. This transfusion of such energies as are manifested in Goethe, Kant, and Schelling into these private lives is a creation not less worthy our admiration, than the forms which the muse has given them to bestow on the world through their immediate working by their chosen means. These are not less the children of the genius than his statue or the exposition of his method. Truly, as regards the artist, the immortal offspring of the Muse,

"Loves where (art) has set its seal,"

are objects of clearer confidence than the lives on which he has breathed; they are safe as the poet tells us death alone can make the beauty of the actual; they will ever bloom as sweet and fair as now, ever thus radiate pure light, nor degrade the prophecy of high moments, by compromise, fits of inanity, or folly, as the living poems do. But to the universe, which will give time and room to correct the bad lines in those living poems, it is given to wait as the artist with his human feelings cannot, though secure that a true thought never dies, but once gone forth must work and live forever.

We know that cant and imitation must always follow a bold expression of thought in any wise, and reconcile ourself as well as we can to those insects called by the very birth of the rose to prey upon its sweetness. But pleasure is unmingled, where thought has done its proper work and fertilized while it modified each being in its own kind. Let him who has seated himself beneath the great German oak, and gazed upon the growth of poesy, of philosophy, of criticism, of historic painting, of the drama, till the life of the last fifty years seems well worth man's living, pick up also these little acorns which are dropping gracefully on the earth, and carry them away to be planted in his own home, for in each fairy form may be read the story of the national tree, the promise of future growths as noble.

The talisman of this friendship may be found in Günderode's postscript to one of her letters, "If thou findest Musse, write soon again," I have hesitated whether this might not be, "if thou findest Muse (leisure) write soon again;" then had the letters wound up like one of our epistles here in America. But, in fine, I think there can be no mistake. They waited for the Muse. Here the pure products of public and private literature are on a par. That inspiration which the poet finds in the image of the ideal man, the man of the ages, of whom nations are but features, and Messiahs the voice, the friend finds in the thought of his friend, a nature in whose positive existence and illimitable tendencies he finds the mirror of his desire, and the spring of his conscious growth. For those who write in the spirit of sincerity, write neither to the public nor the individual, but to the soul made manifest in the flesh, and publication or correspondence only furnish them with the occasion for bringing their thoughts to a focus.

The day was made rich to Bettine and her friend by hoarding its treasures for one another. If we have no object of the sort, we cannot live at all in the day, but thoughts stretch out into eternity and find no home. We feel of these two that they were enough to one another to be led to indicate their best thoughts, their fairest visions, and therefore theirs was a true friendship. They needed not "descend to meet."

Sad are the catastrophes of friendships, for they are mostly unequal, and it is rare that more than one party keeps true to the original covenant.

Happy the survivor if in losing his friend, he loses not the idea of friendship, nor can be made to believe, because those who were once to him the
angels of his life, sustaining the aspiration of his nobler nature, and calming
his soul by the gleams of pure beauty that for a time were seen in their
deeds, in their desires, unexpectedly grieve the spirit, and baffle the trust
which had singled them out as types of excellence amid a sullied race, by
infirmity of purpose, shallowness of heart and mind, selfish absorption or
worldly timidity, that there is no such thing as true intimacy, as harmonious development of mind by mind, two souls prophesying to one another, two minds feeding one another, two human hearts sustaining and
pardoning one another! Be not faithless, thou whom I see wandering alone
amid the tombs of thy buried loves. The relation thou hast thus far sought
in vain is possible even on earth to calm, profound, tender, and unselfish
natures; it is assured in heaven, where only chastened spirits can enter,—
pilgrims dedicate to Perfection.

As there is no drawback upon the beauty of this intimacy—there
being sufficient nearness of age to give Günderode just the advantage
needful with so daring a child as Bettine, and a sufficient equality in every
other respect—so is every detail of their position attractive and picturesque. There is somewhat fantastic or even silly in some of the scenes with
Goethe; there is a slight air of travestie and we feel sometimes as if we saw
rather a masque aiming to express nature, than nature's self. Bettine's
genius was excited to idealize life for Goethe, and gleams of the actual will
steal in and give a taint of the grotesque to the groupes. The aim is to meet
as nymph and Apollo, but with sudden change the elderly prime minister
and the sentimental maiden are beheld instead. But in the intercourse with
Günderode there is no effort; each mind being at equal expense of keeping
up its fires. We think with unmingled pleasure of the two seated together
beside the stove in Günderode's little room, walking in Madame La
Roche's garden, where they "*founded a religion for a young prince,*" or on the
Rhine, or in the old castle on the hill, as described in the following beautiful letters. . . .

SUMMER ON THE LAKES

Summer days of busy leisure,
Long summer days of dear-bought pleasure,
You have done your teaching well;
Had the scholar means to tell
How grew the vine of bitter-sweet,
What made the path for truant feet,
Winter nights would quickly pass,
Gazing on the magic glass
O'er which the new-world shadows pass;
But, in fault of wizard spell,
Moderns their tale can only tell
In dull words, with a poor reed
Breaking at each time of need.
But those to whom a hint suffices
Mottoes find for all devices,
See the knights behind their shields,
Through dried grasses, blooming fields.

TO A FRIEND

Some dried grass-tufts from the wide flowery plain,
A muscle shell from the lone fairy shore,
Some antlers from tall woods which never more
To the wild deer a safe retreat can yield,
An eagle's feather which adorned a Brave,
Well-nigh the last of his despairing band,
For such slight gifts wilt thou extend thy hand
When weary hours a brief refreshment crave?
I give you what I can, not what I would,
If my small drinking-cup would hold a flood,
As Scandinavia sung those must contain
With which the giants gods may entertain;
In our dwarf day we drain few drops, and soon must thirst again.

CHAPTER I

Niagara, June 10, 1843

SINCE you are to share with me such foot-notes as may be made on the pages of my life during this summer's wanderings, I should not be quite silent as to this magnificent prologue to the, as yet, unknown drama. Yet I, like others, have little to say where the spectacle is, for once, great enough to fill the whole life, and supersede thought, giving us only its own presence. "It is good to be here," is the best as the simplest expression that occurs to the mind.

We have been here eight days, and I am quite willing to go away. So great a sight soon satisfies, making us content with itself, and with what is less than itself. Our desires, once realized, haunt us again less readily. Having "lived one day" we would depart, and become worthy to live another.

We have not been fortunate in weather, for there cannot be too much, or too warm sunlight for this scene, and the skies have been lowering, with cold, unkind winds. My nerves, too much braced up by such an atmosphere, do not well bear the continual stress of sight and sound. For here there is no escape from the weight of a perpetual creation; all other forms and motions come and go, the tide rises and recedes, the wind, at its mightiest, moves in gales and gusts, but here is really an incessant, an indefatigable motion. Awake or asleep, there is no escape, still this rushing round you and through you. It is in this way I have most felt the grandeur—somewhat eternal, if not infinite.

At times a secondary music rises; the cataract seems to seize its own rhythm and sing it over again, so that the ear and soul are roused by a double vibration. This is some effect of the wind, causing echoes to the thundering anthem. It is very sublime, giving the effect of a spiritual repetition through all the spheres.

When I first came I felt nothing but a quiet satisfaction. I found that drawings, the panorama, &c. had given me a clear notion of the position and proportions of all objects here; I knew where to look for everything, and everything looked as I thought it would.

Long ago, I was looking from a hill-side with a friend at one of the finest sunsets that ever enriched this world. A little cow-boy, trudging along, wondered what we could be gazing at. After spying about some time, he found it could only be the sunset, and looking, too, a moment, he said approvingly "that sun looks well enough;" a speech worthy of Shakspeare's Cloten,[1] or the infant Mercury, up to everything from the cradle, as you please to take it.

Even such a familiarity, worthy of Jonathan, our national hero, in a prince's palace, or "stumping" as he boasts to have done, "up the Vatican stairs, into the Pope's presence, in my old boots," I felt here; it looks really *well enough*, I felt, and was inclined, as you suggested, to give my approbation as to the one object in the world that would not disappoint.

But all great expression, which, on a superficial survey, seems so easy as well as so simple, furnishes, after a while, to the faithful observer its own standard by which to appreciate it. Daily these proportions widened and towered more and more upon my sight, and I got, at last, a proper foreground for these sublime distances. Before coming away, I think I really saw the full wonder of the scene. After awhile it so drew me into itself as to inspire an undefined dread, such as I never knew before, such as may be felt when death is about to usher us into a new existence. The perpetual trampling of the waters seized my senses. I felt that no other sound, however near, could be heard, and would start and look behind me for a foe. I realized the identity of that mood of nature in which these waters were poured down with such absorbing force, with that in which the Indian was shaped on the same soil. For continually upon my mind came, unsought and unwelcome, images, such as never haunted it before, of naked savages stealing behind me with uplifted tomahawks;[2] again and again this illusion recurred, and even after I had thought it over, and tried to shake it off, I could not help starting and looking behind me.

As picture, the Falls can only be seen from the British side. There they are seen in their veils, and at sufficient distance to appreciate the magical effects of these, and the light and shade. From the boat, as you cross, the effects and contrasts are more melodramatic. On the road back from the whirlpool, we saw them as a reduced picture with delight. But what I liked best was to sit on Table Rock, close to the great fall. There all power of observing details, all separate consciousness, was quite lost.

Once, just as I had seated myself there, a man came to take his first look. He walked close up to the fall, and, after looking at it a moment, with an air as if thinking how he could best appropriate it to his own use, he spat into it.

This trait seemed wholly worthy of an age whose love of *utility* is such that the Prince Puckler Muskau [3] suggests the probability of men coming to put the bodies their dead parents in the fields to fertilize them, and of a country such as Dickens has described; but these will not, I hope, be seen on the historic page to be truly the age or truly the America. A little leaven is leavening the whole mass for other bread.

The whirlpool I like very much. It is seen to advantage after the great falls; it is so sternly solemn. The river cannot look more imperturbable, almost sullen in its marble green, than it does just below the great fall; but the slight circles that mark the hidden vortex, seem to whisper mysteries the thundering voice above could not proclaim,—a meaning as untold as ever.

It is fearful, too, to know, as you look, that whatever has been swallowed by the cataract, is like to rise suddenly to light here, whether uprooted tree, or body of man or bird.

The rapids enchanted me far beyond what I expected; they are so swift that they cease to seem so; you can think only of their beauty. The fountain beyond the Moss Islands, I discovered for myself, and thought it for some time an accidental beauty which it would not do to leave, lest I might never see it again. After I found it permanent, I returned many times to watch the play of its crest. In the little waterfall beyond, nature seems, as she often does, to have made a study for some larger design. She delights in this,—a sketch within a sketch, a dream within a dream. Wherever we see it, the lines of the great buttress in the fragment of stone, the hues of the waterfall, copied in the flowers that star its bordering mosses, we are delighted; for all the lineaments become fluent, and we mould the scene in congenial thought with its genius.

People complain of the buildings at Niagara, and fear to see it further deformed. I cannot sympathize with such an apprehension: the spectacle is capable to swallow up all such objects; they are not seen in the great whole, more than an earthworm in a wide field.

The beautiful wood on Goat Island is full of flowers; many of the fairest love to do homage here. The Wake Robin and May Apple are in bloom now; the former, white, pink, green, purple, copying the rainbow of the fall, and fit to make a garland for its presiding deity when he walks the land, for they are of imperial size, and shaped like stones for a diadem. Of the May Apple, I did not raise one green tent without finding a flower beneath.

And now farewell, Niagara. I have seen thee, and I think all who come here must in some sort see thee; thou art not to be got rid of as easily as the stars. I will be here again beneath some flooding July moon and sun. Owing to the absence of light, I have seen the rainbow only two or three times by day; the lunar bow not at all. However, the imperial presence needs not its crown, though illustrated by it.

General Porter and Jack Downing[4] were not unsuitable figures here. The former heroically planted the bridges by which we cross to Goat Island, and the Wake-Robin-crowned genius has punished his temerity with deafness, which must, I think, have come upon him when he sank the first stone in the rapids. Jack seemed an acute and entertaining representative of Jonathan, come to look at his great water-privilege. He told us all about the Americanisms of the spectacle; that is to say, the battles that have been fought here. It seems strange that men could fight in such a place; but no temple can still the personal griefs and strifes in the breasts of its visitors.

No less strange is the fact that, in this neighborhood, an eagle should be chained for a plaything. When a child, I used often to stand at a window from which I could see an eagle chained in the balcony of a museum. The people used to poke at it with sticks, and my childish heart would swell with indignation as I saw their insults, and the mien with which they were borne by the monarch-bird. Its eye was dull, and its plumage soiled and shabby, yet, in its form and attitude, all the king was visible, though sorrowful and dethroned. I never saw another of the family till, when passing through the Notch of the White Mountains, at that moment striding before us in all the panoply of sunset, the driver shouted, "Look there!" and following with our eyes his upward-pointing finger, we saw, soaring slow in majestic poise above the highest summit, the bird of Jove. It was a glorious sight, yet I know not that I felt more on seeing the bird in all its natural freedom and royalty, than when, imprisoned and insulted, he had filled my early thoughts with the Byronic "silent rages" of misanthropy.

Now, again, I saw him a captive, and addressed by the vulgar with the language they seem to find most appropriate to such occasions—that of thrusts and blows. Silently, his head averted, he ignored their existence, as Plotinus or Sophocles might that of a modern reviewer. Probably, he listened to the voice of the cataract, and felt that congenial powers flowed free, and was consoled, though his own wing was broken.

The story of the Recluse of Niagara interested me a little. It is wonderful that men do not oftener attach their lives to localities of great beauty—that, when once deeply penetrated, they will let themselves so easily be borne away by the general stream of things, to live any where and any how. But there is something ludicrous in being the hermit of a showplace, unlike St. Francis in his mountain-bed, where none but the stars and rising sun ever saw him.

There is also a "guide to the falls," who wears his title labeled on his hat; otherwise, indeed, one might as soon think of asking for a gentleman usher to point out the moon. Yet why should we wonder at such, either, when we have Commentaries on Shakspeare, and Harmonies of the Gospels?

And now you have the little all I have to write. Can it interest you? To one who has enjoyed the full life of any scene, of any hour, what thoughts can be recorded about it, seem like the commas and semicolons in the paragraph, mere stops. Yet I suppose it is not so to the absent. At least, I have read things written about Niagara, music, and the like, that interested *me*. Once I was moved by Mr. Greenwood's[5] remark, that he could not realize this marvel till, opening his eyes the next morning after he had seen it, his doubt as to the possibility of its being still there, taught him what he had experienced. I remember this now with pleasure, though, or because, it is exactly the opposite to what I myself felt. For all greatness affects different minds, each in "its own particular kind," and the variations of testimony mark the truth of feeling.

I will add a brief narrative of the experience of another here, as being much better than anything I could write, because more simple and individual.

"Now that I have left this 'Earth-wonder,' and the emotions it excited are past, it seems not so much like profanation to analyze my feelings, to recall minutely and accurately the effect of this manifestation of the Eternal. But one should go to such a scene prepared to yield entirely to its influences, to forget one's little self and one's little mind. To see a miserable

75

worm creep to the brink of this falling world of waters, and watch the trembling of its own petty bosom, and fancy that this is made alone to act upon him excites—derision?—No,—pity."

As I rode up to the neighborhood of the falls, a solemn awe imperceptibly stole over me, and the deep sound of the ever-hurrying rapids prepared my mind for the lofty emotions to be experienced. When I reached the hotel, I felt a strange indifference about seeing the aspiration of my life's hopes. I lounged about the rooms, read the stage bills upon the walls, looked over the register, and, finding the name of an acquaintance, sent to see if he was still there. What this hesitation arose from, I know not; perhaps it was a feeling of my unworthiness to enter this temple which nature has erected to its God.

At last, slowly and thoughtfully I walked down to the bridge leading to Goat Island, and when I stood upon this frail support, and saw a quarter of a mile of tumbling, rushing rapids, and heard their everlasting roar, my emotions overpowered me, a choking sensation rose to my throat, a thrill rushed through my veins, "my blood ran rippling to my finger's ends." This was the climax of the effect which the falls produced upon me— neither the American nor the British fall moved me as did these rapids. For the magnificence, the sublimity of the latter I was prepared by descriptions and by paintings. When I arrived in sight of them I merely felt, "ah, yes, here is the fall, just as I have seen it in picture." When I arrived at the terrapin bridge, I expected to be overwhelmed, to retire trembling from this giddy eminence, and gaze with unlimited wonder and awe upon the immense mass rolling on and on, but, somehow or other, I thought only of comparing the effect on my mind with what I had read and heard. I looked for a short time, and then with almost a feeling of disappointment, turned to go to the other points of view to see if I was not mistaken in not feeling any surpassing emotion at this sight. But from the foot of Biddle's stairs, and the middle of the river, and from below the table rock, it was still "barren, barren all." And, provoked with my stupidity in feeling most moved in the wrong place, I turned away to the hotel, determined to set off for Buffalo that afternoon. But the stage did not go, and, after nightfall, as there was a splendid moon, I went down to the bridge, and leaned over the parapet, where the boiling rapids came down in their might. It was grand, and it was also gorgeous; the yellow rays of the moon made the broken waves appear like auburn tresses twining around the black rocks. But they did not inspire me as before. I felt a foreboding of a mightier emotion to rise up and swallow all others, and I passed on to the terrapin bridge.

Everything was changed, the misty apparition had taken off its many-colored crown which it had worn by day, and a bow of silvery white spanned its summit. The moonlight gave a poetical indefiniteness to the distant parts of the waters, and while the rapids were glancing in her beams, the river below the falls was black as night, save where the reflection of the sky gave it the appearance of a shield of blued steel. No gaping tourists loitered, eyeing with their glasses, or sketching on cards the hoary locks of the ancient river god. All tended to harmonize with the natural grandeur of the scene. I gazed long. I saw how here mutability and unchangeableness were united. I surveyed the conspiring waters rushing against the rocky ledge to overthrow it at one mad plunge, till, like toppling ambition, o'erleaping themselves, they fall on t'other side, expanding into foam ere they reach the deep channel where they creep submissively away.

Then arose in my breast a genuine admiration, and a humble adoration of the Being who was the architect of this and of all. Happy were the first discoverers of Niagara, those who could come unawares upon this view and upon that, whose feelings were entirely their own. With what gusto does Father Hennepin describe "this great downfall of water," "this vast and prodigious cadence of water, which falls down after a surprising and astonishing manner, insomuch that the universe does not afford its parallel. 'Tis true Italy and Swedeland boast of some such things, but we may well say that they be sorry patterns when compared with this of which we do now speak."[6]

CHAPTER II

THE LAKES

SCENE, STEAMBOAT—*About to leave Buffalo—Baggage coming on
board—Passengers bustling for their berths—Little boys persecuting everybody
with their newspapers and pamphlets—J., S. and M.*[1] *huddled up in a forlorn
corner, behind a large trunk—A heavy rain falling.*

M.   Water, water everywhere. After Niagara one would like a dry strip of existence. And at any rate it is quite enough for me to have it under foot without having it over head in this way.

J.   Ah, do not abuse the gentle element. It is hardly possible to have too much of it, and indeed, if I were obliged to choose amid the four, it would be the one in which I could bear confinement best.

S.   You would make a pretty Undine,[2] to be sure!

J.   Nay, I only offered myself as a Triton, a boisterous Triton of the sounding shell. You, M. I suppose, would be a salamander, rather.

M.   No.! that is too equivocal a position, whether in modern mythology, or Hoffman's tales.[3] I should choose to be a gnome.

J.   That choice savors of the pride that apes humility.

M.   By no means; the gnomes are the most important of all the elemental tribes. Is it not they who make the money?

J.   And are accordingly a dark, mean, scoffing,——

M.   You talk as if you had always lived in that wild unprofitable element you are so fond of, where all things glitter, and nothing is gold; all show and no substance. My people work in the secret, and their works praise them in the open light; they remain in the dark because only there such marvels could be bred.[4] You call them mean. They do not spend their energies on their own growth, or their own play, but to feed the veins of mother earth with permanent splendors, very different from what she shows on the surface.

Think of passing a life, not merely in heaping together, but making gold. Of all dreams, that of the alchymist is the most poetical, for he looked at the finest symbol. Gold, says one of our friends, is the hidden light of the earth, it crowns the mineral, as wine the vegetable order, being the last expression of vital energy.

J.   Have you paid for your passage?

M.   Yes! and in gold, not in shells or pebbles.

J.   No really wise gnome would scoff at the water, the beautiful water. "The spirit of man is like the water."

S.   Yes, and like the air and fire, no less.

J.   Yes, but not like the earth, this low-minded creature's chosen dwelling.

M.   The earth is spirit made fruitful,—life. And its heart-beats are told in gold and wine.

J.   Oh! it is shocking to hear such sentiments in these times. I thought that Bacchic energy of yours was long since repressed.

M.   No! I have only learned to mix water with my wine, and stamp upon my gold the heads of kings, or the hieroglyphics of worship. But since

I have learnt to mix with water, let's hear what you have to say in praise of your favorite.

    J.   From water Venus was born, what more would you have? It is the mother of Beauty, the girdle of earth, and the marriage of nations.

    S.   Without any of that high-flown poetry, it is enough, I think, that it is the great artist, turning all objects that approach it to picture.

    J.   True, no object that touches it, whether it be the cart that ploughs the wave for sea-weed, or the boat or plank that rides upon it, but is brought at once from the demesne of coarse utilities into that of picture. All trades, all callings, become picturesque [5] by the water's side, or on the water. The soil, the slovenliness is washed out of every calling by its touch. All river-crafts, sea-crafts, are picturesque, are poetical. Their very slang is poetry.

    M.   The reasons for that are complex.

    J.   The reason is, that there can be no plodding, groping words and motions, on my water as there are on your earth. There is no time, no chance for them where all moves so rapidly, though so smoothly, every-thing connected with water must be like itself, forcible, but clear. That is why sea-slang is so poetical; there is a word for everything and every act, and a thing and an act for every word. Seamen must speak quick and bold, but also with utmost precision. They cannot reef and brace other than in a Homeric dialect—therefore,—(Steamboat bell rings.) But I must say a quick good-by.

    M.   What, going, going back to earth after all this talk upon the other side. Well, that is nowise Homeric, but truly modern.

    J. is borne off without time for any reply, but a laugh—at himself, of course.

    S. and M. retire to their state-rooms to forget the wet, the chill and steamboat smell in their just-bought new world of novels.

    Next day, when we stopped at Cleveland, the storm was just clearing up; ascending the bluff, we had one of the finest views of the lake that could have been wished. The varying depths of these lakes give to their surface a great variety of coloring, and beneath this wild sky and changeful lights, the waters presented kaleidoscopic varieties of hues, rich, but mournful. I admire these bluffs of red, crumbling earth. Here land and water meet under very different auspices from those of the rock-bound coast to which I have been accustomed. There they meet tenderly to challenge, and proudly to refuse, though not in fact repel. But here they meet to mingle, are always rushing together, and changing places; a new creation takes place beneath the eye.

The weather grew gradually clearer, but not bright; yet we could see the shore and appreciate the extent of these noble waters.

Coming up the river St. Clair, we saw Indians for the first time. They were camped out on the bank. It was twilight, and their blanketed forms, in listless groups or stealing along the bank, with a lounge and a stride so different in its wildness from the rudeness of the white settler, gave me the first feeling that I really approached the West.

The people on the boat were almost all New Englanders, seeking their fortunes. They had brought with them their habits of calculation, their cautious manners, their love of polemics. It grieved me to hear these immigrants who were to be the fathers of a new race, all, from the old man down to the little girl, talking not of what they should do, but of what they should get in the new scene. It was to them a prospect, not of the unfolding nobler energies, but of more ease, and larger accumulation. It wearied me, too, to hear Trinity and Unity discussed in the poor, narrow doctrinal way on these free waters; but that will soon cease, there is not time for this clash of opinions in the West, where the clash of material interests is so noisy. They will need the spirit of religion more than ever to guide them, but will find less time than before for its doctrine. This change was to me, who am tired of the war of words on these subjects, and believe it only sows the wind to reap the whirlwind, refreshing, but I argue nothing from it; there is nothing real in the freedom of thought at the West, it is from the position of men's lives, not the state of their minds. So soon as they have time, unless they grow better meanwhile, they will cavil and criticise, and judge other men by their own standard, and outrage the law of love every way, just as they do with us.

We reached Mackinaw the evening of the third day, but, to my great disappointment, it was too late and too rainy to go ashore. The beauty of the island, though seen under the most unfavorable circumstances, did not disappoint my expectations. But I shall see it to more purpose on my return.

As the day has passed dully, a cold rain preventing us from keeping out in the air, my thoughts have been dwelling on a story told when we were off Detroit, this morning, by a fellow passenger, and whose moral beauty touched me profoundly.

Some years ago, said Mrs. L., my father and mother stopped to dine at Detroit. A short time before dinner my father met in the hall Captain P., a friend of his youthful days. He had loved P. extremely, as did many who knew him, and had not been surprised to hear of the distinction and popular esteem which his wide knowledge, talents, and noble temper commanded, as he went onward in the world. P. was every way fitted to succeed; his aims were high, but not too high for his powers, suggested by an instinct of his own capacities, not by an ideal standard drawn from culture. Though steadfast in his course, it was not to overrun others, his wise self-possession was no less for them than himself. He was thoroughly the gentleman, gentle because manly, and was a striking instance that where there is strength for sincere courtesy, there is no need of other adaptation to the character of others, to make one's way freely and gracefully through the crowd.

My father was delighted to see him, and after a shortly parley in the hall—"We will dine together," he cried, "then we shall have time to tell all our stories."

P. hesitated a moment, then said, "My wife is with me."

"And mine with me," said my father, "that's well; they, too, will have an opportunity of getting acquainted and can entertain one another, if they get tired of our college stories."

P. acquiesced, with a grave bow, and shortly after they all met in the dining-room. My father was much surprised at the appearance of Mrs. P. He had heard that his friend married abroad, but nothing further, and he was not prepared to see the calm, dignified P. with a woman on his arm, still handsome, indeed, but whose coarse and imperious expression showed as low habits of mind as her exaggerated dress and gesture did of education. Nor could there be a greater contrast to my mother, who, though understanding her claims and place with the certainty of a lady, was soft and retiring in an uncommon degree.

However, there was no time to wonder or fancy; they sat down, and P. engaged in conversation, without much vivacity, but with his usual ease. The first quarter of an hour passed well enough. But soon it was observable that Mrs. P. was drinking glass after glass of wine, to an extent few gentlemen did, even then, and soon that she was actually excited by it. Before this, her manner had been brusque, if not contemptuous towards her new acquaintance; now it became, towards my mother especially, quite rude. Presently she took up some slight remark made by my mother, which, though it did not naturally mean anything of the sort, could be twisted into some reflection upon England, and made it a handle, first of vulgar sarcasm, and then, upon my mother's defending herself with some surprise and gentle dignity, hurled upon her a volley of abuse, beyond Billingsgate.

My mother, confounded, feeling scenes and ideas presented to her mind equally new and painful, sat trembling; she knew not what to do, tears rushed into her eyes. My father, no less distressed, yet unwilling to outrage the feelings of his friend by doing or saying what his indignation prompted, turned an appealing look on P.

Never, as he often said, was the painful expression of that sight effaced from his mind. It haunted his dreams and disturbed his waking thoughts. P. sat with his head bent forward, and his eyes cast down, pale, but calm, with a fixed expression, not merely of patient wo, but of patient shame, which it would not have been thought possible for that noble countenance to wear, "yet," said my father, "it became him. At other times he was handsome, but then beautiful, though of a beauty saddened and abashed. For a spiritual light borrowed from the worldly perfection of his mien that illustration by contrast, which the penitence of the Magdalen does from the glowing earthliness of her charms."

Seeing that he preserved silence, while Mrs. P. grew still more exasperated, my father rose and led his wife to her own room. Half an hour had passed, in painful and wondering surmises, when a gentle knock was heard at the door, and P. entered equipped for a journey. "We are just going," he said, and holding out his hand, but without looking at them, "Forgive."

They each took his hand, and silently pressed it, then he went without a word more.

Some time passed and they heard now and then of P., as he passed from one army station to another, with his uncongenial companion, who became, it was said, constantly more degraded. Whoever mentioned having seen them, wondered at the chance which had yoked him to such a woman, but yet more at the silent fortitude with which he bore it. Many blamed him for enduring it, apparently without efforts to check her; others answered that he had probably made such at an earlier period, and finding them unavailing, had resigned himself to despair, and was too delicate to meet the scandal that, with such a resistance as such a woman could offer, must attend a formal separation.

But my father, who was not in such haste to come to conclusions, and substitute some plausible explanation for the truth, found something in the look of P. at that trying moment to which none of these explanations offered a key. There was in it, he felt, a fortitude, but not the fortitude of the hero, a religious submission, above the penitent, if not enkindled with the enthusiasm of the martyr.

I have said that my father was not of those who are ready to substitute specious explanations for truth, and those who are thus abstinent rarely lay their hand on a thread without making it a clue. Such an one, like the dexterous weaver, lets not one color go, till he finds that which matches it in the pattern; he keeps on weaving, but chooses his shades, and my father found at last what he wanted to make out the pattern for himself. He met a lady who had been intimate with both himself and P. in early days, and finding she had seen the latter abroad, asked if she knew the circumstances of the marriage. "The circumstances of the act I know," she said, "which sealed the misery of our friend, though as much in the dark as any one about the motives that led to it."

We were quite intimate with P. in London, and he was our most delightful companion. He was then in the full flower of the varied accomplishments, which set off his fine manners and dignified character, joined, towards those he loved, with a certain soft willingness which gives the desirable chivalry to a man. None was more clear of choice where his personal affections were not touched, but where they were, it cost him pain to say no, on the slightest occasion. I have thought this must have had some connexion with the mystery of his misfortunes.

One day he called on me, and, without any preface, asked if I would be present next day at his marriage. I was so surprised, and so unpleasantly surprised, that I did not at first answer a word. We had been on terms so familiar, that I thought I knew all about him, yet had never dreamed of his having an attachment, and, though I had never inquired on the subject, yet this reserve, where perfect openness had been supposed, and really, on my side, existed, seemed to me a kind of treachery. Then it is never pleasant to know that a heart, on which we have some claim, is to be given to another. We cannot tell how it will affect our own relations with a person; it may strengthen or it may swallow up other affections; the crisis is hazardous, and our first thought, on such an occasion, is too often for ourselves, at least, mine was. Seeing me silent, he repeated his question.

To whom, said I, are you to be married?

That, he replied, I cannot tell you. He was a moment silent, then continued with an impassive look of cold self-possession, that affected me with strange sadness.

"The name of the person you will hear, of course, at the time, but more I cannot tell you. I need, however, the presence, not only of legal, but of respectable and friendly witnesses. I have hoped you and your husband would do me this kindness. Will you?"

Something in his manner made it impossible to refuse. I answered before I knew I was going to speak, "We will," and he left me.

I will not weary you with telling how I harassed myself and my husband, who was, however, scarce less interested, with doubts and conjectures. Suffice it that, next morning, P. came and took us in a carriage to a distant church. We had just entered the porch when a cart, such as fruit and vegetables are brought to market in, drove up, containing an elderly woman and a young girl. P. assisted them to alight, and advanced with the girl to the altar.

The girl was neatly dressed and quite handsome, yet something in her expression displeased me the moment I looked upon her. Meanwhile the ceremony was going on, and, at its close, P. introduced us to the bride, and we all went to the door.

Good-by, Fanny, said the elderly woman. The new-made Mrs. P. replied without any token of affection or emotion. The woman got into the cart and drove away.

From that time I saw but little of P. or his wife. I took our mutual friends to see her, and they were civil to her for his sake. Curiosity was very much excited, but entirely baffled; no one, of course, dared speak to P. on the subject, and no other means could be found of solving the riddle.

He treated his wife with grave and kind politeness, but it was always obvious that they had nothing in common between them. Her manners and tastes were not at that time gross, but her character showed itself hard and material. She was fond of riding, and spent much time so. Her style in this, and in dress, seemed the opposite of P.'s; but he indulged all her wishes, while, for himself, he plunged into his own pursuits.

For a time he seemed, if not happy, not positively unhappy; but, after a few years, Mrs. P. fell into the habit of drinking, and then such scenes as you witnessed grew frequent. I have often heard of them, and always that P. sat, as you describe him, his head bowed down and perfectly silent all through, whatever might be done or whoever be present, and always his aspect has inspired such sympathy that no person has questioned him or resented her insults, but merely got out of the way, so soon as possible.

Hard and long penance, said my father, after some minutes musing, for an hour of passion, probably for his only error.

Is that your explanation? said the lady. O, improbable. P. might err, but not be led beyond himself.

I know his cool gray eye and calm complexion seemed to say so, but a different story is told by the lip that could tremble, and showed what flashes might pierce those deep blue heavens; and when these over intellectual beings do swerve aside, it is to fall down a precipice, for their narrow path lies over such. But he was not one to sin without making a brave atonement, and that it had become a holy one, was written on that downcast brow.

The fourth day on these waters, the weather was milder and brighter, so that we could now see them to some purpose. At night was clear moon, and, for the first time, from the upper deck, I saw one of the great steamboats come majestically up. It was glowing with lights, looking many-eyed and sagacious; in its heavy motion it seemed a dowager queen, and this motion, with its solemn pulse, and determined sweep, becomes these smooth waters, especially at night, as much as the dip of the sailship the long billows of the ocean.

But it was not so soon that I learned to appreciate the lake scenery; it was only after a daily and careless familiarity that I entered into its beauty, for nature always refuses to be seen by being stared at. Like Bonaparte, she discharges her face of all expression when she catches the eye of impertinent curiosity fixed on her. But he who has gone to sleep in childish ease on her lap, or leaned an aching brow upon her breast, seeking there comfort with full trust as from a mother, will see all a mother's beauty in the look she bends upon him. Later, I felt that I had really seen these regions, and shall speak of them again.

In the afternoon we went on shore at the Manitou islands, where the boat stops to wood. No one lives here except woodcutters for the steamboats. I had thought of such a position, from its mixture of profound solitude with service to the great world, as possessing an ideal beauty. I think so still, after seeing the woodcutters and their slovenly huts.

In times of slower growth, man did not enter a situation without a certain preparation or adaptedness to it. He drew from it, if not to the poetical extent, at least, in some proportion, its moral and its meaning. The woodcutter did not cut down so many trees a day, that the hamadryads had not time to make their plaints heard; the shepherd tended his sheep, and did no jobs or chores the while; the idyl had a chance to grow up, and modulate his oaten pipe. But now the poet must be at the whole expense of the poetry in describing one of these positions; the worker is a true Midas to the gold he makes. The poet must describe, as the painter sketches Irish peasant girls and Danish fishwives, adding the beauty, and leaving out the dirt.

I come to the west prepared for the distaste I must experience at its mushroom growth. I know that where "go ahead" is the only motto, the village cannot grow into the gentle proportions that successive lives, and the gradations of experience involuntarily give. In older countries the house of the son grew from that of the father, as naturally as new joints on a bough. And the cathedral crowned the whole as naturally as the leafy summit the tree. This cannot be here. The march of peaceful is scarce less wanton than that of warlike invasion. The old landmarks are broken down, and the land, for a season, bears none, except of the rudeness of conquest and the needs of the day, whose bivouac fires blacken the sweetest forest glades. I have come prepared to see all this, to dislike it, but not with stupid narrowness to distrust or defame. On the contrary, while I will not be so obliging as to confound ugliness with beauty, discord with harmony, and laud and be contented with all I meet, when it conflicts with my best desires and tastes, I trust by reverent faith to woo the mighty meaning of the scene, perhaps to foresee the law by which a new order, a new poetry is to be evoked from this chaos, and with a curiosity as ardent, but not so selfish as that of Macbeth, to call up the apparitions of future kings from the strange ingredients of the witch's caldron. Thus, I will not grieve that all the noble trees are gone already from this island to feed this caldron, but believe it will have Medea's virtue,[6] and reproduce them in the form of new intellectual growths, since centuries cannot again adorn the land with such.

On this most beautiful beach of smooth white pebbles, interspersed with agates and cornelians, for those who know how to find them, we stepped, not like the Indian, with some humble offering, which, if no better than an arrow-head or a little parched corn, would, he judged, please the Manitou,[7] who looks only at the spirit in which it is offered. Our visit was so far for a religious purpose that one of our party went to inquire the fate of some Unitarian tracts left among the woodcutters a year or two before. But the old Manitou, though, daunted like his children by the approach of the fire-ships which he probably considered demons of a new dynasty, he had suffered his woods to be felled to feed their pride, had been less patient of an encroachment, which did not to him seem so authorized by the law of the strongest, and had scattered those leaves as carelessly as the others of that year.

But S. and I, like other emigrants, went not to give, but to get, to rifle the wood of flowers for the service of the fire-ship. We returned with a rich booty, among which was the uva ursi, whose leaves the Indians smoke, with the kinnick-kinnick, and which had then just put forth its highly-finished little blossoms, as pretty as those of the blueberry.

Passing along still further, I thought it would be well if the crowds assembled to stare from the various landings were still confined to the kinnick-kinnick, for almost all had tobacco written on their faces, their cheeks rounded with plugs, their eyes dull with its fumes. We reached Chicago on the evening of the sixth day, having been out five days and a half, a rather longer passage than usual at a favorable season of the year.

Chicago, June 20

There can be no two places in the world more completely thorough-fares than this place and Buffalo. They are the two correspondent valves that open and shut all the time, as the life-blood rushes from east to west, and back again from west to east.

Since it is their office thus to be the doors, and let in and out, it would be unfair to expect from them much character of their own. To make the best provisions for the transmission of produce is their office, and the people who live there are such as are suited for this; active, complaisant, inventive, business people. There are no provisions for the student or idler; to know what the place can give, you should be at work with the rest, the mere traveller will not find it profitable to loiter there as I did.

Since circumstances made it necessary for me so to do, I read all the books I could find about the new region, which now began to become real to me. All the books about the Indians, a paltry collection, truly, yet which furnished material for many thoughts. The most narrow-minded and awkward recital still bears some lineaments of the great features of this nature, and the races of men that illustrated them.

Catlin's book[8] is far the best. I was afterwards assured by those acquainted with the regions he describes, that he is not to be depended on for the accuracy of his facts, and, indeed, it is obvious, without the aid of such assertions, that he sometimes yields to the temptation of making out a story. They admitted, however, what from my feelings I was sure of, that he is true to the spirit of the scene, and that a far better view can be got from him than from any source at present existing, of the Indian tribes of the far west, and of the country where their inheritance lay.

Murray's travels[9] I read, and was charmed by their accuracy and clear broad tone. He is the only Englishman that seems to have traversed these regions, as man, simply, not as John Bull. He deserves to belong to an aristocracy, for he showed his title to it more when left without a guide in the wilderness, than he can at the court of Victoria. He has, himself, no poetic force at description, but it is easy to make images from his hints. Yet we believe the Indian cannot be looked at truly except by a poetic eye. The Pawnees, no doubt, are such as he describes them, filthy in their habits, and treacherous in their character, but some would have seen, and seen truly, more beauty and dignity than he does with all his manliness and fairness of mind. However, his one fine old man is enough to redeem the rest, and is perhaps the relic of a better day, a Phocion among the Pawnees.

Schoolcraft's Algic Researches [10] is a valuable book, though a worse use could hardly have been made of such fine material. Had the mythological or hunting stories of the Indians been written down exactly as they were received from the lips of the narrators, the collection could not have been surpassed in interest, both for the wild charm they carry with them, and the light they throw on a peculiar modification of life and mind. As it is, though the incidents have an air of originality and pertinence to the occasion, that gives us confidence that they have not been altered, the phraseology in which they were expressed has been entirely set aside, and the flimsy graces, common to the style of annuals and souvenirs, substituted for the Spartan brevity and sinewy grasp of Indian speech. We can just guess what might have been there, as we can detect the fine proportions of the Brave whom the bad taste of some white patron has arranged in frock-coat, hat, and pantaloons.

The few stories Mrs. Jameson wrote out,[11] though to these also a sentimental air has been given, offend much less in that way than is common in this book. What would we give for a completely faithful version of some among them. Yet with all these drawbacks we cannot doubt from internal evidence that they truly ascribe to the Indian a delicacy of sentiment and of fancy that justifies Cooper in such inventions as his Uncas.[12] It is a white man's view of a savage hero, who would be far finer in his natural proportions; still, through a masquerade figure, it implies the truth.

Irving's books [13] I also read, some for the first, some for the second time, with increased interest, now that I was to meet such people as he received his materials from. Though the books are pleasing from their grace and luminous arrangement, yet, with the exception of the Tour to the Prairies, they have a stereotype, second-hand air. They lack the breath, the glow, the charming minute traits of living presence. His scenery is only fit to be glanced at from dioramic distance; his Indians are academic figures only. He would have made the best of pictures, if he could have used his own eyes for studies and sketches; as it is, his success is wonderful, but inadequate.

McKenney's Tour to the Lakes [14] is the dullest of books, yet faithful and quiet, and gives some facts not to be met with elsewhere.

I also read a collection of Indian anecdotes and speeches, the worst compiled and arranged book possible, yet not without clues of some value. All these books I read in anticipation of a canoe-voyage on Lake Superior as far as the Pictured Rocks, and, though I was afterwards compelled to give up this project, they aided me in judging of what I afterwards saw and heard of the Indians.

In Chicago I first saw the beautiful prairie flowers. They were in their glory the first ten days we were there—

"The golden and the flame-like flowers."

The flame-like flower I was taught afterwards, by an Indian girl, to call "Wickapee;" and she told me, too, that its splendors had a useful side, for it was used by the Indians as a remedy for an illness to which they were subject.

Beside these brilliant flowers, which gemmed and gilt the grass in a sunny afternoon's drive near the blue lake, between the low oakwood and the narrow beach, stimulated, whether sensuously by the optic nerve, unused to so much gold and crimson with such tender green, or symbolically through some meaning dimly seen in the flowers, I enjoyed a sort of fairyland exultation never felt before, and the first drive amid the flowers gave me anticipation of the beauty of the prairies.

At first, the prairie seemed to speak of the very desolation of dullness. After sweeping over the vast monotony of the lakes to come to this monotony of land, with all around a limitless horizon,—to walk, and walk, and run, but never climb, oh! it was too dreary for any but a Hollander to bear. How the eye greeted the approach of a sail, or the smoke of a steamboat; it seemed that any thing so animated must come from a better land, where mountains gave religion to the scene.

The only thing I liked at first to do, was to trace with slow and unexpecting step the narrow margin of the lake. Sometimes a heavy swell gave it expression; at others, only its varied coloring, which I found more admirable every day, and which gave it an air of mirage instead of the vastness of ocean. Then there was a grandeur in the feeling that I might continue that walk, if I had any seven-leagued mode of conveyance to save fatigue, for hundreds of miles without an obstacle and without a change.

But after I had rode out, and seen the flowers and seen the sun set with that calmness seen only in the prairies, and the cattle winding slowly home to their homes in the "island groves"—peacefullest of sights—I began to love because I began to know the scene, and shrank no longer from "the encircling vastness."

It is always thus with the new form of life; we must learn to look at it by its own standard. At first, no doubt my accustomed eye kept saying, if the mind did not, What! no distant mountains? what, no valleys? But after a while I would ascend the roof of the house where we lived, and pass many hours, needing no sight but the moon reigning in the heavens, or starlight falling upon the lake, till all the lights were out in the island grove of men beneath my feet, and felt nearer heaven that there was nothing but this lovely, still reception on the earth; no towering mountains, no deep tree-shadows, nothing but plain earth and water bathed in light.

Sunset, as seen from that place, presented most generally, low-lying, flaky clouds, of the softest serenity, "like," said S., "the Buddhist tracts."

One night a star shot madly from its sphere, and it had a fair chance to be seen, but that serenity could not be astonished.

Yes! it was a peculiar beauty of those sunsets and moonlights on the levels of Chicago which Chamouny or the Trosachs[15] could not make me forget.

Notwithstanding all the attractions I thus found out by degrees on the flat shores of the lake, I was delighted when I found myself really on my way into the country for an excursion of two or three weeks. We set forth in a strong wagon, almost as large, and with the look of those used elsewhere for transporting caravans of wild beasts, loaded with every thing we might want, in case nobody would give it to us—for buying and selling were no longer to be counted on—with a pair of strong horses, able and willing to force their way through mud holes and amid stumps, and a guide, equally admirable as marshal and companion, who knew by heart the country and its history, both natural and artificial, and whose clear hunter's eye needed neither road nor goal to guide it to all the spots where beauty best loves to dwell.

Add to this the finest weather, and such country as I had never seen, even in my dreams, although these dreams had been haunted by wishes for just such an one, and you may judge whether years of dullness might not, by these bright days, be redeemed, and a sweetness be shed over all thoughts of the West.

The first day brought us through woods rich in the moccasin flower and lupine, and plains whose soft expanse was continually touched with expression by the slow moving clouds which

> "Sweep over with their shadows, and beneath
> The surface rolls and fluctuates to the eye;
> Dark hollows seem to glide along and chase
> The sunny ridges,"

to the banks of the Fox river, a sweet and graceful stream. We reached Geneva just in time to escape being drenched by a violent thunder shower, whose rise and disappearance threw expression into all the features of the scene.

Geneva reminds me of a New England village, as indeed there, and in the neighborhood, are many New Englanders of an excellent stamp, generous, intelligent, discreet, and seeking to win from life its true values. Such are much wanted, and seem like points of light among the swarms of settlers, whose aims are sordid, whose habits thoughtless and slovenly.

With great pleasure we heard, with his attentive and affectionate congregation, the Unitarian clergyman, Mr. Conant, and afterward visited him in his house, where almost everything bore traces of his own handywork or that of his father. He is just such a teacher as is wanted in this region, familiar enough with the habits of those he addresses to come home to their experience and their wants; earnest and enlightened enough to draw the important inferences from the life of every day.

A day or two we remained here, and passed some happy hours in the woods that fringe the stream, where the gentlemen found a rich booty of fish.

Next day, travelling along the river's banks, was an uninterrupted pleasure. We closed our drive in the afternoon at the house of an English gentleman, who has gratified, as few men do, the common wish to pass the evening of an active day amid the quiet influences of country life. He showed us a bookcase filled with books about this country; these he had collected for years, and become so familiar with the localities that, on coming here at last, he sought and found, at once, the very spot he wanted, and where he is as content as he hoped to be, thus realizing Wordsworth's description of the wise man, who "sees what he foresaw."[16]

A wood surrounds the house, through which paths are cut in every direction. It is, for this new country, a large and handsome dwelling; but round it are its barns and farm yard, with cattle and poultry. These, however, in the framework of wood, have a very picturesque and pleasing effect. There is that mixture of culture and rudeness in the aspect of things as gives a feeling of freedom, not of confusion.

I wish it were possible to give some idea of this scene as viewed by the earliest freshness of dewy dawn. This habitation of man seemed like a nest in the grass, so thoroughly were the buildings and all the objects of human care harmonized with what was natural. The tall trees bent and whispered all around, as if to hail with sheltering love the men who had come to dwell among them.

The young ladies were musicians, and spoke French fluently, having been educated in a convent. Here in the prairie, they had learned to take care of the milk-room, and kill the rattlesnakes that assailed their poultry yard. Beneath the shade of heavy curtains you looked out from the high and large windows to see Norwegian peasants at work in their national dress. In the wood grew, not only the flowers I had before seen, and wealth of tall, wild roses, but the splendid blue spiderwort, that ornament of our gardens. Beautiful children strayed there, who were soon to leave these civilized regions for some really wild and western place, a post in the buffalo country. Their no less beautiful mother was of Welsh descent, and the eldest child bore the name of Gwynthleon. Perhaps there she will meet with some young descendants of Madoc,[17] to be her friends; at any rate, her looks may retain that sweet, wild beauty, that is soon made to vanish from eyes which look too much on shops and streets, and the vulgarities of city "parties."

Next day we crossed the river. We ladies crossed on a little foot-bridge, from which we could look down the stream, and see the wagon pass over at the ford. A black thunder cloud was coming up. The sky and waters heavy with expectation. The motion of the wagon, with its white cover, and the laboring horses, gave just the due interest to the picture, because it seemed as if they would not have time to cross before the storm came on. However, they did get across, and we were a mile or two on our way before the violent shower obliged us to take refuge in a solitary house upon the prairie. In this country it is as pleasant to stop as to go on, to lose your way as to find it, for the variety in the population gives you a chance for fresh entertainment in every hut, and the luxuriant beauty makes every path attractive. In this house we found a family "quite above the common," but, I grieve to say, not above false pride, for the father, ashamed of being caught barefoot, told us a story of a man, one of the richest men, he said, in one of the eastern cities, who went barefoot, from choice and taste.

Near the door grew a Provence rose, then in blossom. Other families we saw had brought with them and planted the locust. It was pleasant to see their old home loves, brought into connection with their new splendors. Wherever there were traces of this tenderness of feeling, only too rare among Americans, other things bore signs also of prosperity and intelligence, as if the ordering mind of man had some idea of home beyond a mere shelter, beneath which to eat and sleep.

No heaven need wear a lovelier aspect than earth did this afternoon, after the clearing up of the shower. We traversed the blooming plain, unmarked by any road, only the friendly track of wheels which tracked, not broke the grass. Our stations were not from town to town, but from grove to grove. These groves first floated like blue islands in the distance. As we drew nearer, they seemed fair parks, and the little log houses on the edge, with their curling smokes, harmonized beautifully with them.

One of these groves, Ross's grove, we reached just at sunset. It was of the noblest trees I saw during this journey, for the trees generally were not large or lofty, but only of fair proportions. Here they were large enough to form with their clear stems pillars for grand cathedral aisles. There was space enough for crimson light to stream through upon the floor of water which the shower had left. As we slowly plashed through, I thought I was never in a better place for vespers.

That night we rested, or rather tarried at a grove some miles beyond, and there partook of the miseries so often jocosely portrayed, of bedchambers for twelve, a milk dish for universal handbasin, and expectations that you would use and lend your "hankercher" for a towel. But this was the only night, thanks to the hospitality of private families, that we passed thus, and it was well that we had this bit of experience, else might we have pronounced all Trollopian records of the kind to be inventions of pure malice.[18]

With us was a young lady who showed herself to have been bathed in the Britannic fluid, wittily described by a late French writer, by the impossibility she experienced of accommodating herself to the indecorums of the scene. We ladies were to sleep in the bar-room, from which its drinking visiters could be ejected only at a late hour. The outer door had no fastening to prevent their return. However, our host kindly requested we would call him, if they did, as he had "conquered them for us," and would do so again. We had also rather hard couches; (mine was the supper table,) but we yankees, born to rove, were altogether too much fatigued to stand upon trifles, and slept as sweetly as we would in the "bigly bower" of any baroness. But I think England sat up all night, wrapped in her blanket shawl, and with a neat lace cap upon her head; so that she would have looked perfectly the lady, if any one had come in; shuddering and listening. I know that she was very ill next day, in requital. She watched, as her parent country watches the seas, that nobody may do wrong in any case, and deserved to have met some interruption, she was so well prepared. However, there was none, other than from the nearness of some twenty sets of powerful lungs, which would not leave the night to a deadly still-ness. In this house we had, if not good beds, yet good tea, good bread, and wild strawberries, and were entertained with most free communications of opinion and history from our hosts. Neither shall any of us have a right to say again that we cannot find any who may be willing to hear all we may have to say. "A's fish that comes to the net," should be painted on the sign at Papaw grove.

CHAPTER III

IN THE AFTERNOON of this day we reached the Rock river, in whose neighborhood we proposed to make some stay, and crossed at Dixon's ferry.

This beautiful stream flows full and wide over a bed of rocks, traversing a distance of near two hundred miles, to reach the Mississippi. Great part of the country along its banks is the finest region of Illinois, and the scene of some of the latest romance of Indian warfare. To these beautiful regions Black Hawk[1] returned with his band "to pass the summer," when he drew upon himself the warfare in which he was finally vanquished. No wonder he could not resist the longing, unwise though its indulgence might be, to return in summer to this home of beauty.

Of Illinois, in general, it has often been remarked that it bears the character of country which has been inhabited by a nation skilled like the English in all the ornamental arts of life, especially in landscape gardening. That the villas and castles seem to have been burnt, the enclosures taken down, but the velvet lawns, the flower gardens, the stately parks, scattered at graceful intervals by the decorous hand of art, the frequent deer, and the peaceful herd of cattle that make picture of the plain, all suggest more of the masterly mind of man, than the prodigal, but careless, motherly love of nature. Especially is this true of the Rock river country. The river flows sometimes through these parks and lawns, then betwixt high bluffs, whose grassy ridges are covered with fine trees, or broken with crumbling stone, that easily assumes the forms of buttress, arch and clustered columns. Along the face of such crumbling rocks, swallows' nests are clustered, thick as cities, and eagles and deer do not disdain their summits. One morning, out in the boat along the base of these rocks, it was amusing, and affecting too, to see these swallows put their heads out to look at us. There was something very hospitable about it, as if man had never shown himself a tyrant near them. What a morning that was! Every sight is worth twice as much by the early morning light. We borrow something of the spirit of the hour to look upon them.

The first place where we stopped was one of singular beauty, a beauty of soft, luxuriant wildness. It was on the bend of the river, a place chosen by an Irish gentleman, whose absenteeship seems of the wisest kind, since for a sum which would have been but a drop of water to the thirsty fever of his native land, he commands a residence which has all that is desirable, in its independence, its beautiful retirement, and means of benefit to others.

His park, his deer-chase, he found already prepared; he had only to make an avenue through it. This brought us by a drive, which in the heat of noon seemed long, though afterwards, in the cool of morning and evening, delightful, to the house. This is, for that part of the world, a large and commodious dwelling. Near it stands the log-cabin where its master lived while it was building, a very ornamental accessory.

In front of the house was a lawn, adorned by the most graceful trees. A few of these had been taken out to give a full view of the river, gliding through banks such as I have described. On this bend the bank is high and bold, so from the house or the lawn the view was very rich and command-ing. But if you descended a ravine at the side to the water's edge, you found there a long walk on the narrow shore, with a wall above of the richest hanging wood, in which they said the deer lay hid. I never saw one, but often fancied that I heard them rustling, at daybreak, by these bright clear waters, stretching out in such smiling promise, where no sound broke the deep and blissful seclusion, unless now and then this rustling, or the plash of some fish a little gayer than the others; it seemed not necessary to have any better heaven, or fuller expression of love and freedom than in the mood of nature here.

Then, leaving the bank, you would walk far and far through long grassy paths, full of the most brilliant, also the most delicate flowers. The brilliant are more common on the prairie, but both kinds loved this place.

Amid the grass of the lawn, with a profusion of wild strawberries, we greeted also a familiar love, the Scottish harebell, the gentlest, and most touching form of the flower-world.

The master of the house was absent, but with a kindness beyond thanks had offered us a resting place there. Here we were taken care of by a deputy, who would, for his youth, have been assigned the place of a page in former times, but in the young west, it seems he was old enough for a steward. Whatever be called his function, he did the honors of the place so much in harmony with it, as to leave the guests free to imagine themselves in Elysium. And the three days passed here were days of unalloyed, spotless happiness.

There was a peculiar charm in coming here, where the choice of location, and the unobtrusive good taste of all the arrangements, showed such intelligent appreciation of the spirit of the scene, after seeing so many dwellings of the new settlers, which showed plainly that they had no thought beyond satisfying the grossest material wants. Sometimes they looked attractive, the little brown houses, the natural architecture of the country, in the edge of the timber. But almost always when you came near, the slovenliness of the dwelling and the rude way in which objects around it were treated, when so little care would have presented a charming whole, were very repulsive. Seeing the traces of the Indians, who chose the most beautiful sites for their dwellings, and whose habits do not break in on that aspect of nature under which they were born, we feel as if they were the rightful lords of a beauty they forbore to deform. But most of these settlers do not see it at all; it breathes, it speaks in vain to those who are rushing into its sphere. Their progress is Gothic, not Roman, and their mode of cultivation will, in the course of twenty, perhaps ten, years, obliterate the natural expression of the country.

This is inevitable, fatal; we must not complain, but look forward to a good result. Still, in travelling through this country, I could not but be struck with the force of a symbol. Wherever the hog comes, the rattle-snake disappears; the omnivorous traveller, safe in its stupidity, willingly and easily makes a meal of the most dangerous of reptiles, and one whom the Indian looks on with a mystic awe. Even so the white settler pursues the Indian, and is victor in the chase. But I shall say more upon the subject by-and-by.

While we were here we had one grand thunder storm, which added new glory to the scene.

One beautiful feature was the return of the pigeons every afternoon to their home. Every afternoon they came sweeping across the lawn, positively in clouds, and with a swiftness and softness of winged motion, more beautiful than anything of the kind I ever knew. Had I been a musician, such as Mendelssohn, I felt that I could have improvised a music quite peculiar, from the sound they made, which should have indicated all the beauty over which their wings bore them. I will here insert a few lines left at this house, on parting, which feebly indicate some of the features.

> Familiar to the childish mind were tales
>   Of rock-girt isles amid a desert sea,
> Where unexpected stretch the flowery vales
>   To soothe the shipwrecked sailor's misery.
> Fainting, he lay upon a sandy shore,
> And fancied that all hope of life was o'er;
> But let him patient climb the frowning wall,
> Within, the orange glows beneath the palm tree tall,
> And all that Eden boasted waits his call.

> Almost these tales seem realized to-day,
> When the long dullness of the sultry way,
> Where "independent" settlers' careless cheer
> Made us indeed feel we were "strangers" here,
> Is cheered by sudden sight of this fair spot,
> On which "improvement" yet has made no blot,
> But Nature all-astonished stands, to find
> Her plan protected by the human mind.

> Blest be the kindly genius of the scene;
>   The river, bending in unbroken grace,
> The stately thickets, with their pathways green,
>   Fair lonely trees, each in its fittest place.
> Those thickets haunted by the deer and fawn;
> Those cloudlike flights of birds across the lawn;
> The gentlest breezes here delight to blow,
> And sun and shower and star are emulous to deck the
>   show.

Wondering, as Crusoe, we survey the land;
Happier than Crusoe we, a friendly band;
Blest be the hand that reared this friendly home,
The heart and mind of him to whom we owe
Hours of pure peace such as few mortals know;
May he find such, should he be led to roam;
Be tended by such ministering sprites—
Enjoy such gaily childish days, such hopeful nights!
And yet, amid the goods to mortals given,
To give those goods again is most like heaven.

Hazelwood, Rock River, June 30th, 1843.

The only really rustic feature was of the many coops of poultry near the house, which I understood it to be one of the chief pleasures of the master to feed.

Leaving this place, we proceeded a day's journey along the beautiful stream, to a little town named Oregon. We called at a cabin, from whose door looked out one of those faces which, once seen, are never forgotten; young, yet touched with many traces of feeling, not only possible, but endured; spirited, too, like the gleam of a finely tempered blade. It was a face that suggested a history, and many histories, but whose scene would have been in courts and camps. At this moment their circles are dull for want of that life which is waning unexcited in this solitary recess.

The master of the house proposed to show us a "short cut," by which we might, to especial advantage, pursue our journey. This proved to be almost perpendicular down a hill, studded with young trees and stumps. From these he proposed, with a hospitality of service worthy an Oriental, to free our wheels whenever they should get entangled, also, to be himself the drag, to prevent our too rapid descent. Such generosity deserved trust; however, we women could not be persuaded to render it. We got out and admired, from afar, the process. Left by our guide—and prop! we found ourselves in a wide field, where, by playful quips and turns, an endless "creek," seemed to divert itself with our attempts to cross it. Failing in this, the next best was to whirl down a steep bank, which feat our charioteer performed with an air not unlike that of Rhesus,[2] had he but been as suitably furnished with chariot and steeds!

At last, after wasting some two or three hours on the "short cut," we got out by following an Indian trail,—Black Hawk's! How fair the scene through which it led! How could they let themselves be conquered, with such a country to fight for!

Afterwards, in the wide prairie, we saw a lively picture of non-chalance, (to speak in the fashion of dear Ireland.) There, in the wide sunny field, with neither tree nor umbrella above his head, sat a pedler, with his pack, waiting apparently for customers. He was not disappointed. We bought, what hold in regard to the human world, as unmarked, as mysterious, and as important an existence, as the infusoria to the natural, to wit, pins. This incident would have delighted those modern sages, who, in imitation of the sitting philosophers of ancient Ind, prefer silence to speech, waiting to going, and scornfully smile in answer to the motions of earnest life,

> "Of itself will nothing come,
> That ye must still be seeking?"

However, it seemed to me to-day, as formerly on these sublime occasions, obvious that nothing would come, unless something would go; now, if we had been as sublimely still as the pedler, his pins would have tarried in the pack, and his pockets sustained an aching void of pence!

Passing through one of the fine, park-like woods, almost clear from underbrush and carpeted with thick grasses and flowers, we met, (for it was Sunday,) a little congregation just returning from their service, which had been performed in a rude house in its midst. It had a sweet and peaceful air, as if such words and thoughts were very dear to them. The parents had with them all their little children; but we saw no old people; that charm was wanting, which exists in such scenes in older settlements, of seeing the silver bent in reverence beside the flaxen head.

At Oregon, the beauty of the scene was of even a more sumptuous character than at our former "stopping place." Here swelled the river in its boldest course, interspersed by halcyon isles on which nature had lavished all her prodigality in tree, vine, and flower, banked by noble bluffs, three hundred feet high, their sharp ridges as exquisitely definite as the edge of a shell; their summits adorned with those same beautiful trees, and with buttresses of rich rock, crested with old hemlocks, which wore a touching and antique grace amid the softer and more luxuriant vegetation. Lofty natural mounds rose amidst the rest, with the same lovely and sweeping outline, showing everywhere the plastic power of water,—water, mother of beauty, which, by its sweet and eager flow, had left such lineaments as human genius never dreamt of.

Not far from the river was a high crag, called the Pine Rock, which looks out, as our guide observed, like a helmet above the brow of the country. It seems as if the water left here and there a vestige of forms and materials that preceded its course, just to set off its new and richer designs.

The aspect of this country was to me enchanting, beyond any I have ever seen, from its fullness of expression, its bold and impassioned sweetness. Here the flood of emotion has passed over and marked everywhere its course by a smile. The fragments of rock touch it with a wildness and liberality which give just the needed relief. I should never be tired here, though I have elsewhere seen country of more secret and alluring charms, better calculated to stimulate and suggest. Here the eye and heart are filled.

How happy the Indians must have been here! It is not long since they were driven away, and the ground, above and below, is full of their traces.

"The earth is full of men."

You have only to turn up the sod to find arrowheads and Indian pottery. On an island, belonging to our host, and nearly opposite his house, they loved to stay, and, no doubt, enjoyed its lavish beauty as much as the myriad wild pigeons that now haunt its flower-filled shades. Here are still the marks of their tomahawks, the troughs in which they prepared their corn, their caches.

A little way down the river is the site of an ancient Indian village, with its regularly arranged mounds. As usual, they had chosen with the finest taste. It was one of those soft shadowy afternoons when we went there, when nature seems ready to weep, not from grief, but from an overfull heart. Two prattling, lovely little girls, and an African boy, with glittering eye and ready grin, made our party gay; but all were still as we entered their little inlet and trod those flowery paths. They may blacken Indian life as they will, talk of its dirt, its brutality, I will ever believe that the men who chose that dwelling-place were able to feel emotions of noble happiness as they returned to it, and so were the women that received them. Neither were the children sad or dull, who lived so familiarly with the deer and the birds, and swam that clear wave in the shadow of the Seven Sisters.[3] The whole scene suggested to me a Greek splendor, a Greek sweetness, and I can believe that an Indian brave, accustomed to ramble in such paths, and be bathed by such sunbeams, might be mistaken for Apollo, as Apollo was for him by West.[4] Two of the boldest bluffs are called the Deer's Walk, (not because deer do *not* walk there,) and the Eagle's Nest. The latter I visited one glorious morning; it was that of the fourth of July, and certainly I think I had never felt so happy that I was born in

America. Wo to all country folks that never saw this spot, never swept an enraptured gaze over the prospect that stretched beneath. I do believe Rome and Florence are suburbs compared to this capital of nature's art. The bluff was decked with great bunches of a scarlet variety of the milkweed, like cut coral, and all starred with a mysterious-looking dark flower, whose cup rose lonely on a tall stem. This had, for two or three days, disputed the ground with the lupine and phlox. My companions disliked, I liked it.

Here I thought of, or rather saw, what the Greek expresses under the form of Jove's darling, Ganymede, and the following stanzas took form.

GANYMEDE TO HIS EAGLE,

Suggested by a Work of Thorwaldsen's.[5]

Composed on the height called the Eagle's Nest, Oregon, Rock River, July 4th, 1843.

Upon the rocky mountain stood the boy,
    A goblet of pure water in his hand,
His face and form spoke him one made for joy,
    A willing servant to sweet love's command,
But a strange pain was written on his brow,
And thrilled throughout his silver accents now—

"My bird," he cries, "my destined brother friend,
    O whither fleets to-day thy wayward flight?
Hast thou forgotten that I here attend,
    From the full noon until this sad twilight?
A hundred times, at least, from the clear spring,
    Since the full noon o'er hill and valley glowed,
I've filled the vase which our Olympian king
    Upon my care for thy sole use bestowed;
That at the moment when thou should'st descend,
A pure refreshment might thy thirst attend.

Hast thou forgotten earth, forgotten me,
    Thy fellow bondsman in a royal cause,
Who, from the sadness of infinity,
    Only with thee can know that peaceful pause
In which we catch the flowing strain of love,
Which binds our dim fates to the throne of Jove?

Before I saw thee, I was like the May,
    Longing for summer that must mar its bloom,

Or like the morning star that calls the day,
    Whose glories to its promise are the tomb;
And as the eager fountain rises higher
    To throw itself more strongly back to earth,
Still, as more sweet and full rose my desire,
    More fondly it reverted to its birth,
For, what the rosebud seeks tells not the rose,
The meaning foretold by the boy the man cannot disclose.

I was all Spring, for in my being dwelt
    Eternal youth, where flowers are the fruit,
Full feeling was the thought of what was felt,
    Its music was the meaning of the lute;
But heaven and earth such life will still deny,
For earth, divorced from heaven, still asks the question *Why?*

Upon the highest mountains my young feet
    Ached, that no pinions from their lightness grew,
My starlike eyes the stars would fondly greet,
    Yet win no greeting from the circling blue;
Fair, self-subsistent each in its own sphere,
    They had no care that there was none for me;
Alike to them that I was far or near,
    Alike to them, time and eternity.

But, from the violet of lower air,
    Sometimes an answer to my wishing came,
Those lightning births my nature seemed to share,
    They told the secrets of its fiery frame,
The sudden messengers of hate and love,
The thunderbolts that arm the hand of Jove,
And strike sometimes the sacred spire, and strike the sacred grove.

Come in a moment, in a moment gone,
They answered me, then left me still more lone,
They told me that the thought which ruled the world,
As yet no sail upon its course had furled,
That the creation was but just begun,
New leaves still leaving from the primal one,
But spoke not of the goal to which *my* rapid wheels
    would run.

Still, still my eyes, though tearfully, I strained
To the far future which my heart contained,
And no dull doubt my proper hope profaned.

Summer on the Lakes

At last, O bliss, thy living form I spied,
    Then a mere speck upon a distant sky,
Yet my keen glance discerned its noble pride,
    And the full answer of that sun-filled eye;
I knew it was the wing that must upbear
My earthlier form into the realms of air.

Thou knowest how we gained that beauteous height,
Where dwells the monarch of the sons of light,
Thou knowest he declared us two to be
The chosen servants of his ministry,
Thou as his messenger, a sacred sign
Of conquest, or with omen more benign,
To give its due weight to the righteous cause,
To express the verdict of Olympian laws.

And I to wait upon the lonely spring,
    Which slakes the thirst of bards to whom 'tis given
The destined dues of hopes divine to sing,
    And weave the needed chain to bind to heaven.
Only from such could be obtained a draught
For him who in his early home from Jove's own cup has
    quaffed.

To wait, to wait, but not to wait too long,
Till heavy grows the burthen of a song;
O bird! too long has thou been gone to-day,
My feet are weary of their frequent way,
The spell that opes the spring my tongue no more can say.

If soon thou com'st not, night will fall around,
My head with a sad slumber will be bound,
And the pure draught be spilt upon the ground.

Remember that I am not yet divine,
Long years of service to the fatal Nine
Are yet to make a Delphian vigor mine.

O, make them not too hard, thou bird of Jove,
Answer the stripling's hope, confirm his love,
Receive the service in which he delights,
And bear him often to the serene heights,
Where hands that were so prompt in serving thee,
Shall be allowed the highest ministry,
And Rapture live with bright Fidelity.

The afternoon was spent in a very different manner. The family, whose guests we were, possessed a gay and graceful hospitality that gave zest to each moment. They possessed that rare politeness which, while fertile in pleasant expedients to vary the enjoyment of a friend, leaves him perfectly free the moment he wishes to be so. With such hosts, pleasure may be combined with repose. They lived on the bank opposite the town, and, as their house was full, we slept in the town, and passed three days with them, passing to and fro morning and evening in their boats. (To one of these, called the Fairy, in which a sweet little daughter of the house moved about lighter than any Scotch Ellen ever sung, I should indite a poem, if I had not been guilty of rhyme on the very last page.) At morning this was very pleasant; at evening; I confess I was generally too tired with the excitements of the day to think it so.

Their house—a double log cabin—was, to my eye, the model of a Western villa. Nature had laid out before it grounds which could not be improved. Within, female taste had veiled every rudeness—availed itself of every sylvan grace.

In this charming abode what laughter, what sweet thoughts, what pleasing fancies, did we not enjoy! May such never desert those who reared it and made us so kindly welcome to all its pleasures!

Fragments of city life were dexterously crumbled into the dish prepared for general entertainment. Ice creams followed the dinner drawn by the gentlemen from the river, and music and fireworks wound up the evening of days spent on the Eagle's Nest. Now they had prepared a little fleet to pass over to the Fourth of July celebration, which some queer drumming and fifing, from the opposite bank, had announced to be "on hand."

We found the free and independent citizens there collected beneath the trees, among whom many a round Irish visage dimpled at the usual puffs of Ameriky.

The orator was a New Englander, and the speech smacked loudly of Boston, but was received with much applause, and followed by a plentiful dinner, provided by and for the Sovereign People, to which Hail Columbia served as grace.

Returning, the gay flotilla hailed the little flag which the children had raised from a log-cabin, prettier than any president ever saw, and drank the health of their country and all mankind, with a clear conscience.

Dance and song wound up the day. I know not when the mere local habitation has seemed to me to afford so fair a chance of happiness as this.

To a person of unspoiled tastes, the beauty alone would afford stimulus enough. But with it would be naturally associated all kinds of wild sports, experiments, and the studies of natural history. In these regards, the poet, the sportsman, the naturalist, would alike rejoice in this wide range of untouched loveliness.

Then, with a very little money, a ducal estate may be purchased, and by a very little more, and moderate labor, a family be maintained upon it with raiment, food and shelter. The luxurious and minute comforts of a city life are not yet to be had without effort disproportionate to their value. But, where there is so great a counterpoise, cannot these be given up once for all? If the houses are imperfectly built, they can afford immense fires and plenty of covering; if they are small, who cares?—with such fields to roam in. In winter, it may be borne; in summer, is of no consequence. With plenty of fish, and game, and wheat, can they not dispense with a baker to bring "muffins hot" every morning to the door for their breakfast?

Here a man need not take a small slice from the landscape, and fence it in from the obtrusions of an uncongenial neighbor, and there cut down his fancies to miniature improvements which a chicken could run over in ten minutes. He may have water and wood and land enough, to dread no incursions on his prospect from some chance Vandal that may enter his neighborhood. He need not painfully economise and manage how he may use it all; he can afford to leave some of it wild, and to carry out his own plans without obliterating those of nature.

Here, whole families might live together, if they would. The sons might return from their pilgrimages to settle near the parent hearth; the daughters might find room near their mother. Those painful separations, which already desecrate and desolate the Atlantic coast, are not enforced here by the stern need of seeking bread; and where they are voluntary, it is no matter. To me, too, used to the feelings which haunt a society of struggling men, it was delightful to look upon a scene where nature still wore her motherly smile and seemed to promise room not only for those favored or cursed with the qualities best adapting for the strifes of competition, but for the delicate, the thoughtful, even the indolent or eccentric. She did not say, Fight or starve; nor even, Work or cease to exist; but, merely showing that the apple was a finer fruit than the wild crab, gave both room to grow in the garden.

A pleasant society is formed of the families who live along the banks of this stream upon farms. They are from various parts of the world, and have much to communicate to one another. Many have cultivated minds and refined manners, all a varied experience, while they have in common the interests of a new country and a new life. They must traverse some space to get at one another, but the journey is through scenes that make it a separate pleasure. They must bear inconveniences to stay in one another's houses; but these, to the well-disposed, are only a source of amusement and adventure.

The great drawback upon the lives of these settlers, at present, is the unfitness of the women for their new lot. It has generally been the choice of the men, and the women follow, as women will, doing their best for affection's sake, but too often in heartsickness and weariness. Beside it frequently not being a choice or conviction of their own minds that it is best to be here, their part is the hardest, and they are least fitted for it. The men can find assistance in field labor, and recreation with the gun and fishing-rod. Their bodily strength is greater, and enables them to bear and enjoy both these forms of life.

The women can rarely find any aid in domestic labor. All its various and careful tasks must often be performed, sick or well, by the mother and daughters, to whom a city education has imparted neither the strength nor skill now demanded.

The wives of the poorer settlers, having more hard work to do than before, very frequently become slatterns; but the ladies, accustomed to a refined neatness, feel that they cannot degrade themselves by its absence, and struggle under every disadvantage to keep up the necessary routine of small arrangements.

With all these disadvantages for work, their resources for pleasure are fewer. When they can leave the housework, they have not learnt to ride, to drive, to row, alone. Their culture has too generally been that given to women to make them "the ornaments of society." They can dance, but not draw; talk French, but know nothing of the language of flowers; neither in childhood were allowed to cultivate them, lest they should tan their complexions. Accustomed to the pavement of Broadway, they dare not tread the wildwood paths for fear of rattlesnakes!

Seeing much of this joylessness, and inaptitude, both of body and mind, for a lot which would be full of blessings for those prepared for it, we could not but look with deep interest on the little girls, and hope they would grow up with the strength of body, dexterity, simple tastes, and resources that would fit them to enjoy and refine the western farmer's life.

But they have a great deal to war with in the habits of thought acquired by their mothers from their own early life. Everywhere the fatal spirit of imitation, of reference to European standards, penetrates, and threatens to blight whatever of original growth might adorn the soil.

If the little girls grow up strong, resolute, able to exert their faculties, their mothers mourn over their want of fashionable delicacy. Are they gay, enterprising, ready to fly about in the various ways that teach them so much, these ladies lament that "they cannot go to school, where they might learn to be quiet." They lament the want of "education" for their daughters, as if the thousand needs which call out their young energies, and the language of nature around, yielded no education.

Their grand ambition for their children, is to send them to school in some eastern city, the measure most likely to make them useless and unhappy at home. I earnestly hope that, ere long, the existence of good schools near themselves, planned by persons of sufficient thought to meet the wants of the place and time, instead of copying New York or Boston, will correct this mania. Instruction the children want to enable them to profit by the great natural advantages of their position; but methods copied from the education of some English Lady Augusta, are as ill suited to the daughter of an Illinois farmer, as satin shoes to climb the Indian mounds. An elegance she would diffuse around her, if her mind were opened to appreciate elegance; it might be of a kind new, original, enchanting, as different from that of the city belle as that of the prairie torchflower from the shopworn article that touches the cheek of that lady within her bonnet.

To a girl really skilled to make home beautiful and comfortable, with bodily strength to enjoy plenty of exercise, the woods, the streams, a few studies, music, and the sincere and familiar intercourse, far more easily to be met here than elsewhere, would afford happiness enough. Her eyes would not grow dim, nor her cheeks sunken, in the absence of parties, morning visits, and milliner's shops.

As to music, I wish I could see in such places the guitar rather than the piano, and good vocal more than instrumental music.

The piano many carry with them, because it is the fashionable instrument in the eastern cities. Even there, it is so merely from the habit of imitating Europe, for not one in a thousand is willing to give the labor requisite to ensure any valuable use of the instrument.

But, out here, where the ladies have so much less leisure, it is still less desirable. Add to this, they never know how to tune their own instruments, and as persons seldom visit them who can do so, these pianos are constantly out of tune, and would spoil the ear of one who began by having any.

The guitar, or some portable instrument which requires less practice, and could be kept in tune by themselves, would be far more desirable for most of these ladies. It would give all they want as a household companion to fill up the gaps of life with a pleasant stimulus or solace, and be sufficient accompaniment to the voice in social meetings.

Singing in parts is the most delightful family amusement, and those who are constantly together can learn to sing in perfect accord. All the practice it needs, after some good elementary instruction, is such as meetings by summer twilight, and evening firelight naturally suggest. And, as music is an universal language, we cannot but think a fine Italian duet would be much at home in the log cabin as one of Mrs. Gore's novels.[6]

The sixth July we left this beautiful place. It was one of those rich days of bright sunlight, varied by the purple shadows of large sweeping clouds. Many a backward look we cast, and left the heart behind.

Our journey to-day was no less delightful than before, still all new, boundless, limitless. Kinmont[7] says, that limits are sacred; that the Greeks were in the right to worship a god of limits. I say, that what is limitless is alone divine, that there was neither wall nor road in Eden, that those who walked there lost and found their way just as we did, and that all the gain from the Fall was that we had a wagon to ride in. I do not think, either, that even the horses doubted whether this last was any advantage.

Everywhere the rattlesnake-weed grows in profusion. The antidote survives the bane. Soon the coarser plantain, the "white man's footstep," shall take its place.

We saw also the compass plant, and the western tea plant. Of some of the brightest flowers an Indian girl afterwards told me the medicinal virtues. I doubt not those students of the soil knew a use to every fair emblem, on which we could only look to admire its hues and shape.

After noon we were ferried by a girl, (unfortunately not of the most picturesque appearance) across the Kishwaukie, the most graceful stream, and on whose bosom rested many full-blown water-lilies, twice as large as any of ours. I was told that, *en revanche,*[8] they were scentless, but I still regret that I could not get at one of them to try.

Query, did the lilied fragrance which, in the miraculous times, accompanied visions of saints and angels, proceed from water or garden lilies?

Kishwaukie is, according to tradition, the scene of a famous battle, and its many grassy mounds contain the bones of the valiant. On these waved thickly the mysterious purple flower, of which I have spoken before. I think it springs from the blood of the Indians, as the hyacinth did from that of Apollo's darling.[9]

The ladies of our host's family at Oregon, when they first went there, after all the pains and plagues of building and settling, found their first pastime in opening one of these mounds, in which they found, I think, three of the departed, seated in the Indian fashion.

One of these same ladies, as she was making bread one winter morning, saw from the window a deer directly before the house. She ran out, with her hands covered with dough, calling the others, and they caught him bodily before he had time to escape.

Here (at Kishwaukie) we received a visit from a ragged and barefoot, but bright-eyed gentleman, who seemed to be the intellectual loafer, the walking Will's coffeehouse of the place. He told us many charming snake stories; among others, of himself having seen seventeen young ones reenter the mother snake, on the intrusion of a visiter.

This night we reached Belvidere, a flourishing town in Boon county, where was the tomb, now despoiled, of Big Thunder.[10] In this later day we felt happy to find a really good hotel.

From this place, by two days of very leisurely and devious journeying, we reached Chicago, and thus ended a journey, which one at least of the party might have wished unending.

I have not been particularly anxious to give the geography of the scene, inasmuch as it seemed to me no route, nor series of stations, but a garden interspersed with cottages, groves and flowery lawns, through which a stately river ran. I had no guidebook, kept no diary, do not know how many miles we travelled each day, nor how many in all. What I got from the journey was the poetic impression of the country at large; it is all I have aimed to communicate.

The narrative might have been made much more interesting, as life was at the time, by many piquant anecdotes and tales drawn from private life. But here courtesy restrains the pen, for I know those who received the stranger with such frank kindness would feel ill requited by its becoming the means of fixing many spy-glasses, even though the scrutiny might be one of admiring interest, upon their private homes.

For many of these, too, I was indebted to a friend, whose property they more lawfully are. This friend was one of those rare beings who are equally at home in nature and with man. He knew a tale of all that ran and swam, and flew, or only grew, possessing that extensive familiarity with things which shows equal sweetness of sympathy and playful penetration. Most refreshing to me was his unstudied lore, the unwritten poetry which common life presents to a strong and gentle mind. It was a great contrast to the subtleties of analysis, the philosophic strainings of which I had seen too much. But I will not attempt to transplant it. May it profit others as it did me in the region where it was born, where it belongs. The evening of our return to Chicago the sunset was of a splendor and calmness beyond any we saw at the West. The twilight that succeeded was equally beautiful; soft, pathetic, but just so calm. When afterwards I learned this was the evening of Allston's death,[11] it seemed to me as if this glorious pageant was not without connection with that event; at least, it inspired similar emotions,—a heavenly gate closing a path adorned with shows well worthy Paradise.

> Farewell, ye soft and sumptuous solitudes!
> Ye fairy distances, ye lordly woods,
> Haunted by paths like those that Poussin[12] knew,
> When after his all gazers eyes he drew;
> I go,—and if I never more may steep
> An eager heart in your enchantments deep,
> Yet ever to itself that heart may say,
> Be not exacting; thou hast lived one day;
> Hast looked on that which matches with thy mood,
> Impassioned sweetness of full being's flood,
> Where nothing checked the bold yet gentle wave,
> Where nought repelled the lavish love that gave.
> A tender blessing lingers o'er the scene,
> Like some young mother's thought, fond, yet serene,
> And through its life new-born our lives have been.
> Once more farewell,—a sad, a sweet farewell;
> And, if I never must behold you more,
> In other worlds I will not cease to tell
> The rosary I here have numbered o'er;
> And bright-haired Hope will lend a gladdened ear,
> And Love will free him from the grasp of Fear,
> And Gorgon[13] critics, while the tale they hear,
> Shall dew their stony glances with a tear,
> If I but catch one echo from your spell;—
> And so farewell,—a grateful, sad farewell!

CHAPTER IV

Chicago Again

CHICAGO had become interesting to me now, that I knew it as the portal to so fair a scene. I had become interested in the land, in the people, and looked sorrowfully on the lake on which I must soon embark, to leave behind what I had just begun to enjoy.

Now was the time to see the lake. The July moon was near its full, and night after night it rose in a cloudless sky above this majestic sea. The heat was excessive, so that there was no enjoyment of life, except in the night, but then the air was of that delicious temperature, worthy of orange groves. However, they were not wanted;—nothing was, as that full light fell on the faintly rippling waters which then seemed boundless.

A poem received shortly after, from a friend in Massachusetts,[1] seemed to say that the July moon shone there not less splendid, and may claim insertion here.

TRIFORMIS

I

So pure her forehead's dazzling white;
　So swift and clear her radiant eyes,
Within the treasure of whose light
　Lay undeveloped destinies,—
Of thoughts repressed such hidden store
　Was hinted by each flitting smile,
I could but wonder and adore,
　Far off, in awe, I gazed the while.

I gazed at her, as at the moon,
　Hanging in lustrous twilight skies,
Whose virgin crescent, sinking soon,
　Peeps through the leaves before it flies.
Untouched Diana, flitting dim,
　While sings the wood its evening hymn.

II

Again we met. O joyful meeting!
   Her radiance now was all for me,
Like kindly airs her kindly greeting,
   So full, so musical, so free.
Within romantic forest aisles,
   Within romantic paths we walked,
I bathed me in her sister smiles,
   I breathed her beauty as we talked.

So full-orbed Cynthia walks the skies,
   Filling the earth with melodies,
Even so she condescends to kiss
   Drowsy Endymions, coarse and dull,
Or fills our waking souls with bliss,
   Making long nights too beautiful.

III

O fair, but fickle lady-moon,
   Why must thy full form ever wane?
O love! O friendship! why so soon
   Must your sweet light recede again?
I wake me in the dead of night,
   And start,—for through the misty gloom
Red Hecate stares—a boding sight!—
   Looks in, but never fills my room.

Thou music of my boyhood's hour!
   Thou shining light on manhood's way!
No more dost thou fair influence shower
   To move my soul by night or day.
O strange! that while in hall and street
   Thy hand I touch, thy grace I meet,
Such miles of polar ice should part
   The slightest touch of mind and heart!
But all thy love has waned, and so
   I gladly let thy beauty go.

Now that I am borrowing, I will also give a letter received at this
time, and extracts from others from an earlier traveller, and in a different
region of the country from that I saw, which, I think, in different ways,
admirably descriptive of the country.

"And you, too, love the Prairies, flying voyager of a summer hour; but *I* have only there owned the wild forest, the wide-spread meadows; there only built my house, and seen the livelong day the thoughtful shadows of the great clouds color, with all-transient browns, the untrampled floor of grass; there has Spring pranked the long smooth reaches with those golden flowers, whereby became the fields a sea too golden to o'erlast the heats. Yes! and with many a yellow bell she gilded our unbounded path, that sank in the light swells of the varied surface, skirted the untilled barrens, nor shunned the steep banks of rivers darting merrily on. There has the white snow frolicsomely strown itself, till all that vast, outstretched distance glittered like a mirror in which only the heavens were reflected, and among these drifts our steps have been curbed. Ah! many days of precious weather are on the Prairies!

"You have then found, after many a weary hour, when Time has locked your temples as in a circle of heated metal, some cool, sweet, swift-gliding moments, the iron ring of necessity ungirt, and the fevered pulses at rest. You have also found this where fresh nature suffers no ravage, amid those bowers of wild-wood, those dream-like, bee-sung, murmuring and musical plains, swimming under their hazy distances, as if there, in that warm and deep back ground, stood the fairy castle of our hopes, with its fountains, its pictures, its many mystical figures in repose. Ever could we rove over those sunny distances, breathing that modulated wind, eyeing those so well-blended, imaginative, yet thoughtful surfaces, and above us wide—wide a horizon effortless and superb as a young divinity.

"I was a prisoner where you glide, the summer's pensioned guest, and my chains were the past and the future, darkness and blowing sand. There, very weary, I received from the distance a sweet emblem of an incorruptible, lofty and pervasive nature, but was I less weary? I was a prisoner, and you, plains, were my prison bars.

"Yet never, O never, beautiful plains, had I any feeling for you but profoundest gratitude, for indeed ye are only fair, grand and majestic, while I had scarcely a right there. Now, ye stand in that past day, grateful images of unshattered repose, simple in your tranquillity, strong in your self-possession, yet ever musical and springing as the footsteps of a child.

"Ah! that to some poet, whose lyre had never lost a string, to whom mortality, kinder than is her custom, had vouchsafed a day whose down had been untouched,—that to him these plains might enter, and flow forth in airy song. And you, forests, under whose symmetrical shields of dark green the colors of the fawns move, like the waters of the river under its spears,—its cimeters of flag, where, in gleaming circles of steel, the breasts of the wood-pigeons flash in the playful sunbeam, and many sounds, many notes of no earthly music, come over the well-relieved glades,—should not your depth pass into that poet's heart,—in your depths should he not fuse his own?"

The other letters show the painter's eye, as this the poet's heart.

"Springfield, Illinois, May 20, 1840.

"Yesterday morning I left Griggsville, my knapsack at my back, pursued my journey all day on foot, and found so new and great delight in this charming country, that I must needs tell you about it. Do you remember our saying once, that we never found the trees tall enough, the fields green enough. Well, the trees are for once tall, and fair to look upon, and one unvarying carpet of the tenderest green covers these marvellous fields, that spread out their smooth sod for miles and miles, till they even reach the horizon. But, to begin my day's journey. Griggsville is situated on the west side of the Illinois river, on a high prairie; between it and the river is a long range of bluffs which reaches a hundred miles north and south, then a wide river bottom, and then the river. It was a mild, showery morning, and I directed my steps toward the bluffs. They are covered with forest, not like our forests, tangled and impassable, but where the trees stand fair and apart from one another, so that you might ride every where about on horseback, and the tops of the hills are generally bald, and covered with green turf, like our pastures. Indeed, the whole country reminds me perpetually of one that has been carefully cultivated by a civilized people, who had been suddenly removed from the earth, with all the works of their hands, and the land given again into nature's keeping. The solitudes are not savage; they have not that dreary, stony loneliness that used to affect me in our own country; they never repel; there are no lonely heights, no isolated spots, but all is gentle, mild, inviting,—all is accessible. In following this winding, hilly road for four or five miles, I think I counted at least a dozen new kinds of wild flowers, not timid, retiring little plants like ours, but bold flowers of rich colors, covering the ground in abundance. One very common flower resembles our cardinal flower, though not of so deep a color, another is very like rocket or phlox, but smaller and of various colors, white, blue and purple. Beautiful white lupines I find too, violets white and purple. The vines and parasites are magnificent. I followed on this road till I came to the prairie which skirts the river, and this, of all the beauties of this region, is the most peculiar and wonderful. Imagine a vast and gently-swelling pasture of the brightest green grass, stretching away from you on every side, behind, toward these hills I have described, in all other directions, to a belt of tall trees, all growing up with noble proportions, from the generous soil. It is an unimagined picture of abundance and peace. Somewhere about, you are sure to see a huge herd of cattle, often white, and generally brightly marked, grazing. All looks like the work of man's hand, but you see no vestige of man, save perhaps an almost imperceptible hut on the edge of the prairie. Reaching the river, I ferried myself across, and then crossed over to take the Jacksonville railroad, but, finding there was no train, passed the night at a farm house." And here may find its place this converse between the solitary old man and the young traveller.[2]

SOLITARY

My son, with weariness thou seemest spent,
And toiling on the dusty road all day,
Weary and pale, yet with inconstant step,
Hither and thither turning,—seekest thou
To find aught lost, or what dark care pursues thee?
If thou art weary, rest, if hungry, eat.

TRAVELLER

Oh rather, father, let me ask of thee
What is it I do seek, what thing I lack?
These many days I've left my father's hall,
Forth driven by insatiable desire,
That, like the wind, now gently murmuring,
Enticed me forward with its own sweet voice
Through many-leaved woods, and valleys deep,
Yet ever fled before me. Then with sound
Stronger than hurrying tempest, seizing me,
Forced me to fly its power. Forward still,
Bound by enchanted ties, I seek its source.
Sometimes it is a something I have lost,
Known long since, before I bent my steps
Toward this beautiful broad plane of earth.
Sometimes it is a spirit yet unknown,
In whose dim-imaged features seem to smile
The dear delight of these high-mansioned thoughts,
That sometimes visit me. Like unto mine
Her lineaments appear, but beautiful,

115

As of a sister in a far-off world,
Waiting to welcome me. And when I think
To reach and clasp the figure, it is gone,
And some ill-omened ghastly vision comes
To bid beware, and not too curiously
Demand the secrets of that distant world,
Whose shadow haunts me.—On the waves below
But now I gazed, warmed with the setting sun,
Who sent his golden streamers to my feet,
It seemed a pathway to a world beyond,
And I looked round, if that my spirit beckoned
That I might follow it.

SOLITARY

Dreams all, my son. Yes, even so I dreamed
And even so was thwarted. You must learn
To dream another long and troublous dream,
The dream of life. And you shall think you wake,
And think the shadows substance, love and hate,
Exchange and barter, joy, and weep, and dance,
And this too shall be dream.

TRAVELLER

Oh who can say
Where lies the boundary? What solid things
That daily mock our senses, shall dissolve
Before the might within, while shadowy forms
Freeze into stark reality, defying
The force and will of man. These forms I see,
They may go with me through eternity,
And bless or curse with ceaseless company,
While yonder man, that I met yesternight,
Where is he now? He passed before my eyes,
He is gone, but these stay with me ever.

That night the young man rested with the old,
And, grave or gay, in laughter or in tears,
They wore the night in converse. Morning came,
The dreamer took his solitary way;
And, as he pressed that old man's hand, he sighed,
Must this too be a dream?

Afterwards, of the rolling prairie. "There was one of twenty miles in extent, not flat, but high and rolling, so that when you arrived at a high part, by gentle ascents, the view was beyond measure grand; as far as the eye could reach, nothing but the green, rolling plain, and at a vast distance, groves, all looking gentle and cultivated, yet all uninhabited. I think it would impress you, as it does me, that these scenes are truly sublime. I have a sensation of vastness which I have sought in vain among high mountains. Mountains crowd one sensation on another, till all is excitement, all is surprise, wonder, enchantment. Here is neither enchantment or disappointment, but expectation fully realized. I have always had an attachment for a plain. The Roman Campagna is a prairie. Peoria is in a most lovely situation. In fact I am so delighted that I am as full of superlatives as the Italian language. I could, however, find fault enough, if you ask what I dislike."

But no one did ask; it is not worth while where there is so much to admire. Yet the following is a good statement of the shadow side.

"As to the boasts about the rapid progress here, give me rather the firm fibre of a slow and knotty growth. I could not help thinking as much when I was talking to E. the other day, whom I met on board the boat. He quarrelled with Boston for its slowness; said it was a bad place for a young man. He could not make himself felt, could not see the effects of his exertions as he could here.—To be sure he could not. Here he comes, like a yankee farmer, with all the knowledge that our hard soil and laborious cultivation could give him, and what wonder if he is surprised at the work of his own hands, when he comes to such a soil as this. But he feeds not so many mouths, though he tills more acres. The plants he raises have not so exquisite a form, the vegetables so fine a flavor. His cultivation becomes more negligent, he is not so good a farmer. Is not this a true view? It strikes me continually. The traces of a man's hand in a new country are rarely productive of beauty. It is a cutting down of forest trees to make zigzag fences."

The most picturesque objects to be seen from Chicago on the inland side were the lines of Hoosier wagons. These rude farmers, the large first product of the soil, travel leisurely along, sleeping in their wagons by night, eating only what they bring with them. In the town they observe the same plan, and trouble no luxurious hotel for board and lodging. In the town they look like foreign peasantry, and contrast well with the many Germans, Dutch, and Irish. In the country it is very pretty to see them prepared to "camp out" at night, their horses taken out of harness, and they lounging under the trees, enjoying the evening meal.

On the lake side it is fine to see the great boats come panting in from their rapid and marvellous journey. Especially at night the motion of their lights is very majestic.

When the favorite boats, the Great Western and Illinois, are going out, the town is thronged with people from the south and farther west, to go in them. These moonlight nights I would hear the French rippling and fluttering familiarly amid the rude ups and downs of the Hoosier dialect.

At the hotel table were daily to be seen new faces, and new stories to be learned. And any one who has a large acquaintance may be pretty sure of meeting some of them here in the course of a few days.

Among those whom I met was Mrs. Z., the aunt of an old school-mate, to whom I impatiently hastened, as soon as the meal was over, to demand news of Mariana.[3] The answer startled me. Mariana, so full of life, was dead. That form, the most rich in energy and coloring of any I had ever seen, had faded from the earth. The circle of youthful associations had given way in the part, that seemed the strongest. What I now learned of the story of this life, and what was by myself remembered, may be bound together in this slight sketch.

At the boarding-school to which I was too early sent, a fond, a proud, and timid child, I saw among the ranks of the gay and graceful, bright or earnest girls, only one who interested my fancy or touched my young heart; and this was Mariana. She was, on the father's side, of Spanish Creole blood, but had been sent to the Atlantic coast, to receive a school education under the care of her aunt, Mrs. Z.

This lady had kept her mostly at home with herself, and Mariana had gone from her house to a dayschool; but the aunt, being absent for a time in Europe, she had now been unfortunately committed for some time to the mercies of a boarding-school.

A strange bird she proved there,—a lonely swallow that could not make for itself a summer. At first, her schoolmates were captivated with her ways; her love of wild dances and sudden song, her freaks of passion and of wit. She was always new, always surprising, and, for a time, charming.

But, after awhile, they tired of her. She could never be depended on to join in their plans, yet she expected them to follow out hers with their whole strength. She was very loving, even infatuated in her own affections, and exacted from those who had professed any love for her, the devotion she was willing to bestow.

Yet there was a vein of haughty caprice in her character; a love of solitude, which made her at times wish to retire entirely, and at these times she would expect to be thoroughly understood, and let alone, yet to be welcomed back when she returned. She did not thwart others in their humors, but she never doubted of great indulgence from them.

Some singular habits she had which, when new, charmed, but, after acquaintance, displeased her companions. She had by nature the same habit and power of excitement that is described in the spinning dervishes of the East. Like them, she would spin until all around her were giddy, while her own brain, instead of being disturbed, was excited to great action. Pausing, she would declaim verse of others or her own; act many parts, with strange catch-words and burdens that seemed to act with mystical power on her own fancy, sometimes stimulating her to convulse the hearer with laughter, sometimes to melt him to tears. When her power began to languish, she would spin again till fired to recommence her singular drama, into which she wove figures from the scenes of her earlier childhood, her companions, and the dignitaries she sometimes saw, with fantasies unknown to life, unknown to heaven or earth.

This excitement, as may be supposed, was not good for her. It oftenest came on in the evening, and often spoiled her sleep. She would wake in the night, and cheat her restlessness by inventions that teazed, while they sometimes diverted her companions.

She was also a sleep-walker; and this one trait of her case did somewhat alarm her guardians, who, otherwise, showed the same profound stupidity as to this peculiar being, usual in the overseers of the young. They consulted a physician, who said she would outgrow it, and prescribed a milk diet.

Meantime, the fever of this ardent and too early stimulated nature was constantly increased by the restraints and narrow routine of the boarding school. She was always devising means to break in upon it. She had a taste which would have seemed ludicrous to her mates, if they had not felt some awe of her, from a touch of genius and power that never left her, for costume and fancy dresses, always some sash twisted about her, some drapery, something odd in the arrangement of her hair and dress, so that the methodical preceptress dared not let her go out without a careful scrutiny and remodelling, whose soberizing effects generally disappeared the moment she was in the free air.

At last, a vent for her was found in private theatricals. Play followed play, and in these and the rehearsals she found entertainment congenial with her. The principal parts, as a matter of course, fell to her lot; most of the good suggestions and arrangements came from her, and for a time she ruled masterly and shone triumphant.

During these performances the girls had heightened their natural bloom with artificial red; this was delightful to them—it was something so out of the way. But Mariana, after the plays were over, kept her carmine saucer on the dressing-table, and put on her blushes regularly as the morning.

When stared and jeered at, she at first said she did it because she thought it made her look prettier; but, after a while, she became quite petulant about it,—would make no reply to any joke, but merely kept on doing it.

This irritated the girls, as all eccentricity does the world in general, more than vice or malignity. They talked it over among themselves, till they got wrought up to a desire of punishing, once for all, this sometimes amusing, but so often provoking nonconformist.

Having obtained the leave of the mistress, they laid, with great glee, a plan one evening, which was to be carried into execution next day at dinner.

Among Mariana's irregularities was a great aversion to the meal-time ceremonial. So long, so tiresome she found it, to be seated at a certain moment, to wait while each one was served at so large a table, and one where there was scarcely any conversation; from day to day it became more heavy to her to sit there, or go there at all. Often as possible she excused herself on the ever-convenient plea of headache, and was hardly ever ready when the dinnerbell rang.

To-day it found her on the balcony, lost in gazing on the beautiful prospect. I have heard her say afterwards, she had rarely in her life been so happy,—and she was one with whom happiness was a still rapture. It was one of the most blessed summer days; the shadows of great white clouds empurpled the distant hills for a few moments only to leave them more golden; the tall grass of the wide fields waved in the softest breeze. Pure blue were the heavens, and the same hue of pure contentment was in the heart of Mariana.

Suddenly on her bright mood jarred the dinner bell. At first rose her usual thought, I will not, cannot go; and then the *must,* which daily life can always enforce, even upon the butterflies and birds, came, and she walked reluctantly to her room. She merely changed her dress, and never thought of adding the artificial rose to her cheek.

When she took her seat in the dining-hall, and was asked if she would be helped, raising her eyes, she saw the person who asked her was deeply rouged, with a bright glaring spot, perfectly round, in either cheek. She looked at the next, same apparition! She then slowly passed her eyes down the whole line, and saw the same, with a suppressed smile distorting every countenance. Catching the design at once, she deliberately looked along her own side of the table, at every schoolmate in turn; every one had joined in the trick. The teachers strove to be grave, but she saw they enjoyed the joke. The servants could not suppress a titter.

When Warren Hastings stood at the bar of Westminster Hall[4]— when the Methodist preacher walked through a line of men, each of whom greeted him with a brickbat or a rotten egg, they had some preparation for the crisis, and it might not be very difficult to meet it with an impassive brow. Our little girl was quite unprepared to find herself in the midst of a world which despised her, and triumphed in her disgrace.

She had ruled, like a queen, in the midst of her companions; she had shed her animation through their lives, and loaded them with prodigal favors, nor once suspected that a powerful favorite might not be loved. Now, she felt that she had been but a dangerous plaything in the hands of those whose hearts she never had doubted.

Yet, the occasion found her equal to it, for Mariana had the kind of spirit, which, in a better cause, had made the Roman matron truly say of her death-wound, "It is not painful, Poetus." She did not blench—she did not change countenance. She swallowed her dinner with apparent composure. She made remarks to those near her, as if she had no eyes.

The wrath of the foe of course rose higher, and the moment they were freed from the restraints of the dining-room, they all ran off, gaily calling, and sarcastically laughing, with backward glances, at Mariana, left alone.

She went alone to her room, locked the door, and threw herself on the floor in strong convulsions. These had sometimes threatened her life, as a child, but of later years, she had outgrown them. School–hours came, and she was not there. A little girl, sent to her door, could get no answer. The teachers became alarmed, and broke it open. Bitter was their penitence and that of her companions at the state in which they found her. For some hours, terrible anxiety was felt; but, at last, nature, exhausted, relieved herself by a deep slumber.

From this Mariana rose an altered being. She made no reply to the expressions of sorrow from her companions, none to the grave and kind, but undiscerning comments of her teacher. She did not name the source of her anguish, and its poisoned dart sank deeply in. It was this thought which stung her so. What, not one, not a single one, in the hour of trial, to take my part, not one who refused to take part against me. Past words of love, and caresses, little heeded at the time, rose to her memory, and gave fuel to her distempered thoughts. Beyond the sense of universal perfidy, of burning resentment, she could not get. And Mariana, born for love, now hated all the world.

The change, however, which these feelings made in her conduct and appearance bore no such construction to the careless observer. Her gay freaks were quite gone, her wildness, her invention. Her dress was uniform, her manner much subdued. Her chief interest seemed now to lie in her studies, and in music. Her companions she never sought, but they, partly from uneasy remorseful feelings, partly that they really liked her much better now that she did not oppress and puzzle them, sought her continually. And here the black shadow comes upon her life, the only stain upon the history of Mariana.

They talked to her, as girls, having few topics, naturally do, of one another. And the demon rose within her, and spontaneously, without design, generally without words of positive falsehood, she became a genius of discord among them. She fanned those flames of envy and jealousy which a wise, true word from a third will often quench forever; by a glance, or a seemingly light reply, she planted the seeds of dissension, till there was scarce a peaceful affection, or sincere intimacy in the circle where she lived, and could not but rule, for she was one whose nature was to that of the others as fire to clay.

It was at this time that I came to the school, and first saw Mariana. Me she charmed at once, for I was a sentimental child, who, in my early ill health, had been indulged in reading novels, till I had no eyes for the common greens and browns of life. The heroine of one of these, "The Bandit's Bride,"[5] I immediately saw in Mariana. Surely the Bandit's Bride had just such hair, and such strange, lively ways, and such a sudden flush of the eye. The Bandit's Bride, too, was born to be "misunderstood" by all but her lover. But Mariana, I was determined, should be more fortunate, for, until her lover appeared, I myself would be the wise and delicate being who could understand her.

It was not, however, easy to approach her for this purpose. Did I offer to run and fetch her handkerchief, she was obliged to go to her room, and would rather do it herself. She did not like to have people turn over for her the leaves of the music book as she played. Did I approach my stool to her feet, she moved away, as if to give me room. The bunch of wild flowers which I timidly laid beside her plate was left there.

After some weeks my desire to attract her notice really preyed upon me, and one day meeting her alone in the entry, I fell upon my knees, and kissing her hand, cried, "O Mariana, do let me love you, and try to love me a little." But my idol snatched away her hand, and, laughing more wildly than the Bandit's Bride was ever described to have done, ran into her room. After that day her manner to me was not only cold, but repulsive; I felt myself scorned, and became very unhappy.

Perhaps four months had passed thus, when, one afternoon, it became obvious that something more than common was brewing. Dismay and mystery were written in many faces of the older girls; much whispering was going on in corners.

In the evening, after prayers, the principal bade us stay; and, in a grave, sad voice, summoned forth Mariana to answer charges to be made against her.

Mariana came forward, and leaned against the chimney-piece. Eight of the older girls came forward, and preferred against her charges, alas, too well-founded, of calumny and falsehood.

My heart sank within me, as one after the other brought up their proofs, and I saw they were too strong to be resisted. I could not bear the thought of this second disgrace of my shining favorite. The first had been whispered to me, though the girls did not like to talk about it. I must confess, such is the charm of strength to softer natures, that neither of these crises could deprive Mariana of hers in my eyes.

At first, she defended herself with self-possession and eloquence. But when she found she could no more resist the truth, she suddenly threw herself down, dashing her head, with all her force, against the iron hearth, on which a fire was burning, and was taken up senseless.

The affright of those present was great. Now that they had perhaps killed her, they reflected it would have been as well, if they had taken warning from the former occasion, and approached very carefully a nature so capable of any extreme. After awhile she revived, with a faint groan, amid the sobs of her companions. I was on my knees by the bed, and held her cold hand. One of those most aggrieved took it from me to beg her pardon, and say it was impossible not to love her. She made no reply.

Neither that night, nor for several days, could a word be obtained from her, nor would she touch food; but, when it was presented to her, or any one drew near for any cause, she merely turned away her head, and gave no sign. The teacher saw that some terrible nervous affection had fallen upon her, that she grew more and more feverish. She knew not what to do.

Meanwhile a new revolution had taken place in the mind of the passionate, but nobly-tempered child. All these months nothing but the sense of injury had rankled in her heart. She had gone on in one mood, doing what the demon prompted, without scruple and without fear.

But, at the moment of detection, the tide ebbed, and the bottom of her soul lay revealed to her eye. How black, how stained and sad. Strange, strange that she had not seen before the baseness and cruelty of falsehood, the loveliness of truth. Now, amid the wreck, uprose the moral nature which never before had attained the ascendant. "But," she thought, "too late, sin is revealed to me in all its deformity, and, sin-defiled, I will not, cannot live. The mainspring of life is broken."

And thus passed slowly by her hours in that black despair of which only youth is capable. In older years men suffer more dull pain, as each sorrow that comes drops its leaden weight into the past, and, similar features of character bringing similar results, draws up a heavy burden buried in those depths. But only youth has energy, with fixed unwinking gaze, to contemplate grief, to hold it in the arms and to the heart, like a child which makes it wretched, yet is indubitably its own.

The lady who took charge of this sad child had never well understood her before, but had always looked on her with great tenderness. And now love seemed, when all around were in greatest distress, fearing to call in medical aid, fearing to do without it, to teach her where the only balm was to be found that could have healed this wounded spirit.

One night she came in, bringing a calming draught. Mariana was sitting, as usual, her hair loose, her dress the same robe they had put on her at first, her eyes fixed vacantly upon the whited wall. To the proffers and entreaties of her nurse she made no reply.

The lady burst into tears, but Mariana did not seem even to observe it.

The lady then said, "O my child, do not despair, do not think that one great fault can mar a whole life. Let me trust you, let me tell you the griefs of my sad life. I will tell to you, Mariana, what I never expected to impart to any one."

And so she told her tale: it was one of pain, of shame, borne, not for herself, but for one near and dear as herself. Mariana knew the lady, knew the pride and reserve of her nature; she had often admired to see how the cheek, lovely, but no longer young, mantled with the deepest blush of youth, and the blue eyes were cast down at any little emotion. She had understood the proud sensibility of the character. She fixed her eyes on those now raised to hers, bright with fast falling tears. She heard the story to the end, and then, without saying a word, stretched out her hand for the cup. She returned to life, but it was as one who has passed through the valley of death. The heart of stone was quite broken in her. The fiery life fallen from flame to coal. When her strength was a little restored, she had all her companions summoned, and said to them; "I deserved to die, but a generous trust has called me back to life. I will be worthy of it, nor ever betray the truth, or resent injury more. Can you forgive the past?"

And they not only forgave, but, with love and earnest tears, clasped in their arms the returning sister. They vied with one another in offices of humble love to the humbled one; and, let it be recorded as an instance of the pure honor of which young hearts are capable, that these facts, known to forty persons, never, so far as I know, transpired beyond those walls.

It was not long after this that Mariana was summoned home. She went thither a wonderfully instructed being, though in ways those who had sent her forth to learn little dreamed of.

Never was forgotten the vow of the returning prodigal. Mariana could not resent, could not play false. The terrible crisis, which she so early passed through, probably prevented the world from hearing much of her. A wild fire was tamed in that hour of penitence at the boarding school, such as has oftentimes wrapped court and camp in its destructive glow.

But great were the perils she had yet to undergo, for she was one of those barks which easily get beyond soundings, and ride not lightly on the plunging billow.

Her return to her native climate seconded the effects of inward revolutions. The cool airs of the north had exasperated nerves too suscep-tible for their tension. Those of the south restored her to a more soft and indolent state. Energy gave place to feeling, turbulence to intensity of character.

At this time love was the natural guest, and he came to her under a form that might have deluded one less ready for delusion.

Sylvain was a person well proportioned to her lot in years, family, and fortune. His personal beauty was not great, but of a noble character. Repose marked his slow gesture, and the steady gaze of his large brown eye, but it was a repose that would give way to a blaze of energy when the occasion called. In his stature, expression, and heavy coloring, he might not unfitly be represented by the great magnolias that inhabit the forests of that climate. His voice, like everything about him, was rich and soft, rather than sweet or delicate.

Mariana no sooner knew him than she loved, and her love, lovely as she was, soon excited his. But, oh! it is a curse to woman to love first, or most. In so doing she reverses the natural relations, and her heart can never, never be satisfied with what ensues.

Mariana loved first, and loved most, for she had most force and variety to love with. Sylvain seemed, at first, to take her to himself, as the deep southern night might some fair star. But it proved not so.

Mariana was a very intellectual being, and she needed companionship. This she could only have with Sylvain, in the paths of passion and action. Thoughts he had none, and little delicacy of sentiment. The gifts she loved to prepare of such for him, he took with a sweet, but indolent smile; he held them lightly, and soon they fell from his grasp. He loved to have her near him, to feel the glow and fragrance of her nature, but cared not to explore the little secret paths whence that fragrance was collected.

Mariana knew not this for a long time. Loving so much, she imagined all the rest, and, where she felt a blank, always hoped that further communion would fill it up. When she found this could never be; that there was absolutely a whole province of her being to which nothing in his answered, she was too deeply in love to leave him. Often after passing hours together, beneath the southern moon, when, amid the sweet intoxication of mutual love, she still felt the desolation of solitude, and a repression of her finer powers, she had asked herself, can I give him up? But the heart always passionately answered, no! I may be miserable with him, but I cannot live without him.

And the last miserable feeling of these conflicts was, that if the lover, soon to be the bosom friend, could have dreamed of these conflicts, he would have laughed, or else been angry, even enough to give her up.

Ah weakness of the strong. Of these strong only where strength is weakness. Like others she had the decisions of life to make, before she had light by which to make them. Let none condemn her. Those who have not erred as fatally, should thank the guardian angel who gave them more time to prepare for judgment, but blame no children who thought at arm's length to find the moon. Mariana, with a heart capable of highest Eros, gave it to one who knew love only as a flower or plaything, and bound her heartstrings to one who parted his as lightly as the ripe fruit leaves the bough. The sequel could not fail. Many console themselves for the one great mistake with their children, with the world. This was not possible to

Mariana. A few months of domestic life she still was almost happy. But Sylvain then grew tired. He wanted business and the world; of these she had no knowledge, for them no faculties. He wanted in her the head of his house; she to make her heart his home. No compromise was possible between natures of such unequal poise, and which had met only on one or two points. Through all its stages she

> "felt
> The agonizing sense
> Of seeing love from passion melt
> Into indifference;
> The fearful shame that, day by day,
> Burns onward, still to burn,
> To have thrown her precious heart away,
> And met this black return,"

till death at last closed the scene. Not that she died of one downright blow on the heart. That is not the way such cases proceed. I cannot detail all the symptoms, for I was not there to watch them, and aunt Z. was neither so faithful an observer or narrator as I have shown myself in the school-day passages; but, generally, they were as follows.

Sylvain wanted to go into the world, or let it into his house. Mariana consented; but, with an unsatisfied heart, and no lightness of character, she played her part ill there. The sort of talent and facility she had displayed in early days, were not the least like what is called out in the social world by the desire to please and to shine. Her excitement had been muse-like, that of the improvisatrice,[6] whose kindling fancy seeks to create an atmosphere round it, and makes the chain through which to set free its electric sparks. That had been a time of wild and exuberant life. After her character became more tender and concentrated, strong affection or a pure enthusiasm might still have called out beautiful talents in her. But in the first she was utterly disappointed. The second was not roused within her thought. She did not expand into various life, and remained unequal; sometimes too passive, sometimes too ardent, and not sufficiently occupied with what occupied those around her to come on the same level with them and embellish their hours.

Thus she lost ground daily with her husband, who, comparing her with the careless shining dames of society, wondered why he had found her so charming in solitude.

At intervals, when they were left alone, Mariana wanted to open her heart, to tell the thoughts of her mind. She was so conscious of secret riches within herself, that sometimes it seemed, could she but reveal a glimpse of them to the eye of Sylvain, he would be attracted near her again, and take a path where they could walk hand in hand. Sylvain, in these intervals, wanted an indolent repose. His home was his castle. He wanted no scenes too exciting there. Light jousts and plays were well enough, but no grave encounters. He liked to lounge, to sing, to read, to sleep. In fine, Sylvain became the kind, but preoccupied husband, Mariana, the solitary and wretched wife. He was off continually, with his male companions, on excursions or affairs of pleasure. At home Mariana found that neither her books nor music would console her.

She was of too strong a nature to yield without a struggle to so dull a fiend as despair. She looked into other hearts, seeking whether she could there find such home as an orphan asylum may afford. This she did rather because the chance came to her, and it seemed unfit not to seize the proffered plank, than in hope, for she was not one to double her stakes, but rather with Cassandra power to discern early the sure course of the game. And Cassandra whispered that she was one of those.

"Whom men love not, but yet regret,"

And so it proved. Just as in her childish days, though in a different form, it happened betwixt her and these companions. She could not be content to receive them quietly, but was stimulated to throw herself too much into the tie, into the hour, till she filled it too full for them. Like Fortunio, who sought to do homage to his friends by building a fire of cinnamon, not knowing that its perfume would be too strong for their endurance, so did Mariana. What she wanted to tell, they did not wish to hear; a little had pleased, so much overpowered, and they preferred the free air of the street, even, to the cinnamon perfume of her palace.

However, this did not signify; had they staid, it would not have availed her! It was a nobler road, a higher aim she needed now; this did not become clear to her.

She lost her appetite, she fell sick, had fever. Sylvain was alarmed, nursed her tenderly; she grew better. Then his care ceased, he saw not the mind's disease, but left her to rise into health and recover the tone of her spirits, as she might. More solitary than ever, she tried to raise herself, but she knew not yet enough. The weight laid upon her young life was a little too heavy for it. One long day she passed alone, and the thoughts and presages came too thick for her strength. She knew not what to do with them, relapsed into fever, and died.

Notwithstanding this weakness, I must ever think of her as a fine sample of womanhood, born to shed light and life on some palace home. Had she known more of God and the universe, she would not have given way where so many have conquered. But peace be with her; she now, perhaps, has entered into a larger freedom, which is knowledge. With her died a great interest in life to me. Since her I have never seen a Bandit's Bride. She, indeed, turned out to be only a merchant's.—Sylvain is married again to a fair and laughing girl, who will not die, probably, till their marriage grows a "golden marriage."

Aunt Z. had with her some papers of Mariana's, which faintly shadow forth the thoughts that engaged her in the last days. One of these seems to have been written when some faint gleam had been thrown across the path, only to make its darkness more visible. It seems to have been suggested by remembrance of the beautiful ballad, *Helen of Kirconnel Lee,*[7] which once she loved to recite, and in tones that would not have sent a chill to the heart from which it came.

> "Death
> Opens her sweet white arms, and whispers Peace;
> Come, say thy sorrows in this bosom!   This
> Will never close against thee, and my heart,
> Though cold, cannot be colder much than man's."

> "I wish I were where Helen lies,"
> A lover in the times of old,
>   Thus vents his grief in lonely sighs,
> And hot tears from a bosom cold.

> But, mourner for thy martyred love,
> Could'st thou but know what hearts must feel,
>   Where no sweet recollections move,
> Whose tears a desert fount reveal.

> When "in thy arms lyred Helen fell,"
> She died, sad man, she died for thee,
>   Nor could the films of death dispel
> Her loving eye's sweet radiancy.

> Thou wert beloved, and she had loved,
> Till death alone the whole could tell,

Death every shade of doubt removed,
And steeped the star in its cold well.

On some fond breast the parting soul
Relies,—earth has no more to give;
Who wholly loves has known the whole,
The wholly loved doth truly live.

But some, sad outcasts from this prize,
Wither down to a lonely grave,
All hearts their hidden love despise,
And leave them to the whelming wave.

They heart to heart have never pressed,
Nor hands in holy pledge have given,
By father's love were ne'er caressed,
Nor in a mother's eye saw heaven.

A flowerless and fruitless tree,
A dried up stream, a mateless bird,
They live, yet never living be,
They die, their music all unheard.

I wish I were where Helen lies,
For there I could not be alone;
But now, when this dull body dies,
The spirit still will make its moan.

Love passed me by, nor touched my brow;
Life would not yield one perfect boon;
And all too late it calls me now,
O all too late, and all too soon.

If thou couldst the dark riddle read
Which leaves this dart within my breast,
Then might I think thou lov'st indeed,
Then were the whole to thee confest.

Father, they will not take me home,
To the poor child no heart is free;
In sleet and snow all night I roam;
Father,—was this decreed by thee?

I will not try another door,
To seek what I have never found;

Now, till the very last is o'er,
Upon the earth I'll wander round.

I will not hear the treacherous call
That bids me stay and rest awhile,
For I have found that, one and all,
They seek me for a prey and spoil.

They are not bad, I know it well;
I know they know not what they do;
They are the tools of the dread spell
Which the lost lover must pursue.

In temples sometimes she may rest,
In lonely groves, away from men,
There bend the head, by heats distrest,
Nor be by blows awoke again.

Nature is kind, and God is kind,
And, if she had not had a heart,
Only that great discerning mind,
She might have acted well her part.

But oh this thirst, that none can still,
Save those unfounden waters free;
The angel of my life should fill
And soothe me to Eternity!

It marks the defect in the position of woman that one like Mariana should have found reason to write thus. To a man of equal power, equal sincerity, no more!—many resources would have presented themselves. He would not have needed to seek, he would have been called by life, and not permitted to be quite wrecked through the affections only. But such women as Mariana are often lost, unless they meet some man of sufficiently great soul to prize them.

Van Artevelde's Elena,[8] though in her individual nature unlike my Mariana, is like her in a mind whose large impulses are disproportioned to the persons and occasions she meets, and which carry her beyond those reserves which mark the appointed lot of woman. But, when she met Van Artevelde, he was too great not to revere her rare nature, without regard to the stains and errors of its past history; great enough to receive her entirely and make a new life for her; man enough to be a lover! But as such men come not so often as once an age, their presence should not be absolutely needed to sustain life.

At Chicago I read again Philip Van Artevelde, and certain passages in it will always be in my mind associated with the deep sound of the lake, as heard in the night. I used to read a short time at night, and then open the blind to look out. The moon would be full upon the lake, and the calm breath, pure light, and the deep voice harmonized well with the thought of the Flemish hero. When will this country have such a man? It is what she needs; no thin Idealist, no coarse Realist, but a man whose eye reads the heavens while his feet step firmly on the ground, and his hands are strong and dexterous for the use of human implements. A man religious, virtuous and—sagacious; a man of universal sympathies, but self-possessed; a man who knows the region of emotion, though he is not its slave; a man to whom this world is no mere spectacle, or fleeting shadow, but a great solemn game to be played with good heed, for its stakes are of eternal value, yet who, if his own play be true, heeds not what he loses by the falsehood of others. A man who hives from the past, yet knows that its honey can but moderately avail him; whose comprehensive eye scans the present, neither infatuated by its golden lures, nor chilled by its many ventures; who possesses prescience, as the wise man must, but not so far as to be driven mad to-day by the gift which discerns to-morrow. When there is such a man for America, the thought which urges her on will be expressed.

Now that I am about to leave Illinois, feelings of regret and admiration come over me, as in parting with a friend whom we have not had the good sense to prize and study, while hours of association, never perhaps to return, were granted. I have fixed my attention almost exclusively on the picturesque beauty of this region; it was so new, so inspiring. But I ought to have been more interested in the housekeeping of this magnificent state, in the education she is giving her children, in their prospects.

Illinois is, at present, a by-word of reproach among the nations, for the careless, prodigal course, by which, in early youth, she has endangered her honor. But you cannot look about you there, without seeing that there are resources abundant to retrieve, and soon to retrieve, far greater errors, if they are only directed with wisdom.

Might the simple maxim, that honesty is the best policy be laid to heart! Might a sense of the true aims of life elevate the tone of politics and trade, till public and private honor become identical! Might the western man in that crowded and exciting life which develops his faculties so fully for to-day, not forget that better part which could not be taken from him! Might the western woman take that interest and acquire that light for the education of the children, for which she alone has leisure!

This is indeed the great problem of the place and time. If the next generation be well prepared for their work, ambitious of good and skilful to achieve it, the children of the present settlers may be leaven enough for the mass constantly increasing by emigration. And how much is this needed where those rude foreigners can so little understand the best interests of the land they seek for bread and shelter. It would be a happiness to aid in this good work, and interweave the white and golden threads into the fate of Illinois. It would be a work worthy the devotion of any mind.

In the little that I saw, was a large proportion of intelligence, activity, and kind feeling; but, if there was much serious laying to heart of the true purposes of life, it did not appear in the tone of conversation.

Having before me the Illinois guide-book, I find there mentioned, as a "visionary," one of the men I should think of as able to be a truly valuable settler in a new and great country—Morris Birkbeck,[9] of England. Since my return, I have read his journey to, and letters from, Illinois. I see nothing promised there that will not surely belong to the man who knows how to seek for it.

Mr. Birkbeck was an enlightened philanthropist, the rather that he did not wish to sacrifice himself to his fellow men, but to benefit them with all he had, and was, and wished. He thought all the creatures of a divine love ought to be happy and ought to be good, and that his own soul and his own life were not less precious than those of others; indeed, that to keep these healthy, was his only means of a healthy influence.

But his aims were altogether generous. Freedom, the liberty of law, not license; not indolence, work for himself and children and all men, but under genial and poetic influences;—these were his aims. How different from those of the new settlers in general! And into his mind so long ago shone steadily the two thoughts, now so prevalent in thinking and aspiring minds, of "Resist not evil," and "Every man his own priest, and the heart the only true church."

He has lost credit for sagacity from accidental circumstances. It does not appear that his position was ill chosen, or his means disproportioned to his ends, had he been sustained by funds from England, as he had a right to expect. But through the profligacy of a near relative, commissioned to collect these dues, he was disappointed of them, and his paper protested and credit destroyed in our cities, before he became aware of his danger.

Still, though more slowly and with more difficulty, he might have succeeded in his designs. The English farmer might have made the English settlement a model for good methods and good aims to all that region, had not death prematurely cut short his plans.

I have wished to say these few words, because the veneration with which I have been inspired for his character by those who knew him well, makes me impatient of this careless blame being passed from mouth to mouth and book to book. Success is no test of a man's endeavor, and Illinois will yet, I hope, regard this man, who knew so well what *ought* to be, as one of her true patriarchs, the Abraham of a promised land.

He was one too much before his time to be soon valued; but the time is growing up to him, and will understand his mild philanthropy and clear, large views.

I subjoin the account of his death, given me by a friend, as expressing, in fair picture, the character of the man.

"Mr. Birkbeck was returning from the seat of government, whither he had been on public business, and was accompanied by his son Bradford, a youth of sixteen or eighteen. It was necessary to cross a ford, which was rendered difficult by the swelling of the stream. Mr. B.'s horse was unwilling to plunge into the water, so his son offered to go first, and he followed. Bradford's horse had just gained footing on the opposite shore, when he looked back and perceived his father was dismounted, struggling in the water, and carried down by the current.

"Mr. Birkbeck could not swim; Bradford could; so he dismounted, and plunged into the stream to save his father. He got to him before he sank, held him up above water, and told him to take hold of his collar, and he would swim ashore with him. Mr. B. did so, and Bradford exerted all his strength to stem the current and reach the shore at a point where they could land; but, encumbered by his own clothing and his father's weight, he made no progress; and when Mr. B. perceived this, he, with his characteristic calmness and resolution, gave up his hold of his son, and, motioning to him to save himself, resigned himself to his fate. His son reached the shore, but was too much overwhelmed by his loss to leave it. He was found by some travellers, many hours after, seated on the margin of the stream, with his head in his hands, stupefied with grief.

"The body was found, and on the countenance was the sweetest smile; and Bradford said, 'just so he smiled upon me when he let go and pushed me away from him.'"

Many men can choose the right and best on a great occasion, but not many can, with such ready and serene decision, lay aside even life, when it is right and best. This little narrative touched my imagination in very early youth, and often has come up, in lonely vision, that face, serenely smiling above the current which bore him away to another realm of being.

CHAPTER V

Wisconsin

A TERRITORY, not yet a state; still, nearer the acorn than we were.

It was very pleasant coming up. These large and elegant boats are so well arranged that every excursion may be a party of pleasure. There are many fair shows to see on the lake and its shores, almost always new and agreeable persons on board, pretty children playing about, ladies singing, (and if not very well, there is room to keep out of the way.) You may see a great deal here of Life, in the London sense, if you know a few people; or if you do not, and have the tact to look about you without seeming to stare.

We came to Milwaukie, where we were to pass a fortnight or more.

This place is most beautifully situated. A little river, with romantic banks, passes up through the town. The bank of the lake is here a bold bluff, eighty feet in height. From its summit, you enjoyed a noble outlook on the lake. A little narrow path wound along the edge of the lake below. I liked this walk much. Above me this high wall of rich earth, garlanded on its crest with trees, the long ripples of the lake coming up to my feet. Here, standing in the shadow, I could appreciate better its magnificent changes of color, which are the chief beauties of the lake-waters; but these are indescribable.

It was fine to ascend into the lighthouse, above this bluff, and watch from thence the thunder-clouds which so frequently rose over the lake, or the great boats coming in. Approaching the Milwaukie pier, they made a bend, and seemed to do obeisance in the heavy style of some dowager duchess entering a circle she wishes to treat with especial respect.

These boats come in and out every day, and still afford a cause for general excitement. The people swarm down to greet them, to receive and send away their packages and letters. To me they seemed such mighty messengers, to give, by their noble motion, such an idea of the power and fullness of life, that they were worthy to carry despatches from king to king. It must be very pleasant for those who have an active share in carrying on the affairs of this great and growing world to see them come in. It must be very pleasant to those who have dearly loved friends at the next station. To those who have neither business nor friends, it sometimes gives a desolating sense of insignificance.

The town promises to be, some time, a fine one, as it is so well situated; and they have good building material—a yellow brick, very pleasing to the eye. It seems to grow before you, and has indeed but just emerged from the thickets of oak and wild roses. A few steps will take you into the thickets, and certainly I never saw so many wild roses, or of so beautiful a red. Of such a color were the first red ones the world ever saw, when, says the legend, Venus flying to the assistance of Adonis, the rose-bushes kept catching her to make her stay, and the drops of blood the thorns drew from her feet, as she tore herself away, fell on the white roses, and turned them this beautiful red.

I will here insert, though with no excuse, except that it came to memory at the time, this description of Titian's Venus and Adonis.[1]

"This picture has that perfect balance of lines and forms that it would, (as was said of all Raphael's) 'seen at any distance have the air of an ornamental design.' It also tells its story at the first glance, though, like all beautiful works, it gains by study.

"On one side slumbers the little God of Love, as an emblem, I suppose, that only the love of man is worth embodying, for surely Cytherea's is awake enough. The quiver of Cupid, suspended to a tree, gives sportive grace to the scene which softens the tragedy of a breaking tie. The dogs of Adonis pull upon his hand; he can scarce forbear to burst from the detaining arms of Beauty herself, yet he waits a moment to coax her—to make an unmeaning promise. 'A moment, a moment, my love, and I will return; a moment only.' Adonis is not beautiful, except in his expression of eager youth. The Queen of Beauty does not choose Apollo. Venus herself is very beautiful; especially the body is lovely as can be; and the soft, imploring look, gives a conjugal delicacy to the face which purifies the whole picture. This Venus is not as fresh, as moving and breathing as Shakspeare's, yet lovelier to the mind if not to the sense. 'T is difficult to look at this picture without indignation, because it is, in one respect, so true. Why must women always try to detain and restrain what they love? Foolish beauty; let him go; it is thy tenderness that has spoiled him. Be less lovely—less feminine; abandon thy fancy for giving thyself wholly; cease to love so well, and any Hercules will spin among thy maids, if thou wilt. But let him go this time; thou canst not keep him. Sit there, by thyself, on that bank, and, instead of thinking how soon he will come back, think how thou may'st love him no better than he does thee, for the time has come."

It was soon after this moment that the poor Queen, hearing the frightened hounds, apprehended the rash huntsman's danger, and, flying through the woods, gave their hue to the red roses.

To return from the Grecian isles to Milwaukie. One day, walking along the river's bank in search of a waterfall to be seen from one ravine, we heard tones from a band of music, and saw a gay troop shooting at a mark, on the opposite bank. Between every shot the band played; the effect was very pretty.

On this walk we found two of the oldest and most gnarled hemlocks that ever afforded study for a painter. They were the only ones we saw; they seemed the veterans of a former race.

At Milwaukie, as at Chicago, are many pleasant people, drawn together from all parts of the world. A resident here would find great piquancy in the associations,—those he met having such dissimilar histories and topics. And several persons I saw evidently transplanted from the most refined circles to be met in this country. There are lures enough in the West for people of all kinds;—the enthusiast and the cunning man; the naturalist, and the lover who needs to be rich for the sake of her he loves.

The torrent of emigration swells very strongly towards this place. During the fine weather, the poor refugees arrive daily, in their national dresses, all travel-soiled and worn. The night they pass in rude shantees, in a particular quarter of the town, then walk off into the country—the mothers carrying their infants, the fathers leading the little children by the hand, seeking a home where their hands may maintain them.

One morning we set off in their track, and travelled a day's journey into this country,—fair, yet not, in that part which I saw, comparable, in my eyes, to the Rock River region. It alternates rich fields, proper for grain, with oak openings, as they are called; bold, various and beautiful were the features of the scene, but I saw not those majestic sweeps, those boundless distances, those heavenly fields; it was not the same world.

Neither did we travel in the same delightful manner. We were now in a nice carriage, which must not go off the road, for fear of breakage, with a regular coachman, whose chief care was not to tire his horses, and who had no taste for entering fields in pursuit of wild flowers, or tempting some strange wood path in search of whatever might befall. It was pleasant, but almost as tame as New England.

But charming indeed was the place where we stopped. It was in the vicinity of a chain of lakes, and on the bank of the loveliest little stream, called the Bark river, which flowed in rapid amber brightness, through fields, and dells, and stately knolls, of most idyllic beauty.

The little log cabin where we slept, with its flower garden in front, disturbed the scene no more than a stray lock on the fair cheek. The hospitality of that house I may well call princely; it was the boundless hospitality of the heart, which, if it has no Aladdin's lamp to create a palace for the guest, does him still higher service by the freedom of its bounty up to the very last drop of its powers.

Sweet were the sunsets seen in the valley of this stream, though here, and, I grieve to say, no less near the Rock River, the fiend, who has ever liberty to tempt the happy in this world, appeared in the shape of mosquitoes, and allowed us no bodily to enjoy our mental peace.

One day we ladies gave, under the guidance of our host, to visiting all the beauties of the adjacent lakes—Nomabbin, Silver, and Pine Lakes. On the shore of Nomabbin had formerly been one of the finest Indian villages. Our host said that, one day, as he was lying there beneath the bank, he saw a tall Indian standing at gaze on the knoll. He lay a long time, curious to see how long the figure would maintain its statue-like absorption. But, at last, his patience yielded, and, in moving, he made a slight noise. The Indian saw him, gave a wild, snorting sound of indignation and pain, and strode away.

What feelings must consume their heart at such moments! I scarcely see how they can forbear to shoot the white man where he stands.

But the power of fate is with the white man, and the Indian feels it. This same gentleman told of his travelling through the wilderness with an Indian guide. He had with him a bottle of spirit which he meant to give him in small quantities, but the Indian, once excited, wanted the whole at once. I would not, said Mr. —, give it him, for I thought if he got really drunk, there was an end to his services as a guide. But he persisted, and at last tried to take it from me. I was not armed; he was, and twice as strong as I. But I knew an Indian could not resist the look of a white man, and I fixed my eye steadily on his. He bore it for a moment, then his eye fell; he let go the bottle. I took his gun and threw it to a distance. After a few moments' pause, I told him to go and fetch it, and left it in his hands. From that moment he was quite obedient, even servile, all the rest of the way.

This gentleman, though in other respects of most kindly and liberal heart, showed the aversion that the white man soon learns to feel for the Indian on whom he encroaches, the aversion of the injurer for him he has degraded. After telling the anecdote of his seeing the Indian gazing at the seat of his former home,

"A thing for human feelings the most trying,"

and which, one would think, would have awakened soft compassion— almost remorse—in the present owner of that fair hill, which contained for the exile the bones of his dead, the ashes of his hopes,—he observed, "They cannot be prevented from straggling back here to their old haunts. I wish they could. They ought not to be permitted to drive away *our* game." OUR game—just heavens!

The same gentleman showed, on a slight occasion, the true spirit of the sportsman, or, perhaps I might say of Man, when engaged in any kind of chase. Showing us some antlers, he said, "This one belonged to a majestic creature. But this other was the beauty. I had been lying a long time at watch, when at last I heard them come crackling along. I lifted my head cautiously, as they burst through the trees. The first was a magnificent fellow; but then I saw coming one, the prettiest, the most graceful I ever beheld—there was something so soft and beseeching in its look. I chose him at once; took aim, and shot him dead. You see the antlers are not very large; it was young, but the prettiest creature!"

In the course of this morning's drive, we visited the gentlemen on their fishing party. They hailed us gaily, and rowed ashore to show us what fine booty they had. No disappointment there, no dull work. On the beautiful point of land from which we first saw them, lived a contented woman, the only one I heard of out there. She was English, and said she had seen so much suffering in her own country that the hardships of this seemed as nothing to her. But the others—even our sweet and gentle hostess— found their labors disproportioned to their strength, if not to their patience; and, while their husbands and brothers enjoyed the country in hunting or fishing, they found themselves confined to a comfortless and laborious indoor life. But it need not be so long.

This afternoon, driving about on the banks of these lakes, we found the scene all of one kind of loveliness; wide, graceful woods, and then these fine sheets of water, with fine points of land jutting out boldly into them. It was lovely, but not striking or peculiar.

All woods suggest pictures. The European forest, with its long glades and green sunny dells, naturally suggested the figures of armed knight on his proud steed, or maiden, decked in gold and pearl, pricking along them on a snow white palfrey. The green dells, of weary Palmer sleeping there beside the spring with his head upon his wallet. Our minds, familiar with such figures, people with them the New England woods, wherever the sunlight falls down a longer than usual cart-track, wherever a cleared spot has lain still enough for the trees to look friendly, with their exposed sides cultivated by the light, and the grass to look velvet warm, and be embroidered with flowers. These western woods suggest a different kind of ballad. The Indian legends have, often, an air of the wildest solitude, as has the one Mr. Lowell has put into verse, in his late volume.[2] But I did not see those wild woods; only such as suggest little romances of love and sorrow, like this:

> A maiden sat beneath the tree,
> Tear-bedewed her pale cheeks be,
> And she sigheth heavily.
>
> From forth the wood into the light,
> A hunter strides with carol light,
> And a glance so bold and bright.
>
> He careless stopped and eyed the maid;
> "Why weepest thou?" he gently said,
> "I love thee well; be not afraid."
>
> He takes her hand, and leads her on;
> She should have waited there alone,
> For he was not her chosen one.
>
> He leans her head upon his breast,
> She knew 't was not her home of rest,
> But ah! she had been sore distrest.
>
> The sacred stars looked sadly down;
> The parting moon appeared to frown,
> To see thus dimmed the diamond crown.
>
> Then from the thicket starts a deer,
> The huntsman, seizing on his spear,
> Cries, "Maiden, wait thou for me here."
>
> She sees him vanish into night,
> She starts from sleep in deep affright,
> For it was not her own true knight.

Though but in dream Gunhilda failed;
Though but a fancied ill assailed,
Though she but fancied fault bewailed.

Yet thought of day makes dream of night:
She is not worthy of the knight,
The inmost altar burns not bright.

If loneliness thou canst not bear,
Cannot the dragon's venom dare,
Of the pure meed thou shouldst despair.

Now sadder that lone maiden sighs,
Far bitterer tears profane her eyes,
Crushed in the dust her heart's flower lies.

On the bank of Silver Lake we saw an Indian encampment. A shower
threatened us, but we resolved to try if we could not visit it before it came
on. We crossed a wide field on foot, and found them amid the trees on a
shelving bank; just as we reached them the rain began to fall in torrents,
with frequent thunder claps, and we had to take refuge in their lodges.
These were very small, being for temporary use, and we crowded the
occupants much, among whom were several sick, on the damp ground, or
with only a ragged mat between them and it. But they showed all the
gentle courtesy which marks them towards the stranger, who stands in any
need; though it was obvious that the visit, which inconvenienced them,
could only have been caused by the most impertinent curiosity, they made
us as comfortable as their extreme poverty permitted. They seemed to
think we would not like to touch them: a sick girl in the lodge where I was,
persisted in moving so as to give me the dry place; a woman with the sweet
melancholy eye of the race, kept off the children and wet dogs from even
the hem of my garment.

Without, their fires smouldered, and black kettles, hung over them
on sticks, smoked and seethed in the rain. An old theatrical looking Indian
stood with arms folded, looking up to the heavens, from which the rain
dashed and the thunder reverberated; his air was French-Roman, that is,
more romanesque than Roman. The Indian ponies, much excited, kept
careering through the wood, around the encampment, and now and then
halting suddenly, would thrust in their intelligent, though amazed, phizzes,
as if to ask their masters when this awful pother would cease, and then,
after a moment, rush and trample off again.

At last we got off, well wetted, but with a picturesque scene for memory. At a house where we stopped to get dry, they told us that this wandering band (of Pottawattamies,) who had returned on a visit, either from homesickness, or need of relief, were extremely destitute. The women had been there to see if they could barter their head bands with which they club their hair behind into a form not unlike a Grecian knot, for food. They seemed, indeed, to have neither food, utensils, clothes, nor bedding; nothing but the ground, the sky, and their own strength. Little wonder if they drove off the game!

Part of the same band I had seen in Milwaukie, on a begging dance. The effect of this was wild and grotesque. They wore much paint and feather head-dresses. "Indians without paint are poor coots," said a gentleman who had been a great deal with, and really liked, them; and I like the effect of the paint on them; it reminds of the gay fantasies of nature. With them in Milwaukie, was a chief, the finest Indian figure I saw, more than six feet in height, erect, and of a sullen, but grand gait and gesture. He wore a deep red blanket, which fell in large folds from his shoulders to his feet, did not join in the dance, but slowly strode about through the streets, a fine sight, not a French-Roman, but a real Roman. He looked unhappy, but listlessly unhappy, as if he felt it was of no use to strive or resist.

While in the neighborhood of these lakes, we visited also a foreign settlement of great interest. Here were minds, it seemed, to "comprehend the trusts," of their new life; and if they can only stand true to them, will derive and bestow great benefits therefrom.

But sad and sickening to the enthusiast who comes to these shores, hoping the tranquil enjoyment of intellectual blessings, and the pure happiness of mutual love, must be a part of the scene that he encounters at first. He has escaped from the heartlessness of courts, to encounter the vulgarity of a mob; he has secured solitude, but it is a lonely, a deserted solitude. Amid the abundance of nature he cannot, from petty, but insuperable obstacles, procure, for a long time, comforts, or a home.

But let him come sufficiently armed with patience to learn the new spells which the new dragons require, (and this can only be done on the spot,) he will not finally be disappointed of the promised treasure; the mob will resolve itself into men, yet crude, but of good dispositions, and capable of good character; the solitude will become sufficiently enlivened and home grow up at last from the rich sod.

In this transition state we found one of these homes. As we approached it seemed the very Eden which earth might still afford to a pair willing to give up the hackneyed pleasures of the world, for a better and more intimate communion with one another and with beauty: the wild road led through wide beautiful woods, to the wilder and more beautiful shores of the finest lake we saw. On its waters, glittering in the morning sun, a few Indians were paddling to and fro in their light canoes. On one of those fair knolls I have so often mentioned, stood the cottage, beneath trees which stooped as if they yet felt brotherhood with its roof tree. Flowers waved, birds fluttered round, all had the sweetness of a happy seclusion; all invited on entrance to cry, All hail ye happy ones! to those who inhabited it.

But on entrance to those evidently rich in personal beauty, talents, love, and courage, the aspect of things was rather sad. Sickness had been with them, death, care, and labor; these had not yet blighted them, but had turned their gay smiles grave. It seemed that hope and joy had given place to resolution. How much, too, was there in them, worthless in this place, which would have been so valuable elsewhere. Refined graces, cultivated powers, shine in vain before field laborers, as laborers are in this present world; you might as well cultivate heliotropes to present to an ox. Oxen and heliotropes are both good, but not for one another.

With them were some of the old means of enjoyment, the books, the pencil, the guitar; but where the wash-tub and the axe are so constantly in requisition, there is not much time and pliancy of hand for these.

In the inner room the master of the house was seated; he had been sitting there long, for he had injured his foot on ship-board, and his farming had to be done by proxy. His beautiful young wife was his only attendant and nurse, as well as a farm housekeeper; how well she performed hard and unaccustomed duties, the objects of her care shewed; everything that belonged to the house was rude but neatly arranged; the invalid, confined to an uneasy wooden chair, (they had not been able to induce any one to bring them an easy chair from the town,) looked as neat and elegant as if he had been dressed by the valet of a duke. He was of northern blood, with clear full blue eyes, calm features, a tempering of the soldier, scholar, and man of the world, in his aspect; whether that various intercourses had given himself that thorough-bred look never seen in Americans, or that it was inherited from a race who had known all these disciplines. He formed a great but pleasing contrast to his wife, whose glowing complexion and dark mellow eye bespoke an origin in some climate more familiar with the sun. He looked as if he could sit there a great while patiently, and live on his own mind, biding his time; she, as if she could bear anything for affection's sake, but would feel the weight of each moment as it passed.

Seeing the album full of drawings and verses which bespoke the circle of elegant and affectionate intercourse they had left behind, we could not but see that the young wife sometimes must need a sister, the husband a companion, and both must often miss that electricity which sparkles from the chain of congenial minds.

For man, a position is desirable in some degree proportioned to his education. Mr. Birkbeck was bred a farmer, but these were nurslings of the court and city; they may persevere, for an affectionate courage shone in their eyes, and, if so, become true lords of the soil, and informing geniuses to those around; then, perhaps, they will feel that they have not paid too dear for the tormented independence of the new settler's life. But, generally, damask roses will not thrive in the wood, and a ruder growth, if healthy and pure, we wish rather to see there.

I feel very differently about these foreigners from Americans; American men and women are inexcusable if they do not bring up children so as to be fit for vicissitudes; that is the meaning of our star, that here all men being free and equal, all should be fitted for freedom and an independence by his own resources wherever the changeful wave of our mighty stream may take him. But the star of Europe brought a different horoscope, and to mix destinies breaks the thread of both. The Arabian horse will not plough well, nor can the plough-horse be rode to play the jereed. But a man is a man wherever he goes, and something precious cannot fail to be gained by one who knows how to abide by a resolution of any kind, and pay the cost without a murmur.

Returning, the fine carriage at last fulfilled its threat of breaking down. We took refuge in a farm house. Here was a pleasant scene. A rich and beautiful estate, several happy families, who had removed together, and formed a natural community, ready to help and enliven one another. They were farmers at home, in western New York, and both men and women knew how to work. Yet even here the women did not like the change, but they were willing, "as it might be best for the young folks." Their hospitality was great, the housefull of women and pretty children seemed all of one mind.

Returning to Milwaukie much fatigued, I entertained myself for a day or two with reading. The book I had brought with me was in strong contrast with the life around me. Very strange was this vision of an exalted and sensitive existence, which seemed to invade the next sphere, in contrast with the spontaneous, instinctive life, so healthy and so near the ground I had been surveying. This was the German book entitled: Die Seherin von Prevorst.—Eröffnungen über das innere Leben des Menschen und über das hereinragen einer Geisterwelt in die unsere. Mitgetheilt von Justinus Kerner. The Seeress of Prevorst.—Revelations concerning the inward life of man, and the projection of a world of spirits into ours, communicated by Justinus Kerner.[3]

This book, published in Germany some twelve years since, and which called forth there plenteous dews of admiration, as plenteous hail-storms of jeers and scorns, I never saw mentioned till some year or two since, in any English publication. Then a playful, but not sarcastic account of it, in the Dublin Magazine, so far excited my curiosity that I procured the book intending to read it so soon as I should have some leisure days, such as this journey has afforded.

Dr. Kerner, its author, is a man of distinction in his native land, both as a physician and a thinker, though always on the side of reverence, marvel, and mysticism. He was known to me only through two or three little poems of his in Catholic legends, which I much admired for the fine sense they showed of the beauty of symbols.

He here gives a biography, mental and physical, of one of the most remarkable cases of high nervous excitement that the age, so interested in such, yet affords, with all its phenomena of clairvoyance and susceptibility of magnetic influences. I insert some account of this biography at the request of many who have been interested by slight references to it. The book, a thick and heavy volume, written with true German patience, some would say clumsiness, has not, probably, and may not be translated into other languages. As to my own mental position on these subjects it may be briefly expressed by a dialogue between several persons who honor me with a portion of friendly confidence and of criticism, and myself expressed as *Free Hope*. The others may be styled *Old Church, Good Sense,* and *Self-Poise*.

Good Sense. I wonder you can take any interest in such observations or experiments. Don't you see how almost impossible it is to make them with any exactness, how entirely impossible to know anything about them unless made by yourself, when the least leaven of credulity, excited fancy, to say nothing of willing or careless imposture, spoils the whole loaf. Beside, allowing the possibility of some clear glimpses into a higher state of being, what do we want of it now? All around us lies what we neither understand nor use. Our capacities, our instincts for this our present sphere are but half developed. Let us confine ourselves to that till the lesson be learned; let us be completely natural, before we trouble ourselves with the supernatural. I never see any of these things but I long to get away and lie under a green tree and let the wind blow on me. There is marvel and charm enough in that for me.

    Free Hope. And for me also. Nothing is truer than the Wordsworthian creed, on which Carlyle lays such stress, that we need only look on the miracle of every day, to sate ourselves with thought and admiration every day. But how are our faculties sharpened to do it? Precisely by apprehending the infinite results of every day.

    Who sees the meaning of the flower uprooted in the ploughed field? The ploughman who does not look beyond its boundaries and does not raise his eyes from the ground? No—but the poet who sees that field in its relations with the universe, and looks oftener to the sky than on the ground. Only the dreamer shall understand realities, though, in truth, his dreaming must not be out of proportion to his waking!

    The mind, roused powerfully by this existence, stretches of itself into what the French sage calls the "aromal state."[4] From the hope thus gleaned it forms the hypothesis, under whose banner it collects its facts.

    Long before these slight attempts were made to establish as a science what is at present called animal magnetism, always, in fact men were occupied more or less with this vital principle, principle of flux and influx, dynamic of our mental mechanics, human phase of electricity. Poetic observation was pure, there was no quackery in its free course, as there is so often in this wilful tampering with the hidden springs of life, for it is tampering unless done in a patient spirit and with severe truth; yet it may be, by the rude or greedy miners, some good ore is unearthed. And some there are who work in the true temper, patient and accurate in trial, not rushing to conclusions, feeling there is a mystery, not eager to call it by name, till they can know it as a reality: such may learn, such may teach.

    Subject to the sudden revelations, the breaks in habitual existence caused by the aspect of death, the touch of love, the flood of music, I never lived, that I remember, what you call a common natural day. All my days are touched by the supernatural, for I feel the pressure of hidden causes, and the presence, sometimes the communion, of unseen powers.[5] It needs not that I should ask the clairvoyant whether "a spirit-world projects into ours." As to the specific evidence, I would not tarnish my mind by hasty reception. The mind is not, I know, a highway, but a temple, and its doors should not be carelessly left open. Yet it were sin, if indolence or coldness excluded what had a claim to enter; and I doubt whether, in the eyes of pure intelligence, an ill-grounded hasty rejection be not a greater sign of weakness than an ill-grounded and hasty faith.

I will quote, as my best plea, the saying of a man old in years, but not in heart, and whose long life has been distinguished by that clear adaptation of means to ends which gives the credit of practical wisdom. He wrote to his child, "I have lived too long, and seen too much to be *incredulous*." Noble the thought, no less so its frank expression, instead of saws of caution, mean advices, and other modern instances. Such was the romance of Socrates when he bade his disciples "sacrifice a cock to Æsculapius."

Old Church. You are always so quick-witted and voluble, Free Hope, you don't get time to see how often you err, and even, perhaps, sin and blaspheme. The Author of all has intended to confine our knowledge within certain boundaries, has given us a short span of time for a certain probation, for which our faculties are adapted. By wild speculation and intemperate curiosity we violate his will and incur dangerous, perhaps fatal, consequences. We waste our powers, and, becoming morbid and visionary, are unfitted to obey positive precepts, and perform positive duties.

Free Hope. I do not see how it is possible to go further beyond the results of a limited human experience than those do who pretend to settle the origin and nature of sin, the final destiny of souls, and the whole plan of the causal spirit with regard to them. I think those who take your view, have not examined themselves, and do not know the ground on which they stand.

I acknowledge no limit, set up by man's opinion, as to the capacities of man. "Care is taken," I see it, "that the trees grow not up into heaven," but, to me it seems, the more vigorously they aspire the better. Only let it be a vigorous, not a partial or sickly aspiration. Let not the tree forget its root.

So long as the child insists on knowing where its dead parent is, so long as bright eyes weep at mysterious pressures, too heavy for the life, so long as that impulse is constantly arising which made the Roman emperor address his soul in a strain of such touching softness, vanishing from the thought, as the column of smoke from the eye, I know of no inquiry which the impulse of man suggests that is forbidden to the resolution of man to pursue. In every inquiry, unless sustained by a pure and reverent spirit, he gropes in the dark, or falls headlong.

Self-Poise.[6]　All this may be very true, but what is the use of all this straining? Far-sought is dear-bought. When we know that all is in each, and that the ordinary contains the extraordinary, why should we play the baby, and insist upon having the moon for a toy when a tin dish will do as well. Our deep ignorance is a chasm that we can only fill up by degrees, but the commonest rubbish will help us as well as shred silk. The God Brahma, while on earth, was set to fill up a valley, but he had only a basket given him in which to fetch earth for this purpose; so is it with us all. No leaps, no starts will avail us, by patient crystallization alone the equal temper of wisdom is attainable. Sit at home and the spirit-world will look in at your window with moonlit eyes; run out to find it, and rainbow and golden cup will have vanished and left you the beggarly child you were. The better part of wisdom is a sublime prudence, a pure and patient truth that will receive nothing it is not sure it can permanently lay to heart. Of our study there should be in proportion two-thirds of rejection to one of acceptance. And, amid the manifold infatuations and illusions of this world of emotion, a being capable of clear intelligence can do no better service than to hold himself upright, avoid nonsense, and do what chores lie in his way, acknowledging every moment that primal truth, which no fact exhibits, nor, if pressed by too warm a hope, will even indicate. I think, indeed, it is part of our lesson to give a formal consent to what is farcical, and to pick up our living and our virtue amid what is so ridiculous, hardly deigning a smile, and certainly not vexed. The work is done through all, if not by every one.

Free Hope.　Thou art greatly wise, my friend, and ever respected by me, yet I find not in your theory or your scope, room enough for the lyric inspirations, or the mysterious whispers of life. To me it seems that it is madder never to abandon oneself, than often to be infatuated; better to be wounded, a captive, and a slave, than always to walk in armor.[7] As to magnetism, that is only a matter of fancy. You sometimes need just such a field in which to wander vagrant, and if it bear a higher name, yet it may be that, in last result, the trance of Pythagoras might be classed with the more infantine transports of the Seeress of Prevorst.

What is done interests me more than what is thought and supposed. Every fact is impure, but every fact contains in it the juices of life. Every fact is a clod, from which may grow an amaranth or a palm.

Do you climb the snowy peaks from whence come the streams,

where the atmosphere is rare, where you can see the sky nearer, from which you can get a commanding view of the landscape. I see great disadvantages as well as advantages in this dignified position. I had rather walk myself through all kinds of places, even at the risk of being robbed in the forest, half drowned at the ford, and covered with dust in the street.

I would beat with the living heart of the world, and understand all the moods, even the fancies or fantasies, of nature. I dare to trust to the interpreting spirit to bring me out all right at last—to establish truth through error.

Whether this be the best way is of no consequence, if it be the one individual character points out.

> For one, like me, it would be vain
> From glittering heights the eyes to strain;
> I the truth can only know,
> Tested by life's most fiery glow.
> Seeds of thought will never thrive
> Till dews of love shall bid them live.

Let me stand in my age with all its waters flowing round me. If they sometimes subdue, they must finally upbear me, for I seek the universal—and that must be the best.

The Spirit, no doubt, leads in every movement of my time: if I seek the How, I shall find it, as well as if I busied myself more with the Why.

Whatever is, is right, if only men are steadily bent to make it so, by comprehending and fulfilling its design.

May not I have an office, too, in my hospitality and ready sympathy? If I sometimes entertain guests who cannot pay with gold coin, with "fair rose nobles," that is better than to lose the chance of entertaining angels unawares.

You, my three friends, are held in heart-honor, by me. You, especially, Good-Sense, because where you do not go yourself, you do not object to another's going, if he will. You are really liberal. You, Old Church, are of use, by keeping unforgot the effigies of old religion, and reviving the tone of pure Spenserian sentiment, which this time is apt to stifle in its childish haste. But you are very faulty in censuring and wishing to limit others by your own standard. You, Self-Poise, fill a priestly office. Could but a larger intelligence of the vocations of others, and a tender sympathy with their individual natures be added, had you more of love, or more of apprehensive genius, (for either would give you the needed expansion and delicacy) you would command my entire reverence. As it is, I must at times deny and oppose you, and so must others, for you tend, by your influence, to exclude us from our full, free life. We must be content when you censure, and rejoiced when you approve; always admonished to good by your whole being, and sometimes by your judgment. And so I pass on to interest myself and others in the memoir of the Seherin von Prevorst.

Aside from Löwenstein, a town of Wirtemberg, on mountains whose highest summit is more than eighteen hundred feet above the level of the sea, lies in romantic seclusion, surrounded on all sides by woods and hills, the hamlet of Prevorst.

Its inhabitants number about four hundred and fifty, most of whom support themselves by wood-cutting, and making charcoal, and collecting wood seed.

As is usual with those who live upon the mountains, these are a vigorous race, and generally live to old age without sickness. Diseases that infest the valley, such as ague, never touch them; but they are subject in youth to attacks upon the nerves, which one would not expect in so healthy a class. In a town situated near to, and like Prevorst, the children were often attacked with a kind of St. Vitus's dance. They would foresee when it would seize upon them, and, if in the field, would hasten home to undergo the paroxysms there. From these they rose, as from magnetic sleep, without memory of what had happened.

Other symptoms show the inhabitants of this region very susceptible to magnetic and sidereal[8] influences.

On the mountain, and indeed in the hamlet of Prevorst, was, in 1801, a woman born, in whom a peculiar inner life discovered itself from early childhood. Frederica Hauffe, whose father was gamekeeper of this district of forest, was, as the position and solitude of her birthplace made natural, brought up in the most simple manner. In the keen mountain air and long winter cold, she was not softened by tenderness either as to dress or bedding, but grew up lively and blooming; and while her brothers and sisters, under the same circumstances, were subject to rheumatic attacks, she remained free from them. On the other hand, her peculiar tendency displayed itself in her dreams. If anything affected her painfully, if her mind was excited by reproof, she had instructive warning or prophetic dreams.

While yet quite young, her parents let her go, for the advantages of instruction, to her grand-father, Johann Schmidgall, in Löwenstein.

Here were discovered in her the sensibility to magnetic and ghostly influences, which, the good Kerner assures us, her grand-parents deeply lamented, and did all in their power to repress. But, as it appears that her grandfather, also, had seen a ghost, and there were evidently legends in existence about the rooms in which the little Frederika saw ghosts, and spots where the presence of human bones caused her sudden shivering, we may be allowed to doubt whether indirect influence was not more powerful than direct repression upon these subjects.

There is the true German impartiality with regard to the scene of appearance for these imposing visitors; sometimes it is "a room in the Castle of Löwenstein, long disused," à la Radcliffe,[9] sometimes "a deserted kitchen."

This "solemn, unhappy gift," brought no disturbance to the childish life of the maiden, she enjoyed life with more vivacity than most of her companions. The only trouble she had was the extreme irritability of the optic nerve, which, though without inflammation of the eyes, sometimes confined her to a solitary chamber. "This," says Dr. K. "was probably a sign of the development of the spiritual in the fleshly eye."

Sickness of her parents at last called her back to the lonely Prevorst, where, by trouble and watching beside sick beds, her feelings were too much excited, so that the faculty for prophetic dreams and the vision of spirits increased upon her.

From her seventeenth to her nineteenth year, when every outward relation was pleasant for her, this inward life was not so active, and she was distinguished from other girls of her circle only by the more intellectual nature, which displayed itself chiefly in the eyes, and by a greater liveliness which, however, never passed the bounds of grace and propriety.

She had none of the sentimentality so common at that age, and it can be proved that she had never an attachment, nor was disappointed in love, as has been groundlessly asserted.

In her nineteenth year, she was by her family betrothed to Herr H. The match was desirable on account of the excellence of the man, and the sure provision it afforded for her comfort through life.

But, whether from presentiment of the years of suffering that were before her, or from other hidden feelings, of which we only know with certainty that, if such there were, they were not occasioned by another attachment, she sank into a dejection, inexplicable to her family; passed whole days in weeping; scarcely slept for some weeks, and thus the life of feeling which had been too powerful in her childhood was called up anew in full force.

On the day of her solemn betrothal, took place, also, the funeral of T., the preacher of Oberstenfeld, a man of sixty and more years, whose preaching, instruction, and character, (he was goodness itself,) had had great influence upon her life. She followed the dear remains, with others, to the church-yard. Her heart till then so heavy, was suddenly relieved and calmed, as she stood beside the grave. She remained there long, enjoying her new peace, and when she went away found herself tranquil, but indifferent to all the concerns of this world. Here began the period, not indeed as yet of sickness, but of her peculiar inward life, which knew afterward no pause.

Later, in somnambulic state, she spoke of this day in the following verses. The deceased had often appeared to her as a shape of light, protecting her from evil spirits.

(These are little simple rhymes; they are not worth translating into verse, though, in the original, they have a childish grace.)

> What was once so dark to me,
> I see now clearly.
> In that day
> When I had given in marriage myself away,
>
> I stood quite immersed in thee,
> Thou angel figure above thy grave mound.
> Willingly would I have exchanged with thee,
> Willingly given up to thee my earthly luck,
> Which those around praised as the blessing of heaven.
>
> I prayed upon thy grave
> For one blessing only,
> That the wings of this angel
> Might henceforward
> On the hot path of life,
> Waft around me the peace of heaven.
> There standest thou, angel, now; my prayer was heard.

She was, in consequence of her marriage, removed to Kürnbach, a place on the borders of Würtemberg and Baden. Its position is low, gloomy, shut in by hills; opposite in all the influences of earth and atmosphere to those of Prevorst and its vicinity.

Those of electrical susceptibility are often made sick or well by change of place. Papponi, (of whom Amoretti[10] writes,) a man of such susceptibility, was cured of convulsive attacks by change of place. Pennet could find repose while in one part of Calabria, only by wrapping himself in an oil-cloth mantle, thus, as it were, isolating himself. That great sense of sidereal and imponderable influences, which afterward manifested itself so clearly in the Seherin, probably made this change of place very unfavorable to her. Later, it appeared, that the lower she came down from the hills, the more she suffered from spasms, but on the heights her tendency to the magnetic state was the greatest.

But also mental influences were hostile to her. Already withdrawn from the outward life, she was placed, where, as consort and housekeeper to a laboring man, the calls on her care and attention were incessant. She was obliged hourly to forsake her inner home, to provide for an outer, which did not correspond with it.

She bore this seven months, though flying to solitude, whenever outward relations permitted. But longer it was not possible to conceal the inward verity by an outward action, "the body sank beneath the attempt, and the spirit took refuge in the inner circle."

One night she dreamed that she awoke and found the dead body of the preacher T. by her side; that at the same time her father, and two physicians were considering what should be done for her in a severe sickness. She called out that "the dead friend would help her; she needed no physician." Her husband, hearing her cry out in sleep, woke her.

This dream was presage of a fever, which seized her next morning. It lasted fourteen days with great violence, and was succeeded by attacks of convulsion and spasm. This was the beginning of that state of bodily suffering and mental exaltation in which she passed the remaining seven years of her life.

She seems to have been very injudiciously treated in the first stages of her illness. Bleeding was resorted to, as usual in cases of extreme suffering where the nurses know not what else to do, and, as usual, the momentary relief was paid for by an increased nervousness, and capacity for suffering.

Magnetic influences from other persons were of frequent use to her, but they were applied without care as to what characters and constitutions were brought into connexion with hers, and were probably in the end just as injurious to her as the loss of blood. At last she became so weak, so devoid of all power in herself, that her life seemed entirely dependent on artificial means and the influence of other men.

There is a singular story of a woman in the neighborhood, who visited her once or twice, apparently from an instinct that she should injure her, and afterwards, interfered in the same way, and with the same results, in the treatment of her child.

This demoniacal impulse and power, which were ascribed to the Canidias[11] of ancient superstition, may be seen subtly influencing the members of every-day society. We see persons led, by an uneasy impulse, towards the persons and the topics where they are sure they can irritate and annoy. This is constantly observable among children, also in the closest relations between grown up people who have not yet the government of themselves, neither are governed by the better power.

There is also an interesting story of a quack who treated her with amulets, whose parallel may be found in the action of such persons in common society. It is an expression of the power that a vulgar and self-willed nature will attain over one delicate, poetical, but not yet clear within itself; outwardly it yields to a power which it inwardly disclaims.

A touching little passage is related of a time in the first years, when she seemed to be better, so much so as to receive an evening visit from some female friends. They grew merry and began to dance; she remained sad and thoughtful. When they stopped, she was in the attitude of prayer. One of her intimates, observing this, began to laugh. This affected her so much, that she became cold and rigid like a corpse. For some time they did not hear her breathe, and, when she did, it was with a rattling noise. They applied mustard poultices, and used foot and hand baths; she was brought back to life, but to a state of great suffering.

She recognized as her guardian spirit, who sometimes magnetized her or removed from her neighborhood substances that were hurtful to her, her grand-mother; thus coinciding with the popular opinion that traits reappear in the third generation.

Now began still greater wonders; the second sight, numerous and various visits from spirits and so forth.

The following may be mentioned in connection with theories and experiments current among ourselves.

"A friend, who was often with her at this time, wrote to me (Kerner): When I, with my finger, touch her *on the forehead between the eyebrows,* she says each time something that bears upon the state of my soul. Some of these sentences I record.

"Keep thy soul so that thou mayst bear it in thy hands."

"When thou comest into a world of bustle and folly, hold the Lord fast in thy heart."

"If any seek to veil from thee thy true feeling, pray to God for grace."
"Permit not thyself to stifle the light that springs up within thyself."
"Think often of the cross of Jesus; go forth and embrace it."
"As the dove found a resting-place in Noah's ark, so wilt thou, also, find a resting-place which God has appointed for thee."

When she was put under the care of Kerner, she had been five years in this state, and was reduced to such weakness, that she was, with difficulty, sustained from hour to hour.

He thought at first it would be best to take no notice of her magnetic states and directions, and told her he should not, but should treat her, with regard to her bodily symptoms, as he would any other invalid.

"At this time she fell every evening into magnetic sleep, and gave orders about herself; to which, however, those round her no longer paid attention.

I was now called in. I had never seen this woman, but had heard many false or perverted accounts of her condition. I must confess that I shared the evil opinion of the world as to her illness; that I advised to pay no attention to her magnetic situation, and the orders she gave in it; in her spasms, to forbear the laying of hands upon her; to deny her the support of persons of stronger nerves; in short, to do all possible to draw her out of the magnetic state, and to treat her with attention, but with absolutely none but the common medical means.

These views were shared by my friend, Dr. Off, of Löwenstein, who continued to treat her accordingly. But without good results. Hemorrhage, spasms, night-sweats continued. Her gums were scorbutically affected, and bled constantly; she lost all her teeth. Strengthening remedies affected her like being drawn up from her bed by force; she sank into a fear of all men, and a deadly weakness. Her death was to be wished, but it came not. Her relations, in despair, not knowing themselves what they could do with her, brought her, almost against my will, to me at Weinsberg.

She was brought hither an image of death, perfectly emaciated, unable to raise herself. Every three or four minutes, a teaspoonful of nourishment must be given her, else she fell into faintness or convulsion. Her somnambulic situation alternated with fever, hemorrhage, and night-sweats. Every evening, about seven o'clock, she fell into magnetic sleep. She then spread out her arms, and found herself, from that moment, in a clairvoyant state; but only when she brought them back upon her breast, did she begin to speak. (Kerner mentions that her child, too, slept with its hands and feet crossed.) In this state her eyes were shut, her face calm and bright. As she fell asleep, the first night after her arrival, she asked for me, but I bade them tell her that I now, and in future, should speak to her only when awake.

After she awoke, I went to her and declared, in brief and earnest terms, that I should pay no attention to what she said in sleep, and that her somnambulic state, which had lasted so long to the grief and trouble of her family, must now come to an end. This declaration I accompanied by an earnest appeal, designed to awaken a firm will in her to put down the excessive activity of brain that disordered her whole system. Afterwards, no address was made to her on any subject when in her sleep-waking state. She was left to lie unheeded. I pursued a homœopathic treatment of her case. But the medicines constantly produced effects opposite to what I expected. She now suffered less from spasm and somnambulism, but with increasing marks of weakness and decay. All seemed as if the end of her sufferings drew near. It was too late for the means I wished to use. Affected so variously and powerfully by magnetic means in the first years of her illness, she had now no life more, so thoroughly was the force of her own organization exhausted, but what she borrowed from others. In her now more infrequent magnetic trance, she was always seeking the true means of her cure. It was touching to see how, retiring within herself, she sought for help. The physician who had aided her so little with his drugs, must often stand abashed before this inner physician, perceiving it to be far better skilled than himself."

After some weeks forbearance, Kerner did ask her in her sleep what he should do for her. She prescribed a magnetic treatment, which was found of use. Afterwards, she described a machine, of which there is a drawing in this book, which she wished to have made for her use; it was so, and she derived benefit from it. She had indicated such a machine in the early stages of her disease, but at that time no one attended to her. By degrees she grew better under this treatment, and lived at Weinsberg, nearly two years, though in a state of great weakness, and more in the magnetic and clairvoyant than in the natural human state.

How his acquaintance with her affected the physician, he thus expresses:

"During those last months of her abode on the earth, there remained to her only the life of a sylph. I have been interested to record, not a journal of her sickness, but the mental phenomena of such an almost disembodied life. Such may cast light on the period when also our Psyche[12] may unfold her wings, free from bodily bonds, and the hindrances of space and time. I give facts; each reader may interpret them in his own way.

The manuals of animal magnetism and other writings have proposed many theories by which to explain such. All these are known to me. I shall make no reference to them, but only, by use of parallel facts here and there, show that the phenomena of this case recall many in which there is nothing marvellous, but which are manifestly grounded in our common existence. Such apparitions cannot too frequently, if only for moments, flash across that common existence, as electric lights from the higher world.

Frau H. was, previous to my magnetic treatment, in so deep a somnambulic life, that she was, in fact, never rightly awake, even when she seemed to be; or rather, let us say, she was at all times more awake than others are; for it is strange to term sleep this state which is just that of the clearest wakefulness. Better to say she was immersed in the inward state.

In this state and the consequent excitement of the nerves, she had almost wholly lost organic force, and received it only by transmission from those of stronger condition, principally from their eyes and the ends of the fingers. The atmosphere and nerve communications of others, said she, bring me the life which I need; they do not feel it; these effusions on which I live, would flow from them and be lost, if my nerves did not attract them; only in this way can I live.

She often assured us that others did not suffer by loss of what they imparted to her; but it cannot be denied that persons were weakened by constant intercourse with her, suffered from contraction in the limbs, trembling, &c. They were weakened also in the eyes and pit of the stomach. From those related to her by blood, she could draw more benefit than from others, and, when very weak, from them only; probably on account of a natural affinity of temperament. She could not bear to have around her nervous and sick persons; those from whom she could gain nothing made her weaker.

Even so it is remarked that flowers soon lose their beauty near the sick, and suffer peculiarly under the contact or care of some persons.

Other physicians, beside myself, can vouch that the presence of some persons affected her as pabulum vitæ,[13] while, if left with certain others or alone, she was sure to grow weaker.

From the air, too, she seemed to draw a peculiar ethereal nourishment of the same sort; she could not remain without an open window in the severest cold of winter.*

The spirit of things, about which we have no perception, was sensible to her, and had influence on her; she showed this sense of the spirit of metals, plants, animals, and men. Imponderable existences, such as the various colors of the ray, showed distinct influences upon her. The electric fluid was visible and sensible to her when it was not to us. Yea! what is incredible! even the written words of men she could discriminate by touch.†

These experiments are detailed under their several heads in the book.

From her eyes flowed a peculiar spiritual light which impressed even those who saw her for a very short time. She was in each relation more spirit than human.

Should we compare her with anything human, we would say she was as one detained at the moment of dissolution, betwixt life and death; and who is better able to discern the affairs of the world that lies before, than that behind him.

She was often in situations when one who had, like her, the power of discerning spirits, would have seen her own free from the body, which at all times enveloped it only as a light veil. She saw herself often out of the body; saw herself double. She would say, "I seem out of myself, hover above my body, and think of it as something apart from myself. But it is not a pleasant feeling, because I still sympathize with my body. If only my soul were bound more firmly to the nerve-spirit, it might be bound more closely with the nerves themselves; but the bond of my nerve-spirit is always becoming looser."

She makes a distinction between spirit as the pure intelligence; soul, the ideal of this individual man; and nerve-spirit, the dynamic of his temporal existence. Of this feeling of double identity, an invalid, now wasting under nervous disease, often speaks to me. He has it when he first awakes from sleep. Blake, the painter, whose life was almost as much a series of trances as that of our Seherin, in his designs of the Resurrection, represents spirits as rising from, or hovering over, their bodies in the same way.

---

* Near us, this last winter, a person who suffered, and finally died, from spasms like those of the Seherin, also found relief from having the windows open, while the cold occasioned great suffering to his attendants.

† Facts of the same kind are asserted of late among ourselves, and believed, though "incredible."

Often she seemed quite freed from her body, and to have no more sense of its weight.

As to artificial culture, or dressing, (dressur,) Frau H. had nothing of it. She had learned no foreign tongue, neither history, nor geography, nor natural philosophy, nor any other of those branches now imparted to those of her sex in their schools. The Bible and hymn-book were, especially in the long years of her sickness, her only reading: her moral character was throughout blameless; she was pious without fanaticism. Even her long suffering, and the peculiar manner of it, she recognized as the grace of God; as she expresses in the following verses:

> Great God! how great is thy goodness,
> To me thou hast given faith and love,
> Holding me firm in the distress of my sufferings.
>
> In the darkness of my sorrow,
> I was so far led away,
> As to beg for peace in speedy death.
>
> But then came to me the mighty strong faith;
> Hope came; and came eternal love;
> They shut my earthly eyelids.
> When, O bliss!
>
> Dead lies my bodily frame,
> But in the inmost mind a light burns up,
> Such as none knows in the waking life.
> Is it a light? no! but a sun of grace!

Often in the sense of her sufferings, while in the magnetic trance, she made prayers in verse, of which this is one:

> Father, hear me!
> Hear my prayer and supplication.
> Father, I implore thee,
> Let not thy child perish!
> Look on my anguish, my tears.
>
> Shed hope into my heart, and still its longing,
> Father, on thee I call; have pity!
> Take something from me, the sick one, the poor one.
>
> Father, I leave thee not,
> Though sickness and pain consume me.
> If I the spring's light,

See only through the mist of tears,
Father, I leave thee not.

These verses lose their merit of touching simplicity in an unrhymed translation; but they will serve to show the habitual temper of her mind.

"As I was a maker of verses," continues Dr. Kerner, "it was easy to say, Frau H. derived this talent from my magnetic influence; but she made these little verses before she came under my care." Not without deep significance was Apollo distinguished as being at once the God of poesy, of prophecy, and the medical art. Sleep-waking develops the powers of seeing, healing, and poesy. How nobly the ancients understood the inner life; how fully is it indicated in their mysteries?

I know a peasant maiden, who cannot write, but who, in the magnetic state, speaks in measured verse.

Galen [14] was indebted to his nightly dreams for a part of his medical knowledge.

The calumnies spread about Frau H. were many and gross; this she well knew. As one day she heard so many of these as to be much affected by them, we thought she would express her feelings that night in the magnetic sleep, but she only said "they can affect my body, but not my spirit." Her mind, raised above such assaults by the consciousness of innocence, maintained its tranquillity and dwelt solely on spiritual matters.

Once in her sleep-waking she wrote thus:

When the world declares of me
Such cruel ill in calumny,
And to your ears it finds a way,
Do you believe it, yea or nay?

I answered:

To us thou seemest true and pure,
Let others view it as they will;
We have our assurance still
If our own sight can make us sure.

People of all kinds, to my great trouble, were always pressing to see her. If we refused them access to the sick room, they avenged themselves by the invention of all kinds of falsehoods.

She met all with an equal friendliness, even when it cost her bodily pain, and those who defamed her, she often defended. There came to her both good and bad men. She felt the evil in men clearly, but would not censure; lifted up a stone to cast at no sinner, but was rather likely to awake, in the faulty beings she suffered near her, faith in a spiritual life which might make them better.

Years before she was brought to me, the earth, with its atmosphere, and all that is about and upon it, human beings not excepted, was no more for her. She needed, not only a magnetizer, not only a love, an earnestness, an insight, such as scarce lies within the capacity of any man, but also what no mortal could bestow upon her, another heaven, other means of nourishment, other air than that of this earth. She belonged to the world of spirits, living here herself, as more half spirit. She belonged to the state after death, into which she had advanced more than half way.

It is possible she might have been brought back to an adaptation for this world in the second or third year of her malady; but, in the fifth, no mode of treatment could have effected this. But by care she was aided to a greater harmony and clearness of the inward life; she enjoyed at Weinsberg, as she after said, the richest and happiest days of this life, and to us her abode here remains a point of light.

As to her outward form, we have already said it seemed but a thin veil about her spirit. She was little, her features of an oriental cast, her eye had the penetrating look of a seer's eye, which was set off by the shade of long dark eyelashes. She was a light flower that only lived on rays.

Eschenmayer writes thus of her in his "Mysteries."[15]

"Her natural state was a mild, friendly earnestness, always disposed to prayer and devotion; her eye had a highly spiritual expression, and remained, notwithstanding her great sufferings, always bright and clear. Her look was penetrating, would quickly change in the conversation, seem to give forth sparks, and remain fixed on some one place,—this was a token that some strange apparition fettered it,—then would she resume the conversation. When I first saw her, she was in a situation which showed that her bodily life could not long endure, and that recovery to the common natural state was quite impossible. Without visible derangement of the functions, her life seemed only a wick glimmering in the socket. She was, as Kerner truly describes her, like one arrested in the act of dying and detained in the body by magnetic influences. Spirit and soul seemed often divided, and the spirit to have taken up its abode in other regions, while the soul was yet bound to the body."

I have given these extracts as being happily expressive of the relation between the physician and the clairvoyant, also of her character.

It seems to have been one of singular gentleness, and grateful piety, simple and pure, but not at all one from which we should expect extraordinary development of brain in any way; yet the excitement of her temperament from climate, scenery, the influence of traditions which evidently flowed round her, and a great constitutional impressibility did develop in her brain the germs both of poetic creation and science.

I say poetic creation, for, to my mind, the ghosts she saw were projections of herself into objective reality. The Hades she imagines is based in fact, for it is one of souls, who, having neglected their opportunities for better life, find themselves left forlorn, helpless, seeking aid from beings still ignorant and prejudiced, perhaps much below themselves in natural powers. Having forfeited their chance of direct access to God, they seek mediation from the prayers of men. But in the coloring and dress* of these ghosts, as also in their manner and mode of speech, there is a great deal which seems merely fanciful—local and peculiar.

To me, these interviews represent only prophecies of her mind; yet, considered in this way, they are, if not ghostly, spiritual facts of high beauty, and which cast light on the state of the soul after its separation from the body. Her gentle patience with them, her steady reference to a higher cause, her pure joy, when they became white in the light of happiness obtained through aspiration, are worthy of a more than half enfranchised angel.

As to the stories of mental correspondence and visits to those still engaged in this world, such as are told of her presentiment of her father's death, and connexion with him in the last moments, these are probably pure facts. Those who have sufficient strength of affection to be easily disengaged from external impressions and habits, and who dare trust their mental impulses are familiar with such.

Her invention of a language seems a simply natural motion of the mind when left to itself. The language we habitually use is so broken, and so hackneyed by ages of conventional use, that, in all deep states of being, we crave one simple and primitive in its stead. Most persons make one more or less clear from looks, tones, and symbols:—this woman, in the long leisure of her loneliness, and a mind bent upon itself, attempted to compose one of letters and words. I look upon it as no gift from without, but a growth from her own mind.

Her invention of a machine, of which she made a drawing, her power

---

*The women ghosts all wear veils, put on the way admired by the Italian poets, of whom, however, she could know nothing.

of drawing correctly her life-circle, and sun-circle, and the mathematical feeling she had of her existence, in correspondent sections of the two, are also valuable as mental facts. These figures describe her history and exemplify the position of mathematics toward the world of creative thought.

Every fact of mental existence ought to be capable of similar demonstration. I attach no especial importance to her circles:—we all live in such; all who observe themselves have the same sense of exactness and harmony in the revolutions of their destiny. But few attend to what is simple and invariable in the motions of their minds, and still fewer seek out means clearly to express them to others.

Goethe has taken up these facts in his Wanderjahre, where he speaks of his Macaria;[16] also, one of these persons who are compensated for bodily infirmity by a more concentrated and acute state of mind, and consequent accesses of wisdom, as being bound to a star. When she was engaged by a sense of these larger revolutions, she seemed to those near her on the earth, to be sick; when she was, in fact, lower, but better adapted to the details and variations of an earthly life, these said she was well. Macaria knew the sun and life circles, also, the lives of spirit and soul, as did the forester's daughter of Prevorst.

Her power of making little verses was one of her least gifts. Many excitable persons possess this talent at versification, as all may possess it. It is merely that a certain exaltation of feeling raises the mode of expression with it, in the same way as song differs from speech. Verses of this sort do not necessarily demand the high faculties that constitute the poet,—the creative powers. Many verses, good ones, are personal or national merely. Ballads, hymns, love-lyrics, have often no claim differing from those of common prose speech, to the title of poems, except a greater keenness and terseness of expression.

The verses of this Seherin are of the simplest character, the natural garb for the sighs or aspirations of a lonely heart. She uses the shortest words, the commonest rhymes, and the verses move us by their nature and truth alone.

The most interesting of these facts to me, are her impressions from minerals and plants. Her impressions coincide with many ancient superstitions.

The hazel woke her immediately and gave her more power, therefore the witch with her hazel wand, probably found herself superior to those around her. We may also mention, in reference to witchcraft, that Dr. K. asserts that, in certain moods of mind, she had no weight, but was upborne upon water, like cork, thus confirming the propriety, and justice of our forefathers' ordeal for witchcraft!

The laurel produced on her the highest magnetic effect, therefore the Sibyls had good reasons for wearing it on their brows.

"The laurel had on her, as on most sleep-wakers, a distinguished magnetic effect. We thus see why the priestess at Delphi, previous to uttering her oracles, shook a laurel tree, and then seated herself on a tripod covered with laurel boughs. In the temple of Æsculapius, and others, the laurel was used to excite sleep and dream."

From grapes she declared impressions, which corresponded with those caused by the wines made from them. Many kinds were given her, one after the other, by the person who raised them, and who gives a certificate as to the accuracy of her impressions, and his belief that she could not have derived them from any cause, but that of the touch.

She prescribed vegetable substances to be used in her machine, (as a kind of vapor bath,) and with good results to herself.

She enjoyed contact with minerals, deriving from those she liked a sense of concentrated life. Her impressions of the precious stones, corresponded with many superstitions of the ancients, which led to the preference of certain gems for amulets, on which they had engraved talismanic figures.[17]

The ancients, in addition to their sense of the qualities that distinguish the diamond above all gems, venerated it as a talisman against wild beasts, poison, and evil spirits, thus expressing the natural influence of what is so enduring, bright, and pure. Townshend, speaking of the effect of gems on one of his sleep-wakers, said, she loved the diamond so much that she would lean her forehead towards it, whenever it was brought near her.[18]

It is observable that these sleep-wakers, in their prescriptions, resemble the ancient sages, who culled only simples for the sick. But if they have this fine sense, also, for the qualities of animal and mineral substances, there is no reason why they should not turn bane to antidote, and prescribe at least homeopathic doses of poison, to restore the diseased to health.

The Seherin ascribed different states to the right and left sides of every body, even of the lady moon. The left is most impressible. Query: Is this the reason why the left hand has been, by the custom of nations, so almost disused, because the heart is on the left side?

She also saw different sights in the left from the right eye. In the left, the bodily state of the person; in the right, his real or destined self, how often unknown to himself, almost always obscured or perverted by his present ignorance or mistake. She had also the gift of second sight. She saw the coffins of those about to die. She saw in mirrors, cups of water; in soap-bubbles, the coming future.

We are here reminded of many beautiful superstitions and legends; of the secret pool in which the daring may, at mid-moon of night, read the future; of the magic globe, on whose pure surface Britomart sees her future love, whom she must seek, arrayed in knightly armor, through a difficult and hostile world.

> A looking-glass, right wondrously aguized,
> Whose virtues through the wyde world soon were solemnized.
> It vertue had to show in perfect sight,
> Whatever thing was in the world contayned,
> Betwixt the lowest earth and hevens hight;
> So that it to the looker appertayned,
> Whatever foe had wrought, or friend had fayned,
> Herein discovered was, ne ought mote pas,
> Ne ought in secret from the same remayned;
> Forthy it round and hollow shaped was,
> Like to the world itselfe, and seemed a World of Glas.

Faerie Queene, Book III

Such mirrors had Cornelius Aggrippa [19] and other wizards. The soap-bubble is such a globe; only one had need of second sight or double sight to see the pictures on so transitory a mirror. Perhaps it is some vague expectation of such wonders, that makes us so fond of blowing them in childish years. But, perhaps, it is rather as a prelude to the occupation of our lives, blowing bubbles where all things may be seen, that, "to the looker apper-tain," if we can keep them long enough or look quick enough.

In short, were this biography of no other value, it would be most interesting as showing how the floating belief of nations, always no doubt shadowing forth in its imperfect fashion the poetic facts with their specific exposition, is found to grow up anew in a simple, but high-wrought nature.

The fashioning spirit, working upwards from the clod to man, proffers as its last, highest essay, the brain of man. In the lowest zoöphyte it aimed at this; some faint rudiments may there be discerned: but only in man has it perfected that immense galvanic battery that can be loaded from above, below, and around;—that engine, not only of perception, but of conception and consecutive thought,—whose right hand is memory, whose life is idea, the crown of nature, the platform from which spirit takes wing.

Yet, as gradation is the beautiful secret of nature, and the fashioning spirit, which loves to develop and transcend, loves no less to moderate, to modulate, and harmonize, it did not mean by thus drawing man onward to the next state of existence, to destroy his fitness for this. It did not mean to destroy his sympathies with the mineral, vegetable, and animal realms, of whose components he is in great part composed; which were the preface to his being, of whom he is to take count, whom he should govern as a reasoning head of a perfectly arranged body. He was meant to be the historian, the philosopher, the poet, the king of this world, no less than the prophet of the next.

These functions should be in equipoise, and when they are not, when we see excess either on the natural (so called as distinguished from the spiritual,) or the spiritual side, we feel that the law is transgressed. And, if it be the greatest sorrow to see brain merged in body, to see a man more hands or feet than head, so that we feel he might, with propriety, be on all fours again, or even crawl like the serpent; it is also sad to see the brain, too much excited on some one side, which we call madness, or even unduly and prematurely, so as to destroy in its bloom, the common human existence of the person, as in the case before us, and others of the poetical and prophetical existence.

We would rather minds should foresee less and see more surely, that death should ensue by gentler gradation, and the brain be the governor and interpreter, rather than the destroyer, of the animal life. But, in cases like this, where the animal life is prematurely broken up, and the brain prematurely exercised, we may as well learn what we can from it, and believe that the glimpses thus caught, if not as precious as the full view, are bright with the same light, and open to the same scene.

There is a family character about all the German ghosts. We find the same features in these stories as in those related by Jung Stilling [20] and others. They bear the same character as the pictures by the old masters, of a deep and simple piety. She stands before as, this piety, in a full, high-necked robe, a simple, hausfrauish cap, a clear, straightforward blue eye. These are no terrible, gloomy ghosts with Spanish mantle or Italian dagger. We feel quite at home with them, and sure of their good faith.

To the Seherin, they were a real society, constantly inspiring good thoughts. The reference to them in these verses, written in her journal shortly before her death, is affecting, and shows her deep sense of their reality. She must have felt that she had been a true friend to them, by refusing always, as she did, requests she thought wrong, and referring them to a Saviour.

> Farewell, my friends,
> All farewell,
> God bless you for your love—
> Bless you for your goodness.
>   All farewell!
>
> And you, how shall I name you?
>   Who have so saddened me,
> I will name you also—Friends;
> You have been discipline to me.
>   Farewell! farewell!
>
> Farewell! you my dear ones,
> Soon will you know*
> How hard have been my sufferings
>   In the Pilgrim land.
>   Farewell!
>
>   Let it not grieve you,
> That my woes find an end;
>   Farewell, dear ones,
> Till the second meeting;
>   Farewell! Farewell!

In this journal her thoughts dwell much upon those natural ties which she was not permitted to enjoy. She thought much of her children, and often fancied she had saw the one who had died, growing in the spirit land. Any allusion to them called a sweet smile on her face when in her trance.

Other interesting poems are records of these often beautiful visions, especially of that preceding her own death; the address to her life-circle, the thought of which is truly great, (this was translated in the Dublin Magazine,) and descriptions of her earthly state as an imprisonment. The

---

*The physician thought she here referred to the examination of her body that would take place after her death. The brain was found to be sound, though there were marks of great disease elsewhere.

story of her life, though stained like others, by partialities, and prejudices, which were not justly distinguished from what was altogether true and fair, is a poem of so pure a music, presents such gentle and holy images, that we sympathize fully in the love and gratitude Kerner and his friends felt towards her, as the friend of their best life. She was a St. Theresa [21] in her way.

His address to her, with which his volume closes, may thus be translated in homely guise. In the original it has no merit, except as uttering his affectionate and reverent feeling towards his patient, the peasant girl,— "the sick one, the poor one." But we like to see how, from the mouths of babes and sucklings, praise may be so perfected as to command this reverence from the learned and worldly-wise.

> Farewell; the debt I owe thee
>   Ever in heart I bear;
> My soul sees, since I know thee,
>   The spirit depths so clear.
>
> Whether in light or shade,
>   Thy soul now dwelling hath;
> Be, if my faith should fade,
>   The guide upon my path.
>
> Livest thou in mutual power,
>   With spirits blest and bright,
> O be, in death's dark hour,
>   My help to heaven's light.
>
> Upon thy grave is growing,
>   The plant by thee beloved,*
> St. Johns-wort golden glowing,
>   Like St. John's thoughts of love.
>
> Witness of sacred sorrow,
>   Whene'er thou meet'st my eye,
> O flower, from thee I borrow,
>   Thoughts for eternity.
>
> Farewell! the woes of earth
>   No more my soul affright;

---

*She received great benefit from decoctions of this herb, and often prescribed it to others.

Who knows their temporal birth
Can easy bear their weight.

I do confess this is a paraphrase, not a translation, also, that in the other extracts, I have taken liberties with the original for the sake of condensation, and clearness. What I have written must be received as a slight and conversational account of the work.

Two or three other remarks, I had forgotten, may come in here.

The glances at the spirit-world have none of that large or universal significance, none of that value from philosophical analogy, that is felt in any picture by Swedenborg, or Dante, of permanent relations.[22] The mind of the forester's daughter was exalted and rapidly developed; still the wild cherry tree bore no orange; she was not transformed into a philosophic or poetic organization.

Yet many of her untaught notions remind of other seers of a larger scope. She, too, receives this life as one link in a long chain; and thinks that immediately after death, the meaning of the past life will appear to us as one word.

She tends to a belief in the aromal state, and in successive existences on this earth; for behind persons she often saw another being, whether their form in the state before or after this, I know not; behind a woman a man, equipped for fight, and so forth. Her perception of character, even in cases of those whom she saw only as they passed her window, was correct.

Kerner aims many a leaden sarcasm at those who despise his credulity. He speaks of those sages as men whose brain is a glass table, incapable of receiving the electric spark, and who will not believe, because, in their mental isolation, they are incapable of feeling these facts.

Certainly, I think he would be dull, who could see no meaning or beauty in the history of the forester's daughter of Prevorst. She lived but nine-and-twenty years, yet, in that time, had traversed a larger portion of the field of thought than all her race before, in their many and long lives.

Of the abuses to which all these magical implements are prone, I have an instance, since leaving Milwaukie, in the journal of a man equally sincere, but not equally inspired, led from Germany hither by signs and wonders, as a commissioned agent of Providence, who, indeed, has arranged every detail of his life with a minuteness far beyond the promised care of the sparrow. He props himself by spiritual aid from a maiden now in this country, who was once an attendant on the Seeress, and who seems to have caught from her the contagion of trance, but not its revelations.

DO NOT blame me that I have written so much about Germany and Hades, while you were looking for news of the West. Here, on the pier, I see disembarking the Germans, the Norwegians, the Swedes, the Swiss. Who knows how much of old legendary lore, of modern wonder, they have already planted amid the Wisconsin forests? Soon, soon their tales of the origin of things, and the Providence which rules them, will be so mingled with those of the Indian, that the very oak trees will not know them apart,—will not know whether itself be a Runic, a Druid, or a Winnebago oak.

Some seeds of all growths that have ever been known in this world might, no doubt, already be found in these Western wilds, if we had the power to call them to life.

I saw, in the newspaper, that the American Tract Society[23] boasted of their agents' having exchanged, at a Western cabin door, tracts for the Devil on Two Sticks, and then burnt that more entertaining than edifying volume. No wonder, though, they study it there. Could one but have the gift of reading the dreams dreamed by men of such various birth, various history, various mind, it would afford much more extensive amusement than did the chambers of one Spanish city!

Could I but have flown at night through such mental experiences, instead of being shut up in my little bedroom at the Milwaukie boarding house, this chapter would have been worth reading. As it is, let us hasten to a close.

Had I been rich in money, I might have built a house, or set up in business, during my fortnight's stay at Milwaukie, matters move on there at so rapid a rate. But, being only rich in curiosity, I was obliged to walk the streets and pick up what I could in casual intercourse. When I left the street, indeed, and walked on the bluffs, or sat beside the lake in their shadow, my mind was rich in dreams congenial to the scene, some time to be realized, though not by me.

A boat was left, keel up, half on the sand, half in the water, swaying with each swell of the lake. It gave a picturesque grace to that part of the shore, as the only image of inaction—only object of a pensive character to be seen. Near this I sat, to dream my dreams and watch the colors of the lake, changing hourly, till the sun sank. These hours yielded impulses, wove webs, such as life will not again afford.

Returning to the boarding house, which was also a boarding school, we were sure to be greeted by gay laughter.

This school was conducted by two girls of nineteen and seventeen years; their pupils were nearly as old as themselves; the relation seemed very pleasant between them. The only superiority—that of superior knowledge—was sufficient to maintain authority—all the authority that was needed to keep daily life in good order.

In the West, people are not respected merely because they are old in years; people there have not time to keep up appearances in that way; when they cease to have a real advantage in wisdom, knowledge, or enterprise, they must stand back, and let those who are oldest in character "go ahead," however few years they may count. There are no banks of established respectability in which to bury the talent there; no napkin of precedent in which to wrap it. What cannot be made to pass current, is not esteemed coin of the realm.

To the windows of this house, where the daughter of a famous "Indian fighter," i.e. fighter against the Indians, was learning French and the piano, came wild, tawny figures, offering for sale their baskets of berries. The boys now, instead of brandishing the tomahawk, tame their hands to pick raspberries.

Here the evenings were much lightened by the gay chat of one of the party, who, with the excellent practical sense of mature experience, and the kindest heart, united a naiveté and innocence such as I never saw in any other who had walked so long life's tangled path. Like a child, she was everywhere at home, and like a child, received and bestowed entertainment from all places, all persons. I thanked her for making me laugh, as did the sick and poor, whom she was sure to find out in her briefest sojourn in any place, for more substantial aid. Happy are those who never grieve, and so often aid and enliven their fellow men!

This scene, however, I was not sorry to exchange for the much celebrated beauties of the Island of Mackinaw.

CHAPTER VI

Mackinaw

LATE AT NIGHT we reached this island, so famous for its beauty, and to which I proposed a visit of some length. It was the last week in August, when a large representation from the Chippewa and Ottowa tribes are here to receive their annual payments from the American government. As their habits make travelling easy and inexpensive to them, neither being obliged to wait for steamboats, or write to see whether hotels are full, they come hither by thousands, and those thousands in families, secure of accommodation on the beach, and food from the lake, to make a long holiday out of the occasion. There were near two thousand encamped on the island already, and more arriving every day.

As our boat came in, the captain had some rockets let off. This greatly excited the Indians, and their yells and wild cries resounded along the shore. Except for the momentary flash of the rockets, it was perfectly dark, and my sensations as I walked with a stranger to a strange hotel, through the midst of these shrieking savages, and heard the pants and snorts of the departing steamer, which carried away all my companions, were somewhat of the dismal sort; though it was pleasant, too, in the way that everything strange is; everything that breaks in upon the routine that so easily incrusts us.

I had reason to expect a room to myself at the hotel, but found none, and was obliged to take up my rest in the common parlor and eating-room, a circumstance which ensured my being an early riser.

With the first rosy streak, I was out among my Indian neighbors, whose lodges honey-combed the beautiful beach, that curved away in long, fair outline on either side the house. They were already on the alert, the children creeping out from beneath the blanket door of the lodge; the women pounding corn in their rude mortars, the young men playing on their pipes. I had been much amused, when the strain proper to the Winnebago courting flute was played to me on another instrument, at any one fancying it a melody; but now, when I heard the notes in their true tone and time, I thought it not unworthy comparison, in its graceful sequence, and the light flourish, at the close, with the sweetest bird-songs;

and this, like the bird-song, is only practised to allure a mate. The Indian, become a citizen and a husband, no more thinks of playing the flute than one of the "settled down" members of our society would of choosing the "purple light of love" as dye-stuff for a surtout.

Mackinaw has been fully described by able pens, and I can only add my tribute to the exceeding beauty of the spot and its position. It is charming to be on an island so small that you can sail round it in an afternoon, yet large enough to admit of long secluded walks through its gentle groves. You can go round it in your boat; or, on foot, you can tread its narrow beach, resting, at times, beneath the lofty walls of stone, richly wooded, which rise from it in various architectural forms. In this stone, caves are continually forming, from the action of the atmosphere; one of these is quite deep, and with a fragment left at its mouth, wreathed with little creeping plants, that looks, as you sit within, like a ruined pillar.

The arched rock surprised me, much as I had heard of it, from the perfection of the arch. It is perfect whether you look up through it from the lake, or down through it to the transparent waters. We both ascended and descended, no very easy matter, the steep and crumbling path, and rested at the summit, beneath the trees, and at the foot upon the cool mossy stones beside the lapsing wave. Nature has carefully decorated all this architecture with shrubs that take root within the crevices, and small creeping vines. These natural ruins may vie for beautiful effect with the remains of European grandeur, and have, beside, a charm as of a playful mood in nature.

The sugar-loaf rock is a fragment in the same kind as the pine rock we saw in Illinois. It has the same air of a helmet, as seen from an eminence at the side, which you descend by a long and steep path. The rock itself may be ascended by the bold and agile. Half way up is a niche, to which those, who are neither, can climb by a ladder. A very handsome young officer and lady who were with us did so, and then, facing round, stood there side by side, looking in the niche, if not like saints or angels wrought by pious hands in stone, as romantically, if not as holily, worthy the gazer's eye.

The woods which adorn the central ridge of the island are very full in foliage, and, in August, showed the tender green and pliant leaf of June elsewhere. They are rich in beautiful mosses and the wild raspberry.

From Fort Holmes, the old fort, we had the most commanding view of the lake and straits, opposite shores, and fair islets. Mackinaw, itself, is best seen from the water. Its peculiar shape is supposed to have been the origin of its name, Michilimackinac, which means the Great Turtle. One person whom I saw, wished to establish another etymology, which he fancied to be more refined; but, I doubt not, this is the true one, both because the shape might suggest such a name, and that the existence of an island in this commanding position, which did so, would seem a significant fact to the Indians. For Henry gives the details of peculiar worship paid to the Great Turtle, and the oracles received from this extraordinary Apollo of the Indian Delphos.[1]

It is crowned most picturesquely, by the white fort, with its gay flag. From this, on one side, stretches the town. How pleasing a sight, after the raw, crude, staring assemblage of houses, everywhere else to be met in this country, an old French town, mellow in its coloring, and with the harmonious effect of a slow growth, which assimilates, naturally, with objects round it. The people in its streets, Indian, French, half-breeds, and others, walked with a leisure step, as of those who live a life of taste and inclination, rather than of the hard press of business, as in American towns elsewhere.

On the other side, along the fair, curving beach, below the white houses scattered on the declivity, clustered the Indian lodges, with their amber brown matting, so soft, and bright of hue, in the late afternoon sun. The first afternoon I was there, looking down from a near height, I felt that I never wished to see a more fascinating picture. It was an hour of the deepest serenity; bright blue and gold, rich shadows. Every moment the sunlight fell more mellow. The Indians were grouped and scattered among the lodges; the women preparing food, in the kettle or frying-pan, over the many small fires; the children, half-naked, wild as little goblins, were playing both in and out of the water. Here and there lounged a young girl, with a baby at her back, whose bright eyes glanced, as if born into a world of courage and of joy, instead of ignominious servitude and slow decay. Some girls were cutting wood, a little way from me, talking and laughing, in the low musical tone, so charming in the Indian women. Many bark canoes were upturned upon the beach, and, by that light, of almost the same amber as the lodges. Others, coming in, their square sails set, and with almost arrowy speed, though heavily laden with dusky forms, and all the apparatus of their household. Here and there a sail-boat glided by, with a different, but scarce less pleasing motion.

It was a scene of ideal loveliness, and these wild forms adorned it, as looking so at home in it. All seemed happy, and they were happy that day, for they had no firewater to madden them, as it was Sunday, and the shops were shut.

From my window, at the boarding house, my eye was constantly attracted by these picturesque groups. I was never tired of seeing the canoes come in, and the new arrivals set up their temporary dwellings. The women ran to set up the tent-poles, and spread the mats on the ground. The men brought the chests, kettles, &c.; the mats were then laid on the outside, the cedar boughs strewed on the ground, the blanket hung up for a door, and all was completed in less than twenty minutes. Then they began to prepare the night meal, and to learn of their neighbors the news of the day.

The habit of preparing food out of doors, gave all the gipsy charm and variety to their conduct. Continually I wanted Sir Walter Scott to have been there. If such romantic sketches were suggested to him, by the sight of a few gipsies, not a group near one of these fires but would have furnished him material for a separate canvass. I was so taken up with the spirit of the scene, that I could not follow out the stories suggested by these weather-beaten, sullen, but eloquent figures.

They talked a great deal, and with much variety of gesture, so that I often had a good guess at the meaning of their discourse. I saw that, whatever the Indian may be among the whites, he is anything but taciturn with his own people. And he often would declaim, or narrate at length, as indeed it is obvious, that these tribes possess great power that way, if only from the fables taken from their stores, by Mr. Schoolcraft.

I liked very much to walk or sit among them. With the women I held much communication by signs. They are almost invariably coarse and ugly, with the exception of their eyes, with a peculiarly awkward gait, and forms bent by burthens. This gait, so different from the steady and noble step of the men, marks the inferior position they occupy. I had heard much eloquent contradiction of this. Mrs. Schoolcraft [2] had maintained to a friend, that they were in fact as nearly on a par with their husbands as the white woman with hers. "Although," said she, "on account of inevitable causes, the Indian woman is subjected to many hardships of a peculiar nature, yet her position, compared with that of the man, is higher and freer than that of the white woman. Why will people look only on one side? They either exalt the Red man into a Demigod or degrade him into a beast. They say that he compels his wife to do all the drudgery, while he does nothing but hunt and amuse himself; forgetting that, upon his activity and power of endurance as a hunter, depends the support of his family; that this is labor of the most fatiguing kind, and that it is absolutely necessary that he should keep his frame unbent by burdens and unworn by toil, that he may be able to obtain the means of subsistence. I have witnessed scenes of conjugal and parental love in the Indian's wigwam from which I have often, often thought the educated white man, proud of his superior civilization, might learn an useful lesson. When he returns from hunting, worn out with fatigue, having tasted nothing since dawn, his wife, if she is a good wife, will take off his moccasons and replace them with dry ones, and will prepare his game for their repast, while his children will climb upon him, and he will caress them with all the tenderness of a woman; and in the evening the Indian wigwam is the scene of the purest domestic pleasures. The father will relate for the amusement of the wife, and for the instruction of the children, all the events of the day's hunt, while they will treasure up every word that falls, and thus learn the theory of the art whose practice is to be the occupation of their lives.

Mrs. Grant [3] speaks thus of the position of woman amid the Mohawk Indians:

"Lady Mary Montague says, that the court of Vienna was the paradise of old women, and that there is no other place in the world where a woman past fifty excites the least interest. Had her travels extended to the interior of North America, she would have seen another instance of this inversion of the common mode of thinking. Here a woman never was of consequence, till she had a son old enough to fight the battles of his country. From that date she held a superior rank in society; was allowed to live at ease, and even called to consultations on national affairs. In savage and warlike countries, the reign of beauty is very short, and its influence comparatively limited. The girls in childhood had a very pleasing appearance; but excepting their fine hair, eyes, and teeth, every external grace was soon banished by perpetual drudgery, carrying burdens too heavy to be borne, and other slavish employments considered beneath the dignity of the men. These walked before erect and graceful, decked with ornaments which set off to advantage the symmetry of their well-formed persons, while the poor women followed, meanly attired, bent under the weight of the children and utensils, which they carried everywhere with them, and disfigured and degraded by ceaseless toils. They were very early married, for a Mohawk had no other servant but his wife, and, whenever he commenced hunter, it was requisite he should have some one to carry his load, cook his kettle, make his moccasons, and, above all, produce the young warriors who were to succeed him in the honors of the chase and of the tomahawk. Wherever man is a mere hunter, woman is a mere slave. It is domestic intercourse that softens man, and elevates woman; and of that there can be but little, where the employments and amusements are not in common; the ancient Caledonians honored the fair; but then it is to be observed, they were fair huntresses, and moved in the light of their beauty to the hill of roes; and the culinary toils were entirely left to the rougher sex. When the young warrior made his appearance, it softened the cares of his mother, who well knew that, when he grew up, every deficiency in tenderness to his wife would be made up in superabundant duty and affection to her. If it were possible to carry filial veneration to excess, it was done here; for all other charities were absorbed in it. I wonder this system of depressing the sex in their early years, to exalt them when all their juvenile attractions were flown, and when mind alone can distinguish them, has not occurred to our modern reformers. The Mohawks took good care not to admit their women to share their prerogatives, till they approved themselves good wives and mothers."

The observations of women upon the position of woman are always more valuable than those of men; but, of these two, Mrs. Grant's seems much nearer the truth than Mrs. Schoolcraft's, because, though her opportunities for observation did not bring her so close, she looked more at both sides to find the truth.

Carver, in his travels among the Winnebagoes,[4] describes two queens, one nominally so, like Queen Victoria; the other invested with a genuine royalty, springing from her own conduct.

In the great town of the Winnebagoes, he found a queen presiding over the tribe, instead of a sachem. He adds, that, in some tribes, the descent is given to the female line in preference to the male, that is, a sister's son will succeed to the authority, rather than a brother's son.

The position of this Winnebago queen, reminded me forcibly of Queen Victoria's.

"She sat in the council, but only asked a few questions, or gave some trifling directions in matters relative to the state, for women are never allowed to sit in their councils, except they happen to be invested with the supreme authority, and then it is not customary for them to make any formal speeches, as the chiefs do. She was a very ancient woman, small in stature, and not much distinguished by her dress from several young women that attended her. These, her attendants, seemed greatly pleased whenever I showed any tokens of respect to their queen, especially when I saluted her, which I frequently did to acquire her favor."

The other was a woman, who being taken captive, found means to kill her captor, and make her escape, and the tribe were so struck with admiration at the courage and calmness she displayed on the occasion, as to make her chieftainess in her own right.

Notwithstanding the homage paid to women, and the consequence allowed her in some cases, it is impossible to look upon the Indian women, without feeling that they *do* occupy a lower place than women among the nations of European civilization. The habits of drudgery expressed in their form and gesture, the soft and wild but melancholy expression of their eye, reminded me of the tribe mentioned by Mackenzie,[5] where the women destroy their female children, whenever they have a good opportunity; and of the eloquent reproaches addressed by the Paraguay woman to her mother, that she had not, in the same way, saved her from the anguish and weariness of her lot.

More weariness than anguish, no doubt, falls to the lot of most of these women. They inherit submission, and the minds of the generality accommodate themselves more or less to any posture. Perhaps they suffer less than their white sisters, who have more aspiration and refinement, with little power of self-sustenance. But their place is certainly lower, and their share of the human inheritance less.

Their decorum and delicacy are striking, and show that when these are native to the mind, no habits of life make any difference. Their whole gesture is timid, yet self-possessed. They used to crowd round me, to inspect little things I had to show them, but never press near; on the contrary, would reprove and keep off the children. Anything they took from my hand, was held with care, then shut or folded, and returned with an air of lady-like precision. They would not stare, however curious they might be, but cast sidelong glances.

A locket that I wore, was an object of untiring interest; they seemed to regard it as a talisman. My little sun-shade was still more fascinating to them; apparently they had never before seen one. For an umbrella they entertain profound regard, probably looking upon it as the most luxurious superfluity a person can possess, and therefore a badge of great wealth. I used to see an old squaw, whose sullied skin and coarse, tanned locks, told that she had braved sun and storm, without a doubt or care, for sixty years at the least, sitting gravely at the door of her lodge, with an old green umbrella over her head, happy for hours together in the dignified shade. For her happiness pomp came not, as it so often does, too late; she received it with grateful enjoyment.

One day, as I was seated on one of the canoes, a woman came and sat beside me, with her baby in its cradle set up at her feet. She asked me by a gesture, to let her take my sun-shade, and then to show her how to open it. Then she put it into her baby's hand, and held it over its head, looking at me the while with a sweet, mischievous laugh, as much as to say, "you carry a thing that is only fit for a baby;" her pantomime was very pretty. She, like the other women, had a glance, and shy, sweet expression in the eye; the men have a steady gaze.

That noblest and loveliest of modern Preux, Lord Edward Fitz-gerald,[6] who came through Buffalo to Detroit and Mackinaw, with Brant, and was adopted into the Bear tribe by the name of Eghnidal, was struck, in the same way, by the delicacy of manners in the women. He says, "Notwithstanding the life they lead, which would make most women rough and masculine, they are as soft, meek and modest, as the best brought up girls in England. Somewhat coquettish too! Imagine the man-ners of Mimi in a poor *squaw,* that has been carrying packs in the woods all her life."

McKenney mentions that the young wife, during the short bloom of her beauty, is an object of homage and tenderness to her husband. One Indian woman, the Flying Pigeon, a beautiful, an excellent woman, of whom he gives some particulars, is an instance of the power uncommon characters will always exert of breaking down the barriers custom has erected round them. She captivated by her charms, and inspired with reverence for her character, her husband and son. The simple praise with which the husband indicates the religion, the judgment, and the generosity he saw in her, are as satisfying as Count Zinzendorf's[7] more labored eu-logium on his "noble consort." The conduct of her son, when, many years after her death, he saw her picture at Washington, is unspeakably affecting. Catlin gives anecdotes of the grief of a chief for the loss of a daughter, and the princely gifts he offers in exchange for her portrait, worthy not merely of European, but of Troubadour sentiment. It is also evident that, as Mrs. Schoolcraft says, the women have great power at home. It can never be otherwise, men being dependent upon them for the comfort of their lives. Just so among ourselves, wives who are neither esteemed nor loved by their husbands, have great power over their conduct by the friction of every day, and over the formation of their opinions by the daily opportunities so close a relation affords, of perverting testimony and instilling doubts. But these sentiments should not come in brief flashes, but burn as a steady flame, then there would be more women worthy to inspire them. This power is good for nothing, unless the woman be wise to use it aright. Has the Indian, has the white woman, as noble a feeling of life and its uses, as religious a self-respect, as worthy a field of thought and action, as man? If not, the white woman, the Indian woman, occupies an inferior position to that of man. It is not so much a question of power, as of privilege.

The men of these subjugated tribes, now accustomed to drunkenness and every way degraded, bear but a faint impress of the lost grandeur of the race. They are no longer strong, tall, or finely proportioned. Yet as you see them stealing along a height, or striding boldly forward, they remind you of what *was* majestic in the red man.

On the shores of lake Superior, it is said, if you visit them at home, you may still see a remnant of the noble blood. The Pillagers—(Pilleurs)—a band celebrated by the old travellers, are still existant there.

"Still some, 'the eagles of their tribe,' may rush."

I have spoken of the hatred felt by the white man for the Indian: with white women it seems to amount to disgust, to loathing. How I could endure the dirt, the peculiar smell of the Indians, and their dwellings, was a great marvel in the eyes of my lady acquaintance; indeed, I wonder why they did not quite give me up, as they certainly looked on me with great distaste for it. "Get you gone, you Indian dog," was the felt, if not the breathed, expression towards the hapless owners of the soil. All their claims, all their sorrows quite forgot, in abhorrence of their dirt, their tawny skins, and the vices the whites have taught them.

A person who had seen them during great part of a life, expressed his prejudices to me with such violence, that I was no longer surprised that the Indian children threw sticks at him as he passed. A lady said, "do what you will for them, they will be ungrateful. The savage cannot be washed out of them. Bring up an Indian child and see if you can attach it to you." The next moment, she expressed, in the presence of one of those children whom she was bringing up, loathing at the odor left by one of her people, and one of the most respected, as he passed through the room. When the child is grown she will consider it basely ungrateful not to love her, as it certainly will not; and this will be cited as an instance of the impossibility of attaching the Indian.

Whether the Indian could, by any efforts of love and intelligence from the white man, have been civilized and made a valuable ingredient in the new state, I will not say; but this we are sure of; the French Catholics, at least, did not harm them, nor disturb their minds merely to corrupt them. The French they loved. But the stern Presbyterian, with his dogmas and his task-work, the city circle and the college, with their niggard concessions and unfeeling stare, have never tried the experiment. It has not been tried. Our people and our government have sinned alike against the first-born of the soil, and if they are the fated agents of a new era, they have done nothing—have invoked no god to keep them sinless while they do the hest of fate.

Worst of all, when they invoke the holy power only to mask their iniquity; when the felon trader, who, all the week, has been besotting and degrading the Indian with rum mixed with red pepper, and damaged tobacco, kneels with him on Sunday before a common altar, to tell the rosary which recalls the thought of him crucified for love of suffering men, and to listen to sermons in praise of "purity"!!

My savage friends, cries the old fat priest, you must, above all things, aim at *purity*.

Oh, my heart swelled when I saw them in a Christian church. Better their own dog-feasts and bloody rites than such mockery of that other faith.

"The dog," said an Indian, "was once a spirit; he has fallen for his sin, and was given by the Great Spirit, in this shape, to man, as his most intelligent companion. Therefore we sacrifice it in highest honor to our friends in this world,—to our protecting geniuses in another."

There was religion in that thought. The white man sacrifices his own brother, and to Mammon, yet he turns in loathing from the dog-feast.

"You say," said the Indian of the South to the missionary, "that Christianity is pleasing to God. How can that be?—Those men at Savannah are Christians."

Yes! slave-drivers and Indian traders are called Christians, and the Indian is to be deemed less like the Son of Mary than they! Wonderful is the deceit of man's heart!

I have not, on seeing something of them in their own haunts, found reason to change the sentiments expressed in the following lines, when a deputation of the Sacs and Foxes visited Boston in 1837, and were, by one person at least, received in a dignified and courteous manner.[8]

GOVERNOR EVERETT RECEIVING THE INDIAN CHIEFS

November, 1837

Who says that Poesy is on the wane,
And that the Muses tune their lyres in vain?
'Mid all the treasures of romantic story,
When thought was fresh and fancy in her glory,
Has ever Art found out a richer theme,
More dark a shadow, or more soft a gleam,
Than fall upon the scene, sketched carelessly,
In the newspaper column of to-day?

American romance is somewhat stale.
Talk of the hatchet, and the faces pale,
Wampum and calumets and forests dreary,
Once so attractive, now begins to weary.
Uncas and Magawisca⁹ please us still,
Unreal, yet idealized with skill;
But every poetaster scribbling witling,
From the majestic oak his stylus whittling,
Has helped to tire us, and to make us fear
The monotone in which so much we hear
Of "stoics of the wood," and "men without a tear."

Yet Nature, ever buoyant, ever young,
If let alone, will sing as erst she sung;
The course of circumstance gives back again
The Picturesque, erewhile pursued in vain;
Shows us the fount of Romance is not wasted—
The lights and shades of contrast not exhausted.

Shorn of his strength, the Samson now must sue
    For fragments from the feast his fathers gave,¹⁰
The Indian dare not claim what is his due,
    But as a boon his heritage must crave;
His stately form shall soon be seen no more
Through all his father's land, th' Atlantic shore,
Beneath the sun, to *us* so kind, *they* melt,
More heavily each day our rule is felt;
The tale is old,—we do as mortals must:
Might makes right here, but God and Time are just.

Summer on the Lakes

So near the drama hastens to its close,
On this last scene awhile your eyes repose;
The polished Greek and Scythian meet again,
The ancient life is lived by modern man—
The savage through our busy cities walks,—
He in his untouched grandeur silent stalks.
Unmoved by all our gaieties and shows,
Wonder nor shame can touch him as he goes;
He gazes on the marvels we have wrought,
But knows the models from whence all was brought;
In God's first temples he has stood so oft,
And listened to the natural organ loft—
Has watched the eagle's flight, the muttering thunder heard,
Art cannot move him to a wondering word;
Perhaps he sees that all this luxury
Brings less food to the mind than to the eye;
Perhaps a simple sentiment has brought
More to him than your arts had ever taught.
What are the petty triumphs Art has given,
To eyes familiar with the naked heaven?

All has been seen—dock, railroad, and canal,
Fort, market, bridge, college, and arsenal,
Asylum, hospital, and cotton mill,
The theatre, the lighthouse, and the jail.
The Braves each novelty, reflecting, saw,
And now and then growled out the earnest *yaw.*
And now the time is come, 't is understood,
When, having seen and thought so much, a *talk* may do some good.

A well-dressed mob have thronged the sight to greet,
And motley figures throng the spacious street;
Majestical and calm through all they stride,
Wearing the blanket with a monarch's pride;
The gazers stare and shrug, but can't deny
Their noble forms and blameless symmetry.

If the Great Spirit their morale has slighted,
And wigwam smoke their mental culture blighted,
Yet the physique, at least, perfection reaches,
In wilds where neither Combe nor Spurzheim teaches;[11]
Where whispering trees invite man to the chase,
And bounding deer allure him to the race.

Would thou hadst seen it! That dark, stately band,
Whose ancestors enjoyed all this fair land,
Whence they, by force or fraud, were made to flee,
Are brought, the white man's victory to see.
Can kind emotions in their proud hearts glow,
As through these realms, now decked by Art, they go?
The church, the school, the railroad and the mart—
Can these a pleasure to their minds impart?
All once was theirs—earth, ocean, forest, sky—
How can they joy in what now meets the eye?
Not yet Religion has unlocked the soul,
Nor Each has learned to glory in the Whole!

Must they not think, so strange and sad their lot,
That they by the Great Spirit are forgot?
From the far border to which they are driven,
They might look up in trust to the clear heaven;
But *here*—what tales doth every object tell
Where Massasoit sleeps—where Philip fell! [12]

We take our turn, and the Philosopher
Sees through the clouds a hand which cannot err,
An unimproving race, with all their graces
And all their vices, must resign their places;
And Human Culture rolls its onward flood
Over the broad plains steeped in Indian blood.

Such thoughts steady our faith; yet there will rise
Some natural tears into the calmest eyes—
Which gaze where forest princes haughty go,
Made for a gaping crowd a raree show.

But *this* a scene seems where, in courtesy,
The pale face with the forest prince could vie,
For One presided, who, for tact and grace,
In any age had held an honored place,—
In Beauty's own dear day, had shone a polished Phidian vase!

Oft have I listened to his accents bland,
    And owned the magic of his silvery voice,
In all the graces which life's arts demand,
    Delighted by the justness of his choice.
Not his the stream of lavish, fervid thought,—
The rhetoric by passion's magic wrought;

Summer on the Lakes

Not his the massive style, the lion port,
Which with the granite class of mind assort;
But, in a range of excellence his own,
With all the charms to soft persuasion known,
Amid our busy people we admire him—"elegant and lone."

He scarce needs words, so exquisite the skill
Which modulates the tones to do his will,
That the mere sound enough would charm the ear,
And lap in its Elysium all who hear.
The intellectual paleness of his cheek,
    The heavy eyelids and slow, tranquil smile,
The well cut lips from which the graces speak,
    Fit him alike to win or to beguile;
Then those words so well chosen, fit, though few,
Their linked sweetness as our thoughts pursue,
We deem them spoken pearls, or radiant diamond dew.

And never yet did I admire the power
    Which makes so lustrous every threadbare theme—
Which won for Lafayette one other hour,
    And e'en on July Fourth could cast a gleam—
As now, when I behold him play the host,
With all the dignity which red men boast—
With all the courtesy the whites have lost;—
Assume the very hue of savage mind,
Yet in rude accents show the thought refined;—
Assume the naiveté of infant age,
And in such prattle seem still more a sage;
The golden mean with tact unerring seized,
A courtly critic shone, a simple savage pleased;
The stoic of the woods his skill confessed,
As all the Father answered in his breast,
To the sure mark the silver arrow sped,
The man without a tear a tear has shed;
And thou hadst wept, hadst thou been there, to see
How true one sentiment must ever be,
In court or camp, the city or the wild,
To rouse the Father's heart, you need but name his Child.

'T was a fair scene—and acted well by all;
So here's a health to Indian braves so tall—
Our Governor and Boston people all!

I will copy the admirable speech of Governor Everett on that occasion, as I think it the happiest attempt ever made to meet the Indian in his own way, and catch the tone of his mind. It was said, in the newspapers, that Keokuck did actually shed tears when addressed as a father. If he did not with his eyes, he well might in his heart.

Everett's Speech [13]

CHIEFS and warriors of the Sauks and Foxes, you are welcome to our hall of council.

Brothers! you have come a long way from home to visit your white brethren; we rejoice to take you by the hand.

Brothers! we have heard the names of your chiefs and warriors; our brothers, who have travelled into the West, have told us a great deal of the Sauks and Foxes; we rejoice to see you with our own eyes, and take you by the hand.

Brothers! we are called the Massachusetts. This is the name of the red men that once lived here. Their wigwams filled yonder field; their council fire was kindled on this spot. They were of the same great race as the Sauks and Misquakuiks.

Brothers! when our fathers came over the great waters, they were a small band. The red man stood upon the rock by the seaside, and saw our fathers. He might have pushed them into the water and drowned them. But he stretched out his arm to our fathers and said, "Welcome, white men!" Our fathers were hungry, and the red men gave them corn and venison. Our fathers were cold, and the red man wrapped them up in his blanket. We are now numerous and powerful, but we remember the kindness of the red man to our fathers. Brothers, you are welcome; we are glad to see you.

Brothers! our faces are pale, and your faces are dark; but our hearts are alike. The Great Spirit has made his children of different colors, but he loves them all.

Brothers! you dwell between the Mississippi and the Missouri. They are mighty rivers. They have one branch far East in the Alleghanies, and the other far West in the Rocky Mountains; but they flow together at last into one great stream, and run down together into the sea. In like manner, the red man dwells in the West, and the white man in the East, by the great waters; but they are all one branch, one family; it has many branches and one head.

Brothers! as you entered our council house, you beheld the image of our great Father Washington. It is a cold stone—it cannot speak. But he was the friend of the red man, and had his children live in peace with their red brethren. He is gone to the world of spirits. But his words have made a very deep print in our hearts, like the step of a strong buffalo on the soft clay of the prairie.

Brother! I perceive your little son between your knees. God preserve his life, my brother. He grows up before you like the tender sapling by the side of the mighty oak. May the oak and the sapling flourish a long time together. And when the mighty oak is fallen to the ground, may the young tree fill its place in the forest, and spread out its branches over the tribe like the parent trunk.

Brothers! I make you a short talk and again bid you welcome to our council hall.

NOT OFTEN have they been addressed with such intelligence and tact. The few who have not approached them with sordid rapacity, but from love to them, as men, and souls to be redeemed, have most frequently been persons intellectually too narrow, too straightly bound in sects or opinions, to throw themselves into the character or position of the Indians, or impart to them anything they can make available. The Christ shown them by these missionaries, is to them but a new and more powerful Manito; the signs of the new religion, but the fetiches that have aided the conquerors.

Here I will copy some remarks made by a discerning observer, on the methods used by the missionaries, and their natural results.

"Mr.—and myself had a very interesting conversation, upon the subject of the Indians, their character, capabilities, &c. After ten years' experience among them, he was forced to acknowledge, that the results of the missionary efforts had produced nothing calculated to encourage. He thought that there was an intrinsic disability in them, to rise above, or go beyond the sphere in which they had so long moved. He said, that even those Indians who had been converted, and who had adopted the habits of civilization, were very little improved in their real character; they were as selfish, as deceitful, and as indolent, as those who were still heathens. They had repaid the kindnesses of the missionaries with the basest ingratitude, killing their cattle and swine, and robbing them of their harvests, which they wantonly destroyed. He had abandoned the idea of effecting any general good to the Indians. He had conscientious scruples, as to promoting an enterprise so hopeless, as that of missions among the Indians, by sending accounts to the east, that might induce philanthropic individuals to contribute to their support. In fact, the whole experience of his intercourse with them, seemed to have convinced him of the irremediable degradation of the race. Their fortitude under suffering, he considered the result of physical and mental insensibility; their courage, a mere animal excitement, which they found it necessary to inflame, before daring to meet a foe. They have no constancy of purpose; and are, in fact, but little superior to the brutes, in point of moral development. It is not astonishing, that one looking upon the Indian character, from Mr.——'s point of view, should entertain such sentiments. The object of his intercourse with them was, to make them apprehend the mysteries of a theology, which, to the most enlightened, is an abstruse, metaphysical study; and it is not singular they should prefer their pagan superstitions, which address themselves more directly to the senses. Failing in the attempt to christianize, before civilizing them, he inferred, that, in the intrinsic degradation of their faculties, the obstacle was to be found."

Thus the missionary vainly attempts, by once or twice holding up the cross, to turn deer and tigers into lambs; vainly attempts to convince the red man that a heavenly mandate takes from him his broad lands. He bows his head, but does not at heart acquiesce. He cannot. It is not true; and if it were, the descent of blood through the same channels, for centuries, had formed habits of thought not so easily to be disturbed.

Amalgamation [14] would afford the only true and profound means of civilization. But nature seems, like all else, to declare, that this race is fated to perish. Those of mixed blood fade early, and are not generally a fine race. They lose what is best in either type, rather than enhance the value of each, by mingling. There are exceptions, one or two such I know of, but this, it is said, is the general rule.

A traveller observes, that the white settlers, who live in the woods, soon become sallow, lanky, and dejected; the atmosphere of the trees does not agree with Caucasian lungs; and it is, perhaps, in part, an instinct of this, which causes the hatred of the new settlers towards trees. The Indian breathed the atmosphere of the forests freely; he loved their shade. As they are effaced from the land, he fleets too; a part of the same manifestation, which cannot linger behind its proper era.

The Chippewas have lately petitioned the state of Michigan, that they may be admitted as citizens; but this would be vain, unless they could be admitted, as brothers, to the heart of the white man. And while the latter feels that conviction of superiority, which enabled our Wisconsin friend to throw away the gun, and send the Indian to fetch it, he had need to be very good, and very wise, not to abuse his position. But the white man, as yet, is a half-tamed pirate, and avails himself, as much as ever, of the maxim, "Might makes right." All that civilization does for the generality, is to cover up this with a veil of subtle evasions and chicane, and here and there to rouse the individual mind to appeal to heaven against it.

I have no hope of liberalizing the missionary, of humanizing the sharks of trade, of infusing the conscientious drop into the flinty bosom of policy, of saving the Indian from immediate degradation, and speedy death. The whole sermon may be preached from the text, "Needs be that offences must come, yet wo them by whom they come." Yet, ere they depart, I wish there might be some masterly attempt to reproduce, in art or literature, what is proper to them, a kind of beauty and grandeur, which few of the every-day crowd have hearts to feel, yet which ought to leave in the world its monuments, to inspire the thought of genius through all ages. Nothing in this kind has been done masterly; since it was Clevenger's ambition, 'tis pity he had not opportunity to try fully his powers.[15] We hope some other mind may be bent upon it, ere too late.

At present the only lively impress of their passage through the world is to be found in such books as Catlin's and some stories told by the old travellers, of which I purpose a brief account.

First, let me give another brief tale of the power exerted by the white man over the savage in a trying case, but, in this case, it was righteous, was moral power.

"We were looking over McKenney's trip to the Lakes, and, on observing the picture of Key-way-no-wut, or the Going Cloud, Mr. B. observed "Ah, that is the fellow I came near having a fight with," and he detailed at length the circumstances. This Indian was a very desperate character, and whom all the Leech lake band stood in fear of. He would shoot down any Indian who offended him, without the least hesitation, and had become quite the bully of that part of the tribe. The trader at Leech lake warned Mr. B. to beware of him, and said that he once, when he (the trader) refused to give up to him his stock of wild rice, went and got his gun and tomahawk, and shook the tomahawk over his head saying, "*Now,* give me your wild rice." The trader complied with his exaction, but not so did Mr. B. in the adventure which I am about to relate. Key-way-no-wut came frequently to him with furs, wishing him to give for them cotton cloth, sugar, flour, &c. Mr. B. explained to him that he could not trade for furs, as he was sent there as a teacher, and that it would be like putting his hand into the fire to do so, as the traders would inform against him, and he would be sent out of the country. At the same time, he *gave* him the articles which he wished. Key-way-no-wut found this a very convenient way of getting what he wanted, and followed up this sort of game, until, at last, it became insupportable. One day the Indian brought a very large otter skin, and said "I want to get for this ten pounds of sugar, and some flour and cloth," adding, "I am not like other Indians, *I* want to pay for what I get." Mr. B. found that he must either be robbed of all he had by submitting to these exactions, or take a stand at once. He thought, however, he would try to avoid a scrape, and told his customer he had not so much sugar to spare. "Give me then," said he, "what you can spare," and Mr. B. thinking to make him back out, told him he would give him five pounds of sugar for his skin. "Take it," said the Indian. He left the skin, telling Mr. B. to take good care of it. Mr. B. took it at once to the trader's store, and related the circumstance, congratulating himself that he had got rid of the Indian's exactions. But, in about a month, Key-way-no-wut appeared bringing some dirty Indian sugar, and said "I have brought back the sugar that I borrowed of you, and I want my otter skin back." Mr. B. told him, "I *bought* an otter skin of you, but if you will return the other articles you have got for it, perhaps I can get it for you." "Where is the skin?" said he very quickly, "what have you done with it?" Mr. B. replied it was in the trader's store, where he (the Indian) could not get it. At this information he was furious, laid his hands on his knife and tomahawk, and commanded Mr. B. to bring it at once. Mr. B. found this was the crisis, where he must take a stand or be "rode over rough shod" by this man; his wife, who was present was much alarmed, and begged he would get the skin for the Indian, but he told her that "either he or the Indian would soon be master of his house, and if she was afraid to see it decided which was to be so, she had better retire." He turned to Key-way-no-wut, and addressed him in a stern voice as follows: "I will *not* give you the skin. How often have you come to my house, and I have shared with you what I had. I gave you tobacco when you were well, and medicine when you were sick, and you never went away from my wigwam with your hands empty. And this is the way you return my treatment to you. I had thought you were a man and a chief, but you are not, you are nothing but an old woman. Leave this house, and never enter it again." Mr. B. said he expected the Indian would attempt his life when he said this, but that he had placed himself in a position so that he could defend himself, and he looked straight into the Indian's eye, and like other wild beasts he quailed before the glance of mental and moral courage. He calmed down at once, and soon began to make apologies. Mr. B. then told him kindly, but firmly, that, if he wished to walk in the same path with him, he must walk as straight as the crack on the floor before them; adding that he would not walk with anybody who would jostle him by walking so crooked as he had done. He was perfectly tamed, and Mr. B. said he never had any more trouble with him."

The conviction here livingly enforced of the superiority on the side of the white man, was thus expressed by the Indian orator at Mackinaw while we were there. After the customary compliments about sun, dew, &c., "This," said he, "is the difference between the white and the red man; the white man looks to the future and paves the way for posterity." This is a statement uncommonly refined for an indian; but one of the gentlemen present, who understood the Chippeway, vouched for it as a literal rendering of his phrases; and he did indeed touch the vital point of difference. But the Indian, if he understands, cannot make use of his intelligence. The fate of his people is against it, and Pontiac and Philip have no more chance, than Julian in the times of old.[16]

Now that I am engaged on this subject, let me give some notices of writings upon it, read either at Mackinaw or since my return.

Mrs. Jameson made such good use of her brief visit to these regions, as leaves great cause to regret she did not stay longer and go farther; also, that she did not make more use of her acquaintance with, indeed, adoption by, the Johnson family. Mr. Johnson seems to have been almost the only white man who knew how to regard with due intelligence and nobleness, his connexion with the race. Neither French or English, of any powers of sympathy, or poetical apprehension, have lived among the Indians without high feelings of enjoyment. Perhaps no luxury has been greater, than that experienced by the persons, who, sent either by trade or war, during the last century, into these majestic regions, found guides and shelter amid the children of the soil, and recognized in a form so new and of such varied, yet simple, charms, the tie of brotherhood.

But these, even Sir William Johnson,[17] whose life, surrounded by the Indians in his castle on the Mohawk, is described with such vivacity by Mrs. Grant, have been men better fitted to enjoy and adapt themselves to this life, than to observe and record it. The very faculties that made it so easy for them to live in the present moment, were likely to unfit them for keeping its chronicle. Men, whose life is full and instinctive, care little for the pen. But the father of Mrs. Schoolcraft seems to have taken pleasure in observation and comparison, and to have imparted the same tastes to his children. They have enough of European culture to have a standard, by which to judge their native habits and inherited lore.

By the premature death of Mrs. Schoolcraft was lost a mine of poesy, to which few had access, and from which Mrs. Jameson would have known how to coin a series of medals for the history of this ancient people. We might have known in clear outline, as now we shall not, the growths of religion and philosophy, under the influences of this climate and scenery, from such suggestions as nature and the teachings of the inward mind presented.

Now we can only gather that they had their own theory of the history of this globe; had perceived a gap in its genesis, and tried to fill it up by the intervention of some secondary power, with moral sympathies. They have observed the action of fire and water upon this earth; also that the dynasty of animals has yielded to that of man. With these animals they have profound sympathy, and are always trying to restore to them their lost honors. On the rattlesnake, the beaver, and the bear, they seem to look with a mixture of sympathy and veneration, as on their fellow settlers in these realms. There is something that appeals powerfully to the imagination in the ceremonies they observe, even in case of destroying one of these animals. I will say more of this by-and-by.

The dog they cherish as having been once a spirit of high intelligence; and now in its fallen and imprisoned state, given to man as his special companion. He is therefore to them a sacrifice of peculiar worth: whether to a guardian spirit or a human friend. Yet nothing would be a greater violation than giving the remains of a sacrificial feast to the dogs, or even suffering them to touch the bones.

Similar inconsistences may be observed in the treatment of the dog by the white man. He is the most cherished companion in the familiar walks of many men; his virtues form the theme of poetry and history; the nobler races present grand traits, and are treated with proportionate respect. Yet the epithets dog and hound, are there set apart to express the uttermost contempt.

Goethe, who abhorred dogs, has selected that animal for the embodiment of the modern devil, who, in earlier times, chose rather the form of the serpent.

There is, indeed, something that peculiarly breaks in on the harmony of nature, in the bark of the dog, and that does not at all correspond with the softness and sagacity observable in his eye. The baying the moon, I have been inclined to set down as an unfavorable indication; but, since Fourier has found out that the moon is dead, and "no better than carrion;" and the Greeks have designated her as Hecate, the deity of suicide and witchcraft, the dogs are perhaps in the right.

They have among them the legend of the carbuncle, so famous in oriental mythos. Adair[18] states that they believe this fabulous gem may be found on the spot where the rattlesnake has been destroyed.

If they have not the archetypal man, they have the archetypal animal, "the grandfather of all beavers;" to them, who do not know the elephant, this is the symbol of wisdom, as the rattlesnake and bear of power.

I will insert here a little tale about the bear, which has not before appeared in print, as representing their human way of looking on these animals, even when engaged in their pursuit. To me such stories give a fine sense of the lively perceptions and exercise of fancy, enjoyed by them in their lives of woodcraft:

Muckwa, or the Bear

A YOUNG INDIAN, who lived a great while ago, when he was quite young killed a bear; and the tribe from that circumstance called him Muckwa. As he grew up he became an expert hunter, and his favorite game was the bear, many of which he killed. One day he started off to a river far remote from the lodges of his tribe, and where berries and grapes were very plenty, in pursuit of bears. He hunted all day but found nothing; and just at night he came to some lodges which he thought to be those of some of his tribe. He approached the largest of them, lifted the curtain at its entrance, and went in, when he perceived the inmates to be bears, who were seated around the fire smoking. He said nothing, but seated himself also and smoked the pipe which they offered him, in silence. An old grey bear, who was the chief, ordered supper to be brought for him, and after he had eaten it, addressed him as follows: "My son, I am glad to see you come among us in a friendly manner. You have been a great hunter, and all the she-bears of our tribe tremble when they hear your name. But cease to trouble us, and come and live with me; we have a very pleasant life, living upon the fruits of the earth; and in the winter, instead of being obliged to hunt and travel through the deep snow, we sleep soundly until the sun unchains the streams, and makes the tender buds put forth for our subsistence. I will give you my daughter for a wife, and we will live happily together." Muckwa was inclined to accept the old bear's offer; but when he saw the daughter, who came and took off his wet moccasins, and gave him dry ones, he thought that he had never seen any Indian woman so beautiful. He accepted the offer of the chief of the bears, and lived with his wife very happily for some time. He had by her two sons, one of whom was like an Indian, and the other like a bear. When the bear-child was oppressed with heat, his mother would take him into the deep cool caves, while the Indian-child would shiver with cold, and cry after her in vain. As the autumn advanced, the bears began to go out in search of acorns, and then the she-bear said to Muckwa, "Stay at home here and watch our house, while I go to gather some nuts." She departed and was gone for some days with her people. By-and-by Muckwa became tired of staying at home, and thought that he would go off to a distance and resume his favorite bear-hunting. He accordingly started off, and at last came to a grove of lofty oaks, which were full of large acorns. He found signs of bear, and soon espied a fat she-bear on the top of a tree. He shot at her with a good aim, and she fell, pierced by his unerring arrow. He went up to her, and found it was his sister-in-law, who reproached him with his cruelty, and told him to return to his own people. Muckwa returned quietly home, and pretended not to have left his lodge. However, the old chief understood, and was disposed to kill him in revenge; but his wife found means to avert her father's anger. The winter season now coming on, Muckwa prepared to accompany his wife into winter quarters; they selected a large tamarack tree, which was hollow, and lived there comfortably until a party of hunters discovered their retreat. The she-bear told Muckwa to remain quietly in the tree, and that she would decoy off the hunters. She came out of the hollow, jumped from a bough of the tree, and escaped unharmed, although the hunters shot after her. Some time after, she returned to the tree, and told Muckwa that he had better go back to his own people. "Since you have lived among us," said she, "we have nothing but ill-fortune; you have killed my sister; and now your friends have followed your footsteps to our retreats to kill us. The Indian and the bear cannot live in the same lodge, for the Master of Life has appointed for them different habitations." So Muckwa returned with his son to his own people; but he never after would shoot a she-bear, for fear that he should kill his wife."

I admire this story for the *savoir faire,* the nonchalance, the Vivian Greyism of Indian life.[19] It is also a poetical expression of the sorrows of unequal relations; those in which the Master of Life was not consulted. Is it not pathetic; the picture of the mother carrying off the child that was like herself into the deep, cool caves, while the other, shivering with cold, cried after her in vain? The moral, too, of Muckwa's return to the bear lodges, thinking to hide his sin by silence, while it was at once discerned by those connected with him, is fine.

We have a nursery tale, of which children never weary, of a little boy visiting a bear house and holding intercourse with them on terms as free as Muckwa did. So, perhaps, the child of Norman-Saxon blood, no less than the Indian, finds some pulse of the Orson in his veins.

As they loved to draw the lower forms of nature up to them, divining their histories, and imitating their ways, in their wild dances and paintings; even so did they love to look upward and people the atmosphere that enfolds the earth, with fairies and manitoes. The sister, obliged to leave her brother on the earth, bids him look up at evening, and he will see her painting her face in the west.

All places, distinguished in any way by nature, aroused the feelings of worship, which, however ignorant, are always elevating. See as instances in this kind, the stories of Nanabojou, and the Winnebago Prince, at the falls of St. Anthony.

As with the Greeks, beautiful legends grow up which express the aspects of various localities. From the distant sand-banks in the lakes, glittering in the sun, come stories of enchantresses combing, on the shore, the long golden hair of a beautiful daughter. The Lorelei of the Rhine, [20] with her syren song, and the sad events that follow, is found on the lonely rocks of Lake Superior.

The story to which I now refer, may be found in a book called Life on the Lakes, or, a Trip to the Pictured Rocks. [21] There are two which purport to be Indian tales; one is simply a romantic narrative, connected with a spot at Mackinaw, called Robinson's Folly. This, no less than the other, was unknown to those persons I saw on the island; but as they seem entirely beyond the powers of the person who writes them down, and the other one has the profound and original meaning of Greek tragedy, I believe they must be genuine legends.

The one I admire is the story of a young warrior, who goes to keep, on these lonely rocks, the fast which is to secure him vision of his tutelary spirit. There the loneliness is broken by the voice of sweet music from the water. The Indian knows well that to break the fast, which is the crisis of his life, by turning his attention from seeking the Great Spirit, to any lower

object, will deprive him through life of heavenly protection, probably call
down the severest punishment.

But the temptation is too strong for him; like the victims of the
Lorelei, he looks, like them beholds a maiden of unearthly beauty, to him
the harbinger of earthly wo.

The development of his fate, that succeeds; of love, of heart-break, of
terrible revenge, which back upon itself recoils, may vie with anything I
have ever known of stern tragedy, is altogether unlike any other form, and
with all the peculiar expression we see lurking in the Indian eye. The
demon is not frightful and fantastic, like those that haunt the German
forest; but terribly human, as if of full manhood, reared in the shadow of
the black forests. An Indian sarcasm vibrates through it, which, with Indian fortitude, defies the inevitable torture.

The Indian is steady to that simple creed, which forms the basis of all
this mythology; that there is a God, and a life beyond this; a right and
wrong which each man can see, betwixt which each man should choose;
that good brings with it its reward and vice its punishment. Their moral
code, if not refined as that of civilized nations, is clear and noble in the
stress laid upon truth and fidelity. And all unprejudiced observers bear
testimony that the Indians, until broken from their old anchorage by intercourse with the whites, who offer them, instead, a religion of which they
furnish neither interpretation nor example, were singularly virtuous, if
virtue be allowed to consist in a man's acting up to his own ideas of right.

Old Adair, who lived forty years among the Indians; not these tribes,
indeed, but the southern Indians, does great justice to their religious aspiration. He is persuaded that they are Jews, and his main object is to identify
their manifold ritual, and customs connected with it, with that of the
Jews.[22] His narrative contains much that is worthless, and is written in the
most tedious manner of the folios. But his devotion to the records of
ancient Jewry, has really given him power to discern congenial traits elsewhere, and for the sake of what he has expressed of the noble side of Indian
character, we pardon him our having to wade through so many imbecilities.

An infidel, he says, is, in their language, "one who has shaken hands
with the accursed speech;" a religious man, "one who has shaken hands
with the beloved speech." If this be a correct definition, we could wish
Adair more religious.

He gives a fine account of their methods of purification. These show
a deep reliance on the sustaining Spirit. By fasting and prayer they make
ready for all important decisions and actions. Even for the war path, on

which he is likely to endure such privations, the brave prepares by a solemn fast. His reliance is on the spirit in which he goes forth.

We may contrast with the opinion of the missionary, as given on a former page, the testimony of one, who knew them as Adair did, to their heroism under torture.

He gives several stories, illustrative both of their courage, fortitude, and resource in time of peril, of which I will cite only the two first.

"The Shawano Indians took a Muskohge warrior, known by the name of "Old Scrany;" they bastinadoed him in the usual manner, and condemned him to the fiery torture. He underwent a great deal, without showing any concern; his countenance and behavior were as if he suffered not the least pain, and was formed beyond the common laws of nature. He told them, with a bold voice, that he was a very noted warrior, and gained most of his martial preferments at the expense of their nation, and was desirous of showing them in the act of dying that he was still as much their superior, as when he headed his gallant countrymen against them. That, although he had fallen into their hands, in forfeiting the protection of the divine power, by some impurity or other, yet he had still so much virtue remaining, as would enable him to punish himself more exquisitely than all their despicable, ignorant crowd could possibly do, if they gave him liberty by untying him, and would hand to him one of the red hot gun-barrels out of the fire. The proposal, and his method of address, appeared so exceedingly bold and uncommon, that his request was granted. Then he suddenly seized one end of the red hot barrel, and, brandishing it from side to side, he found his way through the armed and surprised multitude, and leaped down a prodigious steep and high bank into a branch of the river, dived through it, ran over a small island, passed the other branch amidst a shower of bullets, and, though numbers of his eager enemies were in close pursuit of him, he got to a bramble swamp, and in that naked, mangled condition, reached his own country. He proved a sharp thorn in their side afterwards, to the day of his death.

The Shawano also captivated a warrior of the Anantooiah, and put him to the stake, according to their usual cruel solemnities. Having unconcernedly suffered much sharp torture, he told them with scorn, they did not know how to punish a noted enemy, therefore he was willing to teach them, and would confirm the truth of his assertion, if they allowed him the opportunity. Accordingly he requested of them a pipe and some tobacco, which was given him; as soon as he lighted it, he sat down, naked as he was, on the women's burning torches, that were within his circle, and continued smoking his pipe without the least discomposure. On this a head warrior leaped up, and said they had seen, plain enough, that he was a warrior, and not afraid of dying; nor should he have died, but that he was both spoiled by the fire, and devoted to it by their laws; however, though he was a very dangerous enemy, and his nation a treacherous people, it should appear they paid a regard to bravery, even in one, who was marked over the body with war streaks at the cost of many lives of their beloved kindred. And then, by way of favor, he, with his friendly tomahawk, put an end to all his pains: though this merciful but bloody instrument was ready some minutes before it gave the blow, yet, I was assured, the spectators could not perceive the sufferer to change, either his posture, or his steady, erect countenance in the least."

Some stories as fine, but longer, follow. In reference to which Adair says, "The intrepid behavior of these red stoics, their surprising contempt of and indifference to life or death, instead of lessening, helps to confirm our belief of that supernatural power, which supported the great number of primitive martyrs, who sealed the christian faith with their blood. The Indians have as much belief and expectation of a future state, as the greater part of the Israelites seem to have. But the christians of the first centuries, may justly be said to exceed even the most heroic American Indians, for they bore the bitterest persecution with steady patience, in imitation of their divine leader Messiah, in full confidence of divine support and of a glorious recompense of reward; and, instead of even wishing for revenge on their cruel enemies and malicious tormentors, (which is the chief principle that actuates the Indians,) they not only forgave them, but, in the midst of their tortures, earnestly prayed for them, with composed countenances, sincere love, and unabated fervor. And not only men of different conditions, but the delicate women and children suffered with constancy, and died praying for their tormentors: the Indian women and children, and their young men untrained to war, are incapable of displaying the like patience and magnanimity."

Thus impartially looks the old trader. I meant to have inserted other passages, that of the encampment at Yowanne, and the horse race to which he challenged them, to show how well he could convey in his garrulous fashion the whole presence of Indian life. That of Yowanne, especially, takes my fancy much, by its wild and subtle air, and the old-nurse fashion in which every look and gesture is detailed. His enjoyment, too, at outwitting the Indians in their own fashion is contagious. There is a fine history of a young man driven by a presentiment to run upon his death. But I find, to copy these stories, as they stand, would half fill this little book, and compression would spoil them, so I must wait some other occasion.

The story, later, of giving an Indian liquid fire to swallow, I give at full length, to show how a kind-hearted man and one well disposed towards them, can treat them, and view his barbarity as a joke. It is not then so much wonder, if the trader, with this same feeling that they may be treated, (as however brutes should not be,) brutally, mixes red pepper and damaged tobacco with the rum, intending in their fever to fleece them of all they possess.

Like Murray and Henry, he has his great Indian chief, who represents what the people should be, as Pericles and Phocion what the Greek people should be.[23] If we are entitled to judge by its best fruits of the goodness of the tree, Adair's Red Shoes, and Henry's Wawatam, should make us respect the first possessors of our country, and doubt whether we are in all ways worthy to fill their place. Of the whole tone of character, judgment may be formed by what is said of the death of Red Shoes.

"This chief, by his several transcendent qualities had arrived at the highest pitch of the red glory. . . .

He was murdered, for the sake of a French reward, by one of his own countrymen. He had the misfortune to be taken very sick on the road, and to lodge apart from the camp, according to their custom. A Judas, tempted by the high reward of the French for killing him, officiously pretended to take great care of him. While Red Shoes kept his face toward him, the barbarian had such feelings of awe and pity that he had not power to perpetrate his wicked design; but when he turned his back, then gave the fatal shot. In this manner fell this valuable brave man, by hands that would have trembled to attack him on an equality."

Adair, with all his sympathy for the Indian, mixes quite unconsciously some white man's views of the most decided sort. For instance, he recommends that the tribes be stimulated as much as possible to war with each other, that they may the more easily and completely be kept under the dominion of the whites, and he gives the following record of brutality as quite a jocose and adroit procedure.

"I told him, on his importuning me further, that I had a full bottle of the water of *ane hoome,* "bitter ears," meaning long pepper, of which he was ignorant. We were of opinion that his eager thirst for liquor, as well as his ignorance of the burning quality of the pepper, would induce the bacchanal to try it. He accordingly applauded my generous disposition, and said his heart had all along told him I would not act beneath the character I bore among his country people. The bottle was brought, I laid it on the table, and then told him, as he was spitting very much, (a general custom among the Indians when they are eager for anything,) if I drank it all at one sitting it would cause me to spit in earnest, as I used it only when I ate, and then very moderately; but though I loved it, if his heart was very poor for it, I should be silent, and not the least grudge him for pleasing his mouth. He said, 'your heart is honest, indeed; I thank you, for it is good to my heart, and makes it greatly to rejoice.' Without any further ceremony he seized the bottle, uncorked it, and swallowed a large quantity of the burning liquid, till he was nearly strangled. He gasped for a considerable time, and as soon as he recovered his breath, he said *Hah,* and soon after kept stroking his throat with his right hand. When the violence of this burning draught was pretty well over, he began to flourish away in praise of the strength of the liquor and bounty of the giver. He then went to his companion and held the liquor to his mouth according to custom, till he took several hearty swallows. This Indian seemed rather more sensible of its fiery quality than the other, for it suffocated him for a considerable time; but as soon as he recovered his breath, he tumbled about the floor like a drunken person. In this manner they finished the whole bottle, into which two others had been decanted. The burning liquor so highly inflamed their bodies, that one of the Choctaws, to cool his inward parts, drank water till he almost burst; the other, rather than bear the ridicule of the people, and the inward fire that distracted him, drowned himself the second night after in a broad and shallow clay hole. . . . .

There was an incident similar, which happened among the Cherokees. When all the liquor was expended the Indians went home, leading with them, at my request, those that were drunk. One, however, soon came back, and earnestly importuned me for more Nawahti, which signifies both physic and spirituous liquor. They, as they are now become great liars, suspect all others of being infected with their own disposition and principles. The more I excused myself, the more anxious he grew, so as to become offensive. I then told him I had only one quarter of a bottle of strong physic, which sick people might drink in small quantities, for the cure of inward pains: and, laying it down before him, I declared I did not on any account choose to part with it, but as his speech had become very long and troublesome, he might do just as his heart directed him concerning it. He took it up, saying, his heart was very poor for physic, but he would cure it, and make it quite straight. The bottle contained three gills of strong spirits of turpentine, which, in a short time he drank off. Such a quantity would have demolished me or any white person. The Indians, in general, are either capable of suffering exquisite pain longer than we are, or of showing more constancy and composure in their torments. The troublesome visiter soon tumbled down and foamed prodigiously. I then sent for some of his relations to carry him home. They came; I told them he drank greedily, and too much of the physic. They said, it was his usual custom, when the red people bought the English physic. They gave him a decoction of proper herbs and roots, the next day sweated him, repeated the former draught, and he got well. As these turpentine spirits did not inebriate him, but only inflamed his intestines, he well remembered the burning quality of my favorite physic, and cautioned the rest from ever teasing me for any physic I had concealed in any sort of bottles for my own use; otherwise they might be sure it would spoil them like the eating of fire."

We are pleased to note that the same white man, who so resolutely resisted the encroachments of Key-way-no-wut, devised a more humane experiment in a similar dilemma.

"Mr. B. told me that, when he first went into the Indian country, they got the taste of his peppermint, and, after that, colics prevailed among them to an alarming extent, till Mrs. B. made a strong decoction of flagroot, and gave them in place of their favorite medicine. This effected, as might be supposed, a radical cure."

I am inclined to recommend Adair to the patient reader, if such may be found in these United States, with the assurance that, if he will have tolerance for its intolerable prolixity and dryness, he will find, on rising from the book, that he has partaken of an infusion of real Indian bitters, such as may not be drawn from any of the more attractive memoirs on the same subject.

Another book of interest, from its fidelity and candid spirit, though written without vivacity, and by a person neither of large mind nor prepared for various inquiry, is Carver's Travels, "for three years throughout the interior parts of America, for more than five thousand miles."

He set out from Boston in "June, 1786, and proceeded, by way of Albany and Niagara, to Michilimackinac, a fort situated between the Lakes Huron and Michigan, and distant from Boston 1300 miles."

It is interesting to follow his footsteps in these localities, though they be not bold footsteps.

He mentions the town of the Sacs, on the Wisconsin, as the largest and best built he saw, "composed of ninety houses, each large enough for several families. These are built of hewn plank, neatly jointed, and covered with bark so compactly as to keep out the most penetrating rains. Before the doors are placed comfortable sheds, in which the inhabitants sit, when the weather will permit, and smoke their pipes. The streets are regular and spacious. In their plantations, which lie adjacent to their houses, and which are neatly laid out, they raise great quantities of Indian corn, beans and melons."

Such settlements compare very well with those which were found on the Mohawk. It was of such that the poor Indian was thinking, whom our host saw gazing on the shore of Nomabbin lake.

He mentions the rise and fall of the lake-waters, by a tide of three feet, once in seven years,—a phenomenon not yet accounted for.

His view of the Indian character is truly impartial. He did not see it so fully drawn out by circumstances as Henry did, (of whose narrative we shall presently speak,) but we come to similar results from the two witnesses. They are in every feature Romans, as described by Carver, and patriotism their leading impulse. He deserves the more credit for the justice he is able to do them, that he had undergone the terrors of death at their hands, when present at the surrender of one of the forts, and had seen them in that mood which they express by drinking the blood and eating the hearts of their enemies, yet is able to understand the position of their minds, and allow for their notions of duty.

No selfish views, says he, influence their advice, or obstruct their consultations.

Let me mention here the use they make of their vapor baths. "When about to decide on some important measure, they go into them, thus cleansing the skin and carrying off any peccant humors, so that the body may, as little as possible, impede the mind by any ill conditions."

They prepare the bath for one another when any arrangement is to be made between families, on the opposite principle to the whites, who make them drunk before bargaining with them. The bath serves them instead of a cup of coffee, to stimulate the thinking powers.

He mentions other instances of their kind of delicacy, which, if different from ours, was, perhaps, more rigidly observed.

Lovers never spoke of love till the daylight was quite gone.

"If an Indian goes to visit any particular person in a family, he mentions for whom his visit is intended, and the rest of the family, immediately retiring to the other end of the hut or tent, are careful not to come near enough to interrupt them during the whole of the conversation."

In cases of divorce, which was easily obtained, the advantage rested with the woman. The reason given is indeed contemptuous toward her, but a chivalric direction is given to the contempt.

"The children of the Indians are always distinguished by the name of the mother, and, if a woman marries several husbands, and has issue by each of them, they are called after her. The reason they give for this is, that, 'as their offspring are indebted to the father for the soul, the invisible part of their essence, and to the mother for their corporeal and apparent part, it is most rational that they should be distinguished by the name of the latter, from whom they indubitably derive their present being.'"

This is precisely the division of functions made by Ovid, as the father sees Hercules perishing on the funeral pyre.

> "Nec nisi materna Vulcanum parte potentem
> Sentiet. Æternuum est a me quod traxit et expers
> Atque immune necis, nullaqe domabile flamma." [24]

He is not enough acquainted with natural history to make valuable observations. He mentions, however, as did my friend, the Indian girl, that those splendid flowers, the Wickapee and the root of the Wake-Robin, afford valuable medicines. Here, as in the case of the Lobelia, nature has blazoned her drug in higher colors than did ever quack doctor.

He observes some points of resemblance between the Indians and Tartars, but they are trivial, and not well considered. He mentions that the Tartars have the same custom, with some of these tribes, of shaving all the head except a tuft on the crown. Catlin says this is intended to afford a convenient means by which to take away the scalp; for they consider it a great disgrace to have the foeman neglect this, as if he considered the conquest, of which the scalp is the certificate, no addition to his honors.

"The Tartars," he says, "had a similar custom of sacrificing the dog; and among the Kamschatkans was a dance resembling the dog-dance of our Indians."

My friend, who joined me at Mackinaw, happened, on the homeward journey, to see a little Chinese girl, who had been sent over by one of the missions, and observed that, in features, complexion, and gesture, she was a counterpart to the little Indian girls she had just seen playing about on the lake shore.

The parentage of these tribes is still an interesting subject of speculation, though, if they be not created for this region, they have become so assimilated to it as to retain little trace of any other. To me it seems most probable, that a peculiar race was bestowed on each region, as the lion on one latitude and the white bear on another. As man has two natures—one, like that of the plants and animals, adapted to the uses and enjoyments of this planet, another, which presages and demands a higher sphere—he is constantly breaking bounds, in proportion as the mental gets the better of the mere instinctive existence. As yet, he loses in harmony of being what he gains in height and extension; the civilized man is a larger mind, but a more imperfect nature than the savage.

It is pleasant to meet, on the borders of these two states, one of those persons who combines some of the good qualities of both; not, as so many of these adventurers do, the rapaciousness and cunning of the white, with the narrowness and ferocity of the savage, but the sentiment and thoughtfulness of the one, with the boldness, personal resource, and fortitude of the other.

Such a person was Alexander Henry, who left Quebec in 1760, for Mackinaw and the Sault St. Marie, and remained in those regions, of which he has given us a most lively account, sixteen years.

His visit to Mackinaw was premature; the Indians were far from satisfied; they hated their new masters. From the first, the omens were threatening, and before many months passed, the discontent ended in the seizing of the fort at Mackinaw and massacre of its garrison; on which occasion Henry's life was saved by a fine act of Indian chivalry.

Wawatam, a distinguished chief, had found himself drawn, by strong affinity, to the English stranger. He had adopted him as a brother, in the Indian mode. When he found that his tribe had determined on the slaughter of the whites, he obtained permission to take Henry away with him, if he could. But not being able to prevail on him, as he could not assign the true reasons, he went away deeply saddened, but not without obtaining a promise that his brother should not be injured. The reason he was obliged to go, was, that his tribe felt his affections were so engaged, that his self-command could not be depended on to keep their secret. Their promise was not carefully observed, and, in consequence of the baseness of a French Canadian in whose house Henry took refuge,—baseness such as has not, even by their foes, been recorded of any Indian, his life was placed in great hazard. But Wawatam returned in time to save him. The scene in which he appears, accompanied by his wife—who seems to have gone hand in hand with him in this matter—lays down all his best things in a heap, in the middle of the hall, as a ransom for the captive, and his little, quiet speech, are as good as the Iliad. They have the same simplicity, the same lively force and tenderness.

Henry goes away with his adopted brother, and lives for some time among the tribe. The details of this life are truly interesting. One time he is lost for several days while on the chase. The description of these weary, groping days, the aspect of natural objects and of the feelings thus inspired, and the mental change after a good night's sleep, form a little episode worthy the epic muse. He stripped off the entire bark of a tree for a coverlet in the snow-storm, going to sleep with "the most distracted thoughts in the world, while the wolves around seemed to know the distress to which he was reduced;" but he waked in the morning another man, clear-headed, able to think out the way to safety.

When living in the lodge, he says: "At one time much scarcity of food prevailed. We were often twenty-four hours without eating; and when in the morning we had no victuals for the day before us, the custom was to black our faces with grease and charcoal, and exhibit, through resignation, a temper as cheerful as in the midst of plenty." This wise and dignified proceeding reminds one of a charming expression of what is best in French character, as described by Rigolette, in the Mysteries of Paris,[25] of the household of Père Cretu and Ramonette.

He bears witness to much virtue among them. Their superstitions, as described by him, seem childlike and touching. He gives with much humor, traits that show their sympathy with the lower animals, such as I have mentioned. He speaks of them as, on the whole, taciturn, because their range of topics is so limited, and seems to have seen nothing of their talent for narration. Catlin, on the contrary, describes them as lively and garrulous, and says, that their apparent taciturnity among the whites is owing to their being surprised at what they see, and unwilling, from pride, to show that they are so, as well as that they have little to communicate on their side, that they think will be valuable.

After peace was restored, and Henry lived long at Mackinaw and the Sault St. Marie, as a trader, the traits of his biography and intercourse with the Indians, are told in the same bold and lively style. I wish I had room for many extracts, as the book is rare.

He made a journey one winter on snow shoes, to Prairie du Chien, which is of romantic interest as displaying his character. His companions could not travel nearly so fast as he did, and detained him on the way. Provisions fell short; soon they were ready to perish of starvation. Apprehending this, on a long journey, in the depth of winter, broken by no hospitable station, Henry had secreted some chocolate. When he saw his companions ready to lie down and die, he would heat water, boil in it a square of this, and give them. By the heat of the water and the fancy of nourishment, they would be revived, and induced to proceed a little further. At last they saw antlers sticking up from the ice, and found the body of an elk, which had sunk in and been frozen there, and thus preserved to save their lives. On this "and excellent soup" made from bones they found they were sustained to their journey's end; thus furnishing, says Henry, one other confirmation of the truth, that "despair was not made for man;" this expression, and his calm consideration for the Canadian women that was willing to betray him to death, denote the two sides of a fine character.

He gives an interesting account of the tribe called "The Weepers," on account of the rites with which they interrupt their feasts in honor of their friends.

He gives this humorous notice of a chief, called "The Great Road."

"The chief, to whose kindly reception we were so much indebted, was of a complexion rather darker than that of the Indians in general. His appearance was greatly injured by the condition of his hair, and this was the result of an extraordinary superstition.

"The Indians universally fix upon a particular object as sacred to themselves—as the giver of prosperity and as their preserver from evil. The choice is determined either by a dream or some strong predilection of fancy, and usually falls upon an animal, part of an animal, or something else which is to be met with by land, or by water; but the Great Road had made choice of his hair, placing, like Samson, all his safety in this portion of his proper substance! His hair was the fountain of all his happiness; it was his strength and his weapon—his spear and his shield. It preserved him in battle, directed him in the chase, watched over him in the march, and gave length of days to his wives and children. Hair, of a quality like this, was not to be profaned by the touch of human hands. I was assured that it never had been cut nor combed from his childhood upward, and that when any part of it fell from his head, he treasured that part with care; meanwhile, it did not escape all care, even while growing on the head, but was in the especial charge of a spirit, who dressed it while the owner slept. The spirit's style of hair-dressing was peculiar, the hair being matted into ropes, which spread in all directions."

I insert the following account of a visit from some Indians to him at Mackinaw, with a design to frighten him, and one to Carver, for the same purpose, as very descriptive of Indian manners:

"At two o'clock in the afternoon, the Chippeways came to my house, about sixty in number, and headed by Mina-va-va-na, their chief. They walked in single file, each with his tomahawk in one hand, and scalping knife in the other. Their bodies were naked, from the waist upwards, except in a few examples, where blankets were thrown loosely over the shoulders. Their faces were painted with charcoal, worked up with grease; their bodies with white clay in patterns of various fancies. Some had feathers thrust through their noses, and their heads decorated with the same. It is unnecessary to dwell on the sensations with which I beheld the approach of this uncouth, if not frightful, assemblage."

"Looking out, I saw about twenty naked young Indians, the most perfect in their shape, and by far the handsomest I had ever seen, coming towards me, and dancing as they approached to the music of their drums. At every ten or twelve yards they halted, and set up their yells and cries.

When they reached my tent I asked them to come in, which, without deigning to make me any answer, they did. As I observed they were painted red and black, as they are when they go against an enemy, and perceived that some parts of the war-dance were intermixed with their other movements, I doubted not but they were set on by the hostile chief who refused my salutation. I therefore determined to sell my life as dearly as possible. To this purpose I received them sitting on my chest, with my gun and pistols beside me; and ordered my men to keep a watchful eye on them, and be also on their guard.

The Indians being entered, they continued their dance alternately, singing at the same time of their heroic exploits, and the superiority of their race over every other people. To enforce their language, though it was uncommonly nervous and expressive, and such as would of itself have carried terror to the firmest heart; at the end of every period they struck their war-clubs against the poles of my tent with such violence, that I expected every moment it would have tumbled upon us. As each of them in dancing round passed by me, they placed their right hands over their eyes, and coming close to me, looked me steadily in the face, which I could not construe into a token of friendship. My men gave themselves up for lost; and I acknowledge for my own part, that I never found my apprehensions more tumultuous on any occasion."

He mollified them, however, in the end by presents.

It is pity that Lord Edward Fitzgerald did not leave a detailed account of his journey through the wilderness, where he was pilot of an unknown course for twenty days, as Murray and Henry have of theirs. There is nothing more interesting than to see the civilized man thus thrown wholly on himself and his manhood, and *not* found at fault.

McKenney and Hall's book upon the Indians [26] is a valuable work. The portraits of the chiefs alone would make a history, and they are beautifully colored.

Most of the anecdotes may be found again in Drake's Book of the Indians;[27] which will afford a useful magazine to their future historian.

I shall, however, cite a few of them, as especially interesting to myself.

Of Guess, the inventor of the Cherokee alphabet,[28] it was observable in the picture, and observed in the text, that his face had an oriental cast. The same, we may recall, was said of that of the Seeress of Prevorst, and the circumstance presents pleasing analogies. Intellect dawning through features still simple and national, presents very different apparitions from the "expressive" and "historical" faces of a broken and cultured race, where there is always more to divine than to see.

Of the picture of the Flying Pigeon, the beautiful and excellent woman mentioned above, a keen observer said, "If you cover the forehead, you would think the face that of a Madonna, but the forehead is still savage; the perceptive faculties look so sharp, and the forehead not moulded like a European forehead." This is very true; in her the moral nature was most developed, and the effect of a higher growth upon her face is entirely different from that upon Guess.

His eye is inturned, while the proper Indian eye gazes steadily, as if on a distant object. That is half the romance of it, that it makes you think of dark and distant places in the forest.

Guess always preferred inventing his implements to receiving them from others: and, when considered as mad by his tribe, while bent on the invention of his alphabet, contented himself with teaching it to his little daughter; an unimpeachable witness.

Red Jacket's [29] face, too, is much more intellectual than almost any other. But, in becoming so, it loses nothing of the peculiar Indian stamp, but only carries these traits to their perfection. Irony, discernment, resolution, and a deep smouldering fire, that disdains to flicker where it cannot blaze, may there be read. Nothing can better represent the sort of unfeelingness the whites have towards the Indians, than their conduct towards his remains. He had steadily opposed the introduction of white religion, or manners, among the Indians. He believed that for them to break down the barriers was to perish. On many occasions he had expressed this with all the force of his eloquence. He told the preachers, "if the Great Spirit had meant your religion for the red man, he would have given it to them. What they (the missionaries) tell us, we do not understand; and the light they ask for us, makes the straight and plain path trod by our fathers dark and dreary."

When he died, he charged his people to inter him themselves. "Dig my grave yourselves, and let not the white man pursue me there." In defiance of this last solemn request, and the invariable tenor of his life, the missionaries seized the body and performed their service over it, amid the sullen indignation of his people, at what, under the circumstances, was sacrilege.

Of Indian religion a fine specimen is given in the conduct of one of the war chiefs, who, on an important occasion, made a vow to the sun of entire renunciation in case he should be crowned with success. When he was so, he first went through a fast, and sacrificial dance, involving great personal torment, and lasting several days; then, distributing all his property, even his lodges, and mats, among the tribe, he and his family took up their lodging upon the bare ground, beneath the bare sky.

The devotion of the Stylites and the hair-cloth saints, is in act, though not in motive, less noble, because this great chief proposed to go on in common life, where he had lived as a prince—a beggar.

The memoir by Corn Plant of his early days is beautiful.

Very fine anecdotes are told of two of the Western chiefs, father and son, who had the wisdom to see the true policy toward the whites, and steadily to adhere to it.

A murder having taken place in the jurisdiction of the father, he delivered himself up, with those suspected, to imprisonment. One of his companions chafed bitterly under confinement. He told the chief, if they ever got out, he would kill him, and did so. The son, then a boy, came in his rage and sorrow, to this Indian, and insulted him in every way. The squaw, angry at this, urged her husband "to kill the boy at once." But he only replied with "the joy of the valiant," "He will be a great Brave," and then delivered himself up to atone for his victim, and met his death with the noblest Roman composure.

This boy became rather a great chief than a great brave, and the anecdotes about him are of signal beauty and significance.

There is a fine story of an old mother, who gave herself to death instead of her son. The son, at the time, accepted the sacrifice, seeing, with Indian coolness, that it was better she should give up her few solitary and useless days, than he a young existence full of promise. But he could not abide by this view, and after suffering awhile all the anguish of remorse, he put himself solemnly to death in the presence of the tribe, as the only atonement he could make. His young wife stood by, with her child in her arms, commanding her emotions, as he desired, for, no doubt, it seemed to her also, a sacred duty.

But the finest story of all is that of Petalesharro, in whose tribe at the time, and not many years since, the custom of offering human sacrifices still subsisted. The fire was kindled, the victim, a young female captive, bound to the stake, the tribe assembled round. The young brave darted through them, snatched the girl from her peril, placed her upon his horse, and both had vanished before the astonished spectators had thought to interpose.

He placed the girl in her distant home, and then returned. Such is the might of right, when joined with courage, that none ventured a word of resentment or question. His father, struck by truth, endeavored, and with success, to abolish the barbarous custom in the tribe. On a later occasion, Petalesharro again offered his life, if required, but it was not.

This young warrior visiting Washington, a medal was presented him in honor of these acts. His reply deserves sculpture: "When I did it, I knew not that it was good. I did it in ignorance. This medal makes me know that it was good."

The recorder, through his playful expressions of horror at a declaration so surprising to the civilized Good, shows himself sensible to the grand simplicity of heroic impulse it denotes. Were we, too, so good, as to need a medal to show us that we are!

The half-breed and half-civilized chiefs, however handsome, look vulgar beside the pure blood. They have the dignity of neither race.

The death of Osceola,[30] (as described by Catlin,) presents a fine picture in the stern, warlike kind, taking leave with kindness, as a private friend, of the American officers; but, as a foe in national regards, he raised himself in his dying bed, and painted his face with the tokens of eternal enmity.

The historian of the Indians should be one of their own race, as able to sympathize with them, and possessing a mind as enlarged and cultivated as John Ross,[31] and with his eye turned to the greatness of the past, rather than the scanty promise of the future. Hearing of the wampum belts, supposed to have been sent to our tribes by Montezuma, on the invasion of the Spaniard, we feel that an Indian who could glean traditions familiarly from the old men, might collect much that we could interpret.

Still, any clear outline, even of a portion of their past, is not to be hoped, and we shall be well contented if we can have a collection of genuine fragments, that will indicate as clearly their life, as a horse's head from the Parthenon the genius of Greece.

Such, to me, are the stories I have cited above. And even European sketches of this greatness, distant and imperfect though they be, yet convey the truth, if made in a sympathizing spirit. Adair's Red Shoes, Murray's old man, Catlin's noble Mandan chief, Henry's Wa-wa-tam, with what we know of Philip, Pontiac, Tecumseh [32] and Red Jacket, would suffice to give the ages a glimpse at what was great in Indian life and Indian character.

We hope, too, there will be a national institute, containing all the remains of the Indians,—all that has been preserved by official intercourse at Washington, Catlin's collection, and a picture gallery as complete as can be made, with a collection of skulls from all parts of the country. To this should be joined the scanty library that exists on the subject.

I have not mentioned Mackenzie's Travels. He is an accurate observer, but sparing in his records, because his attention was wholly bent on his own objects. This circumstance gives a heroic charm to his scanty and simple narrative. Let what will happen, or who will go back, he cannot; he must find the sea, along those frozen rivers, through those starving countries, among tribes of stinted men, whose habitual interjection was "edui, it is hard, uttered in a querulous tone," distrusted by his followers, deserted by his guides, on, on he goes, till he sees the sea, cold, lowering, its strand bristling with foes; but he does see it.

His few observations, especially on the tribes who lived on fish, and held them in such superstitious observance, give a lively notion of the scene.

A little pamphlet has lately been published, giving an account of the massacre at Chicago, [33] which I wish much I had seen while there, as it would have imparted an interest to spots otherwise barren. It is written with animation, and in an excellent style, telling just what we want to hear, and no more. The traits given of Indian generosity are as characteristic as those of Indian cruelty. A lady, who was saved by a friendly chief holding her under the waters of the lake, while the balls were whizzing around, received also, in the heat of the conflict, a reviving draught from a squaw, who saw she was exhausted; and, as she lay down, a mat was hung up between her and the scene of butchery, so that she was protected from the sight, though she could not be from sounds, full of horror.

I have not wished to write sentimentally about the Indians, however moved by the thought of their wrongs and speedy extinction. I know that

the Europeans who took possession of this country, felt themselves justified by their superior civilization and religious ideas. Had they been truly
civilized or Christianized, the conflicts which sprang from the collision of
the two races, might have been avoided; but this cannot be expected in
movements made by masses of men. The mass has never yet been human-
ized, though the age may develop a human thought.

Since those conflicts and differences did arise, the hatred which
sprang, from terror and suffering, on the European side, has naturally
warped the whites still farther from justice.

The Indian, brandishing the scalps of his friends and wife, drinking
their blood and eating their hearts, is by him viewed as a fiend, though, at a
distant day, he will no doubt be considered as having acted the Roman or
Carthaginian part of heroic and patriotic self-defence, according to the
standard of right and motives prescribed by his religious faith and education. Looked at by his own standard, he is virtuous when he most injures
his enemy, and the white, if he be really the superior in enlargement of
thought, ought to cast aside his inherited prejudices enough to see this,—
to look on him in pity and brotherly goodwill, and do all he can to mitigate
the doom of those who survive his past injuries.

In McKenney's book, is proposed a project for organizing the Indians
under a patriarchal government, but it does not look feasible, even on
paper. Could their own intelligent men be left to act unimpeded in their
behalf, they would do far better for them than the white thinker, with all
his general knowledge. But we dare not hope the designs of such will not
always be frustrated by the same barbarous selfishness they were in
Georgia. There was a chance of seeing what might have been done, now
lost forever.

Yet let every man look to himself how far this blood shall be required
at his hands. Let the missionary, instead of preaching to the Indian, preach
to the trader who ruins him, of the dreadful account which will be demanded of the followers of Cain, in a sphere where the accents of purity
and love come on the ear more decisively than in ours. Let every legislator
take the subject to heart, and if he cannot undo the effects of past sin, try
for that clear view and right sense that may save us from sinning still more
deeply. And let every man and every woman, in their private dealings with
the subjugated race, avoid all share in embittering, by insult or unfeeling
prejudice, the captivity of Israel.

CHAPTER VII

✻✻✻✻✻

Sault St. Marie

NINE DAYS I passed alone at Mackinaw, except for occasional visits from kind and agreeable residents at the fort, and Mr. and Mrs. A. Mr. A., long engaged in the fur-trade, is gratefully remembered by many travellers. From Mrs. A., also, I received kind attentions, paid in the vivacious and graceful manner of her nation.

The society at the boarding house entertained, being of a kind entirely new to me. There were many traders from the remote stations, such as La Pointe, Arbre Croche,—men who had become half wild and wholly rude, by living in the wild; but good-humored, observing, and with a store of knowledge to impart, of the kind proper to their place.

There were two little girls here, that were pleasant companions for me. One gay, frank, impetuous, but sweet and winning. She was an American, fair, and with bright brown hair. The other, a little French Canadian, used to join me in my walks, silently take my hand, and sit at my feet when I stopped in beautiful places. She seemed to understand without a word; and I never shall forget her little figure, with its light, but pensive motion, and her delicate, grave features, with the pale, clear complexion and soft eye. She was motherless, and much left alone by her father and brothers, who were boatmen. The two little girls were as pretty representatives of Allegro and Penseroso,[1] as one would wish to see.

I had been wishing that a boat would come in to take me to the Sault St. Marie, and several times started to the window at night in hopes that the pant and dusky-red light crossing the waters belonged to such an one; but they were always boats for Chicago or Buffalo, till, on the 28th of August, Allegro, who shared my plans and wishes, rushed in to tell me that the General Scott had come, and, in this little steamer, accordingly, I set off the next morning.

I was the only lady, and attended in the cabin by a Dutch girl and an Indian woman. They both spoke English fluently, and entertained me much by accounts of their different experiences.

The Dutch girl told me of a dance among the common people at

Amsterdam, called the shepherd's dance. The two leaders are dressed as shepherd and shepherdess; they invent to the music all kinds of movements, descriptive of things that may happen in the field, and the rest were obliged to follow. I have never heard of any dance which gave such free play to the fancy as this. French dances merely describe the polite movements of society; Spanish and Neapolitan, love; the beautiful Mazurkas, &c., are warlike or expressive of wild scenery. But in this one is great room both for fun and fancy.

The Indian was married, when young, by her parents, to a man she did not love. He became dissipated, and did not maintain her. She left him, taking with her their child; for whom and herself she earns a subsistence by going as chambermaid in these boats. Now and then, she said, her husband called on her, and asked if he might live with her again; but she always answered, no. Here she was far freer than she would have been in civilized life.

I was pleased by the nonchalance of this woman, and the perfectly national manner she had preserved after so many years of contact with all kinds of people. The two women, when I left the boat, made me presents of Indian work, such as travellers value, and the manner of the two was characteristic of their different nations. The Indian brought me hers, when I was alone, looked bashfully down when she gave it, and made an almost sentimental little speech. The Dutch girl brought hers in public, and, bridling her short chin with a self-complacent air, observed she had *bought* it for me. But the feeling of affectionate regard was the same in the minds of both.

Island after island we passed, all fairly shaped and clustering friendly, but with little variety of vegetation.

In the afternoon the weather became foggy, and we could not proceed after dark. That was as dull an evening as ever fell.

The next morning the fog still lay heavy, but the captain took me out in his boat on an exploring expedition, and we found the remains of the old English fort on Point St. Joseph's. All around was so wholly unmarked by anything but stress of wind and weather, the shores of these islands and their woods so like one another, wild and lonely, but nowhere rich and majestic, that there was some charm in the remains of the garden, the remains even of chimneys and a pier. They gave feature to the scene.

Here I gathered many flowers, but they were the same as at Mackinaw.

The captain, though he had been on this trip hundreds of times, had never seen this spot, and never would, but for this fog, and his desire to entertain me. He presented a striking instance how men, for the sake of getting a living, forget to live. It is just the same in the most romantic as the most dull and vulgar places. Men get the harness on so fast, that they can never shake it off, unless they guard against this danger from the very first. In Chicago, how many men, who never found time to see the prairies or learn anything unconnected with the business of the day, or about the country they were living in!

So this captain, a man of strong sense and good eyesight, rarely found time to go off the track or look about him on it. He lamented, too, that there had been no call which induced him to develop his powers of expression, so that he might communicate what he had seen, for the enjoyment or instruction of others.

This is a common fault among the active men, the truly living, who could tell what life is. It should not be so. Literature should not be left to the mere literati—eloquence to the mere orator. Every Cæsar should be able to write his own commentary.[2] We want a more equal, more thorough, more harmonious development, and there is nothing to hinder from it the men of this country, except their own supineness, or sordid views.

When the weather did clear, our course up the river was delightful. Long stretched before us the island of St. Joseph's, with its fair woods of sugar maple. A gentleman on board, who belongs to the Fort at the Sault, said their pastime was to come in the season of making sugar, and pass some time on this island,—the days at work, and the evening in dancing and other amusements.

I wished to extract here Henry's account of this, for it was just the same sixty years ago as now, but have already occupied too much room with extracts. Work of this kind done in the open air, where everything is temporary, and every utensil prepared on the spot, gives life a truly festive air. At such times, there is labor and no care—energy with gaiety, gaiety of the heart.

I think with the same pleasure of the Italian vintage, the Scotch harvest-home, with its evening dance in the barn, the Russian cabbage-feast even, and our huskings and hop-gatherings—the hop-gatherings where the groups of men and girls are pulling down and filling baskets with the gay festoons, present as graceful pictures as the Italian vintage.

I should also like to insert Henry's descriptions of the method of catching trout and white fish, the delicacies of this region, for the same reason as I want his account of the Gens de Terre, the savages among savages, and his tales, dramatic, if not true, of cannibalism.

I have no less grieved to omit Carver's account of the devotion of a Winnebago prince at the Falls of St. Anthony, which he describes with a simplicity and intelligence, that are very pleasing.

I take the more pleasure in both Carver and Henry's power of appreciating what is good in the Indian character, that both had run the greatest risk of losing their lives during their intercourse with the Indians, and had seen them in the utmost exasperation, with all its revolting circumstances.

I wish I had a thread long enough to string on it all these beads that take my fancy; but, as I have not, I can only refer the reader to the books themselves, which may be found in the library of Harvard College, if not elsewhere.

How pleasant is the course along a new river, the sight of new shores; like a life, would but life flow as fast, and upbear us with as full a stream. I hoped we should come in sight of the rapids by daylight; but the beautiful sunset was quite gone, and only a young moon trembling over the scene, when we came within hearing of them.

I sat up long to hear them merely. It was a thoughtful hour. These two days, the 29th and 30th August, are memorable in my life; the latter is the birth-day of a near friend. I pass them alone, approaching Lake Superior; but I shall not enter into that truly wild and free region; shall not have the canoe voyage, whose daily adventure, with the camping out at night beneath the stars, would have given an interlude of such value to my existence. I shall not see the Pictured Rocks, their chapels and urns. It did not depend on me; it never has, whether such things shall be done or not.

My friends! may they see, and do, and be more, especially those who have before them a greater number of birthdays, and of a more healthy and unfettered existence:

TO EDITH, ON HER BIRTHDAY

If the same star our fates together bind,
Why are we thus divided, mind from mind?
If the same law one grief to both impart,
How could'st thou grieve a trusting mother's heart?

Our aspiration seeks a common aim,
Why were we tempered of such differing frame?
—But 'tis too late to turn this wrong to right;
Too cold, too damp, too deep, has fallen the night.

And yet, the angel of my life replies,
Upon that night a Morning Star shall rise,
Fairer than that which ruled the temporal birth,
Undimmed by vapors of the dreamy earth;

It says, that, where a heart thy claim denies,
Genius shall read its secret ere it flies;
The earthly form may vanish from thy side,
Pure love will make thee still the spirit's bride.

And thou, ungentle, yet much loving child,
Whose heart still shows the "untamed haggard wild,"
A heart which justly makes the highest claim,
Too easily is checked by transient blame;

Ere such an orb can ascertain its sphere,
The ordeal must be various and severe;
My prayers attend thee, though the feet may fly,
I hear thy music in the silent sky.

I should like, however, to hear some notes of earthly music to-night.
By the faint moonshine I can hardly see the banks; how they look I have no
guess, except that there are trees, and, now and then, a light lets me know
there are homes with their various interests. I should like to hear some
strains of the flute from beneath those trees, just to break the sound of the
rapids.

When no gentle eyebeam charms;
No fond hope the bosom warms;
Of thinking the lone mind is tired—
Nought seems bright to be desired;

Music, be thy sails unfurled,
Bear me to thy better world;
O'er a cold and weltering sea,
Blow thy breezes warm and free;

By sad sighs they ne'er were chilled,
By sceptic spell were never stilled;
Take me to that far-off shore,
Where lovers meet to part no more;
There doubt, and fear and sin are o'er,
The star of love shall set no more.

With the first light of dawn I was up and out, and then was glad I had not seen all the night before; it came upon me with such power in its dewy freshness. O! they are beautiful indeed, these rapids! The grace is so much more obvious than the power. I went up through the old Chippeway burying ground to their head, and sat down on a large stone to look. A little way off was one of the home lodges, unlike in shape to the temporary ones at Mackinaw, but these have been described by Mrs. Jameson. Women, too, I saw coming home from the woods, stooping under great loads of cedar boughs, that were strapped upon their backs. But in many European countries women carry great loads, even of wood, upon their backs. I used to hear the girls singing and laughing as they were cutting down boughs at Mackinaw; this part of their employment, though laborious, gives them the pleasure of being a great deal in the free woods.

I had ordered a canoe to take me down the rapids, and presently I saw it coming, with the two Indian canoe-men in pink calico shirts, moving it about with their long poles, with a grace and dexterity worthy fairy land. Now and then they cast the scoop-net; all looked just as I had fancied, only far prettier.

When they came to me, they spread a mat in the middle of the canoe; I sat down, and in less than four minutes we had descended the rapids, a distance of more than three quarters of a mile. I was somewhat disappointed in this being no more of an exploit than I found it. Having heard such expressions used as of "darting," or, "shooting down," these rapids, I had fancied there was a wall of rock somewhere, where descent would somehow be accomplished, and that there would come some one gasp of terror and delight, some sensation entirely new to me; but I found myself in smooth water, before I had time to feel anything but the buoyant pleasure of being carried so lightly through this surf amid the breakers. Now and then the Indians spoke to one another in a vehement jabber, which, however, had no tone that expressed other than pleasant excitement. It is, no doubt, an act of wonderful dexterity to steer amid these jagged rocks, when one rude touch would tear a hole in the birch canoe; but these men are evidently so used to doing it, and so adroit, that the silliest person could not feel afraid. I should like to have come down twenty times, that I might have had leisure to realize the pleasure. But the fog which had detained us on the way, shortened the boat's stay at the Sault, and I wanted my time to walk about.

While coming down the rapids, the Indians caught a white-fish for my breakfast; and certainly it was the best of breakfasts. The white-fish I found quite another thing caught on this spot, and cooked immediately, from what I had found it at Chicago or Mackinaw. Before, I had had the bad taste to prefer the trout, despite the solemn and eloquent remonstrances of the Habitués, to whom the superiority of white fish seemed a cardinal point of faith.

I am here reminded that I have omitted that indispensable part of a travelling journal, the account of what we found to eat. I cannot hope to make up, by one bold stroke, all my omissions of daily record; but that I may show myself not destitute of the common feelings of humanity, I will observe that he whose affections turn in summer towards vegetables, should not come to this region, till the subject of diet be better understood; that of fruit, too, there is little yet, even at the best hotel tables; that the prairie chickens require no praise from me, and that the trout and white-fish are worthy the transparency of the lake waters.

In this brief mention I by no means mean to give myself an air of superiority to the subject. If a dinner in the Illinois woods, on dry bread and drier meat, with water from the stream that flowed hard by, pleased me best of all, yet at one time, when living at a house where nothing was prepared for the table fit to touch, and even the bread could not be partaken of without a headach in consequence, I learnt to understand and sympathize with the anxious tone in which fathers of families, about to take their innocent children into some scene of wild beauty, ask first of all, "Is there a good table?" I shall ask just so in future. Only those whom the Powers have furnished small travelling cases of ambrosia, can take exercise all day, and be happy without even bread morning or night.

Our voyage back was all pleasure. It was the fairest day. I saw the river, the islands, the clouds to the greatest advantage.

On board was an old man, an Illinois farmer, whom I found a most agreeable companion. He had just been with his son, and eleven other young men, on an exploring expedition to the shores of lake Superior. He was the only old man of the party, but he had enjoyed, most of any, the journey. He had been the counsellor and playmate, too, of the young ones. He was one of those parents,—why so rare?—who understand and live a new life in that of their children, instead of wasting time and young happiness in trying to make them conform to an object and standard of their own. The character and history of each child may be a new and poetic experience to the parent, if he will let it. Our farmer was domestic, judicious, solid; the son, inventive, enterprising, superficial, full of follies, full of resources, always liable to failure, sure to rise above it. The father conformed to, and learnt from, a character he could not change, and won the sweet from the bitter.

His account of his life at home, and of his late adventures among the Indians, was very amusing, but I want talent to write it down. I have not heard the slang of these people intimately enough. There is a good book about Indiana, called the New Purchase,[3] written by a person who knows the people of the country well enough to describe them in their own way. It is not witty, but penetrating, valuable for its practical wisdom and good-humored fun.

There were many sportsman stories told, too, by those from Illinois and Wisconsin. I do not retain any of these well enough, nor any that I heard earlier, to write them down, though they always interested me from bringing wild, natural scenes before the mind. It is pleasant for the sportsman to be in countries so alive with game; yet it is so plenty that one would think shooting pigeons or grouse would seem more like slaughter, than the excitement of skill to a good sportsman. Hunting the deer is full of adventure, and needs only a Scrope to describe it to invest the western woods with *historic* associations.[4]

How pleasant it was to sit and hear rough men tell pieces out of their own common lives, in places of the frippery talk of some fine circle with its conventional sentiment, and timid, second-hand criticism. Free blew the wind, and boldly flowed the stream, named for Mary mother mild.

A fine thunder shower came on in the afternoon. It cleared at sunset, just as we came in sight of beautiful Mackinaw, over which a rainbow bent in promise of peace.

I have always wondered, in reading travels, at the childish joy travellers felt at meeting people they knew, and their sense of loneliness when they did not, in places where there was everything new to occupy the attention. So childish, I thought, always to be longing for the new in the old, and the old in the new. Yet just such sadness I felt, when I looked on the island, glittering in the sunset, canopied by the rainbow, and thought no friend would welcome me there; just such childish joy I felt, to see unexpectedly on the landing, the face of one whom I called friend.

The remaining two or three days were delightfully spent, in walking or boating, or sitting at the window to see the Indians go. This was not quite so pleasant as their coming in, though accomplished with the same rapidity; a family not taking half an hour to prepare for departure, and the departing canoe a beautiful object. But they left behind, on all the shore, the blemishes of their stay—old rags, dried boughs, fragments of food, the marks of their fires. Nature likes to cover up and gloss over spots and scars, but it would take her some time to restore that beach to the state it was in before they came.

S. and I had a mind for a canoe excursion, and we asked one of the traders to engage us two good Indians, that would not only take us out, but be sure and bring us back, as we could not hold converse with them. Two others offered their aid, beside the chief's son, a fine looking youth of about sixteen, richly dressed in blue broadcloth, scarlet sash and leggins, with a scarf of brighter red than the rest, tied around his head, its ends falling gracefully on one shoulder. They thought it, apparently, fine amusement to be attending two white women; they carried us into the path of the steamboat, which was going out, and paddled with all their force,—rather too fast, indeed, for there was something of a swell on the lake, and they sometimes threw water into the canoe. However, it flew over the waves, light as a sea-gull. They would say, "Pull away," and "Ver' warm," and, after these words, would laugh gaily. They enjoyed the hour, I believe, as much as we.

The house where we lived belonged to the widow of a French trader, an Indian by birth, and wearing the dress of her country. She spoke French fluently, and was very ladylike in her manners. She is a great character among them. They were all the time coming to pay her homage, or to get her aid and advice; for she is, I am told, a shrewd woman of business. My companion carried about her sketch-book with her, and the Indians were interested when they saw her using her pencil, though less so than about the sun-shade. This lady of the tribe wanted to borrow the sketches of the beach, with its lodges and wild groups, "to show to the *savages,*" she said.

Of the practical ability of the Indian women, a good specimen is given by McKenney, in an amusing story of one who went to Washington, and acted her part there in the "first circles," with a tact and sustained dissimulation worthy of Cagliostro.[5] She seemed to have a thorough love of intrigue for its own sake, and much dramatic talent. Like the chiefs of her nation, when on an expedition among the foe, whether for revenge or profit, no impulses of vanity or wayside seductions had power to turn her aside from carrying out her plan as she had originally projected it.

Although I have little to tell, I feel that I have learnt a great deal of the Indians, from observing them even in this broken and degraded condition. There is a language of eye and motion which cannot be put into words, and which teaches what words never can. I feel acquainted with the soul of this race; I read its nobler thought in their defaced figures. There *was* a greatness, unique and precious, which he who does not feel will never duly appreciate the majesty of nature in this American continent.

I have mentioned that the Indian orator, who addressed the agents on this occasion, said, the difference between the white man and the red man is this: "the white man no sooner came here, than he thought of preparing the way for his posterity; the red man never thought of this." I was assured this was exactly his phrase; and it defines the true difference. We get the better because we do

"Look before and after."

But, from the same cause, we

"Pine for what is not."

The red man, when happy, was thoroughly happy; when good, was simply good. He needed the medal, to let him know that he *was* good.

These evenings we were happy, looking over the old-fashioned garden, over the beach, over the waters and pretty island opposite, beneath the growing moon; we did not stay to see it full at Mackinaw. At two o'clock, one night, or rather morning, the Great Western came snorting in, and we must go; and Mackinaw, and all the north-west summer, is now to me no more than picture and dream;—

"A dream within a dream."

These last days at Mackinaw have been pleasanter than the "lonesome" nine, for I have recovered the companion with whom I set out from the East, one who sees all, prizes all, enjoys much, interrupts never.

At Detroit we stopped for half a day. This place is famous in our history, and the unjust anger at its surrender is still expressed by almost every one who passes there.[6] I had always shared the common feeling on this subject; for the indignation at a disgrace to our arms that seemed so unnecessary, has been handed down from father to child, and few of us have taken the pains to ascertain where the blame lay. But now, upon the spot, having read all the testimony, I felt convinced that it should rest solely with the government, which, by neglecting to sustain General Hull, as he had a right to expect they would, compelled him to take this step, or sacrifice many lives, and of the defenceless inhabitants, not of soldiers, to the cruelty of a savage foe, for the sake of his reputation.

I am a woman, and unlearned in such affairs; but, to a person with common sense and good eyesight, it is clear, when viewing the location, that, under the circumstances, he had no prospect of successful defence, and that to attempt it would have been an act of vanity, not valor.

I feel that I am not biased in this judgment by my personal relations, for I have always heard both sides, and, though my feelings had been moved by the picture of the old man sitting down, in the midst of his children, to a retired and despoiled old age, after a life of honor and happy intercourse with the public, yet tranquil, always secure that justice must be done at last, I supposed, like others, that he deceived himself, and deserved to pay the penalty for failure to the responsibility he had undertaken. Now on the spot, I change, and believe the country at large must, ere long, change from this opinion. And I wish to add my testimony, however trifling its weight, before it be drowned in the voice of general assent, that I may do some justice to the feelings which possessed me here and now.

A noble boat, the Wisconsin, was to be launched this afternoon, the whole town was out in many-colored array, the band playing. Our boat swept round to a good position, and all was ready but—the Wisconsin, which could not be made to stir. This was quite a disappointment. It would have been an imposing sight.

In the boat many signs admonished that we were floating eastward. A shabbily dressed phrenologist[7] laid his hand on every head which would bend, with half-conceited, half-sheepish expression, to the trial of his skill. Knots of people gathered here and there to discuss points of theology. A bereaved lover was seeking religious consolation in—Butler's Analogy, which he had purchased for that purpose. However, he did not turn over many pages before his attention was drawn aside by the gay glances of certain damsels that came on board at Detroit, and, though Butler might afterwards be seen sticking from his pocket, it had not weight to impede him from many a feat of lightness and liveliness. I doubt if it went with him from the boat. Some there were, even, discussing the doctrines of Fourier.[8] It seemed pity they were not going to, rather than from, the rich and free country where it would be so much easier, than with us, to try the great experiment of voluntary association, and show, beyond a doubt, that "an ounce of prevention is worth a pound of cure," a maxim of the "wisdom of nations," which has proved of little practical efficacy as yet.

Better to stop before landing at Buffalo, while I have yet the advantage over some of my readers.

THE BOOK TO THE READER

Who opens, as American readers often do, at the end,
with doggerel submission

To see your cousin in her country home,
If at the time of blackberries you come,
"Welcome, my friends," she cries with ready glee,
"The fruit is ripened, and the paths are free.
But, madam, you will tear that handsome gown;
The little boy be sure to tumble down;
And, in the thickets where they ripen best,
The matted ivy, too, its bower has drest.
And then, the thorns your hands are sure to rend,
Unless with heavy gloves you will defend;
Amid most thorns the sweetest roses blow,
Amid most thorns the sweetest berries grow."

If, undeterred, you to the fields must go,
    You tear your dresses and you scratch your hands;
But, in the places where the berries grow,
    A sweeter fruit the ready sense commands,
Of wild, gay feelings, fancies springing sweet—
Of bird-like pleasures, fluttering and fleet.

Another year, you cannot go yourself,
    To win the berries from the thickets wild,
And housewife skill, instead, has filled the shelf
    With blackberry jam, "by best receipts compiled,—
Not made with country sugar, for too strong
The flavors that to maple juice belong;
But foreign sugar, nicely mixed 'to suit
The taste,' spoils not the fragrance of the fruit."

"'T is pretty good," half-tasting, you reply,
"I scarce should know it from fresh blackberry.
But the best pleasure such a fruit can yield,
Is to be gathered in the open field;
If only as an article of food,
Cherry or crab-apple are quite as good;

And, for occasions of festivity,
West India sweetmeats you had better buy."

Thus, such a dish of homely sweets as these
In neither way may chance the taste to please.

Yet try a little with the evening-bread;
Bring a good needle for the spool of thread;
Take fact with fiction, silver with the lead,
And, at the mint, you can get gold instead;
In fine, read me, even as you would be read.

Now wandering on a tangled way—
Is their lost child pure spirits say
    The diamond marshal thee by day,
By night the carbuncle defend
    Hearts-blood of a bosom-friend;
On thy brow the amethyst
    Violet of secret earth.
When by fullest sunlight kissed
    Best reveals its regal worth;
And when that haloed moment flies
    Shall keep thee steadfast, chaste and wise.

Sunday 5th May 1844

Four times the form upon the dreamer's eye
Has dawned;—a fateful form well known by day,
    But not with such deep presage on the mind
When still and lone discerned;
    First, on a sunny slope
I seemed to stand; the trees were gently moved
    As if in expectation:—sudden there he stood:
I cannot paint him as it was that day,
    But a deep sense of what the glory was
Is with me still, as fresh as when I woke

And named the boon was given in that hour
   "The Revelation of all Poesy"!
Then came the key-note of that special strain
   Which must reveal the entire harmony
To me. I ne'er have doubted, doubt not now
   That all my Delphos[1] centred in that hour.

   The second time was in the blossom-time
When Nature's wealth should make the human heart
   Be blest in prodigal beauty. . . .

   Yet once again it came,
Here, in the scene of those sad youthful days,
   Several nights of the full harvest moon
I had walked forth alone, seeking in vain
   After dull days of many petty cares,
Of petty, seemingly of useless cares,
   To find again my nobler life,—again
To weave the web which, from the frosty ground,
   Should keep the tender feet of prisoned Queen,
Or wrap the breast of weeping beggar child,
   Or curtain from the saint a wicked world,
Or,—if but rightly woven were this web
   For any, for all uses it were fit:
But I had lost the shuttle from my hand. . . .

∽

Let me gather from the Earth, one full grown fragrant flower,
Let it bloom within my bosom through its one blooming hour.
Let it die within my bosom and to its parting breath
Mine shall answer, *having lived,* I shrink not now from death.
It is this niggard halfness that turns my heart to stone,
'Tis the cup seen, not tasted, that makes the infant moan.
Let me for once press firm my lips upon the moment's brow,
Let me for once distinctly feel *I am all happy now,*
And bliss shall seal a blessing upon that moment's brow.

∽

   Boding raven of the breast
   Dost call the vulture to thy nest
   Through broken hearted trusting love

That vulture may become a Dove
Yet scare the vulture from my breast
These days have brought too much unrest
Let the humble linnet sing
Of the assured, if distant Spring;
While I baptize in the pure wave,
Then prepare a deep safe grave.
Where the plighted hand may bring
Violets from that other spring.
Whence the soul may take its flight
Lark-like spiral seeking light
Seeking secure the source of light.

On the boundless plain careering
By an unseen compass steering
   Wildly flying, re-appearing,
With untamed fire their broad eyes glowing
   In every step a grand pride showing,
Of no servile moment knowing,
   Happy as the trees & flowers
In their instinct-cradled hours,
   Happier in fuller powers,
   See the wild horse nobly ranging
Nature varying not changing
   Lawful in their lawless ranging.
   But hark, what boding crouches near?
On the horizon now appear
Centaur forms of force & fear.

On their enslaved brethren borne
With bit & whip of tyrant scorn,
   To make new captives as forlorn.
   Wildly snort the astonished throng
Stamp & wheel & fly along
   Those Centaur powers they know are strong.
   But the lasso, skilful-cast,
Holds one only captive fast
   Youngest, weakest, left the last.
   How thou trembledst then, Konic!
Thy full breath came short & thick,

Thy heart to bursting beat so quick;
Thy strange brethren peering round,
By those tyrants held & bound,
Tyrants fell whom falls confound;
With rage & pity fill thy heart
Death shall be thy chosen part,
Ere such slavery tame thy heart.
But strange unexpected joy!
They seem to mean him no annoy
Gallop off, both man & boy.

Let the wild horse freely go,
Almost he shames it should be so,
So lightly prized himself to know.
All delusion 'tis, O steed!
Never again, upon the mead
Shalt thou a free wild horse feed.
The mark of man doth blot thy side
The fear of man hath dulled thy pride
Thy master soon shall on thee ride.
Thy brethren of the free plain,
Joyful speeding back again
With proud career & flowing mane,
Find thee branded, left alone,
And their hearts are turned to stone,
They keep thee in their midst alone.
Cruel the intervening years,
Seeming freedom stained by fears,
Till the captor re-appears,
Finding thee with thy broken pride,
Amid thy peers still left aside,
Unbeloved & unallied;
Finds thee ready for thy fate;
For joy & hope 'tis all too late,
Thou'rt wedded to the sad estate.

Would'st have the princely spirit bowed
Whisper only, speak not loud,
Mark & leave him in the crowd.
Thou need'st not spies nor jailors have,
The free will serve thee like the slave,
Coward shrinking from the brave.

And thy cohorts, when they come,
    To take the weary captive home
    Need only beat the retreating drum.

Sometime, on a fairer plain[2]
    May those captives live again
    Where no tyrant stigmas stain.
Marriage will then have broke the rod
    Where wicked foot has never trod
    The verdure sacred to a God.

Only, Konic, that noble heart
    To the dark predestined part
    Its own temper must impart.
Move as nobly, Centaur-driven,
    As when, ungiving & ungiven,
    Thou didst greet thy native heaven.
To the trumpet cry ha ha
    Scent the battle-field afar[3]
    Thy day dawn from that bloody war.
Day of hope as day of doom,
    Opening realms, where will be room
    For all to live, & need no tomb!

           ∾

TO SARAH.

Our friend has likened thee to the sweet fern,[4]
    Which with no flower salutes the ardent day,
    Yet, as the wanderer pursues his way
    While the dews fall, & hues of sunset burn,
    Sheds forth a fragrance from the deep green brake
Sweeter than the rich scents that gardens make.

Like thee, the fern loves well the hallowed shade
Of trees that quietly aspire on high,
    Amid such groves was consecration made
Of vestals tranquil as the vestal sky;
    Like thee, the fern doth better love to hide
Beneath the leaf the treasure of its seed
    Than to display it, with an idle pride,

To any but the careful gatherer's heed;
  A treasure known to philosophic ken,
Garnered in nature, asking nought of men;
Nay! can invisible the wearer make
Who would, unnoted, in life's game partake.

But I will liken thee to the sweet bay,
  Which I just learned in the Cohasset woods⁵
To name upon a sweet, though pensive day
  Passed in their minstreling solitudes.
I had grown weary of the anthem high
  Of the full wave cheering the patient rocks,
I had grown weary of the sob & sigh
  Of the dull ebb after emotion's shocks;
My eye was weary of the glittering blue
  And the unbroken horizontal line,
My mind was weary, tempted to pursue
  The circling waters in their wide design;
Like snowy sea-gulls, stooping to the wave,
  Or, rising buoyant to the utmost air,
To dart, to circle, airily to lave,
  Or wave-like, float in foam-born lightness fair;
I had swept onward like the wave so full,
Like sea-weed, now, left on the shore so dull.

  I turned my steps to the retreating hills,
Rejected sand from that great haughty sea,
  Watered by nature with consoling rills
And gradual dressed with grass, & shrub, & tree;
  They seemed to welcome me with timid smile
That said, "We'd like to soothe you for a while,
You seem to have been treated by the sea
In the same way that long ago were we."

They had not much to boast, those gentle slopes;
  For the wild gambols of the sea-sent breeze
Had mocked at many of their quiet hopes
  And bent & dwarfed their fondly cherished trees;
Yet even in those marks of by past wind
There was a tender stirring for my mind.

  Hiding within a small, but thick set wood,
  I soon forget the haughty chiding flood;

The sheep bell's tinkle on the drowsy ear
With the birds' chirp, so short, & light, & clear,
Composed a melody that filled my heart
With flower-like growths of childish artless art
And of the tender tranquil life I lived a part.

It was an hour of pure tranquillity
Like to the autumn sweetness of thine eye
Which pries not, seeks not, & yet clearly sees,
Which woos not, beams not, yet is sure to please.
Hours passed, & sunset called me to return
Where its sad glories on the cold wave burn.
Rising from my kind bed of thick-strewn leaves,
A fragrance the astonished sense receives
Ambrosial, searching, yet untiring mild
Of that soft scene the soul was it, or child?
'Twas the sweet bay I had unwitting spread
A pillow for my senseless throbbing head
And which, like all the sweetest things, demands
To make it speak, the grasp of alien hands.

All that this scene did in that moment tell
I since have read, O wise mild friend, in thee;
Pardon the rude grasp its sincerity,
And feel that I, at least, have known thee well;
Grudge not the green leaves ravished from thy stem
Their music should I live, muse-like to tell,
Thou wilt, in fresher green forgetting them,
Send others to console me for farewell
Thou wilt see why the dim wood of regret
Was made the one to rhyme with Margaret.

But to the Oriental parent tongue
Sunrise of Nature, does my chosen name
My name of Leila, as a spell belong
Teaching the meaning of each temporal blame;
I chose it by the sound, not knowing why,
But, since I know that Leila stands for night,
I own that sable mantle of the sky
Through which pierce, gem-like, points of distant light.
"As sorrow truths, so night brings out her stars."
(O add not, Bard! that "those stars shine too late")

While Earth grows green amid the ocean jars
And trumpets yet shall wake the slain of her long century wars.

∽

  Leila in the Arabian zone
 Dusky, languishing and lone
  Yet full of light are her deep eyes
 And her gales are lovers sighs.

  Io in Egyptian clime [6]
 Grows an Isis calm sublime [7]
  Blue black is her robe of night
 But blazoned o'er with points of light
  The horns that Io's brow deform
 With Isis take a crescent form
 And as a holy moon inform.
The magic Sistrum arms her hand
  And at her deep eye's command
  Brutes are raised to thinking men
Soul growing to her soul filled ken.

  Dian of the lonely life
 Hecate fed on gloom and strife
 Phebe on her throne of air
 Only Leila's children are. [8]

∽

DOUBLE TRIANGLE, SERPENT AND RAYS

  Patient serpent, circle round,
 Till in death thy life is found;
  Double form of godly prime
 Holding the whole thought of time,
  When the perfect two embrace,
 Male & female, black & white,
  Soul is justified in space,
 Dark made fruitful by the light;
  And, centred in the diamond Sun,
  Time & Eternity are one. [9]

∽

WINGED SPHYNX

Through brute nature upward rising,
  Seed up-striving to the light,
Revelations still surprising,
  My inwardness is grown insight.
  Still I slight not those first stages,
Dark but God-directed Ages;
  In my nature leonine
Labored & learned a Soul divine;
  Put forth an aspect Chaste, Serene,
Of nature virgin mother queen;
  Assumes at last the destined wings,
Earth & heaven together brings;
  While its own form the riddle tells
That baffled all the wizard spells
  Drawn from intellectual wells,
Cold waters where truth never dwells:
  —It was fable told you so;—
  Seek her in common daylight's glow. [10]

MY SEAL RING

Mercury [11] has cast aside
  The signs of intellectual pride,
Freely offers thee the soul,
  Art thou noble to receive?
Canst thou give or take the whole?
  Nobly promise and believe?
Then thou wholly human art
A spotless radiant ruby heart
And the golden chain of love
Has bound thee to the realm above.
  If there be one small mean doubt
One serpent thought that fled not out
Take, instead, the serpent rod
Thou art neither man nor god;
Guard thee from the powers of evil,
Who cannot trust vows to the Devil;
Walk thy slow and spell-bound way,

Keep on thy mask, or shun the day,
Let go my hand upon the way.

∾

SISTRUM

Triune shaping restless power
Life-flow from life's natal hour,
  No music chords are in thy sound
By some thou'rt but a rattle found,
  Yet, without thy ceaseless motion
To ice would turn their dead devotion.
Life-flow of my natal hour
I will not weary of thy power,
Till, in the changes of thy sound,
  A chord, three parts distinct are found;
I will faithful move with thee,
  God-ordained, self-fed Energy
Nature in Eternity.[12]

∾

Lead, lunar ray:
To the crossing of the way
Where to secret rite
Rises the armed knight
My champion for the fight.

Fall heavier still, sweet rain!
Free from their pain
Plants which still in earth
Are prisoned back from birth
Teach the sun their worth.

Soul, long lie thus still,
Cradled in the will,
Which to this motley ball,
Sphere so great, so small,
  Did thee call.

Suns have shone on thee
Brooding thy mystery;

Now this sweet rain
Frees from the pain
Of birth the golden grain.

Yet within the nest
Patience still were best.
Birds of my thought!
Food shall be brought
To you by mother thought.

Let your wings grow strong,
For the way is long
To the distant zone
Where glows the throne
Of your phoenix king so lone.

Nestle still, keep still,
Cradled by the will
Which must daily ye fill,
If while callow, ye keep still.

∾

SUB ROSA — CRUX.

In times of old, as we are told
When men more childlike at the feet
    Of Jesus sat, than now;
A chivalry was known more bold
    Than ours, yet of stricter vow
    Of worship more complete.

Knights of the Rosy Cross,[13] they bore
Its weight within the heart, but wore
    Without, devotion's sign in glistening ruby bright
The gall and vinegar they drank alone,
    But to the world at large would only own
The wine of faith, sparkling with rosy light.

They knew the secret of the sacred oil
Which, poured upon the prophet's head,
    Could keep him wise and pure for aye
Apart from all that might distract or soil;

With this their lamps they fed,
Which burn in their sepulchral shrines, unfading night and day.

The password now is lost
To that initiation full and free,
        Daily we pay the cost
Of our slow schooling for divine degree:
We know no means to feed an undying lamp;
Our lights go out in every wind or damp.

We wear the cross of ebony and gold,
Upon a dark background a form of light
        A heavenly hope upon a bosom cold,
        A starry promise in a frequent night,
The dying lamp must often trim again,
For we are conscious, thoughtful, striving men.

Yet be we faithful to this present trust,
Clasp to a heart resigned the fatal *Must,*
Though deepest dark our efforts should enfold,
        Unwearied mine to find the vein of gold,
Forget not oft to lift the hope on high,
        The rosy dawn again shall fill the sky.

And, by that lovely light all truth revealed,
The cherished forms which sad distrust concealed
        Transfigured, yet the same, will round us stand,
        The kindred angels of a faithful band;
Ruby and ebon cross both cast aside,
No lamp is needed for the night has died.

Happy be those who seek the distant day,
With feet that from the appointed way
        Could never stray;
Yet happy too be those who, more and more,
As beams the beacon of that only shore,
        Strive at the laboring oar!

Be to the best thou knowest ever true
        Is all the creed;
Then, be thy talisman of rosy hue,
Or fenced with thorns that, wearing, thou must bleed,
Or gentle pledge of Love's prophetic view
The faithful steps it will securely lead.

Happy are all who reach that shore
And bathe in heavenly day;
Happiest are those who high the banner bore
To marshal others on the way;
Or waited for them, fainting and way-worn,
By burdens over borne.

❧

RAPHAEL'S DEPOSITION FROM THE CROSS

I

Penitential Psalm

Virgin Mother, Mary Mild!
It was thine to see the child,
Gift of the Messiah dove,
Pure blossom of ideal love,
Break, upon the "guilty cross"
The seeming promise of his life;
Of faith, of hope, of love a loss
Deepened all thy bosom's strife,
Brow, down-bent, and heart-strings torn,
Fainting by frail arms upborne.

But 'tis mine, oh Mary mild,
To tremble lest the heavenly child,
Crucified within my heart
Ere of earth he take his part,
Leave my life that horror wild
The mother who has slain her child.

Let me to the tomb repair,
Find the angel watching there,
Ask his aid to walk again
Undefiled with brother men.
Once my heart within me burned
At the least whisper of thy voice;
Though my love was unreturned,
Happy in a holy choice;
Once my lamp was constant trimmed,
And my fond resolve undimmed.

Fan again the Parsee fire,
Let it light my funeral pyre
Purify the veins of Earth,
Temper for a Phenix birth.

II

Meditation

Virgin Mother, Mary Mild!
It was thine to see the child,
Gift of the Messiah dove,
Pure blossom of ideal love,
Break, upon the "guilty cross"
The seeming promise of his life;
Of faith, of hope, of love a loss
Deepened all thy bosom's strife,
Brow, down-bent, and heart-strings torn,
Fainting by frail arms upborne.

All those startled figures show
That they did not apprehend
The thought of him who there lies low,
On whom those sorrowing eyes they bend;
They do not feel this holiest hour,
Their hearts soar not to reach the power
Which this deepest of distress
Alone could give to save and bless.

Soul of that fair now ruined form,
Thou who hadst force to bide the storm
Must again descend to tell
Of thy life the hidden spell;
"Maiden, wrap thy mantle round thee"
Night is coming, clear cold night;
Fate, that in the cradle bound thee,
In the coffin hides thy blight;
Angels weeping, dirges singing,
Rosemary with hearts-ease bringing,
Softly spread the fair green sod,
Thou escape and bathe in God.

Margaret! shed no idle tears;
In the far perspective bright

A muse-like form as thine appears
As thine new-born in primal light.

Leila, take thy wand again;
Upon thy arm no longer rest;
   Listen to the thrilling brain;
   Listen to the throbbing breast;
      There nightingales have made their nest
   Shall shoothe with song the night's unrest.

Slowly drop the beaded years;
Slowly drop the pearly tears;
   At last the Rosary appears
A Ruby heart its clasp appears
      With cross of gold and diamond
      Like to that upon the wand.

"Maiden wrap thy mantle round thee"
Night is coming, starlit night,
   Fate that in the cradle bound thee,
In the coffin hides thy blight;
   All transfused the orb now glowing,
Full-voiced and free the music growing
      Planted in a senseless sod
      The life is risen to flower a God.[14]

❧

TO THE FACE SEEN IN THE MOON

Oft, from the shadows of my earthly sphere
I looked to thee, orb of pale pearly light,
   To loose the weariness of doubt and fear
In thy soft Mother's smile so pensive bright,
   Thou seemedst far and safe and chastely living
Graceful and thoughtfull, loving, beauty giving,
   But, if I stedfast gaze upon thy face
A human secret, like my own, I trace,
   For through the woman's smile looks the male eye
So mildly, stedfastly but mournfully
   He holds the bush to point us to his cave,
Teaching anew the truth so bright, so grave
   Escape not from the middle of the earth

Through mortal pangs to win immortal birth,
   Both man and woman, from the natural womb,
Must slowly win the secrets of the tomb,
   And then, together rising fragrant, clear,
The worthy Angel of a better sphere,
   Diana's beauty shows how Hecate wrought,
Apollo's lustre rays the zodiac thought
(In Leo regal, as in Virgo fair
   As Scorpio's secret, as the Archer rare,)
   In unpolluted beauty mutual shine
Earth, Moon and Sun the Human thought Divine.
For Earth is purged by tameless central fire,
And Moon in Man has told her hid desire,
And Time has found himself eternal Sire,
And the Sun sings All on his ray-strung lyre.

   Steady bear me on,
Counting life's pulses thus alone,
   Till all is felt and known and done.
Thus far have I conquered Fate
   I have learned to wait,
Nor in these early days snatch
    at the fruits of late.
The Man from the Moon
Looks not for an instant Noon,
   But from its secret heart
   Slow evolves the Art
Of that full consummation needed part.

   For thee, my Apollo,[15]
   The girdle I weave,
   From whose splendid hollow
Thy young heart shall its impulse receive.
   I am the mother of thy spirit-life
And so in law thy wife,
And thou art my sire
   For all this treasured fire
   Learnt from thee
    Its destiny;
And our full mutual birth
Must free this earth;
From our union shall spring
   The promised King

Who with white sail unfurled
Shall steer through the heaven
    Of soul—an unpolluted world.

  In that world,
Earth's tale shall be
  A valued page
  Of poesy.
As Grecian bards
  Knew how to praise
The kingly woes
  Of darker days;
And Tantalus [16] soaring, where the mist
  Is overblown
Meets on his hard won throne a Juno
  Of his own.

WOMAN IN THE NINETEENTH CENTURY

"Frei durch Vernunft, stark durch Gesetze,
Durch Sanftmuth gross, und reich durch Schätze,
Die lange Zeit dein Busen dir verschwieg." [1]

~

"I meant the day-star should not brighter rise,
Nor lend like influence from its lucent seat;
  I meant she should be courteous, facile, sweet,
Free from that solemn vice of greatness, pride;
  I meant each softest virtue there should meet,
Fit in that softer bosom to reside;
  Only a (heavenward and instructed) soul
I purposed her, that should, with even powers,
  The rock, the spindle, and the shears control
Of destiny, and spin her own free hours." [2]

THE FOLLOWING ESSAY is a reproduction, modified and expanded, of an article published in "The Dial, Boston, July, 1843," under the title of "The Great Lawsuit. Man versus Men: Woman versus Women."

This article excited a good deal of sympathy, and still more interest. It is in compliance with wishes expressed from many quarters, that it is prepared for publication in its present form.

Objections having been made to the former title, as not sufficiently easy to be understood, the present has been substituted as expressive of the main purpose of the essay; though, by myself, the other is preferred, partly for the reason others do not like it, *i. e.,* that it requires some thought to see what it means, and might thus prepare the reader to meet me on my own ground. Beside, it offers a larger scope, and is, in that way, more just to my desire. I meant, by that title, to intimate the fact that, while it is the destiny of Man, in the course of the Ages, to ascertain and fulfil the law of his being, so that his life shall be seen, as a whole, to be that of an angel or messenger, the action of prejudices and passions, which attend, in the day, the growth of the individual, is continually obstructing the holy work that is to make the earth a part of heaven. By Man I mean both man and woman: these are the two halves of one thought. I lay no especial stress on the welfare of either. I believe that the development of the one cannot be effected without that of the other. My highest wish is that this truth should be distinctly and rationally apprehended, and the conditions of life and freedom recognized as the same for the daughters and the sons of time; twin exponents of a divine thought.

I solicit a sincere and patient attention from those who open the following pages at all. I solicit of women that they will lay it to heart to ascertain what is for them the liberty of law. It is for this, and not for any, the largest, extension of partial privileges that I seek. I ask them, if interested by these suggestions, to search their own experience and intuitions for better, and fill up with fit materials the trenches that hedge them in. From men I ask a noble and earnest attention to any thing that can be offered on this great and still obscure subject, such as I have met from many with whom I stand in private relations.

And may truth, unpolluted by prejudice, vanity, or selfishness, be granted daily more and more, as the due inheritance, and only valuable conquest for us all!

November, 1844.

WOMAN IN THE NINETEENTH CENTURY

"Frailty, thy name is Woman."[3]

"The Earth waits for her Queen."

THE CONNECTION between these quotations may not be obvious, but it is strict. Yet would any contradict us, if we made them applicable to the other side, and began also

Frailty, thy name is MAN.
The Earth waits for its King.

Yet man, if not yet fully installed in his powers, has given much earnest of his claims. Frail he is indeed, how frail! how impure! Yet often has the vein of gold displayed itself amid the baser ores, and Man has appeared before us in princely promise worthy of his future.

If, oftentimes, we see the prodigal son feeding on the husks in the fair field no more his own, anon, we raise the eyelids, heavy from bitter tears, to behold in him the radiant apparition of genius and love, demanding not less than the all of goodness, power and beauty.[4] We see that in him the largest claim finds a due foundation. That claim is for no partial sway, no exclusive possession. He cannot be satisfied with any one gift of life, any one department of knowledge or telescopic peep at the heavens. He feels himself called to understand and aid nature, that she may, through his intelligence, be raised and interpreted; to be a student of, and servant to, the universe-spirit; and king of his planet, that as an angelic minister, he may bring it into conscious harmony[5] with the law of that spirit.

In clear triumphant moments, many times, has rung through the spheres the prophecy of his jubilee, and those moments, though past in time, have been translated into eternity by thought; the bright signs they left hang in the heavens, as single stars or constellations, and, already, a thickly sown radiance consoles the wanderer in the darkest night. Other heroes since Hercules have fulfilled the zodiac of beneficent labors, and then given up their mortal part to the fire without a murmur; while no God dared deny that they should have their reward.

> Siquis tamen, Hercule, siquis
> Forte Deo doliturus erit, data præmia nollet,
> Sed meruise dari sciet, invitus que probabit,
> Assensere Dei.[6]

Sages and lawgivers have bent their whole nature to the search for truth, and thought themselves happy if they could buy, with the sacrifice of all temporal ease and pleasure, one seed for the future Eden. Poets and priests have strung the lyre with the heartstrings, poured out their best blood upon the altar, which, reared anew from age to age shall at last sustain the flame pure enough to rise to highest heaven. Shall we not name with as deep a benediction those who, if not so immediately, or so consciously, in connection with the eternal truth, yet, led and fashioned by a divine instinct, serve no less to develope and interpret the open secret of love passing into life, energy creating for the purpose of happiness; the artist whose hand, drawn by a pre-existent harmony to a certain medium, moulds it to forms of life more highly and completely organized than are seen elsewhere, and, by carrying out the intention of nature, reveals her meaning to those who are not yet wise enough to divine it; the philosopher who listens steadily for laws and causes, and from those obvious, infers those yet unknown; the historian who, in faith that all events must have their reason and their aim, records them, and thus fills archives from which the youth of prophets may be fed. The man of science dissects the statements, tests the facts, and demonstrates order, even where he cannot its purpose.

Lives, too, which bear none of these names, have yielded tones of no less significance. The candlestick set in a low place has given light as faithfully, where it was needed, as that upon the hill.[7] In close alleys, in dismal nooks, the Word has been read as distinctly, as when shown by angels to holy men in the dark prison. Those who till a spot of earth scarcely larger than is wanted for a grave, have deserved that the sun should shine upon its sod till violets answer.

So great has been, from time to time, the promise, that, in all ages, men have said the gods themselves came down to dwell with them; that the All-Creating wandered on the earth to taste, in a limited nature, the sweetness of virtue; that the All-Sustaining incarnated himself to guard, in space and time, the destinies of this world; that heavenly genius dwelt among the shepherds, to sing to them and teach them how to sing. Indeed

"Der stets den Hirten gnadig sich bewies."

"He has constantly shown himself favorable to shepherds."

And the dwellers in green pastures and natural students of the stars were selected to hail, first among men, the holy child, whose life and death were to present the type of excellence, which has sustained the heart of so large a portion of mankind in these later generations.

Such marks have been made by the footsteps of *man,* (still alas! to be spoken of as the *ideal* man,) wherever he has passed through the wilderness of *men,* and whenever the pigmies stepped in one of those they felt dilate within the breast somewhat that promised nobler stature and purer blood. They were impelled to forsake their evil ways of decrepit scepticism, and covetousness of corruptible possessions. Conviction flowed in upon them. They, too, raised the cry; God is living, now, to-day; and all beings are brothers, for they are his children. Simple words enough, yet which only angelic nature, can use or hear in their full free sense.

These were the triumphant moments, but soon the lower nature took its turn, and the era of a truly human life was postponed.

Thus is man still a stranger to his inheritance, still a pleader, still a pilgrim. Yet his happiness is secure in the end. And now, no more a glimmering consciousness, but assurance begins to be felt and spoken, that the highest ideal man can form of his own powers, is that which he is destined to attain. Whatever the soul knows how to seek, it cannot fail to obtain. This is the law and the prophets. Knock and it shall be opened, seek and ye shall find.[8] It is demonstrated; it is a maxim. Man no longer paints his proper nature in some form and says, "Prometheus had it; it is God-like;" but "Man must have it; it is human." However disputed by many, however ignorantly used, or falsified by those who do receive it, the fact of an universal, unceasing revelation has been too clearly stated in words to be lost sight of in thought, and sermons preached from the text, "Be ye perfect," are the only sermons of a pervasive and deep-searching influence.

But, among those who meditate upon this text, there is a great difference of view, as to the way in which perfection shall be sought.

Through the intellect, say some. Gather from every growth of life its seed of thought; look behind every symbol for its law; if thou canst *see* clearly, the rest will follow.

Through the life, say others. Do the best thou knowest to-day. Shrink not from frequent error in this gradual fragmentary state. Follow thy light for as much as it will show thee, be faithful as far as thou canst, in hope that faith presently will lead to sight. Help others, without blaming their need of thy help. Love much and be forgiven.

It needs not intellect, needs not experience, says a third. If you took the true way, your destiny would be accomplished in a purer and more natural order. You would not learn through facts of thought or action, but express through them the certainties of wisdom. In quietness yield thy soul to the causal soul. Do not disturb thy apprenticeship by premature effort; neither check the tide of instruction by methods of thy own. Be still, seek not, but wait in obedience. Thy commission will be given.

Could we indeed say what we want, could we give a description of the child that is lost, he would be found.[9] As soon as the soul can affirm clearly that a certain demonstration is wanted, it is at hand. When the Jewish prophet described the Lamb, as the expression of what was required by the coming era,[10] the time drew nigh. But we say not, see not as yet, clearly, what we would. Those who call for a more triumphant expression of love, a love that cannot be crucified, show not a perfect sense of what has already been given. Love has already been expressed, that made all things new, that gave the worm its place and ministry as well as the eagle; a love to which it was alike to descend into the depths of hell, or to sit at the right hand of the Father.[11]

Yet, no doubt, a new manifestation is at hand, a new hour in the day of man. We cannot expect to see any one sample of completed being, when the mass of men still lie engaged in the sod, or use the freedom of their limbs only with wolfish energy.[12] The tree cannot come to flower till its root be free from the cankering worm, and its whole growth open to air and light. While any one is base, none can be entirely free and noble. Yet something new shall presently be shown of the life of man, for hearts crave, if minds do not know how to ask it.

Among the strains of prophecy, the following, by an earnest mind of a foreign land, written some thirty years ago, is not yet outgrown; and it has the merit of being a positive appeal from the heart, instead of a critical declaration what man should *not* do.

"The ministry of man implies, that he must be filled from the divine fountains which are being engendered through all eternity, so that, at the mere name of his master, he may be able to cast all his enemies into the abyss; that he may deliver all parts of nature from the barriers that imprison them; that he may purge the terrestrial atmosphere from the poisons that infect it; that he may preserve the bodies of men from the corrupt influences that surround, and the maladies that afflict them; still more, that he may keep their souls pure from the malignant insinuations which pollute, and the gloomy images that obscure them; that he may restore its serenity to the Word, which false words of men fill with mourning and sadness; that he may satisfy the desires of the angels, who await from him the development of the marvels of nature; that, in fine, his world may be filled with God, as eternity is." *[13]

Another attempt we will give, by an obscure observer of our own day and country, to draw some lines of the desired image. It was suggested by seeing the design of Crawford's Orpheus,[14] and connecting with the circumstance of the American, in his garret at Rome, making choice of this subject, that of Americans here at home, showing such ambition to represent the character, by calling their prose and verse "Orphic sayings"[15]— "Orphics." We wish we could add that they have shown that musical apprehension of the progress of nature through her ascending gradations which entitled them so to do, but their attempts are frigid, though sometimes grand; in their strain we are not warmed by the fire which fertilized the soil of Greece.

Orpheus was a law-giver by theocratic commission. He understood nature, and made her forms move to his music. He told her secrets in the form of hymns, nature as seen in the mind of God. His soul went forth toward all beings, yet could remain sternly faithful to a chosen type of excellence. Seeking what he loved, he feared not death nor hell, neither could any shape of dread daunt his faith in the power of the celestial harmony that filled his soul.[16]

It seemed significant of the state of things in this country, that the sculptor should have represented the seer at the moment when he was obliged with his hand to shade his eyes.

---

*St. Martin.

Each Orpheus must to the depths descend,
For only thus the Poet can be wise,
   Must make the sad Persephone his friend,[17]
And buried love to second life arise;
   Again his love must lose through too much love,
Must lose his life by living life too true,
   For what he sought below is passed above,
Already done is all that he would do;
   Must tune all being with his single lyre,[18]
Must melt all rocks free from their primal pain,
   Must search all nature with his one soul's fire,
Must bind anew all forms in heavenly chain.
   If he already sees what he must do,
Well may he shade his eyes from the far-shining view.

A better comment could not be made on what is required to perfect man, and place him in that superior position for which he was designed, than by the interpretation of Bacon[19] upon the legends of the Syren coast. When the wise Ulysses passed, says he, he caused his mariners to stop their ears with wax, knowing there was in them no power to resist the lure of that voluptuous song.[20] But he, the much experienced man, who wished to be experienced in all, and use all to the service of wisdom, desired to hear the song that he might understand its meaning. Yet, distrusting his own power to be firm in his better purpose, he caused himself to be bound to the mast, that he might be kept secure against his own weakness. But Orpheus passed unfettered, so absorbed in singing hymns to the gods that he could not even hear those sounds of degrading enchantment.

Meanwhile not a few believe, and men themselves have expressed the opinion, that the time is come when Eurydice is to call for an Orpheus, rather than Orpheus for Eurydice: that the idea of Man, however imperfectly brought out, has been far more so than that of Woman, that she, the other half of the same thought, the other chamber of the heart of life, needs now to take her turn in the full pulsation, and that improvement in the daughters will best aid in the reformation of the sons of this age.

It should be remarked that, as the principle of liberty is better understood, and more nobly interpreted, a broader protest is made in behalf of Woman. As men become aware that few men have had a fair chance, they are inclined to say that no women have had a fair chance. The French Revolution, that strangely disguised angel, bore witness in favor of woman, but interpreted her claims no less ignorantly than those of man. Its idea of happiness did not rise beyond outward enjoyment, unobstructed by the tyranny of others. The title it gave was citoyen, citoyenne,[21] and it is not unimportant to woman that even this species of equality was awarded her. Before, she could be condemned to perish on the scaffold for treason, not as a citizen, but as a subject. The right with which this title then invested a human being, was that of bloodshed and license. The Goddess of Liberty was impure. As we read the poem addressed to her not long since, by Beranger,[22] we can scarcely refrain from tears as painful as the tears of blood that flowed when "such crimes were committed in her name." Yes! man, born to purify and animate the unintelligent and the cold, can, in his madness, degrade and pollute no less the fair and the chaste. Yet truth was prophesied in the ravings of that hideous fever, caused by long ignorance and abuse. Europe is conning a valued lesson from the blood-stained page. The same tendencies, farther unfolded, will bear good fruit in this country.

Yet, by men in this country, as by the Jews, when Moses was leading them to the promised land, every thing has been done that inherited depravity could do, to hinder the promise of heaven from its fulfilment. The cross here as elsewhere, has been planted only to be blasphemed by cruelty and fraud. The name of the Prince of Peace has been profaned by all kinds of injustice toward the Gentile whom he said he came to save. But I need not speak of what has been done towards the red man, the black man. Those deeds are the scoff of the world; and they have been accompanied by such pious words that the gentlest would not dare to intercede with "Father, forgive them, for they know not what they do."[23]

Here, as elsewhere, the gain of creation consists always in the growth of individual minds, which live and aspire, as flowers bloom and birds sing, in the midst of morasses; and in the continual development of that thought, the thought of human destiny, which is given to eternity adequately to express, and which ages of failure only seemingly impede. Only seemingly, and whatever seems to the contrary, this country is as surely destined to elucidate a great moral law, as Europe was to promote the mental culture of man.

Though the national independence be blurred by the servility of individuals, though freedom and equality have been proclaimed only to leave room for a monstrous display of slave-dealing and slave-keeping; though the free American so often feels himself free, like the Roman, only to pamper his appetites and his indolence through the misery of his fellow beings, still it is not in vain, that the verbal statement has been made, "All men are born free and equal."[24] There it stands, a golden certainty wherewith to encourage the good, to shame the bad. The new world may be called clearly to perceive that it incurs the utmost penalty, if it reject or oppress the sorrowful brother. And, if men are deaf, the angels hear. But men cannot be deaf. It is inevitable that an external freedom, an independence of the encroachments of other men, such as has been achieved for the nation, should be so also for every member of it. That which has once been clearly conceived in the intelligence cannot fail sooner or later to be acted out. It has become a law as irrevocable as that of the Medes in their ancient dominion; men will privately sin against it, but the law, as expressed by a leading mind of the age,[25]

> "Tutti fatti a sembianza d'un Solo,
> Figli tutti d'un solo riscatto,
> In qual'ora, in qual parte del suolo
> Trascorriamo quest' aura vital,
> Siam fratelli, siam stretti ad un patto:
> Maladetto colui cho lo infrango,
> Che s'innalza sul fiacco che piange
> Che contrista uno spirto immortal."*

> "All made in the likeness of the One,
> All children of one ransom,
> In whatever hour, in whatever part of the soil,
> We draw this vital air,
> We are brothers; we must be bound by one compact,
> Accursed he who infringes it,
> Who raises himself upon the weak who weep,
> Who saddens an immortal spirit."

This law cannot fail of universal recognition. Accursed be he who willingly saddens an immortal spirit, doomed to infamy in later, wiser ages, doomed in future stages of his own being to deadly penance, only short of death. Accursed be he who sins in ignorance, if that ignorance be caused by sloth.

We sicken no less at the pomp than the strife of words. We feel that never were lungs so puffed with the wind of declamation, on moral and religious subjects, as now. We are tempted to implore these "word-

---

*Manzoni.

heroes," these word-Catos, word-Christs, to beware of cant* above all things; to remember that hypocrisy is the most hopeless as well as the meanest of crimes, and that those must surely be polluted by it, who do not reserve a part of their morality and religion for private use. Landor[26] says that he cannot have a great deal of mind who cannot afford to let the larger part of it lie fallow, and what is true of genius is not less so of virtue. The tongue is a valuable member, but should appropriate but a small part of the vital juices that are needful all over the body. We feel that the mind may "grow black and rancid in the smoke" even "of altars." We start up from the harangue to go into our closet and shut the door. There inquires the spirit, "Is this rhetoric the bloom of healthy blood or a false pigment artfully laid on ?" And yet again we know where is so much smoke, must be some fire; with so much talk about virtue and freedom, must be mingled some desire for them; that it cannot be in vain that such have become the common topics of conversation among men, rather than schemes for tyranny and plunder, that the very newspapers see it best to proclaim themselves Pilgrims, Puritans, Heralds of Holiness. The king that maintains so costly a retinue cannot be a mere boast, or Carabbas fiction.[27] We have waited here long in the dust; we are tired and hungry, but the triumphal procession must appear at last.

Of all its banners, none has been more steadily upheld, and under none have more valor and willingness for real sacrifices been shown, than that of the champions of the enslaved African. And this band it is, which, partly from a natural following out of principles, partly because many women have been prominent in that cause, makes, just now, the warmest appeal in behalf of woman.

Though there has been a growing liberality on this subject, yet society at large is not so prepared for the demands of this party, but that they are and will be for some time, coldly regarded as the Jacobins[28] of their day.

"Is it not enough," cries the irritated trader, "that you have done all you could to break up the national union, and thus destroy the prosperity of our country, but now you must be trying to break up family union, to take my wife away from the cradle and the kitchen hearth to vote at polls, and preach from a pulpit? Of course, if she does such things, she cannot

---

*Dr. Johnson's one piece of advice should be written on every door; "Clear your mind of cant." But Byron, to whom it was so acceptable, in clearing away the noxious vine, shook down the building. Sterling's emendation is worthy of honor:

"Realize your cant, not cast it off."[29]

attend to those of her own sphere. She is happy enough as she is. She has more leisure than I have, every means of improvement, every indulgence."

"Have you asked her whether she was satisfied with these indulgences?" [30]

"No, but I know she is. She is too amiable to wish what would make me unhappy, and too judicious to wish to step beyond the sphere of her sex. I will never consent to have our peace disturbed by any such discussions."

"'Consent—you?' it is not consent from you that is in question, it is assent from your wife."

"Am not I the head of my house?"

"You are not the head of your wife. God has given her a mind of her own."

"I am the head and she the heart."

"God grant you play true to one another then. I suppose I am to be grateful that you did not say she was only the hand. If the head represses no natural pulse of the heart, there can be no question as to your giving your consent. Both will be of one accord, and there needs but to present any question to get a full and true answer. There is no need of precaution, of indulgence, or consent. But our doubt is whether the heart does consent with the head, or only obeys its decrees with a passiveness that precludes the exercise of its natural powers, or a repugnance that turns sweet qualities to bitter, or a doubt that lays waste the fair occasions of life. It is to ascertain the truth, that we propose some liberating measures."

Thus vaguely are these questions proposed and discussed at present. But their being proposed at all implies much thought and suggests more. Many women are considering within themselves, what they need that they have not, and what they can have, if they find they need it. Many men are considering whether women are capable of being and having more than they are and have, *and,* whether, if so, it will be best to consent to improvement in their condition.

This morning, I open the Boston "Daily Mail," and find in its "poet's corner," a translation of Schiller's "Dignity of Woman." [31] In the advertisement of a book on America, I see in the table of contents this sequence, "Republican Institutions. American Slavery. American Ladies."

I open the "*Deutsche Schnellpost,*" [32] published in New-York, and find at the head of a column, *Juden und Frauen-emancipation in Ungarn.* Emancipation of Jews and Women in Hungary.

The past year has seen action in the Rhode-Island legislature, to

(281)398-9561

secure married women rights over their own property, where men showed that a very little examination of the subject could teach them much; an article in the Democratic Review on the same subject more largely considered,[33] written by a woman, impelled, it is said, by glaring wrong to a distinguished friend having shown the defects in the existing laws, and the state of opinion from which they spring; and an answer from the revered old man, J. Q. Adams, in some respects the Phocion[34] of his time, to an address made him by some ladies. To this last I shall again advert in another place.

These symptoms of the times have come under my view quite accidentally: one who seeks, may, each month or week, collect more.

The numerous party, whose opinions are already labelled and adjusted too much to their mind to admit of any new light, strive, by lectures on some model-woman of bride-like beauty and gentleness, by writing and lending little treatises, intended to mark out with precision the limits of woman's sphere, and woman's mission, to prevent other than the rightful shepherd from climbing the wall, or the flock from using any chance to go astray.

Without enrolling ourselves at once on either side, let us look upon the subject from the best point of view which to-day offers. No better, it is to be feared, than a high house-top. A high hill-top, or at least a cathedral spire, would be desirable.

It may well be an Anti-Slavery party that pleads for woman, if we consider merely that she does not hold property on equal terms with men; so that, if a husband dies without making a will, the wife, instead of taking at once his place as head of the family, inherits only a part of his fortune, often brought him by herself, as if she were a child, or ward only, not an equal partner.

We will not speak of the innumerable instances in which profligate and idle men live upon the earnings of industrious wives; or if the wives leave them, and take with them the children, to perform the double duty of mother and father, follow from place to place, and threaten to rob them of the children, if deprived of the rights of a husband, as they call them, planting themselves in their poor lodgings, frightening them into paying tribute by taking from them the children, running into debt at the expense of these otherwise so overtasked helots. Such instances count up by scores within my own memory. I have seen the husband who had stained himself by a long course of low vice, till his wife was wearied from her heroic forgiveness, by finding that his treachery made it useless, and that if she would provide bread for herself and her children, she must be separate

257

from his ill fame. I have known this man come to instal himself in the chamber of a woman who loathed him and say she should never take food without his company. I have known these men steal their children whom they knew they had no means to maintain, take them into dissolute company, expose them to bodily danger, to frighten the poor woman, to whom, it seems, the fact that she alone had borne the pangs of their birth, and nourished their infancy, does not give an equal right to them. I do believe that this mode of kidnapping, and it is frequent enough in all classes of society, will be by the next age viewed as it is by Heaven now, and that the man who avails himself of the shelter of men's laws to steal from a mother her own children, or arrogate any superior right in them, save that of superior virtue, will bear the stigma he deserves, in common with him who steals grown men from their mother land, their hopes, and their homes.

I said, we will not speak of this now, yet I have spoken, for the subject makes me feel too much. I could give instances that would startle the most vulgar and callous, but I will not, for the public opinion of their own sex is already against such men, and where cases of extreme tyranny are made known, there is private action in the wife's favor. But she ought not to need this, nor, I think, can she long. Men must soon see that, on their own ground, that woman is the weaker party, she ought to have legal protection, which would make such oppression impossible. But I would not deal with "atrocious instances" except in the way of illustration, neither demand from men a partial redress in some one matter, but go to the root of the whole. If principles could be established, particulars would adjust themselves aright. Ascertain the true destiny of woman, give her legitimate hopes, and a standard within herself; marriage and all other relations would by degrees be harmonized with these.

But to return to the historical progress of this matter. Knowing that there exists in the minds of men a tone of feeling towards women as towards slaves, such as is expressed in the common phrase, "Tell that to women and children," that the infinite soul can only work through them in already ascertained limits; that the gift of reason, man's highest prerogative, is allotted to them in much lower degree; that they must be kept from mischief and melancholy by being constantly engaged in active labor, which is to be furnished and directed by those better able to think, &c. &c.; we need not multiply instances, for who can review the experience of last week without recalling words which imply, whether in jest or earnest, these views or views like these; knowing this, can we wonder that many reformers think that measures are not likely to be taken in behalf of women, unless their wishes could be publicly represented by women?

That can never be necessary, cry the other side. All men are privately influenced by women; each has his wife, sister, or female friends, and is too much biased by these relations to fail of representing their interests, and, if this is not enough, let them propose and enforce their wishes with the pen. The beauty of home would be destroyed, the delicacy of the sex be violated, the dignity of halls of legislation degraded by an attempt to introduce them there. Such duties are inconsistent with those of a mother; and then we have ludicrous pictures of ladies in hysterics at the polls, and senate chambers filled with cradles.

But if, in reply, we admit as truth that woman seems destined by nature rather for the inner circle, we must add that the arrangements of civilized life have not been, as yet, such as to secure it to her. Her circle, if the duller, is not the quieter. If kept from "excitement," she is not from drudgery. Not only the Indian squaw carries the burdens of the camp, but the favorites of Louis the Fourteenth accompany him in his journeys, and the washerwoman stands at her tub and carries home her work at all seasons, and in all states of health. Those who think the physical circumstances of woman would make a part in the affairs of national government unsuitable, are by no means those who think it impossible for the negresses to endure field work, even during pregnancy, or the sempstresses to go through their killing labors.

As to the use of the pen, there was quite as much opposition to woman's possessing herself of that help to free agency, as there is now to her seizing on the rostrum or the desk; and she is likely to draw, from a permission to plead her cause that way, opposite inferences to what might be wished by those who now grant it.

As to the possibility of her filling with grace and dignity, any such position, we should think those who had seen the great actresses, and heard the Quaker preachers of modern times,[35] would not doubt, that woman can express publicly the fulness of thought and creation, without losing any of the peculiar beauty of her sex. What can pollute and tarnish is to act thus from any motive except that something needs to be said or done. Women could take part in the processions, the songs, the dances of old religion; no one fancied their delicacy was impaired by appearing in public for such a cause.

As to her home, she is not likely to leave it more than she now does for balls, theatres, meetings for promoting missions, revival meetings, and others to which she flies, in hope of an animation for her existence, commensurate with what she sees enjoyed by men. Governors of ladies' fairs are no less engrossed by such a change, than the Governor of the state by his; presidents of Washingtonian societies no less away from home than presidents of conventions. If men look straitly to it, they will find that, unless their lives are domestic, those of the women will not be. A house is no home unless it contain food and fire for the mind as well as for the body. The female Greek, of our day, is as much in the street as the male to cry, What news? We doubt not it was the same in Athens of old. The women, shut out from the market place, made up for it at the religious festivals. For human beings are not so constituted that they can live without expansion. If they do not get it one way, they must another, or perish.

As to men's representing women fairly at present, while we hear from men who owe to their wives not only all that is comfortable or graceful, but all that is wise in the arrangement of their lives, the frequent remark, "You cannot reason with a woman," when from those of delicacy, nobleness, and poetic culture, the contemptuous phrase "women and children," and that in no light sally of the hour, but in works intended to give a permanent statement of the best experiences, when not one man, in the million, shall I say? no, not in the hundred million, can rise above the belief that woman was made *for man,* when such traits as these are daily forced upon the attention, can we feel that man will always do justice to the interests of woman? Can we think that he takes a sufficiently discerning and religious view of her office and destiny, *ever* to do her justice, except when prompted by sentiment, accidentally or transiently, that is, for the sentiment will vary according to the relations in which he is placed. The lover, the poet, the artist, are likely to view her nobly. The father and the philosopher have some chance of liberality; the man of the world, the legislator for expediency, none.

Under these circumstances, without attaching importance, in themselves, to the changes demanded by the champions of woman, we hail them as signs of the times. We would have every arbitrary barrier thrown down. We would have every path laid open to woman as freely as to man. Were this done and a slight temporary fermentation allowed to subside, we should see crystallizations more pure and of more various beauty. We believe the divine energy would pervade nature to a degree unknown in the history of former ages, and that no discordant collision, but a ravishing harmony of the spheres would ensue.

Yet, then and only then, will mankind be ripe for this, when inward and outward freedom for woman as much as for man shall be acknowledged as a right, not yielded as a concession. As the friend of the negro assumes that one man cannot by right, hold another in bondage, so should the friend of woman assume that man cannot, by right, lay even well-meant restrictions on woman. If the negro be a soul, if the woman be a soul, appareled in flesh, to one Master only are they accountable. There is but one law for souls, and if there is to be an interpreter of it, he must come not as man, or son of man, but as son of God.

Were thought and feeling once so far elevated that man should esteem himself the brother and friend, but nowise the lord and tutor of woman, were he really bound with her in equal worship, arrangements as to function and employment would be of no consequence. What woman needs is not as a woman to act or rule, but as a nature to grow, as an intellect to discern, as soul to live freely and unimpeded, to unfold such powers as were given her when we left our common home. If fewer talents were given her, yet if allowed the free and full employment of these, so that she may render back to the giver his own with usury[36] she will not complain; nay I dare to say she will bless and rejoice in her earthly birth-place, her earthly lot. Let us consider what obstructions impede this good era, and what signs give reason to hope that it draws near.

I was talking on this subject with Miranda, a woman, who, if any in the world could, might speak without heat and bitterness of the position of her sex. Her father was a man who cherished no sentimental reverence for woman, but a firm belief in the equality of the sexes. She was his eldest child, and came to him at an age when he needed a companion. From the time she could speak and go alone, he addressed her not as a plaything, but as a living mind. Among the few verses he ever wrote was a copy addressed to this child, when the first locks were cut from her head, and the reverence expressed on this occasion for that cherished head, he never belied. It was to him the temple of immortal intellect. He respected his child, however, too much to be an indulgent parent. He called on her for clear judgment, for courage, for honor and fidelity; in short, for such virtues as he knew. In so far as he possessed the keys to the wonders of this universe, he allowed free use of them to her, and by the incentive of a high expectation, he forbade, as far as possible, that she should let the privilege lie idle.[37]

Thus this child was early led to feel herself a child of the spirit. She took her place easily, not only in the world of organized being, but in the world of mind. A dignified sense of self-dependence was given as all her portion, and she found it a sure anchor. Herself securely anchored, her relations with others were established with equal security. She was fortunate in a total absence of those charms which might have drawn to her bewildering flatteries, and in a strong electric nature, which repelled those who did not belong to her, and attracted those who did.[38] With men and women her relations were noble, affectionate without passion, intellectual without coldness. The world was free to her, and she lived freely in it. Outward adversity came, and inward conflict, but that faith and self-respect had early been awakened which must always lead at last, to an outward serenity and an inward peace.

Of Miranda I had always thought as an example, that the restraints upon the sex were insuperable only to those who think them so, or who noisily strive to break them. She had taken a course of her own, and no man stood in her way. Many of her acts had been unusual, but excited no uproar. Few helped, but none checked her, and the many men, who knew her mind and her life, showed to her confidence, as to a brother, gentleness as to a sister. And not only refined, but very coarse men approved and aided one in whom they saw resolution and clearness of design. Her mind was often the leading one, always effective.

When I talked with her upon these matters, and had said very much what I have written, she smilingly replied: "and yet we must admit that I have been fortunate, and this should not be. My good father's early trust gave the first bias, and the rest followed of course. It is true that I have had less outward aid, in after years, than most women, but that is of little consequence. Religion was early awakened in my soul, a sense that what the soul is capable to ask it must attain, and that, though I might be aided and instructed by others, I must depend on myself as the only constant friend. This self dependence, which was honored in me, is deprecated as a fault in most women. They are taught to learn their rule from without, not to unfold it from within.

"This is the fault of man, who is still vain, and wishes to be more important to woman than, by right, he should be."

"Men have not shown this disposition toward you," I said.

"No! because the position I early was enabled to take was one of self-reliance.[39] And were all women as sure of their wants as I was, the result would be the same. But they are so overloaded with precepts by guardians, who think that nothing is so much to be dreaded for a woman as originality of thought or character, that their minds are impeded by doubts till they lose their chance of fair free proportions. The difficulty is to get them to the point from which they shall naturally develope self-respect, and learn self-help.

"Once I thought that men would help to forward this state of things more than I do now. I saw so many of them wretched in the connections they had formed in weakness and vanity. They seemed so glad to esteem women whenever they could.

"The soft arms of affection," said one of the most discerning spirits, "will not suffice for me, unless on them I see the steel bracelets of strength."

But early I perceived that men never, in any extreme of despair, wished to be women. On the contrary they were ever ready to taunt one another at any sign of weakness with,

"Art thou not like the women, who"—

The passage ends various ways, according to the occasion and rhetoric of the speaker. When they admired any woman they were inclined to speak of her as "above her sex." Silently I observed this, and feared it argued a rooted scepticism, which for ages had been fastening on the heart, and which only an age of miracles could eradicate. Ever I have been treated with great sincerity; and I look upon it as a signal instance of this, that an intimate friend of the other sex said, in a fervent moment, that I "deserved in some star to be a man." He was much surprised when I disclosed my view of my position and hopes, when I declared my faith that the feminine side, the side of love, of beauty, of holiness, was now to have its full chance, and that, if either were better, it was better now to be a woman, for even the slightest achievement of good was furthering an especial work of our time. He smiled incredulous. "She makes the best she can of it," thought he. "Let Jews believe the pride of Jewry, but I am of the better sort, and know better."

Another used as highest praise, in speaking of a character in literature, the words "a manly woman."

So in the noble passage of Ben Jonson:

"I meant the day-star should not brighter ride,
  Nor shed like influence from its lucent seat;
I meant she should be courteous, facile, sweet,
  Free from that solemn vice of greatness, pride;
I meant each softest virtue there should meet,
  Fit in that softer bosom to abide,

Only a learned and a *manly* soul,
    I purposed her, that should with even powers,
The rock, the spindle, and the shears control
    Of destiny, and spin her own free hours." [40]

"Methinks," said I, "you are too fastidious in objecting to this. Jonson in using the word 'manly' only meant to heighten the picture of this, the true, the intelligent fate, with one of the deeper colors." 'And yet,' said she, 'so invariable is the use of this word where a heroic quality is to be described, and I feel so sure that persistence and courage are the most womanly no less than the most manly qualities, that I would exchange these words for others of a larger sense at the risk of marring the fine tissue of the verse. Read, 'a heavenward and instructed soul,' and I should be satisfied. Let it not be said, wherever there is energy or creative genius, 'She has a masculine mind.''

This by no means argues a willing want of generosity toward woman. Man is as generous toward her, as he knows how to be.

Wherever she has herself arisen in national or private history, and nobly shone forth in any form of excellence, men have received her, not only willingly, but with triumph. Their encomiums indeed, are always, in some sense, mortifying; they show too much surprise. Can this be you? he cries to the transfigured Cinderella; well I should never have thought it, but I am very glad. We will tell every one that you have "*surpassed your sex*."

In every-day life the feelings of the many are stained with vanity. Each wishes to be lord in a little world, to be superior at least over one; and he does not feel strong enough to retain a life-long ascendancy over a strong nature. Only a Theseus could conquer before he wed the Amazonian Queen. Hercules wished rather to rest with Dejanira, and received the poisoned robe, as a fit guerdon. [41] The tale should be interpreted to all those who seek repose with the weak.

But not only is man vain and fond of power, but the same want of development, which thus affects him morally, prevents his intellectually discerning the destiny of woman. The boy wants no woman, but only a girl to play ball with him, and mark his pocket handkerchief.

Thus, in Schiller's Dignity of Woman, beautiful as the poem is, there is no "grave and perfect man," but only a great boy to be softened and restrained by the influence of girls. Poets, the elder brothers of their race, have usually seen farther; but what can you expect of every-day men, if Schiller was not more prophetic as to what women must be? Even with

Richter,[42] one foremost thought about a wife was that she would "cook him something good." But as this is a delicate subject, and we are in constant danger of being accused of slighting what are called "the functions," let me say in behalf of Miranda and myself, that we have high respect for those who cook something good, who create and preserve fair order in houses, and prepare therein the shining raiment for worthy inmates, worthy guests. Only these "functions" must not be a drudgery, or enforced necessity, but a part of life. Let Ulysses drive the beeves home while Penelope there piles up the fragrant loaves; they are both well employed if these be done in thought and love, willingly. But Penelope is no more meant for a baker or weaver solely, than Ulysses for a cattle-herd.

The sexes should not only correspond to and appreciate, but prophesy to one another. In individual instances this happens. Two persons love in one another the future good which they aid one another to unfold. This is imperfectly or rarely done in the general life. Man has gone but little way; now he is waiting to see whether woman can keep step with him, but instead of calling out, like a good brother, "you can do it, if you only think so," or impersonally; "any one can do what he tries to do;" he often discourages with school-boy brag: "Girls can't do that; girls can't play ball." But let any one defy their taunts, break through and be brave and secure, they rend the air with shouts.

This fluctuation was obvious in a narrative I have lately seen, the story of the life of Countess Emily Plater, the heroine of the last revolution in Poland.[43] The dignity, the purity, the concentrated resolve, the calm, deep enthusiasm, which yet could, when occasion called, sparkle up a holy, an indignant fire, make of this young maiden the figure I want for my frontispiece. Her portrait is to be seen in the book, a gentle shadow of her soul. Short was the career—like the maid of Orleans,[44] she only did enough to verify her credentials, and then passed from a scene on which she was, probably, a premature apparition.

When the young girl joined the army where the report of her exploits had preceded her, she was received in a manner that marks the usual state of feeling. Some of the officers were disappointed at her quiet manners; that she had not the air and tone of a stage-heroine. They thought she could not have acted heroically unless in buskins; had no idea that such deeds only showed the habit of her mind. Others talked of the delicacy of her sex, advised her to withdraw from perils and dangers, and had no comprehension of the feelings within her breast that made this impossible. The gentle irony of her reply to these self-constituted tutors, (not one of whom showed himself her equal in conduct or reason,) is as good as her indignant reproof at a later period to the general, whose perfidy ruined all.

But though, to the mass of these men, she was an embarrassment and a puzzle, the nobler sort viewed her with a tender enthusiasm worthy of her. "Her name," said her biographer, "is known throughout Europe. I paint her character that she may be as widely loved."

With pride, he shows her freedom from all personal affections; that, though tender and gentle in an uncommon degree, there was no room for a private love in her consecrated life. She inspired those who knew her with a simple energy of feeling like her own. We have seen, they felt, a woman worthy the name, capable of all sweet affections, capable of stern virtue.

It is a fact worthy of remark, that all these revolutions in favor of liberty have produced female champions that share the same traits, but Emily alone has found a biographer. Only a near friend could have performed for her this task, for the flower was reared in feminine seclusion, and the few and simple traits of her history before her appearance in the field could only have been known to the domestic circle. Her biographer has gathered them up with a brotherly devotion.

No! man is not willingly ungenerous. He wants faith and love, because he is not yet himself an elevated being. He cries, with sneering skepticism, Give us a sign. But if the sign appears, his eyes glisten, and he offers not merely approval, but homage.

The severe nation which taught that the happiness of the race was forfeited through the fault of a woman, and showed its thought of what sort of regard man owed her, by making him accuse her on the first question to his God; who gave her to the patriarch as a handmaid, and by the Mosaical law, bound her to allegiance like a self; even they greeted, with solemn rapture, all great and holy women as heroines, prophetesses, judges in Israel; and if they made Eve listen to the serpent, gave Mary as a bride to the Holy Spirit.[45] In other nations it has been the same down to our day. To the woman who could conquer, a triumph was awarded. And not only those whose strength was recommended to the heart by association with goodness and beauty, but those who were bad, if they were steadfast and strong, had their claims allowed. In any age a Semiramis, an Elizabeth of England, a Catharine of Russia,[46] makes her place good, whether in a large or small circle. How has a little wit, a little genius, been celebrated in a woman! What an intellectual triumph was that of the lonely Aspasia,[47] and how heartily acknowledged! She, indeed, met a Pericles. But what annalist, the rudest of men, the most plebeian of husbands, will spare from his page one of the few anecdotes of Roman women—Sappho! Eloisa![48] The names are of threadbare celebrity. Indeed they were not more suitably met in their own time than the Countess Colonel Plater on her first joining the army. They had much to mourn, and their great impulses did not find due scope. But with time enough, space enough, their kindred appear on the scene. Across the ages, forms lean, trying to touch the hem of their retreating robes. The youth here by my side cannot be weary of the fragments from the life of Sappho. He will not believe they are not addressed to himself, or that he to whom they were addressed could be ungrateful. A recluse of high powers devotes himself to understand and explain the thought of Eloisa; he asserts her vast superiority in soul and genius to her master; he curses the fate that cast his lot in another age than hers. He could have understood her: he would have been to her a friend, such as Abelard never could. And this one woman he could have loved and reverenced, and she, alas! lay cold in her grave hundreds of years ago. His sorrow is truly pathetic. These responses that come too late to give joy are as tragic as any thing we know, and yet the tears of later ages glitter as they fall on Tasso's prison bars.[49] And we know how elevating to the captive is the security that somewhere an intelligence must answer to this.

The man habitually most narrow towards women will be flushed, as by the worst assault on Christianity, if you say it has made no improvement in her condition. Indeed, those most opposed to new acts in her favor, are jealous of the reputation of those which have been done.

We will not speak of the enthusiasm excited by actresses, improvisatrici, female singers, for here mingles the charm of beauty and grace; but female authors, even learned women, if not insufferably ugly and slovenly, from the Italian professor's daughter, who taught behind the curtain, down to Mrs. Carter and Madame Dacier,[50] are sure of an admiring audience, and what is far better, chance to use what they have learned, and to learn more, if they can once get a platform on which to stand.

But how to get this platform, or how to make it of reasonably easy access is the difficulty. Plants of great vigor will almost always struggle into blossom, despite impediments. But there should be encouragement, and a free genial atmosphere for those of more timid sort, fair play for each in its own kind. Some are like the little, delicate flowers which love to hide in the dripping mosses, by the sides of mountain torrents, or in the shade of tall trees. But others require an open field, a rich and loosened soil, or they never show their proper hues.

It may be said that man does not have his fair play either; his energies are repressed and distorted by the interposition of artificial obstacles. Ay, but he himself has put them there; they have grown out of his own imperfections. If there *is* a misfortune in woman's lot, it is in obstacles being interposed by men, which do *not* mark her state; and, if they express her past ignorance, do not her present needs. As every man is of woman born, she has slow but sure means of redress, yet the sooner a general justness of thought makes smooth the path, the better.

Man is of woman born, and her face bends over him in infancy with an expression he can never quite forget. Eminent men have delighted to pay tribute to this image, and it is an hacknied observation, that most men of genius boast some remarkable development in the mother. The rudest tar brushes off a tear with his coat-sleeve at the hallowed name. The other day, I met a decrepit old man of seventy, on a journey, who challenged the stage-company to guess where he was going. They guessed aright, "To see your mother." "Yes," said he, "she is ninety-two, but has good eye-sight still, they say. I have not seen her these forty years, and I thought I could not die in peace without." I should have liked his picture painted as a companion piece to that of a boisterous little boy, whom I saw attempt to declaim at a school exhibition—

> "O that those lips had language. Life has passed
> With me but roughly since I heard thee last."[51]

He got but very little way before sudden tears shamed him from the stage.

Some gleams of the same expression which shone down upon his infancy, angelically pure and benign, visit man again with hopes of pure love, of a holy marriage. Or, if not before, in the eyes of the mother of his child they again are seen, and dim fancies pass before his mind, that woman may not have been born for him alone, but have come from heaven, a commissioned soul, a messenger of truth and love; that she can only make for him a home in which he may lawfully repose, in so far as she is

> "True to the kindred points of Heaven and home."[52]

In gleams, in dim fancies, this thought visits the mind of common men. It is soon obscured by the mists of sensuality, the dust of routine, and he thinks it was only some meteor, or ignis fatuus[53] that shone. But, as a Rosicrucian lamp,[54] it burns unwearied, though condemned to the solitude of tombs; and to its permanent life, as to every truth, each age has in some form borne witness. For the truths, which visit the minds of careless men only in fitful gleams, shine with radiant clearness into those of the poet, the priest, and the artist.

Whatever may have been the domestic manners of the ancients, the idea of woman was nobly manifested in their mythologies and poems, where she appears as Sita in the Ramayana, a form of tender purity, as the Egyptian Isis,* of divine wisdom never yet surpassed. In Egypt, too, the Sphynx,[55] walking the earth with lion tread, looked out upon its marvels in the calm, inscrutable beauty of a virgin's face, and the Greek could only add wings to the great emblem. In Greece, Ceres, and Proserpine,[56] significantly termed "the great goddesses," were seen seated, side by side. They needed not to rise for any worshipper or any change; they were prepared for all things, as those initiated to their mysteries knew. More obvious is the meaning of these three forms, the Diana, Minerva, and Vesta.[57] Unlike in the expression of their beauty, but alike in this,—that each was self-sufficing. Other forms were only accessories and illustrations, none the complement to one like these. Another might, indeed, be the companion, and the Apollo and Diana set off one another's beauty. Of the Vesta, it is to be observed, that not only deep-eyed, deep-discerning Greece, but ruder Rome, who represents the only form of good man, (the always busy warrior), that could be indifferent to woman, confided the permanence of its glory to a tutelary goddess, and her wisest legislator spoke of meditation as a nymph.

Perhaps in Rome the neglect of woman was a reaction on the manners of Etruria, where the priestess Queen, warrior Queen, would seem to have been so usual a character.

An instance of the noble Roman marriage, where the stern and calm nobleness of the nation was common to both, we see in the historic page through the little that is told us of Brutus and Portia. Shakspeare has seized on the relation in its native lineaments, harmonizing the particular with the universal; and, while it is conjugal love, and no other, making it unlike the same relation, as seen in Cymbeline, or Othello, even as one star differeth from another in glory.

"By that great vow
Which did incorporate and make us one,

---

* For an adequate description of the Isis, see Appendix A.

Unfold to me, yourself, your half,
Why you are heavy. * * *
             Dwell I but in the suburbs
Of your good pleasure? If it be no more,
Portia is Brutus' harlot, not his wife."

Mark the sad majesty of his tone in answer. Who would not have lent a life-long credence to that voice of honor?

"You are my true and honorable wife,
    As dear to me as are the ruddy drops
    That visit this sad heart."

It is the same voice that tells the moral of his life in the last words—

"Countrymen,
My heart doth joy, that yet in all my life,
I found no man but he was true to me."

It was not wonderful that it should be so.

Shakespeare, however, was not content to let Portia rest her plea for confidence on the essential nature of the marriage bond;

"I grant I am a woman; but withal,
  A woman that lord Brutus took to wife.
I grant that I am a woman; but withal,
  A woman well reputed—Cato's daughter.
Think you I am *no stronger than my sex,*
Being so fathered and so husbanded?"

And afterwards in the very scene where Brutus is suffering under that "insupportable and touching loss," the death of his wife, Cassius pleads—

"Have you not love enough to bear with me,
When that rash humor which my mother gave me
Makes me forgetful?
Brutus.—Yes, Cassius; and henceforth,
When you are over-earnest with your Brutus,
He'll think your mother chides and leave you so." [58]

As indeed it was a frequent belief among the ancients, as with our Indians, that the *body* was inherited from the mother, the *soul* from the father. As in that noble passage of Ovid, already quoted, where Jupiter, as his divine synod are looking down on the funeral pyre of Hercules, thus triumphs—

> Nic nisi *maternâ* Vulcanum parte potentem.
> Sentiet. Aeternum est, à me quod traxit, et expers
> At que immune necis, nullaque domabile flamma
> Idque ego defunctum terrâ cœlestibus oris
> Accipiam, cunctisque meum lætabile factum
> Dis fore confido.
> "The part alone of gross *maternal* frame
> Fire shall devour, while that from me he drew
> Shall live immortal and its force renew;
> That, when he's dead, I'll raise to realms above;
> Let all the powers the righteous act approve." [59]

It is indeed a god speaking of his union with an earthly woman, but it expresses the common Roman thought as to marriage, the same which permitted a man to lend his wife to a friend, as if she were a chattel.

> "She dwelt but in the suburbs of his good pleasure." [60]

Yet the same city as I have said leaned on the worship of Vesta, the Preserver, and in later times was devoted to that of Isis. In Sparta, thought, in this respect as in all others, was expressed in the characters of real life, and the women of Sparta were as much Spartans as the men. The citoyen, citoyenne of France was here actualized. Was not the calm equality they enjoyed as honorable as the devotion of chivalry? They intelligently shared the ideal life of their nation.

Like the men they felt

> "Honor gone, all's gone,
> Better never have been born."

They were the true friends of men. The Spartan, surely, would not think that he received only his body from his mother. The sage, had he lived in that community, could not have thought the souls of "vain and foppish men will be degraded after death, to the forms of women, and, if they do not there make great efforts to retrieve themselves, will become birds."

(By the way it is very expressive of the hard intellectuality of the merely *mannish* mind, to speak thus of birds, chosen always by the *feminine* poet as the symbols of his fairest thoughts.)

We are told of the Greek nations in general, that woman occupied there an infinitely lower place than man. It is difficult to believe this when we see such range and dignity of thought on the subject in the mythologies, and find the poets producing such ideals as Cassandra, Iphiginia, Antigone, Macaria,[61] where Sibylline priestesses told the oracle of the highest god, and he could not be content to reign with a court of fewer than nine muses. Even victory wore a female form.

But whatever were the facts of daily life, I cannot complain of the age and nation, which represents its thought by such a symbol as I see before me at this moment. It is a zodiac of the busts of gods and goddesses, arranged in pairs. The circle breathes the music of a heavenly order. Male and female heads are distinct in expression, but equal in beauty, strength and calmness. Each male head is that of a brother and a king—each female of a sister and a queen. Could the thought, thus expressed, be lived out, there would be nothing more to be desired. There would be unison in variety, congeniality in difference.

Coming nearer our own time, we find religion and poetry no less true in their revelations. The rude man, just disengaged from the sod, the Adam, accuses woman to his God, and records her disgrace to their posterity. He is not ashamed to write that he could be drawn from heaven by one beneath him, one made, he says, from but a small part of himself. But in the same nation, educated by time, instructed by a succession of prophets, we find woman in as high a position as she has ever occupied. No figure that has ever arisen to greet our eyes has been received with more fervent reverence than that of the Madonna. Heine calls her the *Dame du Comptoir*[62] of the Catholic church, and this jeer well expresses a serious truth.

And not only this holy and significant image was worshipped by the pilgrim, and the favorite subject of the artist, but it exercised an immediate influence on the destiny of the sex. The empresses who embraced the cross, converted sons and husbands. Whole calendars of female saints, heroic dames of chivalry, binding the emblem of faith on the heart of the best-beloved, and wasting the bloom of youth in separation and loneliness, for the sake of duties they thought it religion to assume, with innumerable forms of poesy, trace their lineage to this one. Nor, however imperfect may be the action, in our day, of the faith thus expressed, and though we can scarcely think it nearer this ideal, than that of India or Greece was near their ideal, is it in vain that the truth has been recognized, that woman is not only a part of man, bone of his bone, and flesh of his flesh, born that men might not be lonely, but that women are in themselves possessors of and possessed by immortal souls. This truth undoubtedly received a greater outward stability from the belief of the church that the earthly parent of the Saviour of souls was a woman.

The assumption of the Virgin, as painted by sublime artists, Petrarch's Hymn to the Madonna,*[63] cannot have spoken to the world wholly without result, yet, oftentimes those who had ears heard not.

See upon the nations the influence of this powerful example. In Spain look only at the ballads. Woman in these is "very woman;" she is the betrothed, the bride, the spouse of man, there is on her no hue of the philosopher, the heroine, the savante, but she looks great and noble; why? because she is also, through her deep devotion, the betrothed of heaven. Her upturned eyes have drawn down the light that casts a radiance round her. See only such a ballad as that of "Lady Teresa's Bridal."[64]

Where the Infanta, given to the Moorish bridegroom,[65] calls down the vengeance of Heaven on his unhallowed passion, and thinks it not too much to expiate by a life in the cloister, the involuntary stain upon her princely youth.† It was this constant sense of claims above those of earthly love or happiness that made the Spanish lady who shared this spirit, a guerdon to be won by toils and blood and constant purity, rather than a chattel to be bought for pleasure and service.

Germany did not need to *learn* a high view of woman; it was inborn in that race. Woman was to the Teuton warrior his priestess, his friend, his sister, in truth, a wife. And the Christian statues of noble pairs, as they lie above their graves in stone, expressing the meaning of all the by-gone pilgrimage by hands folded in mutual prayer, yield not a nobler sense of the place and powers of woman, than belonged to the altvater day. The holy love of Christ which summoned them, also, to choose "the better part, that which could not be taken from them," refined and hallowed in this nation a native faith, thus showing that it was not the warlike spirit alone that left the Latins so barbarous in this respect.

But the Germans, taking so kindly to this thought, did it the more justice. The idea of woman in their literature is expressed both to a greater height and depth than elsewhere.

I will give as instances the themes of three ballads.[66]

One is upon a knight who had always the name of the Virgin on his

---

* Appendix B.

† Appendix, C.

lips. This protected him all his life through, in various and beautiful modes, both from sin and other dangers, and, when he died, a plant sprang from his grave, which so gently whispered the Ave Maria that none could pass it by with an unpurified heart.

Another is one of the legends of the famous Drachenfels.[67] A maiden, one of the earliest converts to Christianity, was carried by the enraged populace to this dread haunt of "the dragon's fabled brood," to be their prey. She was left alone, but unafraid, for she knew it whom she trusted. So, when the dragons came rushing towards her, she showed them a crucifix and they crouched reverently at her feet. Next day the people came, and seeing these wonders, are all turned to the faith which exalts the lowly.

The third I have in mind is another of the Rhine legends. A youth is sitting with the maid he loves on the shore of an isle, her fairy kingdom, then perfumed by the blossoming grape vines, which draped its bowers. They are happy; all blossoms with them, and life promises its richest wine. A boat approaches on the tide; it pauses at their feet. It brings, perhaps, some joyous message, fresh dew for their flowers, fresh light on the wave. No! it is the usual check on such great happiness. The father of the Count departs for the crusade; will his son join him, or remain to rule their domain, and wed her he loves? Neither of the affianced pair hesitate a moment. "I must go with my father." "Thou must go with thy father." It was one thought, one word. "I will be here again," he said, "when these blossoms have turned to purple grapes." "I hope so," she sighed, while the prophetic sense said "no."

And there she waited, and the grapes ripened, and were gathered into the vintage, and he came not. Year after year passed thus, and no tidings; yet still she waited.

He, meanwhile, was in a Moslem prison. Long he languished there without hope, till, at last, his patron saint appeared in vision and announced his release, but only on condition of his joining the monastic order for the service of the saint.

And so his release was effected, and a safe voyage home given. And once more he sets sail upon the Rhine. The maiden, still watching beneath the vines, sees at last the object of this patient love approach. Approach, but not to touch the strand to which she, with outstretched arms, has rushed. He dares not trust himself to land, but in low, heart-broken tones, tells her of heaven's will; and that he, in obedience to his vow, is now on his way to a convent on the river bank, there to pass the rest of his earthly life in the service of the shrine. And then he turns his boat, and floats away from her and hope of any happiness in this world, but urged, as he believes, by the breath of heaven.

The maiden stands appalled, but she dares not murmur, and cannot hesitate long. She also bids them prepare her boat. She follows her lost love to the convent gate, requests an interview with the abbot, and devotes her Elysian isle, where vines had ripened their ruby fruit in vain for her, to the service of the monastery where her love was to serve. Then, passing over to the nunnery opposite, she takes the veil, and meets her betrothed at the altar; and for a life long union, if not the one they had hoped in earlier years.

Is not this sorrowful story of a lofty beauty? Does it not show a sufficiently high view of woman, of marriage? This is commonly the chivalric, still more the German view.

Yet, wherever there was a balance in the mind of man of sentiment, with intellect, such a result was sure. The Greek Xenophon[68] has not only painted as a sweet picture of the domestic woman, in his Economics, but in the Cyropedia has given, in the picture of Panthea, a view of woman which no German picture can surpass, whether lonely and quiet with veiled lids, the temple of a vestal loveliness, or with eyes flashing, and hair flowing to the free wind, cheering on the hero to fight for his God, his country, or whatever name his duty might bear at the time. This picture I shall copy by and by. Yet Xenophon grew up in the same age with him who makes Iphigenia say to Achilles—

"Better a thousand women should perish than one man cease to see the light."[69]

This was the vulgar Greek sentiment. Xenophon, aiming at the ideal man, caught glimpses of the ideal woman also. From the figure of a Cyrus, the Pantheas stand not afar. They do not in thought; they would not in life.

I could swell the catalogue of instances far beyond the reader's patience. But enough have been brought forward to show that, though there has been great disparity betwixt the nations as between individuals in their culture on this point, yet the idea of woman has always cast some rays and often been forcibly represented.

Far less has woman to complain that she has not had her share of power. This, in all ranks of society, except the lowest, has been hers to the extent that vanity would crave, far beyond what wisdom would accept. In the very lowest, where man, pressed by poverty, sees in woman only the partner of toils and cares, and cannot hope, scarcely has an idea of, a comfortable home, he often maltreats her, and is less influenced by her. In all ranks, those who are gentle and uncomplaining, too candid to intrigue, too delicate to encroach, suffer much. They suffer long, and are kind; verily, they have their reward. But wherever man is sufficiently raised above extreme poverty or brutal stupidity, to care for the comforts of the fireside, or the bloom and ornament of life, woman has always power enough, if she choose to exert it, and is usually disposed to do so, in proportion to her ignorance and childish vanity. Unacquainted with the importance of life and its purposes, trained to a selfish coquetry and love of petty power, she does not look beyond the pleasure of making herself felt at the moment, and governments are shaken and commerce broken up to gratify the pique of a female favorite. The English shopkeeper's wife does not vote, but it is for her interest that the politician canvasses by the coarsest flattery. France suffers no woman on her throne, but her proud nobles kiss the dust at the feet of Pompadour and Dubarry; for such flare in the lighted foreground where a Roland would modestly aid in the closet. Spain, (that same Spain which sang of Ximena[70] and the Lady Teresa, shuts up her women in the care of duennas, and allows them no book but the Breviary, but the ruin follows only the more surely from the worthless favorite of a worthless queen. Relying on mean precautions, men indeed cry peace, peace, where there is no peace.

It is not the transient breath of poetic incense that women want; each can receive that from a lover. It is not life-long sway; it needs but to become a coquette, a shrew, or a good cook, to be sure of that. It is not money, nor notoriety, nor the badges of authority that men have appropriated to themselves. If demands, made in their behalf, lay stress on any of these particulars, those who make them have not searched deeply into the need. It is for that which at once includes these and precludes them; which would not be forbidden power, lest there be temptation to steal and misuse it; which would not have the mind perverted by flattery from a worthiness of esteem. It is for that which is the birthright of every being capable to receive it,—the freedom, the religious, the intelligent freedom of the universe, to use its means; to learn its secret as far as nature has enabled them, with God alone for their guide and their judge.

Ye cannot believe it, men; but the only reason why women ever assume what is more appropriate to you, is because you prevent them from finding out what is fit for themselves. Were they free, were they wise fully to develop the strength and beauty of woman; they would never wish to be men, or manlike. The well-instructed moon flies not from her orbit to seize on the glories of her partner. No; for she knows that one law rules, one heaven contains, one universe replies to them alike. It is with women as with the slave.

> "Vor dem Sklaven, wenn er die Kette bricht,
> Vor dem freien Meuschen erzittert nicht." [71]

Tremble not before the free man, but before the slave who has chains to break.

In slavery, acknowledged slavery, women are on a par with men. Each is a work-tool, an article of property, no more! In perfect freedom, such as is painted in Olympus, in Swedenborg's angelic state, in the heaven where there is no marrying nor giving in marriage, each is a purified intelligence, an enfranchised soul,—no less! [72]

> Jene himmlische Gestalten
> Sie fragen nicht nach Mann and Weib,
> Und keine kleider, keine Falten
> Umgeben den verklarten Leib. [73]

The child who sang this was a prophetic form, expressive of the longing for a state of perfect freedom, pure love. She could not remain here, but was transplanted to another air. And it may be that the air of this earth will never be so tempered that such can bear it long. But, while they stay, they must bear testimony to the truth they are constituted to demand.

That an era approaches which shall approximate nearer to such a temper than any has yet done, there are many tokens, indeed so many, that only a few of the most prominent can here be enumerated.

The reigns of Elizabeth of England and Isabella of Castile foreboded this era. They expressed the beginning of the new state, while they forwarded its progress. These were strong characters and in harmony with the wants of their time. One showed that this strength did not unfit a woman for the duties of a wife and a mother, the other that it could enable her to live and die alone, a wide energetic life, a courageous death. Elizabeth is certainly no pleasing example. In rising above the weakness, she did not lay aside the weaknesses ascribed to her sex; but her strength must be respected now, as it was in her own time.

Elizabeth and Mary Stuart seem types, [74] moulded by the spirit of the time, and placed upon an elevated platform to show to the coming ages, woman such as the conduct and wishes of man in general is likely to make her, lovely even to allurement, quick in apprehension and weak in judgment, with grace and dignity of sentiment, but no principle; credulous and indiscreet, yet artful; capable of sudden greatness or of crime, but not of a steadfast wisdom, or self-restraining virtue; and woman half-emancipated and jealous of her freedom, such as she has figured before and since in many a combative attitude, mannish, not equally manly, strong and prudent more than great or wise; able to control vanity, and the wish to rule through coquetry and passion, but not to resign these dear deceits, from the very foundation, as unworthy a being capable of truth and nobleness. Elizabeth, taught by adversity, put on her virtues as armor, more than produced them in a natural order from her soul. The time and her position called on her to act the wise sovereign, and she was proud that she could do so, but her tastes and inclinations would have led her to act the weak woman. She was without magnanimity of any kind.

We may accept as an omen for ourselves, that it was Isabella who furnished Columbus with the means of coming hither. This land must pay back its debt to woman, without whose aid it would not have been brought into alliance with the civilized world.

A graceful and meaning figure is that introduced to us by Mr. Prescott, in the Conquest of Mexico, in the Indian girl Marina, who accompanied Cortes, and was his interpreter in all the various difficulties of his career. She stood at his side, on the walls of the besieged palace, to plead with her enraged countrymen. By her name he was known in New Spain, and, after the conquest, her gentle intercession was often of avail to the conquered. The poem of the Future may be read in some features of the story of "Malinche."[75]

The influence of Elizabeth on literature was real, though, by sympathy with its finer productions, she was no more entitled to give name to an era than Queen Anne.[76] It was simply that the fact of having a female sovereign on the throne affected the course of a writer's thoughts. In this sense, the presence of a woman on the throne always makes its mark. Life is lived before the eyes of men, by which their imaginations are stimulated as to the possibilities of woman. "We will die for our King, Maria Theresa," cry the wild warriors, clashing their swords, and the sounds vibrate through the poems of that generation. The range of female character in Spenser alone might content us for one period. Britomart and Belphœbe have as much room on the canvass as Florimel; and where this is the case, the haughtiest amazon will not murmur that Una should be felt to be the fairest type.[77]

Unlike as was the English Queen to a fairy queen, we may yet conceive that it was the image of *a* queen before the poet's mind, that called up this splendid court of women. Shakspeare's range is also great; but he has left out the heroic characters, such as the Macaria of Greece, the Britomart of Spenser. Ford and Massinger[78] have, in this respect, soared to a higher flight of feeling than he. It was the holy and heroic woman they most loved, and if they could not paint an Imogen, a Desdemona, a Rosalind, yet, in those of a stronger mould, they showed a higher ideal, though with so much less poetic power to embody it, than we see in Portia or Isabella. The simple truth of Cordelia, indeed, is of this sort. The beauty of Cordelia is neither male nor female; it is the beauty of virtue.[79]

The ideal of love and marriage rose high in the mind of all the Christian nations who were capable of grave and deep feeling. We may take as examples of its English aspect, the lines,

> "I could not love thee, dear, so much,
> Loved I not honor more."[80]

Or the address of the Commonwealth's man to his wife, as she looked out from the Tower window to see him for the last time, on his way to the scaffold. He stood up in the cart, waved his hat, and cried, "To Heaven, my love, to Heaven, and leave you in the storm?"

Such was the love of faith and honor, a love which stopped, like Colonel Hutchinson's, "on this side idolatry," because it was religious. The meeting of two such souls Donne describes as giving birth to an "abler soul."[81]

Lord Herbert wrote to his love,

> "Were not our souls immortal made,
> Our equal loves can make them such."[82]

In the "Broken Heart" of Ford,[83] Penthea, a character which engages my admiration even more deeply than the famous one of Calanthe, is made to present to the mind the most beautiful picture of what these relations should be in their purity. Her life cannot sustain the violation of what she so clearly felt.

Shakspeare, too, saw that, in true love as in fire, the utmost ardor is coincident with the utmost purity. It is a true lover that exclaims in the agony of Othello,

"If thou art false, O then Heaven mocks itself."

The son, framed like Hamlet, to appreciate truth in all the beauty of relations, sinks into deep melancholy, when he finds his natural expectations disappointed. He has no mother. She to whom he gave the name, disgraces from his heart's shrine all the sex.

"Frailty, thy name is woman."

It is because a Hamlet could find cause to say so, that I have put the line, whose stigma has never been removed, at the head of my work. But, as a lover, surely a Hamlet would not have so far mistook, as to have finished with such a conviction. He would have felt the faith of Othello, and that faith could not, in his more dispassionate mind, have been disturbed by calumny.

In Spain, this thought is arrayed in a sublimity, which belongs to the sombre and passionate genius of the nation. Calderon's Justina[84] resists all the temptation of the Demon, and raises her lover, with her, above the sweet lures of mere temporal happiness. Their marriage is vowed at the stake; their souls are liberated together by the martyr flame into "a purer state of sensation and existence."

In Italy, the great poets wove into their lives an ideal love which answered to the highest wants. It included those of the intellect and the affections, for it was a love of spirit for spirit. It was not ascetic, or superhuman, but, interpreting all things, gave their proper beauty to details of the common life, the common day; the poet spoke of his love, not as a flower to place in his bosom, or hold carelessly in his hand, but as a light towards which he must find wings to fly, or "a stair to heaven." He delighted to speak of her, not only as the bride of his heart, but the mother of his soul; for he saw that, in cases where the right direction had been taken, the greater delicacy of her frame, and stillness of her life, left her more open to spiritual influx than man is. So he did not look upon her as betwixt him and earth, to serve his temporal needs, but, rather, betwixt him and heaven, to purify his affections and lead him to wisdom through love. He sought, in her, not so much the Eve, as the Madonna.

In these minds the thought, which gleams through all the legends of chivalry, shines in broad intellectual effulgence, not to be misinterpreted, and their thought is reverenced by the world, though it lies so far from the practice of the world as yet, so far, that it seems as though a gulf of death yawned between.

Even with such men, the practice was, often, widely different from the mental faith. I say mental, for if the heart were thoroughly alive with it, the practice could not be dissonant. Lord Herbert's was a marriage of convention, made for him at fifteen; he was not discontented with it, but looked only to the advantages it brought of perpetuating his family on the basis of a great fortune. He paid, in act, what he considered a dutiful attention to the bond; his thoughts travelled elsewhere; and while forming a high ideal of the companionship of minds in marriage, he seems never to have doubted that its realization must be postponed to some other state of being. Dante, almost immediately after the death of Beatrice, married a lady chosen for him by his friends, and Boccaccio,[85] in describing the miseries that attended, in this case,

"The form of an union where union is none,"

speaks as if these were inevitable to the connection, and the scholar and poet, especially, could expect nothing but misery and obstruction in a domestic partnership with woman.

Centuries have passed since, but civilized Europe is still in a transition state about marriage; not only in practice, but in thought. It is idle to speak with contempt of the nations where polygamy is an institution, or seraglios a custom, when practices far more debasing haunt, well nigh fill, every city and every town.[86] And so far as union of one with one is believed to be the only pure form of marriage, a great majority of societies and individuals are still doubtful whether the earthly bond must be a meeting of souls, or only supposes a contract of convenience and utility. Were woman established in the rights of an immortal being, this could not be. She would not, in some countries, be given away by her father, with scarcely more respect for her feelings than is shown by the Indian chief, who sells his daughter for a horse, and beats her if she runs away from her new home. Nor, in societies where her choice is left free, would she be perverted, by the current of opinion that seizes her, into the belief that she must marry, if it be only to find a protector, and a home of her own.

Neither would man, if he thought the connection of permanent importance, form it so lightly. He would not deem it a trifle, that he was to enter into the closest relations with another soul, which, if not eternal in themselves, must eternally affect his growth.

Neither, did he believe woman capable of friendship,* would he, by rash haste, lose the chance of finding a friend in the person who might, probably, live half a century by his side. Did love, to his mind, stretch forth into infinity, he would not miss his chance of its revelations, that he might, the sooner, rest from his weariness by a bright fireside, and secure a sweet and graceful attendant "devoted to him alone." Were he a step higher, he would not carelessly enter into a relation where he might not be able to do the duty of a friend, as well as a protector from external ill, to the other party, and have a being in his power pining for sympathy, intelligence and aid, that he could not give.

What deep communion, what real intercourse is implied by the sharing the joys and cares of parentage, when any degree of equality is admitted between the parties! It is true that, in a majority of instances, the man looks upon his wife as an adopted child, and places her to the other children in the relation of nurse or governess, rather than of parent. Her influence with them is sure, but she misses the education which should enlighten that influence, by being thus treated. It is the order of nature that children should complete the education, moral and mental, of parents, by making them think what is needed for the best culture of human beings, and conquer all faults and impulses that interfere with their giving this to these dear objects, who represent the world to them. Father and mother should assist one another to learn what is required for this sublime priesthood of nature. But, for this, a religious recognition of equality is required.

Where this thought of equality begins to diffuse itself, it is shown in four ways.

The household partnership. In our country, the woman looks for a "smart but kind" husband; the man for a "capable, sweet-tempered" wife.

The man furnishes the house; the woman regulates it. Their relation is one of mutual esteem, mutual dependence. Their talk is of business, their affection shows itself by practical kindness. They know that life goes more smoothly and cheerfully to each for the other's aid; they are grateful and content. The wife praises her husband as a "good provider;" the husband, in return, compliments her as a "capital housekeeper." This relation is good, as far as it goes.

Next comes a closer tie, which takes the two forms, either of mutual idolatry, or of intellectual companionship. The first, we suppose, is to no

---

*See Appendix D; Spinoza's view.

one a pleasing subject of contemplation. The parties weaken and narrow one another; they lock the gate against all the glories of the universe, that they may live in a cell together. To themselves they seem the only wise, to all others steeped in infatuation; the gods smile as they look forward to the crisis of cure; to men, the woman seems an unlovely syren; to women, the man an effeminate boy.

The other form, of intellectual companionship, has become more and more frequent. Men engaged in public life, literary men, and artists, have often found in their wives companions and confidants in thought no less than in feeling. And as the intellectual development of woman has spread wider and risen higher, they have, not unfrequently, shared the same employment. As in the case of Roland and his wife, who were friends in the household and in the nation's councils, read, regulated home affairs, or prepared public documents together, indifferently.

It is very pleasant, in letters begun by Roland, and finished by his wife, to see the harmony of mind, and the difference of nature; one thought, but various ways of treating it.[87]

This is one of the best instances of a marriage of friendship. It was only friendship, whose basis was esteem; probably neither party knew love, except by name.

Roland was a good man, worthy to esteem, and be esteemed; his wife as deserving of admiration, as able to do without it. Madame Roland is the fairest specimen we have yet of her class, as clear to discern her aim, as valiant to pursue it, as Spenser's Britomart; austerely set apart from all that did not belong to her, whether as woman or as mind. She is an antetype of a class to which the coming time will afford a field, the Spartan matron,[88] brought by the culture of the age of Books to intellectual consciousness and expansion.

Self-sufficingness, strength, and clear-sightedness were, in her, combined with a power of deep and calm affection. She, too, would have given a son or husband the device for his shield, "Return with it or upon it;" and this, not because she loved little, but much. The page of her life is one of unsullied dignity.

Her appeal to posterity is one against the injustice of those who committed such crimes in the name of Liberty. She makes it in behalf of herself and her husband. I would put beside it, on the shelf, a little volume, containing a similar appeal from the verdict of contemporaries to that of mankind, made by Godwin in behalf of his wife, the celebrated, the, by most men, detested, Mary Wolstonecraft.[89] In his view, it was an appeal from the injustice of those who did such wrong in the name of virtue.

Were this little book interesting for no other cause, it would be so for the generous affection evinced under the peculiar circumstances. This man had courage to love and honor this woman in the face of the world's sentence, and of all that was repulsive in her own past history. He believed he saw of what soul she was, and that the impulses she had struggled to act out were noble, though the opinions to which they had led might not be thoroughly weighed. He loved her, and he defended her for the meaning and tendency of her inner life. It was a good fact.

Mary Wolstonecraft, like Madame Dudevant, (commonly known as George Sand,) in our day, was a woman whose existence better proved the need of some new interpretation of woman's rights, than any thing she wrote. Such beings as these, rich in genius, of most tender sympathies, capable of high virtue and a chastened harmony, ought not to find them-selves, by birth, in a place so narrow, that, in breaking bonds, they become outlaws. Were there as much room in the world for such, as in Spenser's poem for Britomart, they would not run their heads so wildly against the walls, but prize their shelter rather. They find their way, at last, to light and air, but the world will not take off the brand it has set upon them. The champion of the Rights of Woman found, in Godwin, one who would plead that cause like a brother. He who delineated with such purity of traits the form of woman in the Marguerite, of whom the weak St. Leon could never learn to be worthy, a pearl indeed whose price was above rubies, was not false in life to the faith by which he had hallowed his romance. He acted as he wrote, like a brother. This form of appeal rarely fails to touch the basest man. "Are you acting towards other women in the way you would have men act towards your sister?" George Sand smokes, wears male attire, wishes to be addressed as "Mon frère;[90]—perhaps, if she found those who were as brothers, indeed, she would not care whether she were brother or sister.*

We rejoice to see that she, who expresses such a painful contempt for

---

*Since writing the above, I have read with great satisfaction, the following sonnets addressed to George Sand by a woman who has precisely the qualities that the author of Simon and Indiana lacks. It is such a woman, so unblemished in character, so high in aim, and pure in soul, that should address this other, as noble in nature, but clouded by error, and struggling with circumstances. It is such women that will do such justice. They are not afraid to look for virtue and reply to

men in most of her works, as shows she must have known great wrong from them, depicting in "La Roche Mauprat," a man raised by the workings of love, from the depths of savage sensualism, to a moral and intellectual life. It was love for a pure object, for a steadfast woman, one of those who, the Italian said, could make the stair to heaven.

---

aspiration, among those who have *not* "dwelt in decencies forever." It is a source of pride and happiness to read this address from the heart of Elizabeth Barrett.

TO GEORGE SAND

A Desire

Thou large brained woman and large hearted man,
　　Self-called George Sand! whose soul, amid the lions
　　Of thy tumultuous senses moans defiance,
And answers roar for roar, as spirits can:
I would some mild miraculous thunder ran
　　Above the applauded circus, in appliance
　　Of thine own nobler nature's strength and science,
　　Drawing two pinions, white as wings of swan,
From the strong shoulder, to amaze the place
　　With holier light! that thou to woman's claim,
And man's might join, beside, the angel's grace
　　Of a pure genius sanctified from blame;
Till child and maiden pressed to thine embrace,
　　To kiss upon thy lips a stainless fame.

ᔆ✹ᔆ

TO THE SAME

A Recognition

True genius, but true woman! dost deny
　　Thy woman's nature with a manly scorn,
And break away the gauds and armlets worn
　　By weaker women in captivity?
Ah, vain denial! that revolted cry
　　Is sobbed in by a woman's voice forlorn:—
Thy woman's hair, my sister, all unshorn,
　　Floats back dishevelled strength in agony,
Disproving thy man's name, and while before
　　The world thou burnest in a poet-fire,
We see thy woman-heart beat evermore
　　Through the large flame. Beat purer, heart, and higher,

This author, beginning like the many in assault upon bad institutions, and external ills, yet deepening the experience through comparative freedom, sees at last, that the only efficient remedy must come from individual character. These bad institutions, indeed, it may always be replied, prevent individuals from forming good character, therefore we must remove them. Agreed, yet keep steadily the higher aim in view. Could you clear away all the bad forms of society, it is vain, unless the individual begin to be ready for better. There must be a parallel movement in these two branches of life. And all the rules left by Moses availed less to further the best life than the living example of one Messiah.

Still, still the mind of the age struggles confusedly with these problems, better discerning as yet the ill it can no longer bear, than the good by which it may supersede it. But women, like Sand, will speak now and cannot be silenced; their characters and their eloquence alike foretell an era when such as they shall easier learn to lead true lives. But though such forebode, not such shall be the parents of it.* Those who would reform the world must show that they do not speak in the heat of wild impulse; their lives must be unstained by passionate error; they must be severe lawgivers to themselves. They must be religious students of the divine purpose with regard to man, if they would not confound the fancies of a day with the requisitions of eternal good. Their liberty must be the liberty of law and knowledge. But, as to the transgressions against custom which have caused such outcry against those of noble intention, it may be observed, that the resolve of Eloisa to be only the mistress of Abelard, was that of one who saw in practice around her, the contract of marriage made the seal of degradation. Shelley feared not to be fettered, unless so to be was to be false. Wherever abuses are seen, the timid will suffer; the bold with protest. But society has a right to outlaw them till she has revised her law; and this she must be taught to do, by one who speaks with authority, not in anger or haste.

If Godwin's choice of the calumniated authoress of the "Rights of Woman," for his honored wife, be a sign of a new era, no less is an article to

---

> Till God unsex thee on the spirit-shore;
> To which alone unsexing, purely aspire.

This last sonnet seems to have been written after seeing the picture of Sand, which represents her in a man's dress, but with long loose hair, and an eye whose mournful fire is impressive even in the caricatures.

*Appendix, E.

which I have alluded some pages back, published five or six years ago in one of the English Reviews, where the writer, in doing full justice to Eloisa, shows his bitter regret that she lives not now to love him, who might have known better how to prize her love than did the egotistical Abelard.

These marriages, these characters, with all their imperfections, express an onward tendency. They speak of aspiration of soul, of energy of mind, seeking clearness and freedom. Of a like promise are the tracts lately published by Goodwyn Barmby, (the European Pariah, as he calls himself,)[91] and his wife Catharine. Whatever we may think of their measures, we see in them wedlock; the two minds are wed by the only contract that can permanently avail, of a common faith and a common purpose.

We might mention instances, nearer home, of minds, partners in work and in life, sharing together, on equal terms, public and private interests, and which wear not, on any side, the aspect of offence shown by those last-named: persons who steer straight onward, yet, in our comparatively free life, have not been obliged to run their heads against any wall. But the principles which guide them might, under petrified and oppressive institutions, have made them warlike, paradoxical, and in some sense, Pariahs. The phenomena are different, the law is the same, in all these cases. Men and women have been obliged to build up their house anew from the very foundation. If they found stone ready in the quarry, they took it peaceably, other wise they alarmed the country by pulling down old towers to get materials.

These are all instances of marriage as intellectual companionship. The parties meet mind to mind, and a mutual trust is produced, which can buckler them against a million. They work together for a common purpose, and, in all these instances, with the same implement, the pen. The pen and the writing-desk furnish forth as naturally the retirement of woman as of man.

A pleasing expression, in this kind, is afforded by the union in the names of the Howitts. William and Mary Howitt[92] we heard named together for years, supposing them to be brother and sister; the equality of labors and reputation, even so, was auspicious; more so, now we find them man and wife. In his late work on Germany, Howitt mentions his wife, with pride, as one among the constellation of distinguished English-women, and in a graceful simple manner.

Our pleasure, indeed, in this picture, is marred by the vulgar apparition which has of late displaced the image, which we had from her writings cherished of a pure and gentle Quaker poetess. The surprise was painful as that of the little sentimentalist in the tale of "L'Amie Inconnue" when she found her correspondent, the poetess, the "adored Araminta," scolding her servants in Welsh, and eating toasted cheese and garlic. Still, we cannot forget what we have thought of the partnership in literature and affection between the Howitts, the congenial pursuits and productions, the pedestrian tours where the married pair showed that marriage, on a wide enough basis, does not destroy the "inexhaustible" entertainment which lovers found in one another's company.

In naming these instances, I do not mean to imply that community of employment is essential to union of husband and wife, more than to the union of friends. Harmony exists in difference, no less than in likeness, if only the same key-note govern both parts. Woman the poem, man the poet! Woman the heart, man the head! Such divisions are only important when they are never to be transcended. If nature is never bound down, nor the voice of inspiration stifled, that is enough. We are pleased that women should write and speak, if they feel the need of it, from having something to tell; but silence for ages would be no misfortune, if that silence be from divine command, and not from man's tradition.

While Goetz Von Berlichingen[93] rides to battle, his wife is busy in the kitchen; but difference of occupation does not prevent that community of inward life, that perfect esteem, with which he says—

"Whom God loves, to him gives he such a wife."

Manzoni thus dedicates his "Adelchi."[94]

"To his beloved and venerated wife, Enrichetta Luigia Blondel, who, with conjugal affection and maternal wisdom, has preserved a virgin mind, the author dedicates this "Adelchi," grieving that he could not, by a more splendid and more durable monument, honor the dear name, and the memory of so many virtues."

The relation could not be fairer, or more equal, if she, too, had written poems. Yet the position of the parties might have been the reverse as well; the woman might have sung the deeds, given voice to the life of the man, and beauty would have been the result, as we see, in pictures of Arcadia,[95] the nymph singing to the shepherds, or the shepherd, with his pipe, alluring the nymphs; either makes a good picture. The sounding lyre requires, not muscular strength, but energy of soul to animate the hand which would control it. Nature seems to delight in varying the arrangements, as if to show that she will be fettered by no rule, and we must admit the same varieties that she admits.

The fourth and highest grade of marriage union, is the religious, which may be expressed as pilgrimage towards a common shrine. This includes the others; home sympathies and household wisdom, for these pilgrims must know how to assist each other along the dusty way; intellectual communion, for how sad it would be on such a journey to have a companion to whom you could not communicate thoughts and aspirations as they sprang to life; who would have no feeling for the prospects that open, more and more glorious as we advance; who would never see the flowers that may be gathered by the most industrious traveller. It must include all these. Such a fellow-pilgrim Count Zinzendorf[96] seems to have found in his Countess, of whom he thus writes:

"Twenty-five years' experience has shown me that just the helpmate whom I have, is the only one that could suit my vocation. Who else could have so carried through my family affairs? Who lived so spotlessly before the world? Who so wisely aided me in my rejection of a dry morality? Who so clearly set aside the Pharisaism which, as years passed, threatened to creep in among us? Who so deeply discerned as to the spirits of delusion, which sought to bewilder us? Who would have governed my whole economy so wisely, richly, and hospitably, when circumstances commanded? Who have taken indifferently the part of servant or mistress, without, on the one side, affecting an especial spirituality; on the other, being sullied by any worldly pride? Who, in a community where all ranks are eager to be on a level, would, from wise and real causes, have known how to maintain inward and outward distinctions? Who, without a murmur, have seen her husband encounter such dangers by land and sea? Who undertaken with him, and *sustained* such astonishing pilgrimages? Who, amid such difficulties, always held up her head and supported me? Who found such vast sums of money, and acquitted them on her own credit? And, finally, who, of all human beings, could so well understand and interpret to others my inner and outer being as this one, of such nobleness in her way of thinking, such great intellectual capacity, and free from the theological perplexities that enveloped me!"

Let any one peruse, with all their power, the lineaments of this portrait, and see if the husband had not reason, with this air of solemn rapture and conviction, to challenge comparison? We are reminded of the majestic cadence of the line whose feet step in the just proportions of Humanity,

"Daughter of God and Man, accomplished Eve!"[97]

An observer* adds this testimony:

"We may, in many marriages, regard it as the best arrangement, if the man has so much advantage over his wife, that she can, without much thought of her own, be, by him, led and directed as by a father. But it was not so with the Count and his consort. She was not made to be a copy; she was an original; and, while she loved and honored him, she thought for herself, on all subjects, with so much intelligence, that he could and did look on her as sister and friend also."

Compare with this refined specimen of a religiously civilized life, the following imperfect sketch of a North American Indian, and we shall see that the same causes will always produce the same results. The Flying Pigeon (Ratchewaine)[98] was the wife of a barbarous chief, who had six others, but she was his only true wife, because the only one of a strong and pure character, and, having this, inspired a veneration, as like as the mind of the man permitted, to that inspired by the Countess Zinzendorf. She died when her son was only four years old, yet left on his mind a feeling of reverent love worthy the thought of Christian chivalry. Grown to manhood, he shed tears on seeing her portrait.

The Flying Pigeon

"RATCHEWAINE was chaste, mild, gentle in her disposition, kind, generous, and devoted to her husband. A harsh word was never known to proceed from her mouth; nor was she ever known to be in a passion. Mahaskah used to say of her, after her death, that her hand was shut, when those, who did not want, came into her presence; but when the really poor came in, it was like a strainer full of holes, letting all she held in it pass through. In the exercise of generous feeling she was uniform. It was not indebted for its exercise to whim, or caprice, or partiality. No matter of what nation the applicant for her bounty was, or whether at war or peace with her nation; if he were hungry, she fed him; if naked, she clothed him; and if houseless, she gave him shelter. The continued exercise of this generous feeling kept her poor. And she has been known to give away her last blanket—all the honey that was in the lodge, the last bladder of bear's oil, and the last piece of dried meat.

"She was scrupulously exact in the observance of all the religious

---

*Spangenberg.

rites which her faith imposed upon her. Her conscience is represented to have been extremely tender. She often feared that her acts were displeasing to the Great Spirit, when she would blacken her face, and retire to some lone place, and fast and pray."

To these traits should be added, but for want of room, anecdotes which show the quick decision and vivacity of her mind. Her face was in harmony with this combination. Her brow is as ideal and the eyes and lids as devout and modest as the Italian pictures of the Madonna, while the lower part of the face has the simplicity and childish strength of the Indian race. Her picture presents the finest specimen of Indian beauty we have ever seen.

Such a woman is the sister and friend of all beings, as the worthy man is their brother and helper.

With like pleasure we survey the pairs wedded on the eve of missionary effort. They, indeed, are fellow pilgrims on a well-made road, and whether or no they accomplish all they hope for the sad Hindoo, or the nearer savage, we feel that, in the burning waste, their love is like to be a healing dew, in the forlorn jungle, a tent of solace to one another. They meet, as children of one Father, to read together one book of instruction.

We must insert in this connection the most beautiful picture presented by ancient literature of wedded love under this noble form.

It is from the romance in which Xenophon, the chivalrous Greek, presents his ideal of what human nature should be.

The generals of Cyrus had taken captive a princess, a woman of unequalled beauty, and hastened to present her to the prince as the part of the spoil he would think most worthy of his acceptance.

Cyrus visits the lady, and is filled with immediate admiration by the modesty and majesty with which she receives him. He finds her name is Panthea, and that she is the wife of Abradatus, a young king whom she entirely loves. He protects her as a sister, in his camp, till he can restore her to her husband.

After the first tranports of joy at this re-union, the heart of Panthea is bent on showing her love and gratitude to her magnanimous and delicate protector. And as she has nothing so precious to give as the aid of Abradatus, that is what she most wishes to offer. Her husband is of one soul with her in this, as in all things.

The description of her grief and self-destruction, after the death which ensued upon this devotion, I have seen quoted, but never that of their parting when she sends him forth to battle. I shall copy both. If they have been read by any of my readers, they may be so again with profit in this connexion, for never were the heroism of a true woman, and the purity of love, in a true marriage, painted in colors more delicate or more lively.

"The chariot of Abradatus, that had four perches and eight horses, was completely adorned for him; and when he was going to put on his linen corslet, which was a sort of armor used by those of his country, Panthea brought him a golden helmet, and arm-pieces, broad bracelets for his wrists, a purple habit that reached down to his feet, and hung in folds at the bottom, and a crest dyed of a violet color. These things she had made unknown to her husband, and by taking the measure of his armor. He wondered when he saw them, and inquired thus of Panthea: 'And have you made me these arms, woman, by destroying your own ornaments?' 'No, by Jove,' said Panthea, 'not what is the most valuable of them; for it is you, if you appear to others to be what I think you, that will be my greatest ornament.' And, saying that, she put on him the armor, and, though she endeavored to control it, the tears poured down her cheeks. When Abradatus, who was before a man of fine appearance, was set out in those arms, he appeared the most beautiful and noble of all, especially, being likewise so by nature. Then, taking the reins from the driver, he was just preparing to mount the chariot, when Panthea, after she had desired all that were there to retire, thus said:

'O Abradatus! if ever there was a woman who had a greater regard to her husband than to her own soul, I believe you know that I am such an one; what need I therefore speak of things in particular? for I reckon that my actions have convinced you more than any words I can now use. And yet, though I stand thus affected towards you, as you know I do, I swear by this friendship of mine and yours, that I certainly would rather choose to be put under ground jointly with you, approving yourself a brave man, than to live with you in disgrace and shame; so much do I think you and myself worthy of the noblest things. Then I think that we both lie under great obligations to Cyrus, that, when I was a captive, and chosen out for himself, he thought fit to treat me neither as a slave, nor, indeed, as a woman of mean account, but he took and kept me for you, as if I were his brother's wife. Besides, when Araspes, who was my guard, went away from him, I promised him, that, if he would allow me to send for you, you would come to him, and approve yourself a much better and more faithful friend than Araspes.'

"Thus she spoke; and Abradatus being struck with admiration at her discourse, laying his hand gently on her head, and lifting up his eyes to heaven, made this prayer: 'Do thou, O greatest Jove! grant me to appear a husband worthy of Panthea, and a friend worthy of Cyrus, who has done us so much honor!'

"Having said this, he mounted the chariot by the door of the driver's seat; and, after he had got up, when the driver shut the door, Panthea, who had now no other way to salute him, kissed the seat of the chariot. The chariot then moved, and she, unknown to him, followed, till Abradatus turning about, and seeing her, said: 'Take courage, Panthea! Fare you happily and well, and now go your ways.' On this her women and servants carried her to her conveyance, and, laying her down, concealed her by throwing the covering of a tent over her. The people, though Abradatus and his chariot made a noble spectacle, were not able to look at him till Panthea was gone."

AFTER THE BATTLE—

"Cyrus calling to some of his servants, 'Tell me,' said he, 'has any one seen Abradatus? for I admire that he now does not appear.' One replied, 'My sovereign, it is because he is not living, but died in the battle as he broke in with his chariot on the Egyptians. All the rest, except his particular companions, they say, turned off when they saw the Egyptians' compact body. His wife is now said to have taken up his dead body, to have placed it in the carriage that she herself was conveyed in, and to have brought it hither to some place on the river Pactolus, and her servants are digging a grave on a certain elevation. They say that his wife, after setting him out with all the ornaments she has, is sitting on the ground with his head on her knees.' Cyrus, hearing this, gave himself a blow on the thigh, mounted his horse at a leap, and taking with him a thousand horse, rode away to this scene of affliction; but gave orders to Gadatas and Gobryas to take with them all the rich ornaments proper for a friend and an excellent man deceased, and to follow after him; and whoever had herds of cattle with him, he ordered them to take both oxen, and horses, and sheep in good number, and to bring them away to the place where, by inquiry, they should find him to be, that he might sacrifice these to Abradatus.

"As soon as he saw the woman sitting on the ground, and the dead body there lying, he shed tears at the afflicting sight, and said: 'Alas! thou brave and faithful soul, hast thou left us, and art thou gone?' At the same time he took him by the right hand, and the hand of the deceased came away, for it had been cut off, with a sword, by the Egyptians. He, at the sight of this, became yet much more concerned than before. The woman shrieked out in a lamentable manner, and, taking the hand from Cyrus, kissed it, fitted it to its proper place again, as well as she could, and said, 'The rest, Cyrus, is in the same condition, but what need you see it? And I know that I was not one of the least concerned in these his sufferings, and, perhaps you were not less so, for I, fool that I was! frequently exhorted him to behave in such a manner as to appear a friend to you, worthy of notice; and I know he never thought of what he himself should suffer, but of what he should do to please you. He is dead, therefore,' said she, 'without reproach, and I, who urged him on, sit here alive.' Cyrus, shedding tears for some time in silence, then spoke—'He has died, woman, the noblest death; for he has died victorious! do you adorn him with these things that I furnish you with.' (Gobryas and Gadatas were then come up and had brought rich ornaments in great abundance with them.) 'Then,' said he, 'be assured that he shall not want respect and honor in all other things: but, over and above, multitudes shall concur in raising him a monument that shall be worthy of us, and all the sacrifices shall be made him that are proper to be made in honor of a brave man. You shall not be left destitute, but, for the sake of your modesty and every other virtue, I will pay you all other honors, as well as place those about you who will conduct you wherever you please. Do you but make it known to me where it is that you desire to be conveyed to.' And Panthea replied, 'Be confident, Cyrus,' said she, 'I will not conceal from you to whom it is that I desire to go.'

"He, having said this, went away with great pity for her that she should have lost such a husband, and for the man that he should have left such a wife behind him, never to see her more. Panthea then gave orders for her servants to retire, 'Till such time,' said she, 'as I shall have lamented my husband, as I please.' Her nurse she bid to stay, and gave orders that, when she was dead, she would wrap her and her husband up in one mantle together. The nurse, after having repeatedly begged her not to do this, and meeting with no success, but observing her to grow angry, sat herself down, breaking out into tears. She, being before-hand provided with a sword, killed herself, and, laying her head down on her husband's breast, she died. The nurse set up a lamentable cry, and covered them both as Panthea had directed.

"Cyrus, as soon as he was informed of what the woman had done, being struck with it, went to help her if he could. The servants, three in number, seeing what had been done, drew their swords and killed themselves, as they stood at the place where she had ordered them. And the monument is now said to have been raised by continuing the mount on to the servants; and on a pillar above, they say, the names of the man and woman were written in Syriac letters.

"Below were three pillars, and they were inscribed thus, "Of the servants." Cyrus, when he came to this melancholy scene, was struck with admiration of the woman, and, having lamented over her, went away. He took care, as was proper, that all the funeral rites should be paid them in the noblest manner, and the monument, they say, was raised up to a very great size."

These be the ancients, who, so many assert had no idea of the dignity of woman, or of marriage. Such love Xenophon could paint as subsisting between those who after death "would see one another never more." Thousands of years have passed since, and with the reception of the cross, the nations assume the belief that those who part thus, may meet again and forever, if spiritually fitted to one another, as Abradatus and Panthea were, and yet do we see such marriages among them? If at all, how often?

I must quote two more short passages from Xenophon, for he is a writer who pleases me well.

Cyrus receiving the Armenians whom he had conquered.

"Tigranes," said he, "at what rate would you purchase the regaining of your wife?" Now Tigranes happened to be *but lately married,* and had a very great love for his wife," (that clause perhaps sounds *modern.*)

"Cyrus," said he, "I would ransom her at the expense of my life."

"Take then your own to yourself," said he.***

When they came home, one talked of Cyrus' wisdom, another of his patience and resolution, another of his mildness. One spoke of his beauty and the smallness of his person, and, on that, Tigranes asked his wife, "And do you, Armenian dame, think Cyrus handsome?" "Truly," said she, "I did not look at him." "At whom, then, did you look?" said Tigranes. "At him who said that, to save me from servitude, he would ransom me at the expense of his own life."

FROM THE BANQUET.[99]—

Socrates, who observed her with pleasure, said, "This young girl has confirmed me in the opinion I have had, for a long time, that the female sex are nothing inferior to ours, excepting only in strength of body, or, perhaps, in steadiness of judgment."

In the Economics, the manner in which the husband gives counsel to his young wife, presents the model of politeness and refinement. Xenophon is thoroughly the gentleman, gentle in breeding and in soul. All the men he describes are so, while the shades of manner are distinctly marked. There is the serene dignity of Socrates, with gleams of playfulness thrown across its cool religious shades, the princely mildness of Cyrus, and the more domestic elegance of the husband in the Economics.

There is no way that men sin more against refinement, as well as discretion, than in their conduct towards their wives. Let them look at the men of Xenophon. Such would know how to give counsel, for they would know how to receive it. They would feel that the most intimate relations claimed most, not least, of refined courtesy. They would not suppose that confidence justified carelessness, nor the reality of affection want of delicacy in the expression of it.

Such men would be too wise to hide their affairs from the wife and then expect her to act as if she knew them. They would know that if she is expected to face calamity with courage, she must be instructed and trusted in prosperity, or, if they had failed in wise confidence such as the husband shows in the Economics, they would be ashamed of anger or querulous surprise at the results that naturally follow.

Such men would not be exposed to the bad influence of bad wives, for all wives, bad or good, loved or unloved, inevitably influence their husbands, from the power their position not merely gives, but necessitates, of coloring evidence and infusing feelings in hours when the patient, shall I call him? is off his guard. Those who understand the wife's mind, and think it worth while to respect her springs of action, know better where they are. But to the bad or thoughtless man who lives carelessly and irreverently so near another mind, the wrong he does daily back upon himself recoils. A Cyrus, an Abradatus knows where he stands.

But to return to the thread of my subject.

Another sign of the times is furnished by the triumphs of female authorship. These have been great and constantly increasing. Women have taken possession of so many provinces for which men had pronounced them unfit, that though these still declare there are some inaccessible to them, it is difficult to say just *where* they must stop.

The shining names of famous women have cast light upon the path of the sex, and many obstructions have been removed. When a Montague could learn better than her brother, and use her lore afterward to such purpose, as an observer, it seemed amiss to hinder women from preparing themselves to see, or from seeing all they could, when prepared. Since Somerville[100] has achieved so much, will any young girl be prevented from seeking a knowledge of the physical sciences, if she wishes it? De Stael's[101] name was not so clear of offence; she could not forget the woman in the thought; while she was instructing you as a mind, she wished to be admired as a woman; sentimental tears often dimmed the eagle glance. Her intellect too, with all its splendor, trained in a drawing-room, fed on flattery, was tainted and flawed; yet its beams make the obscurest schoolhouse in New-England warmer and lighter to the little rugged girls, who are gathered together on its wooden bench. They may never through life hear her name, but she is not the less their benefactress.

The influence has been such, that the aim certainly is, now, in arranging school instruction for girls, to give them as fair a field as boys. As yet, indeed, these arrangements are made with little judgment or reflection; just as the tutors of Lady Jane Grey, and other distinguished women of her time, taught them Latin and Greek,[102] because they knew nothing else themselves, so now the improvement in the education of girls is to be made by giving them young men as teachers, who only teach what has been taught themselves at college, while methods and topics need revision for these new subjects, which could better be made by those who had experienced the same wants. Women are, often, at the head of these institutions, but they have, as yet, seldom been thinking women, capable to organize a new whole for the wants of the time, and choose persons to officiate in the departments. And when some portion of instruction is got of a good sort from the school, the far greater proportion which is infused from the general atmosphere of society contradicts its purport. Yet books and a little elementary instruction are not furnished, in vain. Women are better aware how great and rich the universe is, not so easily blinded by narrowness or partial views of a home circle. "Her mother did so before her," is no longer a sufficient excuse. Indeed, it was never received as an excuse to mitigate the severity of censure, but was adduced as a reason, rather, why there should be no effort made for reformation.

Whether much or little has been done or will be done, whether women will add to the talent of narration, the power of systematizing, whether they will carve marble, as well as draw and paint, is not important. But that it should be acknowledged that they have intellect which needs developing, that they should not be considered complete, if beings of affection and habit alone, is important.

Yet even this acknowledgment, rather conquered by woman than proffered by man, has been sullied by the usual selfishness. So much is said of women being better educated, that they may become better companions and mothers *for men*. They should be fit for such companionship, and we have mentioned, with satisfaction, instances where it has been established. Earth knows no fairer, holier relation than that of a mother. It is one which, rightly understood, must both promote and require the highest attainments. But a being of infinite scope must not be treated with an exclusive view to any one relation. Give the soul free course, let the organization, both of body and mind, be freely developed, and the being will be fit for any and every relation to which it may be called. The intellect, no more than the sense of hearing, is to be cultivated merely that she may be a more valuable companion to man, but because the Power who gave a power, by its mere existence, signifies that it must be brought out towards perfection.

In this regard of self-dependence, and a greater simplicity and fulness of being, we must hail as a preliminary the increase of the class contemptuously designated as old maids.

We cannot wonder at the aversion with which old bachelors and old maids have been regarded. Marriage is the natural means of forming a sphere, of taking root on the earth; it requires more strength to do this without such an opening; very many have failed, and their imperfections have been in every one's way. They have been more partial, more harsh, more officious and impertinent than those compelled by severer friction to render themselves endurable. Those, who have a more full experience of the instincts, have a distrust, as to whether they can be thoroughly human and humane, such as is hinted in the saying, "Old maids' and bachelors' children are well cared for," which derides at once their ignorance and their presumption.

Yet the business of society has become so complex, that it could now scarcely be carried on without the presence of these despised auxiliaries; and detachments from the army of aunts and uncles are wanted to stop gaps in every hedge. They rove about, mental and moral Ishmaelites,[103] pitching their tents amid the fixed and ornamented homes of men.

In a striking variety of forms, genius of late, both at home and abroad, has paid its tribute to the character of the Aunt, and the Uncle, recognizing in these personages the spiritual parents, who had supplied defects in the treatment of the busy or careless actual parents.

They also gain a wider, if not so deep existence. Those who are not intimately and permanently linked with others, are thrown upon themselves, and, if they do not there find peace and incessant life, there is none to flatter them that they are not very poor and very mean.

A position which so constantly admonishes, may be of inestimable benefit. The person may gain, undistracted by other relationships, a closer

communion with the one. Such a use is made of it by saints and sybils. Or
she may be one of the lay sisters of charity, a Canoness, bound by an inward
vow! Or the useful drudge of all men, the Martha, much sought, little
prized![104] Or the intellectual interpreter of the varied life she sees; the
Urania of a half-formed world's twilight.[105]

Or she may combine all these. Not "needing to care that she may
please a husband," a frail and limited being, her thoughts may turn to the
centre, and she may, by steadfast contemplation entering into the secret of
truth and love, use it for the use of all men, instead of a chosen few, and
interpret through it all the forms of life. It is possible, perhaps, to be at
once a priestly servant, and a loving muse.

Saints and geniuses have often chosen a lonely position in the faith
that if, undisturbed by the pressure of near ties, they would give themselves up to the inspiring spirit, it would enable them to understand and
reproduce life better than actual experience could.

How many old maids take this high stand, we cannot say: it is an
unhappy fact, that too many who have come before the eye are gossips
rather, and not always good-natured gossips. But if these abuse, and none
make the best of their vocation, yet it has not failed to produce some good
results. It has been seen by others, if not by themselves, that beings, likely
to be left alone, need to be fortified and furnished within themselves, and
education and thought have tended more and more to regard these beings
as related to absolute Being, as well as to other men. It has been seen that,
as the breaking of no bond ought to destroy a man, so ought the missing of
none to hinder him from growing. And thus a circumstance of the time,
which springs rather from its luxury than its purity, has helped to place
women on the true platform.

Perhaps the next generation, looking deeper into this matter, will
find that contempt is put upon old maids, or old women at all, merely
because they do not use the elixir which would keep them always young.
Under its influence a gem brightens yearly which is only seen to more
advantage through the fissures Time makes in the casket.* No one thinks
of Michael Angelo's Persican Sibyl, or St. Theresa, or Tasso's Leonora, or
the Greek Electra, as an old maid, more than of Michael Angelo or Canova
as old bachelors, though all had reached the period in life's course appointed to take that degree.[106]

See a common woman at forty; scarcely has she the remains of

---

*Appendix, F.

beauty, of any soft poetic grace which gave her attraction as woman, which kindled the hearts of those who looked on her to sparkling thoughts, or diffused round her a roseate air of gentle love. See her, who was, indeed, a lovely girl, in the coarse full-blown dahlia flower of what is commonly called matron-beauty, fat, fair, and forty, showily dressed, and with manners as broad and full as her frill or satin cloak. People observe, "how well she is preserved;" "she is a fine woman still," they say. This woman, whether as a duchess in diamonds, or one of our city dames in mosaics, charms the poet's heart no more, and would look much out of place kneeling before the Madonna. She "does well the honors of her house," "leads society," is, in short, always spoken and thought of upholstery-wise.

Or see that care-worn face, from which every soft line is blotted, those faded eyes from which lonely tears have driven the flashes of fancy, the mild white beam of a tender enthusiasm. This woman is not so ornamental to a tea party; yet she would please better, in picture. Yet surely she, no more than the other, looks as a human being should at the end of forty years. Forty years! have they bound those brows with no garland? shed in the lamp no drop of ambrosial oil?

Not so looked the Iphigenia in Aulis.[107] Her forty years had seen her in anguish, in sacrifice, in utter loneliness. But those pains were borne for her father and her country; the sacrifice she had made pure for herself and those around her. Wandering alone at night in the vestal solitude of her imprisoning grove, she has looked up through its "living summits" to the stars, which shed down into her aspect their own lofty melody. At forty she would not misbecome the marble.

Not so looks the Persica.[108] She is withered, she is faded; the drapery that enfolds her has, in its dignity and angularity, too, that tells of age, of sorrow, of a stern composure to the *must*. But her eye, that torch of the soul, is untamed, and in the intensity of her reading, we see a soul invincibly young in faith and hope. Her age is her charm, for it is the night of the Past that gives this beacon fire leave to shine. Wither more and more, black Chrysalid! thou dost but give the winged beauty time to mature its splendors.

Not so looked Victoria Colonna,[109] after her life of a great hope, and of true conjugal fidelity. She had been, not merely a bride, but a wife, and each hour had helped to plume the noble bird. A coronet of pearls will not shame her brow; it is white and ample, a worthy altar for love and thought.

Even among the North American Indians, a race of men as completely engaged in mere instinctive life as almost any in the world, and where each chief, keeping many wives as useful servants, of course looks with no kind eye on celibacy in woman, it was excused in the following instance mentioned by Mrs. Jameson.[110] A woman dreamt in youth that she was betrothed to the Sun. She built her a wigwam apart, filled it with emblems of her alliance, and means of an independent life. There she passed her days, sustained by her own exertions, and true to her supposed engagement.

In any tribe, we believe, a woman, who lived as if she was betrothed to the Sun, would be tolerated, and the rays which made her youth blossom sweetly, would crown her with a halo in age.

There is, on this subject, a nobler view than heretofore, if not the noblest, and improvement here must coincide with that in the view taken of marriage.

We must have units before we can have union, says one of the ripe thinkers of the times.

If larger intellectual resources begin to be deemed needful to woman, still more is a spiritual dignity in her, or even the mere assumption of it, looked upon with respect. Joanna Southcott and Mother Anne Lee are sure of a band of disiples; Ecstatica, Dolorosa, of enraptured believers who will visit them in their lowly huts, and wait for days to revere them in their trances.[111] The foreign noble traverses land and sea to hear a few words from the lips of the lowly peasant girl, whom he believes especially visited by the Most High. Very beautiful, in this way, was the influence of the invalid of St. Petersburg, as described by De Maistre.[112]

Mysticism, which may be defined as the brooding soul of the world, cannot fail of its oracular promise as to woman. "The mothers"—"The mother of all things," are expressions of thought which lead the mind towards this side of universal growth.[113] Whenever a mystical whisper was heard, from Behmen down to St. Simon,[114] sprang up the thought, that, if it be true, as the legend says, that humanity withers through a fault committed by and a curse laid upon woman, through her pure child, or influence, shall the new Adam, the redemption, arise. Innocence is to be replaced by virtue, dependence by a willing submission, in the heart of the Virgin Mother of the new race.

The spiritual tendency is towards the elevation of woman, but the intellectual by itself is not so. Plato sometimes seems penetrated by that high idea of love, which considers man and woman as the two-fold expression of one thought.[115] This the angel of Swedenborg, the angel of the coming age, cannot surpass, but only explain more fully. But then again

Plato, the man of intellect, treats woman in the Republic as property, and, in the Timaeus, says that man, if he misuse the privileges of one life, shall be degraded into the form of woman, and then, if he do not redeem himself, into that of a bird. This, as I said above, expresses most happily how anti-poetical is this state of mind. For the poet, contemplating the world of things, selects various birds as the symbols of his most gracious and ethe-real thoughts, just as he calls upon his genius, as muse, rather than as God. But the intellect, cold, is ever more masculine than feminine; warmed by emotion, it rushes towards mother earth, and puts on the forms of beauty.

The electrical, the magnetic element in woman has not been fairly brought out at any period.[116] Every thing might be expected from it; she has far more of it than man. This is commonly expressed by saying that her intuitions are more rapid and more correct. You will often see men of high intellect absolutely stupid in regard to the atmospheric changes, the fine invisible links which connect the forms of life around them, while common women, if pure and modest, so that a vulgar self do not overshadow the mental eye, will seize and delineate these with unerring discrimination.

Women who combine this organization with creative genius, are very commonly unhappy at present. They see too much to act in confor-mity with those around them, and their quick impulses seem folly to those who do not discern the motives. This is an usual effect of the apparition of genius, whether in man or woman, but is more frequent with regard to the latter, because a harmony, an obvious order and self-restraining decorum, is most expected from her.

Then women of genius, even more than men, are likely to be enslaved by an impassioned sensibility. The world repels them more rudely, and they are of weaker bodily frame.

Those, who seem overladen with electricity, frighten those around them. "When she merely enters the room, I am what the French call *hérissé*,"[117] said a man of petty feelings and worldly character of such a woman, whose depth of eye and powerful motion announced the conduc-tor of the mysterious fluid.[118]

Wo to such a woman who finds herself linked to such a man in bonds too close. It is the cruellest of errors. He will detest her with all the bitterness of wounded self-love. He will take the whole prejudice of man-hood upon himself, and to the utmost of his power imprison and torture her by its imperious rigors.

Yet, allow room enough, and the electric fluid will be found to invigorate and embellish, not destroy life. Such women are the great actresses, the songsters. Such traits we read in a late searching, though too French analysis of the character of Mademoiselle Rachel, by a modern La Roche-foucauld.[119] The Greeks thus represent the muses; they have not the golden serenity of Apollo; they are *over*-flowed with thought; there is something tragic in their air. Such are the Sibyls of Guercino,[120] the eye is over-full of expression, dilated and lustrous; it seems to have drawn the whole being into it.

Sickness is the frequent result of this over-charged existence. To this region, however misunderstood, or interpreted with presumptuous care-lessness, belong the phenomena of magnetism, or mesmerism, as it is now often called, where the trance of the Ecstatica purports to be produced by the agency of one human being on another, instead of, as in her case, direct from the spirit.

The worldling has his sneer at this as at the services of religion. "The churches can always be filled with women." "Show me a man in one of your magnetic states, and I will believe."

Women are, indeed, the easy victims both of priest-craft and self-delusion, but this would not be, if the intellect was developed in propor-tion to the other powers. They would, then, have a regulator, and be more in equipoise, yet must retain the same nervous susceptibility, while their physical structure is such as it is.

It is with just that hope, that we welcome every thing that tends to strengthen the fibre and develope the nature on more sides. When the intellect and affections are in harmony; when intellectual consciousness is calm and deep; inspiration will not be confounded with fancy.

> Then, "she who advances
> With rapturous, lyrical glances,
> Singing the song of the earth, singing
> Its hymn to the Gods,"

will not be pitied, as a madwoman, nor shrunk from as unnatural.

The Greeks, who saw every thing in forms, which we are trying to ascertain as law, and classify as cause, embodied all this in the form of Cassandra. Cassandra was only unfortunate in receiving her gift too soon. The remarks, however, that the world still makes in such cases, are well expressed by the Greek dramatist.

In the Trojan Dames,[121] there are fine touches of nature with regard to Cassandra. Hecuba shows that mixture of shame and reverence that prosaic kindred always do towards the inspired child, the poet, the elected sufferer for the race.

When the herald announces that Cassandra is chosen to be the mistress of Agamemnon, Hecuba answers, with indignation, betraying the pride and faith she involuntarily felt in this daughter.

> Hec. 'The maiden of Phoebus, to whom the golden haired
> Gave as a privilege a virgin life!
> Tal. Love of the inspired maiden hath pierced him.
> Hec. Then cast away, my child, the sacred keys, and from thy person
> The consecrated garlands which thou wearest.'

Yet, when a moment after, Cassandra appears, singing, wildly, her inspired song, Hecuba calls her, "My *frantic* child."

Yet how graceful she is in her tragic *raptus*,[122] the chorus shows.

> Chor. 'How sweetly at thy house's ills thou smil'st,
> Chanting what, haply, thou wilt not show true.'

If Hecuba dares not trust her highest instinct about her daughter, still less can the vulgar mind of the herald Talthybius, a man not without feeling, but with no princely, no poetic blood, abide the wild prophetic mood which insults all his prejudices.

> Tal. 'The venerable, and that accounted wise,
> Is nothing better than that of no repute,
> For the greatest king of all the Greeks,
> The dear son of Atreus, is possessed with the love
> Of this madwoman. I, indeed, am poor,
> Yet, I would not receive her to my bed.'

The royal Agamemnon could see the beauty of Cassandra, HE was not afraid of her prophetic gifts.

The best topic for a chapter on this subject in the present day, would be the history of the Seeress of Prevorst, the best observed subject of magnetism in our present times, and who, like her ancestresses of Delphos, was roused to ecstacy or phrenzy by the touch of the laurel.

I observe in her case, and in one known to me here, that, what might have been a gradual and gentle disclosure of remarkable powers, was broken and jarred into disease by an unsuitable marriage. Both these persons were unfortunate in not understanding what was involved in this relation, but acted ignorantly as their friends desired. They thought that this was the inevitable destiny of woman. But when engaged in the false position, it was impossible for them to endure its dissonances, as those of less delicate perceptions can, and the fine flow of life was checked and sullied. They grew sick, but, even so, learnt and disclosed more than those in health are wont to do.

In such cases, worldlings sneer, but reverent men learn wondrous news, either from the person observed, or by thoughts caused in themselves by the observation. Fenelon learns from Guyon,[123] Kerner, from his Seeress, what we fain would know. But to appreciate such disclosures one must be a child, and here the phrase, "women and children" may, perhaps, be interpreted aright, that only little children shall enter into the kingdom of heaven.

All these motions of the time, tides that betoken a waxing moon, overflow upon our land.[124] The world, at large, is readier to let woman learn and manifest the capacities of her nature than it ever was before, and here is a less encumbered field and freer air than any where else. And it ought to be so; we ought to pay for Isabella's jewels.[125]

The names of nations are feminine—religion, virtue, and victory are feminine. To those who have a superstition, as to outward reigns, it is not without significance that the name of the queen of our mother-land should at this crisis be Victoria—Victoria the First. Perhaps to us it may be given to disclose the era thus outwardly presaged.

Another Isabella too at this time ascends the throne. Might she open a new world to her sex! But, probably, these poor little women are, least of any, educated to serve as examples or inspirers for the rest. The Spanish queen is younger; we know of her that she sprained her foot the other day, dancing in her private apartments; of Victoria, that she reads aloud, in a distinct voice and agreeable manner, her addresses to parliament on certain solemn days, and, yearly, that she presents to the nation some new prop of royalty. These ladies have, very likely, been trained more completely to the puppet life than any other. The queens, who have been queens indeed, were trained by adverse circumstances to know the world around them and their own powers.

It is moving, while amusing, to read of the Scottish peasant measuring the print left by the queen's foot as she walks, and priding himself on its beauty. It is so natural to wish to find what is fair and precious in high places, so astonishing to find the Bourbon a glutton, or the Guelph a dullard or gossip.[126]

In our own country, women are, in many respects, better situated than men. Good books are allowed, with more time to read them. They are not so early forced into the bustle of life, nor so weighed down by demands for outward success. The perpetual changes, incident to our society, make the blood circulate freely through the body politic, and, if not favorable at present to the grace and bloom of life, they are so to activity, resource, and would be to reflection, but for a low materialist tendency, from which the women are generally exempt in themselves, though its existence, among the men, has a tendency to repress their impulses and make them doubt their instincts, thus, often, paralyzing their action during the best years.

But they have time to think, and no traditions chain them, and few conventionalities compared with what must be met in other nations. There is no reason why they should not discover that the secrets of nature are open, the revelations of the spirit waiting for whoever will seek them. When the mind is once awakened to this consciousness, it will not be restrained by the habits of the past, but fly to seek the seeds of a heavenly future.

Their employments are more favorable to meditation than those of men.

Woman is not addressed religiously here, more than elsewhere. She is told she should be worthy to be the mother of a Washington, or the companion of some good man. But in many, many instances, she has already learnt that all bribes have the same flaw; that truth and good are to be sought solely for their own sakes. And, already, an ideal sweetness floats over many forms, shines in many eyes.

Already deep questions are put by young girls on the great theme: What shall I do to enter upon the eternal life?

Men are very courteous to them. They praise them often, check them seldom. There is chivalry in the feeling towards "the ladies," which gives them the best seats in the stage-coach, frequent admission, not only to lectures of all sorts, but to courts of justice, halls of legislature, reform conventions. The newspaper editor "would be better pleased that the Lady's Book should be filled up exclusively by ladies. It would then, indeed, be a true gem, worthy to be presented by young men to the mistresses of their affections." Can gallantry go further?

In this country is venerated, wherever seen, the character which Goethe spoke of an Ideal, which he saw actualized in his friend and patroness, the Grand Duchess Amelia. "The excellent woman is she, who, if the husband dies, can be a father to the children." And this, if read aright, tells a great deal.

Women who speak in public, if they have a moral power, such as has been felt from Angelina Grimke and Abby Kelley;[127] that is, if they speak for conscience' sake, to serve a cause which they hold sacred, invariably subdue the prejudices of their hearers, and excite an interest proportionate to the aversion with which it had been the purpose to regard them.

A passage in a private letter so happily illustrates this, that it must be inserted here.

Abby Kelley in the Town-House of ————.

"The scene was not unheroic—to see that woman, true to humanity and her own nature, a centre of rude eyes and tongues, even gentlemen feeling licensed to make part of a species of mob around a female out of her sphere. As she took her seat in the desk amid the great noise, and in the throng, full, like a wave, of something to ensue, I saw her humanity in a gentleness and unpretension, tenderly open to the sphere around her, and, had she not been supported by the power of the will of genuineness and principle, she would have failed. It led her to prayer, which, in woman especially, is childlike; sensibility and will going to the side of God and looking up to him; and humanity was poured out in aspiration.

"She acted like a gentle hero, with her mild decision and womanly calmness. All heroism is mild and quiet and gentle, for it is life and possession, and combativeness and firmness show a want of actualness. She is as earnest, fresh, and simple as when she first entered the crusade. I think she did much good, more than the men in her place could do, for woman feels more as being and reproducing, this brings the subject more into home relations. Men speak through, and mostly from intellect, and this addresses itself in others, which creates and is combative."

Not easily shall we find elsewhere, or before this time, any written observations on the same subject, so delicate and profound.

The late Dr. Channing,[128] whose enlarged and tender and religious nature, shared every onward impulse of his time, though his thoughts followed his wishes with a deliberate caution, which belonged to his habits and temperament, was greatly interested in these expectations for women. His own treatment of them was absolutely and thoroughly religious. He regarded them as souls, each of which had a destiny of its own, incalculable to other minds, and whose leading it must follow, guided by the light of a private conscience. He had sentiment, delicacy, kindness, taste; but they were all pervaded and ruled by this one thought, that all beings had souls, and must vindicate their own inheritance. Thus all beings were treated by him with an equal, and sweet, though solemn, courtesy. The young and unknown, the woman and the child, all felt themselves regarded with an infinite expectation, from which there was no reaction to vulgar prejudice. He demanded of all he met, to use his favorite phrase, "great truths."

His memory, every way dear and reverend, is, by many, especially cherished for this intercourse of unbroken respect.

At one time, when the progress of Harriet Martineau[129] through this country, Angelina Grimke's appearance in public, and the visit of Mrs. Jameson had turned his thoughts to this subject, he expressed high hopes as to what the coming era would bring to woman. He had been much pleased with the dignified courage of Mrs. Jameson in taking up the defence of her sex, in a way from which women usually shrink, because, if they express themselves on such subjects with sufficient force and clearness to do any good, they are exposed to assaults whose vulgarity makes them painful. In intercourse with such a woman, he had shared her indignation at the base injustice, in many respects, and in many regions, done to the sex; and been led to think of it far more than ever before. He seemed to think that he might some time write upon the subject. That his aid is withdrawn from the cause is a subject of great regret, for, on this question as on others, he would have known how to sum up the evidence and take, in the noblest spirit, middle ground. He always furnished a platform on which opposing parties could stand, and look at one another under the influence of his mildness and enlightened candor.

Two younger thinkers, men both, have uttered noble prophecies, auspicious for woman. Kinmont,[130] all whose thoughts tended towards the establishment of the reign of love and peace, thought that the inevitable means of this would be an increased predominance given to the idea of woman. Had he lived longer, to see the growth of the peace party, the reforms in life and medical practice which seek to substitute water for wine and drugs, pulse for animal food, he would have been confirmed in his view of the way in which the desired changes are to be effected.

In this connection, I must mention Shelley, who, like all men of genius, shared the feminine development, and, unlike many, knew it. His life was one of the first pulse-beats in the present reform-growth. He, too, abhorred blood and heat, and, by his system and his song, tended to reinstate a plant-like gentleness in the development of energy. In harmony with this, his ideas of marriage were lofty, and, of course, no less so of woman, her nature, and destiny.

For woman, if, by a sympathy as to outward condition she is led to aid the enfranchisement of the slave, must be no less so, by inward tendency, to favor measures which promise to bring the world more thoroughly and deeply into harmony with her nature. When the lamb takes place of the lion as the emblem of nations, both women and men will be as children of one spirit, perpetual learners of the word and doers therof, not hearers only.

A writer in the New-York Pathfinder, in two articles headed "Femality," has uttered a still more pregnant word than any we have named. He views woman truly from the soul, and not from society, and the depth and leading of his thoughts are proportionably remarkable. He views the feminine nature as a harmonizer of the vehement elements, and this has often been hinted elsewhere; but what he expresses most forcibly is the lyrical, the inspiring, and inspired apprehensiveness of her being.

This view being identical with what I have before attempted to indicate, as to her superior susceptibility to magnetic or electric influence, I will now try to express myself more fully.

There are two aspects of woman's nature, represented by the ancients as Muse and Minerva.[131] It is the former to which the writer in the Pathfinder looks. It is the latter which Wordsworth has in mind, when he says—

"With a placid brow,
Which woman ne'er should forfeit, keep thy vow.[132]

The especial genius of woman I believe to be electrical in movement, intuitive in function, spiritual in tendency. She excels not so easily in classification, or re-creation, as in an instinctive seizure of causes, and a simple breathing out of what she receives that has the singleness of life, rather than the selecting and energizing of art.

More native is it to her to be the living model of the artist than to set apart from herself any one form in objective reality; more native to inspire and receive the poem, than to create it. In so far as soul is in her completely developed, all soul is the same; but as far as it is modified in her as woman, it flows, it breathes, it sings, rather than deposits soil, or finishes work, and that which is especially feminine flushes, in blossom, the face of earth, and pervades, like air and water, all this seeming solid globe, daily renewing and purifying its life. Such may be the especially feminine element, spoken of as Femality. But it is no more the order of nature that it should be incarnated pure in any form, than that the masculine energy should exist unmingled with it in any form.

Male and female represent the two sides of the great radical dualism. But, in fact, they are perpetually passing into one another. Fluid hardens to solid, solid rushes to fluid. There is no wholly masculine man, no purely feminine woman.

History jeers at the attempts of physiologists to bind great original laws by the forms which flow from them. They make a rule; they say from observation, what can and cannot bē. In vain! Nature provides exceptions to every rule. She sends women to battle, and sets Hercules spinning; she enables women to bear immense burdens, cold, and frost; she enables the man, who feels maternal love, to nourish his infant like a mother. Of late she plays still gayer pranks. Not only she deprives organizations, but organs, of a necessary end. She enables people to read with the top of the head, and see with the pit of the stomach. Presently she will make a female Newton, and a male Syren.

Man partakes of the feminine in the Apollo, woman of the masculine as Minerva.

What I mean by the Muse is the unimpeded clearness of the intuitive powers which a perfectly truthful adherence to every admonition of the higher instincts would bring to a finely organized human being. It may appear as prophecy or as poesy. It enabled Cassandra to foresee the results of actions passing round her; the Seeress to behold the true character of the person through the mask of his customary life. (Sometimes she saw a feminine form behind the man, sometimes the reverse.) It enabled the daughter of Linnæus to see the soul of the flower exhaling from the flower.* It gave a man, but a poet man, the power of which he thus speaks: "Often in my contemplation of nature, radiant intimations, and as it were sheaves of light appear before me as to the facts of cosmogony in which my mind has, perhaps, taken especial part." He wisely adds, "but it is neces-

---

*The daughter of Linneus states, that, while looking steadfastly at the red lily, she saw its spirit hovering above it, as a red flame. It is true, this, like many fair spirit-stories, may be explained away as an optical illusion, but its poetic beauty and meaning would, even then, make it valuable, as an illustration of the spiritual fact.

sary with earnestness to verify the knowledge we gain by these flashes of light." And none should forget this. Sight must be verified by life before it can deserve the honors of piety and genius. Yet sight comes first, and of this sight of the world of causes, this approximation to the region of primitive motions, women I hold to be especially capable. Even without equal freedom with the other sex, they have already shown themselves so, and should these faculties have free play, I believe they will open new, deeper and purer sources of joyous inspiration than have as yet refreshed the earth.

Let us be wise and not impede the soul. Let her work as she will. Let us have one creative energy, one incessant revelation. Let it take what form it will, and let us not bind it by the past to man or woman, black or white. Jove sprang from Rhea, Pallas from Jove.[133] So let it be.

If it has been the tendency of these remarks to call woman rather to the Minerva side,—if I, unlike the more generous writer, have spoken from society no less than the soul,—let it be pardoned! It is love that has caused this, love for many incarcerated souls, that might be freed, could the idea of religious self-dependence be established in them, could the weakening habit of dependence on others be broken up.

Proclus teaches that every life has, in its sphere, a totality or wholeness of the animating powers of the other spheres; having only, as its own characteristic, a predominance of some one power. Thus Jupiter comprises, within himself, the other twelve powers, which stand thus: The first triad is *demiurgic or fabricative,* i.e., Jupiter, Neptune, Vulcan; the second, *defensive,* Vesta, Minerva, Mars; the third, *vivific,* Ceres, Juno, Diana; and the fourth, Mercury, Venus, Apollo, *elevating and harmonic.*[134] In the sphere of Jupiter, energy is predominant—with Venus, beauty; but each comprehends and apprehends all the others.

When the same community of life and consciousness of mind begins among men, humanity will have, positively and finally, subjugated its brute elements and Titanic childhood; criticism will have perished; arbitrary limits and ignorant censure be impossible; all will have entered upon the liberty of law, and the harmony of common growth.

Then Apollo will sing to his lyre what Vulcan forges on the anvil, and the Muse weave anew the tapestries of Minerva.

It is, therefore, only in the present crisis that the preference is given to Minerva. The power of continence must establish the legitimacy of freedom, the power of self-poise the perfection of motion.

Every relation, every gradation of nature is incalculably precious, but only to the soul which is poised upon itself, and to whom no loss, no change, can bring dull discord, for it is in harmony with the central soul.

If any individual live too much in relations, so that he becomes a stranger to the resources of his own nature, he falls, after a while, into a distraction, or imbecility, from which he can only be cured by a time of isolation, which gives the renovating fountains time to rise up. With a society it is the same. Many minds, deprived of the traditionary or instinctive means of passing a cheerful existence, must find help in self-impulse, or perish. It is therefore that, while any elevation, in the view of union, is to be hailed with joy, we shall not decline celibacy as the great fact of the time. It is one from which no vow, no arrangement, can at present save a thinking mind. For now the rowers are pausing on their oars; they wait a change before they can pull together. All tends to illustrate the thought of a wise contemporary. Union is only possible to those who are units. To be fit for relations in time, souls, whether of man or woman, must be able to do without them in the spirit.

It is therefore that I would have woman lay aside all thought, such as she habitually cherishes, of being taught and led by men. I would have her, like the Indian girl, dedicate herself to the Sun, the Sun of Truth, and go no where if his beams did not make clear the path. I would have her free from compromise, from complaisance, from helplessness, because I would have her good enough and strong enough to love one and all beings, from the fulness, not the poverty of being.

Men, as at present instructed, will not help this work, because they also are under the slavery of habit. I have seen with delight their poetic impulses. A sister is the fairest ideal, and how nobly Wordsworth, and even Byron, have written of a sister.[135]

There is no sweeter sight than to see a father with his little daughter. Very vulgar men become refined to the eye when leading a little girl by the hand. At that moment the right relation between the sexes seems established, and you feel as if the man would aid in the noblest purpose, if you ask him in behalf of his little daughter. Once two fine figures stood before me, thus. The father of very intellectual aspect, his falcon eye softened by affection as he looked down on his fair child, she the image of himself, only more graceful and brilliant in expression. I was reminded of Southey's Kehama;[136] when lo, the dream was rudely broken. They were talking of education, and he said,

"I shall not have Maria brought too forward. If she knows too much, she will never find a husband; superior women hardly ever can."

"Surely," said his wife, with a blush, "you wish Maria to be as good and wise as she can, whether it will help her to marriage or not."

"No," he persisted, "I want her to have a sphere and a home, and some one to protect her when I am gone."

It was a trifling incident, but made a deep impression. I felt that the holiest relations fail to instruct the unprepared and perverted mind. If this man, indeed, could have looked at it on the other side, he was the last that would have been willing to have been taken himself for the home and protection he could give, but would have been much more likely to repeat the tale of Alcibiades with his phials.[137]

But men do *not* look at both sides, and women must leave off asking them and being influenced by them, but retire within themselves, and explore the groundwork of life till they find their peculiar secret. Then, when they come forth again, renovated and baptized, they will know how to turn all dross to gold, and will be rich and free though they live in a hut, tranquil, if in a crowd. Then their sweet singing shall not be from passionate impulse, but the lyrical overflow of a divine rapture, and a new music shall be evolved from this many-chorded world.

Grant her, then, for a while, the armor and the javelin. Let her put from her the press of other minds and meditate in virgin loneliness. The same idea shall re-appear in due time as Muse, or Ceres, the all-kindly patient Earth-Spirit.

AMONG THE THRONG of symptoms which denote the present tendency to a crisis in the life of woman, which resembles the change from girlhood with its beautiful instincts, but unharmonized thoughts, its blind pupilage and restless seeking, to self-possessed, wise, and graceful womanhood, I have attempted to select a few.

One of prominent interest is the unison of three male minds, upon the subject, which, for width of culture, power of self-concentration and dignity of aim, take rank as the prophets of the coming age, while their histories and labors are rooted in the past.

Swedenborg came, he tells us, to interpret the past revelation and unfold a new. He announces the new church that is to prepare the way for the New Jerusalem, a city built of precious stones, hardened and purified by secret processes in the veins of earth through the ages.[138]

Swedenborg approximated to that harmony between the scientific and poetic lives of mind, which we hope from the perfected man. The links that bind together the realms of nature, the mysteries that accompany her births and growths, were unusually plain to him. He seems a man to whom insight was given at a period when the mental frame was sufficiently matured to retain and express its gifts.

His views of woman are, in the main, satisfactory. In some details, we may object to them as, in all his system, there are still remains of what is arbitrary and seemingly groundless; fancies that show the marks of old habits, and a nature as yet not thoroughly leavened with the spiritual leaven. At least so it seems to me now. I speak reverently, for I find such reason to venerate Swedenborg, from an imperfect knowledge of his mind, that I feel one more perfect might explain to me much that does not now secure my sympathy.

His idea of woman is sufficiently large and noble to interpose no obstacle to her progress. His idea of marriage is consequently sufficient. Man and woman share an angelic ministry, the union is from one to one, permanent and pure.

As the New Church extends its ranks, the needs of woman must be more considered.

Quakerism also establishes woman on a sufficient equality with man. But though the original thought of Quakerism is pure, its scope is too narrow, and its influence, having established a certain amount of good and made clear some truth, must, by degrees, be merged in one of wider range.* The mind of Swedenborg appeals to the various nature of man and allows room for aesthetic culture and the free expression of energy.

As apostle of the new order, of the social fabric that is to rise from love, and supersede the old that was based on strife, Charles Fourier comes next, expressing, in an outward order, many facts of which Swedenborg saw the secret springs. The mind of Fourier, though grand and clear, was, in some respects, superficial. He was a stranger to the highest experiences. His eye was fixed on the outward more than the inward needs of man. Yet he, too, was a seer of the divine order, in its musical expression, if not in its poetic soul. He has filled one department of instruction for the new era, and the harmony in action, and freedom for individual growth he hopes

---

*In worship at stated periods, in daily expression, whether by word or deed, the Quakers have placed woman on the same platform with man. Can any one assert that they have reason to repent this?

shall exist; and if the methods he proposes should not prove the true ones, yet his fair propositions shall give many hints, and make room for the inspiration needed for such.

He, too, places woman on an entire equality with man, and wishes to give to one as to the other that independence which must result from intellectual and practical development.

Those who will consult him for no other reason, might do so to see how the energies of woman may be made available in the pecuniary way. The object of Fourier was to give her the needed means of self help, that she might dignify and unfold her life for her own happiness, and that of society. The many, now, who see their daughters liable to destitution, or vice to escape from it, may be interested to examine the means, if they have not yet soul enough to appreciate the ends he proposes.

On the opposite side of the advancing army, leads the great apostle of individual culture, Goethe. Swedenborg makes organization and union the necessary results of solitary thought. Fourier, whose nature was, above all, constructive, looked to them too exclusively. Better institutions, he thought, will make better men. Goethe expressed, in every way, the other side. If one man could present better forms, the rest could not use them till ripe for them.

Fourier says, As the institutions, so the men! All follies are excusable and natural under bad institutions.

Goethe thinks, As the man, so the institutions! There is no excuse for ignorance and folly. A man can grow in any place, if he will.

Ay! but Goethe, bad institutions are prison walls and impure air that make him stupid, so that he does not will.

And thou, Fourier, do not expect to change mankind at once, or even "in three generations" by arrangement of groups and series, or flourish of trumpets for attractive industry. If these attempts are made by unready men, they will fail.

Yet we prize the theory of Fourier no less than the profound suggestion of Goethe. Both are educating the age to a clearer consciousness of what man needs, what man can be, and better life must ensue.

Goethe, proceeding on his own track, elevating the human being in the most imperfect states of society, by continual efforts at self-culture, takes as good care of women as of men. His mother, the bold, gay Frau Aja, with such playful freedom of nature; the wise and gentle maiden, known in his youth, over whose sickly solitude "the Holy Ghost brooded as a dove;" his sister, the intellectual woman *par excellence:* the Duchess Amelia; Lili, who combined the character of the woman of the world with the lyrical sweetness of the shepherdess, on whose chaste and noble breast flowers and gems were equally at home; all these had supplied abundant suggestions to his mind, as to the wants and the possible excellencies of woman.[139] And, from his poetic soul, grew up forms new and more admirable than life has yet produced, for whom his clear eye marked out paths in the future.

In Faust, we see the redeeming power, which, at present, upholds woman, while waiting, for a better day, in Margaret. The lovely little girl, pure in instinct, ignorant in mind, is misled and profaned by man abusing her confidence.* To the Mater *Dolorosa* she appeals for aid.[140] It is given to the soul, if not against outward sorrow; and the maiden, enlightened by her sufferings, refusing to receive temporal salvation by the aid of an evil power, obtains the eternal in its stead.

In the second part, the intellectual man, after all his manifold strivings, owes to the interposition of her whom he had betrayed *his* salvation. She intercedes, this time herself a glorified spirit, with the Mater *Gloriosa.*

Leonora, too, is woman, as we see her now, pure, thoughtful, refined by much acquaintaince with grief.[141]

Iphigenia he speaks of in his journals as his "daughter," and she is the daughter† whom a man will wish, even if he has chosen his wife from very mean motives. She is the virgin, steadfast soul, to whom falsehood is more dreadful than any other death.[142]

But it is to Wilhelm Meister's Apprenticeship and Wandering Years that I would especially refer, as these volumes contain the sum of the Sage's observations during a long life, as to what man should do, under present circumstances, to obtain mastery over outward, through an initiation into inward life, and severe discipline of faculty.[143]

As Wilhelm advances in the upward path he becomes acquainted

---

* As Faust says, her only fault was a "Kindly delusion," — "ein guter wahn."

† Goethe was as false to his ideas in practice, as Lord Herbert. And his punishment was the just and usual one of connections formed beneath the standard of right, from the impulses of the baser self. Iphigenia was the worthy daughter of his mind, but the son, child of his degrading connection in actual life, corresponded with that connection. This son, on whom Goethe vainly lavished so much thought and care, was like his mother, and like Goethe's attachment for his mother. "This young man," says a late well informed writer, (M. Henri Blaze,) "Wieland, with good reason, was called the son of the servant, *der Sohn der Magd.* He inherited from his father only his name and his *physique.*"

with better forms of woman by knowing how to seek, and how to prize them when found. For the weak and immature man will, often, admire a superior woman, but he will not be able to abide by a feeling, which is too severe a tax on his habitual existence. But, with Wilhelm, the gradation is natural and expresses ascent in the scale of being. At first he finds charm in Mariana and Philina, very common forms of feminine character, not without redeeming traits, no less than charms, but without wisdom or purity. Soon he is attended by Mignon, the finest expression ever yet given to what I have called the lyrical element in woman. She is a child, but too full-grown for this man; he loves, but cannot follow her; yet is the association not without an enduring influence. Poesy has been domesticated in his life, and, though he strives to bind down her heavenward impulse, as art or apothegm, these are only the tents, beneath which he may sojourn for a while, but which may be easily struck, and carried on limitless wanderings.

Advancing into the region of thought, he encounters a wise philanthropy in Natalia, (instructed, let us observe, by an *uncle*), practical judgment and the outward economy of life in Theresa, pure devotion in the Fair Saint.

Farther and last he comes to the house of Macaria, the soul of a star, *i.e.* a pure and perfected intelligence embodied in feminine form, and the centre of a world whose members revolve harmoniously round her. She instructs him in the archives of a rich human history, and introduces him to the contemplation of the heavens.

From the hours passed by the side of Mariana to these with Macaria, is a wide distance for human feet to traverse. Nor has Wilhelm travelled so far, seen and suffered so much in vain. He now begins to study how he may aid the next generation; he sees objects in harmonious arrangement, and from his observations deduces precepts by which to guide his course as a teacher and a master, "help-full, comfort-full."

In all these expressions of woman, the aim of Goethe is satisfactory to me. He aims at a pure self-subsistence, and free development of any powers with which they may be gifted by nature as much for them as for men. They are units, addressed as souls. Accordingly the meeting between man and woman, as represented by him, is equal and noble, and, if he does not depict marriage, he makes it possible.

In the Macaria, bound with the heavenly bodies in fixed revolutions, the centre of all relations, herself unrelated, he expresses the Minerva side of feminine nature. It was not by chance that Goethe gave her this name.

Macaria, the daughter of Hercules, who offered herself as a victim for the good of her country, was canonized by the Greeks, and worshipped as the Goddess of true Felicity. Goethe has embodied this Felicity as the Serenity that arises from Wisdom, a Wisdom, such as the Jewish wise man venerated, alike instructed in the designs of heaven, and the methods necessary to carry them into effect upon earth.

Mignon is the electrical, inspired, lyrical nature. And wherever it appears we echo in our aspirations that of the child,

> "So let me seem until I be:—
> Take not the *white robe* away."
>
>   *   *   **
>
> "Though I lived without care and toil,
> Yet felt I sharp pain enough,
> Make me again forever young." [144]

All these women, though we see them in relations, we can think of as unrelated. They are all very individual, yet seem, nowhere, restrained. They satisfy for the present, yet arouse an infinite expectation.

The economist Theresa, the benevolent Natalia, the fair Saint, have chosen a path, but their thoughts are not narrowed to it. The functions of life to them are not ends, but suggestions.

Thus, to them, all things are important, because none is necessary. Their different characters have fair play, and each is beautiful in its minute indications, for nothing is enforced or conventional, but every thing, however slight, grows from the essential life of the being.

Mignon and Theresa wear male attire when they like, and it is graceful for them to do so, while Macaria is confined to her arm-chair behind the green curtain, and the Fair Saint could not bear a speck of dust on her robe.

All things are in their places in this little world, because all is natural and free, just as "there is room for everything out of doors." Yet all is rounded in by natural harmony, which will always arise where Truth and Love are sought in the light of Freedom.

Goethe's book bodes an era of freedom like its own of "extraordinary generous seeking," and new revelations. New individualities shall be developed in the actual world, which shall advance upon it as gently as the figures come out upon his canvass.

I have indicated on this point the coincidence between his hopes and those of Fourier, though his are directed by an infinitely higher and deeper knowledge of human nature. But, for our present purpose, it is sufficient to show how surely these different paths have conducted to the same end two earnest thinkers. In some other place I wish to point out similar coincidences between Goethe's model school and the plans of Fourier, which may cast light upon the page of prophecy.

Many women have observed that the time drew nigh for a better care of the sex, and have thrown out hints that may be useful. Among these may be mentioned—

Miss Edgeworth,[145] who, although restrained by the habits of her age and country, and belonging more to the eighteenth than the nineteenth century, has done excellently as far as she goes. She had a horror of sentimentalism, and the love of notoriety, and saw how likely women, in the early stages of culture, were to aim at these. Therefore she bent her efforts to recommending domestic life. But the methods she recommends are such as will fit a character for any position to which it may be called. She taught a contempt of falsehood, no less in its most graceful, than in its meanest apparitions; the cultivation of a clear, independent judgment, and adherence to its dictates; habits of various and liberal study and employment, and a capacity for friendship. Her standard of character is the same for both sexes. Truth, honor, enlightened benevolence, and aspiration after knowledge. Of poetry, she knows nothing, and her religion consists of honor and loyalty to obligations once assumed, in short, in "the great idea of duty which holds us upright." Her whole tendency is practical.

Mrs. Jameson[146] is a sentimentalist, and, therefore, suits us ill in some respects, but she is full of talent, has a just and refined perception of the beautiful, and a genuine courage when she finds it necessary. She does not appear to have thought out, thoroughly, the subject on which we are engaged, and her opinions, expressed as opinions, are sometimes inconsistent with one another. But from the refined perception of character, admirable suggestions are given in her "Women of Shakspeare," and "Loves of the Poets."

But that for which I most respect her is the decision with which she speaks on a subject which refined women are usually afraid to approach, for fear of the insult and scurril jest they may encounter; but on which she neither can nor will restrain the indignation of a full heart. I refer to the degradation of a large portion of women into the sold and polluted slaves of men, and the daring with which the legislator and man of the world lifts his head beneath the heavens, and says "this must be; it cannot be helped; it is a necessary accompaniment of *civilization.*"

So speaks the *citizen.* Man born of woman, the father of daughters, declares that he will and must buy the comforts and commercial advantages of his London, Vienna, Paris, New-York, by conniving at the moral death, the damnation, so far as the action of society can insure it, of thousands of women for each splendid metropolis.

O men! I speak not to you. It is true that your wickedness (for you must not deny that, at least, nine thousand out of the ten fall through the vanity you have systematically flattered, or the promises you have treacherously broken;) yes, it is true that your wickedness is its own punishment. Your forms degraded and your eyes clouded by secret sin; natural harmony broken and fineness of perception destroyed in your mental and bodily organization; God and love shut out from your hearts by the foul visitants you have permitted there; incapable of pure marriage; incapable of pure parentage; incapable of worship; oh wretched men, your sin is its own punishment! You have lost the world in losing yourselves. Who ruins another has admitted the worm to the root of his own tree, and the fuller ye fill the cup of evil, the deeper must be your own bitter draught. But I speak not to you—you need to teach and warn one another. And more than one voice rises in earnestness. And all that *women* say to the heart that has once chosen the evil path, is considered prudery, or ignorance, or perhaps, a feebleness of nature which exempts from similar temptations.

But to you, women, American women, a few words may not be addressed in vain. One here and there may listen.

You know how it was in the Oriental clime. One man, if wealth permitted, had several wives and many hand-maidens. The chastity and equality of genuine marriage, with "the thousand decencies that flow," from its communion, the precious virtues that gradually may be matured, within its enclosure, were unknown.

But this man did not wrong according to his light. What he did, he might publish to God and Man; it was not a wicked secret that hid in vile lurking-places and dens, like the banquets of beasts of prey. Those women were not lost, not polluted in their own eyes, nor those of others. If they were not in a state of knowledge and virtue, they were at least in one of comparative innocence.

You know how it was with the natives of this continent. A chief had many wives whom he maintained and who did his household work; those women were but servants, still they enjoyed the respect of others and their own. They lived together in peace. They knew that a sin against what was in their nation esteemed virtue, would be as strictly punished in man as in woman.

Now pass to the countries where marriage is between one and one. I will not speak of the Pagan nations, but come to those which own the Christian rule. We all know what that enjoins; there is a standard to appeal to.

See now, not the mass of people, for we all know that it is a proverb and a bitter jest to speak of the "down-trodden million." We know that, down to our own time, a principle never had so fair a chance to pervade the mass of the people, but that we must solicit its illustration from select examples.

Take the Paladin,[147] take the Poet. Did *they* believe purity more impossible to man than to woman? Did they wish woman to believe that man was less amenable to higher motives, that pure aspirations would not guard him against bad passions, that honorable employments and temperate habits would not keep him free from slavery to the body. O no! Love was to them a part of heaven, and they could not even wish to receive its happiness, unless assured of being worthy of it. Its highest happiness to them was, that it made them wish to be worthy. They courted probation. They wished not the title of knight, till the banner had been upheld in the heats of battle, amid the rout of cowards.

I ask of you, young girls—I do not mean *you,* whose heart is that of an old coxcomb, though your locks have not yet lost their sunny tinge. Not of you whose whole character is tainted with vanity, inherited or taught, who have early learnt the love of coquettish excitement, and whose eyes rove restlessly in search of a "conquest" or a "beau." You who are ashamed *not* to be seen by others the mark of the most contemptuous flattery or injurious desire. To such I do not speak. But to thee, maiden, who, if not so fair, art yet of that unpolluted nature which Milton saw when he dreamed of Comus and the Paradise.[148] Thou, child of an unprofaned wedlock, brought up amid the teachings of the woods and fields, kept fancy-free by useful employment and a free flight into the heaven of thought, loving to please only those whom thou wouldst not be ashamed to love; I ask of thee, whose cheek has not forgotten its blush nor thy heart its lark-like hopes, if he whom thou mayst hope the Father will send thee, as the companion of life's toils and joys, is not to thy thought pure? Is not manliness to thy thought purity, *not* lawlessness? Can his lips speak falsely?

Can he do, in secret, what he could not avow to the mother that bore him? O say, dost thou not look for a heart free, open as thine own, all whose thoughts may be avowed, incapable of wronging the innocent, or still farther degrading the fallen. A man, in short, in whom brute nature is entirely subject to the impulses of his better self.

Yes! it was thus that thou didst hope, for I have many, many times seen the image of a future life, of a destined spouse, painted on the tablets of a virgin heart.

It might be that she was not true to these hopes. She was taken into what is called "the world," froth and scum as it mostly is on the social caldron. There, she saw fair woman carried in the waltz close to the heart of a being who appeared to her a Satyr. Being warned by a male friend that he was in fact of that class, and not fit for such familiar nearness to a chaste being, the advised replied that "women should know nothing about such things." She saw one fairer given in wedlock to a man of the same class. "Papa and mamma said that 'all men were faulty, at one time in their lives; they had a great many temptations. Frederick would be so happy at home; he would not want to do wrong." She turned to the married women; they, oh tenfold horror! laughed at her supposing "men were like women." Sometimes, I say, she was not true and either sadly accommodated herself to "woman's lot," or acquired a taste for satyr-society, like some of the Nymphs, and all the Bacchanals of old. But to these who could not and would not accept a mess of pottage, or a Circe cup, in lieu of their birthright, and to these others who have yet their choice to make, I say, Courage! I have some words of cheer for you. A man, himself of unbroken purity, reported to me the words of a foreign artist, that "the world would never be better till men subjected themselves to the same laws they had imposed on women;" that artist, he added, was true to the thought. The same was true of Canova, the same of Beethoven. "Like each other demigod, they kept themselves free from stain," and Michael Angelo, looking over here from the loneliness of his century, might meet some eyes that need not shun his glance.

In private life, I am assured by men who are not so sustained and occupied by the worship of pure beauty, that a similar consecration is possible, is practiced. That many men feel that no temptation can be too strong for the will of man, if he invokes the aid of the Spirit instead of seeking extenuation from the brute alliances of his nature. In short, what the child fancies is really true, though almost the whole world declares it a lie. Man is a child of God; and if he seek His guidance to keep the heart with diligence, it will be so given that all the issues of life may be pure. Life will then be a temple.[149]

> The temple round
> Spread green the pleasant ground;
> The fair colonnade
> Be of pure marble pillars made;
> Strong to sustain the roof,
> Time and tempest proof,
> Yet, amidst which, the lightest breeze
> Can play as it please;
> The audience hall
> Be free to all
> Who revere
> The Power worshipped here,
> Sole guide of youth
> Unswerving Truth:
> In the inmost shrine
> Stands the image divine,
> Only seen
> By those whose deeds have worthy been—
> Priestlike clean.
> Those, who initiated are,
> Declare,
> As the hours
> Usher in varying hopes and powers;
> It changes its face,
> It changes its age,
> Now a young beaming Grace,
> Now Nestorian Sage:
> But, to the pure in heart,
> This shape of primal art
> In age is fair,
> In youth seems wise,
> Beyond compare,
> Above surprise;
> What it teaches native seems
> Its new lore our ancient dreams;
> Incense rises from the ground,
> Music flows around;
> Firm rest the feet below, clear gaze the eyes above,
> When Truth to point the way through Life assumes the wand of Love;

But, if she cast aside the robe of green,
Winter's silver sheen,
White, pure as light,
Makes gentle shroud as worthy weed as bridal robe had been.*

We are now in a transition state, and but few steps have yet been taken. From polygamy, Europe passed to the marriage *de convenance*.[150] This was scarcely an improvement. An attempt was then made to substitute genuine marriage, (the mutual choice of souls inducing a permanent union,) as yet baffled on every side by the haste, the ignorance, or the impurity of man.

Where man assumes a high principle to which he is not yet ripened; it will happen, for a long time, that the few will be nobler than before; the many worse. Thus now. In the country of Sidney and Milton, the metropolis is a den of wickedness, and a stye of sensuality; in the country of Lady Russell,[151] the custom of English Peeresses, of selling their daughters to the highest bidder, is made the theme and jest of fashionable novels by unthinking children who would stare at the idea of sending them to a Turkish slave dealer, though the circumstances of the bargain are there less degrading, as the will and thoughts of the person sold are not so degraded by it, and it is not done in defiance of an acknowledged law of right in the land and the age.

I must here add that I do not believe there ever was put upon record more depravation of man, and more despicable frivolity of thought and aim in woman, than in the novels which purport to give the picture of English fashionable life, which are read with such favor in our drawing rooms, and give the tone to the manners of some circles. Compared with the hardhearted cold folly there described, crime is hopeful, for it, at least, shows some power remaining in the mental constitution.

To return: Attention has been awakened among men to the stains of celibacy, and the profanations of marriage. They begin to write about it

---

*(*As described by the historian.*)

The temple of Juno is like what the character of woman should be.
Columns! graceful decorums, attractive yet sheltering.
Porch! noble inviting aspect of the life.
Kaos! receives the worshippers. See here the statue of the Divinity.
Ophistodomos! Sanctuary where the most precious possessions were kept safe from the hand of the spoiler and the eye of the world.

and lecture about it. It is the tendency now to endeavor to help the erring by showing them the physical law. This is wise and excellent; but forget not the better half. Cold bathing and exercise will not suffice to keep a life pure, without an inward baptism and noble and exhilarating employment for the thoughts and the passions. Early marriages are desirable, but if, (and the world is now so out of joint that there are a hundred thousand chances to one against it,) a man does not early, or at all, find the person to whom he can be united in the marriage of souls, will you give him the marriage *de convenance,* or if not married, can you find no way for him to lead a virtuous and happy life? Think of it well, ye who think yourselves better than pagans, for many of *them* knew this sure way.*

To you, women of America, it is more especially my business to address myself on this subject, and my advice may be classed under three heads:

Clear your souls from the taint of vanity.

Do not rejoice in conquests, either that your power to allure may be seen by other women, or for the pleasure of rousing passionate feelings that gratify your love of excitement.

It must happen, no doubt, that frank and generous women will excite love they do not reciprocate, but, in nine cases out of ten, the woman has, half consciously, done much to excite. In this case she shall not be held guiltless, either as to the unhappiness or injury to the lover. Pure love, inspired by a worthy object, must ennoble and bless, whether mutual or not; but that which is excited by coquettish attraction of any grade of refinement, must cause bitterness and doubt, as to the reality of human goodness, so soon as the flush of passion is over. And that you may avoid all taste for these false pleasures

> "Steep the soul
> In one pure love, and it will last thee long."

---

*The Persian sacred books, the Desatir, describe the great and holy prince Ky Khosrou, as being "an angel, and the son of an angel," one to whom the Supreme says, "Thou art not absent from before me for one twinkling of an eye. I am never out of thy heart. And I am contained in nothing but in thy heart, and in a heart like thy heart. And I am nearer unto thee than thou art to thyself." This Prince had in his Golden Seraglio three ladies of surpassing beauty, and all four, in this royal monastery, passed their lives, and left the world, as virgins.

The Persian people had no scepticism when the history of such a mind was narrated. They were Catholics.

The love of truth, the love of excellence, which, whether you clothe them in the person of a special object or not, will have power to save you from following Duessa, and lead you in the green glades where Una's feet have trod.[152]

It was on this one subject that a venerable champion of good, the last representative of the spirit which sanctified the revolution and gave our country such a sunlight of hope in the eyes of the nations, the same who lately in Boston offered anew to the young men the pledge taken by the young men of his day, offered, also, his counsel, on being addressed by the principal of a girl's school, thus:

Reply of Mr. Adams

MR. ADAMS was so deeply affected by the address of Miss Foster,[153] as to be for some time inaudible. When heard, he spoke as follows:

"This is the first instance in which a lady has thus addressed me personally; and I trust that all the ladies present will be able sufficiently to enter into my feelings to know, that I am more affected by this honor, than by any other I could have received.

You have been pleased, Madam, to allude to the character of my father, and the history of my family, and their services to the country. It is indeed true, that from the existence of the Republic as an independent nation, my father and myself have been in the public service of the country, almost without interruption. I came into the world, as a person having personal responsibilities, with the Declaration of Independence, which constituted us a nation. I was a child at that time, and had then perhaps the greatest of blessings that can be bestowed on man—a mother who was anxious and capable to form her children to what they ought to be. From that mother I derived whatever instruction—religious especially, and moral—has pervaded a long life; I will not say perfectly, and as it ought to be; but I will say, because it is justice only to the memory of her whom I revere, that if, in the course of my life, there has been any imperfection, or deviation from what she taught me, the fault is mine, and not hers.

"With such a mother, and such other relations with the sex, of sister, wife, and daughter, it has been the perpetual instruction of my life to love and revere the female sex. And in order to carry that sentiment of love and reverence to its highest degree of perfection, I know of nothing that exists in human society better adapted to produce that result, than institutions of the character that I have now the honor to address.

"I have been taught, as I have said, through the course of my life, to love and to revere the female sex; but I have been taught, also—and that lesson has perhaps impressed itself on my mind even more strongly, it may be, than the other—I have been taught not to flatter them. It is not unusual in the intercourse of man with the other sex—and especially for young men—to think, that the way to win the hearts of ladies is by flattery.—To love and to revere the sex, is what I think the duty of man; but *not to flatter them;* and this I would say to the young ladies here; and if they, and others present, will allow me, with all the authority which nearly four score years may have with those who have not yet attained one score—I would say to them what I have no doubt they say to themselves, and are taught here, not to take the flattery of men as proof of perfection.

"I am now, however, I fear, assuming too much of a character that does not exactly belong to me. I therefore conclude, by assuring you, Madam, that your reception of me has affected me, as you perceive, more than I can express in words; and that I shall offer my best prayers, till my latest hour, to the Creator of us all, that this institution especially, and all others of a similar kind, designed to form the female mind to wisdom and virtue, may prosper to the end of time."

It will be interesting to add here the character of Mr. Adams's mother, as drawn by her husband, the first John Adams, in a family letter* written just before his death.

"I have reserved for the last the life of Lady Russell. This I have not yet read, because I read it more than forty years ago. On this hangs a tale which you ought to know and communicate it to your children. I bought the life and letters of Lady Russell, in the year 1775, and sent it to your grandmother, with an express intent and desire, that she should consider it a mirror in which to contemplate herself; for, at that time, I thought it extremely probable, from the daring and dangerous career I was determined to run, that she would one day find herself in the situation of Lady Russell, her husband without a head. This lady was more beautiful than Lady Russell, had a brighter genius, more information, a more refined taste, and, at least, her equal in the virtues of the heart; equal fortitude and firmness of character, equal resignation to the will of Heaven, equal in all the virtues and graces of the christian life. Like Lady Russell, she never, by

---

* Journal and Correspondence of Miss Adams, vol. i. p. 246.

word or look, discouraged me from running all hazards for the salvation of my country's liberties; she was willing to share with me, and that her children should share with us both, in all the dangerous consequences we had to hazard."

Will a woman who loves flattery or an aimless excitement, who wastes the flower of her mind on transitory sentiments, ever be loved with a love like that, when fifty years trial have entitled to the privileges of "the golden marriage?"

Such was the love of the iron-handed warrior for her, not his hand-maid, but his help-meet:

"Whom God loves, to him gives he such a wife."

I find the whole of what I want in this relation, in the two epithets by which Milton makes Adam address *his* wife.

In the intercourse of every day he begins:

> "Daughter of God and man, *accomplished* Eve." *

In a moment of stronger feeling,

> "Daughter of God and man, IMMORTAL EVE." [154]

What majesty in the cadence of the line; what dignity, what reverence in the attitude, both of giver and receiver!

The woman who permits, in her life, the alloy of vanity; the woman who lives upon flattery, coarse or fine, shall never be thus addressed. She is *not* immortal as far as her will is concerned, and every woman who does so creates miasma, whose spread is indefinite. The hand, which casts into the waters of life a stone of offence, knows not how far the circles thus caused, may spread their agitations.

A little while since, I was at one of the most fashionable places of public resort. I saw there many women, dressed without regard to the season or the demands of the place, in apery, or, as it looked, in mockery of European fashions. I saw their eyes restlessly courting attention. I saw the way in which it was paid, the style of devotion, almost an open sneer, which it pleased those ladies to receive from men whose expression marked their own low position in the moral and intellectual world. Those women went to their pillows with their heads full of folly, their hearts of jealousy, or gratified vanity: those men, with the low opinion they already entertained of woman confirmed. These were American *ladies;* i. e., they

---

* See Appendix, H.

were of that class who have wealth and leisure to make full use of the day, and confer benefits on others. They were of that class whom the possession of external advantages makes of pernicious example to many, if these advantages be misused.

Soon after, I met a circle of women, stamped by society as among the most degraded of their sex. "How," it was asked of them, "did you come here?" for, by the society that I saw in the former place, they were shut up in a prison. The causes were not difficult to trace: love of dress, love of flattery, love of excitement. They had not dresses like the other ladies, so they stole them; they could not pay for flattery by distinctions, and the dower of a worldly marriage, so they paid by the profanation of their persons. In excitement, more and more madly sought from day to day, they drowned the voice of conscience.

Now I ask you, my sisters, if the women at the fashionable house be not answerable for those women being in the prison?

As to position in the world of souls, we may suppose the women of the prison stood fairest, both because they had misused less light, and because loneliness and sorrow had brought some of them to feel the need of better life, nearer truth and good. This was no merit in them, being an effect of circumstance, but it was hopeful. But you, my friends, (and some of you I have already met,) consecrate yourselves without waiting for reproof, in free love and unbroken energy, to win and to diffuse a better life. Offer beauty, talents, riches, on the altar; thus shall ye keep spotless your own hearts, and be visibly or invisibly the angels to others.

I would urge upon those women who have not yet considered this subject, to do so. Do not forget the unfortunates who dare not cross your guarded way. If it do not suit you to act with those who have organized measures of reform, then hold not yourself excused from acting in private. Seek out these degraded women, give them tender sympathy, counsel, employment. Take the place of mothers, such as might have saved them originally.

If you can do little for those already under the ban of the world, and the best considered efforts have often failed, from a want of strength in those unhappy ones to bear up against the sting of shame and the prejudices of the world, which makes them seek oblivion again in their old excitements, you will at least leave a sense of love and justice in their hearts that will prevent their becoming utterly imbittered and corrupt. And you may learn the means of prevention for those yet uninjured. There will be found in a diffusion of mental culture, simple tastes, best taught by your example, a genuine self-respect, and above all, what the influence of man tends to hide from woman, the love and fear of a divine, in preference to a human tribunal.

But suppose you save many who would have lost their bodily innocence (for as to mental, the loss of that is incalculably more general,) through mere vanity and folly; there still remain many, the prey and spoil of the brute passions of man. For the stories frequent in our newspapers outshame antiquity, and vie with the horrors of war.

As to this, it must be considered that, as the vanity and proneness to seduction of the imprisoned women represented a general degradation in their sex; so do these acts a still more general and worse in the male. Where so many are weak it is natural there should be many lost, where legislators admit that ten thousand prostitutes are a fair proportion to one city, and husbands tell their wives that it is folly to expect chastity from men, it is inevitable that there should be many monsters of vice.

I must in this place mention, with respect and gratitude, the conduct of Mrs. Child in the case of Amelia Norman.[155] The action and speech of this lady was a straight-forward nobleness, undeterred by custom or cavil from duty towards an injured sister. She showed the case and the arguments the counsel against the prisoner had the assurance to use in their true light to the public. She put the case on the only ground of religion and equity. She was successful in arresting the attention of many who had before shrugged their shoulders, and let sin pass as necessarily a part of the company of men. They begin to ask whether virtue is not possible, perhaps necessary, to man as well as to woman. They begin to fear that the perdition of a woman must involve that of a man. This is a crisis. The results of this case will be important.

In this connection I must mention Eugene Sue, the French novelist, several of whose works have been lately transplanted among us, as having the true spirit of reform as to women.[156] Like every other French writer, he is still tainted with the transmissions of the old regime. Still falsehood may be permitted for the sake of advancing truth, evil as the way to good. Even George Sand, who would trample on every graceful decorum, and every human law for the sake of a sincere life, does not see that she violates it by making her heroines able to tell falsehoods in a good cause. These French writers need ever to be confronted by the clear perception of the English and German mind, that the only good man, consequently the only good reformer, is he

"Who bases good on good alone, and owes
To virtue every triumph that he knows."

Still, Sue has the heart of a reformer, and especially towards women, he sees what they need, and what causes are injuring them. From the histories of Fleur de Marie and La Louve, from the lovely and independent character of Rigolette, from the distortion given to Matilda's mind, by the present views of marriage, and from the truly noble and immortal character of the "hump-backed Sempstress" in the "Wandering Jew," may be gathered much that shall elucidate doubt and direct inquiry on this subject. In reform, as in philosophy, the French are the interpreters to the civilized world. Their own attainments are not great, but they make clear the past, and break down barriers to the future.

Observe that the good man of Sue is pure as Sir Charles Grandison.[157]

Apropos to Sir Charles, women are accustomed to be told by men that the reform is to come *from them*. "You," say the men, "must frown upon vice, you must decline the attentions of the corrupt, you must not submit to the will of your husband when it seems to you unworthy, but give the laws in marriage, and redeem it from its present sensual and mental pollutions."

This seems to us hard. Men have, indeed, been, for more than a hundred years, rating women for countenancing vice. But at the same time, they have carefully hid from them its nature, so that the preference often shown by women for bad men, arises rather from a confused idea that they are bold and adventurous, acquainted with regions which women are forbidden to explore, and the curiosity that ensues, than a corrupt heart in the woman. As to marriage it has been inculcated on women for centuries, that men have not only stronger passions than they, but of a sort that it would be shameful for them to share or even understand. That, therefore, they must "confide in their husbands," i. e., submit implicitly to their will. That the least appearance of coldness or withdrawal, from whatever cause, in the wife is wicked, because liable to turn her husband's thoughts to illicit indulgence; for a man is so constituted that he must indulge his passions or die!

Accordingly a great part of women look upon men as a kind of wild beasts, but "suppose they are all alike;" the unmarried are assured by the married that, "if they knew men as they do," i. e., by being married to them, "they would not expect continence or self-government from them."

I might accumulate illustrations on this theme, drawn from acquaintance with the histories of women, which would startle and grieve all thinking men, but I forbear. Let Sir Charles Grandison preach to his own sex, or if none there be, who feels himself able to speak with authority from a life unspotted in will or deed, let those who are convinced of the practicability and need of a pure life, as the foreign artist was, advise the others, and warn them by their own example, if need be.

The following passage from a female writer on female affairs, expresses a prevalent way of thinking on this subject.

"It may be that a young woman, exempt from all motives of vanity, determines to take for a husband a man who does not inspire her with a very decided inclination. Imperious circumstances, the evident interest of her family, or the danger of a suffering celibacy, may explain such a resolution. If, however, she were to endeavor to surmount a personal repugnance, we should look upon this as *injudicious.* Such a rebellion of nature marks the limit that the influence of parents, or the self-sacrifice of the young girl, should never pass. *We shall be told that this repugnance is an affair of the imagination;* it may be so; but imagination is a power which it is temerity to brave; and its antipathy is more difficult to conquer than its preference." *

Among ourselves, the exhibition of such a repugnance from a woman who had been given in marriage "by advice of friends," was treated by an eminent physician as sufficient proof of insanity. If he had said sufficient cause for it, he would have been nearer right.

It has been suggested by men who were pained by seeing bad men admitted, freely, to the society of modest women, thereby encouraged to vice by impunity, and corrupting the atmosphere of homes; that there should be a senate of the matrons in each city and town, who should decide what candidates were fit for admission to their houses and the society of their daughters.†

Such a plan might have excellent results, but it argues a moral dignity and decision, which does not yet exist, and needs to be induced by knowledge and reflection. It has been the tone to keep women ignorant on these subjects, or when they were not, command that they should seem so. "It is indelicate," says the father or husband, "to inquire into the private charac-

---

* Madame Necker de Saussure.

† See Goethe's Tasso. "A synod of good women should decide,"—if the golden age is to be restored.[158]

ter of such an one. It is sufficient that I do not think him unfit to visit you."
And so, this man, who would not tolerate these pages in his house, "unfit
for family reading," because they speak plainly, introduces there a man
whose shame is written on his brow, as well as the open secret of the whole
town, and, presently, if *respectable* still, and rich enough, gives him his
daughter to wife. The mother affects ignorance, "supposing he is no worse
than most men." The daughter *is* ignorant; something in the mind of the
new spouse seems strange to her, but she supposes it is "woman's lot" not
to be perfectly happy in her affections; she has always heard, "men could
not understand women," so she weeps alone, or takes to dress and the
duties of the house. The husband, of course, makes no avowal, and dreams
of no redemption.

"In the heart of every young woman," says the female writer, above
quoted, addressing herself to the husband, "depend upon it, there is a fund
of exalted ideas; she conceals, represses, without succeeding in smothering
them. *So long as these ideas in your wife are directed to* Y O U, *they are, no doubt,
innocent,* but take care that they be not accompanied with *too much* pain. In
other respects, also, spare her delicacy. Let all the antecedent parts of your
life, if there are such, which would give her pain, be concealed from her;
her happiness and her respect for you would suffer from this misplaced confidence.
Allow her to retain that flower of purity, *which should distinguish her in your
eyes from every other woman.*" We should think so, truly, under this canon.
Such a man must esteem purity an exotic that could only be preserved by
the greatest care. Of the degree of mental intimacy possible, in such a
marriage, let every one judge for himself!

On this subject, let every woman, who has once begun to think,
examine herself, see whether she does not suppose virtue possible and
necessary to man, and whether she would not desire for her son a virtue
which aimed at a fitness for a divine life, and involved, if not asceticism,
that degree of power over the lower self, which shall "not exterminate the
passions, but keep them chained at the feet of reason." The passions, like
fire, are a bad master; but confine them to the hearth and the altar, and
they give life to the social economy, and make each sacrifice meet for
heaven.

When many women have thought upon this subject, some will be fit
for the Senate, and one such Senate in operation would affect the morals of
the civilized world.

At present I look to the young. As preparatory to the Senate, I should
like to see a society of novices, such as the world has never yet seen, bound

by no oath, wearing no badge. In place of an oath they should have a religious faith in the capacity of man for virtue; instead of a badge, should wear in the heart a firm resolve not to stop short of the destiny promisd him as a son of God. Their service should be action and conservatism, not of old habits, but of a better nature, enlightened by hopes that daily grow brighter.

If sin was to remain in the world, it should not be by their connivance at its stay, or one moment's concession to its claims.

They should succor the oppressed, and pay to the upright the reverence due in hero-worship by seeking to emulate them. They would not denounce the willingly bad, but they could not be with them, for the two classes could not breathe the same atmosphere.

They would heed no detention from the time-serving, the worldly and the timid.

They could love no pleasures that were not innocent and capable of good fruit.

I saw, in a foreign paper, the title now given to a party abroad, "Los Exaltados." [159] Such would be the title now given these children by the world: Los Exaltados, Las Exaltadas; but the world would not sneer always, for from them would issue a virtue by which it would, at last, be exalted too.

I have in my eye a youth and a maiden whom I look to as the nucleus of such a class. They are both in early youth, both as yet uncontaminated, both aspiring, without rashness, both thoughtful, both capable of deep affection, both of strong nature and sweet feelings, both capable of large mental development. They reside in different regions of earth, but their place in the soul is the same. To them I look, as, perhaps, the harbingers and leaders of a new era, for never yet have I known minds so truly virgin, without narrowness or ignorance.

When men call upon women to redeem them, they mean such maidens. But such are not easily formed under the present influences of society. As there are more such young men to help give a different tone, there will be more such maidens.

The English, novelist, D'Israeli, has, in his novel of the "Young Duke," [160] made a man of the most depraved stock be redeemed by a woman who despises him when he has only the brilliant mask of fortune and beauty to cover the poverty of his heart and brain, but knows how to encourage him when he enters on a better course. But this woman was educated by a father who valued character in women.

Still there will come now and then, one who will, as I hope of my young Exaltada, be example and instruction to the rest. It was not the opinion of woman current among Jewish men that formed the character of the mother of Jesus.

Since the sliding and backsliding men of the world, no less than the mystics declare that, as through woman man was lost, so through woman must man be redeemed, the time must be at hand. When she knows herself indeed as "accomplished," still more as "immortal Eve," this may be.

As an immortal, she may also know and inspire immortal love, a happiness not to be dreamed of under the circumstances advised in the last quotation. Where love is based on concealment, it must, of course, disappear when the soul enters the scene of clear vision!

And, without this hope, how worthless every plan, every bond, every power!

"The giants," said the Scandinavian Saga, "had induced Loke, (the spirit that hovers between good and ill,) to steal for them Iduna, (Goddess of Immortality,) and her apples of pure gold.[161] He lured her out, by promising to show, on a marvellous tree he had discovered, apples beautiful as her own, if she would only take them with her for a comparison. Thus, having lured her beyond the heavenly domain, she was seized and carried away captive by the powers of misrule.

As now the gods could not find their friend Iduna, they were confused with grief; indeed they began visibly to grow old and gray. Discords arose, and love grew cold. Indeed, Odur, spouse of the goddess of love and beauty, wandered away and returned no more. At last, however, the gods, discovering the treachery of Loke, obliged him to win back Iduna from the prison in which she sat mourning. He changed himself into a falcon, and brought her back as a swallow, fiercely pursued by the Giant King, in the form of an eagle. So she strives to return among us, light and small as a swallow. We must welcome her form as the speck on the sky that assures the glad blue of Summer. Yet one swallow does not make a summer. Let us solicit them in flights and flocks!

Returning from the future to the present, let us see what forms Iduna takes, as she moves along the declivity of centuries to the valley where the lily flower may concentrate all its fragrance.

It would seem as if this time were not very near to one fresh from books, such as I have of late been—no: *not* reading, but sighing over. A crowd of books having been sent me since my friends knew me to be engaged in this way, on Woman's "Sphere," Woman's "Mission," and

Woman"'s "Destiny," I believe that almost all that is extant of formal precept has come under my eye. Among these I read with refreshment, a little one called "The Whole Duty of Women," [162] "indited by a noble lady at the request of a noble lord," and which has this much of nobleness, that the view it takes is a religious one. It aims to fit woman for heaven, the main bent of most of the others is to fit her to please, or, at least, not to disturb a husband.

Among these I select as a favorable specimen, the book I have already quoted, "The Study* of the Life of Woman, by Madame Necker de Saussure, of Geneva, translated from the French." [163] This book was published at Philadelphia, and has been read with much favor here. Madame Necker is the cousin of Madame de Stael, and has taken from her works the motto prefixed to this.

"Cette vie n'a quelque prix que si elle sert à l'education morale de notre cœur." [164]

Mde. Necker is, by nature, capable of entire consistency in the application of this motto, and, therefore, the qualifications she makes, in the instructions given to her own sex, show forcibly the weight which still paralyzes and distorts the energies of that sex.

The book is rich in passages marked by feeling and good suggestions, but taken in the whole the impression it leaves is this:

Woman is, and *shall remain* inferior to man and subject to his will, and, in endeavoring to aid her, we must anxiously avoid any thing that can be misconstrued into expression of the contrary opinion, else the men will be alarmed, and combine to defeat our efforts.

The present is a good time for these efforts, for men are less occupied about women than formerly. Let us, then, seize upon the occasion, and do what we can to make our lot tolerable. But we must sedulously avoid encroaching on the territory of man. If we study natural history, our observations may be made useful, by some male naturalist; if we draw well, we may make our services acceptable to the artists. But our names must not be known, and, to bring these labors to any result, we must take some man for our head, and be his hands.

The lot of woman is sad. She is constituted to expect and need a happiness that cannot exist on earth. She must stifle such aspirations

---

*This title seems to be incorrectly translated from the French. I have not seen the original.

within her secret heart, and fit herself, as well as she can, for a life of resignations and consolations.

She will be very lonely while living with her husband. She must not expect to open her heart to him fully, or that, after marriage, he will be capable of the refined service of love. The man is not born for the woman, only the woman for the man. "Men cannot understand the hearts of women." The life of woman must be outwardly a well-intentioned, cheerful dissimulation of her real life.

Naturally, the feelings of the mother, at the birth of a female child, resemble those of the Paraguay woman, described by Southey as lamenting in such heart-breaking tones that her mother did not kill her the hour she was born. "Her mother, who knew what the life of a woman must be;"—or those women seen at the north by Sir A. Mackenzie,[165] who performed this pious duty towards female infants whenever they had an opportunity.

"After the first delight, the young mother experiences feelings a little different, according as the birth of a son or a daughter has been announced.

"Is it a son? A sort of glory swells at this thought the heart of the mother; she seems to feel that she is entitled to gratitude. She has given a citizen, a defender to her country. To her husband an heir of his name, to herself a protector. And yet the contrast of all these fine titles with this being, so humble, soon strikes her. At the aspect of this frail treasure, opposite feelings agitate her heart; she seems to recognize in him *a nature superior to her own,* but subjected to a low condition, and she honors a future greatness in the object of extreme compassion. Somewhat of that respect and adoration for a feeble child, of which some fine pictures offer the expression in the features of the happy Mary, seem reproduced with the young mother who has given birth to a son.

"Is it a daughter? There is usually a slight degree of regret; so deeply rooted is the idea of the superiority of man in happiness and dignity, and yet, as she looks upon this child, she is more and more *softened* towards it—a deep sympathy—a sentiment of identity with this delicate being takes possesion of her; an extreme pity for so much weakness, a more pressing need of prayer stirs her heart. Whatever sorrows she may have felt, she dreads for her daughter; but she will guide her to become much wiser, much better than herself. And then the gayety, the frivolity of the young woman have their turn. This little creature is a flower to cultivate, a doll to decorate."

Similar sadness at the birth of a daughter I have heard mothers express not unfrequently.

As to this living so entirely for men, I should think when it was proposed to women they would feel, at least, some spark of the old spirit of races allied to our own. If he is to be my bridegroom *and lord,* cries Brunhilda,[166] he must first be able to pass through fire and water. I will serve at the banquet, says the Valkyrie, but only him who, in the trial of deadly combat, has shown himself a hero.

If women are to be bond-maids, let it be to men superior to women in fortitude, in aspiration, in moral power, in refined sense of beauty! You who give yourselves "to be supported," or because "one must love something," are they who make the lot of the sex such that mothers are sad when daughters are born.

It marks the state of feeling on this subject that it was mentioned, as a bitter censure on a woman who had influence over those younger than herself. "She makes those girls want to see heroes?"

"And will that hurt them?"

"Certainly; how *can* you ask? They will find none, and so they will never be married."

"*Get* married" is the usual phrase, and the one that correctly indicates the thought, but the speakers, on this occasion, were persons too outwardly refined to use it. They were ashamed of the word, but not of the thing. Madame Necker, however, sees good possible in celibacy.

Indeed, I know not how the subject could be better illustrated, than by separating the wheat from the chaff in Madame Necker's book; place them in two heaps and then summon the reader to choose; giving him first a near-sighted glass to examine the two; it might be a christian, an astronomical, or an artistic glass, any kind of good glass to obviate acquired defects in the eye. I would lay any wager on the result.

But time permits not here a prolonged analysis. I have given the clues for fault-finding.

As a specimen of the good take the following passage, on the phenomena of what I have spoken of, as the lyrical or electric element in woman.

"Women have been seen to show themselves poets in the most pathetic pantomimic scenes, where all the passions were depicted full of beauty; and these poets used a language unknown to themselves, and the performance once over, their inspiration was a forgotten dream. Without doubt there is an interior development to beings so gifted, but their sole mode of communication with us is their talent. They are, in all besides, the inhabitants of another planet."

Similar observations have been made by those who have seen the women at Irish wakes, or the funeral ceremonies of modern Greece or Brittany, at times when excitement gave the impulse to genius; but, apparently, without a thought that these rare powers belonged to no other planet, but were a high development of the growth of this, and might by wise and reverent treatment, be made to inform and embellish the scenes of every day. But, when woman has her fair chance, they will do so, and the poem of the hour will vie with that of the ages. I come now with satisfaction to my own country, and to a writer, a female writer, whom I have selected as the clearest, wisest, and kindliest, who has as yet, used pen here on these subjects. This is Miss Sedgwick.

Miss Sedgwick, though she inclines to the private path, and wishes that, by the cultivation of character, might should vindicate right, sets limits nowhere, and her objects and inducements are pure. They are the free and careful cultivation of the powers that have been given with an aim at moral and intellectual perfection.[167] Her speech is moderate and sane, but never palsied by fear or sceptical caution.

Herself a fine example of the independent and beneficent existence that intellect and character can give to woman, no less than man, if she know how to seek and prize it; also that the intellect need not absorb or weaken, but rather will refine and invigorate the affections, the teachings of her practical good sense come with great force, and cannot fail to avail much. Every way her writings please me both as to the means and the ends. I am pleased at the stress she lays on observance of the physical laws, because the true reason is given. Only in a strong and clean body can the soul do its message fitly.

She shows the meaning of the respect paid to personal neatness both in the indispensable form of cleanliness, and of that love of order and arrangement, that must issue from a true harmony of feeling.

The praises of cold water seem to me an excellent sign in the age. They denote a tendency to the true life. We are now to have, as a remedy for ills, not orvietan, or opium, or any quack medicine, but plenty of air and water, with due attention to warmth and freedom in dress, and simplicity of diet.

Every day we observe signs that the natural feelings on these subjects are about to be reinstated, and the body to claim care as the abode and organ of the soul, not as the tool of servile labor, or the object of voluptuous indulgence.

A poor woman who had passed through the lowest grades of ignominy, seemed to think she had never been wholly lost, "for," said she, "I would always have good under-clothes;" and, indeed, who could doubt that this denoted the remains of private self-respect in the mind?

A woman of excellent sense said, "it might seem childish, but to her one of the most favorable signs of the times, was that the ladies had been persuaded to give up corsets."

Yes! let us give up all artificial means of distortion. Let life be healthy, pure, all of a piece. Miss Sedgwick, in teaching that domestics must have the means of bathing as much as their mistresses, and time, too, to bathe, has symbolized one of the most important of human rights.

Another interesting sign of the time is the influence exercised by two women, Miss Martineau and Miss Barrett, from their sick rooms.[168] The lamp of life which, if it had been fed only by the affections, depended on precarious human relations, would scarce have been able to maintain a feeble glare in the lonely prison, now shines far and wide over the nations, cheering fellow sufferers and hallowing the joy of the healthful.

These persons need not health or youth, or the charms of personal presence, to make their thoughts available. A few more such, and old woman * shall not be the synonyme for imbecility; nor old maid a term of contempt, nor woman be spoken of as a reed shaken in the wind.

It is time, indeed, that men and women both should cease to grow old in any other way than as the tree does, full of grace and honor. The hair of the artist turns white, but his eye shines clearer than ever, and we feel that age brings him maturity, not decay. So would it be with all were the springs of immortal refreshment but unsealed within the soul, then like these women they would see, from the lonely chamber window, the glories of the universe; or, shut in darkness, be visited by angels.

I now touch on my own place and day, and, as I write, events are occurring that threaten the fair fabric approached by so long an avenue. Week before last the Gentile was requested to aid the Jew to return to Palestine, for the Millennium, the reign of the Son of Mary, was near. Just now, at high and solemn mass, thanks were returned to the Virgin for having delivered O'Connell from unjust imprisonment, in requital of his

---

* An apposite passage is quoted in Appendix F.

having consecrated to her the league formed in behalf of Liberty on Tara's Hill.[169] But, last week brought news which threatens that a cause identical with the enfranchisement of Jews, Irish, women, ay, and of Americans in general, too, is in danger, for the choice of the people threatens to rivet the chains of slavery and the leprosy of sin permanently on this nation, through the annexation of Texas![170]

Ah! if this should take place, who will dare again to feel the throb of heavenly hope, as to the destiny of this country? The noble thought that gave unity to all our knowledge, harmony to all our designs;—the thought that the progress of history had brought on the era, the tissue of prophecies pointed out the spot, where humanity was, at last, to have a fair chance to know itself, and all men be born free and equal for the eagle's flight, flutters as if about to leave the breast, which, deprived of it, will have no more a nation, no more a home on earth.

Women of my country!—Exaltadas! if such there be,—Women of English, old English nobleness, who understand the courage of Boadicea, the sacrifice of Godiva, the power of Queen Emma to tread the red hot iron unharmed. Women who share the nature of Mrs. Hutchinson, Lady Russell, and the mothers of our own revolution: have you nothing to do with this?[171] You see the men, how they are willing to sell shamelessly, the happiness of countless generations of fellow-creatures, the honor of their country, and their immortal souls, for a money market and political power. Do you not feel within you that which can reprove them, which can check, which can convince them? You would not speak in vain; whether each in her own home, or banded in unison.

Tell these men that you will not accept the glittering baubles, spacious dwellings, and plentiful service, they mean to offer you through these means. Tell them that the heart of women demands nobleness and honor in man, and that, if they have not purity, have not mercy, they are no longer fathers, lovers, husbands, sons of yours.[172]

This cause is your own, for as I have before said, there is a reason why the foes of African slavery seek more freedom for women; but put it not upon that ground, but on the ground of right.

If you have a power, it is a moral power. The films of interest are not so close around you as around the men. If you will but think, you cannot fail to wish to save the country from this disgrace. Let not slip the occasion, but do something to lift off the curse incurred by Eve.

You have heard the women engaged in the abolition movement accused of boldness, because they lifted the voice in public, and lifted the latch of the stranger. But were these acts, whether performed judiciously or not, *so* bold as to dare before God and man to partake the fruits of such offence as this?

You hear much of the modesty of your sex. Preserve it by filling the mind with noble desires that shall ward off the corruptions of vanity and idleness. A profligate woman, who left her accustomed haunts and took service in a New-York boarding-house, said "she had never heard talk so vile at the Five Points, as from the ladies at the boarding-house." And why? Because they were idle; because, having nothing worthy to engage them, they dwelt, with unnatural curiosity, on the ill they dared not go to see.

It will not so much injure your modesty to have your name, by the unthinking, coupled with idle blame, as to have upon your soul the weight of not trying to save a whole race of women from the scorn that is put upon *their* modesty.

Think of this well! I entreat, I conjure you, before it is too late. It is my belief that something effectual might be done by women, if they would only consider the subject, and enter upon it in the true spirit, a spirit gentle, but firm, and which feared the offence of none, save One who is of purer eyes than to behold iniquity.

And now I have designated in outline, if not in fullness, the stream which is ever flowing from the heights of my thought.

In the earlier tract, I was told, I did not make my meaning sufficiently clear. In this I have consequently tried to illustrate it in various ways, and may have been guilty of much repetition. Yet, as I am anxious to leave no room for doubt, I shall venture to retrace, once more, the scope of my design in points, as was done in old-fashioned sermons.

Man is a being of two-fold relations, to nature beneath, and intelligence above him. The earth is his school, if not his birth-place: God his object: life and thought, his means of interpreting nature, and aspiring to God.

Only a fraction of this purpose is accomplished in the life of any one man. Its entire accomplishment is to be hoped only from the sum of the lives of men, or man considered as a whole.

As this whole has one soul and one body, any injury or obstruction to a part, or to the meanest member, affects the whole. Man can never be perfectly happy or virtuous, till all men are so.

To address man wisely, you must not forget that his life is partly animal, subject to the same laws with nature.

But you cannot address him wisely unless you consider him still more as soul, and appreciate the conditions and destiny of soul.

The growth of man is two-fold, masculine and feminine.

As far as these two methods can be distinguished they are so as Energy and Harmony.

Power and Beauty.

Intellect and Love.

Or by some such rude classification, for we have not language primitive and pure enough to express such ideas with precision.

These two sides are supposed to be expressed in man and woman, that is, as the more and less, for the faculties have not been given pure to either, but only in preponderance. There are also exceptions in great number, such as men of far more beauty than power, and the reverse. But as a general rule, it seems to have been the intention to give a preponderance on the one side, that is called masculine, and on the other, one that is called feminine.

There cannot be a doubt that, if these two developments were in perfect harmony, they would correspond to and fulfil one another, like hemispheres, or the tenor and bass in music.

But there is no perfect harmony in human nature; and the two parts answer one another only now and then, or, if there be a persistent consonance, it can only be traced, at long intervals, instead of discoursing an obvious melody.

What is the cause of this?

Man, in the order of time, was developed first; as energy comes before harmony; power before beauty.

Woman was therefore under his care as an elder. He might have been her guardian and teacher.

But as human nature goes not straight forward, but by excessive action and then reaction in an undulated course, he misunderstood and abused his advantages, and became her temporal master instead of her spiritual sire.

On himself came the punishment. He educated woman more as a servant than a daughter, and found himself a king without a queen.

The children of this unequal union showed unequal natures, and, more and more, men seemed sons of the hand-maid, rather than princes.

At last there were so many Ishmaelites that the rest grew frightened and indignant. They laid the blame on Hagar, and drove her forth into the wilderness.

But there were none the fewer Ishmaelites for that.

At last men became a little wiser, and saw that the infant Moses was, in every case, saved by the pure instincts of woman's breast. For, as too much adversity is better for the moral nature than too much prosperity, woman, in this respect, dwindled less than man, though in other respects, still a child in leading strings.

So man did her more and more justice, and grew more and more kind.

But yet, his habits and his will corrupted by the past, he did not clearly see that woman was half himself, that her interests were identical with his, and that, by the law of their common being, he could never reach his true proportions while she remained in any wise shorn of hers.

And so it has gone on to our day; both ideas developing, but more slowly than they would under a clearer recognition of truth and justice, which would have permitted the sexes their due influence on one another, and mutual improvement from more dignified relations.

Wherever there was pure love, the natural influences were, for the time, restored.

Wherever the poet or artist gave free course to his genius, he saw the truth, and expressed it in worthy forms, for these men especially share and need the feminine principle. The divine birds need to be brooded into life and song by mothers.

Wherever religion (I mean the thirst for truth and good, not the love of sect and dogma,) had its course, the original design was apprehended in its simplicity, and the dove presaged sweetly from Dodona's oak.[173]

I have aimed to show that no age was left entirely without a witness of the equality of the sexes in function, duty and hope.

Also that, when there was unwillingness or ignorance, which prevented this being acted upon, women had not the less power for their want of light and noble freedom. But it was power which hurt alike them and those against whom they made use of the arms of the servile: cunning, blandishment, and unreasonable emotion.

That now the time has come when a clearer vision and better action are possible. When man and woman may regard one another as brother and sister, the pillars of one porch, the priests of one worship.

I have believed and intimated that this hope would receive an ampler fruition, than ever before, in our own land.

And it will do so if this land carry out the principles from which sprang our national life.

I believe that, at present, women are the best helpers of one another.

Let them think; let them act; till they know what they need.

We only ask of men to remove arbitrary barriers. Some would like to do more. But I believe it needs for woman to show herself in her native dignity, to teach them how to aid her; their minds are so encumbered by tradition.

When Lord Edward Fitzgerald travelled with the Indians,[174] his manly heart obliged him at once, to take the packs from the squaws and carry them. But we do not read that the red men followed his example, though they are ready enough to carry the pack of the white woman, because she seems to them a superior being.

Let woman appear in the mild majesty of Ceres, and rudest churls will be willing to learn from her.

You ask, what use will she make of liberty, when she has so long been sustained and restrained?

I answer; in the first place, this will not be suddenly given. I read yesterday a debate of this year on the subject of enlarging women's rights over property. It was a leaf from the class book that is preparing for the needed instruction. The men leaned visibly as they spoke. The champions of woman saw the fallacy of arguments, on the opposite side, and were startled by their own convictions. With their wives at home, and the readers of the paper, it was the same. And so the stream flows on; thought urging action, and action leading to the evolution of still better thought.

But, were this freedom to come suddenly, I have no fear of the consequences. Individuals might commit excesses, but there is not only in the sex a reverence for decorums and limits inherited and enhanced from generation to generation, which many years of other life could not efface, but a native love, in woman as woman, of proportion, of "the simple art of not too much," a Greek moderation, which would create immediately a restraining party, the natural legislators and instructors of the rest, and would gradually establish such rules as are needed to guard, without impeding life.

The Graces would lead the choral dance, and teach the rest to regulate their steps to the measure of beauty.

But if you ask me what offices they may fill; I reply—any. I do not care what case you put; let them be sea-captains, if you will. I do not doubt there are women well fitted for such an office, and, if so, I should be glad to see them in it, as to welcome the maid of Saragossa, or the maid of Missolonghi, or the Suliote heroine, or Emily Plater.[175]

I think women need, especially at this juncture, a much greater range of occupation than they have, to rouse their latent powers. A party of travellers lately visited a lonely hut on a mountain. There they found an old woman that told them she and her husband had lived there forty years. "Why," they said, "did you choose so barren a spot? She "did not know; *it was the man's notion."*

And, during forty years, she had been content to act, without knowing why, upon "the man's notion." I would not have it so.

In families that I know, some little girls like to saw wood, others to use carpenters' tools. Where these tastes are indulged, cheerfulness and good humor are promoted. Where they are forbidden, because "such things are not proper for girls," they grow sullen and mischievous.

Fourier had observed these wants of women, as no one can fail to do who watches the desires of little girls, or knows the ennui[176] that haunts grown women, except where they make to themselves a serene little world by art of some kind. He, therefore, in proposing a great variety of employments, in manufactures, or the care of plants and animals, allows for one third of women, as likely to have a taste for masculine pursuits, one third of men for feminine.

Who does not observe the immediate glow and serenity that is diffused over the life of women, before restless or fretful, by engaging in gardening, building, or the lowest department of art. Here is something that is not routine, something that draws forth life toward the infinite.

I have no doubt, however, that a large proportion of women would give themselves to the same employments as now, because there are circumstances that must lead them. Mothers will delight to make the nest soft and warm. Nature would take care of that; no need to clip the wings of any bird that wants to soar and sing, or finds in itself the strength of pinion for a migratory flight unusual to its kind. The difference would be that *all* need not be constrained to employments, for which *some* are unfit.

I have urged upon the sex self-subsistence in its two forms of self-reliance and self-impulse, because I believe them to be the needed means of the present juncture.

I have urged on woman independence of man, not that I do not think the sexes mutually needed by one another, but because in woman this fact has led to an excessive devotion, which has cooled love, degraded marriage, and prevented either sex from being what it should be to itself or the other.

I wish woman to live, *first* for God's sake. Then she will not make an imperfect man her god, and thus sink to idolatry. Then she will not take what is not fit for her from a sense of weakness and poverty. Then, if she finds what she needs in man embodied, she will know how to love, and be worthy of being loved.

By being more a soul, she will not be less woman, for nature is perfected through spirit.

Now there is no woman, only an overgrown child.

That her hand may be given with dignity, she must be able to stand alone. I wish to see men and women capable of such relations as are depicted by Landor in his Pericles and Aspasia, where grace is the natural garb of strength, and the affections are calm, because deep. The softness is that of a firm tissue, as when

> "The gods approve
> The depth, but not the tumult of the soul,
> A fervent, not ungovernable love." [177]

A profound thinker has said, "no married woman can represent the female world, for she belongs to her husband. The idea of woman must be represented by a virgin."

But that is the very fault of marriage, and of the present relation between the sexes, that the woman does belong to the man, instead of forming a whole with him. Were it otherwise, there would be no such limitation to the thought.

Woman, self-centered, would never be absorbed by any relation; it would be only an experience to her as to man. It is a vulgar error that love, *a* love to woman is her whole existence; she also is born for Truth and Love in their universal energy. Would she but assume her inheritance, Mary would not be the only virgin mother. Not Manzoni alone would celebrate in his wife the virgin mind with the maternal wisdom and conjugal affections. The soul is ever young, ever virgin.

And will not she soon appear? The woman who shall vindicate their birthright for all women; who shall teach them what to claim, and how to use what they obtain? [178] Shall not her name be for her era Victoria, for her country and life Virginia? Yet predictions are rash; she herself must teach us to give her the fitting name.

An idea not unknown to ancient times has of late been revived, that, in the metamorphoses of life, the soul assumes the form, first of man, then of woman, and takes the chances, and reaps the benefits of either lot. Why then, say some, lay such emphasis on the rights or needs of woman? What she wins not, as woman, will come to her as man.

That makes no difference. It is not woman, but the law of right, the law of growth, that speaks in us, and demands the perfection of each being in its kind, apple as apple, woman as woman. Without adopting your theory I know that I, a daughter, live through the life of man; but what concerns me now is, that my life be a beautiful, powerful, in a word, a complete life in its kind. Had I but one more moment to live, I must wish the same.

Suppose, at the end of your cycle, your great world-year, all will be completed, whether I exert myself or not (and the supposition is *false*,) but suppose it true, am I to be indifferent about it? Not so! I must beat my own pulse true in the heart of the world; for *that* is virtue, excellence, health.

Thou, Lord, of Day! didst leave us to-night so calmly glorious, not dismayed that cold winter is coming, not postponing thy beneficence to the fruitful summer! Thou didst smile on thy day's work when it was done, and adorn thy down-going as thy up-rising, for thou art loyal, and it is thy nature to give life, if thou canst, and shine at all events!

I stand in the sunny noon of life. Objects no longer glitter in the dews of morning, neither are yet softened by the shadows of evening. Every spot is seen, every chasm revealed. Climbing the dusty hill, some fair effigies that once stood for symbols of human destiny have been broken; those I still have with me, show defects in this broad light. Yet enough is left, even by experience, to point distinctly to the glories of that destiny; faint, but not to be mistaken streaks of the future day. I can say with the bard,

"Though many have suffered shipwreck, still beat noble hearts."

Always the soul says to us all: Cherish your best hopes as a faith, and abide by them in action. Such shall be the effectual fervent means to their fulfilment,

> For the Power to whom we bow
> Has given its pledge that, if not now,
> They of pure and stedfast mind,
> By faith exalted, truth refined,
> *Shall* hear all music loud and clear,
> Whose first notes they ventured here.
> Then fear not thou to wind the horn,
> Though elf and gnome thy courage scorn;
> Ask for the Castle's King and Queen;
> Though rabble rout may rush between,
> Beat thee senseless to the ground,

In the dark beset thee round;
Persist to ask and it will come,
Seek not for rest in humbler home;
So shalt thou see what few have seen,
The palace home of King and Queen.[179]

15th November, 1844.

APPENDIX

※※※※※※

A

APPARITION of the goddess Isis to her votary, from Apuleius.[1]

"Scarcely had I closed my eyes, when behold (I saw in a dream) a divine form emerging from the middle of the sea, and raising a countenance venerable, even to the gods themselves. Afterwards, the whole of the most splendid image seemed to stand before me, having gradually shaken off the sea. I will endeavor to explain to you its admirable form, if the poverty of human language will but afford me the power of an appropriate narration; or if the divinity itself, of the most luminous form, will supply me with a liberal abundance of fluent diction. In the first place, then, her most copious and long hairs, being gradually intorted, and promiscuously scattered on her divine neck, were softly defluous. A multiform crown, consisting of various flowers, bound the sublime summit of her head. And in the middle of the crown, just on her forehead, there was a smooth orb resembling a mirror, or rather a white refulgent light, which indicated that she was the moon. Vipers rising up after the manner of furrows, environed the crown on the right hand and on the left, and Cerealian ears of corn were also extended from above. Her garment was of many colors, and woven from the finest flax, and was at one time lucid with a white splendor, at another yellow from the flower of crocus, and at another flaming with a rosy redness. But that which most excessively dazzled my sight, was a very black robe, fulgid with a dark splendor, and which, spreading round and passing under her right side, and ascending to her left shoulder, there rose protuberant, like the centre of a shield, the dependent part of her robe falling in many folds, and having small knots of fringe, gracefully flowing in its extremities. Glittering stars were dispersed through the embroidered border of the robe, and through the whole of its surface, and the full moon, shining in the middle of the stars, breathed forth flaming fires. A crown, wholly consisting of flowers and fruits of every kind, adhered with indivisible connexion to the border of conspicuous robe, in all its undulating motions.

"What she carried in her hands also consisted of things of a very different nature. Her right hand bore a brazen rattle, through the narrow lamina of which, bent like a belt, certain rods passing, produced a sharp triple sound through the vibrating motion of her arm. An oblong vessel, in the shape of a boat, depended from her left hand, on the handle of which, in that part which was conspicuous, an asp raised its erect head and largely swelling neck. And shoes, woven from the leaves of the victorious palm tree, covered her immortal feet. Such, and so great a goddess, breathing the fragrant odour of the shores of Arabia the happy, deigned thus to address me."

THE FOREIGN ENGLISH of the translator, Thomas Taylor, gives the description the air of being, itself, a part of the Mysteries. But its majestic beauty requires no formal initiation to be enjoyed.

B

I GIVE THIS, in the original, as it does not bear translation. Those who read Italian will judge whether it is not a perfect description of a perfect woman.

LODI E PREGHIERE A MARIA[2]

Vergine bella che di sol vestita,
Coronata di stelle, al sommo Sole
Piacesti si, che'n te sua luce ascose;
Amor mi spinge a dir di te parole:
Ma non so 'ncominciar senza tu' aita,
E di Colui che amando in te si pose.
Invoco lei che ben sempre rispose,
Chi la chiamò con fede.
Vergine, s'a mercede
Miseria extrema dell' smane cose
Giammai ti volse, al mio prego t'inchina:
Soccorri alla mia guerra;
Bench' i' sia terra, e tu del ciel Regina.

Vergine saggia, e del bel numero una
Delle beate vergini prudenti;
Anzi la prima, e con più chiara lampa;
O saldo scudo dell' afflitte gente
Contra colpi di Morte e di Fortuna,

Sotto' l qual si trionfa, non pur scampa:
    O refrigerio alcieco ardor ch' avvampa
Qui fra mortali sciocchi,
    Vergine, que' begli occhi
Che vider tristi la spietata stampa
Ne' dolci membri del tuo caro figlio,
Volgi al mio dubbio stato;
    Che sconsigliato a te vien per consiglio.

Vergine pura, d'ogni parte intera,
Del tuo parto gentil figliuola e madre;
    Che allumi questa vita, e l'altra adorni;
Per te il tuo Figlio e quel del sommo Padre,
    O finestra del ciel lucente altera,
Venne a salvarne in su gli estremi giorni,
    E fra tutt'i terreni altri soggiorni
Sola tu fusti eletta,
    Vergine benedetta;
Che 'l pianto d'Eva in allegrezza torni';
    Fammi; che puoi; della sua grazia degno,
Senza fine o beata,
    Già coronata nel superno regno.

Vergine santa d'ogni grazia piena;
Che per vera e altissima umiltate
    Salisti al ciel, onde miei preghi ascolti;
Tu partoristi il fonte di pietate,
    E di giustizia il Sol, che rasserena
Il secol pien d'erroi ascuri e folti:
    Tre dolci e eari nomi ha' in te raccolti,
Madre, Figliuola, e Sposa;
    Vergine gloriosa,
Donna del Re che nostri lacci ha sciolti,
    E fatto 'l mondo libero e felice;
Nelle cui sante piaghe
    Prego ch'appaghe il cor, vera beatrice.

Vergine sola al mondo senza esempio,
Che 'l ciel di tue bellezze innamorasti,
    Cui nè prima fu simil, nè seconda;
Santi pensieri, atti pietosi e casti
    Al vero Dio sacrato, e vivo tempio
Fecero in tua virginita feconda.

Woman in the Nineteenth Century

Per te può la mia vita esser gioconda,
S' a' tuoi preghi, o MARIA
   Vergine dolce, e pia,
Ove l' fallo abbondò, la grazia abbonda.
Con le ginocchia della mente inchine
Prego che sia mia scorta;
   E la mia torta via drizzi a buon fine.

Vergine chiara, e stabile in eterno,
Di questo tempestoso mare stella;
   D'ogni fedel nocchier fidata guida;
Pon mente in che terribile procella
   I mi ritrovo sol senza governo,
Ed ho gia' da vicin l'ultime strida:
   Ma pur' in te l'anima mia si fida;
Peccatrice; i' nol nego,
   Vergine: ma te prego
Che 'l tuo nemico del mia mal non rida:
Ricorditi che fece il peccar nostro
Prender Dio, per scamparne,
   Umana carne al tuo virginal christro.

Vergine, quante lagrime ho già sparte,
Quante lusinghe, e quanti preghi indarno,
   Pur per mia pena, e per mio grave danno!
Da poi ch' i nacqui in su la riva d' Arno;
   Cercando or questa ed or quell altra parte,
Non è stata mia vita altro ch' affanno.
Mortal bellezza, atti, e parole m' hanno
Tutta ingombrata l' alma.
   Vergine sacra, ed alma,
Non tardar; ch' i' non forse all' ultim'ann,
   I di miei piu correnti che saetta,
Fra miserie e peccati
   Sonsen andati, e sol Morte n'aspetta.

Vergine tale è terra, e posto ha in doglia
Lo mio cor; che vivendo in pianto il tenne;
   E di mille miei mali un non sapea;
E per saperlo, pur quel che n'avvenne,
   Fora avvenuto: ch' ogni altra sua voglia
Era a me morte, ed a lei fama rea
   Or tu, donna del ciel, tu nostra Dea,

Se dir lice, e conviensi;
Vergine d'alti sensi,
Tu vedi il tutto; e quel che non potea
Far altri, è nulla a e la tua gran virtute;
Pon fine al mio dolore;
Ch'a te onore ed a me tia salute.

Vergine, in cui ho tutta mia speranza
Che possi e vogli al gran bisogno aitarme;
Non mi lasciare in su l'estremo passo.
Nun guardar me, ma chi degno crearme;
No'l mio valor, ma l'alta sua sembianza;
Che in me ti mova a curar d'uorm si basso.
Medusa, e l'error mio io han fatto un sasso
D'umor vano stillante;
Vergine, tu di sante
Lagrime, e pie adempi 'l mio cor lasso;
Ch' almen l'ultimo pianto sia divoto,
Senza terrestro limo;
Come fu'l primo non d'insania voto.

Vergine umana, e nemica d'orgoglio,
Del comune principio amor t'induca;
Miserere d' un cor contrito umile;
Che se poca mortal terra caduca
Amar con si mirabil fede soglio;
Che devro far di te cosa gentile?
Se dal mio stato assai misero, e vile
Per le tue man resurgo,
Vergino; è' sacro, e purgo
Al tuo nome e pens ieri e'ngegno, e stile;
La lingua, e'l cor, le lagrime, e i sospiri,
Scorgimi al miglior guado;
E prendi in grado i cangiati desiri.

Il di s'appressa, e non pote esser lunge;
Si corre il tempo, e vola,
Vergine unica, e sola;
E'l cor' or conscienza, or morte punge.
Raccommandami al tuo Figliuol, verace
Uomo, e verace Dio;
Ch accolga l mio spirto ultimo in pace.

As the Scandinavian represented Frigga the Earth, or World mother,[3] knowing all things, yet never herself revealing them, though ready to be called to counsel by the gods. It represents her in action, decked with jewels and gorgeously attended. But, says the Mythos, when she ascended the throne of Odin, her consort (Haaven) she left with mortals, her friend, the Goddess of Sympathy, to protect them in her absence.

Since, Sympathy goes about to do good. Especially she devotes herself to the most valiant and the most oppressed. She consoled the Gods in some degree even for the death of their darling Baldur. Among the heavenly powers she has no consort.

C

"THE WEDDING OF THE LADY THERESA"

From Lockhart's Spanish Ballads[4]

" 'Twas when the fifth Alphonso in Leon held his sway,
   King Abdalla of Toledo an embassy did send;
He asked his sister for a wife, and in an evil day
   Alphonso sent her, for he feared Abdalla to offend;
He feared to move his anger, for many times before
He had received in danger much succor from the Moor.

Sad heart had fair Theresa, when she their paction knew;
   With streaming tears she heard them tell she 'mong the Moors must go;
That she, a Christian damsel, a Christian firm and true,
   Must wed a Moorish husband, it well might cause her wo;
But all her tears and all her prayers they are of small avail;
   At length she for her fate prepares, a victim sad and pale.

The king hath sent his sister to fair Toledo town,
   Where then the Moor Abdalla his royal state did keep;
When she drew near, the Moslem from his golden throne came down,
   And courteously received her, and bade her cease to weep;
With loving words he pressed her to come to his bower within;
With kisses he caressed her, but still she feared the sin.

"Sir King, Sir King, I pray thee,"—'twas thus Theresa spake,
   "I pray thee, have compassion, and do to me no wrong;
For sleep with thee I may not, unless the vows I break,

Whereby I to the holy church of Christ my Lord belong;
For thou hast sworn to serve Mahoun, and if this thing should be,
The curse of God it must bring down upon thy realm and thee.

"The angel of Christ Jesu, to whom my heavenly Lord
    Hath given my soul in keeping, is ever by my side;
If thou dost me dishonor, he will unsheath his sword,
    And smite thy body fiercely, at the crying of thy bride;
Invisible he standeth; his sword like fiery flame,
Will penetrate thy bosom, the hour that sees my shame."

The Moslem heard her with a smile; the earnest words she said,
    He took for bashful maiden's wile, and drew her to his bower:
In vain Theresa prayed and strove,—she pressed Abdalla's bed,
    Perforce received his kiss of love, and lost her maiden flower.
A woful woman there she lay, a loving lord beside,
And earnestly to God did pray, her succor to provide.

The angel of Christ Jesu her sore complaint did hear,
    And plucked his heavenly weapon from out his sheath unseen,
He waved the brand in his right hand, and to the King came near,
    And drew the point o'er limb and joint, beside the weeping Queen:
A mortal weakness from the stroke upon the King did fall;
He could not stand when daylight broke, but on his knees must crawl.

Abdalla shuddered inly, when he this sickness felt,
    And called upon his barons, his pillow to come nigh;
"Rise up," he said "my liegemen," as round his bed they knelt,
    "And take this Christian lady, else certainly I die;
Let gold be in your girdles, and precious stones beside,
    And swiftly ride to Leon, and render up my bride."

When they were come to Leon, Theresa would not go
    Into her brother's dwelling, where her maiden years were spent;
But o'er her downcast visage a white veil she did throw,
    And to the ancient nunnery of Las Huelgas went.
There, long, from worldly eyes retired, a holy life she led;
There she, an aged saint, expired; there sleeps she with the dead."

D

THE FOLLOWING EXTRACT from Spinoza[5] is worthy of attention, as expressing the view which a man of the largest intellectual scope may take of woman, if that part of his life to which her influence appeals, has been left unawakened.

He was a man of the largest intellect, of unsurpassed reasoning powers, yet he makes a statement false to history, for we well know how often men and women have ruled together without difficulty, and one in which very few men even at the present day, I mean men who are thinkers, like him, would acquiesce.

I have put in contrast with it three expressions of the latest literature.

1st. From the poems of W. E. Channing,[6] a poem called "Reverence," equally remarkable for the deep wisdom of its thought and the beauty of its utterance, and containing as fine a description of one class of women as exists in literature.

In contrast with this picture of woman, the happy Goddess of Beauty, the wife, the friend, "the summer queen," I add one by the author of "Festus,"[7] of a woman of the muse, the sybil kind, which seems painted from living experience.

And thirdly, I subjoin Eugene Sue's description of a wicked, but able woman of the practical sort, and appeal to all readers whether a species that admits of three such varieties is so easily to be classed away, or kept within prescribed limits, as Spinoza, and those who think like him, believe.

SPINOZA. TRACTATUS POLITICI, DE DEMOCRATIA, CAPUT XI.

"*PERHAPS* some one will here ask, whether the supremacy of man over woman is attributable to nature or custom? For if it be human institutions alone to which this fact is owing, there is no reason why we should exclude women from a share in government. Experience, however, most plainly teaches that it is woman's weakness which places her under the authority of man. Since it has nowhere happened that men and women ruled together; but wherever men and women are found the world over, there we see the men ruling and the women ruled, and in this order of things men and women live together in peace and harmony. The Amazons, it is true, are reputed formerly to have held the reins of government, but they drove men from their dominions; the male of their offspring they invariably destroyed, permitting their daughters alone to live. Now if women were by nature upon an equality with men, if they equalled men in fortitude, in genius (qualities which give to men might, and consequently, right) it surely would be the case, that among the numerous and diverse nations of the earth, some would be found where both sexes ruled conjointly, and others where the men were ruled by the women, and so educated as to ·be mentally inferior: since this state of things no where exists, it is perfectly fair to infer that the rights of women are not equal to those of men; but that women must be subordinate, and therefore cannot have an equal, far less a superior place in the government. If, too, we consider the passions of men—how the love men feel towards women is seldom any thing but lust and impulse, and much less a reverence for qualities of soul than an admiration of physical beauty, observing, too, how men are afflicted when their sweethearts favor other wooers, and other things of the same character,—we shall see at a glance that it would be, in the highest degree, detrimental to peace and harmony, for men and women to possess an equal share in government."

"REVERENCE"

"As an ancestral heritage revere
All learning, and all thought. The painter's fame
Is thine, whate'er thy lot, who honorest grace.
And need enough in this low time, when they,
Who seek to captivate the fleeting notes
Of heaven's sweet beauty, must despair almost,
So heavy and obdurate show the hearts
Of their companions. Honor kindly then
Those who bear up in their so generous arms
The beautiful ideas of matchless forms;
For were these not portrayed, our human fate,—
Which is to be all high, majestical,
To grow to goodness with each coming age
Till virtue leap and sing for joy to see
So noble, virtuous men,—would brief decay;
And the green, festering slime, oblivious, haunt
About our common fate. Oh honor them!

But what to all true eyes has chiefest charm,
And what to every breast where beats a heart
Framed to one beautiful emotion,—to
One sweet and natural feeling, lends a grace
To all the tedious walks of common life,
This is fair woman,—woman, whose applause
Each poet sings,—woman the beautiful.
Not that her fairest brow, or gentlest form

Woman in the Nineteenth Century

Charm us to tears; not that the smoothest cheek,
Where ever rosy tints have made their home,
So rivet us on her; but that she is
The subtle, delicate grace,—the inward grace,
For words too excellent; the noble, true,
The majesty of earth; the summer queen:
In whose conceptions nothing but what's great
Has any right. And, O! her love for him,
Who does but his small part in honoring her;
Discharging a sweet office, sweeter none,
Mother and child, friend, counsel and repose:—
Nought matches with her, nought has leave with her
To highest human praise. Farewell to him
Who reverences not with an excess
Of faith the beauteous sex: all barren he
Shall live a living death of mockery.

Ah! had but words the power, what could we say
Of woman! We, rude men, of violent phrase,
Harsh action, even in repose inwardly harsh;
Whose lives walk blustering on high stilts, removed
From all the purely gracious influence
Of mother earth. To single from the host
Of angel forms one only, and to her
Devote our deepest heart and deepest mind
Seems almost contradiction. Unto her
We owe our greatest blessings, hours of cheer,
Gay smiles, and sudden tears, and more than these
A sure perpetual love. Regard her as
She walks along the vast still earth; and see!
Before her flies a laughing troop of joys,
And by her side treads old experience,
With never-failing voice admonitory;
The gentle, though infallible, kind advice,
The watchful care, the fine regardfulness,
Whatever mates with what we hope to find,
All consummate in her—the summer queen.

To call past ages better than what now
Man is enacting on life's crowded stage,
Cannot improve our worth; and for the world
Blue is the sky as ever, and the stars
Kindle their crystal flames at soft-fallen eve

Woman in the Nineteenth Century

With the same purest lustre that the east
Worshipped. The river gently flows through fields
Where the broad-leaved corn spreads out, and loads
Its ear as when the Indian tilled the soil.
The dark green pine,—green in the winter's cold,
Still whispers meaning emblems, as of old;
The cricket chirps, and the sweet, eager birds
In the sad woods crowd their thick melodies;
But yet, to common eyes, life's poetry
Something has faded, and the cause of this
May be that man, no longer at the shrine
Of woman, kneeling with true reverence,
In spite of field, wood, river, stars and sea
Goes most disconsolate. A babble now,
A huge and wind-swelled babble, fills the place
Of that great adoration which of old
Man had for woman. In these days no more
Is love the pith and marrow of man's fate.

Thou who in early years feelest awake
To finest impulses from nature's breath,
And in thy walk hearest such sounds of truth
As on the common ear strike without heed,
Beware of men around thee. Men are foul,
With avarice, ambition and deceit;
The worst of all, ambition, This is life
Spent in a feverish chase for selfish ends,
Which has no virtue to redeem its toil
But one long, stagnant hope to arise the self.
The miser's life to this seems sweet and fair;
Better to pile the glittering coin, than seek
To overtop our brothers and our loves.
Merit in this? Where lies it, though thy name
Ring over distant lands, meeting the wind
Even on the extremest verge of the wide world.
Merit in this? Better be hurled abroad
On the vast whirling tide, than in thyself
Concentred, feed upon thy own applause.
Thee shall the good man yield no reverence;
But, while the idle, dissolute crowd are loud
In voice to send thee flattery, shall rejoice

That he has scaped thy fatal doom, and known
How humble faith in the good soul of things
Provides amplest employment. O my brother,
If the Past's counsel any honor claim
From thee, go read the history of those
Who a like path have trod, and see a fate
Wretched with fears, changing like leaves at noon,
When the new wind sings in the white birch wood.
Learn from the simple child the rule of life,
And from the movement of the unconscious tribes
Of animal nature, those that bend the wing
Or cleave the azure tide, content to be,
What the great frame provides,—freedom and grace.
Thee, simple child, do the swift winds obey,
And the white waterfalls with their bold leaps
Follow thy movements. Tenderly the light
Thee watches, girding with a zone of radiance,
And all the swinging herbs love thy soft steps."

DESCRIPTION OF ANGELA, FROM "FESTUS"

"I loved her for that she was beautiful,
And that to me she seemed to be all nature
And all varieties of things in one;
Would set at night in clouds of tears, and rise
All light and laughter in the morning; fear
No petty customs nor appearances,
But think what others only dreamed about;
And say what others did but think; and do
What others would but say; and glory in
What others dared but do; it was these which won me;
And that she never schooled within her breast
One thought or feeling, but gave holiday
To all; and that she told me all her woes
And wrongs and ills; and so she made them mine
In the communion of love; and we
Grew like each other, for we loved each other;
She mild and generous as the sun in spring;
And I, like earth, all budding out with love.

       *   *   *

Woman in the Nineteenth Century

The beautiful are never desolate:
For some one always love them; God or man;
If man abandons, God Himself takes them:
And thus it was. She whom I once loved died,
The lightning loathes its cloud; the soul its clay.
Can I forget that hand I took in mine,
Pale as pale violets; that eye, where mind
And matter met alike divine?—ah, no!
May God that moment judge me when I do!
Oh! she was fair; her nature once all spring
And deadly beauty, like a maiden sword,
Startingly beautiful. I see her now!
Wherever thou art thy soul is in my mind;
Thy shadow hourly lengthens o'er my brain
And peoples all its pictures with thyself;
Gone, not forgotten; passed, not lost; thou wilt shine
In heaven like a bright spot in the sun!
She said she wished to die, and so she died,
For, cloudlike, she poured out her love, which was
Her life, to freshen this parched heart. It was thus;
I said we were to part, but she said nothing;
There was no discord; it was music ceased,
Life's thrilling, bursting, bounding joy. She sate,
Like a house-god, her hands fixed on her knee,
And her dark hair lay loose and long behind her,
Through which her wild bright eye flashed like a flint;
She spake not, moved not, but she looked the more,
As if her eye were action, speech, and feeling.
I felt it all, and came and knelt beside her,
The electric touch solved both our souls together;
Then came the feeling which unmakes, undoes;
Which tears the sealike soul up by the roots,
And lashes it in scorn against the skies.

*   *   *

It is the saddest and the sorest sight,
One's own love weeping. But why call on God?
But that the feeling of the boundless bounds
All feeling; as the welkin does the world;
It is this which ones us with the whole and God.
Then first we wept; then closed and clung together;
And my heart shook this building of my breast

Like a live engine booming up and down:
She fell upon me like a snow-wreath thawing.
Never were bliss and beauty, love and wo,
Ravelled and twined together into madness,
As in that one wild hour to which all else
The past, is but a picture. That alone
Is real, and forever there in front.

     *   *   *

   * * * After that I left her,
And only saw her once again alive."

"Mother Saint Perpetua, the superior of the convent, was a tall woman, of about forty years, dressed in dark gray serge, with a long rosary hanging at her girdle; a white mob cap, with a long black veil, surrounded her thin wan face with its narrow hooded border. A great number of deep transverse wrinkles plowed her brow, which resembled yellowish ivory in color and substance. Her keen and prominent nose was curved like the hooked beak of a bird of prey; her black eye was piercing and sagacious; her face was at once intelligent, firm, and cold.

"For comprehending and managing the material interests of the society, Mother Saint Perpetua could have vied with the shrewdest and most wily lawyer. When women are possessed of what is called *business talent,* and when they apply thereto the sharpness of perception, the indefatigable perseverance, the prudent dissimulation, and above all, the correctness and rapidity of judgment at first sight, which are peculiar to them, they arrive at prodigious results.

"To Mother Saint Perpetua, a woman of a strong and solid head, the vast monied business of the society was but child's play. None better than she understaood how to buy depreciated properties, to raise them to their original value, and sell them to advantage; the average purchase of rents, the fluctuations of exchange, and the current prices of shares in all the leading speculations, were perfectly familiar to her. Never had she directed her agents to make a single false speculation, when it had been the question how to invest funds, with which good souls were constantly endowing the society of Saint Mary. She had established in the house a degree of order, of discipline, and, above all, of economy, that were indeed remarkable; the constant aim of all her exertions being, not to enrich herself, but the community over which she presided; for the spirit of association, when it is directed to an object of *collective selfishness,* gives to corporations all the faults and vices of individuals."

E

THE FOLLOWING is an extract from a letter addressed to me by one of the monks of the 19th century. A part I have omitted, because it does not express my own view, unless with qualifications which I could not make, except by full discussion of the subject.

"Woman in the 19th century should be a pure, chaste, holy being.

This state of being in woman is no more attained by the expansion of her intellectual capacity, than by the augmentation of her physical force.

Neither is it attained by the increase or refinement of her love for man, or for any object whatever, or for all objects collectively; but

This state of being is attained by the reference of all her powers and all her actions to the source of Universal Love, whose constant requisition is a pure, chaste and holy life.

So long as woman looks to man (or to society) for that which she needs, she will remain in an indigent state, for he himself is indigent of it, and as much needs it as she does.

So long as this indigence continues, all unions or relations constructed between man and woman are constructed in indigence, and can produce only indigent results or unhappy consequences.

The unions now constructing, as well as those in which the parties constructing them were generated, being based on self-delight, or lust, can lead to no more happiness in the 20th, than is found in the 19th century.

It is not amended institutions, it is not improved education, it is not another selection of individuals for union, that can meliorate the sad result, but the *basis* of the union must be changed.

If in the natural order Woman and Man would adhere strictly to physiological or natural laws, in physical chastity, a most beautiful amendment of the human race, and human condition, would in a few generations adorn the world.

Still, it belongs to Woman in the spiritual order, to devote herself wholly to her eternal husband, and become the Free Bride of the One who alone can elevate her to her true position, and reconstruct her a pure, chaste, and holy being."

F

I HAVE MISLAID an extract from "The Memoirs of an American Lady"[8] which I wished to use on this subject, but its import is, briefly, this:

Observing of how little consequence the Indian women are in youth, and how much in age, because in that trying life, good counsel and sagacity are more prized than charms, Mrs. Grant expresses a wish that Reformers would take a hint from observation of this circumstance.

In another place she says: "The misfortune of our sex is, that young women are not regarded as the material from which old women must be made."

I quote from memory, but believe the weight of the remark is retained.

G

EURIPIDES. SOPHOCLES.

AS MANY ALLUSIONS are made in the foregoing pages to characters of women drawn by the Greek dramatists, which may not be familiar to the majority of readers, I have borrowed from the papers of Miranda,[9] some notes upon them. I trust the girlish tone of apostrophizing rapture may be excused. Miranda was very young at the time of writing, compared with her present mental age. *Now,* she would express the same feelings, but in a worthier garb—if she expressed them at all.

"Iphigenia! Antigone! you were worthy to live! *We* are fallen on evil times, my sisters! our feelings have been checked; our thoughts questioned; our forms dwarfed and defaced by a bad nurture. Yet hearts, like yours, are in our breasts, living, if unawakened; and our minds are capable of the same resolves. You, we understand at once, those who stare upon us pertly in the street, we cannot—could never understand.

You knew heroes, maidens, and your fathers were kings of men. You believed in your country, and the gods of your country. A great occasion was given to each, whereby to test her character.

You did not love on earth; for the poets wished to show us the force of woman's nature, virgin and unbiassed. You were women; not wives, or lovers, or mothers. Those are great names, but we are glad to see *you* in untouched dower.

Were brothers so dear, then, Antigone? We have no brothers. We see no men into whose lives we dare look steadfastly, or to whose destinies we look forward confidently. We care not for their urns; what inscription could we put upon them? They live for petty successes; or to win daily the bread of the day. No spark of kingly fire flashes from their eyes.

None! are there *none?*

It is a base speech to say it. Yes! there are some such; we have sometimes caught their glances. But rarely have they been rocked in the same cradle as we, and they do not look upon us much; for the time is not yet come.

Thou art so grand and simple! we need not follow thee; thou dost not need our love.

But, sweetest Iphigenia; who knew *thee,* as to me thou art known. I was not born in vain, if only for the heavenly tears I have shed with thee. She will be grateful for them. I have understood her wholly; as a friend should, better than she understood herself.

With what artless art the narrative rises to the crisis. The conflicts in Agamemnon's mind, and the imputations of Menelaus give us, at once, the full image of him, strong in will and pride, weak in virtue, weak in the noble powers of the mind that depend on imagination. He suffers, yet it requires the presence of his daughter to make him feel the full horror of what he is to do.

"Ah me! that breast, those cheeks, those golden tresses!" [10]

It is her beauty, not her misery, that makes the pathos. This is noble. And then, too, the injustice of the gods, that she, this creature of unblemished loveliness, must perish for the sake of a worthless woman. Even Menelaus feels it, the moment he recovers from his wrath.

> "What hath she to do,
> The virgin daughter, with my Helena!
>   *   *   Its former reasonings now
> My soul foregoes.   *   *   *   *
>   For it is not just
> That thou shouldst groan, but my affairs go pleasantly,
> That those of thy house should die, and mine see the light."

Indeed the overwhelmed aspect of the king of men might well move him.

Men. "Brother, give me to take thy right hand,
Aga. I give it, *for* the victory is thine, and I am wretched.
I am, indeed, ashamed to drop the tear,
And not to drop the tear I am ashamed."

How beautifully is Iphigenia introduced; beaming more and more softly on us with every touch of description. After Clytemnestra has given Orestes (then an infant,) out of the chariot, she says:

"Ye females, in your arms,
Receive her, for she is of tender age.
Sit here by my feet, my child,
By thy mother, Iphigenia, and show
These strangers how I am blessed in thee,
And here address thee to thy father.
Iphi. Oh mother, should I run, wouldst thou be angry?
And embrace my father breast to breast?"

With the same sweet timid trust she prefers the request to himself, and as he holds her in his arms, he seems as noble as Guido's Archangel; as if he never could sink below the trust of such a being!

The Achilles, in the first scene, is fine. A true Greek hero; not too good; all flushed with the pride of youth; but capable of god-like impulses. At first, he thinks only of his own wounded pride, (when he finds Iphigenia has been decoyed to Aulis under the pretext of becoming his wife;) but the grief of the queen soon makes him superior to his arrogant chafings. How well he says:—

"*Far as a young man may,* I will repress
So great a wrong."

By seeing him here, we understand why he, not Hector, was the hero of the Iliad. The beautiful moral nature of Hector was early developed by close domestic ties, and the cause of his country. Except in a purer simplicity of speech and manner, he might be a modern and a christian. But Achilles is cast in the largest and most vigorous mould of the earlier day: his nature is one of the richest capabilities, and therefore less quickly unfolds its meaning. The impression it makes at the early period is only of power and pride; running as fleetly with his armor on, as with it off; but sparks of pure lustre are struck, at moments, from the mass of ore. Of this sort is his refusal to see the beautiful virgin he has promised to protect. None of the

Grecians must have the right to doubt his motives. How wise and prudent, too, the advice he gives as to the queen's conduct! He will not show himself, unless needed. His pride is the farthest possible remote from vanity. His thoughts are as free as any in our own time.

> "The prophet? what is he? a man
> Who speaks 'mong many falsehoods, but few truths,
> Whene'er chance leads him to speak true; when false,
> The prophet is no more."

Had Agamemnon possessed like clearness of sight, the virgin would not have perished, but also, Greece would have had no religion and no national existence.

When, in the interview with Agamemnon, the Queen begins her speech, in the true matrimonial style, dignified though her gesture be, and true all she says, we feel that truth, thus sauced with taunts, will not touch his heart, nor turn him from his purpose. But when Iphigenia begins her exquisite speech, as with the breathings of a lute,

> "Had I, my father, the persuasive voice
> Of Orpheus, &c.
>
> Compel me not
> What is beneath to view. I was the first
> To call thee father; me thou first didst call
> Thy child: I was the first that on thy knees
> Fondly caressed thee, and from thee received
> The fond caress: this was thy speech to me:—
> 'Shall I, my child, e'er see thee in some house
> Of splendor, happy in thy husband, live
> And flourish, as becomes my dignity?'
> My speech to thee was, leaning 'gainst thy cheek,
> (Which with my hand I now caress:) 'And what
> Shall I then do for thee? shall I receive
> My father when grown old, and in my house
> Cheer him with each fond office, to repay
> The careful nurture which he gave my youth?'
> These words are in my memory deep impressed,
> Thou hast forgot them and will kill thy child."

Then she adjures him by all the sacred ties, and dwells pathetically on the circumstance which had struck even Menelaus.

"If Paris be enamored of his bride,
His Helen, what concerns it me? and how
Comes he to my destruction?
        Look upon me;
Give me a smile, give me a kiss, my father;
That if my words persuade thee not, in death
I may have this memorial of thy love."

Never have the names of father and daughter been uttered with a holier tenderness than by Euripides, as in this most lovely passage, or in the "Supplicants,"[11] after the voluntary death of Evadne; Iphis says

"What shall this wretch now do? Should I return
To my own house?—and desolation there
I shall behold, to sink my soul with grief.
Or go I to the house of Capaneus?
That was delightful to me, when I found
My daughter there; but she is there no more:
Oft would she kiss my cheek, with fond caress
Oft soothe me. To a father, waxing old,
Nothing is dearer than a daughter! sons
Have spirits of higher pitch, but less inclined
To sweet endearing fondness. Lead me then,
Instantly lead me to my house, consign
My wretched age to darkness, there to pine
And waste away.
        Old age,
Struggling with many griefs, O how I hate thee!"

But to return to Iphigenia,—how infinitely melting is her appeal to Orestes, whom she holds in her robe.

"My brother, small assistance canst thou give
Thy friends; yet for thy sister with thy tears
Implore thy father that she may not die:
Even infants have a sense of ills; and see,
My father! silent though he be, he sues
To thee: be gentle to me; on my life
Have pity: thy two children by this beard
Entreat thee, thy dear children: one is yet
An infant, one to riper years arrived."

The mention of Orestes, then an infant, all through, though slight, is of a domestic charm that prepares the mind to feel the tragedy of his after lot. When the Queen says

> "Dost thou sleep,
> My son? The rolling chariot hath subdued thee;
> Wake to thy sister's marriage happily."

We understand the horror of the doom which makes this cherished child a parricide. And so when Iphigenia takes leave of him after her fate is by herself accepted.

> *Iphi.* "To manhood train Orestes.
> *Cly.* Embrace him, for thou ne'er shalt see him more.
> *Iphi.* (*To Orestes.*) Far as thou couldst, thou didst assist thy friends.

We know now how to blame the guilt of the maddened wife and mother. In her last meeting with Agamemnon, as in her previous expostulations and anguish, we see that a straw may turn the balance, and make her his deadliest foe. Just then, came the suit of Ægisthus, then, when every feeling was uprooted or lacerated in her heart.

Iphigenia's moving address has no further effect than to make her father turn at bay and brave this terrible crisis. He goes out, firm in resolve; and she and her mother abandon themselves to a natural grief.

Hitherto nothing has been seen in Iphigenia, except the young girl, weak, delicate, full of feeling and beautiful as a sunbeam on the full green tree. But, in the next scene, the first impulse of that passion which makes and unmakes us, though unconfessed even to herself, though hopeless and unreturned, raises her at once into the heroic woman, worthy of the goddess who demands her.

Achilles appears to defend her, whom all others clamorously seek to deliver to the murderous knife. She sees him, and fired with thoughts, unknown before, devotes herself at once for the country which has given birth to such a man.

> "To be too fond of life
> Becomes not me; nor for myself alone,
> But to all Greece, a blessing didst thou bear me.
> Shall thousands, when their country's injured, lift
> Their shields; shall thousands grasp the oar, and dare,
> Advancing bravely 'gainst the foe, to die
> For Greece? And shall my life, my single life,

Obstruct all this? Would this be just? What word
Can we reply? Nay more, it is not right
That he with all the Grecians should contest
In fight, should die, *and for a woman.* No:
More than a thousand women is one man
Worthy to see the light of day.
    *   *   *   for Greece I give my life.
  Slay me; demolish Troy: for these shall be
Long time my monuments, my children these,
My nuptials and my glory."

This sentiment marks woman, when she loves enough to feel what a
creature of glory and beauty a true *man* would be, as much in our own time
as that of Euripides. Cooper makes the weak Hetty say to her beautiful
sister:

"Of course, I don't compare you with Harry. A handsome man is
always far handsomer than any woman." [12] True, it was the sentiment of
the age, but it was the first time Iphigenia had felt it. In Agamemnon she
saw *her father,* to him she could prefer her claim. In Achilles she saw *a man,*
the crown of creation, enough to fill the world with his presence, were all
other beings blotted from its spaces.*

The reply of Achilles is as noble. Here is his bride, he feels it now, and
all his vain vauntings are hushed.

"Daughter of Agamemnon, highly blessed
Some god would make me, if I might attain
Thy nuptials. Greece in thee I happy deem,
And thee in Greece.   *   *
   *   *   *   in thy thought
Revolve this well; death is a dreadful thing."

How sweet is her reply, and then the tender modesty with which she
addresses him here and elsewhere as *"stranger."*

"Reflecting not on any, thus I speak:
Enough of wars and slaughters from the charms

---

*Men do not often reciprocate this pure love.

"Her prentice han' she tried on man,
  And then she made the losses o',"

Is a fancy, not a feeling, in their more frequently passionate and strong, than noble
or tender natures.

Of Helen rise; but die not thou for me,
O Stranger, nor distain thy sword with blood,
But let me save my country if I may."

Achilles. "O glorious spirit! nought have I 'gainst this
To urge, since such thy will, for what thou sayst
Is generous. Why should not the truth be spoken?"

But feeling that human weakness may conquer yet, he goes to wait at the altar, resolved to keep his promise of protection thoroughly.

In the next beautiful scene she shows that a few tears might overwhelm her in his absence. She raises her mother beyond weeping them, yet her soft purity she cannot impart.

Iphi. "My father, and thy husband do not hate:
Cly. For thy dear sake fierce contests must he bear.
Iphi. For Greece reluctant me to death he yields;
Cly. Basely, with guile unworthy Atreus' son."

This is truth incapable of an answer and Iphigenia attempts none. She begins the hymn which is to sustain her,

"Lead me; mine the glorious fate,
To o'erturn the Phrygian state."

After the sublime flow of lyric heroism, she suddenly sinks back into the tenderer feeling of her dreadful fate.

"O my country, where these eyes
Opened on Pelasgic skies!
O ye virgins, once my pride,
In Mycenæ who abide!
          CHORUS.
Why of Perseus name the town,
Which Cyclopean ramparts crown?
          IPHIGENIA.
Me you rear'd a beam of light,
Freely now I sink in night."

Freely; as the messenger afterwards recounts it.

*   *   *

"Imperial Agamemnon, when he saw
His daughter, as a victim to the grave,
Advancing, groan'd, and bursting into tears,
Turned from the sight his head, before his eyes,

Holding his robe. The virgin near him stood,
And thus addressed him: 'Father, I to thee
Am present: for my country, and for all
The land of Greece, I freely give myself
A victim: to the altar let them lead me,
Since such the oracle. If aught on me
Depends, be happy, and obtain the prize
Of glorious conquest, and revisit safe
Your country. Of the Grecians, for this cause,
Let no one touch me; with intrepid spirit
Silent will I present my neck.' She spoke,
And all that heard revered the noble soul
And virtue of the virgin."

How quickly had the fair bud bloomed up into its perfection. Had she lived a thousand years, she could not have surpassed this. Goethe's Iphigenia, the mature woman, with its myriad delicate traits, never surpasses, scarcely equals what we know of her in Euripides.

Can I appreciate this work in a translation? I think so, impossible as it may seem to one who can enjoy the thousand melodies, and words in exactly the right place and cadence of the original. They say you can see the Apollo Belvidere in a plaster cast, and I cannot doubt it, so great the benefit conferred on my mind, by a transcript thus imperfect. And so with these translations from the Greek. I can divine the original through this veil, as I can see the movements of a spirited horse by those of his coarse grasscloth muffler. Beside, every translator who feels his subject is inspired, and the divine Aura informs even his stammering lips.

Iphigenia is more like one of the women Shakspeare loved than the others; she is a tender virgin, ennobled and strengthened by sentiment more than intellect, what they call a woman *par excellence.*

Macaria[13] is more like one of Massinger's women. She advances boldly, though with the decorum of her sex and nation:

> *Macaria.* "Impute not boldness to me that I come
> Before you, strangers; this my first request
> I urge; for silence and a chaste reserve
> Is woman's genuine praise, and to remain
> Quiet within the house. But I come forth,
> Hearing thy lamentations, Iolaus:

Though charged with no commission, yet perhaps,
I may be useful."

Her speech when she offers herself as the victim, is reasonable, as one might speak to-day. She counts the cost all through. Iphigenia is too timid and delicate to dwell upon the loss of earthly bliss, and the due experience of life, even as much as Jeptha's daughter[14] did, but Macaria is explicit, as well befits the daughter of Hercules.

> "Should *these* die, myself
> Preserved, of prosperous future could I form
> One cheerful hope?
> A poor forsaken virgin who would deign
> To take in marriage! Who would wish for sons
> From one so wretched? Better then to die,
> Than bear such undeserved miseries:
> One less illustrious thus might more beseem.
>
>   *   *   *
>
> I have a soul that unreluctantly
> Presents itself, and I proclaim aloud
> That for my brothers and myself I die.
> I am not fond of life, but think I gain
> An honorable prize to die with glory."

Still nobler when Iolaus proposes rather that she shall draw lots with her sisters.

> "*By lot* I will not die, for to such death
> No thanks are due, or glory—name it not.
> If you accept me, if my offered life
> Be grateful to you, willingly I give it
> For these, but by constraint I will not die."

Very fine are her parting advice and injunctions to them all:

> "Farewell! revered old man, farewell! and teach
> These youths in all things to be wise, like thee,
> Naught will avail them more."

Macaria has the clear Minerva eye: Antigone's is deeper, and more capable of emotion, but calm. Iphigenia's glistening, gleaming with angel truth, or dewy as a hidden violet.

I am sorry that Tennyson, who spoke with such fitness of all the others in his "Dream of fair women," has not of Iphigenia. Of her alone he has not made a fit picture, but only of the circumstances of the sacrifice. He can never have taken to heart this work of Euripides, yet he was so worthy to feel it. Of Jeptha's daughter, he has spoken as he would of Iphigenia, both in her beautiful song, and when

> "I heard Him, for He spake, and grief became
> A solemn scorn of ills.
>
> It comforts me in this one thought to dwell
> That I subdued me to my father's will;
> Because the kiss he gave me, ere I fell,
> Sweetens the spirit still.
>
> Moreover it is written, that my race
> Hewed Ammon, hip and thigh from Arroer
> Or Arnon unto Minneth. Here her face
> Glow'd as I look'd on her.
>
> She locked her lips; she left me where I stood;
> "Glory to God," she sang, and past afar,
> Thridding the sombre boskage of the woods,
> Toward the morning star." [15]

In the "Trojan dames" [16] there are fine touches of nature with regard to Cassandra. Hecuba shows that mixture of shame and reverence, that prose kindred always do, towards the inspired child, the poet, the elected sufferer for the race.

When the herald announces that she is chosen to be the mistress of Agamemnon, Hecuba answers indignant, and betraying the involuntary pride and faith she felt in this daughter.

> "The virgin of Apollo, whom the God,
> Radiant with golden locks, allowed to live
> In her pure vow of maiden chastity?
> *Tal.* With love the raptured virgin smote his heart.
> *Hec.* Cast from thee, O my daughter, cast away
> Thy sacred wand, rend off the honored wreaths,
> The splendid ornaments that grace thy brows."

Yet the moment Cassandra appears, singing wildly her inspired song, Hecuba calls her

> "My *frantic* child."

Yet how graceful she is in her tragic phrenzy, the chorus shows—

> "How sweetly at thy house's ills thou smil'st,
> Chanting what haply thou wilt not show true?"

But if Hecuba dares not trust her highest instinct about her daughter, still less can the vulgar mind of the herald (a man not without tenderness of heart, but with no princely, no poetic blood,) abide the wild prophetic mood which insults his prejudices both as to country and decorums of the sex. Yet Agamemnon, though not a noble man, is of large mould and could admire this strange beauty which excited distaste in common minds.

> *Tal.* "What commands respect, and is held high
> As wise, is nothing better than the mean
> Of no repute: for this most potent king
> Of all the Grecians, the much honored son
> Of Atreus, is enamored with his prize,
> This frantic raver. I am a poor man,
> Yet would I not receive her to my bed."

Cassandra answers with a careless disdain,

> "This is a busy slave."

With all the lofty decorum of manners among the ancients, how free was their intercourse, man to man, how full the mutual understanding between prince and "busy slave!" Not here in adversity only, but in the pomp of power, it was so. Kings were approached with ceremonious obeisance, but not hedged round with etiquette, they could see and know their fellows.

The Andromache here is just as lovely as that of the Iliad.

To her child whom they are about to murder, the same that was frightened at the "glittering plume."

> "Dost thou weep,
> My son? Hast thou a sense of thy ill fate?
> Why dost thou clasp me with thy hands, why hold
> My robes, and shelter thee beneath my wings,
> Like a young bird? No more my Hector comes,
> Returning from the tomb; he grasps no more
> His glittering spear, bringing protection to thee."

*   *   *

> *   *   "O soft embrace,
> And to thy mother dear. O fragrant breath!
> In vain I swathed thy infant limbs, in vain
> I gave thee nurture at this breast, and toiled,
> Wasted with care. *If ever,* now embrace,
> Now clasp thy mother; throw thine arms around
> My neck and join thy cheek, thy lips to mine."

As I look up I meet the eyes of Beatrice Cenci.[17] Beautiful one, these woes, even, were less than thine, yet thou seemest to understand them all. Thy clear melancholy gaze says, they, at least, had known moments of bliss, and the tender relations of nature had not been broken and polluted from the very first. Yes! the gradations of wo are all but infinite: only good can be infinite.

Certainly the Greeks knew more of real home intercourse, and more of woman than the Americans. It is in vain to tell me of outward observances. The poets, the sculptors always tell the truth. In proportion as a nation is refined, women *must* have an ascendancy, it is the law of nature.

Beatrice! thou wert not "fond of life," either, more than those princesses. Thou wert able to cut it down in the full flower of beauty, as an offering to *the best* known to thee. Thou wert not so happy as to die for thy country or thy brethren, but thou wert worthy of such an occasion.

In the days of chivalry woman was habitually viewed more as an ideal, but I do not know that she inspired a deeper and more home-felt reverence than Iphigenia in the breast of Achilles, or Macaria in that of her old guardian, Iolaus.

We may, with satisfaction, add to these notes the words to which Haydn has adapted his magnificent music in "The Creation."[18]

"In native worth and honor clad, with beauty, courage, strength adorned, erect to heaven, and tall, he stands, a Man!—the lord and king of all! The large and arched front sublime of wisdom deep declares the seat, and in his eyes with brightness shines the soul, the breath and image of his God. With fondness leans upon his breast the partner for him formed, a woman fair, and graceful spouse. Her softly smiling virgin looks, of flowery spring the mirror, bespeak him love, and joy and bliss."

Whoever has heard this music must have a mental standard as to what man and woman should be. Such was marriage in Eden, when "erect to heaven *he* stood," but since, like other institutions, this must be not only reformed, but revived, may be offered as a picture of something intermediate,—the seed of the future growth,—

H

THE SACRED MARRIAGE

And has another's life as large a scope?
It may give due fulfilment to thy hope,
And every portal to the unknown may ope.

If, near this other life, thy inmost feeling
Trembles with fateful prescience of revealing
The future Deity, time is still concealing.

If thou feel thy whole force drawn more and more
To launch that other bark on seas without a shore;
And no still secret must be kept in store;

If meannesses that dim each temporal deed,
The dull decay that mars the fleshly weed,
And flower of love that seems to fall and leave no seed—

Hide never the full presence from thy sight
Of mutual aims and tasks, ideals bright,
Which feed their roots to-day on all this seeming blight.

Twin stars that mutual circle in the heaven,
Two parts for spiritual concord given,
Twin Sabbaths that inlock the Sacred Seven;

Still looking to the centre for the cause,
Mutual light giving to draw out the powers,
And learning all the other groups by cognizance of one another's laws:

The parent love the wedded love includes,
The one permits the two their mutual moods,
The two each other know mid myriad multitudes;

With child-like intellect, discerning love,
And mutual action energizing love,
In myriad forms affiliating love.

A world whose seasons bloom from pole to pole,
A force which knows both starting-point and goal,
A Home in Heaven,—the Union in the Soul.[19]

Emerson's Essays

ESSAYS: SECOND SERIES. By R. W. EMERSON. Boston.
James Munroe and Company, 1844

AT THE DISTANCE of three years this volume follows the first series of Essays, which have already made to themselves a circle of readers, attentive, thoughtful, more and more intelligent, and this circle is a large one if we consider the circumstances of this country, and of England, also, at this time.

In England it would seem there are a larger number of persons waiting for an invitation to calm thought and sincere intercourse than among ourselves. Copies of Mr. Emerson's first published little volume called "Nature," have there been sold by thousands in a short time, while one edition has needed seven years to get circulated here. Several of his Orations and Essays from "The Dial" have also been republished there, and met with a reverent and earnest response.

We suppose that while in England the want of such a voice is as great as here, a larger number are at leisure to recognize that want; a far larger number have set foot in the speculative region and have ears refined to appreciate these melodious accents.

Our people, heated by a partisan spirit, necessarily occupied in these first stages by bringing out the material resources of the land, not generally prepared by early training for the enjoyment of books that require attention and reflection, are still more injured by a large majority of writers and speakers, who lend all their efforts to flatter corrupt tastes and mental indolence, instead of feeling it their prerogative and their duty to admonish the community of the danger and arouse it to nobler energy. The aim of the writer or lecturer is not to say the best he knows in as few and well-chosen words as he can, making it his first aim to do justice to the subject. Rather he seeks to beat out a thought as thin as possible, and to consider what the audience will be most willing to receive.

The result of such a course is inevitable. Literature and Art must become daily more degraded; Philosophy cannot exist. A man who feels within his mind some spark of genius, or a capacity for the exercises of talent, should consider himself as endowed with a sacred commission. He is the natural priest, the shepherd of the people. He must raise his mind as high as he can toward the heaven of truth, and try to draw up with him those less gifted by nature with ethereal lightness. If he does not so, but rather employs his powers to flatter them in their poverty, and to hinder aspiration by useless words, and a mere seeming of activity, his sin is great, he is false to God, and false to man.

Much of this sin indeed is done ignorantly. The idea that literature calls men to the genuine hierarchy is almost forgotten. One, who finds himself able, uses his pen, as he might a trowel, solely to procure himself bread, without having reflected on the position in which he thereby places himself.

Apart from the troop of mercenaries, there is one, still larger, of those who use their powers merely for local and temporary ends, aiming at no excellence other than may conduce to these. Among these, rank persons of honor and the best intentions, but they neglect the lasting for the transient, as a man neglects to furnish his mind that he may provide the better for the house in which his body is to dwell for a few years.

When these sins and errors are prevalent, and threaten to become more so, how can we sufficiently prize and honor a mind which is quite pure from such? When, as in the present case, we find a man whose only aim is the discernment and interpretation of the spiritual laws by which we live and move and have our being, all whose objects are permanent, and whose every word stands for a fact.

If only as a representative of the claims of individual culture in a nation which tends to lay such stress on artificial organization and external results, Mr. Emerson would be invaluable here. History will inscribe his name as a father of the country, for he is one who pleads her cause against herself.

If New-England may be regarded as a chief mental focus to the New World, and many symptoms seem to give her this place, as to other centres the characteristics of heart and lungs to the body politic; if we may believe, as the writer does believe, that what is to be acted out in the country at large is, most frequently, first indicated there, as all the phenomena of the nervous system in the fantasies of the brain, we may hail as an auspicious omen the influence Mr. Emerson has there obtained, which is deep-rooted, increasing, and, over the younger portion of the community, far greater than that of any other person.

His books are received there with a more ready intelligence than elsewhere, partly because his range of personal experience and illustration applies to that region, partly because he has prepared the way for his books to be read by his great powers as a speaker.

The audience that waited for years upon the lectures, a part of which is incorporated into these volumes of Essays, was never large, but it was select, and it was constant. Among the hearers were some, who though, attracted by the beauty of character and manner, they were willing to hear the speaker through, always went away discontented. They were accustomed to an artificial method, whose scaffolding could easily be retraced, and desired an obvious sequence of logical inferences. They insisted there was nothing in what they had heard, because they could not give a clear account of its course and purport. They did not see that Pindar's odes might be very well arranged for their own purpose, and yet not bear translating into the methods of Mr. Locke.[1]

Others were content to be benefitted by a good influence without a strict analysis of its means. "My wife says it is about the elevation of human nature, and so it seems to me;" was a fit reply to some of the critics. Many were satisfied to find themselves excited to congenial thought and nobler life, without an exact catalogue of the thoughts of the speaker.

Those who believed no truth could exist, unless encased by the burrs of opinion, went away utterly baffled. Sometimes they thought he was on their side, then presently would come something on the other. He really seemed to believe there were two sides to every subject, and even to intimate higher ground from which each might be seen to have an infinite number of sides or bearings, an impertinence not to be endured! The partisan heard but once and returned no more.

But some there were, simple souls, whose life had been, perhaps, without clear light, yet still a search after truth for its own sake, who were able to receive what followed on the suggestion of a subject in a natural manner, as a stream of thought. These recognized, beneath the veil of words, the still small voice of conscience, the vestal fires of lone religious hours, and the mild teachings of the summer woods.

The charm of the elocution, too, was great. His general manner was that of the reader, occasionally rising into direct address or invocation in passages where tenderness or majesty demanded more energy. At such times both eye and voice called on a remote future to give a worthy reply. A future which shall manifest more largely the universal soul as it was then manifest to this soul. The tone of the voice was a grave body tone, full and sweet rather than sonorous, yet flexible and haunted by many modulations, as even instruments of wood and brass seem to become after they have been long played on with skill and taste; how much more so the human voice! In the more expressive passages it uttered notes of silvery clearness, winning, yet still more commanding. The words uttered in those tones, floated awhile above us, then took root in the memory like winged seed.

In the union of an even rustic plainness with lyric inspirations, religious dignity with philosophic calmness, keen sagacity in details with boldness of view, we saw what brought to mind the early poets and legislators of Greece—men who taught their fellows to plow and avoid moral evil, sing hymns to the gods and watch the metamorphoses of nature. Here in civic Boston was such a man—one who could see man in his original grandeur and his original childishness, rooted in a simple nature, raising to the heavens the brow and eyes of a poet.

And these lectures seemed not so much lectures as grave didactic poems, theogonies, perhaps, adorned by odes when some Power was in question whom the poet had best learned to serve, and with eclogues wisely portraying in familiar tongue the duties of man to man and "harmless animals."[2]

Such was the attitude in which the speaker appeared to that portion of the audience who have remained permanently attached to him.—They value his words as the signets of reality; receive his influence as a help and incentive to a nobler discipline than the age, in its general aspect, appears to require; and do not fear to anticipate the verdict of posterity in claiming for him the honors of greatness, and, in some respects, of a Master.

In New-England he thus formed for himself a class of readers, who rejoice to study in his books what they already know by heart. For, though the thought has become familiar, its beautiful garb is always fresh and bright in hue.

A similar circle of like-minded the books must and do form for themselves, though with a movement less directly powerful, as more distant from its source.

The Essays have also been obnoxious to many charges. To that of obscurity, or want of perfect articulation. Of 'Euphuism,'[3] as an excess of fancy in proportion to imagination, and an inclination, at times, to subtlety at the expense of strength, has been styled. The human heart complains of inadequacy, either in the nature or experience of the writer, to represent its full vocation and its deeper needs. Sometimes it speaks of this want as "under-development" or a want of expansion which may yet be remedied;

sometimes doubts whether "in this mansion there be either hall or portal to receive the loftier of the Passions." Sometimes the soul is deified at the expense of nature, then again nature at that of man, and we are not quite sure that we can make a true harmony by balance of the statements.— This writer has never written one good work, if such a work be one where the whole commands more attention than the parts. If such an one be produced only where, after an accumulation of materials, fire enough be applied to fuse the whole into one new substance. This second series is superior in this respect to the former, yet in no one essay is the main stress so obvious as to produce on the mind the harmonious effect of a noble river or a tree in full leaf. Single passages and sentences engage our attention too much in proportion. These essays, it has been justly said, tire like a string of mosaics or a house built of medals. We miss what we expect in the work of the great poet, or the great philosopher, the liberal air of all the zones: the glow, uniform yet various in tint, which is given to a body by free circulation of the heart's blood from the hour of birth. Here is, undoubtedly, the man of ideas, but we want the ideal man also; want the heart and genius of human life to interpret it, and here our satisfaction is not so perfect. We doubt this friend raised himself too early to the perpendicular and did not lie along the ground long enough to hear the secret whispers of our parent life. We could wish he might be thrown by conflicts on the lap of mother earth, to see if he would not rise again with added powers.

All this we may say, but it cannot excuse us from benefitting by the great gifts that have been given, and assigning them their due place.

Some painters paint on a red ground. And this color may be supposed to represent the ground work most immediately congenial to most men, as it is the color of blood and represents human vitality. The figures traced upon it are instinct with life in its fulness and depth.

But other painters paint on a gold ground. And a very different, but no less natural, because also a celestial beauty, is given to their works who choose for their foundation the color of the sunbeam, which nature has preferred for her most precious product, and that which will best bear the test of purification, gold.

If another simile may be allowed, another no less apt is at hand. Wine is the most brilliant and intense expression of the powers of earth.—It is her potable fire, her answer to the sun. It exhilarates, it inspires, but then it is liable to fever and intoxicate too the careless partaker.

Mead was the chosen drink of the Northern gods. And this essence of the honey of the mountain bee was not thought unworthy to revive the souls of the valiant who had left their bodies on the fields of strife below.

Nectar should combine the virtues of the ruby wine, the golden mead, without their defects or dangers.

Two high claims our writer can vindicate on the attention of his contemporaries. One from his sincerity. You have his thought just as it found place in the life of his own soul. Thus, however near or relatively distant its approximation to absolute truth, its action on you cannot fail to be healthful. It is a part of the free air.

He belongs to that band of whom there may be found a few in every age, and who now in human history may be counted by hundreds, who worship the one God only, the God of Truth. They worship, not saints, not creeds, nor churches, nor reliques, nor idols in any form. The mind is kept open to truth, and life only valued as a tendency toward it. This must be illustrated by acts and words of love, purity and intelligence. Such are the salt of the earth; let the minutest crystal of that salt be willingly by us held in solution.

The other is through that part of his life, which, if sometimes obstructed or chilled by the critical intellect, is yet the prevalent and the main source of his power. It is that by which he imprisons his hearer only to free him again as a "liberating God" (to use his own words).[4] But indeed let us use them altogether, for none other, ancient or modern, can more worthily express how, making present to use the courses and destinies of nature, he invests himself with her serenity and animates us with her joy.

"Poetry was all written before time was, and whenever we are so finely organized that we can penetrate into that region where the air is music, we hear those primal warblings, and attempt to write them down, but we lose ever and anon a word, or a verse, and substitute something of our own, and thus miswrite the poem. The men of more delicate ear write down these cadences more faithfully, and these transcripts, though imperfect, become the songs of the nations.

"As the eyes of the Lyncæus were said to see through the earth, so the poet turns the world to glass, and shows us all things in their right series and procession. For, through that better perception, he stands one step nearer to things, and sees the flowing or metamorphosis; perceives that thought is multiform; that within the form of every creature is a force impelling it to ascend into a higher form; and following with his eyes the life, uses the forms which express that life, and so the speech flows with the flowing of nature."

Thus have we in a brief and unworthy manner indicated some views of these books. The only true criticism of these, or any good books, may be gained by making them the companions of our lives. Does every accession of knowledge or a juster sense of beauty make us prize them more? Then they are good, indeed, and more immortal than mortal. Let that test be applied to these; essays which will lead to great and complete poems—somewhere.

New-York Daily Tribune
7 Dec. 1844

∾

Our City Charities

VISIT TO BELLEVUE ALMS HOUSE, TO THE FARM SCHOOL, THE ASYLUM FOR THE INSANE, AND PENITENTIARY ON BLACKWELL'S ISLAND.

The aspect of Nature was sad; what is worse, it was dull and dubious, when we set forth on these visits. The sky was leaden and lowering, the air unkind and piercing, the little birds sat mute and astonished at the departure of the beautiful days which had lured them to premature song. It was a suitable day for such visits. The pauper establishments that belong to a great city take the place of the skeleton at the banquets of old. They admonish us of stern realities, which must bear the same explanation as the frequent blight of Nature's bloom. They should be looked at by all, if only for their own sakes, that they may not sink listlessly into selfish ease, in a world so full of disease. They should be looked at by all who wish to enlighten themselves as to the means of aiding their fellow-creatures in any way, public or private. For nothing can really be done till the right principles are discovered, and it would seem they still need to be discovered or elucidated, so little is done, with a great deal of desire in the heart of the community to do what is right. Such visits are not yet calculated to encourage and exhilarate, as does the story of the Prodigal Son; they wear a grave aspect and suit the grave mood of a *cold* Spring day.

At the Alms House there is every appearance of kindness in the guardians of the poor, and there was a greater degree of cleanliness and comfort than we had expected. But the want of suitable and sufficient employment is a great evil. The persons who find here either a permanent or temporary refuge have scarcely any occupation provided except to raise vegetables for the establishment, and prepare clothing for themselves. The men especially have the most vagrant, degraded air, and so much indolence must tend to confirm them in every bad habit. We were told that, as they are under no strict discipline, their labor at the various trades could not be made profitable; yet surely the means of such should be provided, even at some expense. Employments of various kinds must be absolutely needed, if only to counteract the bad effects of such a position. Every establishment in aid of the poor should be planned with a view to their education. There should be instruction, both practical and in the use of books, openings to a better intercourse than they can obtain from their miserable homes, correct notions, as to cleanliness, diet, and fresh air. A great deal of pains would be lost in their case, as with all other arrangements for the good of the many, but here and there the seed would fall into the right places, and some members of the downtrodden million, rising a little from the mud, would raise the whole body with them.

As we saw old women enjoying their dish of gossip and their dish of tea, and mothers able for a while to take care in peace of their poor little children, we longed and hoped for that genius, who shall teach how to make, of these establishments, places of rest and instruction, not of degradation.

The causes which make the acceptance of public charity so much more injurious to the receiver than that of private are obvious, but surely not such that the human mind which has just invented the magnetic telegraph and Anastatic printing,[1] may not obviate them. A deeper religion at the heart of Society would devise such means. Why should it be that the poor may still feel themselves men; paupers not? The poor man does not feel himself injured but benefitted by the charity of the doctor who gives him back the bill he is unable to pay, because the doctor is acting from intelligent sympathy—from love. Let Society do the same. She might raise the man, who is accepting her bounty, instead of degrading him.

Indeed, it requires great nobleness and faith in human nature, and God's will concerning it, for the officials not to take the tone toward these under their care, which their vices and bad habits prompt, but which must confirm them in the same. Men treated with respect are reminded of self-respect, and if there is a sound spot left in the character, the healthy influence spreads.

We were sorry to see mothers with their new-born infants exposed to the careless scrutiny of male visitors. In the hospital, those who had children scarce a day old were not secure from the gaze of the stranger. This cannot be pleasant to them, and, if they have not refinement to dislike it, those who have should teach it to them. But we suppose there is no woman who has so entirely lost sight of the feelings of girlhood as not to dislike the scrutiny of strangers at a time which is sacred, if any in life is. Women they may like to see, even strangers, if they can approach them with delicacy.

In the yard of the hospital, we saw a little Dutch girl, a dwarf, who would have suggested a thousand poetical images and fictions to the mind of Victor Hugo or Sir Walter Scott.[2] She had been brought here to New-York, as we understood, by some showman and then deserted, so that this place was her only refuge. No one could communicate with her or know her feelings, but she showed what they were, by running to the gate whenever it was opened, though treated with familiar kindness and seeming pleased by it. She had a large head, ragged dark hair, a glowering wizard eye, an uncouth yet pleasant smile, like an old child;—she wore a gold ring, and her complexion was as yellow as gold, if not as bright; altogether she looked like a gnome, more than any attempt we have ever known to embody in Art that fabled inhabitant of the mines and secret caves of earth.

From the Alms House we passed in an open boat to the Farm School. We were unprepared to find this, as we did, only a school upon a small farm, instead of one in which study is associated with labor. The children are simply taken care of and taught the common English branches till they are twelve years old, when they are bound out to various kinds of work. We think this plan very injudicious. It is bad enough for the children of rich parents, not likely in after life to bear a hard burden, and who are, at any rate, supplied with those various excitements required to develope the character in the earliest years; it is bad enough, we say, for these to have no kind of useful labor mingled with their plays and studies. Even these children would expand more, and be more variously called forth, and better prepared for common life, if another course were pursued. But, in schools like this at the farm, where the children, on leaving it, will be at once called on for adroitness and readiness of mind and body, and where the absence of natural ties and the various excitements that rise from them inevitably give to life a mechanical routine calculated to cramp and chill the character, it would be peculiarly desirable to provide various occupations, and such as are calculated to prepare for common life. As to economy of time, there is never time lost, by mingling other pursuits with the studies of children; they have vital energy enough for many things at once, and learn more from books when their attention is quickened by other kinds of culture.

Some of these children were pretty, and they were healthy and well-grown, considering the general poverty or vice of the class from which they were taken. That terrible scourge, opthalmia, disfigured many among them. This disease, from some cause not yet detected, has been prevalent here for many years. We trust it may yield to the change of location next summer. There is not water enough here to give the children decent advantages as to bathing. This, too, will be remedied by the change. The Principal, who has been almost all his life connected with this establishment and that at Bellevue, seemed to feel a lively interest in his charge. He has arranged the dormitories with excellent judgment, both as to ventilation and neatness. This, alone, is a great advantage these children have over those of poor families living at home. They may pass the night in healthy sleep, and have thereby a chance for innocent and active days.

We saw with pleasure the little children engaged in the kind of drill they so much enjoy, of gesticulation regulated by singing. It was also pretty to see the babies sitting in a circle and the nurses in the midst feeding them, alternately, with a spoon. It seemed like a nest full of little birds, each opening its bill as the parent returns from her flight.

Hence we passed to the Asylum for the Insane. Only a part of this building is completed, and it is well known that the space is insufficient. Twice as many are inmates here as can be properly accommodated. A tolerable degree, however, of order and cleanliness is preserved. We could not but observe the vast difference between the appearance of the insane here and at Bloomingdale, or other Institutions where the number of attendants and nature of the arrangements permit them to be the objects of individual treatment; that is, where the wants and difficulties of each patient can be distinctly and carefully attended to. At Bloomingdale, the shades of character and feeling were nicely kept up, decorum of manners preserved, and the insane showed in every way that they felt no violent separation betwixt them and the rest of the world, and might easily return to it. The eye, though bewildered, seemed lively, and the tongue prompt. But *here,* insanity appeared in its more stupid, wild, or despairing forms. They crouched in corners; they had no eye for the stranger, no heart for hope, no habitual expectation of light. Just as at the Farm School, where the children show by their unformed features and mechanical movements that they are treated by wholesale, so do these poor sufferers. It is an evil incident to public establishments, and which only a more intelligent public attention can obviate.

One figure we saw, here also, of high poetical interest. It was a woman seated on the floor, in the corner of her cell, with a shawl wrapped gracefully around her head and chest, like a Nun's veil. Her hair was grey, her face attenuated and very pallid, her eyes large, open, fixed and bright with a still fire. She never moved them nor ceased chanting the service of the Church. She was a Catholic, who became insane while preparing to be a Nun. She is surely a Nun now in her heart; and a figure from which a painter might study for some of the most consecrated subjects.

Passing to the Penitentiary, we entered on one of the gloomiest scenes that deforms this great metropolis. Here are the twelve hundred, who receive the punishment due to the vices of so large a portion of the rest. And under what circumstances! Never was punishment treated more simply as a social convenience, without regard to pure right, or a hope of reformation.

Public attention is now so far awake to the state of the Penitentiary that it cannot be long, we trust, before proper means of classification are devised, a temporary asylum provided for those who leave this purgatory, even now, unwilling to return to the inferno from which it has for a time kept them, and means presented likely to lead some, at least, among the many, who seem hardened, to better views and hopes. It must be that the more righteous feeling which has shown itself in regard to the prisons at Sing Sing and elsewhere, must take some effect as to the Penitentiary also. The present Superintendent enters into the necessity of such improvements, and, should he remain there, will do what he can to carry them into effect.

The want of proper matrons, or any matrons, to take the care so necessary for the bodily or mental improvement or even decent condition of the seven hundred women assembled here, is an offence that cries aloud. It is impossible to take the most cursory survey of this assembly of women; especially it is impossible to see them in the Hospital, where the circumstances are a little more favorable, without seeing how many there are in whom the feelings of innocent childhood are not dead, who need only good influences and steady aid to raise them from the pit of infamy and woe into which they have fallen. And, if there was not one that could be helped, at least Society owes them the insurance of a decent condition while here. We trust that interest on this subject will not slumber.

The recognized principles of all such institutions which have any higher object than the punishment of fault, (and we believe few among us are so ignorant as to avow that as the only object, though they may, from want of thought, act as if it were,) are—Classification as the first step, that the bad may not impede those who wish to do well; 2d. Instruction, practical, oral, and by furnishing books which may open entirely new hopes and thoughts to minds oftener darkened than corrupted; 3d. A good Sanitary system, which promotes self-respect, and, through health and purity of body, the same in mind.

In visiting the Tombs the other day, we found the air in the upper galleries unendurable, and felt great regret that those confined there should be constantly subjected to it. Give the free breath of Heaven to all who are still permitted to breathe.—We cannot, however, wonder at finding this barbarity in a prison, having been subjected to it at the most fashionable places of public resort. Dr. Griscom[3] has sent us his excellent lecture on the health of New-York, which we recommend to all who take a vital interest in the city where they live, and have intellect to discern that a cancer on the body must in time affect the head and heart also. We thought, while reading, that it was not surprising typhus fever and opthalmia should be bred in the cellars, while the families of those who live in palaces breathe such infected air at public places, and receive their visitors on New Year's day by candle-light. (That was a sad omen for the New Year—did they mean to class themselves among those who love darkness rather than light?)

We hope to see the two thousand poor people, and the poor children, better situated in their new abode, when we visit them again. The Insane Asylum will gain at once by enlargement of accommodations; but more attendance is also necessary, and, for that purpose, the best persons should be selected. We saw, with pleasure, tame pigeons walking about among the most violent of the insane, but we also saw two attendants with faces brutal and stolid. Such a charge is too delicate to be intrusted to any but excellent persons. Of the Penitentiary we shall write again. All criticism, however imperfect, should be welcome. There is no reason why New-York should not become a model for other States in these things. There is wealth enough, intelligence, and good desire enough, and *surely, need enough.* If she be not the best cared for city in the world, she threatens to surpass in corruption London and Paris. Such bane as is constantly poured into her veins demands powerful antidotes.

But nothing effectual can be achieved while both measures and men are made the sport of political changes. It is a most crying and shameful evil, which does not belong to our institutions, but is a careless distortion of them, that the men and measures are changed in these institutions with changes from Whig to Democrat, from Democrat to Whig. Churches, Schools, Colleges, the care of the Insane, and suffering Poor, should be preserved from the uneasy tossings of this delirium. The Country, the State, should look to it that only those fit for such officers should be chosen for such, apart from all considerations of political party. Let this be thought of; for without an absolute change in this respect no permanent good whatever can be effected; and farther, let not economy but utility be the rule of expenditure, for, here, parsimony is the worst prodigality.

New-York Daily Tribune
19 Mar. 1845

❦

Prevalent Idea that Politeness is too great a Luxury to be given to the Poor

A FEW DAYS AGO, a lady, crossing in one of the ferry boats that ply from this city, saw a young boy, poorly dressed, sitting with an infant in his arms on one of the benches. She observed that the child looked sickly and coughed. This, as the day was raw, made her anxious in its behalf, and she went to the boy and asked whether he was alone there with the baby, and if he did not think the cold breeze dangerous for it. He replied that he was sent out with the child to take care of it, and that his father said the fresh air from the water would do it good.

While he made this simple answer, a number of persons had collected around to listen, and one of them, a well-dressed woman, addressed the boy in a string of such questions and remarks as these:

"What is your name? Where do you live? Are you telling us the truth? It's a shame to have that baby out in such weather; you'll be the death of it. (To the bystanders:) I would go and see his mother and tell her about it, if I was sure he had told us the truth about where he lived. How do you expect to get back? Here, (in the rudest voice,) somebody says you have not told the truth as to where you live."

The child, whose only offence consisted in taking care of the little one in public, and answering when he was spoken to, began to shed tears at the accusations thus grossly preferred against him. The bystanders stared at both; but among them all there was not one with sufficiently clear notions of propriety and moral energy to say to this impudent questioner, "Woman! do you suppose, because you wear a handsome shawl, and that

391

boy a patched jacket, that you have any right to speak to him at all, unless he wishes it, far less to prefer against him those rude accusations. Your vulgarity is unendurable; leave the place or alter your manner."

Many such instances have we seen of insolent rudeness or more insolent affability founded on no apparent grounds, except an apparent difference in pecuniary position, for no one can suppose in such cases the offending party has really enjoyed the benefit of refined education and society, but all present let them pass as matters of course. It was sad to see how the poor would endure—mortifying to see how the purse-proud dared offend. An excellent man who was, in his early years, a missionary to the poor, used to speak afterwards with great shame of the manner in which he had conducted himself towards them.—"When I recollect," said he, "the freedom with which I entered their houses, inquired into all their affairs, commented on their conduct and disputed their statements I wonder I was never horsewhipped and feel that I ought to have been; it would have done me good, for I needed as severe a lesson on the universal obligations of politeness in its only genuine form of respect for man as man, and delicate sympathy with each in his peculiar position."

Charles Lamb, who was indeed worthy to be called a human being from those refined sympathies, said, "You call him a gentleman: does his washerwoman find him so?"[1] We may say, if she did so, she found him a *man,* neither treating her with vulgar abruptness, nor giving himself airs of condescending liveliness, but treating her with that genuine respect which a feeling of equality inspires.

To doubt the veracity of another is an insult which in most *civilized* communities must in the so-called higher classes be atoned for by blood, but, in those same communities, the same men will, with the utmost lightness, doubt the truth of one who wears a ragged coat, and thus do all they can to injure and degrade him by assailing his self-respect, and break-ing the feeling of personal honor—a wound to which hurts a man as a wound to its bark does a tree.

Then how rudely are favors conferred, just as a bone is thrown to a dog. A gentleman indeed will not do *that* without accompanying signs of sympathy and regard. Just as this woman said, "If you have told the truth I will go and see your mother," are many acts performed on which the actors pride themselves as kind and charitable.

All men might learn from the French in these matters. That people, whatever be their faults, are really well-bred, and many acts might be quoted from their romantic annals, where gifts were given from rich to poor with a graceful courtesy, equally honorable and delightful to the giver and the receiver.

In Catholic countries there is more courtesy, for charity is there a duty, and must be done for God's sake; there is less room for a man to give himself the Pharisaical tone about it. A rich man is not so surprised to find himself in contact with a poor one; nor is the custom of kneeling on the open pavement, the silk robe close to the beggar's rags, without profit. The separation by pews, even on the day when all meet nearest, is as bad for the manners as the soul.

Blessed be he or she who has passed through this world, not only with an open purse and willingness to render the aid of mere outward benefits, but with an open eye and open heart, ready to cheer the downcast, and enlighten the dull by words of comfort and looks of love. The wayside charities are the most valuable both as to sustaining hope and diffusing knowledge, and none can render them who has not an expansive nature, a heart alive to affection, and some true notion, however imperfectly developed, of the nature of human brotherhood.

Such an one can never sauce the given meat with taunts, freeze the bread by a cold glance of doubt, or plunge the man who asked for his hand deeper back into the mud by any kind of rudeness.

In the little instance with which we begun, no help *was* asked, unless by the sight of the timid little boy's old jacket. But the license which this seemed to the well-clothed woman to give to rudeness was so characteristic of a deep fault now existing, that a volume of comments might follow and a host of anecdotes be drawn from almost any one's experience in exposition of it. These few words, perhaps, may awaken thought in those who have drawn tears from others eyes through an ignorance brutal, but not hopelessly so, if they are willing to rise above it.

New-York Daily Tribune
31 May 1845

❧

The Wrongs of American Women
The Duty of American Women

THE SAME DAY brought us a copy of Mr. Burdett's little book, in which the sufferings and difficulties that beset the large class of women who must earn their subsistence in a city like New-York are delineated with so much simplicity, feeling and exact adherence to the facts—and a printed circular containing proposals for immediate practical adoption of the plan more fully described in a book published some weeks since under the title "The Duty of American Women to their Country," which was ascribed alternately to Mrs. Stone and Miss Catharine Beecher,[1] but of which we understand both those ladies decline the responsibility. The two matters seemed linked with one another by natural piety. Full acquaintance with the wrong must call forth all manner of inventions for its redress.

The Circular, in showing the vast want that already exists of good means for instructing the children of this nation, especially in the West, states also the belief that among women, as being less immersed in other cares and toils, from the preparation it gives for their task as mothers, and from the necessity in which a great proportion stand of earning a subsistence somehow, at least during the years which precede marriage, if they *do* marry, must the number of teachers wanted be found, which is estimated already at *sixty thousand.*

We cordially sympathize with these views.

Much has been written about Woman's keeping within her sphere, which is defined as the domestic sphere. As a little girl she is to learn the lighter family duties, while she acquires that limited acquaintance with the realm of literature and science that will enable her to superintend the instruction of children in their earliest years. It is not generally proposed that she should be sufficiently instructed and developed to understand the pursuits or aims of her future husband; she is not to be a helpmeet to him, in the way of companionship or counsel, except in the care of his house and children. Her youth is to be passed partly in learning to keep house and the use of the needle, partly in the social circle where her manners may be formed, ornamental accomplishments perfected and displayed, and the husband found who shall give her the domestic sphere for which exclusively she is to be prepared.

Were the destiny of Woman thus exactly marked out, did she invariably retain the shelter of a parent's or a guardian's roof till she married, did marriage give her a sure home and protector, were she never liable to be made a widow, or, if so, sure of finding immediate protection from a brother or new husband, so that she might never be forced to stand alone one moment, and were her mind given for this world only, with no faculties capable of eternal growth and infinite improvement, we would still demand for her a far wider and more generous culture than is proposed by those who so anxiously define her sphere. We would demand it that she might not ignorantly or frivolously thwart the designs of her husband, that she might be the respected friend of her sons no less than her daughters, that she might give more refinement, elevation and attraction to the society which is needed to give the characters of *men* polish and plasticity—no less so than to save them from vicious and sensual habits. But the most fastidious critic on the departure of Woman from her sphere, can scarcely fail to see at present that a vast proportion of the sex, if not the better half, do not, CANNOT, have this domestic sphere. Thousands and scores of thousands in this country no less than in Europe are obliged to maintain themselves alone. Far greater numbers divide with their husbands the care of earning a support for the family. In England, now, the progress of society has reached so admirable a pitch that the position of the sexes is frequently reversed, and the husband is obliged to stay at home and "mind the house and bairns" while the wife goes forth to the employment she alone can secure.

We readily admit that the picture of this is most painful—that Nature made entirely an opposite distribution of functions between the sexes. We believe the natural order to be the best, and that, if it could be followed in an enlightened spirit, it would bring to Woman all she wants, no less for her immortal than her mortal destiny. We are not surprised that men, who do not look deeply or carefully at causes or tendencies, should be led by disgust at the hardened, hackneyed characters which the present state of things too often produces in women to such conclusions as they are. We, no more than they, delight in the picture of the poor woman digging in the mines in her husband's clothes. We, no more than they, delight to hear their voices shrilly raised in the market-place, whether of apples or celebrity. But we see that at present they must do as they do for bread. Hundreds and thousands must step out of that hallowed domestic sphere, with no choice but to work or steal, or belong to men, not as wives, but as the wretched slaves of sensuality.

And this transition state, with all its revolting features, indicates, we do believe, the approach of a nobler era than the world has yet known. We trust that by the stress and emergencies of the present and coming time, the minds of women will be formed to more reflection and higher purposes than heretofore—their latent powers developed, their characters strengthened and eventually beautified and harmonized. Should the state of society then be such that each may remain, as Nature seems to have intended, the tutelary genius of a home, while men manage the out-door business of life, both may be done with a wisdom, a mutual understanding and respect unknown at present. Men will be no less the gainers by this than women, finding in pure and more religious marriages the joys of friendship and love combined—in their mothers and daughters better instruction, sweeter and nobler companionship, and in society at large an excitement to their finer powers and feelings unknown at present except in the region of the fine arts.

Blest be the generous, the wise among them who seek to forward hopes like these, instead of struggling against the fiat of Providence and the march of Fate to bind down rushing Life to the standard of the Past. Such efforts are vain, but those who make them are unhappy and unwise.

It is not, however, to such that we address ourselves, but to those who seek to make the best of things as they are, while they also strive to make them better. Such persons will have seen enough of the state of things in London, Paris, New-York, and manufacturing regions every where, to feel that there is an imperative necessity for opening more avenues of employment to women, and fitting them better to enter them, rather than keeping them back. Women have invaded many of the trades and some of the professions. Sewing, to the present killing extent, they cannot long bear. Factories seem likely to afford them permanent employment. In the culture of fruit, flowers and vegetables, even in the sale of them, we rejoice to see them engaged. In domestic service they will be aided, but can never be supplanted, by machinery. As much room as there is here for woman's mind and woman's labor will always be filled. A few have usurped the martial province, but these must always be few; the nature of woman is opposed to war. It is natural enough to see "Female Physicians," and we believe that the lace cap and workbag are as much at home here as the wig and gold-headed cane. In the priesthood they have from all time shared more or less—in many eras more than at the present. We believe there has been no female lawyer, and probably will be none. The pen, many of the fine arts they have made their own, and, in the more refined countries of the world, as writers, as musicians, as painters, as actors, women occupy as advantageous ground as men. Writing and music may be esteemed professions for them more than any other.

But there are two others where the demand must invariably be immense, and for which they are naturally better fitted than men, for which we should like to see them better prepared and better rewarded than they are. These are the profession of nurse to the sick and of teacher. The first of these professions we have warmly desired to see dignified. It is a noble one, now most unjustly regarded in the light of menial service. It is one which no menial, no servile nature can fitly occupy. We were rejoiced when an intelligent lady of Massachusetts made the refined heroine of a little romance select that calling. This lady (Mrs. George Lee)² has looked on society with unusual largeness of spirit and healthiness of temper. She is well acquainted with the world of conventions, but sees beneath it the world of nature. She is a generous writer and unpretending, as the generous are wont to be. We do not recall the name of the tale, but the circumstance above mentioned marks its temper. We hope to see the time when the refined and cultivated will choose this profession and learn it, not only through experience under the direction of the doctor, but by acquainting themselves with the laws of matter and of mind, so that all they do shall be intelligently done, and afford them the means of developing intelligence as well as the nobler, tenderer feelings of humanity; for even the last part of the benefit they cannot receive if their work be done in a selfish or mercenary spirit.

The other profession is that of teacher, for which women are particularly adapted by their nature, superiority in tact, quickness of sympathy, gentleness, patience, and a clear and animated manner in narration or description. To form a good teacher should be added to this sincere modesty combined with firmness, liberal views with a power and will to liberalize them still further, a good method and habits of exact and thorough investigation. In the two last requisites women are generally deficient, but there are now many shining examples to prove that if they are immethodical and superficial as teachers it is because it is the custom so to teach them, and that when aware of these faults they can and will correct them.

The profession is of itself an excellent one for the improvement of the teacher during that interim between youth and maturity when the mind needs testing, tempering, and to review and rearrange the knowledge it has acquired. The natural method of doing this for one's self is to attempt teaching others; those years also are the best of the practical teacher. The teacher should be near the pupil both in years and feelings— no oracle, but the elder brother or sister of the pupil. More experience and years form the lecturer and the director of studies, but injure the powers as to familiar teaching.

These are just the years of leisure in the lives even of those women who are to enter the domestic sphere, and this calling most of all compatible with a constant progress as to qualifications for that.

Viewing the matter thus it may well be seen that we should hail with joy the assurance that sixty thousand *female* teachers are wanted, and more likely to be, and that a plan is projected which looks wise, liberal and generous, to afford the means of those whose hearts answer to this high calling obeying their dictates.

The plan is to have Cincinnati for a central point, where teachers shall be for a short time received, examined and prepared for their duties. By mutual agreement and cooperation of the various sects funds are to be raised and teachers provided according to the wants and tendencies of the various locations now destitute. What is to be done for them centrally, is for suitable persons to examine into their various kinds of fitness, communicate some general views whose value has been tested, and counsel adapted to the difficulties and advantages of their new positions. The Central Committee are to have the charge of raising funds and finding teachers and places where teachers are wanted.

The passage of thoughts, teachers and funds will be from East to West, the course of sunlight upon this earth.

The plan is offered as the most extensive and pliant means of doing a good and preventing ill to this nation, by means of a national education, whose normal school shall have an invariable object in the search after truth and the diffusion of the means of knowledge, while its form shall be plastic according to the wants of the time. This normal school promises to have good effects, for it proposes worthy aims through simple means, and the motive for its formation and support seems to be disinterested philanthropy.

It promises to eschew the bitter spirit of sectarianism and proselytism, else we, for one party, could have nothing to do with it. Men, no doubt, have been oftentimes kept from absolute famine by the wheat with which such tares are mingled; but we believe the time is come when a purer and more generous food is to be offered to the people at large. We believe the aim of all education to be rouse the mind to action, show it the means of discipline and of information; then leave it free, with God, Conscience, and the love of Truth for its guardians and teachers. Wo be to those who sacrifice these aims of universal and eternal value to the propagation of a set of opinions. But on this subject we can accept such doctrine as is offered by Rev. Calvin Stowe,[3] one of the committee, in the following passage:

> "In judicious practice, I am persuaded there will seldom be any very great difficulty, especially if there be excited in the community anything like

a whole-hearted honesty and enlightened sincerity in the cause of public instruction.

"It is all right for people to suit their own taste and convictions in respect to sect; and by fair means and at proper times to teach their children and those under their influence to prefer the denominations which they prefer; but farther than this no one has any right to go. It is all wrong to hazard the well being of the soul, to jeopardize great public interests for the sake of advancing the interests of a sect. People must learn to practice some self-denial, on Christian principles, in respect to their denominational preferences, as well as in respect to other things, before pure Religion can ever gain a complete victory over every form of human selfishness."

The persons who propose themselves to the examination and instruction of the teachers at Cincinnati, till the plan shall be sufficiently under weigh to provide regularly for the office, are Mrs. Stowe[4] and Miss Catherine Beecher, ladies well known to fame, as possessing unusual qualifications for the task.

As to finding abundance of teachers, who that reads this little book of Mr. Burdett's, or the account of the compensation of female labor in New-York, and the hopeless, comfortless, useless, pernicious lives those who have even the advantage of getting work must live with the sufferings and almost inevitable degradation to which those who cannot are exposed, but must long to snatch such as are capable of this better profession, and among the multitude there must be many who are or could be made so, from their present toils and make them free and the means of freedom and growth to others.

To many books on such subjects, among others to "Woman in the Nineteenth Century," the objection has been made that they exhibit ills without specifying any practical means for their remedy. The writer of the last named essay does indeed think that it contains one great rule which, if laid to heart, would prove a practical remedy for many ills, and of such daily and hourly efficacy in the conduct of life that any extensive observance of it for a single year would perceptibly raise the tone of thought, feeling and conduct throughout the civilized world. But to those who ask not only such a principle, but an external method for immediate use, we say, here is one proposed that looks noble and promising, the proposers offer themselves to the work with heart and hand, with time and purse: Go ye and do likewise.[5]

Those who wish details as to this plan, will find them in the "Duty of

American Women to their Country," published by Harper & Brothers, Cliff-st. The publishers may, probably, be able to furnish also the Circular to which we have referred. At a leisure day we shall offer some suggestions and remarks as to the methods and objects there proposed.

New-York Daily Tribune
30 Sept. 1845

❧

What fits a Man to be a Voter? Is it to be White Within, or White Without?

THE COUNTRY had been denuded of its forests, and men cried—"Come! we must plant anew, or there will be no shade for the homes of our children, or fuel for their hearths. Let us find the best kernels for a new growth."

And a basket of butternuts was offered.

But the planters rejected it with disgust. "What a black, rough coat it has," said they; "it is entirely unfit for the dishes on a nobleman's table, nor have we ever seen it in such places. It must have a greasy, offensive kernel; nor can fine trees grow up from such a nut."

"Friends," said one of the planters, "this decision may be rash. The chestnut has not a handsome outside; it is long encased in troublesome burrs, and, when disengaged, is almost as black as these nuts you despise. Yet from it grow trees of lofty stature, graceful form and long life. Its kernel is white and has furnished food to the most poetic and splendid nations of the older world."

"Don't tell me," says another, "brown is entirely different from black. I like brown very well; there is Oriental precedent for its respectability. Perhaps we will use some of your chestnuts, if we can get fine samples. But for the present I think we should use only English walnuts, such as our fore-fathers delighted to honor. Here are many basketsfull of them, quite enough for the present. We will plant them with a sprinkling between of the chestnut and acorn." "But," rejoined the other, "many butternuts are beneath the sod, and you cannot help a mixture of them being in your wood at any rate."

"Well! we will grub them up and cut them down wherever we find them. We can use the young shrubs for kindlings."

At that moment entered the council two persons of a darker complexion than most of those present, as if born beneath the glow of a more scorching sun. First came a Woman, beautiful in the mild, pure grandeur of her look; in whose large dark eye a prophetic intelligence was mingled with infinite sweetness. She looked at the assembly with an air of surprise, as if its aspect was strange to her. She threw quite back her veil, and stepping aside made room for her companion. His form was youthful, about the age of one we have seen in many a picture, produced by the thought of eighteen centuries, as of one "instructing the Doctors."[1] I need not describe the features; all minds have their own impressions of such an image,

"Severe in youthful beauty."[2]

In his hand, he bore a little white banner on which was embroidered PEACE AND GOOD WILL TO MEN.[3] And the words seemed to glitter and give out sparks, as he paused in the assembly.

"I came hither," said he, "an uninvited guest, because I read sculptured above the door—'All men born Free and Equal,' and in this dwelling hoped to find myself at home. What is the matter in dispute?"

Then they whispered one to another, and murmurs were heard— "He is a mere boy; young people are always foolish and extravagant;" or "He looks like a fanatic." But others said, "He looks like one whom we have been taught to honor. It will be best to tell the matter in dispute."

When he heard it, he smiled and said, "It will be needful first to ascertain which of the nuts is soundest *within*." And with a hammer he broke one, two, and more of the English walnuts, and they were mouldy.

Then he tried the other nuts, but found most of them fresh and *white*, for they were fresh from the bosom of the earth, while the others had been kept in a damp cellar.

And he said, "You had better plant them together, lest none or few of the walnuts be sound. And why are you so reluctant? Has not Heaven permitted them both to grow on the same soil? and does not that show what is intended about it?"

And they said, "But they are black and ugly to look upon." He replied, "They do not seem so to me. What my Father has fashioned in such guise offends not mine eye."

And they said, "But from one of these trees flew a bird of prey who has done great wrong. We meant, therefore, to suffer no such tree among us."

And he replied, "Amid the band of my countrymen and friends there

401

was one guilty of the blackest crime, that of selling for a price the life of his dearest friend, yet all the others of his blood were not put under ban because of his guilt."

Then they said, "But in the Holy Book our teachers tell us, we are bid to keep in exile or distress whatsoever is black and unseemly in our eyes."

Then he put his hand to his brow and cried in a voice of the most penetrating pathos, "Have I been so long among ye and ye have not known me?"[4]—And the Woman turned from them, the majestic hope of her glance, and both forms suddenly vanished, but the banner was left trailing in the dust.

The men stood gazing at one another. After which one mounted on high and said:

"Perhaps, my friends, we carry too far this aversion to objects merely because they are black. I heard, the other day, a wise man say that black was the color of evil—marked as such by God, and that whenever a white man struck a black man he did an act of worship to God. I could not quite believe him. I hope, in what I am about to add, I shall not be misunderstood. I am no Abolitionist. I respect above all things, divine or human, the Constitution framed by our forefathers, and the peculiar institutions[5] hallowed by the usage of their sons. I have no sympathy with the black race in this country. I wish it to be understood that I feel toward negroes the purest personal antipathy. It is a family trait with us. My little son, scarce able to speak, will cry out "Nigger! Nigger!" whenever he sees one, and try to throw things at them. He made a whole omnibus load laugh the other day by his cunning way of doing this. The child of my political antagonist, on the other hand, says "he likes *tullared* children the best." You see he is tainted in his cradle by the loose principles of his parents, even before he can say nigger or pronounce the more refined appellation. But that is no matter. I merely mention this by the way: not to prejudice you against Mr. ———, but that you may appreciate the very different state of things in my family, and not misinterpret what I have to say. I was lately in one of our prisons where a somewhat injudicious indulgence had extended to one of the condemned felons, a lost and wretched outcast from society, the use of materials for painting, that having been his profession. He had completed at his leisure, a picture of the Lord's Supper. Most of the figures were well enough, but Judas he has represented as a black.—Now, gentlemen, I am of opinion that this is an unwarrantable liberty taken with the Holy Scriptures and shows *too much* prejudice in the community. It is my wish to be moderate and fair, and preserve a medium, neither, on the one hand, yielding the wholesome antipathies planted in our breasts as a safe-guard against degradation, and our constitutional obligations, which, as I have before observed, are, with me, more binding than any other; nor on the other hand forgetting that liberality and wisdom which are the pre-rogative of every citizen of this free Commonwealth. I agree then with our young visitor. I hardly know, indeed, why a stranger and one so young was permitted to mingle in this council, but it was certainly thoughtful in him to crack and examine the nuts. I agree that it may be well to plant some of the black nuts among the others, so that, if many of the walnuts fail, we may make use of this inferior tree."

At this moment arose a hubbub, and such a clamor of "dangerous innovation," "political capital," "low-minded demagogue," "infidel who denies the Bible," "lower link in the chain of creation," &c. that it is impossible to say what was the decision.

New-York Daily Tribune,
31 Mar. 1846

∾

Farewell

FAREWELL to New-York City, where twenty months have presented me with a richer and more varied exercise for thought and life than twenty years could in any other part of these United States.

It is the common remark about New-York that it has, at least, nothing petty or provincial in its methods and habits. The place is large enough; there is room enough and occupation enough for men to have no need or excuse for small cavils or scrutinies. A person who is independent and knows what he wants, may lead his proper life here unimpeded by others.

Vice and Crime, if flagrant and frequent, are less thickly coated by Hypocrisy than elsewhere. The air comes sometimes to the most infected subjects.

New-York is the focus, the point where American and European interests converge. There is no topic of general interest to men that will not betimes be brought before the thinker by the quick turning of the wheel.

Too quick that revolution, some object. Life rushes wide and free, but *too fast;* yet it is in the power of every one to avert from himself the evil that accompanies the good. He must build for his study, as did the German poet, a house beneath the bridge, and, then, all that passes above and by him will be heard and seen, but he will not be carried away with it.

Earlier views have been confirmed and many new ones opened. On two great leadings,—the superlative importance of promoting National Education by heightening and deepening the cultivation of individual minds, and the part which is assigned to Woman in the next stage of human progress in this country, where most important achievements are to be effected, I have received much encouragement, much instruction, and the fairest hopes of more.

On various subjects of minor importance, no less than these, I hope for good results from observation with my own eyes of Life in the Old World, and to bring home some packages of seed for Life in the New.

These words I address to my friends, for I feel that I have some. The degree of sympathetic response to the thoughts and suggestions I have offered through the columns of this paper has indeed surprised me, conscious as I am of a natural and acquired aloofness from many, if not most, popular tendencies of my time and place. It has greatly encouraged me, for none can sympathize with thoughts like mine who are permanently ensnared in the meshes of sect or party; none who prefer the formation and advancement of mere opinions to the free pursuit of Truth. I see, surely, that the topmost bubble or sparkle of the cup is no voucher for the nature of its contents throughout, and shall, in future, feel that in our age, nobler in that respect than most of the preceding, each sincere and fervent act or word is secure, not only of a final, but a speedy, response.

I go to behold the wonders of art, and the temples of old religion. But I shall see no forms of beauty and majesty beyond what my Country is capable of producing in myriad variety, if she has but the soul to will it; no temple to compare with what she might erect in the Ages, if the catchword of the time, a sense of DIVINE ORDER, should become, no more a mere word or effigy, but a deeply rooted and pregnant Idea in her life. Beneath the light of a hope that this may be, I ask of my friends once more a kind Farewell.

New-York Daily Tribune,
1 Aug. 1846

THINGS AND THOUGHTS IN EUROPE

No. XVIII
[Dec. 1847]

THIS LETTER will reach the United States about the 1st of January; and it may not be impertinent to offer a few New-Year's reflections. Every new year, indeed, confirms the old thoughts, but also presents them under some new aspects.

The American in Europe, if a thinking mind, can only become more American. In some respects it is a great pleasure to be here. Although we have an independent political existence, our position toward Europe, as to Literature and the Arts, is still that of a colony, and one feels the same joy here that is experienced by the colonist in returning to the parent home. What was but picture to us becomes reality; remote allusions and derivations trouble no more: we see the pattern of the stuff, and understand the whole tapestry. There is a gradual clearing up on many points, and many baseless notions and crude fancies are dropped. Even the post-haste passage of the business American through the great cities, escorted by cheating couriers, and ignorant *valets de place,* unable to hold intercourse with the natives of the country, and passing all his leisure hours with his countrymen, who know no more than himself, clears his mind of some mistakes—lifts some mists from his horizon.

There are three species: first, the servile American—a being utterly shallow, thoughtless, worthless. He comes abroad to spend his money and indulge his tastes. His object in Europe is to have fashionable clothes, good

405

foreign cookery, to know some titled persons, and furnish himself with coffee-house gossip, which he wins importance at home by retailing among those less traveled, and as uninformed as himself.

I look with unspeakable contempt on this class—a class which has all the thoughtlessness and partiality of the exclusive classes in Europe, without any of their refinement, or the chivalric feeling which still sparkles among them here and there. However, though these willing serfs in a free age do some little hurt, and cause some annoyance at present, it cannot last: our country is fated to a grand, independent existence, and, as its laws develop, these parasites of a bygone period must whither and drop away.

Then there is the conceited American, instinctively bristling and proud of—he knows not what.—He does not see, not he, that the history of Humanity for many centuries is likely to have produced results it requires some training, some devotion, to appreciate and profit by. With his great clumsy hands, only fitted to work on a steam-engine, he seizes the old Cremona violin, makes it shriek with anguish in his grasp, and then declares he thought it was all humbug before he came, and now he knows it; that there is not really any music in these old things; that the frogs in one of our swamps make much finer, for they are young and alive. To him the etiquette of courts and camps, the ritual of the Church, seem simply silly— and no wonder, profoundly ignorant as he is of their origin and meaning. Just so the legends which are the subjects of pictures, the profound myths which are represented in the antique marbles, amaze and revolt him; as, indeed, such things need to be judged of by another standard from that of the Connecticut Blue-Laws.[1] He criticizes severely pictures, feeling quite sure that his natural senses are better means of judgment than the rules of connaisseurs—not feeling that to see such objects mental vision as well as fleshly eyes are needed, and that something is aimed at in Art beyond the imitation of the commonest forms of Nature.

This is Jonathan in the sprawling state, the booby truant, not yet aspiring enough to be a good school-boy. Yet in his folly there is meaning; add thought and culture to his independence, and he will be a man of might: he is not a creature without hope, like the thick-skinned dandy of the class first specified.

The Artists form a class by themselves. Yet among them, though seeking special aims by special means, may also be found the lineaments of these two classes, as well as of the third, of which I am now to speak.

3d. The thinking American—a man who, recognizing the immense advantage of being born to a new world and on a virgin soil, yet does not wish one seed from the past to be lost. He is anxious to gather and carry back with him all that will bear a new climate and new culture. Some will dwindle; others will attain a bloom and stature unknown before. He wishes to gather them clean, free from noxious insects. He wishes to give them a fair trial in his new world. And that he may know the conditions under which he may best place them in that new world, he does not neglect to study their history in this.

The history of our planet in some moments seems so painfully mean and little, such trifling bafflings and failures to compensate some brilliant successes—such a crashing of the mass of men beneath the feet of a few, and these, too, often the least worthy—such a small drop of honey to each cup of gall, and, in many cases, so mingled, that it is never one moment in life purely tasted,—above all, so little achieved for Humanity as a whole, such tides of war and pestilence intervening to blot out the traces of each triumph, that no wonder if the strongest soul sometimes pauses aghast! No wonder if the many indolently console themselves with gross joys and frivolous prizes. Yes! those men *are* worthy of admiration who can carry this cross faithfully through fifty years; it is a great while for all the agonies that beset a lover of good, a lover of men; it makes a soul worthy of a speedier ascent, a more productive ministry in the next sphere. Blessed are they who ever keep that portion of pure, generous love with which they began life![2] How blessed those who have deepened the fountains, and have enough to spare for the thirst of others! Some such there are; and, feeling that, with all the excuses for failure, still only the sight of those who triumph gives a meaning to life or makes its pangs endurable, we must arise and follow.

Eighteen hundred years of this Christian culture in these European kingdoms, a great theme never lost sight of, a mighty idea, an adorable history to which the hearts of men invariably cling, yet are genuine results rare as grains of gold in the river's sandy bed! Where is the genuine Democracy to which the rights of all men are holy? where the child-like wisdom learning all through life more and more of the will of God? where the aversion to falsehood in all its myriad disguises of cant, vanity, covetousness, so clear to be read in all the history of Jesus of Nazareth? Modern Europe is the sequel to that history, and see this hollow England, with its monstrous wealth and cruel poverty, its conventional life and low, practical aims; see this poor France, so full of talent, so adroit, yet so shallow and glossy still, which could not escape from a false position with all its baptism of blood; see that lost Poland and this Italy bound down by treacherous hands in all the force of genius; see Russia with its brutal Czar and innumerable slaves; see Austria and its royalty that represents nothing, and its people who, as people, are and have nothing! If we consider the amount of truth that has really been spoken out in the world, and the love that has beat in private hearts—how Genius has decked each spring-time with such splendid flowers, conveying each one enough of instruction in its life of harmonious energy, and how continually, unquenchably the spark of faith has striven to burst into flame and light up the Universe— the public failure seems amazing, seems monstrous.

Still Europe toils and struggles with her idea, and, at this moment, all things bode and declare a new outbreak of the fire, to destroy old palaces of crime![3] May it fertilize also many vineyards!—Here at this moment a successor of St. Peter, after the lapse of near two thousand years, is called "Utopian" by a part of this Europe, because he strives to get some food to the mouths of the *leaner* of his flock. A wonderful state of things, and which leaves as the best argument against despair that men do not, *cannot* despair amid such dark experiences—and thou, my country! will thou not be more true? does no greater success await thee? All things have so conspired to teach, to aid! A new world, a new chance, with oceans to wall in the new thought against interference from the old!—Treasures of all kinds, gold, silver, corn, marble, to provide for every physical need! A noble, constant, starlike soul, an Italian,[4] led the way to its shores, and, in the first days, the strong, the pure, those too brave, too sincere for the life of the Old World hastened to people them. A generous struggle then shook off what was foreign and gave the nation a glorious start for a worthy goal. Men rocked the cradle of its hopes, great firm, disinterested men who saw, who wrote, as the basis of all that was to be done, a statement of the rights, the inborn rights of men, which, if fully interpreted and acted upon, leaves nothing to be desired.

Yet, oh Eagle, whose early flight showed this clear sight of the Sun, how often dost thou near the ground, how show the vulture in these later days! Thou wert to be the advance-guard of Humanity, the herald of all Progress; how often hast thou betrayed this high commission! Fain would the tongue in clear triumphant accents draw example from thy story, to encourage the hearts of those who almost faint and die beneath the old oppressions. But we must stammer and blush when we speak of many things. I take pride here that I may really say the Liberty of the Press works well, and that the checks and balances naturally evolve from it which suffice to its government. I may say the minds of our people are alert, and that Talent has a free chance to rise. It is much. But dare I say that political ambition is not as darkly sullied as in other countries? Dare I say that men of most influence in political life are those who represent most virtue or even intellectual power? Is it easy to find names in that career of which I can speak with enthusiasm? Must I not confess in my country to a bound-less lust of gain? Must I not confess to the weakest vanity, which bristles and blusters at each foolish taunt of the foreign press; and must I not admit that the men who make these undignified rejoinders seek and find popu-larity so? Must I not confess that there is as yet no antidote cordially adopted that will defend even that great, rich country against the evils that have grown out of the commercial system in the old world? Can I say our social laws are generally better, or show a nobler insight to the wants of man and woman? I do, indeed, say what I believe, that voluntary associa-tion[5] for improvement in these particulars will be the grand means for my nation to grow and give a nobler harmony to the coming age. But it is only of a small minority that I can say they as yet seriously take to heart these things; that they earnestly meditate on what is wanted for their coun-try,—for mankind,—for our cause is, indeed, the cause of all mankind at present. Could we succeed, really succeed, combine a deep religious love with practical development, the achievements of Genius with the hap-piness of the multitude, we might believe Man had now reached a com-manding point in his ascent, and would stumble and faint no more. Then there is this horrible cancer of Slavery, and this wicked War,[6] that has grown out of it. How dare I speak of these things here? I listen to the same arguments against the emancipation of Italy, that are used against the emancipation of our blacks; the same arguments in favor of the spoliation of Poland as for the conquest of Mexico. I find the cause of tyranny and wrong everywhere the same—and lo! my Country the darkest offender, because with the least excuse, foresworn to the high calling with which she was called,—no champion of the rights of men, but a robber and a jailor; the scourge hid behind her banner; her eyes fixed, not on the stars, but on the possessions of other men.

How it pleases me here to think of the Abolitionists! I could never endure to be with them at home, they were so tedious, often so narrow, always so rabid and exaggerated in their tone. But, after all, they had a high motive, something eternal in their desire and life; and, if it was not the only thing worth thinking of it was really something worth living and dying for to free a great nation from such a terrible blot, such a threatening plague. God strengthen them and make them wise to achieve their purpose!

I please myself, too, with remembering some ardent souls among the American youth who, I trust, will yet expand and help to give soul to the huge, over fed, too hastily grown-up body. May they be constant. "Were Man but constant he were perfect!" It has been said; and it is true that he who could be constant to those moments in which he has been truly human—not brutal, not mechanical—is on the sure path to his perfection and to effectual service of the Universe.

It is to the youth that Hope addresses itself, to those who yet burn with aspiration, who are not hardened in their sins. But I dare not expect too much of them. I am not very old, yet of those who, in life's morning, I saw touched by the light of a high hope, many have seceded. Some have become voluptuaries; some mere family men, who think it is quite life enough to win bread for half a dozen people and treat them decently; others are lost through indolence and vacillation. Yet some remain constant. "I have witnessed many a shipwreck, yet still beat noble hearts."

I have found many among the youth of England, of France—of Italy also—full of high desire, but will they have courage and purity to fight the battle through in the sacred, the immortal band? Of some of them I believe it and await the proof. If a few succeed amid the trial, we have not lived and loved in vain.

To these, the heart of my country, a Happy New Year! I do not know what I have written; I have merely yielded to my feelings in thinking of America; but something of true love must be in these lines—receive them kindly, my friends; it is, by itself, some merit for printed words to be sincere.

New-York Daily Tribune
1 Jan. 1848

∾

No. XXIII
ROME, 29th March, 1848

It is long since I have written: my health entirely gave way beneath the Roman Winter. The rain was constant, commonly falling in torrents from the 16th December to the 19th March. Nothing could surpass the dirt, the gloom, the desolation of Rome. Let no one fancy he has seen her who comes here only in the Winter. It is an immense mistake to do so. I cannot sufficiently rejoice that I did not first see Italy in the Winter.

The climate of Rome at this time of extreme damp I have found equally exasperating and weakening. I have had constant nervous headache without strength to bear it, nightly fever, want of appetite.[1] Some constitutions bear it better, but the complaint of weakness and extreme dejection of spirits is general among foreigners in the wet season. The English say they become acclimated in two or three years and cease to suffer, though never so strong as at home.

Now this long dark dream—to me the most idle and most suffering season of my life—seems past. The Italian heavens wear again their deep blue; the sun shines gloriously; the melancholy lustres are stealing again over the Campagna, and hundreds of larks sing unwearied above its ruins.

Nature seems in sympathy with the great events that are transpiring: with the emotions which are swelling the hearts of men. The morning sun is greeted by the trumpets of the Roman Legions marching out once more, but now not to oppress but to defend. The stars look down on their jubilees over the good news which nightly reaches them from their brothers of Lombardy. This week has been one of nobler, sweeter feeling of a better hope and faith than Rome in her greatest days ever knew. How much has happened since I wrote!—First the victorious resistance of Sicily and the revolution of Naples.[2] This has led as yet only to half measures, but even these have been of great use to the progress of Italy. The Neapolitans will, probably, have to get rid at last of the stupid crowned head who is at present their puppet, but their bearing with him has led to the wiser sovereigns granting these Constitutions, which, if eventually inadequate to the wants of Italy, will be so useful, are so needed, to educate her to seek better, completer forms of administration.

In the midst of all this serious work came the play of Carnival in which there was much less interest felt than usual, but enough to dazzle and captivate a stranger. One thing, however, had been omitted in the description of the Roman Carnival; i.e. that it rains every day. Almost every day came on violent rain just as the tide of gay masks was fairly engaged in the Corso. This would have been well worth bearing once or twice for the sake of seeing the admirable good humor of this people. Those who had laid out all their savings in the gayest, thinnest dresses, on carriages and chairs for the Corso, and found themselves suddenly drenched, their finery spoiled, and obliged to ride and sit shivering all the afternoon. But they never murmured, never scolded, never stopped throwing their flowers. Their strength of constitution is wonderful. While I, in my shawl and boa, was coughing at the open window from the moment I inhaled the wet sepulchral air, the servant girls of the house had taken off their woolen gowns, and arrayed in white muslins and roses, sat in the drenched street beneath the drenching rain, quite happy, and have suffered nothing in consequence.

The Romans renounced the *moccalletti*,[3] ostensibly as an expression of sympathy for the sufferings of the Milanese, but really because, at that time, there was great disturbance about the Jesuits, and the Government feared that difficulties would arise in the excitement of the evening. But, since, we have had this entertainment in honor of the Revolutions of France and Austria,[4] and nothing could be more beautiful. The fun usually consists in all the people blowing one another's lights out; we had not this, all the little tapers were left to blaze, and the Corso swarmed with tall fire-flies.—Lights crept out over the surface of all the houses, and such merry little twinkling lights, laughing and flickering with each slightest movement of those who held them. Up and down the Corso they twinkled, they swarmed, they streamed, while a surge of gay triumphant sound ebbed and flowed beneath that glittering surface. Here and there danced men carrying aloft *moccoli,* and clanking chains, emblem of the tyrannic power now vanquished by the people. The people, sweet and noble, who, in the intoxication of their joy, were guilty of no rude or unkindly word or act, and who, no signal being given as usual for the termination of their diversion, closed, of their own accord and with one consent, singing the hymns for Pio,[5] by nine o'clock, and retired peacefully to their homes, to dream of hopes they yet scarce understand.

This happened last week. The news of the dethronement of Louis Philippe reached us just after the close of the Carnival. It was just a year from my leaving Paris. I did not think, as I looked with such disgust on the empire of sham he had established in France, and saw the soul of the people imprisoned and held fast as in an iron vice, that it would burst its chains so soon. Whatever be the result, France has done gloriously; she has declared that she will not be satisfied with pretexts while there are facts in the world—that to stop her march is a vain attempt, though the onward path be dangerous and difficult. It is vain to cry Peace, peace, when there is no peace. The news from France, in these days, sounds ominous, though still vague; it would appear that the political is being merged in the social struggle: it is well; whatever blood is to be shed, whatever altars cast down. Those tremendous problems MUST be solved, whatever be the cost! That cost cannot fail to break many a bank, many a heart in Europe, before the good can bud again out of a mighty corruption. To you, people of America, it may perhaps be given to look on and learn in time for a preventive wisdom. You may learn the real meaning of the words FRATERNITY, EQUALITY: you may, despite the apes of the Past, who strive to tutor you, learn the needs of a true Democracy. You may in time learn to reverence, learn to guard, the true aristocracy of a nation, the only real noble—the LABORING CLASSES.

And Metternich, too, is crushed; the seed of the Woman has had his foot on the serpent.[6] I have seen the Austrian arms dragged through the streets of Rome and burned in the Piazza del Popolo.—The Italians embraced one another and cried, *Miracolo, Providenza!* the modern Tribune Ciceronacchio fed the flame with faggots; Adam Mickiewicz,[7] the great Poet of Poland, long exiled from his country or the hopes of a country, looked on, while Polish women, exiled too, or who, perhaps, like one nun who is here, had been daily scourged by the orders of a tyrant, brought little pieces that had been scattered in the street and threw into the flames—an offering received by the Italians with loud plaudits. It was a transport of the people, who found no way to vent their joy, but the symbol, the poesy, natural to the Italian mind; the ever-too-wise "upper classes" regret it, and the Germans choose to resent as an insult to Germany; but it was nothing of the kind; the insult was to the prisons of Spielberg, to those who commanded the massacres of Milan;[8] a base tyranny little congenial to the native German heart, as the true Germans of Germany are at this moment showing by their struggles, by their resolves.

When the double-headed eagle was pulled down from above the lofty portal of the Palazzo di Venezia, the people placed there in its stead one of white and gold inscribed with the name ALTA ITALIA,[9] and quick upon the emblem followed the news that Milan was fighting against her tyrants—that Venice had driven them out and freed from their prisons the courageous Protestants in favor of truth, Tommasseo and Manin[10]—that Manin, descendant of the last Doge, had raised the Republican banner on the Place St. Mark—and that Modena, that Parma, were driving out the unfeeling and imbecile creatures who had mocked Heaven and Man by the pretence of Government there.

With indescribable rapture these news were received in Rome. Men were seen dancing, women weeping with joy along the street. The youth rushed to enrol themselves in regiments to go to the frontier. In the Colosseum their names were received. Father Gavazzi, a truly patriotic monk, gave them the cross to carry on a new, a better, because defensive crusade.

Sterbini,[11] long exiled, addressed them; he said, "Romans, do you wish to go; do you wish to go with all your hearts? If so, you *may,* and those who do not wish to go themselves may give money. To those who will go, the government gives bread and fifteen baiocchi a day." The people cried "We too wish to go, but we do not wish so much; the Government is very poor; we can live on a paul a day." The princes answered by giving, one sixty thousand, others twenty, fifteen, ten thousand dollars. The people answered by giving at the benches which are opened in the piazzas literally everything; street-peddlers gave the gains of each day; women gave every ornament—from the splendid necklace and bracelet down to the poorest bit of coral; servant girls gave five pauls, two pauls, even half a paul, if they had no more; a man all in rags gave two pauls; "it is," said he, "all I have." "Then," said Torlonia, "take from me this dollar;" the man of rags thanked him warmly and handed that also to the bench which refused to receive it. "No! *that* must stay with you," shouted all present. These are the people whom the traveler accuses of being unable to rise above selfish considerations. Nation, rich and glorious by nature as ever, capable, like all nations, all men, of being degraded by slavery, capable as are few nations, few men, of kindling into pure flame at the touch of a ray from the Sun of Truth, of Life.

The two or three days that followed, the troops were marching about by detachments, followed always by the people, to Ponte Malle, often farther. The women wept; for the habits of the Romans are so domestic, that it seemed a great thing to have their sons and lovers gone even for a few months. The English—or, at least, those of the illiberal, bristling nature—too often met here, which casts out its porcupine quills against everything like enthusiasm (of the more generous Saxon blood I know some noble examples,) laughed at all this. They have said that this people would not fight; when the Sicilians, men and women, did so nobly they said, "Oh! the Sicilians are quite unlike the Italians; you will see when the struggle comes on in Lombardy, they cannot resist the Austrian force a moment." I said, "That force is only physical; do not you think a sentiment can sustain them?" They reply, "All stuff and poetry; it will fade the moment their blood flows." When news came that the Milanese, men and women, fight as the Sicilians did, they said, "Well, the Lombards are a better race, but these Romans are good for nothing; it is a farce for a Roman to try to walk even; they never walk a mile; they will not be able to support the first day's march of thirty miles, and not have their usual minestra to eat either." Now the troops were not willing to wait for the Government to make the necessary arrangements for their march, so at the first night's station—Monterosé—they did *not* find food or bedding, yet the second night, at Civita Castellana, they were so well alive as to remain dancing and vivaing Pio Nino in the piazza till after midnight. No, Messieurs, Soul is not quite nothing, if Matter be a clog upon its transports.

The Americans show a better, warmer feeling than they did; the meeting in New-York was of use in instructing the Americans abroad! The dinner given here on Washington's birthday, was marked by fine expressions of sentiment and a display of talent unusual on such occasions. There was a poem from Mr. Story of Boston, which gave great pleasure; a speech by Mr. Hilliard, said to be very good, and one by Mr. Hedge of Bangor, exceedingly admired for the felicity of thought and image and the finished beauty of style.[12]

Next week we shall have more news, and I shall try to write and mention also some interesting things want of time obliges me to omit in this letter. I annex a poem of Cranch's,[13] descriptive of a picture he sends to Mr. Ogden Haggerty of your City, interesting in itself and not irrelevant to this present communication. . . .

April 1

Yesterday I passed at Ostia and Castle Fusano. A million birds sang; the woods teemed with blossoms; the sod grew green hourly over the graves of the mighty Past; the surf rushed in on a fair shore; the Tiber majestically retreated to carry inland her share from the treasures of the deep; the sea breezes burnt my face, but revived my heart; I felt the calm of thought, the sublime hopes of the Future, Nature, Man—so great, though so little—so dear, though incomplete. Returning to Rome, I find the news, pronounced official, that the viceroy Ranieri has capitulated at Verona;[14] that Italy is free, independent, and One. I trust this will prove no April foolery, no premature news; it seems too good, too speedy a realization of hope, to have come on earth, and can only be answered in the words of the proclamation made yesterday by Pius IX.:

The events which these two months past have seen rush after one another in so rapid succession, are no human work. Woe to him who in this wind, which shakes and tears up alike the lofty cedars and humble shrubs, hears not the voice of God! Woe to human pride, if to the fault or merit of any man whatsoever it refer these wonderful changes, instead of adoring the mysterious designs of Providence.

New-York Daily Tribune,
4 May 1848

∾

No. XXVI
ROME December 2, 1848

Not till I saw the snow on the mountains grow rosy in the Autumn sunset did I turn my steps again toward Rome. I was very ready to return. After three or four years of constant excitement this six months of seclusion had been welcome; but not I felt the need of meeting other eyes beside those so bright and so shallow, of the Italian peasant. Indeed, I left what was most precious that I could not take with me; still it was a compensation that I was again to see Rome. Rome that almost killed me with her cold breath of last Winter, yet still with that cold breath whispered a tale of import so divine. Rome so beautiful, so great; her presence stupifies, and one has to withdraw to prize the treasures she has given. City of the Soul! yes, it is *that;* the very dust magnetizes you, and thousand spells have been chaining you in every careless, every murmuring moment. Yes! Rome, however seen, thou must be still adored; and every hour of absence or presence must deepen love with one who has known what it is to repose in thy arms.

Repose! for whatever be the revolutions, tumults, panics, hopes of the present day, still the temper of life here is Repose. The great Past enfolds us, and the emotions of the moment cannot here importantly disturb that impression. From the wild shout and throng of the streets the setting sun recalls us as it rests on a hundred domes and temples—rests on the Campagna, whose grass is rooted in departed human greatness. Burial-place so full of spirit that Death itself seems no longer cold; oh let me rest here, too! Rest, here, seems possible; meseems myriad lives still linger here, awaiting some one great summons.

The rivers had burst their bounds, and beneath the moon the fields round Rome lay, one sheet of silver. Entering the gate while the baggage was under examination I walked to the gate of a villa. Far stretched its overarching shrubberies, its deep-green bowers; two statues with foot

416

advanced and uplifted finger, seemed to greet me; it was near the scene of great revels, great splendors in the old time; there lay the gardens of Sallust, where were combined palace, theater, library, bath and villa. Strange things have happened now, the most attractive part of which—the secret heart—lies buried or has fled to animate other forms: for of that part historians have rarely given a hint, more than they do now of the truest life of our day, that refuses to be embodied by the pen; it craves forms more mutable, more eloquent than the pen can give.

I found Rome empty of foreigners; most of the English have fled in affright—the Germans and French are wanted at home—the Czar has recalled many of his younger subjects; he does not like the schooling they get here. That large part of the population which lives by the visits of foreigners was suffering very much—trade, industry, for every reason, stagnant. The people were every moment becoming more exasperated by the impudent measures of the Minister Rossi, and their mortification at seeing Rome represented and betrayed by a foreigner. And what foreigner? A pupil of Guizot and Louis Philippe.[1] The news had just reached them of the bombardment and storm of Vienna. Zucchi, the Minister-of-War, left Rome to put down over-free manifestations in the Provinces, and impede the entrance of the troops of the Patriot Chief, Garibaldi,[2] into Bologna. From the Provinces came soldiery, called by Rossi to keep order at the opening of the Chamber of Deputies. He reviewed them in the face of the Civic Guard; the Press began to be restrained; men were arbitrarily seized and sent out of the kingdom; the public indignation rose to its hight; the cup overflowed.

The 15th was a beautiful day and I had gone out for a long walk. Returning at night, the old Padrona met me with her usual smile a little clouded, "Do you know," said she, "that the Minister Rossi has been killed?" [No Roman said *murdered*.]

"Killed!"

"Yes—with a thrust in the back. A wicked man, surely, but is that the way to punish CHRISTIANS?"

"I cannot," observed a Philosopher, "sympathize under any circumstances with so immoral a deed; but surely the manner of doing it was *grandiose*."

The people at large was not so refined in their comments as either the Padrona or the Philosopher; but soldiers and populace alike ran up and down singing "Blessed the hand that rids the earth of a tyrant."

"Certainly, the manner *was* grandiose."

The Chamber was awaiting the entrance of Rossi. Had he lived to enter, he would have found the Assembly, without a single exception, ranged upon the Opposition benches. His carriage approached, attended by a howling, hissing multitude. He smiled, affected unconcern, but must have felt relieved when his horses entered the courtyard gate of the *Cancelleria*.[3] He did not know he was entering the place of his execution. The horses stopped; he alighted in the midst of a crowd; it jostled him as if for the purpose of insult; he turned abruptly and received as he did so the fatal blow. It was dealt by a resolute, perhaps experienced, hand; he fell and spoke no word more.

The crowd, as if all previously acquainted with the plan, as no doubt most of them were, issued quietly from the gate and passed through the outside crowd—its members, among whom was he who dealt the blow, dispersing in all directions.—For two or three minutes this outside crowd did not know that anything special had happened.—When they did, the news was at the moment received in silence. The soldiers in whom Rossi had trusted, whom he had hoped to flatter and bribe, stood at their posts and said not a word!—Neither they nor any one asked "Who did this? Where is he gone?" The sense of the people certainly was that it was an act of summary justice on an offender whom the laws could not reach, but they felt it to be indecent to shout or exult on the spot where he was breathing his last. Rome, so long supposed the Capital of Christendom, certainly took a very pagan view of this act, and the piece represented on the occasion at the theaters was "The Death of Nero."

The next morning I went to the church of St. Andrea della Valle, where was to be performed a funeral service, with fine music, in honor of the victims of Vienna; for this they do here for the victims all round— "victims of Milan," "victims of Paris," "victims of Naples," and now "victims of Vienna." But to-day I found the church closed, the service put off—Rome was thinking about her own victims.

I passed into the Ripetta, and entered the church of *San Luigi dei Francesi*. The Republican flag was flying at the door; the young Sacristan said the fine musical service which this church gave formerly on St. Philip's day, in honor of Louis Philippe, would now be transferred to the Republican Anniversary, the 25th of February. I looked at the monument Chateaubriand erected when here, to a poor girl who died last of her family, having seen all the others perish round her. I entered the Domenichino Chapel and gazed anew on those magnificent representations of the Life and Death of St. Cecilia.[4] She and St. Agnes are my favorite saints. I love to think of those angel visits which her husband knew by the fragrance of roses and lilies left behind in the apartment. I love to think of his visit to the Catacombs, and all that followed. In this picture St. Cecilia, as she stretches out her arms toward the suffering multitude, seems as if an immortal fount of purest love sprung from her heart. She gives very strongly the sense of an inexhaustible love—the only love that is much worth thinking about.

Leaving the church I passed along toward the *Piazza del Popolo*. "Yellow Tiber rose," but not high enough to cause "distress," as he does when in a swelling mood rather than "mantle" it. I heard drums beating, and, entering the Piazza, I found the troops of the line already assembled, and the Civic Guard marching in by platoons; each *battaglione* saluted as it entered by trumpets and a fine strain from the hand of the Carbineers.

I climbed the Pincian to see better. There is no place so fine for anything of this kind as the Piazza del Popolo, it is so full of light, so fair and grand, the obelisk and fountain make so fine a center to all kinds of groups.

The object of the present meeting was for the Civic Guard and troops of the line to give pledges of sympathy preparatory to going to the Quirinal to demand a change of Ministry and of measures. The flag of the Union was placed in front of the obelisk; all present saluted it; some officials made addresses; the trumpets sounded, and all moved toward the Quirinal.

Nothing could be gentler than the disposition of the crowd. They were resolved to be played with no longer, but no threat was heard or thought.—They believed that the Court would be convinced by the fate of Rossi that the retrograde movement it had attempted was impracticable. They knew the retrograde party were panic-struck, and hoped to use the occasion to free the Pope from their meshes. All felt that Pius IX. had fallen irrevocably from his high place of the friend of Progress and father of Italy: but still he was personally beloved, and still his name, so often shouted in hope and joy, had not quite lost its *prestige*.

I returned to the house, which is very near the Quirinal. On one side I could see the Palace and gardens of the Pope, on the other the Piazza Barberini and street of the Four Fountains. Presently I saw the carriage of Prince Barberini[5] drive hurriedly into his court-yard gate, the footman signing to close it, a discharge of firearms was heard, and the drums of the Civic Guard beat to arms.

The Padrona ran up and down crying with every round of shot, "Jesu Maria, they are killing the Pope! O! poor Holy Father—Tita, Tita, (out of the window to her husband,) what *is* the matter?"

The lord of creation disdained to reply.

"Oh! Signora, pray, pray, ask Tita what is the matter?" I did so. "I don't know, Signora; nobody knows."

"Why don't you go on the mount and see?"

"It would be an imprudence, Signora; nobody will go."

I was just thinking to go myself when I saw a poor man borne by, badly wounded, and heard that the Swiss were firing on the people. Their doing so was the cause of whatever violence there was, and it was not much.

The people had assembled, as usual, at the Quirinal, only with more form and solemnity than usual. They had taken with them several of the Chamber of Deputies, and they sent an embassy, headed by Galetti, who had been in the late Ministry, to state their wishes. They received a peremptory negative. They then insisted on seeing the Pope, and pressed on the palace. The Swiss became alarmed, and fired from the windows, from the roof. They did this, it is said, without orders, but who could, at the time, suppose that? If it had been planned to exasperate the people to blood, what more could have been done? As it was, very little was shed; but the Pope, no doubt, felt great panic. He heard the report of fire-arms—heard that they tried to burn a door of the palace. I would lay my life that he could have shown himself without the slightest danger; nay, that the habitual respect for his presence would have prevailed, and hushed all tumult. He did not think so, and to still it once more degraded himself and injured his people, by making promises he did not mean to keep.

He protests now against those promises as extorted by violence, a strange plea, indeed, for the representative of St. Peter!

Rome is all full of the effigies of those over whom violence had no power. There is an early Pope about to be thrown into the Tiber; violence had no power to make him say what he did not mean. Delicate girls, men in the prime of hope and pride of power—they were all alike about that. They could be done to death in boiling oil, roasted on coals, or cut to pieces; but they could not say what they did not mean. These formed the true Church; it was these who had power to disseminate the religion of Him, the Prince of Peace, who died a bloody death of torture between sinners, because He never could say what He did not mean.

A little church outside the gate of St. Sebastian commemorates this affecting tradition of the Church; Peter, alarmed at the persecution of the Christians, had gone forth to fly when in this spot he saw a bright figure in his path and recognized his Master traveling toward Rome.

"Lord," he said, "whither goest thou?"

"I go," replied Jesus, "to die, with my people."

Peter comprehended the reproof. He felt that he must not a fourth time deny his Master, yet hope for salvation. He returned to Rome to offer his life in attestation of his faith.

The Roman Catholic Church has risen a monument to the memory of such facts. And has the present Head of that Church quite failed to understand their monition?

Not all the Popes have so failed, though the majority have been intriguing, ambitious men of the world. But even the mob of Rome—and in Rome there *is* a true mob of unheeding cabbage-sellers, who never had a thought before beyond contriving how to satisfy their animal instincts for the day—said, on hearing the protest, "There was another Pius, not long since, who talked in a very different style. When the French threatened him, he said, 'You may do with me as you see fit, but I cannot consent to act against my convictions.'"

In fact, the only dignified course for the Pope to pursue was to resign his temporal power. He could no longer hold it on his own terms; but to that he clung; and the counselors around him were men to wish him to regard *that* as the first of duties. When the question was of waging war for the independence of Italy, they regarded him solely the head of the Church; but when the demand was to satisfy the wants of his people, and ecclesiastical goods were threatened with taxes, then he was the Prince of the State, bound to maintain all the selfish prerogative of by-gone days for the benefit of his successors. Poor Pope! how has his mind been torn to pieces in these later days. It moves compassion. There can be no doubt that all his natural impulses are generous and kind, and in a more private station he would have died beloved and honored; but to this he was unequal; he has suffered bad men to surround; and by their misrepresentations and insidious suggestions, at last entirely to cloud his mind. I believe he really thinks now the Progress movement tends to anarchy, blood, all that looked worst in the first French Revolution. However that may be I cannot forgive him some of the circumstances of this flight. To fly to Naples to throw himself in the arms of the bombarding monarch,[6] blessing him and thanking his soldiery for preserving that part of Italy from anarchy—to protest that all his promises at Rome were null and void, when he thought himself in safety to choose a commission for governing in his absence, composed of men of princely blood, but as to character so null that everybody laughed and said he chose those who could best be spared if they were killed; (but they all ran away directly;) when Rome was thus left without any

Government, to refuse to see any deputation, even the Senator of Rome, whom he had so gladly sanctioned,—these are the acts either of a fool or a foe. They are not his acts, to be sure, but he is responsible, he lets them stand as such in the face of the world, and weeps and prays for their success.

No more of him! His day is over. He has been made, it seems unconsciously, an instrument of good his regrets cannot destroy. Nor can he be made so important an instrument of ill. These acts have not had the effect the foes of freedom hoped. Rome remained quite cool and composed; all felt that they had not demanded more than was their duty to demand, and were willing to accept what might follow. In a few days all began to say, "Well, who would have thought it? The Pope, the Cardinals, the Princes are gone, and Rome is perfectly tranquil, and one does not miss anything, except that there are not so many rich carriages and liveries."

The Pope may regret too late that he ever gave the people a chance to make this reflection. Yet the best fruits of the movement may not ripen for long. It is one which requires radical measures, clear-sighted, resolute men: these last, as yet, do not show themselves in Rome. The new Tuscan Ministry has three men of superior force in various ways: Montanelli, Guerazzi, D'Aguila; such are not as yet to be found in Rome.

But should she fall this time, (and she must either advance with decision and force, or fall—since to stand still is impossible,) the people have learned much; ignorance and servility of thought are lessened—the way is paving for final triumph.

And my country, what does she? You have chosen a new President from a Slave State, representative of the Mexican War.[7] But he seems to be honest, a man that can be esteemed, and is one really known to the people; which is a step upward, after having sunk last time to choosing a mere tool of party.

Pray send here a good Ambassador—one that has experience of foreign life, that he may act with good judgment; and, if possible, a man that has knowledge and views which extend beyond the cause of party politics in the United States; a man of unity in principles, but capable of understanding a variety in forms. And send a man capable to prize the luxury of living in, or knowing Rome: it is one that should not be thrown away on a person who cannot prize or use it. Another century, and I might ask to be made Ambassador myself, ('tis true, like other Ambassadors, I would employ clerks to do the most of the duty,) but woman's day has not come yet. They hold their clubs in Paris, but even George Sand will not act with women as they are. They say she pleads they are too mean, too treacherous. She should not abandon them for that, which is not nature but misfortune. How much I shall have to say on that subject if I live, which I hope I shall not, for I am very tired of the battle with giant wrongs, and would like to have some one younger and stronger arise to say what ought to be said, still more to do what ought to be done. Enough! if I felt these things in privileged America, the cries of mothers and wives beaten at night by sons and husbands for their diversion after drinking, as I have repeatedly heard them these past months, the excuse for falsehood, "I *dare not* tell my husband, he would be ready to kill me," have sharpened my perception as to the ills of Woman's condition and remedies that must be applied. Had I but genius, had I but energy, to tell what I know as it ought to be told! God grant them me, or some other more worthy woman, I pray.

But the hour of sending to the post approaches, and I must leave these great matters for some practical details. I wish to observe to my friends and all others, whom it may concern, that a banking-house here having taken Mr. Hooker, an American, into partnership, some facilities are presented for intercourse with Rome, which they may value. Mr. Hooker undertakes to have pictures copied, and to purchase those little objects of virtu peculiar to Rome, for those who cannot come themselves, as I suppose few would wish to at this time. He has the advantage of a general acquaintance with the artists to be employed, and an experience, that, no doubt, would enable him to do all this with better advantage than any stranger can for himself. It is also an excellent house to have to do with in money matters, reasonable, exact, and where none of the petty trickery or neglect so common at Torlonia's need be apprehended. They have now made arrangements with Livingston, Wells & Co. for the transmission of letters. Many addressed to me have been lost, I know not how; and I should like my friends to send to me when they can through this channel. Men who feel able can pay their letters through in this way, which has been impossible before. I have received many letters marked *paid through,* and I fear my friends in America have often paid what was quite useless, as no arrangements had been made for forwarding the letters post-paid to Rome. These who write now can pay their letters to Florence, if they have friends there, through *Livingston, Wells & Co.* to care *Maquay, Pakenham & Co. Florence.* To us of Rome they can be sent through the same, to care of *Pakenham, Hooker & Co. Rome.*

Those of our friends, (I speak of the poor artists as well as myself,) who cannot afford to pay, should at least forbear to write on thick paper and under an envelop, the unnecessary use of which doubles the expense of the letter. I am surprised to find even those who have been abroad so negligent in these respects. I might have bought all the books of reference I needed, and have been obliged to do without money that could have been saved by attention from my friends to these particulars.

Write us two, three, four sheets if you will, on thin paper, without crossing. Then if one pays a couple of dollars for a letter, at least one has something for the money; and letters are too important to happiness; we cannot afford to be without knowledge of your thoughts, your lives; but it is hard, in people who can scarcely find bread, to pay for coarse paper and an envelop the price of a beautiful engraving, and know at the same time that they are doomed to leave Rome unable to carry away a single copy of what they have most loved here, for possession or for gift. So write, dear friends, much and often, but dont ruin us for nothing.

Don Tirlone, the *Punch* of Rome, has just come in. This number represents the Fortress of Gaeta; outside hangs a cage containing a parrot (Pappagallo), the plump body of the bird is surmounted by a noble large head with benign face and Papal head-dress. He sits on the perch now with folded wings, but the cage door, in likeness of a loggia, shows there is convenience to come forth for the purposes of benediction, when wanted. Outside, the King of Naples, dressed as Harlequin, plays the organ for instruction of the bird (unhappy penitent, doomed to penance,) and grinning with sharp teeth observes: "He speaks in my way now." In the background a young Republican holds ready the match for a barrel of gunpowder, but looks at his watch waiting the moment to ignite it.

A happy New-Year to my country! may she be worthy of the privileges she possesses, while others are lavishing their blood to win them— that is all that need be wished for her at present.

New-York Daily Tribune,
26 Jan. 1849

∾

No. XXXIII
ROME, July 6, 1849

If I mistake not, I closed my last letter just as the news arrived here that the attempt of the Democratic party in France to resist the infamous proceedings of the Government had failed, and thus Rome, as far as human calculation went, had not a hope for her liberties left. An inland city cannot long sustain a siege when there is no hope of aid. Then followed the news of the surrender of Ancona, and Rome found herself quite alone—for, though Venice continued to hold out, all communication was cut off.

The Republican troops, almost to a man, left Ancona, but a long march separated them from Rome.

The extreme heat of these days was far more fatal to the Romans than their assailants, for, as fast as the French troops sickened, their place was taken by fresh arrivals. Ours also not only sustained the exhausting service by day, but were harassed at night by attacks, feigned or real.— These commonly began about 11 or 12 o'clock at night, just when all who meant to rest were fairly asleep. I can imagine the harassing effect upon the troops, from what I feel in my sheltered pavilion, in consequence of not knowing a quiet night's sleep for a month.

The bombardment became constantly more serious. The house where I live was filled as early as the 20th with persons obliged to fly from the *Piazza di Gesu,* where the fiery rain fell thickest. The night of the 21st–22d, we were all alarmed about 2 o'clock A.M. by a tremendous cannonade. It was the moment when the breach was finally made by which the French entered.—They rushed in, and, I grieve to say, that by the only instance of defection known in the course of the siege, those companies of the regiment Union, which had in charge a casino on that point, yielded to panic and abandoned it. The French immediately entered and intrenched themselves. That was the fatal hour for the city. Every day afterward, though obstinately resisted, they gained, till at last, their cannon being well placed, the city was entirely commanded from the Janicular, and all thought of further resistance was idle.

This was true policy to avoid the street fight, in which the Italian, an unpracticed soldier, but full of feeling and sustained from the houses, would have been no match for their disciplined troops. After the 22d, the slaughter of the Romans became every day more fearful. Their defenses were knocked down by the heavy cannon of the French, and, entirely exposed in their valorous onsets, great numbers perished on the spot. Those who were brought into the Hospitals were generally grievously wounded, very commonly subjects for amputation. My heart bled daily more and more at these sights, and I could not feel much for myself, though now the balls and bombs began to fall round me also. The night of the 28th the effect was truly fearful, as they whizzed and burst near me. As many as 30 fell upon or near the *Hotel de Russie,* where Mr. Cass[1] has his temporary abode. The roof of the studio in the pavilion, tenanted by Mr. Stermer, well known to the visitors of Rome, for his highly-finished cabinet pictures, was town to pieces. I sat alone in my much-exposed apartment thinking "if one strikes me, I only hope it will kill me at once, and that God will transport my soul to some sphere where Virtue and Love are not tyrannized over by egotism and brute force, as in this." However, that night passed; the next, we had reason to expect a still more fiery salute to the Pincian, as here alone remained three of four pieces of cannon which could be used. But the morning of the 30th, in a contest at the foot of the Janicular, the line, old Papal troops, naturally not in earnest like the free corps, refused to fight against odds so terrible, the heroic Marara fell, with hundreds of his devoted Lombards. Garibaldi saw his best officers perish, and himself went in the afternoon to say to the Assembly that further resistance was unavailing.

The Assembly sent to Oudinot,[2] but he refused any conditions, refused even to guarantee a safe departure to Garibaldi, his brave foe. Notwithstanding, a great number of men left the other regiments to follow the leader, whose courage had captivated them and whose habit of superiority to difficulties commanded their entire confidence. Toward the evening of Monday, 2d July, it was known that the French were preparing to cross the river and take possession of all the city. I went into the Corso with some friends; it was filled with citizens and military, the carriage was stopped by the crowd near the Doria palace; the lancers of Garibaldi galloped along in full career, I longed for Sir Walter Scott to be on earth again, and see them; all are light athletic, resolute figures, many of the forms of the finest manly beauty of the South, all sparkling with its genius and ennobled by the resolute spirit, ready to dare, to do, to die. We followed them to the piazza of St. John Lateran. Never have I seen a sight so beautiful, so romantic and so sad. Whoever knows Rome knows the peculiar solemn grandeur of that piazza, scene of the first triumph of Rienzi,[3] the magnificence of the "mother of all churches," the Baptistery with its porphyry columns, the Santa Scala with its glittering mosaics of the early ages, the obelisk standing fairest of any of those most imposing monuments of Rome, the view through the gates of the Campagna, on that side so richly strewn with ruins. The sun was setting, the crescent moon rising, the flower of the Italian youth were marshaling in that solemn place. They had been driven from every other spot where they had offered their hearts as bulwarks of Italian Independence; in this last strong hold they had sacrificed hecatombs[4] of their best and bravest in that cause; they must now go or remain prisoners and slaves. *Where* go, they knew not, for except distant Hungary there is not now a spot which would receive them, or where they can act as honor commands. They had all put on the beautiful dress of the Garibaldi legion, the tunic of bright red cloth, the Greek cap, or else round hat with Puritan plume, their long hair was blown back from resolute faces; all looked full of courage; they had counted the cost before they entered on this perilous struggle; they had weighed life and all its material advantages against Liberty, and made their election; they turned not back, nor flinched at this bitter crisis. I saw the wounded, all that could go, laden upon their baggage cars, some were already pale and fainting, still they wished to go. I saw many youths, born to rich inheritance, carrying in a handkerchief all their worldly goods; the women were ready, their eyes too were resolved, if sad. The wife of Garibaldi followed him horseback, he himself was distinguished by the white bournouse; his look was entirely that of a hero of the middle ages, his face still young, for the excitements of his life, though so many, have all been youthful, and there is no fatigue upon his brow or cheek. Fall or stand, one sees in him a man engaged in the career for which he is adapted by nature. He went upon the parapet and looked upon the road with a spy-glass, and, no obstruction being in sight, he turned his face for a moment back upon Rome, then led the way through the gate. Hard was the heart, stony and seared the eye that had no tear for that moment. Go! fated, gallant band, and if God care not indeed for men as for the sparrows,[5] most of ye go forth to perish. And Rome, anew the Niobe![6] Must she lose also these beautiful and brave that prom-ised her regeneration and would have given it, but for the perfidy, the overpowering force of the foreign intervention.

I know that many "respectable" gentlemen would be surprised to hear me speak in this way. Gentlemen who perform their "duties to so-ciety" by buying for themselves handsome clothes and furniture with the interest of their money, speak of Garibaldi and his men as "brigands" and "vagabonds." Such are they, doubtless, in the same sense as Jesus, Eneas and Moses were. To me men who can throw so slightly aside the ease of wealth, the joys of affection, for the sake of what they deem honor, in whatsoever form, are the "respectable." No doubt there are in these bands a number of men of lawless minds, and who follow this banner only be-cause there is for them no other path. But the greater part are the noble youths who have fled from the Austrian conscription, or fly now from the renewal of the Papal suffocation, darkened by the French protection.

As for the protectors, they entirely threw aside the mask, as it was always supposed they would, the moment they had possession of Rome. I do not know whether they were really so bewildered by their priestly councilors as to imagine they would be well received in a city which they had bombarded, and where twelve hundred men were lying wounded by their assault. To say nothing of the justice or injustice of the matter, it could not be supposed that the Roman people, if it had any sense of dignity, would welcome them. However, I was not out, as what countenance I have I would not give on such an occasion; but an English lady, my friend, told me they seemed to look expectingly for the strong party of friends they had always pretended to have within the walls. The French officers looked up to the windows for ladies, and she being the only one they saw, saluted her. She made no reply. They then passed into the Corso. Many were assembled, the softer Romans being unable to control a curiosity the Milanese would have disclaimed, but preserving an icy silence. In an evil hour, a foolish priest dared to break it by the cry of *Viva Pio Nono.* The populace, roused to fury, rushed on him with their knives. He was much wounded; one or two others were killed in the rush. The people howled, then, and hissed at the French, who, advancing their bayonets, and clearing the way before them, fortified themselves in the piazzas. Next day the French troops were marched to and fro through Rome to inspire awe into the people, but it has only created a disgust amounting to loathing, to see that, with such an imposing force, and in great part fresh, the French were not ashamed to use bombs also, and kill women and children in their beds. Oudinot, then seeing the feeling of the people, and finding they pursued as a spy any man who so much as showed the way to his soldiers—that the Italians went out of the cafes if Frenchmen entered; in short, that the people regarded him and his followers in the same light as the Austrians, has declared the state of siege in Rome—the Press is stifled—everybody is to be in the house at 9 1/2 P.M. and, whoever in any way insults his men, or puts any obstacle in their way, is to be shot.

The fruits of all this will be the same as elsewhere: temporary repression will sow the seeds of perpetual resistance; and never was Rome in so fair a way to be educated for the Republican form of Government as now.

Especially could nothing be more irritating for an Italian population, in the month of July, than to drive them to their homes at half-past nine. After the insupportable heat of the day, their only enjoyment and refreshment is found in evening walks, and chats together as they sit before their cafes, or in groups outside some friendly door. Now they must hurry home when the drum beats at 9 o'clock. They are forbidden to stand or sit in groups, and this by their bombarding *protector!* Comment is unnecessary.

French soldiers are daily missing; of some it is known that they have been killed by the Trastevirini[7] for daring to make court to their women.— Of more than a hundred and fifty, it is only known that they cannot be found; and in two days of French "order" more acts of violence have been committed than in two months under the Triumvirate.

The French have taken up their quarters in the court-yards of the Quirinal and Venetian Palaces, which are full of the wounded, many of whom have been driven well nigh mad, and their burning wounds exasperated by the sound of their drums and trumpets—the constant sense of their insulting presence. The wounded have been warned to leave the Quirinal at the end of eight days, though there are many who cannot be moved from bed to bed without causing them great anguish and peril, nor is it known that any other place has been provided as a hospital for them. At the palace of Venice the French have searched for three emigrants that they wished to imprison, even in the apartments where the wounded were lying; they ran their bayonets into the mattresses; they have taken for themselves beds given by the Romans to the hospital—not public property, but private gift. The hospital of Santo Spirito was a Governmental establishment and, in using a part of it for the wounded, its director, Mensignore, had been retained, because he had the reputation of being honest and not illiberal. But as soon as the French entered he, with true priestly baseness, sent away the women nurses, saying he had no longer money to pay them—transported the wounded into a miserable, airless basement, that had before been used as a granary and appropriated the good apartments to the use of the French!

July 8.—The report this morning is that the French yesterday violated the domicile of our Consul, Mr. Brown, pretending to search for persons hidden there; that Mr. Brown, banner in one hand and sword in the other, repelled the assault, and fairly drove them down stairs; that then he made them an appropriate speech, though in a mixed language of English, French and Italian; that the crowd vehemently applauded Mr. Brown, who already was much liked for the warm sympathy he had shown the Romans in their aspirations and their distresses; that he then donned his uniform and went to Oudinot to make his protest. How this was received I know not, but understand Mr. B. departed with his family yesterday evening.

Will America look as coldly on the insult to herself as she has on the struggle of this injured people?

To-day an edict is out to disarm the National Guard. The generous "protectors" wish to take all the trouble upon themselves. Rome is full of them; at every step are met groups in the uniform of France, with faces bronzed in the African war, and so stultified by a life without enthusiasm and without thought, that I do not believe Napoleon would recognize them as French soldiers.—The effect of their appearance compared with that of the Italian free corps is that of body as compared with spirit. It is easy to see how they could be used to purposes so contrary to the legitimate policy of France, for they do not look more intellectual, more fitted to have opinions of their own, than the Austrian soldiery.

July 10.—The plot thickens. The exact facts with regard to the invasion of Mr. Brown's house, I have not been able to ascertain. I suppose they will be published, as Oudinot has promised to satisfy Mr. Cass. I must add in reference to what I wrote sometime ago of the position of our envoy here, that the kind and sympathetic course of Mr. Cass toward the Republicans in these troubles, his very gentlemanly and courteous bearing, have from the minds of most removed all unpleasant feelings. They see that his position was very peculiar; sent to the Papal Government, finding here the Republican, and just at that moment violently assailed. Unless he had extraordinary powers he naturally felt obliged to communicate further with our Government before acknowledging this. I shall always regret, however, that he did not stand free to occupy the high position that belonged to the representative of the United States at that moment, and peculiarly because it was by a Republic that the Roman Republic was betrayed.—But, as I say, the plot thickens. Yesterday three families were carried to prison because a boy crowed like a cock at the French soldiery from the windows of the house they occupied. Another, because a man pursued took refuge in their court yard. Yesterday, the city being mostly disarmed, came the edict to take down the arms of the Republic, "emblems of anarchy." But worst of all they have done is an edict commanding all foreigners who had been in the service of the Republican Government to leave Rome within twenty-four hours. This is the most infamous thing done yet, as it drives to desperation those who stayed because they had so many to go with and no place to go to, or because their relatives lie wounded here: no others wished to remain in Rome under present circumstances.

I am sick of breathing the same air with men capable of a part so utterly cruel and false. As soon as I can I shall take refuge in the mountains, if it be possible to find an obscure nook unpervaded by these convulsions.

Let not my friends be surprised if they do not hear from me for some time. I may not feel like writing. I have seen too much sorrow, and alas! without power to aid. It makes me sick to see the palaces and streets of Rome full of these injurious foreigners, and to see the already changed aspect of her population. The men of Rome had begun, filled with new hopes, to develop unknown energy—they walked quick, their eyes sparkled, they delighted in duty, in responsibility; in a year of such life their effeminacy would have been vanquished—now, dejectedly unemployed, they lounge along the streets, feeling that all the implements of labor, all the ensigns of hope, have been snatched from them. Their hands fall slack, their eyes rove aimless, the beggars begin to swarm again, and the black ravens who delight in the night of ignorance, the slumber of sloth, as the only sureties for their rule, emerge daily more and more frequent from their hiding places.

The following Address has been circulated from hand to hand:

TO THE PEOPLE OF ROME

Misfortune, brothers, has fallen upon us anew. But it is a trial of brief duration—it is the stone of the sepulcher which we shall throw away after three days, rising victorious and renewed, an immortal Nation. For with us are God and Justice—God and Justice, who cannot die, but always triumph, while Kings and Popes, once dead, revive no more.

As you have been great in the combat, be so in the days of sorrow— great in your conduct as citizens, of generous disdain, of sublime silence. Silence is the weapon we have now to use against the Cossacks of France and the Priests, their masters.

In the streets do not look at them; do not answer if they address you.

In the cafes, in the eating-houses, if they enter, rise and go out.

Let your windows remain closed as they pass.

Never attend their feasts, their parades.

The harmony of their musical bands be for you tones of slavery, and, when you hear them, fly.

Let the liberticide soldier be condemned to isolation; let him atone in solitude and contempt for having served priests and kings.

And you, Roman women—master-piece of God's work!—deign no look, no smile to those satellites of an abhorred Pope! Cursed be she who, before the odious satellites of Austria, forgets that she is Italian! Her name shall be published for the execration of all her people! And even the courtezans! let them show love for their country, and thus regain the dignity of citizens!

And our word of order, our cry of reunion and emancipation, be now and ever, VIVA LA REPUBBLICA!

This incessant cry, which not even French slaves can dispute, shall prepare us to administer the bequest of our martyrs, shall be consoling dew to the immaculate and holy bones that repose, sublime holocaust of faith and of love, near our walls, and make doubly divine the Eternal City. In this cry we shall find ourselves always brothers, and we shall conquer. Viva Rome, the Capital of Italy! Viva the Italy of the People! Viva the Roman Republic! A ROMAN.

Dated *Rome, July* 4, 1849.

For this day's anniversary, so joyously celebrated in our land, was that of the entrance of the French into Rome.

I know not whether the Romans will follow out this programme with constancy as the sterner Milanese have done. If they can, it will draw upon them endless persecutions, countless exactions, but at once educate and prove them worthy of a nobler life.

Yesterday I went over the scene of conflict. It was fearful even to *see* the casinos *Quattro Venti* and *Vascello,* where the French and Romans had been several days so near one another, all shattered to pieces, with fragments of rich stucco and painting still sticking to rafters between the great holes made by the cannonade, and think that men had stayed and fought in them when only a mass of ruins. The French, indeed, were entirely sheltered the last days; to my unpracticed eyes the extent and thoroughness of their works seemed miraculous, and gave me first clear idea of the incompetency of the Italians to resist organized armies. I saw their commanders had not even known enough of the art of war to understand how the French were conducting the siege.—It is true their resources were at any rate inadequate to resistance; only continual sorties would have arrested the progress of the foe, and to make them and man the wall their forces were inadequate. I was struck more than ever by the heroic valor of *ours,* let me say, as I have said all along, for go where I may, a large part of my heart will ever remain in Italy. I hope her children will always acknowledge me as a sister, though I drew not my first breath here. A contadini[8] showed me where thirty seven braves are buried beneath a heap of wall that fell upon them in the shock of one cannonade. A marble nymph, with broken arm, looked sadly that way from her sun-dried fountain, some roses were blooming still, some red oleanders amid the ruin. The sun was casting its last light on the mountains on the tranquil, sad Campagna, that sees one leaf turned more in the book of Woe. This was in the Vascello. I then entered the French ground, all mapped and hollowed like a honey-comb. A pair of skeleton legs protruded from a bank of one barricade; lower a dog had scratched away its light covering of earth from the body of a man, and discovered it lying face upward all dressed; the dog stood gazing on it with an air of stupid amazement. I thought at that moment, recalling some letters received, "O men and women of America, spared these frightful sights, these sudden wrecks of every hope, what angel of Heaven do you suppose has time to listen to your tales of morbid woe? If any find leisure to work for men to-day, think you not they have enough to do to care for the victims here."

I see you have meetings, where you speak of the Italians, the Hungarians. I pray you *do something;* let it not end in a mere cry of sentiment. That is better than to sneer at all that is liberal, like the English; than to talk of the holy victims of patriotism as "anarchists" and "brigands,"—but it is not enough. It ought not to content your consciences. Do you owe no tithe to Heaven for the privileges it has showered on you, for whose achievement so many here suffer and perish daily? Deserve to retain them, by helping your fellow-men to acquire them. Our Government must abstain from interference, but private action is practicable, is due. For Italy, it is in this moment too late, but all that helps Hungary helps her also, helps all who wish the freedom of men from an hereditary yoke now become intolerable. Send money, send cheer—acknowledge as the legitimate leaders and rulers those men who represent the people, who understand its wants, who are ready to die or to live for its good. Kossuth[9] I know not, but his people recognize him; Manin I know not, but with what firm nobleness, what persevering virtue, he has acted for Venice!—Mazzini I know, the man and his acts, great, pure and constant,—a man to whom only the next age can do justice, as it reaps the harvest of the seed he has sown in this.— Friends, countrymen, and lovers of virtue, lovers of freedom, lovers of truth!—be on the alert; rest not supine in your easier lives, but remember

> "Mankind is one.
> And beats with one great heart."

❧

Special Correspondence of The Tribune

FLORENCE, Jan. 6, 1850
Last winter began with meteors and the rose-colored Aurora Borealis. All the winter was steady sunshine, and the Spring that followed

no less glorious, as if Nature rejoiced in and daily smiled upon the noble efforts and tender, generous impulses of the Italian people. This winter, Italy is shrouded with snow. Here in Florence the oil congeals in the closet beside the fire—the water in the chamber—just as in our country-houses of New-England, as yet uncomforted by furnaces. I was supposing this to be confined to colder Florence, but a letter, this day received, from Rome says the snow lies there two feet deep, and water freezes instantly if thrown upon the pavement. I hardly know how to believe it—I who never saw but one slight powdering of snow all my two Roman winters, scarce enough to cover a Canary bird's wing.

Thus Nature again sympathizes with this injured people, though, I fear me, many a houseless wanderer wishes she did not. For many want both bread, and any kind of shelter this winter, an extremity of physical deprivation that had seemed almost impossible in this richest land. It had seemed that Italians might be subjected to the extreme of mental and moral suffering, but that the common beggar's plea, "*I am hungry,*" must remain a mere poetic expression. 'Tis no longer so, for it proves possible for the wickedness of man to mar to an indefinite extent the benevolent designs of God. Yet, indeed, if indefinitely not infinitely. I feel now that we are to bless the very extremity of ill with which Italy is afflicted. The cure is sure, else death would follow.

The barbarities of reaction have reached their hight in the kingdom of Naples and Sicily. Bad government grows daily worse in the Roman dominions. The French have degraded themselves there enough to punish them even for the infamous treachery of which they were guilty. Their foolish national vanity, which prefers the honor of the uniform to the honor of the man, has received its due reward, in the numberless derisions and small insults it has received from a bitterer, blacker vice, the arrogance of the priests. President, envoys, ministers, officers, have all debased themselves; have told the most shameless lies; have bartered the fair fame slowly built up by many years of seeming consistency, for a few days of brief authority, in vain. Their schemes, thus far, have ended in disunion, and should they now win any point upon the right reverend cardinal vices, it is too late. The seeds for a vast harvest of hatreds and contempts are sown over every inch of Roman ground, nor can that malignant growth be extirpated, till the wishes of Heaven shall waft a fire that will burn down all, root and branch, and prepare the earth for an entirely new culture. The next revolution, here and elsewhere, will be radical. Not only Jesuitism must go, but the Roman Catholic religion must go. The Pope cannot retain even his spiritual power. The influence of the clergy is too perverting, too foreign to every hope of advancement and health. Not only the Austrian, and every potentate of foreign blood, must be deposed, but every man who assumes an arbitrary lordship over fellow man, must be driven out. It will be an uncompromising revolution. England cannot reason nor ratify nor criticize it—France cannot betray it—Germany cannot bungle it—Italy cannot bubble it away—Russia cannot stamp it down nor hide it in Siberia. The New Era is no longer an embryo: it is born; it begins to walk—this very year sees its first giant steps, and can no longer mistake its features. Men have long been talking of a transition state—it is over—the power of positive, determinate effort is begun. A faith is offered—men are everywhere embracing it; the film is hourly falling from their eyes and they see, not only near but far, duties worthy to be done. God be praised! It was a dark period of that sceptical endeavor and work, only worthy as helping to educate the next generation, was watered with much blood and tears. God be praised! that time is ended, and the noble band of teachers who have passed this last ordeal of the furnace and den of lions,[1] are ready now to enter their followers for the elementary class.

At this moment all the worst men are in power, and the best betrayed and exiled. All the falsities, the abuses of the old political forms, the old social compact, seem confirmed. Yet it is not so: the struggle that is now to begin will be fearful, but even from the first hours not doubtful. Bodies rotten and trembling cannot long contend with swelling life. Tongue and hand cannot be permanently employed to keep down hearts. Sons cannot be long employed in the conscious enslavement of their sires, fathers of their children. That advent called EMMANUEL begins to be understood, and shall no more so foully be blasphemed. Men shall now be represented as souls, not hands and feet, and governed accordingly. A congress of great, pure, loving minds, and not a congress of selfish ambitions, shall preside. Do you laugh, Editor of the "*Times?*" (Times of the Iron Age.) Do you laugh, Roman Cardinal, as you shut the prison-door on woman weeping for her son martyred in the cause of his country? Do you laugh, Austrian officer, as you drill the Hungarian and Lombard youth to tremble at your baton? Soon you, all of you, shall "*believe* and tremble."[2]

I take little interest now in what is going on here in Italy. It is all leavened with the same leaven, and ferments to the same end. Tuscany is stupified. They are not discontented here, if they can fold the hands yet a little while to slumber. The Austrian tutelage is mild. In Lombardy and Venice they would gladly make it so, but the case is too difficult. The sick man tosses and tumbles. The so called Italian moderates are fighting at last, (not battles, they have not energy for that,) but skirmishes in Piedmont. The result cannot be doubtful; we need not waste time and paper in predicting it.

Joy to those born in this day: In America is open to them the easy chance of a noble, peaceful growth, in Europe of a combat grand in its motives, and in its extent beyond what the world ever before so much as dreamed. Joy to them; and joy to those their heralds, who, if their path was desert, their work unfinished, and their heads in the power of a prostituted civilization, to throw as toys at the feet of flushed, triumphant wickedness, yet holy-hearted in masking love, great and entire in their devotion, fall or fade, happy in the thought that these come after them greater than themselves, who may at last string the harp of the world to full concord, in glory to God in the highest, for peace and love from man to man is become the bond of life.

New-York Daily Tribune,
13 Feb. 1850, supp.

EXPLANATORY NOTES

Abbreviations: "AR": "Autobiographical Romance"; *JMN: The Journals and Miscellaneous Notebooks of Ralph Waldo Emerson;* "L": "Leila"; *L: The Letters of Margaret Fuller; M: The Memoirs of Margaret Fuller Ossoli;* MB: Fuller papers, Boston Public Library; MH: Fuller papers, Houghton Library, Harvard University; MHi: Fuller papers, Massachusetts Historical Society; "SD": "Self-Definitions"; *SL: Summer on the Lakes; WNC: Woman in the Nineteenth Century.*

SELF-DEFINITIONS, 1835–42

1. Fuller's friend, Anna Hazard Barker.

2. In "AR" Fuller describes this situation as one of the touchstones of her existence: "it has often seemed since, that . . . I have looked up just so, at times of threatening, of doubt, and distress, and that just so has some being of the next higher order of existence looked down."

3. In 1833 Timothy Fuller moved with his family to Groton, Massachusetts, separating Fuller from her friends in Boston and Cambridge and forcing her to spend much of her time with housework and tutoring her younger sister and brothers.

4. Fuller had made arrangements to travel to Europe with John and Eliza Farrar.

5. Elizabeth may be Fuller's childhood friend Elizabeth Randall. This sketch of forced education is strikingly similar to Fuller's portrait of her own "premature development of the brain" in "AR."

6. E. is Fuller's sister, Ellen Kilshaw Fuller.

7. Fuller had been reading Amariah Brigham's *Remarks on the Influence of Mental Cultivation and Mental Excitement upon Health* (1832).

8. Referring to Adam's "sweat" in Genesis 3.17–19, Fuller describes as a "Fall" Samuel Ward's decision—after his engagement to Anna Barker—to give up his artistic career and join his father's business firm in New York.

9. Isaiah 6.6–7, where the prophet is touched on the lips with a burning coal.

10. Esau sells his birthright to his brother Jacob for pottage in Genesis 25.29–34.

11. In Fuller's "AR" her English friend (Ellen Kilshaw) pledges her friendship to the young Fuller with "golden amaranths or everlasting flowers," associated with immortality in the nineteenth-century language of flowers (Sarah J. Hale, *Flora's Interpreter*, 1833).

12. Probably Samuel Ward, called "Rafaello" by Fuller.

13. Macaria is the daughter of Hercules, who appears in Euripides' *The Heracleidae* (c. 429 BC); she "offered herself as a victim for the good of her country, was canonized by the Greeks, and worshipped as the Goddess of True Felicity" (*WNC*).

14. In *Earths in the Universe,* the Swedish mystic Emanuel Swedenborg (1688–1772) describes childlike spirits who live on the moon.

15. George Sand is the pseudonym of the French novelist Amandine Lucile Aurore Dudevant (1804–76); this phrase refers to "the jeweller's daughter" in Sand's novel *Léone Léoni* (1834) who spent her life "learning to be looked at when dressed, *avec un front impassible . . .*" (with an impassive face, *M* 1: 249).

16. Second sight is the paranormal faculty of clairvoyance.

17. Commenting on Michelangelo's sybils, Fuller observed: "But the *Persica* is my favorite above all. She is the true sibyl. All the grandeur of that wasted frame comes from within. The life of thought has wasted the fresh juices of the body, and hardened the sere leaf of her check to parchment; every lineament is sharp, every tint is tarnished" (*M* 1: 276–77).

18. Saladin (1138–93), sultan of Egypt and Syria who instilled in Muslims the spirit of jihad (holy war) and dealt the Crusaders serious military setbacks.

19. Fuller echoes here John 1.32.

20. Caroline Sturgis (1819–88) was Fuller's closest female friend and confidante during this period. A carbuncle is a red gemstone, either garnet or ruby—a symbol that Fuller learned from Novalis (Friedrich von Hardenberg, 1772–1801). She often associates the carbuncle with the Goddess (as in "Leila"), while at other times she imagines the carbuncle as a talismanic gem—the philosopher's stone—at the end of a spiritual quest.

21. Echoing the annunciation of Mary in Luke 1.35, Fuller uses the ancient symbol of the divine child signifying spiritual rebirth.

22. Shakespeare, *Twelfth Night* I.i.1.

23. The Greeks used the marble from Paros, which was prized for its translucency, in their finest sculptures. The figure of Paria seems to conflate Fuller's image of the recently married Samuel Ward with that of her dead father.

24. Matthew 27.46.

25. Christ's crown of thorns.

26. Matthew 26.42.

27. This refers to the Annunciation to Mary, Luke 1.35.

28. Several differences between these notes and Fuller's posthumously published "Autobiographical Romance" suggest that Fuller either did not finish "AR" or the editors of the *Memoirs* cut out a number of passages when they prepared their text for publication.

29. Probably Samuel Ward.

30. It is only the first step that costs (Fr.).

31. Not yet (Fr.).

32. The German writer Bettina Brentano von Arnim (1785–1859).

33. 1 John 4.8.

34. Mme Jeanne-Françoise Recamier (1777–1849), known for her literary salon. Mme de Staël (1766–1817), née Anne Louise Germaine Necker), French author remembered as a theorist of Romanticism and her novel *Corinne* (1807).

35. Mignon, a character in Goethe's *Wilhelm Meisters Lehrjahre* (1795–96), sings this line in bk. 8 ch. 2 (cf. *WNC* n. 73). Translation: They don't inquire into the difference between man and woman. In other words: They don't pose the question of gender.

36. Alcibiades (c. 450–04 BC), student and lover of Socrates in Plato's *Symposium*. Karl Theodor Korner (1791–1813), German poet whom Fuller praised in the *Western Messenger* as an inspiring and disciplined genius. The love of Wallenstein and Max was portrayed in Friedrich Schiller's *Wallenstein* trilogy (1800). Emerson deleted the name Anna Barker when he reprinted an excerpt of this passage in the *Memoirs*.

37. Fuller identifies the carbuncle (n. 20 above) with Anna Barker, suggesting the ways in which her image of Barker contributed to her symbolization of the Goddess and spiritual quest.

38. Goethe, *Elective Affinities* (*Die Wahlverwandtschaften,* 1809).

AUTOBIOGRAPHICAL ROMANCE

In the *Memoirs* Emerson dates this posthumously published text as 1840. However, Fuller's notes for an autobiography (reprinted in this volume) suggest that she may have been working on "AR" as late as 1841.

1. An admirer of Queen Anne of England, whose reign (1702–14) was marked by the expansion of Britain in the Act of Union with Scotland (1707).

2. After killing the Cyclopes, Apollo was condemned to tend the herds of Admetus for a year (Euripides, *Alcestis*).

3. White toga worn by Roman young men on coming of age (Lat.).

4. According to the legend (recounted by Livy), the founders of Rome—Romulus and Remus—were suckled by a wolf.

5. Ovid's *Metamorphoses* was one of Fuller's most important sources; she used its accounts of Hercules, Isis, Orpheus, and Niobe, among others.

6. Mean, shabby (Fr.).

7. German writer Johann Ludwig Tieck (1773–1853) portrays in several tales characters who pursue their dreams in the mountains.

8. A Jacobin was a radical republican during the French Revolution.

9. Amelia is the title character, distinguished for her fidelity, of *Amelia* (1751) by English novelist Henry Fielding (1701–54).

10. *Specimens of the Table Talk of the Late Samuel Taylor Coleridge* (1835). Reason is Coleridge's term for the direct intuition of spiritual truth, understanding is knowledge gained through the senses.

11. Byron, *Don Juan* 13.11.

12. A reference to *Twelve Lectures on the Natural History of Man, and the Rise and Progress of Philosophy* (1839) by Alexander Kinmont (1799–1838).

13. Perfume distilled from many different flowers (Fr.).

14. Ellen Kilshaw, the daughter of a Liverpool manufacturer.

15. Sir Walter Scott (1771–1832), *Guy Mannering* (1815) ch. 9.

16. Amaranths, see "SD" n. 11.

17. Fuller consistently uses the star as a symbol of an ideal person or being existing on a higher level.

18. Fuller attended Miss Prescott's Young Ladies Seminary at Groton, MA, in 1824–25—an experience that inspired part of the story of Mariana included in *Summer on the Lakes*.

THE MAGNOLIA OF LAKE PONTCHARTRAIN

The germ of this story came from a family friend, William Eustis, who visited the Fuller household in Oct. 1840 and described an account of a Yuca and "the Magnolia of Lake Pontchartrain"—sketches that Fuller thought "harmonize[d] with all legends of Isis, Diana, &c" (*L* 2: 166). By November, she was writing "the companion to the Yuca, the Magnolia, for the Dial" (184).

1. The Queen's "full consciousness of power" corresponds closely to Emerson's doctrine of self-reliance. Emerson commented in a letter to Fuller in Jan. 1841 that this sketch "is of me & mine."

2. A virgin priestess, symbol of female self-reliance.
3. The translation for the Italian passage (unidentified):

> An unknown person walks in front
> On that lonely and deserted street,
> And thinking to himself what he should do,
> Wavers in a great storm of thoughts.

4. Translation:

> A dark shadow takes away from the world
> Various aspects, tinging all color black.

5. Fuller's conception of the "Mothers" is indebted to Goethe's *Faust, Part Two* (see *WNC* n. 113) as well as to nineteenth-century conceptions of the political value of maternal care, exemplified in Fuller's later advice to her female readers on the way to reform the degraded women of New York: "Take the place of mothers, such as might have saved them originally" (*WNC*).

YUCA FILAMENTOSA

1. Diana (Artemis), a dangerous and vengeful virgin goddess, fell in love with Hippolytus, whom she convinced Asclepius to restore to life after his death (Ovid, *Metamorphoses* 15).
2. Watching at the death-bed of a "wretched girl" dying from a botched self-abortion, Fuller had the experience of perceiving "a star . . . mirrored from the very blackness of the yawning gulf" (*L* 2: 168).

LEILA

1. In her poem "To Sarah," Fuller asserts that she chose this name "by the sound" and that it "stands for night"; in her poem "Leila in the Arabian Zone," Fuller uses Leila as her syncretic term for the Goddess.

The epigraph is from William Wordsworth, "Liberty" (beg. "Those breathing Tokens of your kind regard," 1829) line 111.

2. Fetish (Fr.), an object or token embodying magical power.
3. In *WNC*, Fuller describes this maddening power as the "electrical, the magnetic element in woman"—a sexual and psychological charge that sets men on edge.

4. The Roman author Apuleius describes in *The Metamorphosis, or Golden Ass*, trans. Thomas Taylor (1758–1835), "the white veils (by which the image of the Goddess was screened from the view of the profane)." See also *WNC* n. 134.

5. Leila's transcendence of "sex, age, state" and other human "barriers" gives her a supernatural aura, but also connects her with nineteenth-century conceptions of the unconscious.

6. Leila's "mysterious wind" is linked with the "sudden breeze" in "The Magnolia of Lake Pontchartrain." In Romantic literature such manifestations are familiar signs of the nearing of a divine or supernatural power.

7. Fuller's description here parallels accounts of meditative practices that begin with a centering upon a divine image.

8. Carbuncle, see "SD" nn. 20, 37.

9. Leila's "veins of silver" connect with the "silver time" in Fuller's notes for her autobiography—a link between Leila and Fuller's 1840–41 spiritual crisis.

10. Nineteenth-century writers (for example, Emerson and Dickinson) frequently described unconscious forces as a volcanic power that becomes more violent if repressed.

11. Dagon is a Philistine god vanquished by the "ark of God" in 1 Samuel 5.1–4.

12. Derived from Goethe, Fuller's conception of the Demon and Dæmoniacal refer to the "instinctive," an uncanny "fire within the hidden caverns and secret veins of earth" that "refuses to be analyzed by the understanding" (*M* 1: 225–26)—a conception similar to Edgar Allan Poe's "imp of the perverse" and Sigmund Freud's "id."

13. In Plutarch's *Morals* 4, Isis, while in Byblus, became the nurse of the queen's infant whose mortal parts she used to burn away at night.

14. Fuller's use of alchemical imagery to depict processes of psychological transformation is derived in part from Goethe's *Elective Affinities.*

BETTINE BRENTANO AND HER FRIEND GÜNDERODE

1. The translation of Bettina Brentano von Arnim's correspondence with Goethe entitled *Goethe's Correspondence with a Child* dates from 1837.

2. The Juggernaut was believed to contain the bones of the Hindu god Krishna; at his festival, when the idol was drawn in a heavy cart, his worshipers sacrificed themselves by throwing themselves beneath its wheels.

3. A reference to Christ's parable of the prodigal son, Luke 15.11–32.

4. Fuller paraphrases here Emerson's doctrine of "compensation": "Every excess causes a defect; every defect an excess" ("Compensation").

Explanatory Notes

5. In Goethe's *Faust, Part Two,* act III, Euphorion, the son of Helen and Faust, attempts to fly, only to be destroyed like Icarus.

6. Tasso's ill-fated love for Leonora culminated in disillusionment and despair in Goethe's *Torquato Tasso* (1790). Werther's disastrous love for Lotte led to his suicide in Goethe's *The Sorrows of Young Werther* (*Die Leiden des jungen Werthers,* 1774). George Douglass, a character in *The Abbot* by Sir Walter Scott, forms an enthusiastic but unrequited love for Queen Mary. The Greek poet Sappho (c. 610–c. 580 BC) is remembered for her love of other women. Héloïse (c. 1098–1164) married French theologian Abelard, who was castrated by her uncle in retaliation. Julie-Jeanne-Eléonore de Lespinasse (1732–76) was a highly learned hostess remembered for her letters analyzing the French social scene.

7. Anna Brownell Jameson (1794–1860), a popular Irish essayist, discusses apostles, saints, martyrs, and clerical orders in *Sacred and Legendary Art* (1843); see also *SL* ch. II n. 11.

8. Hermia and Helena are Athenian women, whose loves for Lysander and Demetrius are crossed by the fairies in Shakespeare's *A Midsummer-Night's Dream.* The nymphs of Proserpina (Persephone) were gathering flowers in the vale of Enna when she was seized by Death. The three Graces were Greek goddesses personifying charm and beauty; the nine Muses were Greek goddesses of music, literature, and intellectual pursuits in general.

SUMMER ON THE LAKES

CHAPTER I

1. Cloten is a long-winded and somewhat vainglorious character, son of the Queen, in Shakespeare's *Cymbeline.*

2. Fuller's description here of threatening "savages" duplicates the pose found in numerous popular paintings of the period. In Chapter VI Fuller replaces this stereotype with a sympathetic portrait of the Chippewa and Ottowa Indians.

3. Hermann Ludwig Heinrich Pückler-Muskau (1785–1871), a German travel writer and authority on landscape gardening.

4. General Andrew Porter (1743–1813) fought in the American Revolution and in central New York against American Indians; Andrew Jackson Downing (1815–52) was a famous American horticulturalist and landscape architect.

5. John Greenwood (1727–92), born in Boston, executed some of the first genre paintings in America.

6. Louis Hennepin (1640–c. 1701), who served as Robert LaSalle's chaplain on his 1679 expedition through the Great Lakes, published the first printed description of Niagara Falls in *A Description of Louisiana* (1683).

Explanatory Notes

1. James Freeman Clarke (1810–88) escorted Fuller and his sister Sarah Ann Clarke (1808–96) to Buffalo; Sarah and Margaret Fuller completed the remainder of the excursion together.

2. German writer Friedrich Heinrich Karl de la Motte Fouqué (1777–1843) published *Undine* (1811), a fairy tale about a water sylph who gains a soul through her marriage with a human who eventually proves unfaithful to her.

3. The fantastic tales of E. T. A. Hoffmann (1776–1822) were admired by American Romantic authors, as well as later by Sigmund Freud.

4. Echoing the language of the Gnomes in Goethe's *Faust, Part Two*, act I, Fuller here describes the "dæmonic" working of the unconscious. See "L" n. 12.

5. Nineteenth-century theories of the "picturesque" were largely derived from the travel writings of William Gilpin (1724–1804).

6. Medea, a celebrated witch in classical mythology, used her magic to help Jason win the golden fleece.

7. An American Indian term for the immaterial force possessed by all beings and objects and manifesting itself as a person's tutelary spirit.

8. George Catlin (1796–1872) published *Manners, Customs, and Condition of the North American Indians* with about 300 engravings in 1841.

9. Sir Charles Augustus Murray (1806–95), who joined a tribe of wandering Pawnees in 1835 and spent three months with them, published *Travels in North America during the Years 1834, 1835, and 1836. Including a Summer of Residence with the Pawnee Tribe of Indians, in the Remote Prairies of the Missouri* (1841).

10. Henry Rowe Schoolcraft (1793–1864), American explorer and ethnologist, served as federal agent to the Indian tribes of the Lake Superior region, where in 1822 he married the half-Ojibwa daughter of a fur trader; his *Algic Researches, comprising inquiries respecting the mental characteristics of the North American Indians* (1839) inspired both James Russell Lowell's poem "A Chippewa Legend" (1844) and Henry Wadsworth Longfellow's *Song of Hiawatha* (1855).

11. Anna Brownell Jameson, popular Irish essayist known for *Shakespeare's Heroines* (1832), published *Winter Studies and Summer Rambles in Canada* in 1838.

12. Uncas is an American Indian character in James Fenimore Cooper's *The Last of the Mohicans* (1826).

13. Washington Irving (1783–1859) desribed his western travels in *A Tour on the Prairies* (1835) and *Astoria* (1836).

14. Thomas Loraine McKenney (1785–1859) served as head of the newly formed United States Bureau of Indian Affairs (1824–30). His *Sketches of a Tour to the Lakes, of the character and customs of the Chippeway Indians, and of incidents connected with the treaty of Fond du Lac* (1827) describes the expedition on which he helped negotiate the 1826 treaty with the Chippewa, Menominee, and Winnebago tribes which established Indian tribal territories.

15. Chamounix is a valley in eastern France near Mont Blanc described by Wordsworth in his "Descriptive Sketches" and *Prelude* 6; the Trossachs are a woods in central Scotland immortalized by Sir Walter Scott in *Lady of the Lake* (1810) and *Rob Roy* (1818).

16. Wordworth, "Character of the Happy Warrior" line 54.

17. Madoc, a legendary Welsh hero who discovers America 300 years before Columbus, is celebrated in Robert Southey's *Madoc* (1805).

18. The English novelist Anthony Trollope (1815–82) detailed the vicissitudes of rural life in a series of novels comprising the "Barsetshire Chronicles."

CHAPTER III

1. The Sac chieftan Black Hawk (1767–1838) was defeated by U.S. troops in the Black Hawk War (1832), an event recounted in his *Autobiography* (1833).

2. In Homer's *Iliad*, Rhesus is a Thracian king famed for his horses.

3. Seven Sisters, the constellation Pleiades, named for virgin companions of the goddess Artemis, who were changed into stars to avoid rape.

4. The American artist Benjamin West (1738–1820) modeled his painting "The Savage Chief" (c. 1761) on the Apollo Belvedere.

5. Falling in love with Ganymede in Ovid's *Metamorphoses* 10, Jove transforms himself into an eagle and carries him off to Mt. Olympus. The Danish sculptor Bertel Thorwaldsen (c. 1768–1844) executed several statues based on classical mythology, including Jason, Venus, Psyche, and Ganymede.

6. Mrs. Catherine Gore (1799–1861), author of *The Diary of a Desennuyee* (1836) and *Modern Chivalry* (1843).

7. Alexander Kinmont (1799–1838) is remembered for his *Twelve Lectures on the Natural History of Man, and the Rise and Progress of Philosophy* (1839).

8. In return or retaliation (Fr.).

9. In Ovid's *Metamorphoses* 10, Apollo in a game of discus accidentally kills his beloved Hyacinthus, who turns into the hyacinth flower.

10. Possibly Big Thunder, a son of Little Crow (a Sioux chief), killed in 1841 by the Chippewa while on a war expedition.

11. Washington Allston (1779–1843), the first important American Romantic painter, known for his lyric landscapes such as "Moonlit Landscape" (1819). Fuller's companion, Sarah Clarke, had been one of Allston's students.

12. Nicolas Poussin (1594–1665), French painter known for his scriptural and mythological subjects.

13. In Greek mythology the Gorgon, Medusa, who had serpents for hair, turned anyone who looked at her into stone.

Explanatory Notes

CHAPTER IV

1. "Triformis" was written by James Freeman Clarke.

2. Although it uses characters that seem to be modeled upon those in Wordsworth's *The Excursion,* the dialogue between Solitary and Traveller appears to be the composition of one of Fuller's friends.

3. In Goethe's *Wilhelm Meisters Lehrjahre* (1795–96), Mariana is Wilhelm's first love. Fuller's tale of Mariana is loosely autobiographical up to the account of her marriage with Sylvain; see "AR" n. 18.

4. Warren Hastings (1732–1818), the first British governor general of India, was accused of high crimes and misdemeanors, impeached, and then acquitted after a trial before the House of Lords which lasted seven years (1788–95).

5. Louisa Sidney Stanhope, *The Bandit's Bride, or The Maid of Saxony, a Romance* (1807).

6. Literally, a female improviser; a term, derived from Mme de Staël's *Corinne* (see "SD" n. 34), used to define a familiar nineteenth-century female role—that of the wild, impulsive, female genius. While it was applied pejoratively to Fuller by many of her contemporaries, it denotes here the electrical and intuitive qualities that Fuller later celebrated as the "Muse" side of the female personality (*WNC*).

7. This ballad, otherwise known as "O, that I were where Helen lies," presents a lover's lament for the murdered Helen whom he wishes to join in the grave. In Mariana's poem, Fuller adapts the situation to comment on her own sense of abandonment—a topic much on her mind during the early months of 1844 as she completed *Summer on the Lakes* and worked through once again her feeling of having been abandoned by Samuel Ward when he married Anna Barker (1844 Commonplace Book, MHi).

8. In *Philip van Artevelde* (1834), a verse drama by Sir Henry Taylor (1800–86), Elena is an Italian woman killed by French troops as she attempts to protect the body of the slain Flemish leader, van Artevelde.

9. Morris Birkbeck (1764–1825), who emigrated from England to Illinois in 1817, wrote several books that were influential in directing settlers to the prairie lands of the West—for example, *Notes on a Journey in America* (1817) and *Letters from Illinois* (1818).

CHAPTER V

1. The *Venus and Adonis* of the Venetian painter Titian (c. 1487–1576) was based upon Ovid's account (*Metamorphoses* 10) of Venus's love for Adonis, a youth who was killed by a wild boar.

2. James Russell Lowell (1819–91) published "A Chippewa Legend,"

based upon a story from Schoolcraft's *Algic Researches,* in the 1844 edition of *The Liberty Bell,* distributed by the Massachusetts Anti-Slavery Fair, Boston.

3. Andreas Justinus Kerner (1786–1862) was a German physician and spiritualist, as well as friend and biographer of Franz Anton Mesmer, the inventor of "animal magnestism." His *Die Seherin von Prevorst* (1829) records the results of his examination of the somnambulist and clairvoyant Friederike Hauffe from 1826 to 1829.

4. Charles Fourier's "aromal state" resulted when a channel had been opened to release a person's universal, magnetic fluid (a conception of pyschic energy derived from Mesmer's theories).

5. Free Hope's declaration, "All my days are touched by the supernatural," is echoed in Emerson's posthumous account of Fuller's interest in omens, dreams, talismans, the demonic (*M* 1: 219–27).

6. Self-Poise presents a compendium of many of Emerson's favorite aphorisms.

7. Fuller's defense of infatuation echoes the terms in which she debated her spiritual crisis with Emerson in the autumn of 1840; her deepest complaint was that Emerson refused to acknowledge the validity of her spiritual ecstasy.

8. Sidereal, pertaining to the stars.

9. A reference to the Gothic romances of Ann Radcliffe (1764–1823), author of *The Mysteries of Udolpho* (1794) and *The Italian* (1797).

10. Carlo Amoretti (1741–1816) was an Italian naturalist and geographer. Pennet in Calabria (a region in Italy) has not been identified.

11. Canidias, a courtesan denounced as a witch in the *Epodes* and *Satires* of Horace (65–8 BC).

12. In *The Metamorphosis,* Apuleius (see "L" n. 4) tells the story of Cupid and Psyche, who—after a series of trials imposed by Venus—is made immortal.

13. Food of life (Lat.). Galen was a second-century AD Greek physician, whose ideas shaped medical practice until the sixteenth century.

15. Adam Karl August Eschenmayer (1768–1852), a follower of Jung-Stilling (see n. 20 below) published a commentary on Kerner's *Die Seherin von Prevorst*—his *Mysterien des innern Lebens* (*Mysteries of the Inner Life,* 1830).

16. Johann Wolfgang von Goethe (1749–1832), one of Fuller's most important sources and the subject of several of her critical essays, published *Wilhelm Meisters Wanderjahre* from 1821 to 1829.

17. Fuller also shared this belief in the magical properties of gems—see *Memoirs,* the poem for Carrie on the carbuncle, and "SD" n. 20.

18. Chauncey Hare Townshend (1798–1868) describes this phenomenon in *Facts in Mesmerism: With Reasons for a Dispassionate Inquiry into It* (1841)—one of the most popular English books on mesmerism during the nineteenth century.

19. Cornelius Heinrich Agrippa (1486?–1535), German scholar, alchemist, and student of the occult.

20. Johann Heinrich Jung-Stilling (1740–1817), a German writer known
for his autobiography which gives a vivid portrait of village life in a pietistic family,
discussed the mysteries of faith in *Scenes in the World of Spirits* (trans. 1815) and
Theory of Pneumatology (trans. 1834).

21. Saint Theresa (1515–82) was a Spanish Carmelite nun who founded
many convents and monasteries and was famed for her mystical visions.

22. The Swedish mystic, Emanuel Swedenborg (1688–1722); the great Italian poet, Dante Alighieri (1265–1321).

23. The American Tract Society, founded in New York City in May 1825,
quickly became one of the chief interdenominational Christian societies in the
U.S.; it began publishing periodicals as early as 1843.

CHAPTER VI

1. Alexander Henry (1739–1824), taken prisoner after an Indian massacre
in the French and Indian War (1754–63), escaped death through the intervention
of his Chippewa blood brother and later published his experiences in *Travels and
Adventures in Canada and the Indian Territories between the Years 1760 and 1776* (1809).
Delphos was a Greek shrine, devoted to Apollo and famed for the Delphic oracle,
a priestess believed to foretell the future.

2. Jane Schoolcraft was the Ojibwa wife of Henry Rowe Schoolcraft, see
ch. II n. 10.

3. Anne MacVicar Grant (1755–1838) who published *Memoirs of an American Lady: With sketches of manners and scenery as they existed previous to the Revolution*
(1808).

4. Jonathan Carver (1710–80) helped explore the great northwestern territories and published his experiences in *Travels through the Interior Parts of North-
America in the Years 1766, 1767, and 1768* (1778).

5. Sir Alexander Mackenzie (1764–1820), a Scottish fur trader and explorer who traced the course of the 1,100-mile Mackenzie River in northwestern
Canada and described his journeys in *Voyages from Montreal on the River St. Lawrence,
through the continent of North America to the Frozen and Pacific Oceans in the years 1789
and 1793* (1801).

6. Preux, valiant knight, champion (Fr.). Lord Edward Fitzgerald
(1763–98), later a famous Irish rebel and martyr, traveled to Detroit after reading
Jean-Jacques Rousseau's passionate account of the savage life.

7. Nikolaus Ludwig Zinzendorf (1700–60) organized the persecuted
Bohemian Brethran into Moravian Brethren and in 1741 traveled to America to
establish Moravian congregations in eastern Pennsylvania.

8. On 30 Oct. 1837, Keokuk, Black Hawk, and four chiefs of the united
Sac and Fox tribes were received by Governor Everett—a visit described in detail
by Benjamin Drake (1795–1841) in *The Life and Adventures of Black Hawk: with*

sketches of Keokuk, the Sac and Fox Indians, and the late Black Hawk War (1840). Up to this date, he notes, "no public spectacle in the history of Boston, ever assembled so great a number of its citizens."

9. Uncas, heroic Indian in *The Last of the Mohicans;* Magawisca, Indian woman who sacrifices her arm to rescue Everell Fletcher in *Hope Leslie* (1827) by Catharine Maria Sedgwick (1789–1867).

10. In Judges 16 Samson loses his superhuman strength when his hair is cut by Delilah.

11. George Combe (1788–1858), Andrew Combe (1797–1847), and Johann Christoph Spurzheim (1776–1832) were popularizers of phrenology, a pseudoscience that purported to determine a person's psychological faculties and character through an examination of the shape of his or her skull.

12. Massasoit and King Philip were sachems of the Wampanoag Indians in the seventeenth century.

13. The speech of Edward Everett (1794–1865), governor of Massachusetts, is reprinted in Benjamin Drake's *The Life and Adventures of Black Hawk* (see n. 8 above). Fuller probably used this source or the text published in either the 1 Nov. 1837 edition of the *Boston Courier* or the 4 Nov. 1837 edition of the Charlestown *Bunker-Hill Aurora.*

14. Amalgamation, racial intermarriage.

15. Shobail Vail Clevenger (1812–43), Cincinnati sculptor known for his portrait busts, which Fuller had seen at the Boston Atheneum in 1840.

16. Pontiac (c. 1720–69) and Philip (c. 1639–76), chiefs who unsuccessfully waged war on the British (see n. 31 below); Julian (c. 331–63), Roman emperor who was slain in battle.

17. Sir William Johnson (1715–74) left Ireland for America in 1738 and established himself on a New York estate, which became a center of Indian trade and a shelter for the Mohawks. Mrs. Grant, see n. 3 above.

18. James Adair (c. 1709–c. 83), Irish Indian trader known for his *History of the American Indians* (1775).

19. Savoir faire, ability, know-how (Fr.). In her review (*New-York Tribune,* 20 June 1845), of the works of Benjamin Disraeli (1804–81) Fuller praised his novel *Vivian Grey* (1826) for its witty, sparkling, and whimsical qualities.

20. In Germanic mythology the lorelei are sirens of the Rhine whose singing lures sailors to shipwreck.

21. Chandler Robbins Gilman (1802–65), an obstetrician and medical professor in New York, published *Life on the Lakes: Being tales and sketches collected during a trip to the pictured rocks of Lake Superior* (1836).

22. James Adair (see n. 18 above) argued in *History of the American Indians* (1775) that the American Indians were descended from the lost ten tribes of Israel.

23. Murray, see ch. II n. 9; Henry, see n. 1 above; Pericles (c. 495–29 BC), the statesman who most fully developed both the Athenian democracy and em-

pire; Phocion (c. 402–317 BC), Athenian general and statesman remembered for his moderate rule of Athens.

24. Ovid's *Metamorphoses* 9; Fuller cites the continuation of this passage (spoken by Jove) in *WNC* (see nn. 6, 59). Translation: "Only his maternal part [his flesh] shall feel the power of Vulcan. That which he drew from me is exempt and free from death, conquerable by no flames."

25. Rigolette is a kind, hard-working young woman in *The Mysteries of Paris* (1842–43) by Eugène Sue (1804–57).

26. Col. Thomas Loraine McKenney and James Hall published *Catalogue of One Hundred and Fifteen Indian Portraits, Representing Eighteen Different Tribes, Accompanied by a Few Brief Remarks on the Character &c. of Most of Them.* (1836), a popular work reprinted in an expanded edition as *The History of the Indian Tribes of North America, with Biographical Sketches and Anecdotes of the Principal Chiefs* (1838–44).

27. Samuel Gardner Drake (1798–1875), prominent Boston antiquarian and bookseller, published several books on Indians owned by the Harvard Library (which Fuller used for her research). This probably refers to *The book of the Indians of North America; comprising details in the lives of about five hundred chiefs and others* (1833).

28. George Guess (known as Sequoya, c. 1770–1843) was an American Indian scholar who formed a syllabary for the Cherokee language, used to teach thousands of tribal members to read and write.

29. Red Jacket (c. 1758–1830), chief of the Senecas in New York, was known as an orator and for his opposition to the cession of Indian lands to the U.S.

30. Osceola (c. 1800–38) was a leader of the Seminole Indians in Florida during the Second Seminole War (1835–37).

31. John Ross (1790–1866), chief, United Cherokee Nation.

32. Philip of Pokanoket (called King Philip, see nn. 12, 16). Pontiac, an Ottawa chief, led the attack on Detroit (1763) during Pontiac's War. Tecumseh (c. 1768–1813), a Shawnee chief, fought and died with the British in the War of 1812 (see n. 16 above).

33. On 15 Aug. 1812, about 400 Potawatomi massacred most of the garrison being evacuated from Fort Dearborn (Chicago).

CHAPTER VII

1. Allegro and Penseroso are the spirits of joy and melancholy, dramatized in John Milton's poems "L'Allegro" and "Il Penseroso."

2. Julius Caesar (100–44 BC) described the Roman conquest of Gaul (present-day France) in his *Commentary on the Gallic War* (52–51 BC).

3. Baynard Rush Hall (1798–1863), *The New Purchase: or, seven and a half years in the far West. By Robert Carleton, esq. [pseud.]* (1843), a fictitious account of pioneer life in Bloomington, Monroe Co., IN.

4. The English painter and sportsman William Scrope (1772–1852) published *The Art of Deerstalking* in 1838.

5. Count Alessandro di Cagliostro (1743–95) was a notorious Italian imposter who traveled widely in Europe, posing as a physician, alchemist, necromancer, and freemason.

6. General William Hull (1753–1825) was court-martialed and convicted for his surrender of Detroit to the British during the War of 1812.

7. Phrenologists (see ch. VI n. 11). Developed about 1800 by Franz Joseph Gall (1758–1828), phrenology was popularized in America by Orson (1809–87) and Lorenzo Fowler (1811–96). While living in Providence Fuller herself underwent a phrenological examination performed by Orson Fowler in Nov. 1837.

8. The French social theorist Charles Fourier (1772–1837) argued for the establishment through "voluntary association" of utopian communities based on noncompetitive principles. See *WNC* n. 5.

1844 POETRY

1. Delphos, a Greek shrine, devoted to Apollo (see n. 15 below) and famed for the Delphic oracle, a priestess believed to foretell the future.

2. Fuller's brother Arthur omitted the final 18 lines when he printed a heavily edited posthumous version of this poem in *Life Without and Life Within* (1859).

3. Fuller's phrasing echoes Job 39.25—a passage in which the Lord asserts that the horse, like other creations, exceeds human understanding.

4. Sarah Clarke

5. Woods southeast of Boston.

6. In Ovid's *Metamorphoses* 1, Jove, who is filled with desire for Io, transforms her into a cow in order to deceive his wife Juno; Io swam to Egypt where, according to some traditions, she was worshiped as Isis.

7. Isis, the consort of Osiris, was a great Egyptian fertility goddess frequently depicted with cow's horns (her link with Io). Her sistrum (which Fuller chose as a personal talisman) was a rattle used to frighten away Typhon. "I have a great share of Typhon to the Osiris, wild rush and leap, blind force for the sake of force," Fuller is recorded as saying (M 1: 230); this suggests that the sistrum represented for her a talisman of psychic control taming otherwise unruly moods.

8. Diana (Artemis), a very dangerous and powerful Roman nature goddess. Hecate, ancient, pre-Olympian Greek earth goddess of fertility and magic power. Phebe is Phoebe, one of the female Titans, mother of Hecate and grandmother of Diana and Apollo.

9. Fuller used the mystical symbol of the title—interlocking triangles, surrounded by a serpent and the rays of a star—as the frontispiece of *WNC*.

10. In Greek legend the Sphynx was a legendary winged monster, with the body of a lion and the head and breasts of a woman; in *Oedipus Rex,* Oedipus frees Thebes from a devouring Sphynx by answering her riddle: "What has four feet, three feet, two feet, but one voice?"

11. Mercury (Gk. Hermes), messenger of the gods; divinity of "the human intellect" (Fuller's notes, MH).

12. Sistrum, see n. 7 above.

13. Fuller loosely bases this poem on the Rosicrucians, known as the "Order of the Rosy Cross," a mystical and secret society that was popularized in sixteenth-century Germany by a book purporting to give the history of its legendary founder "Christian Rosencreutz." Rosencreutz was supposed to have possessed the philosopher's stone—a legend that inspires here Fuller's ruby/carbuncle imagery.

14. The great Italian painter Raphael (Raffaello Sanzio, 1483–1520) painted numerous works based on the life of Christ.

15. Apollo, son of Jove (Zeus), was god of prophecy and patron of poetry; "the conscious genius of our intellectual being" (Fuller's notes on Coleridge, MH).

16. Tantalus was famed for his punishment after death: he was ever-thirsty while standing in a pool of receding water, ever-hungry beneath a tree filled with ungraspable fruit.

WOMAN IN THE NINETEENTH CENTURY

1. The translation of the German passage is:

> Free through reason, strong through laws,
> Through gentleness great, and rich through treasures,
> This long time your breast conceals you.

2. "On Lucy Countess of Bedford" by Ben Jonson (1572–1637).

3. Hamlet speaks this line, *Hamlet* I.ii.146. The second quotation is unidentified.

4. The story of the prodigal son is told in Luke 15.11–32.

5. French utopian socialist Charles Fourier imagined "Harmony" as an ideal society in which men and woman could escape from the social obstructions caused by capitalist competition. Fuller adds a psychological dimension to the concept by using the term to refer to an ideal state in which the different facets of a person's being are in balance.

6. This passage from Ovid's *Metamorphoses* 9 occurs after Hercules has been killed by his jealous wife Deianira (see nn. 41, 59 below). Translation: "If anyone, any one of you, regrets Hercules' becoming a god, he will not wish honors

to have been given him; yet he will know they deserved to be given, and—though unwilling—will approve. The gods assented."

7. Compare Matthew 5.15.

8. Matthew 7.8, 12.

9. Fuller argues for the recovery of childlike perception of spiritual reality—an idea familiar from her reading of Wordsworth (e.g. "Ode: Intimations of Immortality").

10. Probably the prophecy of the coming prophet in Isaiah 11.1–6, culminating with: "The wolf also shall dwell with the lamb . . ."

11. Compare Matthew 22.44 and Mark 12.36.

12. Fuller associated wolfish energy with Roman aggression, since Rome was founded by Romulus and Remus, who (according to the legend recounted by Livy) were suckled by a wolf.

13. Louis Claude de Saint-Martin (1743–1803), a French mystic philosopher, was originally one of the Illuminati and later devoted himself to the philosophical speculations of Jakob Böhme.

14. Thomas Crawford (1814–57) was an American sculptor who studied in Rome with Thorwaldsen (see *SL* ch. III n. 5). His statue *Orpheus and Cerberus* was bought by the Boston Atheneum in 1840. During the American Renaissance, the mythic poet Orpheus was a widely used symbol for the male artist.

15. Fuller published the "Orphic Sayings" of Amos Bronson Alcott (1799–1888) in the *Dial* (July 1840, Jan. 1841).

16. In the *Metamorphoses* 10 Ovid tells the story of Orpheus, who journeyed into the underworld to rescue his wife Eurydice from Death, only to lose her once again when he looked back at her on their return.

17. The story of Persephone (Proserpina), told in Ovid's *Metamorphoses* 6, parallels that of Eurydice; like Orpheus, her mother Ceres traveled into the underworld to rescue her.

18. Fuller's image of the well-tuned lyre is derived from George Sand's *Les sept cordes de la lyre* (1839).

19. Francis Bacon (1561–1626) anatomized in his works the errors of judgment and learning.

20. Ulysses (Odysseus) passes the sirens, whose singing lured sailors to their death, in the *Odyssey* 12.

21. Citizen (masc. and fem. forms, Fr.).

22. The best-known poem of Pierre-Jean de Bèranger (1780–1857) is "La Liberté."

23. Spoken by Christ on the cross in Luke 23.34.

24. Fuller revises the phrase from "The Declaration of Independence": "all men are created equal."

25. Alessandro Manzoni (1785–1873), Italian poet, novelist, and leader of the Italian Romantic school, is best known for his novel *I promessi sposi* (*The*

Betrothed, 1825–27). In 1847 Fuller met Manzoni, who participated in the 1848 Milan uprising.

26. Fuller admired the *Imaginary Conversations* (1824, 1828, 1829) and *Pericles and Aspasia* (1836) of the English writer, Walter Savage Landor (1775–1864). In her journal (MH) she observes: "In Pericles and Aspasia nothing strikes me than the beauty with which the relations are kept up. What self-respect Yet what tender courting What fine perception of shades in the intellectual commerce of love and friendship."

27. The marquis of Carabbas is the imaginary title that the cat invents for his master, a miller's son, in Charles Perrault's (1628–1703) retelling of "Puss in Boots" in *Contes de ma mère l'oye* (*Mother Goose's Tales,* 1697).

28. Radical republicans during the French Revolution.

29. Fuller's note. The English critic and lexicographer, Samuel Johnson (1709–84); the British essayist and poet, John Sterling (1806–44).

30. In the Catholic Church indulgences are pardons releasing a penitent from temporal punishment due for sin; in this context the word connotes the trader's assumption of a superior position in relation to his wife who is expected to worship him.

31. In "The Dignity of Woman," the German poet Friedrich von Schiller (1759–1805) contrasts man's action and command with woman's rapture and feeling, which—he argues—should win man back "from his trances" to a sense of harmony and concord.

32. The *Deutsche Schnellpost* was a German-language newspaper published in New York beginning in 1842.

33. The anonymous author of the article entitled "The Legal Wrongs of Women" in the *United States Magazine and Democratic Review* 14 (May 1844) argues that free women in the United States "if married, have no more power over their property and earnings than slave-women." She goes on to paint a portrait of an ideal, spiritual marriage in terms that parallel Fuller's views of marriage in "The Great Lawsuit" (1843).

34. Phocion, see *SL* ch. VI n. 23.

35. Fuller may be thinking here of the great French actress Mlle Rachel (1820–58), whom she later saw in Paris in March 1847, and Abby Kelley (1810–87), a Quaker who became a prominent speaker in the antislavery movement.

36. The parable of the talents is told in Luke 25.14–30.

37. Miranda's life history given here parallels that of Fuller, who identified with the portrait of Prospero's accomplished daughter in Shakespeare's *The Tempest.* By comparing her father to Prospero, Fuller is able to acknowledge the beneficial aspects of his instruction, which she had condemned in "AR."

38. Nineteenth-century mesmerists and phrenologists tended to believe that human beings manifested an electrical or magnetic aura that linked them with

others—a force-field manipulated by the male physician to cure his largely female patients. Fuller reverses the polarity here, giving *women* the power to affect those around them.

39. Fuller expands Emerson's concept of "self-reliance," founded upon the intuition and expression of an unconscious masculine power, by arguing that *female* self-reliance depends upon women's discovery and expression of a corresponding core of female energy (an electricity) within.

40. "On Lucy Countess of Bedford."

41. In the myth recounted by Plutarch, Theseus conquered and wed Queen Hippolyte of the Amazons. In Ovid's *Metamorphoses* 9 Hercules is killed by the jealous Deianira, who gives him a poisoned robe that eats away his flesh. A guerdon is a prize or reward won by a knight.

42. The German author Jean Paul Friedrich Richter (known as Jean Paul, 1763–1825) wrote novels, romances, and critical writings.

43. Contess Emily Plater (1806–31) is described in "Emily Plater, the Polish Heroine," *United States Magazine and Democratic Review* 13 (July 1842), as "a noble lady, gifted with the finest qualities of the intellect and the noblest graces of the heart" who "adopt[ed] the apparel of a man, join[ed] the ranks of a rough and ready soldiery, and through the vicissitudes of a disastrous contest, [bore] herself with the energy of a veteran warrior" (23)—attributes that connect her with Fuller's "Minerva" below—see n. 57.

44. Joan of Arc (c. 1412–31), directed by divine voices, put on male armor and successfully led French troops against the English who were besieging Orléans.

45. Eve listens to the serpent in Genesis 3.1–6; Mary becomes the bride of the Holy Spirit in Luke 1.35.

46. Semiramis was the name given by the historian Diodorus Siculus to the ninth-century BC Assyrian queen Sammuramat. Catharine of Russia is Empress Catherine the Great (1729–96).

47. In *Pericles and Aspasia* by Landor; see n. 26 above.

48. Sappho (c. 610–c. 580 BC) was a Greek lyric poet from the isle of Lesbos who celebrated her love for other women. Eloisa is Héloïse (c. 1098–1164), who married the French theologian Abelard.

49. Tasso (1544–95), Italian epic poet and author of *Gerusalemme liberata* (1587), was commemorated in Goethe's drama *Torquato Tasso* (1790), which Fuller translated. Tasso was imprisoned seven years for insanity.

50. Elizabeth Carter (1717–1806) was an English poet, Greek scholar, and translator, and friend of Dr. Johnson. Anne Dacier (1647–1720) was a French classical scholar who translated the *Iliad* and the *Odyssey*.

51. William Cowper (1731–1800), "On the Receipt of My Mother's Picture out of Norfolk," lines 1–2.

52. Wordsworth, "To a Sky-lark," line 18.

53. Ignis fatuus, a phosphorescent light that hovers over swampy ground at night; in other words, something that misleads or deludes.

54. Rosicrucian lamp, see "1844 Poetry" n. 13.

55. Sita, a Hindu goddess of fertility; Isis, see "1844 Poetry" n. 7; Sphynx, see "1844 Poetry" n. 10.

56. Ceres (Gk., Demeter), earth-goddess worshiped in the Eleusinian Mysteries, founded upon the myth of Proserpine's (Gk., Persephone) abduction by Death—"the Isis, the Magna Dea, the feminine principle, par excellence, of all the divinist dynasty" (MH, Fuller's notes; see also n. 17 above).

57. Diana (Gk., Artemis), a very dangerous and powerful Roman nature goddess, whom Fuller associated with Anna Barker (1840 journal, MH). Minerva (Gk., Athena), Roman goddess of war and wisdom, born from the head of her father Jupiter, see also n. 131 below. Vesta, daughter of Rhea, whose shrine in Rome was tended by the vestal virgins.

58. Shakespeare, *Julius Caesar* II.i.272–75, II.i.285–87, II.i.288–90, V.iv.33–35, II.i.292–97, IV.ii.119–24.

59. Ovid's *Metamorphoses* 9; this passage comes immediately before the text cited in n. 6 above.

60. Adapted from *Julius Caesar* II.i.285–86.

61. Cassandra, daughter of Priam, king of Troy, doomed to be a misunderstood prophetess (Euripides, *The Trojan Women,* 415 BC). Iphigenia, daughter sacrificed by the Greek king Agamemnon in order to gain favorable wind for Troy, subject of dramas by Euripides, Goethe, and Racine, see nn. 107, 142 below. Antigone, the heroic niece of Creon who sacrifices her life in order to bury her brother (Sophocles, *Antigone,* 442 BC). Macaria (a model for Fuller's Minerva), the daughter of Hercules in Euripides' *The Heracleidae* (c. 429 BC), as well as a character in Goethe's *Wilhelm Meisters Wanderjahre.*

62. Heinrich Heine (1797–1856), German literary critic and poet, lived most of his life in France. *Dame du Comptoir* (Fr.) is a sales clerk or barmaid (literally, counterwoman).

63. Poem by Francesco Petrarca, see Appendix n. 2.

64. See "The Wedding of Lady Theresa," a ballad reprinted in Appendix C.

65. Infanta, given to the Moorish bridegroom is Lady Theresa, sister of Alfonso V of Asturias, Léon, and Castille (994–1028), celebrated in "The Wedding of Lady Theresa," see Appendix n. 4.

66. Fuller discusses Rhine ballads in detail in her essay "Romaic and Rhine Ballads" (*Dial* 3 [Oct. 1842]).

67. Fuller's description of the Drachenfels is adapted from her essay on "Romaic and Rhine Ballads." In an early poem entitled "Drachenfels" (MB), Fuller focused upon the sublime quality of this legendary landscape. Later associating the dragon with unmanageable instinct, Fuller used the figure of the Drachenfels to explore her sense of the self's victimization by unruly passion, as in

an 1839 letter where she states: "I am on the Drachenfels, and cannot get off; it is one of my naughtiest moods" (*L* 2: 104).

68. Xenophon (c. 434–c. 355 BC), Greek historian, essayist, and student of Socrates.

69. From Euripides' *Iphigenia in Aulis,* spoken by Iphigenia shortly before she is to be taken away and sacrificed.

70. Jeanne Antoinette Poison, marquise de Pompadour (1721–64) and Marie Jeanne Bécu, comtesse du Barry (1746–93) were influential mistresses of Louis XV. Ximena, wife of the famed eleventh-century Spanish military leader, El Cid.

71. From "Words of Faith" (1798), a poem by Friedrich von Schiller. Translation: "The slave, breaking his chains / Not the free man, makes them tremble."

72. Swedenborg argues in *Conjugial Love* that the angels in heaven, experiencing true marriage, feel that their being is completed through a conjugal love that pervades all reality.

73. Mignon sings these lines in *Wilhelm Meisters Lehrjahre* (bk. 8 ch. 2). See also "SD" n. 35. Fuller may also have known Franz Schubert's musical setting ("Lied der Mignon"), composed Jan. 1826. Translation:

> Those celestial forms
> Don't wonder about man and woman,
> And no clothes, no folds
> Surround the transfigured body.

74. Queen Isabella I (1451–1504) of Castille, who married Ferdinand of Aragon, assisted Christopher Columbus. The reign of Mary Stuart (known as Mary Queen of Scots, 1542–87) was marked by violence and intrigue. Because her Catholicism posed a threat to political stability in England, she was imprisoned and eventually executed by Queen Elizabeth I (1558–1603).

75. *The Conquest of Mexico* (1843) by the American historian, William Hickling Prescott (1796–1859). "Malinche" is Marina, the Aztec princess, who was Cortés's slave, mistress, and interpreter.

76. Anne (1665–1714), queen of Great Britain and Ireland (1702–14).

77. Britomart, Belphebe, Florimel, and Una are female figures in Edmund Spenser's *Fairie Queene* (1596).

78. John Ford (1586–?1639) and Philip Massinger (1583–1640), English playwrights in the period immediately after Shakespeare.

79. Imogen, daughter of Cymbeline; Desdemona, wife of Othello; Rosalind, daughter of the banished Duke in *As You Like It;* Portia, wife to Brutus in *Julius Caesar;* Isabella, sister of Claudio in *Measure for Measure;* Cordelia, King Lear's loyal daughter.

80. Richard Lovelace (1618–57), "To *Lucasta,* Going to the Warres" lines 11–12.

81. Thomas Hutchinson (1711–80), pro-British Lieutenant Governor, Chief Justice, and Royal Governor of Massachusetts. The reference to John Donne (1572–1631) is to "The Ecstasy" line 43.

82. Edward, Lord Herbert of Cherbury (1583–1648), "An Ode upon a Question Moved, Whether Love Should Continue Forever" lines 123–24.

83. John Ford (1586–?1639), *The Broken Heart* (1633).

84. A character in *El Magico prodigioso* by the Spanish playwright, Pedro Calderón de la Barca (1600–81).

85. Dante Alighieri (1265–1321), whose greatest works are *La divina commedia* (1308–21) and *La vita nuova* (c. 1293); Giovanni Boccaccio (1313–1375), best known for his *Decameron* (1353), a collection of 100 tales.

86. Polygamy was practiced secretly by the Mormon Church during this period; seraglios are large harems.

87. Jean-Marie Roland de La Platière (1734–93), a French revolutionary who attempted to save the life of Louis XVI, committed suicide when he learned of the execution of his wife, Jeanne-Marie Roland (1754–93), whose salon had been the center of revolutionary activities. Mme Roland's last words were "O Liberty, what crimes are committed in thy name!"

88. The warlike Spartans were renowned for extraordinary self-discipline and fortitude—qualities that link the "Spartan matron" to Countess Emily Plater (n. 43) and Minerva (n. 57).

89. William Godwin (1756–1836) wrote a radical political treatise, *Enquiry Concerning Political Justice* (1793) and the novels, *Caleb Williams* (1794) and *St. Leon* (1799), which contained the noteworthy character Marguerite; Mary Wollstonecraft (1759–97) wrote one of the most famous early treatises on woman's rights, *A Vindication of the Rights of Woman* (1792). They were the parents of Mary Shelley.

90. George Sand is the pseudonym of the French novelist Amandine Lucile Aurore Dudevant (1804–76), whose fiction, cross-dressing, and love affairs scandalized proper Bostonians in the nineteenth century. Her novel *Mauprat* was published in 1837.

91. Goodwyn Barmby (1820–81), Unitarian preacher and Christian socialist, who felt himself a pariah because of his radical views.

92. William (1792–1879) and Mary Howitt (1799–1888) were popular English writers and reformers. He wrote on religion and German culture, while she published poetry, fiction, and translations of Fredrika Bremer's works.

93. Götz von Berlichingen (1480–1562), German knight and source of Goethe's drama, *Götz von Berlichingen* (1773).

94. Manzoni published his tragedy *Adelchi* in 1822.

95. Arcadia, region of ancient Greece regarded as a rural paradise, was

celebrated by English Renaissance writers, including Sir Philip Sidney (1554–86) in *The Arcadia* (c. 1580).

96. Zinzendorf, see *SL* ch. VI n. 7.

97. Adam's manner of addressing Eve before the Fall in *Paradise Lost* (4.660) by John Milton (1608–74).

98. The story of Rantchewaime or "Flying Pigeon," the wife of Mahaskah (an Iowa chief), is quoted from McKenney and Hall's *History of the Indian Tribes of North America,* vol. 1 (see *SL* ch. VI n. 26).

99. Xenophon's "Banquet" and "Economics."

100. Mary Somerville (1780–1872), Scottish writer on mathematics and physical science who turned Laplace's *Mécanique céleste* into popularized English version, *Celestial Mechanism of the Heavens* (1831).

101. Mme. de Staël, see "SD," n. 34.

102. Lady Jane Grey (1537–54), great-granddaughter of Henry VII of England, mastered several languages but not the art of politics—she was beheaded for participating in Wyatt's Rebellion.

103. In Genesis 21.14 Ishmael and his mother Hagar, at the instigation of Sarah, are exiled by his father Abraham; Ishmaelites are wanderers or outcasts.

104. In Luke 10.40 Martha is overwhelmed by household duties.

105. In Greek mythology Urania is the muse of astronomy.

106. For Michelangelo's Sibyl, see "SD" n. 17; St. Theresa, see *SL* ch. V n. 21. Electra conspires with her brother Orestes to revenge her father's murder in *The Libation Bearers* by Aeschylus (525–456 BC) and in *Electra* by Sophocles (c. 496–06 BC). Antonio Canova (1757–1822), Italian sculptor.

107. In a clever revision of the legend that Iphigenia was sacrificed by her father Agamemnon so that his becalmed ships could sail to Troy, Euripides (c. 484–06 BC) in *Iphigenia in Aulis* has her spirited away by Artemis who leaves a deer in her place.

108. Michaelangelo's Persican Sibyl.

109. Vittoria Colonna (1492–1547), Italian noblewoman who wrote sonnets commemorating her dead husband.

110. Irish writer Anna Brownell Jameson (1794–1860) tells the story of this Chippewa woman in *Winter Studies and Summer Rambles in Canada* (1838) 3: 71.

111. Joanna Southcott (1750–1814), an English religious fanatic, declared in *The Book of Wonders* (1813–14) that she would give birth to the second messiah. Mother Ann Lee (1736–84), founder and leader of the Shakers, preached that she embodied the female half of God's dual nature. Ecstatica is probably a reference to the Seeress of Prevorst (see *SL* ch. V n. 3). Dolorosa is a term applied to the Virgin Mary as she grieves over Christ's body, see n. 140 below.

112. Xavier de Maistre (1763–1852), French Christian philosopher who wrote *Voyage autour de ma chambre* (1799), often regarded as an early science fiction novel.

113. Faust searches for the secret realm of the "Mothers" in Goethe's *Faust, Part Two,* act I. The Mothers are also prominent in Scandinavian mythology, which Fuller was studying as she finished *WNC* (see n. 161 below). Fuller created her own vision of the Mother in "The Magnolia of Lake Pontchartrain."

114. Jakob Böhme (Behmen, 1575–1624) was an important German mystic whose writings influenced the Quakers, Pietists, and Romantic writers; Claude-Henri de Rouvroy, comte de Saint-Simon (1760–1825) was a French reformer who founded an influential socialist system known as Saint-Simonianism.

115. In Plato's famous dialogue on love, "The Symposium," Socrates creates a myth of an original, egglike hermaphrodite that combined both male and female and which was cut in half into the two sexes; as a result of this bisection, each man or woman searches for a mate in order to form a perfect whole. For the angel of Swedenborg, see n. 72 above.

116. Fuller read of the "electrical" and "magnetic element in woman" in *The Seeress of Prevorst* (see *SL* ch. V n. 3), one of her most important sources for her conception of the "Muse."

117. Bristling, having one's hair stand on end.

118. Franz Anton Mesmer (1734–1815), the popularizer of "animal magnetism" (hypnotism), believed that a subtle "electric fluid" filled the universe and linked human beings with the world and each other. (Cf. *SL* ch. V n. 4).

119. Mlle Rahcel, see n. 35 above. François, duc de la Rochefoucauld (1630–80), French moralist remembered for his maxims.

120. Guercino is Giovanni Francesco Barbieri (1591–1666), Italian painter known for his frescoes.

121. Euripides' drama, *The Trojan Women* (415 BC) tells the story of Hecuba, queen of Troy, and her prophetess-daughter, Cassandra.

122. Rape, abduction (Lat.), combined here with the English "rapture": Cassandra's prophetic rapture coincides with her abduction by Agamemnon.

123. The French theologian and philosopher François Fénelon (1651–1715), who helped to develop quietism, was influenced by Jean-Marie de la Motte Guyon (1648–1717), a mystic whom he defended.

124. In this context a waxing moon signals the emergence of feminine power, what Fuller calls "the idea of Woman."

125. Queen Isabella allegedly used her jewels to help pay for Christopher Columbus's voyages of discovery.

126. Bourbon, royal family of France; Guelph, a powerful political party in medieval Italy.

127. Both Angelina Grimké (1805–79) and Abby Kelley were Quaker reformers who were early leaders in the abolitionist and woman's rights movements.

128. William Ellery Channing (1780–1842), liberal Congregationalist and one of the organizers of the American Unitarian Association, was the uncle of William Henry Channing (1810–84), one of Fuller's closest friends and most

important correspondents. Fuller's sister Ellen married Ellery Channing, son of Dr. Walker Channing, a distant relative of William Ellery Channing.

129. Harriet Martineau (1802–76) offended many Americans with her travel books, *Society in America* (1837) and *A Retrospect of Western Travel* (1838). In one of her letters Fuller characterized Martineau's style as being "stained with credulity, exaggeration, and man deification" (*L* 2: 48).

130. Kinmont, see "AR" n. 12, *SL* ch. III n. 7.

131. Minerva, warrior-goddess who was born from the head of her father Jupiter Gk. Zeus): she "sprang ready armed from the masculine Will" (Dall, *Margaret and Her Friends*).

132. Wordsworth, "Liberty" lines 133–34; see also "L" n. 1.

133. Jove (Jupiter, Gk. Zeus), chief god of the Romans, identified by Fuller with masculine "will"; Rhea, one of the earliest Greek mother-goddesses; Pallas, an appellation of Minerva (Athena).

134. Proclus (c. 410–85), Greek Neoplatonic philosopher. Fuller's description of the four triads is quoted verbatim from the notes of *The Metamorphosis, or Golden Ass, and Philosophical Works, of Apuleius* (1822), trans. Thomas Taylor (1758–1835)—which provided the description of Isis in her first appendix, as well as with information about the sistrum (rattle) of Isis (her personal talisman).

135. A dutiful sister herself, Fuller admired Wordsworth's poems "To My Sister" and "Tintern Abbey" (addressed to Dorothy Wordsworth) and Byron's "Epistle to Augusta" (to Augusta Leigh, his half-sister).

136. The English poet Robert Southey (1774–1843) published his epic poem *The Curse of Kehama* in 1818. See also *SL* ch. II n. 17.

137. Alcibiades (c. 450–404 BC) was an Athenian aristocrat, general, and unscrupulous politician who was convicted of drunkenly mimicking the sacred rituals of Ceres and Proserpine (the Eleusinian mysteries). To repeat "the tale of Alcibiades" is to miss the value of goddesses such as the Muse and Minerva.

138. Swedenborg, whose followers founded of the Church of the New Jerusalem, describes the new heavenly church in *Apocalypse Revealed.*

139. Goethe's mother, Katharine Elisabeth Textor, was an important intellectual influence on his life; his sister Cornelia inspired an early epistolary novel; at different times, Goethe fell in love with Amelia, duchess of Weimar and Anne Elisabeth (Lili) Schönemann.

140. In her translator's preface of *Eckermann's Conversations with Goethe* (1839), Fuller commends the character of Margaret in Goethe's *Faust, Part One* for "her innocence of heart and resolute aversion to the powers of darkness." *Mater Dolorosa* (the Virgin Mary grieving) and *Mater Gloriosa* (the Virgin Mary glorified after her Annunciation) appear in *Faust, Part One and Part Two* respectively.

141. Leonora is loved by Tasso in Goethe's drama *Torquato Tasso.*

142. In her essay "Goethe" (*Dial* July 1841), Fuller praised Goethe's portrait of Iphigenia in his verse drama *Iphigenia auf Tauris* (1787) as manifesting "the

full beauty of virgin womanhood, solitary but tender, wise and innocent, sensitive and self-collected, sweet as spring, dignified as she becomes the chosen servant of God."

143. In the discussion that follows, Mariana, Philina, Mignon (a model for Fuller's Muse), Natalia, and Theresa are all from Goethe's *Wilhelm Meisters Lehrjahre,* 1795–96); Marcaria (a model for Fuller's Minerva) appears in *Wilhelm Meisters Wanderjahre* (1821–29). During the composition of *WNC,* Fuller contemplated writing "a Lehrjahre for women" (*L* 3: 221).

144. Dressed as an angel, Mignon signs these lines to two girls in *Wilhelm Meisters Lehrjahre* (bk. 8 ch. 2). See also "SD" n. 35 and n. 73 above.

145. Maria Edgeworth (1767–1849), British writer and early Irish regionalist, wrote over twenty volumes, including *Castle Rockrent* (1800), *Belinda* (1801), and *Tales from Fashionable Life* (1809–12).

146. Anna Brownell Jameson wrote several popular books on famous women, both real and literary; see also *SL* ch. II n. 11 and n. 110 above.

147. Paladin, originally one of the twelve peers of Charlemagne's court; here, any knight who serves as a champion.

148. Arguing for the moral power of virginity, Fuller refers to Milton's *Comus* (1634), a masque in which a Lady is protected from the excesses of Comus and his revelers by the spiritual aura of her chastity.

149. Fuller echoes here the language of John 2.21 and the conception expressed in *The Temple: Sacred Poems and Private Ejaculations* by George Herbert (1593–1633). The poem that follows is Fuller's.

150. Of convenience (Fr.).

151. Lady Rachel Russell (1636–1723), author of *Letters of Rachel, Lady Russell* (1773), was an outspoken critic of the immorality and corruption of her time.

152. In Spenser's *Faerie Queene* Duessa represents false religion and chaotic evil; Una represents true religion and the unity of truth.

153. John Quincy Adams (1767–1848), sixth president of the U.S.; Hannah Foster (1759–1840), author of *The Coquette* (1797) and *The Boarding School; or, Lessons of a Preceptress to her Pupils* (1798). In the passage that follows, Adams refers to his mother Abigail Adams (1744–1818), known for her insightful letters (published in 1840).

154. *Paradise Lost* 4.660, 9.291.

155. Lydia Maria Child (1802–80), American reformer active in abolitionist and woman suffrage causes. Joel Myerson has identified Amelia Norman as a woman "acquitted of the charge of stabbing her seducer on the steps of the Astor House in New York" (*Margaret Fuller: Essays on American Life and Letters*).

156. Eugène Sue (1804–57), French author *Les mystères de Paris* (*The Mysteries of Paris,* 1842–43) and *Le juif errant* (*The Wandering Jew,* 1844–45). In the former Fleur-de-Marie is a duke's daughter who maintains her goodness although she is

brought up by criminals, and Rigolette is her friend, a kind and hard-working young woman.

157. The novel *Sir Charles Grandison* (1753) by Samuel Richardson (1689–1761).

158. In Fuller's translation of Goethe's *Torquato Tasso* (II.i), the Princess Leonora and Tasso debate the respective merits of liberty and law. Countering Tasso's arguments in favor of the freedom of a golden age, the princess responds:

> A synod of good *women* should decide;
> It is their province. Like a wall, decorum
> Surrounds and guards the frailer sex. Propriety,
> Morality, are their defence and fortress,
> Their tower of strength; and lawlessness their foe.
> And as man loves bold trials of his strength,
> So woman, graceful bonds, worn with composure.

159. In the 1820s "Los Exaltados" split off from the Liberal party in Spain because of their insistence that the rich, not the poor, should pay taxes.

160. Disraeli published *The Young Duke* in 1831; he later became English prime minister. See also *SL* ch. VI n. 19.

161. In Nov. 1844 as she completed *WNC*, Fuller was reading a handbook to Scandinavian mythology—*Alkuna. Nordische und nordslawische Mythologie* (1831) by Anton Thormond Glückseling (pseud. Von G. Th. Legis, 1806–67). Loki was a Scandinavian deity renowned for his mischief; Idun, wife of Bragi, guarded the golden apples of immortality.

162. Probably *The Whole Duty of a Woman; or, A guide to the female sex. Written by a lady* (1701), a republication of a guide by Richard Allestree (1619–81).

163. Albertine Adrienne Necker de Saussure (1766–1841); this translation was published in 1844.

164. This life only has some worth if it promotes the moral education of our heart (Fr.).

165. Alexander Mackenzie, see *SL* ch. VI n. 5.

166. The Nibelungen Lays (c. 1200) make up a long narrative poem that tells the legends of Siegfried, Brunhilda, and other medieval Germanic figures.

167. Catharine Maria Sedgewick (1789–1867), the author of *Hope Leslie*, later became active in New York prison reform (an interest also shared by Fuller) starting in 1845. Fuller refers either to Sedgwick's *Live and Let Live; or, Domestic Service Illustrated* (1837) or *Means and Ends, or Self-Training* (1839). In a journal (MH) of notes used in *WNC*, Fuller observes: "I agree with Miss S that private education is necessary to enable women to attain these privileges or to use them well. Might must make right.—But then again the reasoning goes two ways as ever. Institutions must be modified to give them a fair chance of establishing these characters.

There will & must be action & reaction from character to institution & vice versa."

168. Harriet Martineau (see n. 129 above); the poet Elizabeth Barrett (1806–61), who later married Robert Browning in 1846, was an invalid.

169. Daniel O'Connell (1775–1847), Irish nationalist leader, was arrested after demanding repeal of the union of Great Britain and Ireland.

170. The annexation of Texas in 1844, the event that precipitated war with Mexico, created enormous controversy in the northern states where it was interpreted as a cynical expansion of U.S. slaveholding territory.

171. Boadicea (d. AD 60), was a British queen who fought valiantly against the Roman conquest of Britain; Lady Godiva (c. 1140–80), according to legend, rode naked through Coventry in order to force her husband to lower taxes; Queen Emma (d. 1052), wife of King Aethelred the Unready and later Cnut, was alleged to have allowed herself to be tortured by hot iron in order to prove her fidelity; Anne Hutchinson (1591–1643) was banished from the Massachusetts Bay Colony for preaching salvation through individual intuition of God's grace; Lady Russell, see n. 151 above.

172. Fuller here advocates that American women duplicate the strike of the Greek women in Aristophanes' comedy *Lysistra* (412 BC).

173. According to legend, a black dove flew from Thebes to Dodona where it landed in an oak tree, spoke in a human voice, and proclaimed that an oracle of Zeus should be founded on that spot.

174. Edward Fitzgerald, see *SL* ch. VI n. 6.

175. Maid of Saragossa, an inhabitant of the Spanish city that was besieged by the French (1808–09) during the Napoleonic Wars; maid of Missolonghi, a woman living in the Greek town besieged twice (1822–23, 1825–26) by the Turks in the Greek War of Independence; a Suliote heroine, resident of the Greek island of Suli which rebelled against Turkist occupation in 1820; Emily Plater, see n. 43 above.

176. In nineteenth-century usage, *ennui* (Fr.) was an extreme form of boredom, bordering on illness and despair.

177. Wordsworth, "Laodamia" lines 74–76.

178. In this passage, Fuller responds to but feminizes Emerson's call in "The Poet" (1844) for an American genius who might know "the value of our incomparable materials."

179. This poem is by Fuller. In her journal (MH) Fuller outlined the final paragraph and poem in the following terms: "Finale will see Goddess Freya with her departing sympathy who cannot herself wed. I stand in the sunny morn &c What I have seen & yet believe Men cannot cure me of hoping for Man Though many shipwreck yet beat noble hearts Ask for the Castle's King & Queen."

Explanatory Notes

1. *The Metamorphosis, or Golden Ass* by Apuleius (see n. 134 above) tells the story of Lucius, who is turned into an ass and experiences numerous adventures, including his overhearing the story of Cupid and Psyche (see *SL* ch. 5 n. 12). He is restored to his human form after Isis, appearing to him in a vision, instructs him to participate in her rites. This tale of a man redeemed from sensuality by a goddess accords well with Fuller's intention to have American women "aid in the reformation of the sons of this age."

2. "Praise and Prayer to Maria" (Hymn to the Madonna) by Francesco Petrarca (1316–20). The opening lines of this poem suggest one source for Fuller's image of the woman "betrothed to the Sun":

> Beautiful Virgin, who clothed with the sun,
> Crowned with stars, the supreme Sun
> Liked, so that he covered you with his light;
> Love urges me to speak some words to you.

3. In Scandinavian mythology, Frig (or Frigga), the wife of Odin, was a fertility goddess known as the weeping mother (after the death of her son Baldur); she was associated with childbirth and with the elusive deities known as the "Mothers" (seen n. 113 above).

4. The Scottish writer and editor John Gibson Lockhart (1794–1854), author of a biography of Sir Walter Scott (his father-in-law), published *Ancient Spanish Ballads* in 1823.

5. Baruch Spinoza (1632–77), Dutch philosopher, published *Tractatus Theologico-Politicus* in 1670.

6. William Ellery Channing (1818–1901), minor Transcendentalist writer who married Fuller's sister Ellen in 1841.

7. Fuller was a great admirer of *Festus* (1839), a narrative poem based on the Faust legend written by Philip James Bailey (1816–1902).

8. Anne MacVicar Grant (1755–1838), *Memoirs of an American Lady: with sketches of manners and scenery in America as they existed previous to the Revolution* (1808).

9. In her May 1844 journal (cited *JMN* 11: 498), Fuller identified herself as the figure of Miranda in "The Great Lawsuit" (which she was revising into *WNC*): "Last year, I wrote of Woman, & proudly painted myself as Miranda."

10. This line and those that follow are from Euripides' *Iphigenia in Aulis* (see n. 107 above).

11. Euripides, *The Suppliant Women* (c. 420–15 BC).

12. James Fenimore Cooper (1789–1851), *The Deerslayer*.

13. Macaria, daughter of Hercules, appears in Euripides' *The Heracleidae* (c. 429 BC).

14. In Judges 11.30–39, Jepthah, praying for victory in battle, vows to sacrifice whoever comes forth first to greet him; it is his virgin daughter, who allows herself to be sacrificed so that her father can fulfill his vow. In its outline, this episode parallels the story of Iphigenia.

15. Alfred, Lord Tennyson (1809–92), "A Dream of Fair Women" lines 227–28, 237–44.

16. The passages immediately following are from Euripides, *The Trojan Women* (415 BC), see n. 121 above.

17. Beatrice Cenci (1577–99) conspired with her mother and stepbrother to murder her vicious father, Francesco Cenci—a crime for which they were all executed. Percy Bysshe Shelley (1792–1822) immortalized her story in his tragedy *The Cenci* (1819).

18. *The Creation* (1798), oratorio by the Austrian composer, Franz Joseph Haydn (1732–1809).

19. Fuller's poem.

NEW-YORK TRIBUNE REVIEWS AND ESSAYS

EMERSON'S ESSAYS

1. The ornate odes of lyric poet Pindar (c. 522–c. 438 BC) are among the most difficult texts in Greek literature to translate; the systematic prose of the British philosopher John Locke (1632–1704), devoted to the exposition of the empirical bases of knowledge, would be incapable of capturing any of their poetic subtlety or mythic enthusiasm.

2. Theogonies (after Hesiod's *Theogony*), literary works portraying the origin and genealogy of the gods; eclogues, formal pastoral poems dealing with shepherd and rustic life.

3. Euphuism, a highly ornate prose style, which took its name from the *Euphues* (1578, 1580) of the English writer John Lyly (c. 1554–1606).

4. This quotation and those following are from Emerson's essay "The Poet," *Essays: Second Series* (1844).

OUR CITY CHARITIES

1. Anastatic printing, technique of printing from etched plates.

2. Victor Hugo (1802–85) and Sir Walter Scott (1771–1832) are both Romantic poets and novelists famed for the range of their characters.

3. The philanthropist John Griscom (1774–1852), one of the founders of the New York Society for the Prevention of Pauperism, was known for his public lectures.

Explanatory Notes

PREVALENT IDEA THAT POLITENESS IS TOO GREAT A LUXURY TO BE GIVEN TO THE POOR

1. Charles Lamb (1775–1834), popular English essayist and critic. This passage repeats in spirit the thesis of his essay "Modern Gallantry"—that a true gentleman treats women of all classes with equal consideration.

THE WRONGS OF AMERICAN WOMEN
THE DUTY OF AMERICAN WOMEN

This review is of Charles Burdett, *Wrongs of American Women. First Series. The Elliott Family; or the Trials of New York Seamstresses* (1845) and of Catharine Beecher, *The Duty of American Women to Their Country* (1845).

1. Lucy Stone (1818–93), prominent American woman suffragist; Catharine Beecher (1800–78), author of *Treatise on Domestic Economy* (1841) and *Letters to Persons Who Are Engaged in Domestic Service* (1842), sister of Harriet Beecher Stowe (see n. 4 below).

2. Hannah Farnham Sawyer Lee (1780–1865) was the author of several educational books, including *Three Experiments of Living* (1837) on the way to live economically.

3. Rev. Calvin Ellis Stowe (1802–86), husband of Harriet Beecher Stowe, was influential in founding the College of Teachers in Cincinnati (1833).

4. The novelist Harriet Beecher Stowe (1811–96) lived in Cincinnati from 1833 to 1850.

5. Luke 10.37, the end of the parable of the Good Samaritan.

WHAT FITS A MAN TO BE A VOTER?

1. Fuller audaciously (for her time) portrays both the Virgin Mary and Jesus as nonwhite. The young Jesus sits in the temple and instructs the doctors in Luke 2.46.

2. Milton, *Paradise Lost*, 4.845.

3. Compare the acclamation of the heavenly host at Christ's birth in Luke 2.14.

4. Compare John 14.9.

5. Peculiar institutions, the institutions of slavery.

THINGS AND THOUGHTS IN EUROPE

NO. XVIII

1. Blue-Laws, laws demanding the closing of businesses on Sunday.

2. Compare Matthew 5.8: "Blessed *are* the pure in heart . . ."

Explanatory Notes

3. Compare Luke 12.49: "I am come to send fire on the earth . . ."

4. Christopher Columbua (1451–1506) was born in Genoa.

5. Voluntary association was the term used to describe utopian communities founded upon the principles of Charles Fourier.

6. The Mexican War (1846–48) extended U.S. slaveholding territory by ensuring the acquisition of Texas.

NO. XXIII

1. Fuller was three and one-half months pregnant and suffering from morning sickness. She hid her pregnancy and the birth of her child until the following year.

2. In the early months of 1848, there were popular uprisings against Ferdinand II, the monarch of Sicily and Naples—the Kingdom of the Two Sicilies.

3. *Moccalletti, moccolli*, wax tapers used in churches.

4. Revolution had broken out in Paris in February and then in Vienna—events that inspired a popular uprising against the Austrian occupation of northern Italy, fueling dreams of Italian unification.

5. Pope Pius IX (1792–1878) originally seemed to support the unification of Italy, but after the declaration of the Republic of Rome he went into exile and enlisted the support of the French government to restore the papacy in Rome.

6. Klemens Metternich (1773–1859), Austrian minister of foreign affairs. In Genesis 2.15, the Lord predicts that the seed of Eve will bruise the head of the serpent.

7. Miracle, Providence! (It.). Angelo Brunetti, one of the leaders of the Roman people, was nicknamed "Ciceruacchio" (Big Boy) because of his size. Adam Mickiewicz (1798–1855), Polish poet and revolutionary, attempted to organize a military unit during the Italian revolution.

8. Metternich's resignation inspired violent street fighting in Milan where the citizens fought to overthrow the Austrian occupation.

9. Northern Italy (It.)—in hope of the liberation of the northern Italian states from foreign rule.

10. The writer Niccolò Tommasseo (1802–74) worked for Italian federation. Daniele Manin (1804–57) led the revolt against the Austrians in Venice.

11. Pietro Sterbini (1795–1863), a Roman minister who was one of the organizers of the assassination of Pellegrino Rossi (see No. XXVI).

12. William Wetmore Story (1819–95), sculptor and man of letters; George Stillman Hilliard (1808–79), later the author of *Six Months in Italy* (1853); Fuller's friend, Frederic Henry Hedge (1805–90), a prominent German scholar who published *Prose Writers of Germany* (1848).

13. Christopher Pearse Cranch (1813–92), "The Castle of the Colonnas."

14. Giuseppe di Asburgo-Lorena Ranieri (1783–1853), viceroy of Lom-

bardy-Venice who was reduced to being an instrument of Austrian policies, relinquished his power during the Milan uprising.

NO. XXVI

1. The Pope had appointed as his minister the unpopular Pellegrino Rossi (1787–1848); François-Pierre-Guillaume Guizot (1787–1874), premier of France forced into retirement by the Revolution of 1848; Louis Philippe (1773–1850), French king overthrown by the revolution.

2. Giuseppe Garibaldi (1807–82), Italian nationalist leader active from the 1830s to the 1860s in the cause of Italian freedom.

3. Chancellery (It.).

4. St. Cecilia (2d or 3d cent. AD), the patron saint of music, was forced to marry a nobleman despite her vow of celibacy; she converted him to Christianity and both were martyred.

5. Prince Francesco-Maria-Barberini-Colona (1772–1853).

6. Ferdinand II (1810–59), king of the Naples, earned the nickname "King Bomba" after his heavy bombardment of his people in order to quell their insurrection.

7. Zachary Taylor (1784–1850) of Virginia, commanding general during the Mexican War, was elected president in 1848.

NO. XXXIII

1. Lewis Cass (1782–1866), prominent military commander, diplomat, and politician, had been a senator from 1845 to 1848 and was the U.S. chargé d'affaires in Rome.

2. Nicolas-Charles-Victor Oudinot (1791–1863) commanded the expedition against Rome which recaptured the city and restored the papacy.

3. Niccolò Rienzo (1313–54) led a revolution that attempted to restore the ancient glory of Rome.

4. Hecatomb, originally a public sacrifice of one hundred oxen; any large-scale sacrifice.

5. Compare Luke 12.7.

6. In Ovid's *Metamorphoses* 6 Niobe is both overly proud of her children and openly critical of the worship of the goddess Latona; out of anger, Latona kills Niobe's seven sons and seven daughters.

7. Trasteverini, inhabitants of the Trastevere section of Rome, on the right bank of the Tiber River.

8. A peasant or rustic (It.).

9. Lajos Kossuth (1802–1894) headed the Hungarian insurrection (1848–49).

Explanatory Notes

1. Shadrach, Meshach, and Abednego endure the ordeal of the fiery furnace in Daniel 3.10–30; Daniel is thrown into a den of lions in Daniel 6.12–24.

2. James 2.19: "The devils also believe, and tremble."

ORDER FORM
■ ■ ■ ■ ■ ■ *AMERICAN WOMEN WRITERS SERIES* ■ ■ ■ ■ ■ ■

☐ Special Boxed-Gift Set Offer!
**All 18 volumes in the Series (in paperback) for only $175.00,
a 30% discount off the list price of $244.95**

Individual volumes in the American Women Writers Series

☐ **Alternative Alcott**, by Louisa May Alcott.
Elaine Showalter, editor
1987. 462 pp. Paper, $15.00.

☐ **"The Amber Gods" and Other Stories**,
by Harriet Prescott Spofford.
Alfred Bendixen, editor
1989. 300 pp. Paper, $14.00.

☐ **American Women Poets of the Nineteenth
Century: An Anthology**.
Cheryl Walker, editor
1992. 350 pp. Paper, $15.00.

☐ **Clovernook Sketches and Other Stories**,
by Alice Cary. Judith Fetterley, editor
1988. 314 pp. Paper, $13.00.

☐ **The Essential Margaret Fuller**, by Margaret
Fuller. Jeffrey Steele, editor
1992. 450 pp. Paper, $16.00.

☐ **Gail Hamilton: Selected Writings**, by Gail
Hamilton. Susan Coultrap-McQuin, editor
1992. 280 pp. Paper, $15.00.

☐ *The Hidden Hand*, by E.D.E.N. Southworth.
Joanne Dobson, editor
1988. 450 pp. Paper, $15.00.

☐ *Hobomok* **and Other Writings on Indians**,
by Lydia Maria Child.
Carolyn L. Karcher, editor
1986. 275 pp. Paper, $12.00.

☐ *Hope Leslie*, by Catharine Maria Sedgwick.
Mary Kelly, editor
1987. 373 pp. Paper, $12.00.

☐ **"How Celia Changed Her Mind" and
Selected Stories**, by Rose Terry Cooke.
Elizabeth Ammons, editor
1986. 265 pp. Paper, $13.00.

☐ *The Lamplighter*, by Maria Susanna
Cummins. Nina Baym, editor
1987. 437 pp. Paper, $15.00.

☐ *Moods*, by Louisa May Alcott.
Sarah Elbert, editor
1991. 284 pp. Paper, $13.00.

☐ *A New Home—Who'll Follow?*,
by Caroline Kirkland.
Sandra A. Zagarell, editor
1990. 250 pp. Paper, $14.00.

☐ *Oldtown Folks*, by Harriet Beecher Stowe.
Dorothy Berkson, editor
1987. 519 pp. Paper, $15.00.

☐ *Quicksand* **and** *Passing*, by Nella Larsen.
Deborah E. McDowell, editor
1986. 246 pp. Paper, $8.95.

☐ *Ruth Hall* **and Other Writings**,
by Fanny Fern. Joyce W. Warren, editor
1986. 380 pp. Paper, $12.00.

☐ **Stories from the Country of Lost Borders**,
by Mary Austin. Marjorie Pryse, editor
1987. 310 pp. Paper, $12.00.

☐ **Women Artists, Women Exiles: "Miss
Grief" and Other Stories**, by Constance
Fenimore Woolson.
Joan Myers Weimer, editor
1988. 292 pp. Paper, $15.00.

Postage: For the boxed-gift set, add $5.00.
For other orders, add $2.25 postage for the
first book, $.50 for each additional book.
New Jersey residents: please add 7% sales
tax.

Copy or tear out this page and send to:

Rutgers University Press
109 Church Street
New Brunswick, New Jersey 08901